Foreign Office.

Here is the report of your Conversation with Cambon of May 17. It referred to several questions. I have marked the passage as to mutual confidence.

THS

I suppose this was the origin of the offensive & defensive alliance.

L

Facsimile of Minutes by Sir T. H. [Lord] Sanderson and the Marquess of Lansdowne, p. 76.

British Documents on the Origins of the War

1898-1914

Edited by G. P. GOOCH, D.Litt., F.B.A., and HAROLD TEMPERLEY, Litt.D., F.B.A.

Vol. III
The Testing of the Entente
1904-6

LONDON:

1928

59—2—3

JOHNSON REPRINT CORPORATION
111 Fifth Avenue, New York, N.Y. 10003

JOHNSON REPRINT COMPANY LTD.
Berkeley Square House, London, W.1

First reprinting, 1967, Johnson Reprint Corporation
Printed in the United States of America

VOLUME III

The Testing of the Entente
1904–6

Edited by

G. P. GOOCH, D.Litt., and HAROLD TEMPERLEY, Litt.D.,

with the assistance of

LILLIAN M. PENSON, Ph.D.

Table of Contents.

Wt. 25035/1683 2000 7/28 F.O.P. [15869]

Foreword to Volume III.

THE decision to publish a selection from the British Documents dealing with the origins of the War was taken by Mr. Ramsay MacDonald, Prime Minister and Secretary of State for Foreign Affairs, in the summer of 1924. It was confirmed and announced by Mr., now Sir, Austen Chamberlain in a letter of the 28th November, 1924 (published in "The Times" on the 3rd December), addressed to Dr. R. W. Seton-Watson. Some extracts from this letter were published by the Editors in the Foreword to Volume XI, and it need only be said here that the Secretary of State for Foreign Affairs referred to "impartiality and accuracy" as being the necessary qualifications for any work which the Editors were to publish.

Volume III covers a very important and much discussed period. It deals with the aftermath of the Anglo-French Agreement and, for the first though not for the last time, with the Morocco problem. This was therefore a period of testing for the Entente. The question of M. Delcassé's resignation in June 1905 is dealt with from the British side, and the opinions of Lord Lansdowne and Lord Sanderson on the whole question are given. The latter half of 1905 is marked by closer diplomatic relations between England and France. The extremely important Anglo-French military and naval conversations of January–April 1906 are described from such materials as exist in the British Archives.([1]) The papers of Colonel Barnardiston, detailing his conversations with Belgian military authorities in January–April 1906, are here for the first time given in full. Certain papers were published from the Belgian Archives by the German Government in 1915, and were referred to in a speech by the German Imperial Chancellor, Herr von Bethmann-Hollweg, on August 19, 1915. Sir Edward Grey replied in a letter to the press on August 26. His statement makes it clear that the Barnardiston papers now published were unknown to him. The documents now printed provide a wealth of detail by which his further contention that the whole negotiation "referred only to the contingency of Belgium being attacked" may be tested.

An outstanding feature of the volume is provided by detailed surveys of German policy from different standpoints, in a memorandum by Mr. [Sir] Eyre Crowe, in a supplementary memorandum by Sir T. H. [Lord] Sanderson, and in certain annexed papers. Another is the full length portrait of the Emperor William II drawn by Sir Frank Lascelles, who, as Lord Lansdowne once stated, "enjoyed so special a position in the confidence of the Emperor." These, together with the written statements of Lord Sanderson and of Lord Lansdowne on the crisis of 1905, of Lord Sydenham on the conversations of 1906, the above-mentioned Barnardiston papers, certain Minutes of King Edward, and the private Diary of Lord Haldane's visit to Berlin are the most valuable unpublished material in the volume.

The opinion expressed by the Editors in Volume I (page vii), that the formal records of the Foreign Office supply more complete information from the year 1901 onwards, is confirmed in the period covered by Volume III. There are various official sources of information which were not available before. The practice instituted in 1906 of demanding Annual Reports from each country, to which Ministers are accredited, results often in general surveys of much value. Some of these are quoted in the present volume. The official summaries of events or questions are more frequent after 1904. The private papers available in the Foreign Office are also more abundant. None the less the Editors cannot be certain that they have not omitted, or failed to find, some important documents; and there are certain negotiations of which no written account exists or as to which the written records are inadequate. Thus the first part of the

([1]) General Huguet's book *L'Intervention Militaire Britannique en* 1914 (Paris, 1928) was published too late for the Editors to consult it.

Diary of Lord Haldane's journey in 1906 has disappeared. In other cases, as for instance the Anglo-French Naval conversations, the written evidence is insufficient to show the actual nature of the business transacted.

In accordance with the practice of the Foreign Office already observed in the case of Volumes I, II and XI of this series, the documents in the present volume containing information supplied or opinions expressed by certain Foreign Governments have been communicated to them for their agreement. The response in this volume has been quite satisfactory.

The Editors have inserted asterisks to indicate gaps or omissions in documents. As a rule these gaps are due to the unimportance of the matter omitted, in which case an indication of subject is usually given. In a few instances, they are due to a desire to consult the susceptibilities of the persons or of the Governments concerned; but the Editors have omitted nothing which they consider essential to the understanding of the history of the period. They think it well here to state, what was already implied in their preface to Volume I, p. viii, that they would feel compelled to resign if any attempt were made to insist on the omission of any document which is in their view vital or essential. In addition to despatches and telegrams there are memoranda and minutes which are properly official documents. No objection has been raised by His Majesty's Secretary of State for Foreign Affairs to the publication in this volume of any documents of the above kind, nor to the publication of certain similar papers or of private letters, which are not properly official documents, but which are preserved in the Foreign Office. Among these is included the private correspondence of Lord Carnock, which becomes fuller from 1905 onwards, that of Lord Grey, which contains much valuable material from the end of 1905, and that of Lord Sanderson, which is fragmentary in character.

His Majesty the King has graciously consented to the publication of Minutes by King Edward. The Editors have also gratefully to acknowledge information and advice given by the late Marquess of Lansdowne in several ways. He was kind enough only a short time before his death to furnish the Editors with an authoritative comment upon a written opinion expressed by Lord Sanderson on the "guarantees" question of 1905, and one of the last letters which he wrote was one authorizing the publication of some of his minutes. Lord Sydenham of Combe has also kindly given to the Editors a written statement elucidating some points in connexion with the Anglo-French conversations of January 1906. Viscount Haldane has kindly permitted the publication of the surviving part of his Diary in Berlin in 1906. Lady Gwendolen Cecil has permitted the publication of a document from the private papers of the late Marquess of Salisbury. In conclusion the Editors desire to acknowledge the friendly assistance and advice of various officials at the Foreign Office, among whom they would like to mention the Librarian, Mr. Stephen Gaselee, C.B.E., Mr. J. W. Headlam-Morley, C.B.E., Historical Adviser, who arranged Volume XI for them, and Mr. J. W. Field. They wish also to thank the officials of the War Office who placed at their disposal the records of the military conversations of 1906, and the officials of the Public Record Office in London, and Mr. Wright, who is in charge of the Diplomatic and Embassy Archives at Cambridge.

G. P. GOOCH.

HAROLD TEMPERLEY.

June 1928.

Note on Arrangement of Documents, &c.

THE arrangement of the material in the present volume follows in the main the same rules as those adopted for Volumes I and II. The scope of the volume is, however, more limited than in the case of the earlier ones. It centres round the Morocco crisis of 1905–6 and deals with the effects produced upon the relations of the Great Powers. More detail is given than in Volumes I and II, but the documents printed are still only a selection from a much larger number in existence. In this volume, as in the others, the documents have been grouped according to the subject with which they deal, and chronological order has been followed within the chapters and their subsections.([1]) Exceptions to this rule are to be found in letters, memoranda or summaries reviewing events at a later date, and these have been printed in small type for purposes of differentiation.

Most of the documents are taken from the official series of Foreign Office papers in the Public Record Office. The classification for the period 1898–1905 was described in the note prefaced to Volumes I (p. ix) and II (p. ix), but may be reproduced here :—

"They are classified mainly by country (F.O. France, etc.), and within countries by years. For each year the diplomatic documents are separated from the commercial and other classes. Within the diplomatic class there are volumes of outgoing and incoming despatches, outgoing and incoming telegrams, communications with the Foreign Ambassador ("Domestic") and with other Government Departments ("Various"). Papers relating to certain subjects have been specially treated. Some have been placed together in a miscellaneous series (F.O. General), as in the case of the Hague Peace Conference. In other instances all papers relating to a certain geographical area have been placed together, as with African affairs (after 1899) and the affairs of Morocco. Correspondence with the British representative at Paris or elsewhere appears in these cases under F.O. Africa and F.O. Morocco. A third method was to separate the correspondence relating to a special aspect of affairs from the other papers of the country concerned, thus removing them from chronological sequence. This was the case with despatches on African affairs down to 1899, which appear in special series of F.O. France (Africa), F.O. Germany (Africa), etc."

A new system was inaugurated at the beginning of the year 1906. From that date all papers, irrespective of country, are first divided into certain general categories, "*Political*" (the former "diplomatic"), *Commercial, Consular, Treaty,* etc. The papers are, however, not removed from their original files, the contents of each file being treated as one document. The files of papers are classified within the general categories according to the country to which their subject most properly belongs. The volumes containing papers relating to any country are therefore in a sub-section of the main series, and these sub-sections are arranged in alphabetical order (*e.g.,* *Political,* Abyssinia, etc.). Previously the correspondence with, say, the British Ambassador at Paris was kept distinct from the communications of the French Ambassador in London, the latter being termed "Domestic." This distinction is now abolished and all papers relating to a subject are placed together in one file or in a series of files. The historian finds many difficulties in this arrangement, as the files are not arranged in the volumes in chronological or alphabetical sequence. The Foreign Office overcomes these difficulties by compiling a manuscript register of the

([1]) The date of the despatch, whether to or from London, and not of its reception, determines its place in the chronological sequence.

contents, but this method cannot be used so satisfactorily by the historian. It is to be feared that the new arrangement makes it more difficult for the historian to be sure he has found all the papers relating to a given incident.

As in the case of the pre-1906 series, documents dealing with certain topics are separately or specially treated. At the end of the series of volumes for each year in any main category (e.g., "1906 Political") there are a number of "case" volumes containing files dealing with important main topics. Thus several such volumes exist on the Algeciras Conference for the year 1906.

As in the previous period some papers appear to be missing from the Foreign Office Archives for the period covered by Volume III. In a few cases these have again been supplied from the Archives of the Embassies, e.g., those of Paris are important for the Anglo-French negotiations of 1905. But after this date the Archives of the Embassies are not available in England, and the Editors cannot therefore guarantee that some missing documents may not be found in future in the Chancery of one or other of our Embassies or Legations. In the period covered by Volumes I and II there were a number of documents, of which the actual text was missing in the files though recoverable from the "Confidential Print." The number of missing documents in the period covered by Volume III appears to be much less.

The year 1906 is memorable not only for a rearrangement of the papers. From that year onwards the British diplomatic representatives abroad were directed to compile and send to the Foreign Office at the end of each year a "General Report for the year . . . ." (commonly quoted as Annual Reports) on the affairs of the country to which they are accredited. Several extracts from these reports are here printed, and they are valuable as showing the importance attached by contemporary diplomatists to the events of each year.

As in the case of Volumes I–II, the private papers of Lord Sanderson now in the Foreign Office have again been used. To these have been added those of Sir Edward (Lord) Grey, and Sir Arthur Nicolson (Lord Carnock), which are less fragmentary than those of Lord Sanderson. They are referred to as "Sanderson MSS," "Grey MSS," and "Carnock MSS," respectively. A written opinion of Lord Sanderson, with a written comment by Lord Lansdowne, a written statement by Lord Sydenham and a portion of the Diary of Lord Haldane, describing his visit to Berlin in 1906, are also reproduced.

The text printed is in every case verbally identical with that given in the source whose reference appears at the head of the document. The text of out-going despatches is therefore that of the draft retained by the Foreign Office, except in a few cases where it is taken from the Embassy Archives. In the case of telegrams the original text is given wherever possible. In cases where the original has not been found, the official paraphase is reproduced, and is indicated by the letter "P" after the number of the telegram. The spelling of proper names, capitalisation, and punctuation in this volume have been made identical with those of the original document. As explained in Volumes I and II, the original texts have many inconsistencies in these matters, but it has not been thought desirable to correct them.

Plan of Volume III.

VOLUME II concluded with the signature of the Anglo-French Agreements of 8 April 1904. The first chapter of Volume III (Chapter XVI) deals with the settlement of points arising after the signature of the Treaties. Those relating to Newfoundland and Siam are described in the first section, which ends with the exchange of ratifications. The second part of the chapter deals with the adherence of the various Powers to the Khedivial Decree, which was an important feature of the Entente Agreement.

Chapter XVII begins the history of the first Morocco crisis. The first section describes the negotiations between France and Spain following on the Anglo-French Declaration, and ends with the Franco-Spanish Agreement of 3 October 1904. The second part, beginning with June 1904, describes the entry of Germany into Moroccan affairs. It ends in May 1905, when the Franco-German crisis had been reached.

The result of the crisis was the Anglo-French negotiation of April–June 1905, raising the so-called " guarantees " question. Chapter XVIII gives the text of all the important documents relating to this matter extant in the Foreign Office Records or in the archives of the British Embassy at Paris. The rumour of an Anglo-French alliance which was current in Germany is discussed in three despatches of June 1905. Some important minutes by King Edward complete the history. A few documents deal with the *Matin* revelations of October 1905. The chapter closes with a written opinion of Lord Sanderson on these negotiations, and a recent comment thereon by the late Lord Lansdowne.

Chapter XIX again deals with the affairs of Morocco, and describes the attitude of the Powers from May 1905 to the eve of the Algeciras Conference.

The renewal of the Anglo-French " conversations " in January 1906, and the opening of " conversations " with Belgium are the subjects of Chapter XX. The records of these in the Foreign Office archives are extremely scanty. Such papers as exist are however given in full, and show that the negotiations of 1906 were fully authorised by the Foreign Office. Detailed reports of the Anglo-Belgian conversations are added from the archives of the War Office, to which the British Military Attaché at Brussels, Colonel Barnardiston, made his reports. They are here printed for the first time, with the omission only of a few personal references; and they give a nearly complete account of these negotiations. The records of the similar conversations with France are very slight. The negotiations were conducted in London with the French Military Attaché, Major Huguet, and no record was left. The War Office file contains only a series of technical notes all emanating from the French side, of which a list is here printed. The contemporary naval negotiations with France were apparently even more informal, and the only record of them that can be found is a document in the Admiralty archives and a private letter from Sir E. Grey to Lord Tweedmouth in the Grey MSS., which are here printed. A written statement on the subject of this chapter made to the Editors by Lord Sydenham (then Secretary to the Committee for Imperial Defence) is also included.

Chapter XXI deals in some detail with the Algeciras Conference and describes every stage of the crisis.

The history of British relations with France and Germany to the end of 1906 is continued in Chapter XXII. Documents describing the meeting of King Edward and the German Emperor at Cronberg, and the second part of an important diary sent by Lord Haldane to King Edward describing his mission to Berlin, are here printed. An extract from the *General Report* on Spain for 1906 sums up the effects of the Moroccan negotiations on Spanish policy and prospects.

In the Appendix the full text is given of Mr. [Sir] Eyre Crowe's *Memorandum on the Present State of British Relations with France and Germany*, dated 1 January 1907, printed at the time for confidential circulation (Appendix A). Lord Sanderson expressed a somewhat different view in a counter-memorandum of which the full text is also given (Appendix B). It is annotated throughout by Mr. [Sir] Eyre Crowe, who defends the statements of his memorandum. This counter-memorandum, dated 21 February 1907, was not printed for confidential circulation until September 1908, but the original in Lord Sanderson's own hand was preserved by Sir Edward Grey among his private papers at the Foreign Office. The Editors have attached to this a document recording Lord Salisbury's opinion on the question of a combination of other Powers against England in 1900. The next document in the Appendix is an extract from the *General Report* on Germany for 1906, of which the most important feature is a long characterisation of Emperor William II by Sir Frank Lascelles, the British diplomatist who knew him best (Appendix C). Together with Lord Haldane's diary these documents supply first-hand evidence as to Anglo-German relations during 1906–7 of an almost unique kind. Appendix D contains the full text of one of the documents recording the results of the Anglo-French military conversations of 1906.

Erratum.

Page 311, No. 363, Line 8...   ...   ... For " French ports " read " eight ports."

xiii

LIST OF EDITORIAL NOTES.

Page.

Editorial notes of a purely formal character are printed on pp. 179, 285, 288, 339, 409.

List of Abbreviations.

A. & P. ... ... British Parliamentary Papers, Accounts and Papers.

B.F.S.P. ... ... British and Foreign State Papers.

G.P. ... ... Die Grosse Politik der Europäischen Kabinette.

Names of Writers of Minutes.

B.A. = Mr. (later Sir) Beilby Alston ... Assistant Clerk, Foreign Office, 1903–6; Acting Senior Clerk, 1906–7.

E.B. = Sir Eric Barrington ... ... Private Secretary to the Marquess of Lansdowne, 1900–5; Assistant Under-Secretary of State for Foreign Affairs, 1906–7.

E.A.C. = Mr. (later Sir) Eyre Crowe ... ... Senior Clerk, Foreign Office, 1906–12; Assistant Under-Secretary of State for Foreign Affairs, 1912–20; Permanent Under-Secretary, 1920–5.

F. = Lord Fitzmaurice ... ... Parliamentary Under-Secretary of State for Foreign Affairs, 1905–8.

E.G. = Sir Edward (later Viscount) Grey ... Secretary of State for Foreign Affairs, 11 December, 1905–11 December, 1916.

C.H. = Mr. (later Sir) Charles Hardinge ... Assistant Under-Secretary of State for Foreign Affairs, 1903–4; Ambassador at St. Petersburg, 1904–6; Permanent Under-Secretary of State, 1906–10; Minister in Attendance on King Edward at Friedrichshof, August, 1906.

L. = The Marquess of Lansdowne ... ... Secretary of State for Foreign Affairs, 12 November, 1900–11 December, 1905.

W.L. = Mr. (later Sir) W. Langley ... ... Senior Clerk, Foreign Office, 1902–7.

C.H.M. = Mr. (later Sir) C. H. Montgomery ... Private Secretary to Earl Percy, 1904–5; to Lord Fitzmaurice, 1905–6; and to Sir C. Hardinge, 1906–7.

O. = The Earl of Onslow ... ... Private Secretary to Sir A. Nicolson (Permanent Under-Secretary of State for Foreign Affairs), 1911–13.

S. = Sir T. H. (later Baron) Sanderson ... Permanent Under-Secretary of State for Foreign Affairs, 1894–1906.

G.S.S. = Mr. G. S. Spicer ... ... Private Secretary to Sir T. H. Sanderson, 1903–1906; Assistant Clerk, Foreign Office, 1906–1912.

List of King Edward's Minutes.

(Attached to the following documents.)

List of Statements by Lord Sanderson, Lord Lansdowne, Lord Sydenham and Lord Salisbury.

LIST OF DOCUMENTS.

Chapter XVI.
The Aftermath of the Anglo-French Treaties, 1904.

I.—The Ratification of the Agreements, May to December 1904.

II.—The Adherence of the Powers to the Khedivial Decree.

Chapter XVII.
Morocco, April 1904–May 1905.
I.—France, Spain and Morocco, April–October 1904.

b 2

Chapter XVIII.

The British "Guarantee" to France, April–October 1905.

Chapter XIX.

Morocco and the Powers, May–December 1905.

Chapter XX.
The Anglo-French and Anglo-Belgian Conversations of January–April 1906.

Chapter XXI.

The Algeciras Conference, January–April 1906.

I.—The Preliminaries.

II.—The Conference.

III.—The Aftermath.

Chapter XXII.

France and Germany after Algeciras.

Appendix A.

Appendix B.

No.	Name.	Date.	Main Subject.	Page
—	*From* Sir C. Hardinge	1907. 25 Feb.	Origin of Memorandum by Lord Sanderson. (*Minutes* by Sir E. Grey and Lord Fitzmaurice)	420
			Enclosure I : Lord Sanderson's *Observations on Mr. E. Crowe's Memorandum,* 21st February, 1907, with annotations by Mr. E. Crowe, Sir C. Hardinge, Sir E. Grey and Lord Fitzmaurice	421
			Ed. Note : Lord Salisbury to the Queen, 10th April, 1900	431
			Enclosure II : Memoranda by Sir L. Mallet of 25th February, 1907	431

Appendix C.

—	*From* Sir F. Lascelles	1907. 24 May	Extract from General Report on Germany for 1906. (*Minutes* by Sir E. Barrington and Mr. Eyre Crowe)	433

Appendix D.

—	*Note* by Major Huguet	1906. 13 Feb.	Military assistance in the event of war. *Text*	438

CHAPTER XVI.

THE AFTERMATH OF THE ANGLO-FRENCH TREATIES, 1904.

I.—THE RATIFICATION OF THE AGREEMENTS, MAY TO DECEMBER 1904.

No. 1.

Sir F. Lascelles to the Marquess of Lansdowne.

F.O. Germany (Prussia) 1593.
(No. 131.) Very Confidential.

My Lord,

Berlin, D. *May* 18, 1904.
R. *May* 23, 1904.

. . . . The Emperor, towards the end of the conversation,([1]) told me that his Government were preparing proposals for an arrangement similar to that recently concluded between England and France for the settlement of all questions pending between the two Governments. I replied that I was now awaiting Your Lordship's instructions on this subject. It appeared to me however that considerable discussion would be required before we could come to terms, or as I put it in the familiar language in which His Majesty allows me to speak to him " we should want a deal of bargaining." There were also some points raised by Baron von Richthofen to which I thought it would be impossible for His Majesty's Government to agree for instance, compensation for losses incurred by Germany during the war in South Africa. His Majesty interrupted me here to say that I should remember that the Bond Holders of the South African Railway had suffered severe loss and deserved compensation, to which I replied that I understood that this question was about to be settled, but the point raised by Baron von Richthofen was a different one and seemed to imply that in certain cases German subjects should receive compensation which, in similar cases had been refused to British subjects. Then, again, the question of the Samoan claims was in itself a matter of very small importance and involved only a small amount of money, but in that question His Majesty's Government and the Government of the United States had been acting together, and it would be necessary to obtain the consent of the latter to a settlement of it. His Majesty observed that he did not anticipate much difficulty on that head as the German and United States' Governments were on very good terms. . . . .

I have, &c.
FRANK C. LASCELLES.

([1]) [At luncheon at the Neues Palais. The first part of this despatch is omitted here as it refers to Mediterranean policy. It will be published in a later volume in a chapter dealing with that subject. A few sentences are omitted at the end; relate to personal details.]

No. 2.

The Marquess of Lansdowne to Sir E. Monson.

F.O. France 3693.
(No. 287.)

Sir,

Foreign Office, June 6, 1904.

The French Ambassador told me to-day that the recently concluded Convention between France and Great Britain in regard to Newfoundland had provoked a considerable amount of opposition in those French constituencies which had an interest

B

in the Newfoundland fisheries. M. Delcassé was to appear to-morrow before the Parliamentary Committee to which the Convention had been referred, and he was extremely anxious for information upon the following points :—

1. How did we intend to define the mouths of the rivers from which the French fishermen are to be excluded?
2. What was intended with regard to the subsidized factories in which the cold storage of bait was resorted to for the supply of the Newfoundland fishermen—a supply which was denied to the French fishermen?
3. Sir Robert Bond was reported to have said in debate in the Newfoundland Assembly that the provision in Article II of the Convention, under which the right of fishing was restricted to the customary season, ending the 20th October, applied only to the French, and that the fishermen of other nationalities would be permitted to take part in the fishery which was pursued later in the year.

I furnished his Excellency with information to the following effect upon these points :—

As to 1, it had been found impossible to give a general definition of the point where a river enters the sea, and it was believed that in each case the point must be settled by a consideration of the local circumstances. An endeavour would be made to indicate the line of separation on a Chart, but probably an examination on the spot by experts on behalf of the two Governments would be necessary.

His Majesty's Government were ready however to state at once that they did not intend to claim such an interpretation of the phrase as would exclude the French fishermen from any waters which have hitherto by common consent been recognized as forming part of Bays in which they had the right to fish.

As to 2, His Majesty's Government were not as yet in possession of the exact terms of the Concession given by the Newfoundland Government for a Company to prepare and store frozen bait.

According to the terms of the Convention of the 8th April, French fishing-vessels resorting to the Treaty Shore would have the right of procuring supplies of frozen bait which may be for sale in the harbours of that portion of the coast, subject to the local Regulations.

His Majesty's Government could not however insist on factories or stores for this purpose being established on this part of the coast, still less on their being assisted by a subsidy from the Newfoundland Government. The Newfoundland Government had clearly the right to arrange that the factories should be established at the places most serviceable to their own fishermen, who were competing at great disadvantage with the bounty-fed French fishery.

As to 3, the meaning which His Majesty's Government attached to the provision of Article II of the Convention in regard to the termination of the usual fishery season on the 20th October of each year was that at that date the general summer fishery, in which alone France has been entitled to share, comes to an end. If for any special reason the season should be prolonged for a few days the French fishermen would share in the prolongation. There was however a subsequent fishery in which the French have never been entitled to take part, and His Majesty's Government continue to reserve this latter fishery for those who have hitherto enjoyed the right to participate in it.

I am, &c.
LANSDOWNE.

P.S.—M. Cambon inquired, with regard to point 2, whether there was anything to prevent a French citizen from acquiring a house or land on the Treaty Shore and establishing there a frozen bait factory. I said that I was unable to tell his Excellency whether such an establishment would be in accordance with the local Regulations or not. At his request I promised to make inquiry.

No. 3.

Sir E. Monson to the Marquess of Lansdowne.

F.O. France 3666.
(No. 347.) Paris, D. June 7, 1904.
My Lord, R. June 9, 1904.

I have the honour to inclose the text, which I have just received, of a Bill for the approval of the Anglo-French Convention of the 8th of April last, respecting Newfoundland and Western and Central Africa. The Bill was laid before the Chamber of Deputies on the 7th instant and referred to the Committee on Foreign Affairs.

I have, &c.
EDMUND MONSON.

Enclosure in No. 3.

Projet de Loi portant approbation d'une Convention concernant Terre-Neuve et l'Afrique Occidentale et Centrale (renvoyé à la Commission des Affaires Extérieures, des Protectorats, et des Colonies), présenté, au nom de M. Émile Loubet, Président de la République Française, par M. Delcassé, Ministre des Affaires Étrangères, et par M. Gaston Doumergue, Ministre des Colonies.

Exposé des Motifs.

Messieurs,

Par la Convention concernant Terre-Neuve et l'Afrique qui est soumise aujourd'hui à l'approbation du Parlement, le Gouvernement de la République, d'accord avec celui de la Grande-Bretagne, s'est appliqué à supprimer un certain nombre de causes de contestation dont on pouvait craindre que la persistance risquât d'altérer les bonnes relations des deux puissances. Animées de dispositions également conciliantes, elles se sont entendues pour mettre fin simultanément à des difficultés qui tendaient à se produire ou à se prolonger sur les points les plus opposés du globe. Grâce à des concessions réciproques qui ménagent les intérêts essentiels de leurs ressortissants, et qui ont été déterminées surtout par les changements qu'a subis l'ancien état des choses, les deux gouvernements ont pu transformer, dans la mesure qui leur a paru indispensable, les conditions dans lesquelles, d'une part, s'exerceront désormais les droits dont nos marins jouissent sur les côtes de Terre-Neuve, et, de l'autre, se développera à l'avenir l'action parallèle de la France et de l'Angleterre sur les territoires de l'Ouest et du Centre africains nouvellement ouverts à nos entreprises et à notre commerce.

Il serait superflu de procéder, dans cet exposé des motifs, à un examen détaillé des stipulations sur lesquelles l'entente s'est établie entre les négociateurs. Le recueil de documents diplomatiques qui vient de vous être distribué débute par une dépêche circulaire aux ambassadeurs de la République, où sont réunis tous les renseignements de nature à pleinement éclairer les membres des deux Assemblées. Vous trouverez notamment, dans ce document, un historique des relations que les pêcheurs Français entretiennent, depuis le 18e siècle, avec les autorités terre-neuviennes. La situation privilégiée qui leur a été consentie par les Traités d'Utrecht et de Versailles, les modifications successives qui résultent de l'accroissement de la population de l'île, non moins que des façons nouvelles de pratiquer la pêche, les conflits d'intérêts qui s'élevaient et s'accusaient chaque année davantage entre nos nationaux et les insulaires, sont relatés de façon à faire clairement comprendre la nécessité où, des deux côtés, on s'est trouvé de modifier l'ancien régime conventionnel.

En échange des avantages à tirer de la mise en exploitation de la partie du littoral terre-neuvien, où nous avions un droit d'usage que nous n'exercions presque plus, le Gouvernement britannique nous cède en Afrique des territoires qui nous seront précieux pour l'œuvre de pénétration et de civilisation à laquelle nos coloniaux consacrent de si vaillants efforts. L'accès à la rivière de Gambie, l'annexion des îles de Los qui commandent notre port de Konakry, l'ouverture d'une route permanente du Niger au Tchad paraîtront, nous n'en saurions douter, des compensations suffisantes aux nouveaux arrangements concernant Terre-Neuve, alors surtout qu'en renonçant à ce qu'il y avait de suranné et de vexatoire dans les anciennes stipulations, nous avons assuré à nos marins les facilités dont ils ont besoin pour continuer de fréquenter les parages de l'île.

C'est pourquoi nous soumettons à votre approbation le projet de Loi suivant :—

Projet de Loi.

Le Président de la République Française

Décrète :

Le projet de loi dont la teneur suit sera présenté à la Chambre des Députés par le Ministre des Affaires Étrangères et par le Ministre des Colonies, qui sont chargés d'en exposer les motifs et d'en soutenir la discussion :—

Article unique.—Le Président de la République est autorisé à ratifier et, s'il y a lieu, à faire exécuter la Convention conclue le 8 Avril, 1904, entre le Gouvernement de la République Française et celui de S[a] M[ajesté] le Roi de Grande-Bretagne et d'Irlande et des territoires britanniques au delà des mers, empereur des Indes, concernant Terre-Neuve et l'Afrique occidentale et centrale.

Une copie authentique de cet acte sera annexée à la présente loi.

Fait à Paris, le 25 Mai, 1904.

(Signé) ÉMILE LOUBET.

Par le Président de la République :

Le Ministre des Affaires étrangères,
(Signé) DELCASSÉ.

Le Ministre des Colonies,
(Signé) GASTON DOUMERGUE.

No. 4.

Colonial Office to Foreign Office.

F.O. France 3693. *Downing Street*, D. *June* 18, 1904.
Sir, R. *June* 24, 1904.

I am directed by Mr. Secretary Lyttelton to acknowledge the receipt of your letter of the 13th instant forwarding copy of a Memorandum([1]) received from the French Ambassador relative to the Act recently passed by the Legislature of Newfoundland confirming a Contract entered into by the Colonial Government with the Newfoundland Cold Storage and Reduction Company, and to the claim of the French to participate in the autumn and winter fishery on the Treaty Shore.

2. I am also to acknowledge the receipt of your letter of the 18th instant, forwarding drafts of the Memoranda which Lord Lansdowne proposes to address to M. Cambon in reply.

3. Mr. Lyttelton concurs in the terms of these Memoranda, and directs me to take this opportunity of transmitting to you, for his Lordship's information, copy of a

([1]) [Not reproduced.]

despatch recently received from the Officer Administering the Government of Newfoundland forwarding copies of the Act in question together with a Report by his Attorney-General on its provisions.

4. While it is true, as stated in the draft Memorandum on the subject of the Cold Storage of Bait, that the Act in question contains no provisions which would prevent persons or companies unassisted by the Government from setting up Cold Bait Factories on the Treaty Shore, Mr. Lyttelton would like to observe, with reference to the inquiry of M. Cambon reported in your letter of the 10th instant, that if there is no frozen bait for sale on the Treaty Shore there is nothing in the Convention which entitles the French to claim that bait prepared in that particular manner should be on sale, any more than salted bait or any particular kind of bait, or to claim the right of erecting Cold Bait factories for themselves. On the other hand, the Convention gives the Colony a free hand in deciding what buildings shall or shall not be erected on the Treaty Shore. It will therefore be possible for the Colonial Government if they choose either to prohibit altogether the erection of Cold Bait factories on the Treaty Shore, or to make the erection of each such factory the subject of special permission. The Bait Act of 1889, which is of general application and can of course be applied to the Treaty Shore as strictly as to the other parts of the Colony provided that the Treaty rights of the French now for the first time clearly defined are not infringed, appears to confer this power, but Mr. Lyttelton will be in a better position to suggest an answer to M. Cambon's inquiry after consulting with Sir R. Bond. In any case, if the Bait Act does not confer the necessary power, there would seem to be nothing to prevent the Colonial Government from obtaining it by legislation.

I am, &c.

H. BERTRAM COX.

No. 5.

Memorandum by Sir T. H. Sanderson.

F.O. France 3693. *Foreign Office, June* 30, 1904.

The French Ambassador and the Comte de Montferrand came by appointment this afternoon, and discussed with me and Captain Montgomerie, R.N., certain questions relating to the provisions of the new Convention for the regulation of the Newfoundland fishery.

The first of these points, of which he had given me a memorandum, related to the question of the fishing implements to be employed on the Treaty Shore. The French Government wished to have some assurance that Seine nets, lobster pots, bultows, salmon nets, and herring nets would not be forbidden the French fishermen. I proposed to him a formula which had been suggested by Sir Robert Bond, as follows :—

" The nets and fishing engines to be used shall be such only as are permitted to Newfoundland fishermen by the competent authority of the Government of Newfoundland. French fishermen will be allowed to use such implements on the same conditions as Newfoundland fishermen, except that they will not be permitted to land or in any way make use of the shore or foreshore."

The French Ambassador and Comte de Montferrand objected strongly to this latter provision. They said that by Article II of the Convention France retained for her citizens the right of fishing on the coast on a footing of equality with British subjects, that the Seine was the net which they most frequently used on the coast, and that it was unduly to strain the provisions of the Convention to forbid to French fishermen in future the necessary right which they had always hitherto enjoyed of dragging the net to the shore. It was an ordinary fishing operation and quite distinct from the use of the shore for other purposes. In reply to an objection on my part that on some portions of the coast the use of the Seine was at certain times forbidden, as it was supposed to interfere with other methods of fishing, the Ambassador stated that they would not object to temporary prohibitions of this nature by the officers charged with the police of the fishery, and he eventually proposed a formula to the following effect :—

> "French fishermen shall be allowed to use on the Treaty Shore such implements as are permitted to Newfoundland fishermen on the rest of the coast. The use of the Seine shall be permitted as heretofore, with power to the officers charged with the police of the fisheries to forbid it when it may prejudice other modes of fishery."

On point 2—the proposal for some general assurance that French fishermen shall not be subjected to treatment in regard to the purchase of bait less favourable than that granted to British fishermen on other parts of the coast—I observed that we were assured by Sir Robert Bond that British fishermen did not buy bait at all, but took it for themselves, and I offered the assurance suggested by Sir Robert Bond, in the following terms :—

> "His Majesty's Government are ready to agree that French fishing vessels shall be allowed to purchase bait on the Treaty coast on terms not less favourable than those at present accorded to other foreign fishing vessels on other parts of the island."

The French Ambassador and Comte de Montferrand objected that this was not what was assured to them by the Convention, which stated that French fishermen might obtain supplies of bait on the same conditions as the inhabitants of Newfoundland. They added that the licences issued to foreign fishing vessels were subject to a very considerable charge of about eight shillings per registered ton of the vessel, and that if licences were to be required of the French fishermen, they had a right to claim licences gratis, as provided for under the regulations for British subjects.

We passed to point 3—the question of the establishment of cold-storage factories for bait on the Treaty Coast.

I said that Sir Robert Bond had stated that it would be quite impossible for the Newfoundland Government to permit the establishment of factories of this description by foreigners on the Treaty Shore, that it would give to the French fishermen a position of perfect equality in regard to the supply of bait, and that, in view of the bounties which were accorded by the French Government, they would then have the means of ruining the fishing industry of the island.

The French Ambassador said that he thought this a most exaggerated view, that in present circumstances the French fishermen had the right of obtaining from the Treaty Shore an unrestricted supply of bait, and that there was nothing to prevent their freezing that bait if they pleased on board a hulk or vessel constructed for the purpose. He added that the Convention plainly indicated that the French would continue in the enjoyment of an unrestricted right of fishing for bait, and that he did not see on what grounds they could be forbidden to freeze it or transfer it to another person for the purpose of being frozen. The Comte de Montferrand said that M. Delcassé had undoubtedly sanctioned the Convention under the impression that it secured this right to French fishermen, and they both agreed that if M. Delcassé was not able to inform the French Chambers that they had secured this right, the Convention would be rejected.

The matter was discussed at some length without our being able to arrive at any further conclusion.

In regard to point 4, concerning the terms on which a point on the south coast might be designated at which French fishermen should be at liberty to purchase bait, I told M. Cambon that I had Sir Robert Bond's authority for saying that if the French would abandon their bounties the Newfoundland Government were ready to concede to them equal fishing rights with those of Newfoundland all over the island.

M. Cambon said he knew this, but that it was absolutely impossible for the French Government to abandon their bounties altogether. What he wished to learn was whether any modification of the bounty system could be suggested as an equivalent for the concession he had mentioned.

I told him that I understood that Sir Robert Bond would consider this question.

Finally, in regard to point 5—the question of the right to share in the herring fishery allowed to American fishermen after the 20th October—I told M. Cambon that this concession was secured by a special Treaty provision with the United States, and that it was impossible for us to admit that the retention by France of her previous fishing rights could be held to have been extended to this perfectly separate fishery in virtue of the introduction of the words "for all persons" in connection with the date of the termination of the summer fishery season. M. Cambon asked to be supplied with a copy of the Treaty under which the United States enjoyed access to this fishery.

T. H. S[ANDERSON].

Foreign Office, June 30, 1904.

No. 6.

The Marquess of Lansdowne to Sir E. Monson.

F.O. France 3694.
(No. 362.)
Sir,   *Foreign Office, July 5, 1904.*

The French Ambassador spoke to me again yesterday with much earnestness as to the difficulties which M. Delcassé was encountering in his endeavours to obtain the acceptance of the Newfoundland Convention by the French Chamber.

His Exc[ellenc]y's arguments were mostly of the kind which he had used in previous conversations upon the same subject. He advanced however one new proposal, namely, that the French Government might give up their fishing rights on the eastern portion of the Treaty Shore between the Straits of Belleisle and Cape St. John in exchange for a "point d'approvisionnement" at which they would procure bait on the south coast. I refused to entertain this proposal, upon the ground that it would be impossible for me to recommend either to my colleagues or to the Government of Newfoundland a condition wholly beyond the scope of the Convention. I repeated, in reply to another suggestion by his Exc[ellenc]y, my objection to discussing the question of allowing the French fishermen to participate in the winter fishery. The discussion eventually narrowed itself to two points :—

1. The right of French fishermen to use seine nets and other implements on the Treaty Shore; and
2. Their right to procure bait.

As to No. 1, I said that it seemed to me that the intention of the Convention was clear. The French fishermen were to retain the rights of fishing which they already enjoyed, but on a footing of equality with British subjects, and subject to the same local regulations. I presumed therefore that whatever implements could be used by British subjects could also be used by French subjects. His Excellency suggested that an enumeration of the different kinds of implements might be desirable. I deprecated any attempt of the kind upon the ground that it would probably be incomplete and that we should be much safer in relying upon the general proposition.

2. With regard to the purchase of bait, I said that it seemed to me that in this case also the words of the Convention were clear. The French were given the right of

entering any port or harbour on the Treaty Shore, and there obtaining supplies of bait on the same conditions as the inhabitants of Newfoundland, but subject to the local regulations in force. It did not seem to be at all probable that these regulations would be framed in such a manner as to oust the French fishermen from their rights, but it would be time enough to raise the question should the French Government hereafter take exception to the Regulations, as being inconsistent with the Convention. I pointed out however that the French fishermen had never been allowed an unrestricted right of buying bait on the Treaty Shore, and that both they and the local fishermen had been restricted to such an amount of bait as would suffice for the equipment of the individual ship. We never should have allowed and never could allow a steamer of two or three thousand tons burthen to come in to the Treaty Shore, take on board a cargo of bait, and then convey it to the Banks.

We renewed our conversation to-day and at the close of it I wrote his Exc[ellenc]y a letter, of which a copy is attached to this despatch.

[I am, &c.]
L[ANSDOWNE].

Enclosure in No. 6.

The Marquess of Lansdowne to M. Cambon.

Dear M. Cambon,   *Foreign Office, July 5,* 1904.

You mentioned to me to-day that M. Delcassé wished to be able to satisfy the French Parliamentary Commission that the rights of the French fishermen upon the Treaty Coast of Newfoundland were sufficiently protected by the recently concluded Convention, and you proposed to me that with this object I shou'd give you certain further assurances as to the manner in which various hypothetical cases might be dealt with.

I ventured in reply to call your Excellency's attention to the wording of Article II of the Convention, under which France retains for her citizens on a footing of equality with British subjects the right of fishing on the Treaty Coast. The same Article gives the French fishermen the right of fishing on that coast for every kind of fish, including bait and shell fish, and of entering into any port or harbour on the said coast, and there obtaining supplies or bait on the same conditions as the inhabitants of Newfoundland, subject to the local regulations in force.

I reminded your Excellency that on the 8th April, in reply to a question which you had put to me, I gave you an assurance that the Article as worded precluded the suppression of the liberty hitherto enjoyed by the French fishermen of purchasing bait on the portion of the coast mentioned.

I also reminded your Excellency that on the 24th June I communicated to you a memorandum in which it was distinctly stated that the Convention preserved to French fishermen the right of purchasing bait on the Treaty Coast, subject to such regulations as are now in force or may hereafter be adopted by the local legislature in respect to the capture and sale of bait fishes. The memorandum went on to say that it was understood that such regulations would be applicable equally to British fishermen, and that this would leave French fishermen in the enjoyment of the same facilities for prosecuting the fishery on the Banks as they hitherto had had.

These declarations seemed to me, I must say, amply sufficient in order to enable M. Delcassé to make out a good Parliamentary case. I see, on the other hand, great objections to assurances dealing with difficulties which have not yet arisen, and with matters of detail with which we are of necessity but imperfectly acquainted. It is therefore with some hesitation that I offer any opinion upon the following points which you raised in your conversation with me to-day. I offer however the following observations for what they are worth :—

(1.) It seems to me that there is nothing to prevent French fishermen who catch bait on the Treaty Coast from taking it away and disposing of it elsewhere. On the other hand the traffic in bait on the Treaty Coast must be, as it has hitherto been, subject to local regulations applicable indiscriminately to French and British fishermen.

I feel no doubt that the Newfoundland Government will honourably respect the Agreement which has been arrived at with regard to the sale and purchase of bait. Should, however, the effect of any local regulations hereafter adopted by them be, in the opinion of the French Government, such as to prejudice the rights of the French fishermen under the Convention, it would be for the French Government to call the attention of His Majesty's Government to the matter with the view to assuring the fulfilment of the terms of the Convention.

(2.) With regard to the use of seines and other fishing implements, I interpret the Convention as laying down that French fishermen shall have the right of using the same implements as they have hitherto been in the habit of using and in the same manner as British fishermen on the Treaty Coast, subject however to any local regulations for the protection or improvement of the fishery. These regulations would of course apply equally to fishermen of both nationalities.

(3.) I am not aware of any reason for which a French subject would be precluded from the right of acquiring or renting land or business premises on the Treaty Coast.

(4.) You suggested to me that we might at some future time enter into an arrangement under which France might give up the rights of French fishermen on the eastern portion of the Treaty Coast in exchange for a "point d'approvisionnement" on the south coast. I feel quite sure that this point could not be raised with any advantage at the present time, and that it would be bad policy to raise it.

I am, &c.
LANSDOWNE.

No. 7.

Sir E. Monson to the Marquess of Lansdowne.

F.O. France 3668.
(No. 567.) Confidential.
My Lord,

Paris, D. *November* 1, 1904.
R. *November* 2, 1904.

I have the honour to transmit herewith to Your Lordship copies of a report([1]) drawn up by M. Deloncle, on behalf of the Foreign Affairs Commission of the Chamber of Deputies, in which he recommends the Chamber to ratify the Convention with Siam signed on the 13th of February, 1904.

This recommendation is hedged in with many reserves and conditions, and it has served M. Deloncle with an opportunity of setting forth once more the views of the extremists of the Colonial Party with regard to the policy of France towards Siam.

It may suffice to call Your Lordship's attention to the following points.

The various frontiers marked in the map which accompanied the text of the Treaty are accepted by M. Deloncle only on the understanding that they may be regarded as merely provisional. In his opinion the boundary to the North of the Great Lake requires ultimate extension westwards, so as to include in the French Dominions the whole of the ancient Cambodian provinces of Battambong, Siem Reap, and Sisophon. Similarly Luang Prabang must be made to embrace a number of districts, excluded by the terms of the Convention but regarded by M. Deloncle as belonging historically to that "Kingdom." As regards the boundary from the Great Lake to the Sea, M. Deloncle is not satisfied with the line marked out in the supplementary Protocol with Siam of June 29, 1904,([2]) as forwarded to Your Lordship in my despatch No. 394 of July 1. He proposes a considerable addition to the country assigned by that instrument to France, and he insists on the necessity of the Port of Krat being secured from Siamese attacks by pushing the frontier back so as to exclude from Siam the whole of the valleys of the rivers falling into the Krat estuary.

([1]) [Not reproduced.]
([2]) [Printed *B.F.S.P.*, Vol. 97, pp. 965–7.]

The evacuation of Chantabun, which was to follow closely upon the surrender to France of the districts designated by the Convention, should be postponed, according to M. Deloncle, until the new arrangements have been formally accepted by the Governor of French Indo China in Council, and until the points on the right bank of the Mekong, assigned to France by the Convention have been completely delimited.

The barracks at Chantabun should be retained by France and a French Consul appointed to reside there, to protect the natives friendly to France.

M. Deloncle calls upon Siam to guarantee that she will never allow a Foreign Power to exercise influence or establish a coaling station at Chantabun.

In the neutral zone along the Mekong, which Monsieur Deloncle regards as still existing, notwithstanding the terms of the Treaty, he includes the territory between the Me Ing and the British Frontier, forming part of the neutralized portion of Siam under the Anglo-French Agreement of 1896. Throughout the zone Siam, he considers, is still precluded, not only from erecting fortifications, but from constructing "Strategic railways."

In order to exercise an effective control over the Military and financial Departments of the Siamese Government, M. Deloncle demands that a French "Adviser" be attached to those Departments. The main object to be secured is the strict observance by Siam of her undertakings in respect of the employment of Siamese troops and native police in the regions adjoining the French Possessions, and in respect of the execution of certain public works in the French sphere as recognised by the Anglo-French Agreement of April 8, 1904.

Article 8 of the Convention refers, among other points, to the construction of railways along the right bank of the Mekong at points where navigation is difficult. M. Deloncle demands under this article the immediate concession by Siam of a trunk line connecting Lakhon on the Upper Mekong with Kranchmar, a point lying a little to the North of Pnom Penh, the Cambodian Capital. This line is to counteract the effect of the British line said to be under contemplation to connect Singapoor [sic] and Burmah.

The Pnom Penh Battambong Railway (Article 9) is stated by M. Deloncle to be merely accessory to a more extensive project, presumably the prolongation to Bangkok.

Much stress is laid on the importance of swelling to the utmost the list of Asiatics in Siam under French protection, and France is called upon to rescue from outrage at the hands of Siam the hundreds of thousands of Laotians, Annamites and Cambodians who, though excluded by Articles 10 and 11 from those lists, must continue nevertheless to be the objects of the special solicitude of the country from which emanated the Declaration of the Rights of Man.

The Convention, in short, is submitted for adoption only as a point of departure requiring unlimited development on the lines laid down by M. Deloncle.

Siam is warned against any failure on her part to accept, in a friendly spirit, these indications of the treatment which the protagonists of the Colonial Party inform her that she is to expect at the hands of France.

I have. &c.
EDMUND MONSON.

MINUTES.

Franco-Siamese Convention.

M. Deloncle, the Reporter of the Committee, recommends the Chamber to adopt the Convention, but has seized the opportunity to suggest an interpretation which in some cases the text does not bear, and to outline a future policy towards Siam which would reopen all the questions which the Convention is supposed to settle.

The Convention is to be treated as a starting point to enable fresh agreements to be forced on Siam and fresh encroachments made, and the policy advocated is as fair to Siam as one would expect from an extreme member of the French Colonial Party.

The report must be read with the map attached to the Convention (annexed), and the complete text of the Convention will be found at p. 34 of the enclosure among the Annexes to the Report.

I annex a short Memo[randum] by Mr. Lampson showing the most important points of M. Deloncle's proposals respecting each article.([1])

It remains to be seen how far the Chamber will adopt M. Deloncle's view and what assurances the Colonial Party can extract from the French Government during the discussion on the Bill.

W. L.

I do not think we are in any way bound to take up M. Deloncle's statements upon this or upon any other points dealt with by the Convention. His interpretation of the Newfoundland portion of it is, *e.g.*, extremely strained. We shall be in a difficult position if the Chamber insists on making terms.

L.

([1]) [The memorandum and map are missing from the volume.]

No. 8.

Sir E. Monson to the Marquess of Lansdowne.

F.O. France 3668.
(No. 576.)
My Lord,

Paris, D. *November* 9, 1904.
R. *November* 10, 1904.

The interest of yesterday's debate on the Anglo-French Agreements centres mainly in the speech delivered by M. Etienne. When the President of the Foreign Affairs Committee rose to defend the Agreement, the Chamber, which had until then been but sparsely attended, immediately filled, and the speaker was listened to with great attention.

In expressing his entire approval of the Agreement, M. Etienne dwelt on the immense importance of an understanding between the two countries which should remove the causes of jealousy, of ill-feeling and of possible conflict necessarily brought into existence by the French Colonial policy of the past thirty years. He spoke with generous appreciation of the work accomplished by England in Egypt, and expressed his firm conviction that France would succeed in establishing her influence in Morocco by methods of "peaceful penetration." At the close of his discourse he declared emphatically that France remained the friend and ally of Russia; and desired to strengthen that friendship because she hoped one day to bring about an understanding between Russia and Great Britain. This sentiment was received with general applause, in which however the Socialist wing of the Left did not join.

The official report of the debate, which will be resumed to-morrow, is enclosed herewith.([1])

I have, &c.
EDMUND MONSON.

([1]) [Not reproduced.]

No. 9.

Sir E. Monson to the Marquess of Lansdowne.

F.O. France 3668.
(No. 577.)
My Lord,

Paris, D. *November* 11, 1904.
R. *November* 12, 1904.

Yesterday's debate on the Anglo-French Agreements was decidedly of greater interest than those of the previous days, including as it did speeches by such recognized authorities on foreign affairs as Mess[ieu]rs de Pressensé and Denys Cochin, by the Socialist leader, M. Jaurès, and by the Minister of Foreign Affairs himself.

The two first-named Deputies both spoke in favour of the ratification of the Agreements, M. de Pressensé approving them unreservedly, while M. Cochin submitted them to a severe criticism. M. Jaurès also warmly defended the Agreements, but the interest of his speech lay, perhaps, not so much in his eloquent remarks upon the Arrangement between Great Britain and France, as in the exposition which he gave of his views regarding the Franco-Russian Alliance, and the Alsace-Lorraine question.

The Minister for Foreign Affairs commenced his discourse by saying that the arrangements now under consideration constituted the result of a policy steadily pursued during the last six years—a policy based upon the Franco-Russian Alliance— as to which he said that it formed "a precious condition of the equilibrium of the greatest forces of the world." He then at once proceeded to reply to the criticisms directed against the Newfoundland Arrangement, with especial reference to the Bait Bill. He explained clearly that the abrogation of the Bait Bill could be obtained only at the price of the abolition of the French Fishing Bounties; and maintained that the solution of the difficulties of the French fishermen with regard to bait was to be found in improved methods of transporting the bait, and of preserving it. Passing to the concessions obtained by France in Africa in return for the abandonment of some of her rights in Newfoundland, he said that she acquired in West and Central Africa advantages for which she had long striven in vain.

Coming to the arrangement regarding Egypt and Morocco, M. Delcassé showed that he had taken ample precautions to safeguard the positive interests which France possessed in Egypt. He went on to say that the prosperity of Algiers and Tunis, which "constituted for France a precious reservoir of economic riches and political force," was of necessity dependent upon the fate of Morocco. Hence the problem which presented itself was "to establish the preponderance of France in Morocco, and in consequence to increase her strength in the Mediterranean, without alienating, but on the contrary while conciliating," the Powers interested. With regard to Spain, international equity, considerations of general policy, and the necessity of guaranteeing the undisturbed fulfilment of French policy in Morocco alike dictated an understanding, which should recognize Spain's titles and interests in Morocco, and at the same time respect the territorial integrity of that country, and the Sovereignty of the Sultan counselled and fortified by France. To these limits the *pourparlers* with the Spanish Government were confined, and on these bases was founded the understanding expressed in the Declaration of October 3, 1904,[1] of which the fundamental provisions had not been modified or even attenuated by anything that had passed either before or after.

It was now, M. Delcassé said, for France to persuade Morocco by acts rather than speeches that she had the will as well as the power, to carry out her task which was, he said: in her own interest to further the interests of Morocco, for her own tranquillity to aid Morocco in establishing tranquillity and order, for her own prosperity to furnish Morocco with the means of developing her resources so that Morocco should know the power of France only by the benefits she received from her.

In conclusion, M. Delcassé said that what France surrendered was of value especially to England and what England surrendered was of value especially to France; on both sides fundamental interests were safeguarded and both parties had reason to be well content. The world was to-day satisfied that France sought her own advantage only in the harmony between her own interests and those of other nations.

On the termination of M. Delcassé's speech the Chamber decided, by 320 votes to 243, to adjourn the discussion until to-morrow, the 12th instant. The official report of the proceedings is inclosed.[2]

I have, &c.
EDMUND MONSON.

[1] [*v. infra* pp. 49-52, No. 59.]
[2] [Not reproduced.]

No. 10.

Sir E. Monson to the Marquess of Lansdowne.

F.O. France 3668.
(No. 582.)   *Paris,* D. *November* 13, 1904.
My Lord,   R. *November* 14, 1904.

I had the honour of informing Your Lordship last night, by telegraph, of the final result of the debate in the Chamber of Deputies on the Anglo-French Agreements.

Yesterday the Chamber having listened to some three or four more speeches, directed mainly against the provisions affecting Newfoundland, proceeded, before voting upon the Bill approving the African and Newfoundland Agreements to deal with various orders of the day and motions which were submitted. By 436 votes to 94 the Deputies adopted an order of the day approving the declarations of the Government, and rejecting any additional suggestion. An order of the day submitted by M. Archdeacon (Nationalist) to the effect that the Chamber would abandon no French territory was refused priority by 435 votes to 60. A motion by M. Riotteau calling on the Government to open supplementary negotiations respecting Newfoundland was repelled by M. Delcassé and was defeated by 385 votes to 174.

The result of these divisions was generally regarded in the Chamber as a foregone conclusion. But a motion which was submitted by M. Denys Cochin (Conservative), M. Deschanel, and M. Etienne gave rise to a slightly more doubtful situation. It ran : " The Chamber, taking note of the declarations made in the Tribune by the Minister of Foreign Affairs, counts on him to open negotiations as early as possible in that sense with the British Government." The declarations alluded to are statements made by M. Delcassé in his speech of the 10th instant to the effect that the Newfoundland Arrangement did not exclude the possibility of new ameliorations, of further improvements.

The Minister of Foreign Affairs was evidently considerably embarrassed by this motion. Probably it was a complete surprise to him, as it was to the greater part of the Chamber, to find the President of the Foreign Affairs Committee associated in it with M. Cochin, an Opposition member, and M. Deschanel, one of the severest critics of the Arrangement. M. Delcassé did not venture, although strongly urged by M. Jaurès to do so, to repel the motion as he had repelled that of M. Riotteau. He said " the motion . . . takes note of my declarations, and calls on me to realize these further ameliorations as soon as possible. In that sense . . . I accept the motion." It was then carried by 457 votes to 5.

Thereupon the Chamber voted the Bill approving the Newfoundland and African Agreements by a majority of 338, there being 443 ayes and 105 noes. The official report of the proceedings is inclosed.(¹)

It is expected that the Agreements will come before the Senate in about ten days.

I have, &c.
EDMUND MONSON.

(¹) [Not reproduced.]

No. 11.

Sir E. Monson to the Marquess of Lansdowne.

F.O. France 3668.
(No. 586.) Confidential.   *Paris,* D. *November* 15, 1904.
My Lord,   R. *November* 16, 1904.

In my despatch No. 582 of the day before yesterday([1]) I had the honour to report what passed at the sitting of the Chamber of Deputies the preceding afternoon and the final adoption of the Anglo-French Agreement and the Convention forming an integral part of that agreement by the more popular division of the Legislature.

I have not yet had an opportunity of seeing M. Delcassé since the deciding vote was taken; but I anticipate his assurance that he is entirely satisfied with the result of the debates. Nevertheless I am disposed to think that he must have passed many anxious hours before the conclusion was reached, and that he found himself confronted with difficulties considerably more threatening than he had admitted to me. His Excellency never fails to impress on me that he has no claim to be a " Parliamentary expert; " and it is notorious that he avoids as much as possible attendance to the ordinary duties of a deputy. He will never go near the Chamber if he can help it; and as the Ministry for Foreign Affairs is only a stone's throw from the Palais Bourbon, he is quite content to confine his attendance to those urgent occasions when his presence can be demanded by telephone. Personally therefore he is not much in touch with the Chamber; and there do not seem to be at his disposal the same facilities for ascertaining and gauging the sentiments of the Deputies at large as are provided for a Minister under our own Parliamentary system. It is true that the method is pursued in France of ranging Parliamentary politicians in groups whose respective presidents act as channels of communication with the Government or with the Opposition leaders; but there is a formality and perhaps a want of elasticity in this system which renders it hardly as efficient as that controlled by the "Whips" officially recognized in our own House of Commons, where political differences do not engender, as they do in Paris, an amount of susceptibility which causes the personal relations between individual Deputies to be less demonstrative in intimacy and comradeship.

M. Delcassé is subject also to the disadvantage of an aloofness between himself and the majority of his colleagues in the Cabinet—including particularly the Prime Minister—which is at this moment not much of a secret, but which deprives him of the authoritative and never-failing support with which his intimate friendship and devoted connection with M. Waldeck-Rousseau supplied him during the years when the latter was at the head of the Government. His Excellency has made no concealment of the fact that in the present Ministry he has asserted and maintained his entire independence in the conduct of the foreign relations of France; and the fact that he has succeeded in keeping a free hand is of course accompanied by a corresponding isolation from the intimacy of colleagues who pay more attention to the inner working of Parliamentary life than to the Ministerial functions which M. Delcassé very naturally regards as dominating in his case all other interests.

His Excellency has nevertheless been exposed to constant harassing on the part of those influential Deputies who have taken up with persistency the Newfoundland Question. His absence from the Chamber has not enabled him to escape their continual invasion of the precincts of the Ministry. He has no doubt pointed out to them over and over again in private that he did his best during the negotiations which resulted in the Agreement of the 8th of April, to induce Your Lordship to give way upon the points upon which they have been insisting; but he has not been successful in persuading them that His Majesty's Government had reached the limit of possible concessions. I cannot but think myself that he would have been well advised during the closing scenes of the Debate if he would have frankly and boldly stated that he could not hold out any hope that it would not be futile to approach His Majesty's Government with a proposal to reopen the negotiations eventually, unless the Chamber

([1]) [*v. supra* p. 13, No. 10.]

were prepared to make on their own side the concession against which the protective instincts of France stand in the way. From what passed in the Chamber during the closing minutes of the Debate it would seem that, overpowered by the expostulations and warnings of a knot of influential politicians who surrounded him he yielded to the impression that his prolonged resistance would jeopardize the whole arrangement, and in view of the character of the combination, and consisting as it did of MM. Denys Cochin, Etienne, and Deschanel, who had brought forward the motion and of the fact that he had previously agreed to the theory that the acceptance of the Convention did not exclude its future revision, I am not so much surprised that he gave way.

I do not believe that his so-called "capitulation" was necessary to save a Government defeat, but perhaps he might well imagine that he had some warrant for apprehension in the recollection of the shocks which have recently shaken the solidarity of M. Combes' administration. It would certainly be disastrous, and would give rise to much outside misinterpretation that that Administration should fall on a question of Foreign Policy so important as that of the cordial understanding between France and England. That the country at large fully appreciates the value of that cordial understanding cannot be doubted. A large proportion of the political opponents of the Administration admit that in this direction M. Delcassé has done the State good service. Much as many of them detest M. Combes, and anxious as they are to seize on any and every chance of upsetting him they have no desire to do so on a question which involves the security of their country's interests in a direction in which there has been heretofore so much to excite apprehension: and this all the more at a moment when the Power in alliance with them is hampered by a vital struggle with a persistent and tenacious enemy.

I have, &c.
EDMUND MONSON

No. 12.

Sir E. Monson to the Marquess of Lansdowne.

F.O. France 3668.
(No. 592.) Confidential.
My Lord, *Paris, November* 17. 1904.

M. Delcassé told me, in answer to my enquiry yesterday, that he was on the whole satisfied with the result of the divisions in the Chamber on the 12th instant as reported in my despatch No. 582 of the following day.(1)

He admitted that he had latterly entertained some apprehension in regard to the fate of the convention; and that he had feared that the majority on which it could be carried would not exceed 30, or at most 35, votes.

He explained that in order to mitigate the opposition to the Newfoundland arrangement he had, in his speech on the 10th instant, stated that he did not consider that the approval of the Chamber of the entire agreement would preclude the eventual resumption by him of negotiations for the purpose of ameliorating the convention in the direction pressed for by those deputies who were interested in the Newfoundland question; but he took credit to himself for having declined to make such a stipulation a condition precedent to the acceptance of the Agreement as a whole.

Having obtained that acceptance "firm," he was prepared to accede to the insertion of the words suggested in the amendment of MM. Etienne, Denys Cochin and Deschanel, as regarded the Convention, with a view to the subsequent resumption of the negotiation.

His Excellency said that he had already laid the agreement and convention before the Senate; where he did not anticipate he should meet with the same sort of opposition that he had encountered in the Chamber; and that he hoped that the Senate would accept the proposals in the first week in December.

(1) [v. *supra* p. 13. No. 10.]

M. Delcassé's language as to the debate in the Chamber was very guarded; but from his manner and deliberate caution in reply to the questions I put him I inferred that he had not dared to reject the draft formula of the order of the day finally voted, although he would have very much preferred to do so.

I have, &c.
EDMUND MONSON.

No. 13.

Sir E. Monson to the Marquess of Lansdowne.

F.O. France 3668.
(No. 634.)
My Lord,

Paris, D. *December* 7, 1904.
R. *December* 9, 1904.

The debate upon the Anglo-French Agreements was resumed yesterday in the Senate.

Both the Senators from the Maritime Department of Ille-et-Vilaine, MM. de la Ville-Moysan and Garreau, criticized the Newfoundland Convention from the point of view of the French fishing interests; and Admiral de Cuverville (Finistère) also attacked that Convention, which he described as being disastrous both to the French fishing industry in the region concerned and to the recruitment of sailors for the French navy. The arguments employed by these speakers were of necessity the same as have been already developed by the Senators who criticized the Convention yesterday, and by Deputies who opposed it in the Chamber.

M. d'Aunay (Nièvre), who followed, referred but briefly to the Newfoundland question, which he said was exhausted, and devoted the greater part of his speech to the subject of Morocco. He expressed some scepticism as to the result of the policy of "peaceful penetration"; urged that the integrity of Morocco should be respected; and called upon M. Delcassé to give the Senate further information as to the arrangement entered into with Spain.(¹) In conclusion M. d'Aunay, who was much applauded by the Left, asked the Senate to ratify the Agreements. Apart from his own special knowledge of foreign affairs, upon which he speaks in the Senate with authority, M. d'Aunay's speech derives particular interest from his close political connection with M. Clémenceau.

The official report of the proceedings is inclosed.(²)

I have, &c.
EDMUND MONSON.

(¹) [*v. infra* pp. 49–52, No. 59.]
(²) [Not reproduced.]

No. 14.

Sir E. Monson to the Marquess of Lansdowne.

F.O. France 3668.
(No. 635.)
My Lord,

Paris, D. *December* 8, 1904.
R. *December* 9, 1904.

As I had the honour to report to your Lordship by telegraph yesterday evening, the Senate adopted by 215 votes to 37 the Bill passed by the Chamber of Deputies for approving the Anglo-French Agreements.

The principal feature of the debate was a set speech delivered by the Minister of Foreign Affairs. M. Delcassé began by dwelling on the importance of a general understanding between Great Britain and France, taking occasion to allude to the

Franco-Russian Alliance as the basis of French foreign policy. Having then dealt in detail with the various objections raised to the Newfoundland arrangement, and recapitulated the compensating advantages obtained by France in Africa, he passed on to the subjects of Siam and Morocco. With regard to the first of these questions his Excellency said that the object attained by France was a free hand in the Mekong Valley. With regard to Morocco he professed his entire belief in the policy of peaceful penetration. He declined to give the Senate any information as to the secret portion of France's arrangement with Spain; but maintained that that arrangement insured the friendship of the two Countries. M. Delcassé concluded his speech with the following intimation, which was received with great applause, that France's peaceful policy abroad did not imply the possibility of her disarmament :—

" But here we must be on our guard against a delusion which might prove dangerous. If it be the part of diplomacy, if it be henceforward diplomacy's peculiar merit, to have secured for the Country which it serves advantages without having to mobilize that Country's Army or its Fleet, let us beware of thinking that diplomacy can henceforth dispense with a solid Army and a powerful Fleet. Let us above all prevent the world from thinking that we hold such a belief. Such is the consideration which the Minister of Foreign Affairs in leaving this tribune is bound to submit to the far-seeing patriotism of the Senate."

The first vote taken was on M. Waddington's Resolution, reported in my despatch No. 633 of the 6th instant, calling for supplementary negotiations with regard to Newfoundland. It was defeated by a majority of 161; and the Senate then divided on the Bill approving the Agreements, which was carried, as stated above, by 215 votes to 37. The official Report of the proceedings is inclosed.(¹)

I have, &c.
EDMUND MONSON.

(¹) [Not reproduced.]

II.—THE ADHERENCE OF THE POWERS TO THE KHEDIVIAL DECREE.(¹)

No. 15.

Sir F. Bertie to the Marquess of Lansdowne.

F.O. Italy 889.
Private.
My dear Lansdowne, *Rome, April 21, 1904.*
I had a pretext for seeing Fusinato to-day, viz., the inquiry which you desired me to make regarding the accrediting of Diplomatic Representatives to Belgrade. I took the opportunity to ask him whether he had read your despatch and the Agreements with France. He said that he had read the latter but not the former (and I am to let him have the Parliamentary Paper containing them) and he thought that on the whole France had gained more than she had given. I asked him whether he thought that the Bondholders would be pleased and whether there were many Italian holders of Egyptian Stock. His answer was that the Bondholders ought to be pleased and there were very few Italian holders, and the number of Italian Employés in the Egyptian Service had

(¹) [" The new Khedivial Decree annexed to the Declaration and accepted by the French Government ", wrote Lord Lansdowne in his covering despatch of April 8, 1904, " will, if it be accepted by the other Powers concerned, have the effect of giving to the Egyptian Government a free hand in the disposal of its own resources so long as the punctual payment of interest on the Debt is assured." See *Gooch and Temperley*, Vol. II, pp. 367–8.]

[15869] c

diminished. He was glad in the interest of the preservation of peace that England and France had come to agreements, but selfishly speaking it had been an advantage to Italy that in Egypt France and England had not been agreed for it had enabled Italy to obtain some advantages from both parties, and that position would disappear. However that was a comparatively small matter from a general European point of view and he was glad that England and France had settled their differences. He did not think that Germany could be pleased and he heard that Spain was very sore as she would not be likely to get much in Morocco—where he thought that we had given France a very free hand. He believed that France was going to allow Spain some railway arrangement but he did not think that Spain would be satisfied. Reverting to Egypt he deplored Italy having refused to join our expedition in 1882 and so deprived herself of any real voice in the destinies of the Country.

Yours v[ery] sincerely,
FRANCIS BERTIE.

[ED. NOTE.—On May 10, 1904, Sir F. Lascelles sent a telegram to Lord Lansdowne (No. 15) reporting a conversation with Baron Richthofen in which the latter raised a number of questions relating to Egypt, colonial frontier problems, Samoan claims, &c. The despatch, from which an extract is given below, dealt with some of these points. A fuller exposition of the British attitude is given in Nos. 18–22, infra pp. 19–23.]

No. 16.

The Marquess of Lansdowne to Sir F. Lascelles.(¹)

F.O. Germany (Prussia) 1592.
(No. 114.)
Extract.   Foreign Office, May 24, 1904.

His Majesty's Government are, however, willing to discuss with the German Government the possibility of arriving at an understanding with regard to their position in Egypt, and if the German Government will give their adhesion to the Decree, and if they will agree not to obstruct the action of Great Britain in Egypt by asking that a limit of time be fixed for the British occupation, or in any other manner, and will agree that certain stipulations in the Suez Canal Convention, the execution of which are incompatible with the British occupation, shall remain in abeyance, His Majesty's Government will undertake :—

1. That German schools in Egypt shall continue to enjoy the same liberty as in the past.
2. That the rights enjoyed by Germany in Egypt in virtue of Treaties, Conventions, and usage shall be maintained.
3. That German commerce in Egypt shall be assured of equality of treatment in Egypt for thirty years, provided that a similar assurance is received as regards British commerce with German Colonies in Africa.
4. The German officials in Egypt shall be treated as favourably as British officials.

The proposal that the post of Director of the Khedivial Library and one post of Conservator of the Cairo Museum shall be reserved for German savants does not seem capable of justification, and His Majesty's Government are not prepared to give any undertaking on the subject, nor can they bind themselves to extend to Germany any additional advantages which might be accorded to Austria, Italy, or Russia.

(¹) [On the negotiations with Germany, cp. G.P. XX, I, Ch. 143.]

No. 17.

Sir E. Monson to the Marquess of Lansdowne.

F.O. France 3666.
(No. 323.)   Most Confidential.   *Paris, D. May* 27, 1904.
My Lord,   R. *May* 28, 1904.

I said to M. Delcassé the day before yesterday that the effect of the prompt acceptation by the Russian Government of the invitation to adhere to the project of the Khedivial Decree forming so important a part in the Anglo-French Arrangement of April 8th last, had not failed to produce considerable satisfaction in London.

His Excellency replied that he hoped that there would be a reciprocity of conciliation on the part of His Majesty's Government. That Russia having taken a step in advance of a friendly nature had a right to expect a corresponding movement from Great Britain.

I said that His Excellency must well know that there was at this moment, and had been for some time past, a very sincere readiness in London to meet with cordiality any genuine evidence of a friendly policy on the part of Russia.

The existing hostilities in which the latter Power is unfortunately engaged render difficult at this moment any material alteration in the relations between the two countries; but the foreign policy of Great Britain is never characterised by any want of generosity; and I could not doubt that the Government of the Emperor Nicholas would give adequate credence to the assurances of that of my Sovereign as to the attitude of Great Britain towards Russia.

M. Delcassé did not pursue the subject.

I have, &c.
EDMUND MONSON.

No. 18.

The Marquess of Lansdowne to Count Metternich.

F.O. Germany (Prussia) 1605.
My dear Ambassador,   *Foreign Office, June* 6, 1904.

We have further considered the proposal which you were good enough to lay before me on behalf of the German Government in regard to the conditions under which they were prepared to give their adhesion to the Egyptian Khedivial Decree.

That proposal was to the following effect :—

1. The German Government would give a Declaration corresponding to that given by the French Government in Article 1 of the Declaration respecting Egypt and Morocco, to the effect that they will not obstruct the action of Great Britain in Egypt by asking that a limit of time be fixed for the British occupation, or in any other manner.

I had the honour of explaining to Your Excellency that if Germany were to accept a similar obligation, she would be bound to give us her unreserved support in the event of our desiring at any future time to obtain the revision of any of the international arrangements which now prevail in Egypt, and I understood Your Excellency to concur in this interpretation.

2. They would in like manner give their assent to the draft Khedivial Decree annexed to the Declaration; and

3. They would, as the French Government has done in Article VI, agree that certain stipulations of the Suez Canal Convention shall remain in abeyance.

[15869]   c 2

On the other hand, His Majesty's Government is asked—

1. To give Germany a Declaration corresponding to that contained in Article IV with regard to the treatment of German commerce in Egypt;

2. To undertake, as they have undertaken in Article III, to respect the rights enjoyed by Germany in Egypt in virtue of Treaties, Conventions, and usages;

3. To undertake that the post of Director of the Khedivial Library shall be held by a German *savant*;

4. To undertake that German schools in Egypt shall continue to enjoy the same liberty as in the past; and

5. To undertake that German officials in Egypt shall be placed under conditions not less advantageous than those applying to British officials in the same service.

The principal difficulty which, in the opinion of His Majesty's Government, stands in the way of an arrangement based on these general lines, arises out of the proposals relating to German commerce in Egypt. The commercial arrangement with France was strictly bilateral. It gave security in Morocco to British commerce, in exchange for security in Egypt to French commerce; and this part of the arrangement between the two Powers might easily have been separated from the rest of the Agreement, and regarded as an equitable settlement of important commercial interests.

The German Government, on the other hand, proposes to obtain for German commerce all that Great Britain has given to French commerce, but to give nothing to British commerce in exchange. This indeed greatly understates the case; for German commerce with Egypt is larger in amount than French commerce, and therefore the security which your Excellency desires to obtain for it is of greater value; while, on the other hand the commerce which this country has, or is likely to have, with German colonies in Africa is smaller than that which she may hope for in Morocco, and the *quid pro quo* is therefore less.

In these circumstances Your Excellency can hardly think it unreasonable if His Majesty's Government are of opinion that there is no parallel possible between the Anglo-French arrangement, in so far as it deals with commercial matters, and the arrangement Your Excellency suggests with regard to German trade in Egypt.

In view of the overwhelming importance which His Majesty's Government attach to these considerations, and as both sides desire a prompt settlement, I cannot help hoping that the German Government may on reflection decide not to withhold their adhesion to the Khedivial Decree. No one can seriously contend that it is injurious to the interests of the other Powers, and of those concerned three have, as you are aware, already given their adhesion to it. The changes which it will effect will on the other hand be in the highest degree beneficial to Egypt: a country to which, as Y[our] E[xcellency] has told me, Germany bears nothing but good will. We should greatly regret if in such circumstances Germany which I believe holds only $\frac{1}{4}$ per cent. of the Egyptian debt were alone to withhold her consent.

With regard to the minor matters referred to by Baron Richthofen, we should be ready to assure you that our influence would be used with the Egyptian Government in order to secure for German officials in the Egyptian Service, and for German schools in Egypt the same fair treatment that they have been accorded in the past, and I feel sure, from what Lord Cromer has said, that the Egyptian Government would be ready to intimate that the claims of a German *savant* to the post of Director of the Khedivial Library would be recognized, at all events for a term of years, or on the occurrence of the next vacancy.([1])

Yours sincerely,
LANSDOWNE.

([1]) [These last two paragraphs, with some very slight differences in punctuation &c., are quoted in *G.P.* XX, I, p. 148 *n.*]

No. 19.

The Marquess of Lansdowne to Count Metternich.(¹)

(Amended Copy.)

F.O. Germany (Prussia) 1605.

Your Excellency,

Foreign Office, June 15, 1904.

I have lately had several conversations with your Excellency on the subject of the adhesion of the German Government to the proposed Khedivial Decree concerning the finances of Egypt. I had expressed the hope that the German Government would find it possible to give their adhesion unreservedly, thereby following the example of the other Powers to whom a similar request was addressed. Your Excellency has however explained to me that in the view of the German Government it would be impossible for them to enter into such an engagement without previously satisfying themselves that His Majesty's Government had no intention of making use of their position in Egypt for the purpose of depriving German commerce of equal treatment. You have also explained to me the great importance which, in view of the extent of German commercial interests in Egypt, the German Government attach to these considerations, and you have told me that the German Government could only give their adhesion if we were able to assure them that the policy of commercial liberty, as affirmed in Article IV of the Anglo-French Declaration, was not designed to be exclusive, a policy to the contrary necessitating a special consent of the German Parliament, which would never be obtained.

In these circumstances your Excellency has suggested to me an arrangement which would, I understand, be upon the following lines :—

It is proposed on the one hand that His Majesty's Government shall declare—

1. That they guarantee to German commerce in Egypt most-favoured-nation treatment for thirty years.
2. That they will respect the rights which Germany, in virtue of Treaties, Conventions, and usage, enjoys in Egypt.
3. That the German schools in Egypt shall continue to enjoy the same liberty as in the past, and that German officials now in the Egyptian service shall not be placed under conditions less advantageous than those applying to the British officials in the same service.

Your Excellency is, I understand, instructed to inform me that, should these conditions be accepted by His Majesty's Government, the German Government will on their side :—

1. Give their assent to the draft Khedivial Decree annexed to the Anglo-French Declaration of April 8th, 1904;
2. Undertake not to obstruct the action of Great Britain in Egypt by asking that a limit of time be fixed for the British occupation or in any other manner; and
3. Agree that the execution of the last sentence of paragraph 1 as well as of paragraph 2 of Article VIII of the Treaty of October 29th, 1888, shall remain in abeyance.

His Majesty's Government are willing to accept this proposal and, assuming that I have correctly interpreted your Excellency's observations, I shall be obliged if, in

(¹) [This and Nos. 20 and 22 are published in *G.P.* XX, I, pp. 155-7 and pp. 160-2. No. 22 is given there (p. 162) in German. There are two versions of No. 19, one on pp. 155-7 and the other on pp. 160-2. The second of these is identical with our text except for some very slight differences in punctuation. This is the final form as amended after consultation with Count Metternich, *v. infra* p. 22, No. 21.]

acknowledging receipt of this communication, you will be good enough to confirm the acceptance by the German Government of the Agreement thus established.

I have, &c.
LANSDOWNE.

[*ED. NOTE.*—The reference to the Treaty of October 29, 1888, appears to be in fact the Anglo-Egyptian Commercial Convention of October 29, 1889, *B.F.S.P.* Vol. 81, pp. 1281-2.]

No. 20.

The Marquess of Lansdowne to Count Metternich.

F.O. Germany (Prussia) 1605.
Confidential.
My dear Ambassador,   *Foreign Office, June 15, 1904.*

With reference to my communication of to-day's date, I ask permission to remind your Excellency that in our conversation of the 6th June upon the subject of the adhesion of the German Government to the Khedivial Decree, I pointed out to your Excellency that if the German Government were to accept an obligation similar to that undertaken by the French Government in Article I of the Declaration respecting Egypt and Morocco, viz., not to obstruct the action of Great Britain in Egypt by asking that a limit of time be fixed for the British occupation, or in any other manner, they would, in our opinion, be bound to give us their unreserved support should we, at any future time, desire to obtain the revision of any of the international arrangements (capitulations) which now prevail in Egypt. I understood your Excellency to concur in this interpretation, and I shall be glad to learn from you that I was not mistaken in this respect.

I am, &c.
LANSDOWNE.

No. 21.

The Marquess of Lansdowne to Mr. Whitehead.

F.O. Germany (Prussia) 1592.
(No. 136.)
Sir,   *Windsor Castle, June 19, 1904.*

The German Ambassador who was staying in this neighbourhood, asked me to receive him during my visit to the King at Windsor today.

He told me that he had been authorised to announce to me the assent of the German Gov[ernmen]t to the Khedivial decree upon the conditions described in my letter of the 15th instant. H[is] E[xcellency] suggested one or two verbal alterations in that part of my letter in which the statements which he had made to me were recapitulated. As these amendments did not affect the sense of the passage in which they occur I accepted them, and I have agreed to substitute for my letter of the 15th instant that which I now enclose with this despatch.(¹)

Passing to my confidential letter of the same date, H[is] E[xcellency] called attention to my use of the word "unreserved" in the passage referring to the support which we expected the German Gov[ernmen]t to give us in the event of our obtaining from them an assurance similar to that given to us by France in Article 1 of the Anglo-French Declaration.

I repeated that I had used the word "unreserved" in order that H[is] E[xcellency] might not be left in any doubt that we should expect the German Representative to support our representative at Cairo to the fullest extent should we hereafter find it desirable to propose a revision of the international agreements affecting the position of the Powers in Egypt.

(¹) [p. 21, No. 19.]

H[is] E[xcellency] did not pursue the subject further but asked me pointedly whether it had been mentioned to the French Gov[ernmen]t.

I replied that I was able to tell H[is] E[xcellency] in confidence that it had been mentioned to them and that we had reason to know that we might expect from France in the event supposed a support corresponding with that which we asked Germany to promise us. H[is] E[xcellency] said that the German G[overnmen]t would object to promise us more than France had promised us and asked me whether he might clearly understand that we were not asking them to do this.

I replied that H[is] E[xcellency] might take it from me that we were not asking more of Germany than we had obtained from France.

H[is] E[xcellency] expressed himself satisfied with this explanation and told me that he would as soon as possible write me a letter in reply to mine of the 15th instant and a second letter in reply to my "confidential" letter of the same date, intimating the acceptance of both proposals by the German Gov[ernmen]t.

[I am. &c.]

L[ANSDOWNE].

No. 22.

Count Metternich to the Marquess of Lansdowne.([1])

F.O. Germany (Prussia) 1605.
Translation.

My Lord,　　　　　　　　*German Embassy, London, June 19, 1904.*

I have the honour to acknowledge the receipt of Your Excellency's note of the 15th instant and to state in reply that the Imperial Gov[ernmen]t accept the agreement proposed therein relative to Egypt. I also venture to confirm the fact that the interpretation given by Your Excellency in your note, of the different points of our discussions agrees with my view.

I have, &c.

P. METTERNICH.

([1]) [The text of Count Metternich's second letter is as follows:—

Dear Lord Lansdowne,　　　　　　　*German Embassy, June 19, 1904.*

I have had the honour to receive your Excellency's confidential communication of the 15th instant relative to Egypt. I venture now to state that the Imperial Gov[ernmen]t accept the interpretation contained therein to the same extent, as has already been done on the part of the French Gov[ernment].

I remain, &c.

P. METTTERNICH.]

No. 23.

The Earl of Cromer to the Marquess of Lansdowne.

F.O. Turkey 5367.
(No. 86.) Confidential.　　　　　　*Cairo, D. July 4, 1904.*
My Lord,　　　　　　　　　　　R. *July 19, 1904.*

I have the honour to enclose copy of a letter addressed to me by Monsieur Jenisch, the German Agent in Cairo, in which he asks that an assurance, more formal than a verbal promise, might be given to him that the Post of Director of the Khedivial Library should continue to be entrusted to a German.

I consequently requested Boutros Pacha Ghali, Egyptian Minister for Foreign Affairs to convey such an assurance to Monsieur Jenisch in a Note of which I have the honour to enclose a copy.

I have, &c.

CROMER.

Enclosure 1 in No. 23.

M. Jenisch to the Earl of Cromer.

Dear Lord Cromer,   *German Consulate, Cairo, July 2, 1904.*

You will remember that in our conversations about the Anglo-French Convention and the Khedivial Decree you promised me that, as soon as all other questions were settled, you would be prepared to meet the wish of the German Government and to agree that the post of Director of the Khedivial Library shall continue to be intrusted to a German.

All other questions with regard to the Anglo-French Convention having, as you know, been settled satisfactorily between the German and the British Governments, and the adhesion of the German Government to the Khedivial Decree having been given, Baron Richthofen would be thankful, if, before we both go on leave, that promise could be brought into some form a little more binding than is a merely verbal assurance.

Awaiting your kind reply, believe me, your, &c.

           JENISCH.

Enclosure 2 in No. 23.

Boutros Ghali to M. Jenisch.

      Ministère des Affaires Étrangères, le Caire,

M. le Ministre,   *le   Juillet, 1904.*(¹)

A la suite des pourparlers qui ont eu lieu entre votre Gouvernement et le Gouvernement de Sa Majesté Britannique, pourparlers qui ont abouti à l'assentiment de l'Allemagne au Décret qui organise sur de nouvelles bases le régime financier égyptien, j'ai l'honneur de vous déclarer que le Gouvernement Égyptien réserve, à l'avenir, à un sujet allemand, le poste de Directeur de la Bibliothèque Khédiviale.

         Veuillez, &c.

         BOUTROS GHALI.

(¹) [The date is not given.]

CHAPTER XVII.

MOROCCO, APRIL 1904-MAY 1905.

I.—FRANCE, SPAIN AND MOROCCO, APRIL-OCTOBER 1904.(¹)

No. 24.

The Marquess of Lansdowne to Sir E. Egerton.

F.O. Spain 2193.
(No. 45.)

Sir,   *Foreign Office, April 11, 1904.*

The Spanish Ambassador called upon me to-day and we had some conversation upon the subject of the recently concluded Agreement between this country and France in regard to Morocco. His Excellency told me that public opinion in Spain was a good deal agitated upon the subject, and that the Spanish Government was perturbed because as lately as Thursday last the Spanish Ambassador had broached the subject at the French Ministry of Foreign Affairs and had found the representative of the French Government quite uncommunicative. I suggested that as this incident had taken place before the signature of the Agreements in London, it was perhaps natural that the French Government should have shown itself reticent.

I said that, as His Excellency was aware, we had throughout the negotiations insisted that the interests of Spain were to be kept in view, and although I did not feel justified in handing him a copy of the Declaration, which had not yet been presented to Parliament, I mentioned to him that it contained a clause in which the French Government declared that it had no intention of disturbing the political status of Morocco, another providing for the principle of commercial equality in that country, and a third under which the two Governments agreed not to permit the erection of fortifications on the coast of Morocco between Melilla and the River Sebou. The two Governments had also agreed to take into special consideration the interests which Spain derived from her geographical position and from her actual possessions on the Moorish coast, and the French Government had undertaken to arrive at an agreement based upon these considerations with that of Spain—an agreement which was to be communicated to the Government of His Majesty.

His Excellency observed that this would leave Spain to fight matters out with the French Government. They would have much preferred that the question should have been dealt with "à trois." Spain would have in that case, as she had on previous occasions, depended on the advice and assistance of Great Britain. I replied that it had taken us nearly a year to come to an understanding with the French Government, and that if the discussion had been triangular it would in my belief have been impossible to arrive at an agreement. I thought it would have been impossible for either of us to have entered into details with the Spanish Government until we had ourselves come to terms, and I had understood from the French Ambassador that, now that we had done so, not a moment would be lost in approaching the Spanish Government. I should be much surprised if this had not been already done. His Excellency admitted that he had no quite recent information either from Paris or Madrid, and could not therefore say whether anything had passed at either of those places since the signature of the Agreement.

H[is] E[xcellency] said that there had been discussions between the French and Spanish Governments in 1902 as to the limits which might be imposed upon the zones

(¹) [Cp. *G.P.* XX, I, Ch. 144, and *Documents Diplomatiques, Affaires du Maroc*, 1901–1905 (Paris 1905).]

within which each Power was to be free to exercise a "peaceful penetration," and he presumed that these discussions might now be resumed.

I said that I could see no objection to this.

H[is] E[xcellency] having expressed a fear as to the effects of allowing France a free hand in preserving order in Morocco and in providing the Moorish Government with financial assistance, I asked H[is] E[xcellency] to bear in mind that the Moorish Government was virtually bankrupt, that its continued existence without money was impossible, and that so far as I was aware neither Spanish nor British financiers were at all inclined to make them further loans. In these circumstances I could not see how we could either of us object to the French Government providing such assistance. I had in fact no doubt whatever that they would have done so whether we had consented to stand aside or not.

I begged H[is] E[xcellency] to remember that we had been careful to avoid any arrangements which could be regarded as prejudicing the rights of Spain to anything which was already hers or to which she had a reversionary claim. All we had done was to undertake that, so far as we were concerned, we would not, in certain respects, stand in the way of France. I did not think it desirable to say anything to H[is] E[xcellency] of the reservations contained in the Secret Clauses of the Agreement, but I could see that he felt considerable anxiety as to the fate of the Moorish sea-board and of the adjoining portions of the Sultan's possessions in the event of a complete collapse of his authority and a "liquidation" of Morocco.

At the conclusion of our conversation H[is] E[xcellency] referred to the British Treaty of 1895, under which the Sultan was bound not to alienate certain portions of Moorish territory in the neighbourhood of Cape Juby. He said that in the event of a liquidation Spain would expect the reversion of these districts, and would look to us to obtain them for her. I said that this was a point which the Spanish Government might, I thought, conveniently discuss with the French Government.

The tone of H[is] E[xcellency]'s observations was throughout of a friendly character, but characterised by a considerable amount of uneasiness as to the situation.

[I am, &c.
LANSDOWNE.]

No. 25.

Sir E. Egerton to the Marquess of Lansdowne.

F.O. Spain 2194.
(No. 40.) Confidential. Madrid, D. *April 11, 1904.*
My Lord, R. *April 18, 1904.*

I met the French Ambassador yesterday who had not seen the text of the agreement most happily come to between the Governments of England and France respecting Egypt and Morocco; and I ventured today when he called to let him take a copy of it, begging him to consider it for his personal use only; as I could not make communication of the text to any one else without instructions.

He told me that he thought that it would probably be Monsieur Delcassé who would inform the Spanish Ambassador of the particulars of the understanding and subsequently enter into negotiations with Monsieur Leon y Castillo for the protection of Spanish interests.

I told him that it seemed the natural wish of my Government that no time should be lost in approaching and settling matters with the Spanish Government.

Monsieur Cambon, who entered at length into the previous history of the Morocco negotiations and agreed with his brother that it would have been hopeless to negotiate "à trois," appeared delighted at the understanding come to between the two countries and thought with me that it was well that pourparlers with Spain should begin as soon as possible; but Monsieur Delcassé had to go for a few days to the country.

As to the prospect of agreement with Spain when I spoke to him yesterday he seemed to anticipate no difficulty; and today when I reverted to the subject, he seemed to think the only obstacle might be the King's military spirit which has been fostered by His Royal Mother, the late Queen Regent and which might make His Majesty desire an opportunity for a brush with the Moors!

As for the other Powers, the German Ambassador's language was that if the same commercial advantages in Morocco were granted to Germany as to France and England, he was pleased at the arrangement.

From Italy no objection is to be expected—the only person who might encourage the Spaniards to make complaints is the Russian Ambassador here, Monsieur Schevitch, who, having no business of his own to transact, out of pure idleness and mischief interferes with his advice to the Spanish Minister of State in all kinds of matters.

I answered that I could not believe that the Spanish Minister would really take seriously anything that Monsieur Schevitch might say on his own account.

Monsieur Cambon regretted that it was never certain here what idea may not be taken up violently by the Press. This I said was an argument for his Government rapidly clinching the question with the present Spanish Government.

His Excellency agreed with me that so far the attitude of the Spanish press is not seriously hostile to our reported arrangement respecting Morocco.

I have, &c.
EDWIN H. EGERTON.

No. 26.

The Marquess of Lansdowne to Sir E. Monson.([1])

F.O. France 3669.

Tel. (No. 43.)

Foreign Office, April 12, 1904.
D. 3·40 P.M.

Spanish Ambassador told me today([2]) that there was considerable agitation in Spain respecting the recently concluded agreement in regard to Morocco. On Thursday last the Spanish Ambassador in Paris had found the French Gover[nmen]t quite uncommunicative : I explained that this was perhaps natural as the signature had not then taken place. I said that we had throughout insisted that Spanish interests should be kept in view, that there were clauses in the agreement denying any intention of disturbing the *status quo*, providing for commercial equality and prohibiting the erection of fortifications on coast in possession of Morocco between Melilla and the Sebou. The two gov[ernmen]ts had also agreed to take into special consideration the interests derived by Spain from her geographical position and from her actual possessions on the coast, and the French Gov[ernmen]t had undertaken to arrive at an agreement with Spain based on these considerations, which agreement was to be communicated to H[is] M[ajesty's] G[overnment].

Spanish Ambassador said that his Gov[ernmen]t would much have preferred that the question should have been dealt with between the three Gov[ernmen]ts. I replied that present understanding with France had taken nearly a year to arrive at and that if discussion had been triangular in my opinion an agreement would have been impracticable. I thought it would have been impossible for either of us to enter into details with the Spanish Gov[ernmen]t until we had ourselves come to terms, and I had understood from the French Ambassador that now we had done so not a moment would be lost in approaching the Spanish Gov[ernmen]t.

I reminded him that Moorish Gov[ernmen]t was virtually bankrupt; that its continued existence without money was impossible, and that so far as I knew neither

([1]) [Also Tel. No. 11 to Sir E. Egerton.]
([2]) [Apparently this refers to the interview of April 11, *v. supra* p. 25, No. 24.]

Spanish nor British financiers were at all disposed to make further loans. I could not see how we could either of us object to the French Government providing such assistance. I had no doubt that they would have done so whether we had consented to stand aside or not.

I said we had carefully avoided any arrangement which could be regarded as prejudicing the rights of Spain to anything already hers or to which she had a reversionary claim. I made no mention of the secret clauses, but he was evidently anxious as to the fate of the Moorish seaboard and the adjoining territories in the event of a liquidation of Morocco. H[is] E[xcellency] said that if this occurred Spain would expect reversion of the districts in the neighbourhood of Cape Juby and would look to us to obtain them for her. I said I thought his Government might conveniently discuss this question with the French Gov[ernmen]t.

No. 27.

The Marquess of Lansdowne to Sir A. Nicolson.

F.O. Morocco 415.   *Foreign Office, April* 19, 1904.
Tel. (No. 12.)   D. 4·10 P.M.

You will have received by last bag copies of our Agreement with France respecting Morocco.

You are authorised whenever you think it advisable to send a message to the Sultan, explaining its provisions and reassuring him as to the intention of the arrangement.

No. 28.

The Marquess of Lansdowne to Sir E. Monson.

F.O. France 3662.
(No. 199.)   Confidential.
Sir,   *Foreign Office, April* 20, 1904.

The French Ambassador called upon me to-day on his return from Paris. His Excellency expressed himself much pleased with the manner in which the Agreements recently concluded between this country and the French Republic had been received in France. Criticisms were directed against points of detail, but the general principles of the Agreements received almost universal commendation.

His Excellency said that M. Delcassé had been distressed by the premature publication in France of the text of the Agreements, but that it was impossible to prevent indiscretions, and, by one means or another, the Agreements had become public property. He trusted however that no great harm had been done.

His Excellency went on to say, with reference to my conversation with him on the 6th instant, that M. Delcassé desired to do all that was possible in order to obtain the adhesion of Russia for the new Khedivial Decree, and had, in fact, already sounded the Russian Government upon the subject. He found Count Lamsdorff thoroughly well disposed towards this country, and not averse to the idea of accepting the Khedivial Decree. His position however was a somewhat difficult one, for it was of no use to conceal the fact that there was a powerful anti-English party in Russia, and that its influence in the immediate neighbourhood of the Emperor was considerable. Count Lamsdorff was not unnaturally apprehensive of finding himself attacked if he were to take a pronounced step, in advance of the other Powers concerned, at the present moment in order to make himself agreeable to this country. If, however, he was to take such a step, it was desirable that we should strengthen his hands as much as possible, and it had occurred to M. Delcassé that this might be done if I would authorize Count Lamsdorff to say([1]) something reassuring to the Russian Government as to the intentions of Great Britain with regard to Tibet. It was true, His Excellency said, that assurances had been given in both Houses of Parliament upon this subject, assurances which, His Excellency said, seemed to him of a very satisfactory character. When M. Delcassé spoke to him, and suggested that I might say something to Count Benckendorff on the subject, he had of course not seen the statement which I had made yesterday in the House of Lords. His Excellency thought that I might perhaps find it possible to repeat what I had said in the House of Lords to Count Benckendorff. This would enable him to make a report to Count Lamsdorff, who, with such a report in his possession, would be in a stronger position to help us in regard to the Khedivial Decree. I promised that I would consider H[is] E[xcellency]'s suggestion. He added that, if Russia fell into line, Austria was not likely to stand out.

His Excellency then said a few words with regard to Spain and the recently concluded Agreements. He told me that he had not forgotten the strong desire which I had expressed that the French Government should lose no time in taking the Spanish Government into its confidence. There had been a meeting between M. Delcassé and the Spanish Ambassador on Friday last, but each side had apparently expected the other to offer suggestions, and the conversation had not led to any results. The discussion was however to be resumed yesterday. His Excellency told me, explaining that he was not authorized to do so, that a proposal would probably be made to Spain upon the following lines. Spain would be offered a sphere of influence extending behind the neutralized portion of the Morocco sea-board and reaching from Melilla to the Atlantic Ocean. Further to the south it was proposed to offer to Spain a second sphere of influence in the neighbourhood of Cape Juby. It would probably reach from Cape Bojador on the south to a point above the Wadi Draa, where the 11th parallel of longitude strikes the coast of Morocco. These regions would in the first instance be spheres of Spanish influence, but would, in the event of a liquidation of Morocco, pass under the actual administration of Spain. His Excellency thought that the Spanish Government would very likely haggle over the terms of the arrangement. It seemed to him however to be one with which in principle they could not be otherwise than pleased. I expressed my thanks to His Excellency for this communication, and told him that I had endeavoured some days ago to reassure the Spanish Ambassador here as to M. Delcassé's intentions, although, in view of the approaching discussions at Paris, I had thought it better not to mention to him the secret portion of the Agreement.

I am, &c.
LANSDOWNE.

([1]) [The despatch was corrected in draft in Lord Lansdowne's hand, and the existing wording was substituted by him for " if we were able to place Count Lamsdorff in a position to say."]

No. 29.

The Marquess of Lansdowne to Sir E. Egerton.

F.O. Spain 2193.
(No. 48.) Confidential.
Sir,   *Foreign Office, April 20, 1904.*

Immediately after my conversation with the French Ambassador, recorded in my despatch to Sir E. Monson No. 199 of April 20th I received a visit from the Spanish Ambassador, who informed me that the Spanish Government was much perturbed because nothing had yet been said to them by the French Government on the subject of the recently concluded Agreement with regard to Morocco. His Excellency had gathered from what I had said to him on previous occasions that no time would be lost by the French Government in making a communication to them. No such communication had, however, he believed, yet been made.

I told His Excellency that I had not been at all surprised that the French Government should have said nothing before the Agreement between France and Great Britain was concluded. I had however just seen the French Ambassador, and I had learned from him that M. Delcassé and the Spanish Ambassador had met on Friday last, and were to meet again yesterday. M. Cambon had assured me that proposals, which seemed to me to offer a reasonable basis for discussion would be made to the Ambassador. I told the Duc de Mandas that M. Cambon had made this announcement to me unsolicited, and that I felt convinced that there was no desire on M. Delcassé's part to evade the question. I added that I had every reason to hope that the communication which the French Government would make would be found in principle acceptable to the Spanish Government.

[I am, &c.
LANSDOWNE.]

<hr>

No. 30.

Sir E. Monson to the Marquess of Lansdowne.

F.O. France 3669.
Tel. (No. 25.)
Spain and Morocco.
Very Confidential.

Paris, *April 22, 1904.*
D. 2·10 P.M.
R. 4·30 P.M.

Spanish Ambassador states that an agreement was drawn up in Paris more than a year ago as to the eventual partition of Morocco which was never signed because Spain insisted that it must first be submitted to approval of Great Britain.

This agreement is now repudiated by M. Delcassé who offers greatly diminished advantages.

Spanish Ambassador considers that M. Delcassé has been guilty of bad faith, and their personal relations are now very strained indeed

Spanish Ambassador does not think his colleague in London is acquainted with all the details of what has passed.

He again asserts that the document which I sent you yesterday is entirely apocryphal.(¹)

Further details by messenger tonight.

(¹) [In his despatch No. 230 of April 21, 1904 (F.O. France 3665), Sir E. Monson enclosed a copy of *Le Maroc Français* of March 24. It contained on p. 17 the text of a document purporting to be a Secret Treaty between France and Spain of November 11, 1902, for the partition of Morocco. The despatch is minuted by King Edward: "*The statement reporting a Secret Treaty seems v[ery] suspicious[?].*"

A translation of the alleged treaty had appeared in the *Morning Post* of April 16, 1904.]

<hr>

No. 31.

Sir M. Gosselin to the Marquess of Lansdowne.

F.O. Portugal 1411.
(No. 48.) Confidential.
My Lord,

Lisbon, D. *April 23, 1904.*
R. *May 2, 1904.*

With reference to my despatch No. 41 Confidential of the 11th Instant, I have the honour to report that Senhor Wenceslau de Lima, at our last interview again alluded to the Anglo-French Agreement recently concluded by Your Lordship and Monsieur Cambon, and said that the more he studied it, the more he realized its great importance and the advantages which would result, directly to the two Signatory Powers, and indirectly to all the world, by the removal of so many causes of possible misunderstanding, and he heartily rejoiced at the success of the negotiations.

He thought that the only Power which might not share the general satisfaction was "our next door neighbour"; he gathered that there was considerable anxiety at

Madrid as to the issue of the negotiations with the French Government about Morocco; Your Lordship's despatch to His Majesty's Ambassador at Paris acknowledges the special interest of Spain in that country([1]); but Spanish Ministers are aware that they have no power to protect those interests, and they realize that the dream of a great Spanish dominion across the Straits is now quite unrealizable.

Monsieur Rouvier, my French colleague, whom I met to-day, was equally hearty in his congratulations, and said that France owes a great debt of gratitude to the King, for having made " Une entente cordiale " between the two countries possible, and to Your Lordship for having conducted the negotiations to a successful issue.

He hoped the agreement with France would be the forerunner of a similar under-standing between His Majesty's and the Russian Governments, and he knew that this was Monsieur Delcassé's very earnest desire.

The full text of the agreement only hardly reached Lisbon just as the typographers' strike commenced, and the issue of all Lisbon newspapers has since then been suspended; but the telegraphic summary of the Agreement was cordially welcomed by all organs of public opinion, and the *Seculo* of the 17th Instant, in commenting on " one of the most notable facts of modern times," hails His Majesty as the Sovereign of Peace, and declares that " God Save the King " should in future be a universal hymn of concord.

I have, &c.
MARTIN GOSSELIN.

([1]) [*v. Gooch & Temperley*, II, p. 367. This is the despatch of April 8, 1904, which was published in *A. & P.* (1904), CX, (*Cd.* 1952), pp. 313–22.]

No. 32.

The Marquess of Lansdowne to Sir E. Egerton.

F.O. Spain 2193.
(No. 52.) Confidential.
Sir, *Foreign Office, April 27, 1904.*

The Spanish Ambassador called upon me today, and we resumed our conversation with regard to the negotiations between France and Spain as to Morocco.

His Excellency said that the course of events had been somewhat different to what I had been led to suppose. He told me that the negotiations which had taken place between France and Spain in 1902 had resulted in an Agreement which had in fact been arrived at (*établi*), although it was never signed. He was able to tell me in strict confidence that Spain had refused to sign it because the French Government had refused to let them communicate it to us. They had received a distinct intimation that this was not agreeable to the French Government, and the matter had therefore been altogether dropped.

In 1902 the French had offered to Spain a sphere of influence commencing at the mouth of the Muluya River, following its course for some distance, then running to the south of Fez and to the mouth of the Sebou. The present offer was much less advantageous. It was suggested that the line should be drawn not from the mouth of the Muluya but from Melilla, that it should run to the south-west through Ulad-abu-Rima, thence to the north of Fez, and thence to the Moulay-Bou-Selham (Muley-Abu-Sallum) on the Atlantic Coast.

Again in 1902 Spain was offered a second sphere of influence commencing at Cape Bogador and including Sus. The present offer, instead of going as far north as Sus, stopped short at Ras Agula, a good deal further to the south. Both spheres of influence were therefore considerably curtailed under the new offer. The curtailment on the Mediterranean Coast was a most serious matter. Melilla was an important Spanish fortress, and Spain also owned the Zafarin Islands, nearly opposite to the mouth of the Muluya. It would be intolerable that the sea-board between Melilla and the Muluya should be within the French sphere. The Spanish Government thought that a mistake must have been made and had asked for explanations, but had not yet received them.

The curtailment on the Atlantic sea-board had the effect of depriving Spain of territory in the neighbourhood of Santa Cruz which she had acquired in 1870 from the Moors.

I asked His Excellency whether I was right in my impression that nothing had been said to us by the Spanish Government as to the negotiations which took place in 1902 and the reasons for which they had been abortive. His Excellency said that it was quite true that no communication had been made to us. I also asked His Excellency whether I was not right in supposing that the present French proposal did not imply that the French frontier was to be actually advanced to Muluya, but only that the region between the Algerian frontier and Melilla should fall within the French sphere of influence. His Excellency replied that this was the case. It seemed to him however quite wrong that Spain should be asked by France to accept less advantageous conditions at the present time merely because Great Britain had now entered upon the scene. Feeling in Spain upon the subject would be extremely strong, and if the French refused to modify their terms there would be considerable popular excitement.

I told His Excellency that it was at any rate satisfactory to find that the French Government was prepared to provide for extensive spheres of Spanish influence in those parts of Morocco which might be regarded as most important to Spain. As for the precise extent of those spheres, that seemed to me to be a matter for discussion between the two Governments, the course of which I should follow with friendly interest.

I am, &c.
LANSDOWNE.

No. 33.

Memorandum handed to M. Cambon.

F.O. France 3686.   *Foreign Office, April* 27, 1904.
In the course of the discussions between Lord Lansdowne and the French Ambassador respecting the declaration with regard to Morocco, signed on the 8th of April, the French Ambassador drew attention to the agreement between the British and Moorish Gov[ernment]s of the 13th March, 1895, in which H[is] M[ajesty's] G[overnment] have recognised the territory in the neighbourhood of Cape Juby as belonging to Morocco on condition that no part of it shall be alienated without their concurrence.

L[or]d Lansdowne assured H[is] E[xcellency] that H[is] M[ajesty's] G[overnment] have no intention of claiming for Great Britain in consideration of that agreement, any special position or influence in the territory in question, and that they will not oppose any arrangements in regard to it, which may be found desirable in furtherance of the objects described in the Declaration.

He added that H[is] M[ajesty's] G[overnment] made this declaration with the less hesitation because they understood that the French Gov[ernmen]t are negotiating with the Spanish Government on the basis that this territory shall fall within the sphere of influence of Spain should the Sultan ever cease to exercise authority over it.

To such an arrangement H[is] M[ajesty's] G[overnment] would give their cordial approval.

No. 34.

The Marquess of Lansdowne to Sir E. Monson.

F.O. France 3662.
(No. 220.)   Confidential.
Sir,   *Foreign Office, April 29, 1904.*

The French Ambassador asked me to see him to-day on his return from Paris.
He brought with him maps of Morocco showing the territories which the French
Gov[ernmen]t proposed to recognize as falling within the Spanish sphere of influence.
His Excellency was subsequently good enough to send me tracings of these maps.
The limits of the two spheres as described on them do not differ materially from
those indicated to me by the Spanish Ambassador on the 27th instant.

His Excellency, after explaining these proposals, referred to the negotiations
which had taken place between the French and Spanish Governments in 1902. He
told me that upon that occasion M. Delcassé had been careful to explain that the
suggestions which he then made for the definition of the Spanish sphere of influence
were put forward on his own responsibility as a basis for discussion, and that he could
not make official proposals on behalf of the French Government until he had some
knowledge of the terms upon which the Spanish Government were prepared to deal.
M. Delcassé's suggestions had been "noted," and referred by M. Leon y Castillo to
the Spanish Government, but without any result. A change of Government at Madrid
had supervened, and the new Minister of Foreign Affairs, M. Abarsuza, had intimated
that Spain was not prepared to pursue the subject further without taking other Powers
into their confidence. Not only Great Britain but Germany would, the Minister had
said, have to be consulted. The matter had not been further pursued by the Spanish
Gov[ernmen]t at the time, and, more recently, no attempt had been made to reöpen
the discussion, although it was well known that negotiations were proceeding between
France and Great Britain.

I told his Excellency that I had listened with the greatest interest to his statement,
and I repeated to him what had been said to me on the 27th by the Spanish
Ambassador as to the inferiority of the terms now offered by M. Delcassé, as compared
with those alleged to have been offered in 1902. M. Cambon assured me positively
that there had never been any idea of bringing Fez within the Spanish sphere. It
was true that the boundary of the northern sphere had been traced in 1902 further to
the south than it was now intended to trace it, but there was at that time no question
of a second sphere in the neighbourhood of Cape Juby.([1]) The offer of the southern
sphere, to which the Spanish Government, as I was aware, attached great importance,
seemed to M. Delcassé an ample compensation for the contraction of the northern
sphere.

I told M. Cambon that I had found the Duc de Mandas greatly concerned at the
omission from the northern sphere of the territory between Melilla and the Muluya
River, and I called H[is] E[xcellency]'s attention to the fact that the line as shown
on the map which he had brought with him would leave the shore of the Mediterranean
at a point so close to Melilla that the French sphere would extend up to the very walls
of that place. I also pointed out that the Spaniards, naturally, resented an arrangement which would bring the coast in the immediate neighbourhood of the Zafarin
islands within the French sphere. I could not help hoping that M. Delcassé would
find it possible to make a concession at this point. I was convinced that such a
concession would have an excellent effect. His Excellency took my suggestion in
very good part, and promised to bear it in mind.

I am, &c.
LANSDOWNE.

([1]) [*v. infra* p. 35, No. 37.]

No. 35.

Sir E. Egerton to the Marquess of Lansdowne.

F.O. Spain 2194.
(No. 62.) Confidential.   *Madrid, D. May* 6, 1904.
My Lord,   *R. May* 14, 1904.

Señor Rodriguez San Pedro, when I saw him today, told me that Monsieur Delcassé had now recognized the justice of the Spanish claim that in the eventual spheres of influence in Morocco the French should not advance theirs to the mainland immediately opposite to the Zaffarine Islands beyond the Muluya River.

He attributed this change to the friendly aid of Your Lordship and expressed gratitude.

I did not say more than what I had already told him that I saw no reason whatever for uneasiness on the Spanish side in these negotiations or for suspicion of want of faith on the side of France.

His Excellency agreed, but he said there was a display of a bargaining spirit. This, I answered, one has to be prepared for in most negotiations.

I may mention incidentally to Your Lordship that a few days ago, the French Ambassador said to me that Señor San Pedro and the Spanish Government appeared to be rather difficult or prone to alarm, (I forget the exact word) in the negotiations going on in Paris respecting Morocco, with which negotiations he (Monsieur Cambon) had nothing to do.

I told him that though I do not interfere in what is not my business and discuss the matter with the Spaniards or others; my personal opinion is that the Spanish Government would have a grievance if the French sphere of influence were extended beyond the Muluya to the immediate rear of the Zaffarines thus cutting them off from communication with the mainland.

Monsieur Jules Cambon said this was his opinion too and that he was about to telegraph to Paris in that sense. Unfortunately Monsieur Etienne, the head of the Colonial party, was from Oran and felt strongly on the question.

I confided to His Excellency that as regards Spanish feeling on the subject of the Morocco arrangement—(though from my slight experience here my opinion may be fallacious), I have never considered—unless provoked by some glaring want of tact— that it is likely to be seriously excited by the turn events have taken or that opposition to the Anglo-French arrangement will injure the Government; moreover I consider Señor San Pedro to be a sensible unexcitable man and that the person on the Spanish side who has shewn most agitation has been the Ambassador in Paris.

I have, &c.
EDWIN H. EGERTON.

No. 36.

The Marquess of Lansdowne to Sir E. Monson.

F.O. France 3663.
(No. 248.) Confidential.
Sir,   *Foreign Office, May* 13, 1904.

The French Ambassador told me today, with reference to the conversation recorded in my despatch No. 220 of the 29th ultimo,([1]) that he had informed M. Delcassé that in the opinion of His Majesty's Government the Spanish Government were justified in claiming to have the region between Melilla and the Muluya River included in the Spanish sphere of influence. M. Delcassé was disposed to admit that there was something to be said for this view of the case, and he had accordingly sent for the Ambassador and told him that he was prepared to draw the frontier of the northern sphere of Spanish

([1]) [*v. supra* p. 33, No. 34.]

influence so that it should start near the mouth of the Muluya, and follow that river for some distance before turning to the west. M. Delcassé had also offered to extend the boundary of the southern sphere of Spanish influence further to the north, so that the line should start, not at Ras Agula as had been at first proposed, but at the mouth of the River Mesa. M. Delcassé had however explained to the Spanish Ambassador that these concessions were offered upon condition that the remainder of the French terms were accepted. He was not prepared to prolong the discussion of these details, and his offer was "à prendre ou à laisser." The Ambassador was apparently inclined to raise difficulties, but H[is] E[xcellency] thought that the matter would probably be arranged.

[I am, &c.
LANSDOWNE.]

No. 37.

The Marquess of Lansdowne to Sir E. Monson.

F.O. France 3663.
(No. 258.)
Sir, *Foreign Office, May* 13, 1904.(¹)
    The French Ambassador informed me during the course of our conversation today that he had been mistaken when on the 29th of April he told me that during the 1902 negotiations between France and Spain as to their interests in Morocco there had been no question of giving Spain a second sphere in the neighbourhood of Cape Juby. M. Delcassé had told him that a second sphere had in fact been then offered to Spain in that neighbourhood. His Excellency had however been unaware of the fact when he spoke to me on the subject.

[I am, &c.]
L[ANSDOWNE].

(¹) [The date of this despatch was queried on the draft retained by the Foreign Office by Lord Lansdowne. It was retained however on the final copy, now in the Embassy archives (F.O. France 3791). There it is endorsed as received on May 18, and this provides some confirmation for the conclusion that it was not actually despatched until the 15th or 16th.]

No. 38.

The Marquess of Lansdowne to Sir E. Egerton.

F.O. Spain 2193.
(No. 60.)
Sir, *Foreign Office, May* 16, 1904.
    The Spanish Ambassador asked me to give him an interview today, and told me that the Spanish Government had been much disappointed at M. Delcassé's attitude with regard to the definition of the Spanish spheres of influence in Morocco.
    It was true that the French Government had given up the idea of making the western frontier of the northern sphere begin at Melilla, but they had not moved it back to the actual mouth of the Muluya River, but to some heights of land situated between the river and Melilla. His Excellency pointed to a spot on the map which would apparently have placed the beginning of the frontier within about 20 miles of the latter place, but he was evidently in ignorance of the precise nature of the French proposal. He insisted however that it would have the effect of giving the whole valley of the Muluya to France, as well as the coast opposite the Zafarin Islands.
    On the Atlantic coast, the southern limit of the same sphere, instead of commencing at the mouth of the Sebou River, was, H[is] E[xcellency] said, to be fixed at a point considerably further to the north.
    Passing to the southern sphere, the northern boundary, instead of reaching, as was proposed in 1902 the River Sus, was to be drawn considerably further to the

[15869] D 2

south.   I said that I had been informed that the French Government were now willing that the line should start at the mouth of the Mesa instead of at Ras Agula, as they had at first proposed.   H[is] E[xcellency] was apparently not aware of this modification.   He pointed out to me however with much earnestness that the effect of the French proposals was to close to Spain the valleys of the Muluya, the Sebou and the Sus, thus denying to her these "voies de pénétration."

I told H[is] E[xcellency] that I would mention what he had said to his French colleague when I next saw him, but that it seemed to me that there must be other "voies de pénétration" within the regions which were to be recognized as falling under Spanish influence.

I am, &c.
LANSDOWNE.

No. 39.

The Marquess of Lansdowne to Sir E. Monson.

F.O. France 3663.
(No. 260.)
Sir,   *Foreign Office, May* 16, 1904.

I repeated to the French Ambassador this evening the substance of the observations which the Spanish Ambassador made to me this morning with regard to the manner in which the French Government was attempting to describe the two Spanish spheres of influence in Morocco.   I told him that I could not help thinking that there was some force in the Duc de Mandas' observation that the Spaniards would under the proposed arrangement be excluded from three important valleys, which they naturally regarded as "voies de pénétration" into the interior.   His Excellency told me that the Duc de Mandas was entirely mistaken in supposing that it was desired to commence the boundary of the northern sphere at a point distant from the River Muluya and within a few miles of Melilla.   The Muluya was a stream which sometimes ran dry, and it had been thought preferable that the frontier should follow a line of low hills running parallel with the river.   I begged his Excellency to repeat to M. Delcassé what I had said in support of the Spanish contention, and in regard to the Muluya I expressed a hope that it would be found possible to adopt the river itself as the frontier.   The point could not be one of great importance to the French Government.   His Excellency said that he would not fail to communicate my observations to M. Delcassé, and gave me to understand that in his own opinion it might be found possible to adopt the bed of the stream as the frontier if the Spaniards were not obstructive at other points.   It was however out of the question to give them Wazan, with the Chief of which France had entered into arrangements, and therefore the valley of the Sebou could not possibly be included in their sphere.

In the southern sphere liberal provision had, he thought, already been made for the satisfaction of Spanish interests.

I am, &c.
LANSDOWNE.

No. 40.

The Marquess of Lansdowne to Sir E. Monson.

F.O. France 3663.
(No. 262.)
Sir,   *Foreign Office, May* 18, 1904.

The French Ambassador told me to-day, with reference to what I had said to him on the 16th instant as to the limits of the Spanish sphere of influence in the north of Morocco, that on the morning after our conversation he had received from

M. Delcassé a letter informing him that he had decided to allow the Spanish sphere to extend up to the river Muluya, in the hope that this concession, to which the Spanish Government attached much importance, would terminate the discussion.

I am, &c.

LANSDOWNE.

No. 41.

Sir E. Monson to the Marquess of Lansdowne.

F.O. France 3666.

(No. 304.) Confidential. *Paris*, D. *May* 20, 1904.

My Lord, R. *May* 21, 1904.

I had a few minutes conversation the day before yesterday with M. Leon y Castillo at the Ministry of Foreign Affairs before the opening of the meeting for the signature of the Protocol, relating to the International White Slave Trade Agreement.

My Spanish colleague asked me whether I had had any instructions regarding the Franco-Spanish Negotiations on the Morocco question; and, on my telling him that I had none, he said that in that case he feared that Spain would be done out of half her rights in that country.

I, in my turn, asked him whether he had any fresh orders from Madrid; but it did not appear from his answer that he had received any.

He saw M. Delcassé immediately after our meeting, above referred to, broke up; and I have not seen him since.

I confess to being puzzled by the contradictions and inconsistencies which have cropped up in the various discussions which have taken place on this subject; but I am inclined to think that M. Leon y Castillo's version of the 1902 negotiations is fairly correct. The Ministry for Foreign Affairs at Madrid seems neither to have kept the Spanish Ambassador in London well informed; nor to have been able to keep in mind accurately for itself what had really occurred in Paris.

As for M. Leon y Castillo himself he lost sight of the difference in value between a signed and an unsigned understanding; and was led by his sanguine belief in his own achievements to overlook the maxim that "there is no such thing as sentiment in business transactions."

I have, &c.

EDMUND MONSON.

No. 42.

Sir E. Egerton to the Marquess of Lansdowne.

F.O. Spain 2194.

(No. 83.) *Madrid*, D. *June* 12, 1904.

My Lord, R. *June* 16, 1904.

In the Senate yesterday there was a short debate on the Morocco question initiated by Señor Groizard of the Liberal Party alluding to the supposed Treaty between France and Spain in 1902.

He was answered by the Minister for Foreign Affairs, who assured him that there was no Treaty of the kind—there had been mere negotiations on the part of the Liberal Government—but in the main even Señor Sagasta, as well as Señor Silvela or Señor Maura maintained the same attitude.

The treaty as published by the "Globo" was purely imaginary.

Señor Abarzuza confirmeu this, and said Señor Silvela had entered into no secret negotiations, the policy of his Government was the *status quo* in Morocco.

When the "Times" and the "Diplomatic Review" alluded to a Treaty of the kind, he at the time denied the truth of the statement here, as did Monsieur Delcassé in the French Chamber.

Even the negotiations of the Duke of Almodóvar cannot be said to have had a real being as they were born without conditions of life, and, as Señor Maura well said, wanted what was necessary for existence, and the Duke was ill-advised in alluding to them.

I have, &c.
EDWIN H. EGERTON.

No. 43.

Sir E. Egerton to the Marquess of Lansdowne.

Madrid, *July* 1, 1904.

F.O. Spain 2195.   D. 7·30 P.M.
Tel. (No. 32.) Confidential.   R. 10·15 P.M.

Franco-Spanish negotiations.

Spanish Minister for Foreign Affairs much disturbed at M. Delcassé's language, reported three days ago, to the effect that until the Empire of Morocco came to an end the influence of Spain over the territory to be allotted to her did not exist.

Spanish Minister for Foreign Affairs seemed to think that if France exercised police influence in Morocco, Spain in her future sphere must do likewise.

I answered that I did not think that it was a question at present of either Power exercising any police influence. French money was being advanced to save the Empire, which for many years to come might continue to exist.

The whole question, I said, is a delicate one, and should be treated without unnecessary mistrust.

He said there was nothing he wished more than the continuance of *status quo*, but he would not sign an Agreement which abandoned Spanish rights. He had telegraphed to London yesterday.

France would have no right, he repeated, to arrange for the police of Tangier.

I held that a diplomatic and not a contentious spirit was the great essential in the present negotiation.

No. 44.

The Marquess of Lansdowne to Sir E. Egerton.

F.O. Spain 2193.
(No. 86.)
Sir,   *Foreign Office, July* 2, 1904.

The Spanish Ambassador asked me to give him an interview today. Your telegram No. 32 of the 1st instant had prepared me for the communication which His Excellency made to me. It was to the effect that the negotiations between the Spanish Ambassador at Paris and M. Delcassé had been virtually concluded, when at the last moment M. Delcassé intimated that he desired the addition of a new clause under which the Spanish Government were to be precluded from taking any action within the sphere of influence which was to be allotted to Spain until such time as the *status quo* in Morocco had come to an end. His Excellency said that the Spanish Government regarded this as a very grave announcement, and entirely inconsistent with the intention of the Declaration respecting Egypt and Morocco made by the British and French Governments. If such a clause as M. Delcassé proposed were to be accepted, it would result that France would for an indefinite period have an exclusive title to establish her influence in Morocco, and she would do so in such a manner that Spain would never be given an opportunity of claiming that the political status of Morocco had been altered, and that the moment had come for the assertion of her rights to a sphere of influence in that country. His Excellency reminded me of the passage in my despatch of April 8th, 1904 to Sir Edmund Monson in which I wrote as follows :—

" An adequate and satisfactory recognition of Spanish interests, political and territorial, has been from the first in the view of His Majesty's Government an essential element in any settlement of the Morocco question. Spain has possessions on the Moorish coast, and the close proximity of the two countries has led to a reasonable expectation on the part of the Spanish Government and people that Spanish interests would receive special consideration in any arrangement affecting the future of Morocco."

I told His Excellency that without knowing more precisely what M. Delcassé had proposed it was difficult for me to express an opinion. I reminded His Excellency however that in Article II of the Declaration—an Article to which, so far as I was aware, the Spanish Government had never taken exception—His Majesty's Government had recognized " that it appertains to France more particularly as a Power whose dominions are coterminous for a great distance with those of Morocco, to preserve order in that country and to provide assistance for the purpose of all administrative, economic, financial, and military reforms which it may require." It seemed to me clear that this Article contemplated a state of things in which France would exercise a preponderating influence in the Sultan's councils—an influence which could not fail to react upon all parts of His Highness's dominions. What seemed to me to be of real importance was that in the event of a disintegration of Morocco the interests of Spain should not be overlooked, and I understood that M. Delcassé had agreed to provide for this contingency to the satisfaction of the Spanish Government. I asked His Excellency whether he could give me an idea of the manner in which Spain hoped in the immediate future to exercise her influence in certain portions of Morocco. Did the Spanish Government desire to construct railways, or to create a force of police, or to advance money to the Moorish Government? His Excellency did not seem able to answer my question, and I ventured to add that I thought the Spanish Government would do well to avoid preferring a claim to do these things, and endeavouring to prevent another Power from doing them unless they were really in a position to undertake in certain territories of Morocco the responsibilities which the French Government were about to assume in the greater portion of the country. If they really desired to effect improvements in the districts adjoining their own possessions, I thought it would be well that they should make a concrete proposal to that effect and see how it was received. I added that I would endeavour to ascertain the views of the French Government, and that I should be glad to speak to H[is] E[xcellency] again upon the subject next week.

His Excellency told me that he regarded the incident as one of the gravest importance. The increase or diminution of the Spanish sphere by a few miles of not very valuable country mattered comparatively little, but this was a direct denial of rights which Spain could not abandon. He believed that nothing would induce the Spanish Government to sign such an Article, and that if they were pressed to do so they would probably make an appeal to the Powers.

Your Excellency will recollect a statement made to me on the 1st ultimo by the German Ambassador as to the possibility of intervention by the German Government in the event of Spain receiving less than justice at the hands of France.([1]) It occurred to me that the Duc de Mandas' observation not improbably pointed to an attempt to obtain German support, should the French Government prove obdurate.

I am, &c
LANSDOWNE.

([1]) [v. infra p. 53, No. 61.]

No. 45.

The Marquess of Lansdowne to Sir E. Monson.

F.O. France 3663.
(No. 361.)
Sir, Foreign Office, July 4, 1904.

I mentioned to the French Ambassador to-day in strict confidence the observations which had been made to me on the 2nd instant by the Spanish Ambassador. I told him that, even if it were recognized that Spain had an immediate right of exercising a kind of peaceful penetration within the sphere of influence assigned to her by the Anglo-French Declaration, I thought it unlikely that the Spanish Government would be able to turn its opportunities to account. It would however be a pity not to recognize, in theory at all events, her aspirations in this direction : a peremptory refusal would have a bad effect, and possibly lead to international difficulties. His Excellency told me that the accounts which he had received from Paris did not at all agree with the Duc de Mandas' statement, and that he had understood that the difficulty had arisen in consequence of the demand of the Spanish Ambassador for leave to publish an Agreement as to the manner in which the possessions of the Sultan were to be disposed of in the event of the disintegration of Morocco. So far as the immediate future was concerned, M. Delcassé had been ready to humour the Spanish Government, and had made certain proposals to them with this object.

I am, &c
LANSDOWNE.

No. 46.

The Marquess of Lansdowne to Sir E. Egerton.

F.O. Spain 2193.
(No. 93.)
Sir, Foreign Office, July 6, 1904.

The Spanish Ambassador spoke to me again today with regard to the negotiations now proceeding between Spain and France as to the influence of those two Powers in Morocco. In the course of his observations, which were upon the same lines as those recorded in my despatch No. 86 of the 2nd instant,([1]) His Excellency observed that if any police were to be sent to Tangier for the purpose of restoring public confidence, those police ought in his opinion to be supplied by the Spanish Government. I told His Excellency that it seemed to me very doubtful whether Spain would be well advised in attempting to undertake a task of the kind, but that I did not see why the Spanish Government should not raise specifically the question of their right to the construction of railways or other useful works for developing the resources of the country within the sphere of influence which it was proposed to assign to them.

I am, &c
LANSDOWNE.

([1]) [v. supra pp. 38–40, No. 44.]

No. 47.

The Marquess of Lansdowne to Sir E. Monson.

F.O. France 3663.
(No. 368.)
Sir,   *Foreign Office, July* 8, 1904.

The French Ambassador asked me to see him this morning. He told me that in consequence of the observations which I had addressed to him on the 4th instant, he had informed M. Delcassé of the nature of the apprehensions which the Duc de Mandas had expressed with regard to the Spanish interests in Morocco.

M. Delcassé had authorized his Excellency to read to me a letter which he had lately addressed to the French Ambassador at Madrid. His Excellency accordingly proceeded to do so. In this letter M. Delcassé expressed his readiness to associate Spanish officials with the French officials in two out of the three ports of which the customs revenues would be affected as security for the new French loan. Besides this it was explained that Spain was to have a share in the economic development of the country; a share the nature of which was explained in the VIIIth Article of a draft Convention to which the French Government were ready to give its adherence.

M. Cambon explained to me that this economic participation had reference *e.g.*, to the construction of railways or "voies de pénétration." It was, therefore, his Excellency said, clear that the French Government were fully disposed to have regard to Spanish susceptibilities in these matters. As for Police, there was no question of imposing the presence of a French police force upon the Moorish Government. M. Delcassé's idea, on the contrary, was that it might be possible at the instance of the Sultan himself to lend the Moorish Government a French Agent to assist in reorganizing the Moorish Police. The statement in the newspapers that a force of Algerian Police was to be sent to Tangier no doubt originated in the fact that the European population at Tangier had been clamouring for such a step. It would, however, M. Cambon said, be most unwise to send Spanish police to Tangier or elsewhere, for their presence would be resented by the native population and the Sultan would be indignant.

His Excellency authorized me to communicate the substance of what he had said to me to the Duc de Mandas, and I did so at an interview which took place between the Duke and myself later in the day.

I am, &c.
LANSDOWNE.

No. 48.

Sir E. Egerton to the Marquess of Lansdowne.

F.O. Spain 2194.
(No. 109.)   Confidential.   *San Sebastian, D. July* 22, 1904.
My Lord,   R. *July* 27, 1904.

Señor Maura, the Prime Minister, arrived here yesterday to see the King prior to His Majesty's departure to-day, and has left for the South.

To those who questioned him on the subject of the Franco-Spanish negotiations respecting Morocco, he answered that Monsieur Delcassé being about to take a short leave of absence, there was an arrest for the moment in them.

Nobody appears more anxious on the subject than the German Ambassador, who, it seems, though desirous to join his family in Germany, has orders—he says—to await the conclusion of the negotiations.

This would at first sight point to exceptional interest on the part of the German

Emperor's Government in the question, but I venture to repeat that I believe it to be prompted by the fussy curiosity of timid agents rather than by serious political design.

I have in a few months been long enough in Spain to understand the remarkable dilatoriness of Spanish action; but neither my French Colleague nor myself have any certain ground for explaining the present delay in concluding an agreement so advantageous as the present appears to be for Spain.

The most influential person, in my opinion, at this Court perfectly agrees with me as to the danger of leaving the Morocco question pendant between France and Spain, and I am driven to the supposition—not of my own invention—that the injured vanity of Señor Leon y Castillo, who is trusted by the Queen, largely contributes to the delay in the understanding with France about Morocco.

I have, &c.
EDWIN H. EGERTON.

No. 49.

The Marquess of Lansdowne to Sir E. Monson.

F.O. France 3663.
(No. 410.)
Sir, *Foreign Office, July 29, 1904.*

The French Ambassador told me today that M. Delcassé had now come to terms with the Spanish Ambassador in regard to the position of the two Powers in Morocco, except upon a single point.

M. Delcassé had proposed that Spain should agree to an Article identical with Article III in our secret Agreement which runs as follows :—

"She would also have to undertake not to alienate the whole, or a part, of the territories placed under her authority or in her sphere of influence."

The Spanish Government considered that it would be derogatory to their dignity to accept such an obligation and proposed an alternative running as follows :—

"If at any time Spain decided to alienate or cede the whole or part of the territories indicated in Articles 1, 2 and 3, she would, on equal conditions, give the preference to France, whether it was a question of a definite cession or a temporary one."

M. Delcassé had replied that it was impossible for him to agree to this proposal, which was inconsistent with the Agreement at which he had arrived with H[is] M[ajesty's] Government, and he would be glad to know how I regarded the matter.

I replied that I certainly could not approve the adoption of the Spanish proposal without consulting my colleagues, and I felt little doubt that they would disapprove of it. I could not see that it was beneath the dignity of the Spanish Government to accept the stipulation which the French Government had seen its way to accept, and the stipulation was itself one of great importance.

I promised His Excellency that I would telegraph to Sir E. Egerton and ask him to impress this view of the case upon the Spanish Government. His Excellency readily accepted my proposal.

I subsequently addressed to H[is] M[ajesty's] Minister at Madrid the telegram of which a copy is attached to this despatch.(¹)

I have, &c.
LANSDOWNE.

(¹) [See next document.]

No. 50.

The Marquess of Lansdowne to Sir E. Egerton.

F.O. Spain 2195.   *Foreign Office, July 29, 1904.*
Tel. (No. 32.)   D. 11·20 P.M.

The French Ambassador informed me to-day that the Spanish Government consider it undignified to accept an Article identical with Article 3 of our Secret Agreement and that they propose the following alternative :—

"Si à un moment quelconque l'Espagne se décidait à aliéner ou à céder tout ou partie des territoires désignés aux Articles 1, 2 et 3, elle donnerait à condition égale la préférence à la France, qu'il s'agisse d'une cession définitive ou à titre temporaire."

The French Minister for Foreign Affairs has informed the Spanish Ambassador that he cannot accept this proposal, as it is inconsistent with the Anglo-French Agreement, and he has asked for my views on the subject.

I have said, in reply, that I could not approve to the Spanish proposal without consulting my colleagues and that I felt little doubt that they would disapprove of it.

Inform the Spanish Minister for Foreign Affairs, and impress upon him that I am quite unable to see that it is inconsistent with the dignity of the Spanish Government to accept the stipulation to which the French Government have agreed, or in what respect the Article which they propose is more favourable to them. Say that I attach great importance to stipulation as originally worded, and express the hope that they will see their way to accept it.

(Confidential.)

It is obviously undesirable that France should be given a preferential claim to the Spanish sphere in the event of Spain being unable to hold it.

No. 51.

Sir E. Egerton to the Marquess of Lansdowne.

F.O. Spain 2194.
(No. 113.) Confidential.
Decypher despatch.   *San Sebastian, D. July 29, 1904.*
My Lord,   R. *August 1, 1904.*

On July 25th I learned that Monsieur Delcassé had informed Spanish Ambassador, on his return from San Sebastian that he would defer leaving Paris for his Province if he could see hope of concluding the present negotiations respecting Morocco.

I was afraid from what I gathered that on the part of Spanish Government there was insistence on the publication of the understanding at a fixed date and a disposition to insist unduly on what the Minister termed the "rights" of Spain.

To-day I asked Minister for Foreign Affairs if Monsieur Delcassé were still in Paris and His Excellency replied in the affirmative that the French Minister for Foreign Affairs was awaiting the answer from Rome on the pending ecclesiastical difficulty.

On further questioning His Excellency, I was glad to learn that he was not without hope of a speedy arrangement being come to on the Morocco question. He entirely agreed with me as to the necessity for this, in the interest of general tranquillity, and explained that the difficulty about the publication was a constitutional one, the King could conclude no treaty with a secret clause. On my saying that this hindrance might be got over, he said that though he could not take it on his own responsibility to do so, he thought that there might, in view of the great importance of the result, be a solution and he had therefore submitted the matter to the Council of Ministers.

I have, &c.

EDWIN H. EGERTON.

No. 52.

Sir E. Egerton to the Marquess of Lansdowne.

F.O. Spain 2194.

(No. 115.)   *San Sebastian,* D. *July* 31, 1904.

My Lord,   R. *August* 6, 1904.

I saw Señor San Pedro to-day and spoke to him in the sense of the instructions of Your Lordship's telegram No. 32 received yesterday on the subject of a change proposed by the Spanish negotiator in Paris respecting Morocco.

I told His Excellency that Your Lordship had learnt that Señor Leon y Castillo had proposed to substitute—instead of a formal assent to the provisions of Article IV and VII of the Anglo-French declaration of the 8th of April last with the engagement not to alienate all or a portion of the territories placed under its authority or in its sphere of influence—an article stating that should Spain decide to alienate or cede the whole or part of the territories indicated in Articles 1, 2 or 3 she would on equal conditions give preference to France, whether it was a question of a definitive cession or a temporary one.

That Your Lordship could not understand that it should be incompatible with the dignity of Spain to accept the engagement to which France has assented nor that the Article proposed by Señor Leon y Castillo would be more favourable to the Spanish Government.

That I was charged by Your Lordship to declare that you attach the highest importance to the original text of the article, and to express Your Lordship's hope that the Government of His Catholic Majesty would find it possible to accept it.

His Excellency answered that in compliance with Your Lordship's wishes the proposal—a mere incident in the course of Señor Leon y Castillo's negotiation—has been dropped. It was made for no purpose but for mutual facility of minor exchanges—the occasion arising; but from the moment that England objected the Spanish Government abandoned it.

He had informed the Duke of Mandas of this and had also instructed him on the subject of a proposed French modification of the original agreement to which he most strongly objected.

Monsieur Delcassé proposed—in view of the difficulty of carrying out the arrangements under the agreement which it is hoped may be arrived at—that Spain should for a period of fifteen years (his first proposal was thirty) abandon the exercise of her influence in the zone allotted to her, and France was thus given the control of the African coast for that period.

This, I said, was new to me and I thought there must be some misunderstanding which might be cleared up—I had no reason to think the French Government harboured any sinister design, but were only anxious to avoid disturbances and bloodshed and were deeply impressed with the danger of the position. An immense number of minor matters had no doubt to be arranged, but these could be settled as they arose without attempting to settle them now.

His Excellency trusted that Your Lordship, as on previous occasions, might be willing and able to put this difficulty right and he left me under the impression that if it were got over the arrangement might be concluded shortly.

I have, &c.

EDWIN H. EGERTON.

No. 53.

Sir E. Egerton to the Marquess of Lansdowne.

San Sebastian, July 31, 1904.

F.O. Spain 2195.
Tel. (No. 39.)

D. 7 P.M.
R. 10 P.M.

Your telegram No. 32.

From the moment Spanish M[inister for] F[oreign] A[ffairs] learnt that Y[our] L[ordship] disapproved of suggestion made by Spanish Ambassador at Paris for alteration of stipulation forbidding alienation of Spanish sphere, His Exc[ellenc]y has abandoned it.

On the other hand he hopes for assistance from Y[our] L[ordship] in opposing a French proposal that Spain should abandon for 15 years the exercise of the duties of her future sphere of influence : this would give, he said, France the control of the Coast for that period.

He has instructed Spanish Ambassador in London to speak to Y[our] L[ordship] on the subject.

I told him that it was evident there was some misunderstanding which Y[our] L[ordship] might clear up.

Confidential. Spanish M[inister for] F[oreign] A[ffairs] is apparently so suspicious of French intentions that reference to Y[our] L[ordship] is necessary to reassure him. I gathered from H[is] E[xcellency] that this may be the last difficulty in the negotiations.

No. 54.

The Marquess of Lansdowne to Sir E. Egerton.

F.O. Spain 2193.
(No. 109.)

Sir,

Foreign Office, August 3, 1904.

The Spanish Ambassador spoke to me again today upon the subject of the negotiations which have for some time been proceeding between the French and Spanish Governments as to the position of Spain in Morocco. He told me that the French Government had proposed that Spain should not be at liberty to commence the process of " peaceful penetration," even in those districts with which she was most concerned, until after the lapse of a long period, say 15 or 20 years. The Spanish Government was far from desiring to resort to precipitate action in Morocco, but they resented this indefinite postponement of the realisation of their hopes. I told His Excellency that I could not help thinking that the French and Spanish Governments had been at cross purposes. I had certainly understood from M. Cambon that it had been clearly understood that at certain points Spain was to be allowed to assert herself at once, although it was, and in my opinion very properly, desired to postpone as long as possible, and perhaps for ever, such a disintegration of the Moorish Kingdom as would lead to the partition of the country between France and Spain.

Later in the afternoon I mentioned the subject to M. Cambon, who entirely confirmed the view which I had expressed. He told me that M. Delcassé had found the Spanish Minister unwilling to accept any arrangement which did not hold out to Spain the prospect of entering into possession of the Spanish sphere of influence within a period, the duration of which could be announced. M. Delcassé had strongly objected to such a premature " liquidation," and it was this which had led the Spanish Government to propose that they should be allowed to announce that after the lapse of 15 years they would be entitled to claim the reversion. The policy of the French

Government was to avoid a partition of the country, and to render the process of "peaceful penetration," either upon the Spanish or upon the French side, as gradual and unobtrusive as possible.

I have, &c.
LANSDOWNE.

No. 55.

The Marquess of Lansdowne to Sir E. Egerton.

F.O. Spain 2193.
(No. 116.)
Sir,   *Foreign Office, August* 16, 1904.
The Spanish Ambassador told me today that the negotiations between France and Spain with regard to the position of those two Powers in Morocco were still dragging on. The Spanish Government was most anxious to bring them to a conclusion, and had no desire to prefer unreasonable claims. His Excellency told me that they were ready to agree to a Clause running as follows :—

(Clause de délimitation.)
"Puis après :—

"Il est réservée à l'Espagne, dans la zone dont la délimitation vient d'être fixée ci-dessus, une action égale à celle qui est reconnue à la France par le paragraphe 2 de l'article 2 de la Déclaration du 8 Avril, 1904 relative au Maroc et à l'Égypte.
"Cependant en considération des difficultés actuelles et de l'avantage réciproque de les aplanir, l'Espagne déclare qu'elle se propose de ne pas faire usage de cette action si ce n'est d'accord avec la France et par les moyens dont pourront convenir les deux Gouvernements pendant la première période d'application de la présente Convention, période qui ne pourra pas excéder de quinze ans à compter du jour de la signature du présent acte ; et la France de son côté, pour l'action qu'elle aura à exercer près du gouvernement du Maroc tant que le *statu quo* durera, devra procéder d'accord avec le Gouvernement espagnol en ce qui touche la zone d'influence réservée à l'Espagne."

I said that the Clause seemed to me, *primâ facie*, a very reasonable one, and I asked whether it had been rejected by the French Government. His Excellency said that it had not yet been offered to M. Delcassé, but that your Excellency was aware of the nature of the proposal. I promised the Duc de Mandas that I would endeavour to find an opportunity of ascertaining how the French Government regarded the proposed clause. M. Cambon was however unfortunately absent from England, and I might not have the chance of speaking to him on the subject for some time.

Should your Excellency have an opportunity of discussing the subject with your French colleague, you might endeavour to ascertain whether the French Government would be likely to raise any objection to the terms proposed.

I am, &c
LANSDOWNE.

No. 56.

Sir E. Monson to the Marquess of Lansdowne.

F.O. France 3667.
(No. 507.) Confidential.
My Lord,

Paris, D. *September* 14, 1904.
R. *September* 16, 1904.

I had the honour to report to Your Lordship by my telegram No. 72 Confidential of yesterday([1]) the fact that the Marquis del Muni, Spanish Ambassador in Paris, had made inquiry as to whether I had received instructions to support the new clause defining the conditions under which Spain should be allowed to exercise her influence during the next fifteen years in the sphere allotted to her in Northern Morocco which has been now put forward by the Spanish Government.([2])

His Excellency asked this question in the course of an interview with Mr. de Bunsen, whom he had requested to call at the Spanish Embassy.

The allusion being clearly to the clause communicated to Your Lordship by the Spanish Ambassador in London, Mr. de Bunsen said that he believed Your Lordship had expressed to the Duc de Mandas a favourable opinion of its terms, which you had regarded, *primâ facie*, as reasonable. He added that he understood that your Lordship had promised to endeavour to find an opportunity of ascertaining the views of the French Government on the question, and that he imagined that Your Lordship was dealing with the question in an official manner with the French Embassy in London.

In giving this reply to the Marquis del Muni, Mr. de Bunsen had in mind the contents of Your Lordship's despatches No. 116 to Sir Edwin Egerton of the 16th, and No. 452, Confidential, to myself of the 17th of last month.([3])

The Marquis del Muni, as usual, expressed himself as being thoroughly dissatisfied with the spirit in which the French Government had carried on the negotiations. He had found M. Delcassé hard and unsympathetic from the first, and he despaired of getting him to take a fair view of the position in which Spain was placed and of the demands which her past relations with Morocco compelled her to make. Spain still counted, he said, mainly on the support of England to obtain what she wanted. England, he hoped, would be led by her own interest to assist Spain in frustrating the evident aim of France, which was to exclude Spain from all participation in the work of civilizing Morocco. France, it was true, had been obliged by the terms of her Agreement with England to recognize an eventual sphere of Spanish influence in Morocco; but Spain was not to exercise her influence there for fifteen years, and it was clear that by that time France would be so firmly established along the coast, as well as in the interior of the country, that it would be impossible for Spain to take her legitimate place in the zone allotted to her.

Thus M. Delcassé would have secured for his country, by indirect means, the control of Northern Morocco, which it had been the avowed object of the Anglo-French Agreement to reserve to her weaker neighbour.

I have, &c.
(For the Ambassador),
M. DE BUNSEN.

([1]) [Not reproduced.]
([2]) [The Duc de Mandas made an enquiry as to the progress of negotiations at the Foreign Office on September 7. He was informed that no communication had yet been received from France, and that the absence of Lord Lansdowne from London, and M. Delcassé from Paris, and of the French Ambassador at Madrid from Madrid had prevented further negotiations.]
([3]) [Despatch No. 452 to Sir E. Monson (F.O. France 3663) records an interview between Sir E. Gorst and M. Geoffray at which the former communicated the substance of Despatch No. 116 to Sir E. Egerton, and at which a copy of the clause proposed by the Duc de Mandas was given privately to M. Geoffray.]

No. 57.

Sir E. Monson to the Marquess of Lansdowne.

F.O. France 3667.
(No. 509.)   Confidential.   *Paris,* D. *September* 16, 1904.
My Lord,   R. *September* 17, 1904.

I had the honour to report to Your Lordship, in my telegram No. 73 Confidential
of the 14th instant,(¹) the unsatisfactory result, as declared by the Spanish Ambassador
in Paris, of the latter's first interview with the French Minister of Foreign Affairs
on the subject of the recent proposals of the Spanish Government in respect of the
partition of French and Spanish interests in Morocco.

The Marquis del Muni was closeted with M. Delcassé for an hour and a-half.
On returning into the waiting-room he informed Mr. de Bunsen that his Excellency
has been as discouraging as ever. Far from accepting a settlement on the basis
proposed by Spain, which is to the effect that for the next fifteen years Spain shall
take no action within her sphere in Northern Morocco without a previous understanding
with France, M. Delcassé scouted entirely the idea of any Spanish penetration
whatever into that sphere during the period in question, and would go no further
than to offer that France would take no steps within the Spanish Sphere without
giving previous notice to Spain.

His Excellency said his Government could never accept such a proposal as this,
and that he saw at present no way out of the difficulty.

I have, &c.
(For the Ambassador),
M. DE BUNSEN.

(¹) [Not reproduced, but *cf.* No. 56 *supra.*]

No. 58.

M. Cambon to the Marquess of Lansdowne.(¹)

F.O. France 3686.
Secret,   *Ambassade de France à Londres,*
Cher Lord Lansdowne,   *le* 6 *octobre* 1904.

Je suis chargé de vous communiquer les arrangements qui viennent d'être conclus
entre la France et l'Espagne au sujet du Maroc—Ils ont été signés le 3 c[ouran]t par
notre ministre des affaires Etrangères et l'Ambassadeur d'Espagne à Paris; ils se
composent d'une déclaration générale destinée à être publiée et d'une convention qui
doit rester secrète.

En me prescrivant de vous remettre le texte de cet accord, conformément aux
dispositions de l'article VIII de notre déclaration du 8 avril 1904, M. Delcassé a
insisté sur le caractère confidentiel de cette communication et m'a chargé de vous prier
de vouloir bien tenir la convention absolument secrète.

Veuillez agréer, Cher Lord Lansdowne, l'expression de mes sentiments dévoués.
PAUL CAMBON.

Enclosure 1 in No. 58.(²)

Declaration signed at Paris, October 3, 1904.

F.O. France 3686.

Le Gouvernement de la République Française et le Gouvernement de Sa
Majesté le Roi d'Espagne, s'étant mis d'accord pour fixer l'étendue des droits et la
garantie des intérêts qui résultent pour la France de ses possessions algériennes, et
pour l'Espagne de ses possessions sur la Côte du Maroc, et, le Gouvernement de Sa

(¹) [Printed, *A. & P.* (1912–3), CXXII, (*Cd.* 6010), p. 36.]
(²) [Printed, *ibid.*, p. 31. For enclosure No. 2, see next document.]

Majesté le Roi d'Espagne ayant en conséquence donné son adhésion à la Déclaration Franco-Anglaise du 8 Avril, 1904, relative au Maroc et à l'Égypte dont communication lui avait été faite par le Gouvernement de la République Française, DÉCLARENT qu'ils demeurent fermement attachés à l'intégrité de l'Empire Marocain sous la souveraineté du Sultan.

En foi de quoi, les soussignés, son Excellence le Ministre des Affaires Étrangères et son Excellence l'Ambassadeur Extraordinaire et Plénipotentiaire de Sa Majesté le Roi d'Espagne près le Président de la République Française, dûment autorisés à cet effet, ont dressé la présente Déclaration, qu'ils ont revêtue de leurs cachets.

Fait, en double exemplaire, à Paris, le 3 Octobre, 1904.

(Signé)   DELCASSÉ.

F. DE LÉON Y CASTILLO.

No. 59.

Convention between France and Spain, signed at Paris, October 3, 1904.([1])

F.O. France 3686.
(Secret.)

Le Président de la République Française et Sa Majesté le Roi d'Espagne, voulant fixer l'étendue des droits et la garantie des intérêts qui résultent, pour la France, de ses possessions algériennes, et, pour l'Espagne, de ses possessions sur la Côte du Maroc, ont décidé de conclure une Convention et ont nommé, à cet effet, pour leurs Plénipotentiaires, savoir :

Le Président de la République Française, S[on] Exc[ellence] M. Th. Delcassé,
    Député, Ministre des Affaires Étrangères de la République Française, &c. ; et
Sa Majesté le Roi d'Espagne, S[on] Exc[ellence] M. de Léon y Castillo, Marquis
    del Muni, son Ambassadeur Extraordinaire et Plénipotentiaire près le
    Président de la République Française, &c. ;

Lesquels, après s'être communiqués leurs pleins pouvoirs, trouvés en bonne et due forme, sont convenus des articles suivants :—

ARTICLE I.

L'Espagne adhère, aux termes de la présente Convention, à la Déclaration Franco-Anglaise du 8 Avril 1904 relative au Maroc et à l'Égypte.

ARTICLE II.

La région située à l'ouest et au nord de la ligne ci-après déterminée constitue la sphère d'influence, qui résulte pour l'Espagne de ses possessions sur la Côte Marocaine de la Méditerranée.

Dans cette zône, est réservée à l'Espagne la même action qui est reconnue à la France par le 2ᵃᵐᵉ paragraphe de l'article II de la Déclaration du 8 Avril, 1904, relative au Maroc et à l'Égypte.

Toutefois, tenant compte des difficultés actuelles et de l'intérêt réciproque qu'il y a à les applanir, l'Espagne déclare qu'elle n'exercera cette action qu'après accord avec la France pendant la première période d'application de la présente Convention, période qui ne pourra pas excéder quinze ans à partir de la signature de la Convention.

([1]) [Published in *Le Matin*, November 1911. It was presented to both Houses of Parliament in December of the same year as Morocco No. 4 of 1911 and published as *A. & P.* (1912–3), CXXII, (*Cd.* 6010), pp. 29–37.]

De son côté, pendant la même période, la France, désirant que les droits et les intérêts reconnus à l'Espagne par la présente Convention soient toujours respectés, fera part préalablement au Gouvernement du Roi de son action près du Sultan du Maroc en ce qui concerne la sphère d'influence espagnole.

Cette première période expirée, et tant que durera le *statu quo*, l'action de la France près du Gouvernement Marocain, en ce qui concerne la sphère d'influence réservée à l'Espagne, ne s'exercera qu'après accord avec le Gouvernement Espagnol.

Pendant la première période, le Gouvernement de la République Française fera son possible pour que, dans deux des ports à douane de la région ci-après déterminée, le délégué du Représentant Général des porteurs de l'emprunt marocain du 12 Juillet 1904 soit de nationalité espagnole.

Partant de l'embouchure de la Moulouia dans la mer Méditerranée, la ligne visée ci-dessus remontera le thalweg de ce fleuve jusqu'à l'alignement de la crête des hauteurs les plus rapprochées de la rive gauche de l'Oued Defla. De ce point, et sans pouvoir, en aucun cas, couper le cours de la Moulouia, la ligne de démarcation gagnera, aussi directement que possible, la ligne de faîte séparant les bassins de la Moulouia et de l'Oued Inaouen de celui de l'Oued Kert, puis elle continuera vers l'Ouest par la ligne de faîte séparant les bassins de l'Oued Inaouen et de l'Oued Sebou de ceux de l'Oued Kert et de l'Oued Ouergha pour gagner par la crête la plus septentrionale le Djebel Moulai Bou Chta. Elle remontera ensuite vers le Nord, en se tenant à une distance d'au moins vingt-cinq kilomètres à l'Est de la route de Fez à Kçar-el-Kébir par Ouezzan jusqu'à la rencontre de l'Oued Loukkos ou Oued-el-Kous, dont elle descendra le thalweg jusqu'à une distance de cinq kilomètres en aval du croisement de cette rivière avec la route précitée de Kçar-el-Kébir par Ouezzan. De ce point, elle gagnera, aussi directement que possible, le rivage de l'Océan Atlantique au dessus de la lagune de Ez Zerga.

Cette délimitation est conforme à la délimitation tracée sur la carte annexée à la présente Convention sous le No. 1.([1])

ARTICLE III.

Dans le cas où l'état politique du Maroc et le Gouvernement Chérifien ne pourraient plus subsister ou si, par la faiblesse de ce gouvernement et par son impuissance persistante à assurer la sécurité et l'ordre publics ou pour toute autre cause à constater d'un commun accord, le maintien du *statu quo* devenait impossible, l'Espagne pourrait exercer librement son action dans la région délimitée à l'article précédent et qui constitue dès à présent sa sphère d'influence.

ARTICLE IV.

Le Gouvernement Marocain ayant, par l'article VII du traité du 26 Avril, 1860,([1]) concédé à l'Espagne un établissement à Santa Cruz de mar Pequeña (Ifni), il est entendu que le territoire de cet établissement ne dépassera pas le cours de l'Oued Tazeroualt depuis sa source jusqu'à son confluent avec l'Oued Mesa, et le cours de l'Oued Mesa depuis ce confluent jusqu'à la mer, selon la carte No. 2 annexée à la présente Convention.([2])

ARTICLE V.

Pour compléter la délimitation indiquée par l'article I de la Convention du 27 Juin 1900,([3]) il est entendu que la démarcation entre les sphères d'influence française et espagnole partira de l'intersection du méridien 14° 20' Ouest de Paris avec le 26° de latitude Nord qu'elle suivra vers l'Est jusqu'à sa rencontre avec le méridien 11° Ouest de Paris. Elle remontera ce méridien jusqu'à sa rencontre avec l'Oued Draa, puis le thalweg de l'Oued Draa jusqu'à sa rencontre avec le méridien 10° Ouest de Paris, enfin le méridien 10° Ouest de Paris jusqu'à la ligne de faîte entre

---

([1]) [Printed *B.F.S.P.*, Vol. 51, p. 930.]
([2]) [Not reproduced.]
([3]) [Printed *B.F.S.P.*, Vol. 92, pp. 1014–5.]

les bassins de l'Oued Draa et de l'Oued Sous, et suivra, dans la direction de l'Ouest, la ligne de faîte entre les bassins de l'Oued Draa et de l'Oued Sous, puis entre les bassins côtiers de l'Oued Mesa et de l'Oued Noun jusqu'au point le plus rapproché de la source de l'Oued Tazeroualt.

Cette délimitation est conforme à la délimitation tracée sur la carte No. 2 déjà citée et annexée à la présente Convention.

ARTICLE VI.

Les articles IV et V seront applicables en même temps que l'article II de la présente Convention.

Toutefois, le Gouvernement de la République Française admet que l'Espagne s'établisse à tout moment dans la partie définie par l'Article IV, à la condition de s'être préalablement entendue avec le Sultan.

De même, le Gouvernement de la République Française reconnaît dès maintenant au Gouvernement espagnol pleine liberté d'action sur la région comprise entre les 26° et 27° 40′ de latitude Nord et le méridien 11° Ouest de Paris qui sont en dehors du territoire marocain.

ARTICLE VII.

L'Espagne s'engage à n'aliéner ni à céder sous aucune forme, même à titre temporaire, tout ou partie des territoires désignés aux articles II, IV, et V de la présente Convention.

ARTICLE VIII.

Si, dans l'application des articles II, IV, et V de la présente Convention, une action militaire s'imposait à l'une des deux parties contractantes, elle en avertirait aussitôt l'autre partie. En aucun cas il ne sera fait appel au concours d'une Puissance étrangère.

ARTICLE IX.

La ville de Tanger gardera le caractère spécial que lui donnent la présence du corps diplomatique et ses institutions municipale et sanitaire.

ARTICLE X.

Tant que durera l'état politique actuel, les entreprises de travaux publics, chemins de fer, routes, canaux partant d'un point du Maroc pour aboutir dans la région visée à l'article II et *vice versâ*, seront exécutées par des Sociétés que pourront constituer des français et des espagnols.

De même, il sera loisible aux français et aux espagnols au Maroc de s'associer pour l'exploitation des Mines, carrières, et généralement d'entreprises d'ordre économique.

ARTICLE XI.

Les écoles et établissements espagnols actuellement existants au Maroc seront respectés. La circulation de la monnaie espagnole ne sera ni empêchée ni entravée. Les espagnols continueront de jouir au Maroc des droits que leur assurent les Traités, Conventions, et usages en vigueur, y compris le droit de navigation et de pêche, dans les eaux et ports marocains.

ARTICLE XII.

Les Français jouiront, dans les régions désignées aux articles II, IV, et V de la présente Convention, des mêmes droits qui sont, par l'article précédent, reconnus aux Espagnols dans le reste du Maroc.

ARTICLE XIII.

Dans le cas où le Gouvernement Marocain en interdirait la vente sur son territoire, les deux Puissances Contractantes s'engagent à prendre, dans leurs possessions d'Afrique, les mesures nécessaires pour empêcher que les armes et les munitions soient introduites en contrebande au Maroc.

ARTICLE XIV.

Il est entendu que la zone visée au paragraphe 1 de l'article VII de la Déclaration Franco-Anglaise du 8 Avril 1904, relative au Maroc et à l'Égypte, commence sur la côte à trente kilom[ètres] au Sud-Est de Melilla.

ARTICLE XV.

Dans le cas où la dénonciation prévue par le paragraphe III de l'article IV de la Déclaration Franco-Anglaise, relative au Maroc et à l'Égypte, aurait eu lieu, les Gouvernements français et espagnol se concerteront pour l'établissement d'un régime économique qui réponde particulièrement à leurs intérêts réciproques.

ARTICLE XVI.

La présente Convention sera publiée lorsque les deux Gouvernements jugeront, d'un commun accord, qu'elle peut l'être sans inconvénients.

En tous cas, elle pourra être publiée par l'un des deux Gouvernements à l'expiration de la première période de son application, période qui est définie au paragraphe III de l'article II.

En foi de quoi, les Plénipotentiaires respectifs ont signé la présente Convention et l'ont revêtue de leurs cachets.

Fait, en double exemplaire, à Paris, le 3 Octobre, 1904.

(L.S.)   (Signé)   DELCASSÉ.
(L.S.)   (Signé)   F. DE LÉON Y CASTILLO.

No. 60.

The Marquess of Lansdowne to Mr. Adam.

F.O. Spain 2193.
(No. 131.)
Sir,   *Foreign Office, October 5, 1904.*

The Spanish Ambassador told me today that he was glad to be able to inform me that an Agreement between France and Spain with regard to their interests in Morocco had now been actually signed. It was not however to be published yet. His Excellency was good enough to say that the close watch which His Majesty's Government had kept upon the proceedings had been of the greatest service to the Spanish Government, who were extremely grateful to us.

I am, &c.
LANSDOWNE.

II.—GERMANY AND MOROCCO, JUNE 1904-MAY 1905.([1])

No. 61.

The Marquess of Lansdowne to Sir F. Lascelles.

F.O. Germany (Prussia) 1592.
(No. 126.)
Sir,   *Foreign Office, June 1, 1904.*

The German Ambassador spoke to me today at some length in regard to that part of the recently concluded Agreement between Great Britain and France which specially affected Morocco. I had no doubt, His Excellency observed, noticed the consternation which the conclusion of the Agreement had created in Spain. The shock had been so great that it might occasion the fall of the Monarchy and the establishment of a Republic. Monarchical institutions were not, His Excellency thought, securely established, either in Spain or in Italy, and it would be a serious thing if all the three Latin Powers were to become Republican. His Excellency expressed serious apprehension as to the outcome of the negotiation said to be in progress between France and Spain in regard to Morocco. Germany could not remain indifferent if the result of these should be to give France access to the coast-line of the Mediterranean in the neighbourhood of the Straits of Gibraltar, and if the claim of Spain to have her existing rights maintained and her reversionary interests taken into account were to be ignored, it might become necessary for Germany to give Spain diplomatic support.

I told His Excellency that I had not seen either his French or Spanish colleagues since my return, and that I did not therefore know what stage the negotiations had reached. My impression when I left London had however been that they were likely to lead to a solution which Spain would be able to accept. I reminded His Excellency of the terms of Article VII of the Anglo-French Declaration, under which the two Powers are precluded from permitting the erection of fortifications or strategic works on that portion of the coast of Morocco which lies between Melilla and the River Sebou, and I pointed out that irrespective of this stipulation no one had proposed that Spain should be ousted from the positions which she at present occupied in Morocco. I had myself no doubt that the negotiations would end in securing for her a sphere of influence not only comprising a considerable portion of the coastline, but also a certain extent of hinterland lying in the rear of it.

His Excellency explained that his observations were to be regarded as made to me unofficially.([2])

I am, &c
LANSDOWNE.

([1]) [*Cf. G.P.* XX, I, Chs. 145 and 146.]
([2]) [For Count Metternich's report, see *G.P.* XX, I, pp. 177–8.]

No. 62.

The Marquess of Lansdowne to Sir F. Lascelles.

F.O. Germany (Prussia) 1592.
(No. 170.)
Sir,   *Foreign Office, August 15, 1904.*

The German Ambassador called upon me this afternoon and told me, explaining that he did so unofficially, that the German Government was anxiously watching the course of events in Morocco, to which he had called my attention on the 1st of June last. They desired that the *status quo* should, so far as possible, be maintained in that country, that the Sultan should remain independent, and that the policy of the open door should prevail. They observed that markets were being closed to German trade all over the world, and they were anxious that the Moorish markets should not be so closed. They had a Commercial Treaty with Morocco which entitled them for all time to most-favoured-nation treatment,(¹) and they imagined that this was sufficient to prevent their trade being unfairly treated. They were however not so sure that they could depend upon fair treatment in regard to concessions and industrial enterprises. They thought they saw symptoms of an intention on the part of France to monopolise these, and they had some doubts as to the manner in which we should regard attempts of the kind. They observed that under Article IX of the Declaration respecting Egypt and Morocco the two Governments agree to afford to one another their diplomatic support in order to obtain the execution of the Declaration. Did this, His Excellency went on to say, mean that, supposing a German concessionnaire was unfairly treated by the Moorish Government at the instance of France, we should support the French Government in their action, and what was the intention of the words at the end of Article IV in which France and Great Britain reserve to themselves in Egypt and Morocco the right to see that concessions for roads, railways, ports, &c., "are only granted on such conditions as will maintain intact the authority of the State over these great undertakings of public interest?"

I told His Excellency that I did not much like expressing an opinion upon an hypothetical case, but that the whole spirit of the Anglo-French Agreement was indicated by the opening words of Article IV, in which it was announced that the two Governments were equally attached to the principle of commercial liberty both in Egypt and Morocco. His Excellency should not forget that in our Agreement with France we made no attempt to dispose of the rights of other Powers, although we made certain concessions in respect of the rights and opportunities to which we were ourselves entitled. I could at any rate say that it was not at all probable that, if any third Power were to have occasion to uphold its Treaty rights, we should use our influence in derogation of them. His Excellency made it clear to me that Germany intended to uphold any rights which she was entitled to claim in Morocco under existing Treaties.(²)

I am, &c
LANSDOWNE.

(¹) [This is the treaty of 1890, published in *B.F.S.P.*, Vol. 82, pp. 968–72.]
(²) [For Count Metternich's report, *v. G.P.* XX, I, pp. 219–222.]

No. 63.

Sir E. Monson to the Marquess of Lansdowne.

F.O. France 3667.
(No. 529.)   *Paris*, D. *October* 7, 1904.
My Lord,   R. *October* 8, 1904.

In all recent discussions concerning French action in Morocco, a distinction has been drawn between the policy which it is expedient to adopt respectively in the regions adjoining the Algerian frontier and in the remaining parts of the country. Whereas, as regards Morocco as a whole, the French Government aim at "pacific penetration" to be pursued in the name of the Sultan and with the assistance of French officers and advisers dependent on the French Legation at Tangiers or placed by the latter at the Sultan's disposal, the frontier districts have been the subject of special arrangements between the representative of the Sultan and the Governor General of Algeria negotiating at Algiers. The upshot of these arrangements has been the establishment of a free zone along the frontier at which markets are held and goods exchanged without payment of customs duties, and further the fixing of a new frontier-line in the Figuig region and southwards, lying considerably to the west of the line generally accepted before the recent attack on French troops and the raids on the

French lines of communication to the south which followed that attack. The French posts on the route to Touat and Tidikelt have also been considerably strengthened and rendered more mobile.

A further development of the frontier policy indicated above appears to be now in contemplation, and advantage has been taken of the presence in Paris of M. Jonnart, Governor General of Algeria, General Lyantey [*sic*], commanding the French troops at Ain-Sefra, in Southern Oran, and M. Saint-René Taillandier, French Minister at Tangiers, to hold consultations with a view to deciding on the best course to be pursued.

I have the honour to forward herewith an article from the " Temps "(¹) offering suggestions on this point, to the effect, mainly, that a French military post be established at Ras-el-Aïn, in order to overawe the neighbouring tribes, and that the Sultan be induced to appoint a Governor over the frontier districts not reached by the authority of the existing Moorish Governors at Oudjda and Figuig. The Moorish frontier authorities should be encouraged, in the writer's opinion, to institute gradually a settled system of government, and to bring the tribes under some scheme of taxation as has been done in Tunis. For this purpose it is essential that they should be supported by an armed force, receiving regular pay.

I have, &c.
EDMUND MONSON.

(¹) [Not reproduced.]

No. 64.

Sir E. Monson to the Marquess of Lansdowne.

F.O. France 3668.
(No. 660.)   *Paris*, D. *December* 26, 1904.
My Lord,   R. *December* 27, 1904.

The news of the dismissal by the Sultan of Morocco of his foreign advisers and " employés," including the French Military Mission, has attracted, as is natural, great attention in France. It has been hailed by the prophets of evil in respect of the responsibilities undertaken by France in Morocco, under the Anglo-French Understanding of the 8th of April last, as an early confirmation of their warnings. The Government Press however is not yet prepared to admit that the policy of " pacific penetration " will have to be abandoned. It agrees with the Opposition newspapers in declaring loudly that the slight put upon the Power which is to be henceforward the predominant one in Morocco must be resented and punished. But it holds that the measures to be taken with this end in view must be such as not to impair the Sultan's authority, which is still to be the main instrument of the French pacific advance into the country. In the article herewith transmitted to your Lordship, the " Temps " hints at two possible alternatives.(¹) Either the Oujda district may be annexed, or the eight ports open to foreign commerce may be seized and held pending compliance with the French demands.

The latter course, however, might prove dangerous to the Sultan himself, and should only be adopted, in the opinion of the " Temps," in the event of the Sultan's folly compelling the French Government to take the most thorough-going measures. Meanwhile there is general approval of M. Delcassé's action in withdrawing all the French citizens residing in Fez.

I have, &c.
EDMUND MONSON.

(¹) [Not reproduced.]

No. 65.

[*ED. NOTE.*—The two following despatches from Sir F. Lascelles give the views of Count Bülow and Herr von Holstein upon Anglo-German relations at this period.]

(a.)

Sir F. Lascelles to the Marquess of Lansdowne.

F.O. Germany (Prussia) 1594.
(No. 299.) Confidential. *Berlin,* D. *December* 28, 1904.
My Lord, R. *January* 2, 1905.

On the evening of the 24th instant I called by appointment on Count Bülow, whom I had not had a previous opportunity of seeing since my return to Berlin on the 19th instant. After an exchange of ordinary civilities I told His Excellency that the King had charged me with a personal message to him :—viz., that His Majesty had read with interest and satisfaction the report which Mr. Whitehead had addressed to Your Lordship of His Excellency's recent speech in the Reichstag, and had complete confidence in the sincerity of His Excellency's desire for a good understanding between our two Countries. Count Bülow, who was evidently highly gratified by this gracious message begged me to convey his warmest thanks to His Majesty.

His Excellency went on to say that sincere as his desire was to cultivate friendly relations with England, he found it no easy task to do so as England did not seem inclined to reciprocate. On the contrary the constant attacks in the English press, which had met with no official disapproval, and the new scheme for the reorganization of the British navy had given rise to a belief, which had become very prevalent in Germany, that England had the intention of attacking her. So strong had this belief become that His Excellency had thought it advisable to consult Count Metternich on the subject, and he had therefore requested him to come to Berlin. Count Bülow requested me to consider this information as strictly confidential, as, in order to avoid creating suspicion, it had been given out that urgent private affairs had been the cause of Count Metternich's sudden arrival in Berlin.

Count Metternich, speaking under the full responsibility which his position as German Ambassador in London imposed upon him, stated his conviction that there was absolutely no ground for the alarm that had been felt in Germany. He was convinced that neither His Majesty's Government nor the vast majority of the English people had the remotest intention of attacking Germany. Count Metternich's statements had given great satisfaction to the Emperor, who had become suspicious in consequence of his attention having been drawn to a recent article in the "Army and Navy Gazette" and a suggestion in "Vanity Fair" that England should treat the German fleet in 1904 as she treated the Danish fleet in 1808.

I said that the two papers he mentioned were without any practical importance and I thought it a pity that the Emperor should have paid any attention to them. I had seen Count Metternich who had asked me whether I thought he had gone too far in giving such positive assurances to the Emperor and I had replied that I not only fully endorsed what he had said, but should have been inclined to go a good deal further and say that I did not believe there was a sane man in England who seriously contemplated the possibility of England's attacking Germany. Such an idea appeared to me so preposterous that I thought I should have some difficulty in making your Lordship believe that it was really entertained in Germany. It might perhaps be said that the scheme for the reorganization of the British fleet was directed against Germany, and this was true to the extent that it was probable that the scheme would not have been considered necessary if the German Fleet had not been built. His Excellency should remember that a great number of my countrymen regarded the construction of the German Fleet as a direct menace to England.

Count Bülow laughed at the idea that the German fleet could be considered a danger to England when one compared its size with that of the English Fleet, but I assured him that it was argued in England that a powerful and constantly-increasing squadron, which hitherto had been concentrated in home waters whilst the English Fleet was scattered all over the world, might, if it became hostile, prove a serious danger to England, against which it was considered necessary to take precautions. However ridiculous the English apprehensions with regard to the possible action of the German Fleet might seem to him, they seemed to me to be less ridiculous than the German apprehensions of an intention on the part of England to attack Germany.

Count Bülow said that the Emperor would certainly be amused to hear that any alarm was felt in England at the possible action of the German Fleet. He was relieved at hearing my confirmation of Count Metternich's statement that there was no danger of England attacking Germany and he was inclined to agree with Count Metternich in thinking that the present situation was the result of a huge misunderstanding.

I replied that in my last interview with him, I found Count Metternich less pessimistic than formerly, and that he had noticed an improvement in the tone of the English Press, which had ceased its unreasoning attacks against Germany. I said I hoped this improvement might continue, but that it was too much to expect a complete change at once, and any real improvement must necessarily be a work of time.

Count Bülow said that Count Metternich had said the same thing to him. He understood that one of the reasons for the hostility of the English Press was the belief that Germany and Russia had concluded an arrangement with regard to their action in the Far East at the conclusion of the War. He could assure me most positively that no such arrangement had been come to, nor would it be to Germany's advantage to limit her complete liberty of action when the terrible War in the Far East should come to an end. He would be ready to sign a Treaty with any Power in the World providing that each of the Contracting Powers should bind itself not to attack the other, but he was not prepared to tie Germany's hands as to the action she should take either in the Far East or anywhere else at the conclusion of the War. He hoped that the improvement in the tone of the English Press might continue for he was anxious as he always had been to establish a good understanding with England. Should he unfortunately be driven to the conclusion that this was impossible, he would be compelled by the force of circumstances to lean towards Russia.

This led his Excellency to speak of the internal state of Russia, and he asked me what news I had received from my son-in-law, Mr. Spring-Rice, who had just arrived from St. Petersburg. I replied that Mr. Spring-Rice had told me that it was greatly to be feared that the extreme revolutionary party would now resume their activity. They had held their hand so long as there was any hope of reform being granted, but now that a reactionary movement had set in, and all hope of reform had vanished, it was probable that they would revert to their former methods and that their ranks would be swelled by members of the more moderate Parties who would now despair of reforms being brought about by peaceful means.

Count Bülow said that this tallied exactly with the reports he had received from St. Petersburg, and that he feared that attempts at assassination would become frequent.

I said there was another point to which Mr. Spring-Rice had called my attention. It was believed in St. Petersburg, or perhaps it would be more correct to say that it was wished that it should be believed that the advice of the German Emperor was to a great extent the cause of the decisions taken by the Emperor of Russia, and the constant journeys of messengers between Berlin and St. Petersburg was cited as a confirmation of this belief.

Count Bülow said that he had, some time ago, received a report to this effect from the German Chargé d'Affaires, and he could tell me most confidentially that the Emperor had written on the margin of the telegram a minute to the effect that he prayed that God might preserve him from ever interfering in the internal affairs of Russia. They were affairs with which he was not acquainted, which did not concern him and with which he was determined not to be mixed up.

At the conclusion of a long interview I asked Count Bülow to inform the Emperor that I was the bearer of a very friendly message to His Majesty from the King, which I proposed to deliver to His Majesty at the usual reception on New Year's Day. As I understood I should have that opportunity of obeying the King's commands, I had not thought it necessary to trouble the Emperor with a request for a special audience.(¹)

I have, &c.

FRANK C. LASCELLES.

(¹) [For Count Bülow's report, see G.P. XIX, II, pp. 372–3, where the conversation is assigned to Christmas Day.]

(b.)

Sir F. Lascelles to the Marquess of Lansdowne.

F.O. Germany (Prussia) 1594.
(No. 303.) Confidential.   Berlin, D. December 30, 1904.
My Lord,   R. January 2, 1905.

In a long conversation which I had with Herr von Holstein on the evening of the 26th instant, we discussed at considerable length the relations between our two countries. His Excellency's language was very similar to that held by Count Bülow on the 24th instant, which formed the subject of my despatch No. 299 of the 28th instant. He said that the alarm which existed in England of the possible action of the German Fleet seemed to him to be absurd, but I pointed out to him that it was no more absurd than the alarm felt in Germany of the intention of England to attack her. What was the position? England was an Island and was bound to take every possible precaution against a foreign invasion which would be disastrous for her. The German Fleet was a recent institution, it was concentrated in home waters and was continually growing in size and power. It was conceivable that it might one day become hostile and England was bound to take every possible precaution for her protection. There was no menace to Germany in the scheme for the reorganization of the navy which was a purely defensive measure.

Herr von Holstein replied that Germany had certainly a right to be suspicious. For a long time past a regular campaign had been carried on by the English Press against her, and as His Majesty's Government had taken no sort of measures to check this campaign it could only be supposed that they did not disapprove of it. The English Government certainly had the power of influencing the Press and he knew of cases in which they had used it effectually. He cited a case in which Lord Palmerston had interfered to prevent the collection of money for the construction of the Suez Canal. I replied that I believed that on certain occasions attempts had been made to induce some of the newspapers to adopt a different tone, but very rarely with success, and I had every reason to believe that His Majesty's present Government deliberately avoided any interference with the Press. Herr von Holstein said that he feared that in that case they did not fully realize their responsibilities. In the present instance a situation had been created by the action of the Press which was fraught with the gravest of all dangers, viz : that of two great nations being involved in war, for if any untoward incident had arisen which gave rise to an acrimonious discussion between the two Governments it would have been almost impossible to have settled it owing to the atmosphere which the Press campaign had created.

I observed that if such a calamity as a war between our two countries were to be brought about, it would certainly be the Germans who would begin it, as we should never attack them, although we should naturally have to fight if they attacked us. Herr von Holstein replied that it was not always the Power who attacked who was really responsible for the war, but, however that might be, he was glad that Count Metternich had so strongly expressed the opinion that England had no intention of making war on Germany, an opinion which he personally shared. On my observing that Count

Metternich had also noticed an improvement in the tone of the English Press, Herr von Holstein said that the improvement had coincided with my arrival in England and had been entirely due to me. I earnestly begged his Excellency not to run away with the impression that I possessed the very slightest means of exercising any sort of influence over the Press. It was true that I had pointed out to some of my personal friends who were connected with the Press that the constant attacks on Germany had created a situation which was becoming dangerous, but the fact was that the cessation of these attacks had begun before I arrived in England. Herr von Holstein replied that in any case he was glad that an improvement had taken place, He hoped it would continue and he believed that if no incident should occur to revive the animosity of the two nations, the present agitation would gradually die out.

I have, &c.
FRANK C. LASCELLES.

No. 66.

Sir A. Nicolson to the Marquess of Lansdowne.

F.O. Spain 2209.
(No. 25.) Confidential.   *Madrid,* D. *February* 12, 1905.
My Lord,   R. *March* 4, 1905.

 I enquired of the French Ambassador this morning whether he had received any news of interest from Morocco, especially with regard to the despatch of a German man of war to Tangier Bay. M. Cambon informed me that he gathered from telegrams which he had received that the French Mission at Fez was meeting with a satisfactory reception there, and that as yet the prospects were fairly favourable. With respect to German movements he asked for my views.

 I told M. Cambon that my impression was that the German Government were desirous of showing that, so far as they were concerned, the Anglo-French Convention had introduced no alteration in the *status quo ante;* and that as they had no official cognizance of the above instrument they were at liberty to ignore its existence. I imagined that the attitude assumed by the German Government in response to the petition of their subjects in Morocco was an invitation to the French Government to initiate some discussion with a view to obtain their concurrence with the provisions of the Convention. When at Tangier I had some ground for believing that the German Government were prepared to recognise the Convention provided their commercial interests were secured for the future on the same footing as the British. I had detected some anxiety on the part of the German Chargé d'Affaires, who probably reflected the views of his Government, lest hereafter, when France had obtained a firm footing in Morocco, foreign commerce with the exception of British might be placed at a disadvantage with French trade. I begged M. Cambon to understand that the above were simply personal views, based perhaps on slender foundations, but I regarded the recent action of the German Government, which indeed was a perfectly legitimate one, in the light of a reminder that in respect of Morocco German hands were perfectly free.

 M. Cambon said it was quite possible my view was correct: and he did not anticipate that there would be any great difficulty in satisfying Germany in the direction I had indicated. He was, however, afraid that Spain might be encouraged to view with complacency any separate action in Morocco on the part of another Power, and might, so far as her restricted means permitted, endeavour to raise jealousies and difficulties. She was not entirely satisfied with the terms she had secured under the Franco-Spanish Agreement, and might hope to acquire, indirectly and with the aid of Germany, some further concessions.

As no member of the Spanish Government has as yet spoken to me on Moorish affairs, and as the Press is practically silent on the subject, I am unable to express an opinion as to Spanish aspirations in Morocco : but I should have thought that the concessions she has secured would have amply satisfied her.

I have, &c.
A. NICOLSON.

No. 67.

Sir F. Bertie to the Marquess of Lansdowne.

F.O. France 3705.
(No. 101A.)   *Paris*, D. *March* 22, 1905.
My Lord,   R. *March* 23, 1905.

In the course of conversation with Monsieur Delcassé to-day I asked him whether he could tell me anything about the German Emperor's intended visit to Tangier.

His Excellency could not, he said, understand what it was that Germany wanted. When the negotiations between the French and British Governments were being carried on in March last the German Ambassador had made enquiries of him as to their subjects and objects, and he had told the Ambassador, that, as he had supposed, they related to Egypt, Newfoundland and Morocco and, as regarded Morocco, he reminded Prince Radolin of the Declarations which he had made in the Senate and the Chamber as to the objects to be secured, viz., the restoration of order with the assistance of France and respect for the political interests of Spain and the commercial interests of Foreign Countries. The German Ambassador had made no objection and appeared to be satisfied.

In the autumn before the publication of the Franco-Spanish Agreement the text of it was communicated to the German Government by the French Embassy at Berlin. No objection was raised to it. In that Agreement, the Agreement between France and England was referred to, and if the German Government had felt concerned in the Morocco questions they would naturally have asked to have the actual text of the Anglo-French Agreement. They did not, however, ask for such communication nor did they raise any objection to the Franco-Spanish Agreement. The Commercial interests of Germany having been duly respected by the Agreements made by France with England and Spain and Count von Bülow having publicly declared that Germany had no territorial ambitions but only commercial interests in Morocco, what could the German Government desire to obtain by the Emperor's visit to Tangier? It raised expectations amongst the Moors.

Monsieur Delcassé showed by his manner and the tone of his conversation that he was uneasy about German policy as regards Morocco.

I have, &c.
FRANCIS BERTIE.

No. 68.

Mr. White to the Marquess of Lansdowne.

                                                              Tangier, March 23, 1905.
F.O. Morocco 424.   D. 7·5 P.M.
Tel. (No. 12.)   R. 10 P.M.

Great preparations are being made by the Moorish authorities for the reception of German Emperor.

His Majesty's visit causes the liveliest satisfaction to the native population, who look upon it as a check to French designs. It is commonly believed throughout country that Germany is willing to assist Sultan to withstand French, and His Majesty's approaching visit will tend to confirm this belief.

No. 69.

Sir F. Lascelles to the Marquess of Lansdowne.

F.O. Germany (Prussia) **1616.**
(No. 75.) Confidential.   *Berlin,* D. *March* 23, 1905.
My Lord,   R. *March* 27, 1905.

The French Ambassador called upon me yesterday and spoke of the approaching visit of the Emperor to Tangier. He had been informed that His Majesty would only remain a few hours in the port and it was even doubtful if he would land. Mr. Bihourd said that he was convinced that the Emperor would land, and he thought it quite natural that he should do so. It would certainly interest His Majesty to see something of Tangier, and he was not inclined to attribute much political importance to His Majesty's visit.

There was however a point in connection with Morocco upon which Mr. Bihourd wished to ask my opinion confidentially. A report had reached him some time ago that the German Chargé d'Affaires at Tangier had stated that Germany knew nothing of the Anglo-French Agreement of the 8th of April last with regard to Egypt and Morocco, and was not in any way bound by it. Mr. Bihourd had asked Herr von Mühlberg whether this report was correct, and had received the reply that he had no knowledge of the statement attributed to the Chargé d'Affaires but that, as a matter of fact, the Agreement had not been communicated to the German Government. Mr. Bihourd was not satisfied with this reply and had therefore drawn up a memorandum asking what meaning was to be attached to the statement said to have been made by the German Chargé d'Affaires. He had communicated this memorandum unofficially to Herr von Mühlberg but had received no reply. The German Government might be technically correct in stating that as the agreement had not been officially communicated to them, they had no knowledge of its contents, but it had been published in the newspapers, and it was a matter of common knowledge that negotiations had been carried on between the British and German Governments as to the modifications which had been brought about by the Agreement in the position in Egypt. If the German Government had thought it necessary to apply to His Majesty's Government with regard to the position in Egypt, in respect of which he understood the German Government had obtained certain concessions, why should they have refrained from applying to the French Government in respect of Morocco.

I replied that the cases were not quite similar. It was necessary to obtain the consent of the German Government to the Khedivial Decree which caused certain modifications in the former position of Egypt. The German Government thereupon demanded certain concessions or rather the recognition of certain rights which they had hitherto enjoyed, and which were very similar to the concessions which were granted to France. In the case of Morocco there had been no necessity to ask the German Government to agree to a Decree modifying the former state of things, and the German Government had probably not thought it necessary to approach the French Government on the subject.

I have. &c.
FRANK C. LASCELLES.

No. 70.

Sir A. Nicolson to the Marquess of Lansdowne.

F.O. Spain 2209.
(No. 46.)   *Madrid*, D. *March* 23, 1905.
My Lord,   R. *April* 1, 1905.

A portion of the Madrid Press, following apparently journals in other countries, is commencing to discuss the visit of the German Emperor to Tangier, and interpreting it in various lights. The German Ambassador spoke to me this afternoon on the subject, and said that it was absurd to attribute any "arrière pensée" to the visit, which was directed solely by simple curiosity.

I told Monsieur de Radowitz that the German Military Attaché to his Embassy. who is to accompany His Majesty to Tangier and Gibraltar, had asked me a few days back whether, in my opinion, there was any personal risk to the Emperor if he landed at Tangier. I had told Baron de Senden that I did not think that there was any fear of anything in the nature of personal risk : but that I considered that His Majesty would find the landing a little embarrassing and that it would be difficult to organize any reception of a dignified character. In my opinion it would be impossible for the Emperor to land incognito and, knowing the topography and all arrangements at the Tangier landing stage I was afraid that His Majesty might be considerably hampered. Moreover the Moors, accustomed to see their Sultan invested with a certain pomp, would be surprised to witness a great European Sovereign making a progress through the Tangier streets, amid the usual Oriental crowd, as a simple tourist. In short, as he had asked for my opinion, I should think on the whole it would be better if His Majesty were to view Tangier from his vessel.

Monsieur de Radowitz said that he quite agreed with me in this view, but that the Emperor was always desirous of inspecting strange places. It was unfortunate, he added, that importance had been given in the Press to a very simple and natural desire on the part of the Emperor.

I have, &c.
A. NICOLSON.

No. 71.

Mr. White to the Marquess of Lansdowne.

                                                                  Tangier, April 1, 1905.
F.O. Morocco 424.   D. 5·15 P.M.
Tel. (No. 26.)   R. 9 P.M.

Secret. Kaid Maclean tells me secretly that when he was presented to the Emperor His Majesty said "I do not acknowledge any agreement that has been come to. I come here as one Sovereign paying a visit to another perfectly independent sovereign. You can tell Sultan this."

Absolute secrecy has been maintained as to what passed between the Emperor and the Sultan's great-uncle.

So far as I have been able to learn it would appear that the Emperor in addressing the German subjects here expressed his pleasure at the increase of German commerce and the hope that it would soon attain great importance. His Majesty referred to the recent statement of Count von Bülow in the Reichstag and said that they might rest assured that both His Majesty and his Gov[ernmen]t were determined that this country should remain free both in itself and in its commerce, as it has been in the past and is at present, and that there should be no favour to any special country.

No. 72.

Mr. White to the Marquess of Lansdowne.

F.O. Morocco 421.
(No. 53.)
My Lord,

Tangier, D. *April* 2, 1905.
R. *April* 10, 1905.

In continuation of my despatch No. 49 of yesterdays' date([1]) I have the honour to report that when the German Emperor landed on the pier he was warmly greeted by Mulai Abdelmalek, who saluted him in the Sultan's name and stated that His Shereefian Majesty's joy at receiving the visit was not only on His Majesty's own account but also on that of his subjects.([2])

The Emperor replied that it gave him great pleasure and satisfaction to salute a near relative of the Sultan, and he requested him to convey to the Sultan his thanks for having sent the special embassy to greet him, and also for the magnificent preparations made for his reception. His Imperial Majesty added that he was deeply interested in the welfare and prosperity of the Moorish Empire. It was to the Sultan as an independent sovereign, that he was paying a visit and he trusted that, under His Shereefian Majesty's sovereignty, Morocco would remain free, and open to the peaceful competition of all nations without monopolies or exclusion.

When later on at the German Legation Mulai Abdelmalek handed to the Emperor the Sultan's letter, his Highness said : " His Shereefian Majesty, recalling the friendship which has always existed between His Majesty's illustrious ancestors and the German Government, is animated by the desire to strengthen and extend that friendship by all means as far as possible. I fulfil the orders I have received in conveying to Your Majesty the message with which I have been charged by the Sultan. His Shereefian Majesty's friendship with Your Imperial Majesty is already well known to all. I beg Your Majesty to receive this message with gracious clemency in accordance with the bonds of strong friendship."

The Emperor in reply thanked Mulai Abdelmalek more especially for the expressions of sincere friendship contained in the message. He entirely concurred in the Sultan's sentiments. It proved emphatically the omnipotence of the divine wisdom, which, as the Ambassador knew, directed the fate of nations. He personally most sincerely wished the development and the prosperity of the Moorish Empire as much as for the good of His Shereefian Majesty's own subjects as for that of the nations of Europe trading in this country, as he hoped, on a footing of perfect equality.

His Imperial Majesty added that he had visited Tangier resolved to do all that lay in his power to efficiently safeguard German Interests in Morocco. He considered the Sultan an absolutely independent Sovereign and it was with His Majesty that he desired to come to an understanding as to a means of safeguarding those interests.

In regard to the reforms the Sultan intended to introduce the Emperor expressed the opinion that His Shereefian Majesty should proceed with great caution and with due regard to the religious sentiments of the people in order to avoid the disturbance of the public peace.

The Emperor handed the Grand Cross of the Order of the Crown of Prussia to Mulai Abdelmalek and bestowed the order of the Red Eagle of the Second Class on the Secretaries.

I am informed that the foregoing account of the speeches exchanged between Mulai Abdelmalek and the German Emperor was furnished to a Journalist by the German Chargé d'Affaires.

I have, &c.
HERBERT E. WHITE.

([1]) [Not reproduced. It gives details of the Kaiser's visit.]
([2]) [The Kaiser's own account of his reception was given to Sir C. Hardinge on 15 August, 1906, *v. infra* p. 369. King Edward's criticism is given in Sir Sidney Lee : *King Edward VII* (1927), II, p. 340.]

No. 73.

The Marquess of Lansdowne to Sir E. Egerton.

F.O. Italy 905.
(No. 53.)

Sir,   *Foreign Office, April 5, 1905.*

The Italian Ambassador told me today, in strict confidence, that he had spoken to Count Metternich in regard to the recent visit of the German Emperor to Tangier, which seemed to him (Signor Pansa) to require some explanation. Count Metternich had said that since the conclusion of the Anglo-French Agreement a "fait nouveau" had arisen in regard to Morocco. The new fact was this. M. Saint-René Taillandier had announced to the Moorish Government that he spoke as the mouthpiece of all Europe. The Sultan had thereupon made enquiries at Berlin as to the correctness of M. Saint-René Taillandier's statement. The German Emperor's visit had been the rejoinder.

I am, &c.
LANSDOWNE.

No. 74.

Mr. White to the Marquess of Lansdowne.

F.O. Morocco 424.
Tel. (No. 31.)

Tangier, April 6, 1905.
D. 11·55 A.M.
R. 2·30 P.M.

Confidential. My Tel[egram] No. 29.(¹)

French Chargé d'Affaires has now communicated to me privately what the German Emperor said to him. After referring to the difficulties experienced by commerce here mentioning as an example the unsatisfactory lighter service at ports which delayed shipping H[is] I[mperial] M[ajesty] said "I hope European nations will do what is necessary to safeguard their commercial interests here." Then after a pause H[is] M[ajesty] added in a louder voice and speaking deliberately "As far as I am concerned I am decided to cause the interests of German commerce to be respected." H[is] M[ajesty] bowed to close the conversation. French Chargé d'Affaires however before retiring replied "But, sir [*sic*], that is entirely in accordance with the desires of the French Gov[ernmen]t."

(¹) [Not reproduced. It relates to a previous conversation with the French Chargé d'Affaires, in which the Kaiser's views were reported in less detail.]

No. 75.

Question asked in the House of Commons, April 6, 1905.

[*Parl. Deb., 4th Ser., Vol. 144, pp. 641–2.*]

Mr. Labouchere (Northampton): I beg to ask the Under-Secretary of State for Foreign Affairs whether the Convention entered into by His Majesty's Government with the French Republic, dated 8th April, 1904, was officially communicated to the German Government, and when; whether, if so, any reply to the communication was received by His Majesty's Government, and, if so received, will he lay it upon the Table of the House; whether any subsequent communications have passed between this Government and Germany in regard to the said Convention; and, if so, will he lay them upon the Table of the House; whether Germany has any Treaty with Morocco securing to it any special commercial rights and privileges; and, if so, whether they are analogous to the rights and privileges secured to this country by the Convention of Commerce and Navigation concluded between this country and Morocco in 1856, and confirmed by the Convention between this country and France, dated 8th April, 1904; and whether the Sultan of Morocco still retains the right to enter into Treaties or Conventions granting commercial rights and privileges with countries which were not parties to the Convention of 8th April, 1904.

Answer by the Under-Secretary of State for Foreign Affairs
(Earl Percy, Kensington, S.):

The Declaration of 8th April, 1904, between the United Kingdom and France was not officially communicated to the German Government, and there were no communications between His Majesty's Government and that of Germany in regard to it so far as it had reference to Morocco. The Sultan of Morocco was not a party to the Declaration, which was an independent arrangement between the British and French Governments having reference to their respective interests in that country. The Treaty between Germany and Morocco of 1890(1) is analogous to that of 1856(2) between this country and Morocco.

(1) [Printed *B.F.S.P.*, Vol. 82, pp. 968–72.]
(2) [Printed *B.F.S.P.*, Vol. 46, pp. 176–87.]

No. 76.

Sir E. Egerton to the Marquess of Lansdowne.

Rome, April 8, 1905.
D. 1·15 P.M.
R. 6 P.M.

F.O. Italy 907.
Tel. (No. 33.)
Morocco.
My tel[egram] No. 28.
Italian M[inister for] F[oreign] A[ffairs] told German Emperor that he had been assured in March of last year (that) German Ambassador in Paris had been informed of the nature of the Agreement by French Min[iste]r for F[oreign] A[ffairs].

No. 77.

Sir M. Durand to the Marquess of Lansdowne.

Washington, April 8, 1905.
D. [*sic*].
R. 9·45 P.M.

F.O. America 2581.
Tel. (No. 2.) Morocco.
Secretary Taft informs me that German Amb[assado]r has called upon him and delivered message from the Emperor to the effect that Germany, not having been consulted with regard to Anglo-French arrangement, holds herself free to consult her own interests and is specially determined to insist on open door in matters of trade. Opinion of U[nited] S[tates] Gov[ernmen]t has not been given or asked.

No. 78.

Sir E. Egerton to the Marquess of Lansdowne.

Rome, April 12, 1905.

F.O. Morocco 434.   D. 3 P.M.
Tel. Private and Confidential.   R. 7 P.M.

In consequence of telegram from M. Delcassé, French Ambassador questioned Italian Minister for Foreign Affairs to-day as to whether German Emperor had suggested conference of Powers respecting affairs of Morocco and other questions.

Denial of Italian Minister appeared so hesitating that French Ambassador stated in strong terms that, in view of previous assurances to France, Italian Government could entertain no such proposal any more than could French Government.

Personally, I consider French suspicions exaggerated if not entirely groundless, and do not suspect Italian Minister for Foreign Affairs.

I have no doubt that Emperor spoke on all manner of subjects with Italian Minister for Foreign Affairs. I know he made allusion to Prince George and Crete.

Personally, I am glad your Lordship does not think Conference respecting Crete called for at present.

No. 79.

Sir A. Nicolson to the Marquess of Lansdowne.

F.O. Morocco 434.
(No. 66.)   *Madrid,* D. *April* 14, 1905.
My Lord,   R. *April* 18, 1905.

The Minister for Foreign Affairs informed me this afternoon that the Italian Ambassador had called on him in the morning to communicate to him confidentially the substance of a telegram which he had received from Monsieur Tittoni. Monsieur Silvestrelli stated that the German Government had enquired of that of Italy in which [*sic*] light the latter would regard the convocation of a Conference to discuss the affairs of Morocco, and that his Government before giving a reply desired to ascertain the views of the Spanish Government on the subject.

Monsieur de Villaurrutia informed Monsieur Silvestrelli that in his personal opinion a Conference on Morocco was inopportune and unnecessary, and likely to lead to grave difficulties. In view of the Agreements which Spain had with France, and of the fact that she had recognized the Anglo-French declaration, the Spanish Government could not possibly adhere to the proposal of a Conference unless both France and Great Britain agreed to the project. The action of Spain must be in harmony with that of the two above mentioned Powers.

The conversation appears to have terminated with this declaration : and Monsieur de Villaurrutia had no opportunity of judging what were the views of the Italian Government.

I have, &c.
A. NICOLSON.

No. 80.

The Marquess of Lansdowne to Sir F. Lascelles.

F.O. Germany (Prussia) 1618.   *Foreign Office, April 23,* 1905.
Tel. (No. 59.)   D. 11 A.M.

My immediately preceding tel[egram] (repeating Sir A. Nicolson's Tel[egram] No. 24, Morocco).

I feel considerable doubts as to the wisdom of this suggestion, and should like to know exactly what you think of it. If it were possible for you to say anything which might help to convince the Emperor that German interests were in no way threatened French Gov[ernmen]t would be grateful, but nothing has yet been said to me on the subject by M. Delcassé.(¹)

(¹) [This telegram was founded on a draft by Lord Lansdowne written by him as a minute on the back of Sir A. Nicolson's telegram No. 24 of April 21, 1905. (F.O. Spain 2211.) Sir A. Nicolson's telegram reported a suggestion from the French Ambassador at Madrid that Sir F. Lascelles might "privately speak to the Emperor in regard to the Morocco difficulty, especially as to suggesting suspension of the German Mission to Fez pending discussion between Paris and Berlin." For Sir F. Lascelles' reply see p. 73, *ed. note.* It is missing from the F.O. archives.]

No. 81.

Mr. Lowther to the Marquess of Lansdowne.

                         Fez, April 26, 1905.
F.O. Morocco. 424.   D. 11·30 A.M.
Tel. (No. 42.) Confidential.   R. 1·30 P.M.

German Legation here assert that they warned French Minister here last November that Germany expected France to come to an agreement with her on Morocco Question. Telegram to that effect in "Times" of today communicated to Correspondent by German Minister.

I have been confidentially informed that this statement is correct but that French Minister not attaching any value to warning of the Chargé d'Affaires and thinking it a very unusual channel for such a communication did not repeat it to his Gov[ernmen]t. It was however reported early in February by the French Chargé d'Affaires here.

No. 82.

Sir M. Durand to the Marquess of Lansdowne.

F.O. America 2581.   *Washington, April 26,* 1905.
Tel. (No. 35.) Secret and Confidential.   R. 11 P.M.

I have just had visit from Secretary Taft, who came by desire of President. The German Emperor has been in communication with President, and has intimated that Germany fears England is going to support France in some important declaration of policy with regard to Morocco. The President thinks England and Germany are unduly suspicious of each other's intentions, and he wishes, if possible, to help in removing any friction which exists. Mr. Taft says that America does not care a cent about Morocco, and has no desire whatever to take sides between Germany and France.

He read me passage from President's letter, asking him to make it clear to me that President's sole desire was to bring about better feeling between England and Germany, and make each believe neither means "to attack" the other. I asked

Mr. Taft to thank the President, and assured him, that, so far as I knew, we had not the slightest apprehension of an attack by Germany, believing that she was much too weak at sea to attempt anything of the kind, even if she wished it. I said I would telegraph at once the substance of his remarks.

My impression is that President wants to know your views about the situation in Morocco, probably for communication to German Emperor. If you could let me have an early reply I should be obliged, as I leave Washington on Friday for England, and should like to let Mr. Taft know your views at farewell interview tomorrow afternoon. Of course if you would prefer my postponing leave it is a matter of indifference to me.

No. 83.

The Marquess of Lansdowne to Sir M. Durand.

F.O. America 2581.　　　　　　　　　　　　*Foreign Office, April 27, 1905.*
Tel. (No. 50.)　　　　　　　　　　　　　　　　　　D. 8 P.M.
　　Your tel. No. 35.

So far as we are concerned you may safely reassure President, we have not and never have had any idea of attacking Germany, nor do we anticipate that she will be so foolish as to attack us. There is at this moment so far as I am aware no subject of dispute between the two Powers, or any reason why their relations should not be of a friendly description.

As to Morocco we are quite unable to understand why any trouble should arise— Anglo-French Agreement contained nothing detrimental to interests of other Powers, and in spite of provocative talk of German Emperor and officials, attitude of French Gov[ernmen]t is most forbearing and conciliatory.

I cannot see why any international complication should be created, unless German Gov[ernmen]t is determined to take advantage of what was at most a diplomatic oversight in order to make mischief or to disturb the *status quo*, e.g., by demanding cession of a Moorish port.

Private.

Be careful to say nothing which could be interpreted as an invitation to the President to act as mediator between us and Germany.

There is no reason why you should postpone your leave.

No. 84.

Sir F. Bertie to the Marquess of Lansdowne.

F.O. France 3705.
(No. 158.)　Confidential.　　　　　　　　　　*Paris, D. April 27, 1905.*
My Lord,　　　　　　　　　　　　　　　　　　　R. *April 29, 1905.*

I asked Monsieur Delcassé today whether there had been any result from the offers which he had made to the German Ambassador and to the German Foreign Office through the French Embassy at Berlin of explanations in regard to the Morocco policy of the French Government, if there should be anything respecting which the German Government desired to be informed.

His Excellency told me that the German Government had not given any sign whatever of what they wanted. There had been no response to his offers and he could not understand what objects the German Emperor had in view.

　　　　　　　　　　　　　　　　I have, &c.
　　　　　　　　　　　　　　　　FRANCIS BERTIE.

No. 85.

Mr. Lowther to the Marquess of Lansdowne.

F.O. Morocco 424.
Tel. (No. 43.)

Your tel. No. 23.(¹)

Tangier, April 28, 1905.
D. 12˙5 P.M.
R. 2˙35 P.M.

It is not thought probable here that German Min[iste]r will make any demand for a Port while at Fez. The ultimate idea of Germany would seem to be to acquire a "sphere of economic influence" about which they would be prepared later to negotiate with France, but it is obviously impossible for them to do so now.

French Ch[argé] d'Aff[aire]s seems quite discouraged about mission obtaining anything now.

(¹) [Not reproduced.]

No. 86.

The Marquess of Lansdowne to Sir F. Bertie.

F.O. France 3703.
(No. 258.)
Sir,

Foreign Office, May 3, 1905.

I had a long conversation today with the French Ambassador upon the Morocco question. His Excellency, who had just returned from Paris, said that the French Government was entirely unable to understand the attitude which the German Government had lately taken up. It might be due to momentary irritation on the part of the German Emperor, or, on the other hand, might point to the desire of the German Government to press for special advantages in Morocco. It could, however, certainly not be justified upon the ground that Germany had been kept in the dark with regard to the Anglo-French Agreement and its effects upon the position of France in Morocco. On the 27th of March of last year, more than a fortnight before the signature of the Declaration, Prince Radolin had questioned M. Delcassé upon the subject of the negotiations then proceeding between Great Britain and France. M. Delcassé had admitted that such negotiations were in progress. Prince Radolin had asked whether they had reference to Morocco, and M. Delcassé had answered in the affirmative, adding that they were based upon the recognition of the *status quo* in that country and upon complete commercial liberty. A report of this conversation had been furnished at the time to the French Ambassador at Berlin.

After the signature of the Declaration, on the 12th and 14th of April, 1904, Count Bülow had made a speech upon the subject in the Reichstag, in the course of which he had said that he could see nothing prejudicial to German interests in the Agreement, those interests being mainly of a commercial character. Prince Radolin had afterwards met M. Delcassé, and had told him distinctly that he could see nothing detrimental to German interests in the Agreement, which M. Delcassé did not therefore think it necessary to notify officially to Germany. Then came the publication of the documents in this country and in France, and their presentation to Parliament.

The German Government were given a further opportunity of expressing their opinion in October, when, as I would remember, the French Government was negotiating with that of Spain a separate Agreement as to Morocco. This Agreement was actually communicated to the German Government, and Baron Richthofen had told the French Ambassador that he presumed that under it commercial liberty would be fully respected. The French Ambassador had replied in the affirmative, and had telegraphed to M. Delcassé asking permission to make a formal announcement upon this point. M. Delcassé had authorised such an announcement, and had referred specially to the fourth Article of the Agreement as bearing upon the point at issue. No further objection was made by Baron Richthofen.

Besides all this the German Government had given its adhesion to the new Khedivial Decree, which formed an integral part of the Anglo-French Agreement and could not be treated apart from the other provisions embodied in it.

When M. Delcassé became aware that the German Government or the German Emperor intended to make a grievance out of the Morocco affair, he announced in the Senate on the 31st of March and in the Chamber on the 19th of April, that he was ready to supply explanations if there was any *mal-entendu* with regard to Morocco, and M. Rouvier had used similar language. M. Delcassé had, soon after this, dined with Prince RadoliL, and had gone out of his way to speak to him about Morocco, asking him what his *polémique* in the press meant, and reminding him that he had already spoken to him upon the subject in the month of March. Prince Radolin had replied that he had no instructions, and could not be got to say anything. The French Ambassador at Berlin had also been instructed to offer explanations, and had offered them to M. Mühlberg, the other members of the German Foreign Office being absent. That gentleman had replied that there was no misunderstanding, and had suggested that the whole question might well be discussed by a European Conference.

Altogether, the conduct of the German Government appeared to His Excellency quite incomprehensible. It might be the outcome of a *mouvement irréfléchi* on the part of the German Emperor, or, more probably, of an attempt to get rid of M. Delcassé— an attempt which had signally failed. There was a third possibility, namely that the German Government hoped to avail themselves of this opportunity in order to obtain possession of a port on the Moorish coast. It was rather remarkable, His Excellency said, that two years ago a son of the German Ambassador at Madrid had, in the course of an after-dinner conversation, announced that Germany intended to ask for the cession of Mogador.[1]

His Excellency expressed great satisfaction at the intimation which had been made by you to M. Delcassé, in compliance with the instructions contained in my telegram No. 61 of the 23rd ultimo.[2] For the present, he said, all we could do was to watch events, and the French Government would not fail to keep us fully informed of any new developments which might take place.

I am, &c.
LANSDOWNE.

[1] [German interests in Morocco had apparently been recognised in the negotiations between France and Spain in 1902. The text of the alleged secret agreement of November 11, 1902 (as given in the *Morning Post* of April 16, 1904), contained the following Article:

Article VII. " The Government of his Majesty the King of Spain undertakes to give effect to the following restrictive clauses: (a) In consideration of the considerable commercial interests of the subjects of his Majesty the German Emperor, and on an *acte de désintéresse-ment* being formally demanded by the German Government, the Government of his Majesty the King of Spain engages to lease for a term to be determined a port on the Atlantic seaboard. A subsequent agreement between the cabinets of Madrid and Berlin will determine the point on the coast, which may be either Casablanca or Rabat."]

[2] [*v. infra* pp. 72–4, Nos. 90–1.]

No. 87.

Sir A. Nicolson to the Marquess of Lansdowne.

Madrid, May 5, 1905.

F.O. Spain 2211.
Tel. (No. 27.)

D. 9 P.M.
R. 11·30 P.M.

Morocco and Germany. My despatch No. 83.[1]

Minister for Foreign Affairs told me to-day that the German Ambassador had informed him this morning that he had instructions to announce that if Spanish Minister proceeded to Fez, Emperor and German Government would regard such a proceeding as an unfriendly act. Minister for Foreign Affairs observed that Spanish Minister would leave for Tangier on (?) 10th May, and that no date had as yet been

[1] [Not reproduced. It relates to the departure of Señor Llaveria, the new Spanish Minister for Fez.]

fixed for his mission to Fez, but he did not see why he should not proceed to present his credentials.

His Excellency added he could not understand why a Spanish Mission should be regarded as an unfriendly act, as he believed German Mission was not intended to be viewed and was not viewed, by other Powers in that character.

German Ambassador replied that it would be wise for Spain not to intervene in the present Moorish difficulties, and that it was to her interest to be on friendly terms with Germany, who could be of greater assistance to her than any other Power.

I told Minister for Foreign Affairs it seemed to me to be going too far to dictate when or when not a Spanish Minister proceeds to present his credentials. I had, I said, (?) told your Lordship as his Excellency had desired me, that he wished Minister should proceed as soon as possible, but that I would now telegraph what had passed. I did not press point of Mission, as I did not think that it would be of much assistance at Fez, and I doubt if Spanish Minister, who is delicate, could make journey in summer.

Language of German Ambassador has evidently made an impression, and caused alarm.

No. 88.

Sir E. Egerton to the Marquess of Lansdowne.

F.O. Italy 906.
(No. 72.) Confidential.
My Lord,

Rome, D. *May* 5, 1905.
R. *May* 9, 1905.

A leading Italian Statesman not now in office spoke to me yesterday with the utmost seriousness of the menacing language with regard to France held to him by the German Ambassador.

As Count Monts appears to me a moderate and sensible man I cannot doubt that he is conforming to orders, though I make allowance for exaggeration on the part of my informant.

Even the possibility of war, unpopular as it would be in Germany, was hinted at, and also the slight hope of practical aid from England, whilst Russia was no longer of use.

I answered my Italian friend that I could not share his anxiety, for though I wondered at the apparent futility of the move made by the German Emperor with regard to Morocco, which seemed to point to a demand for some equivalent elsewhere, I did not doubt that any misunderstanding between France and Germany would easily be removed by diplomatic means.

The doubts I seemed to cast on the gravity of the situation appeared to distress my friend, who assured me that those here with most means of knowing the truth were alarmed.

Today Monsieur Barrère called on me. He began by repeating to me at some length the warnings of the same person of whose language I have just given the gist— to which I answered that, though I had no doubt of the latter's good faith, I had made great allowance for exaggeration.

Monsieur Barrère went on to say that he had also heard similar language from others, one of whom, a former Minister for Foreign Affairs, dwelt on the causes of the Emperor's grievances against Monsieur Loubet and the French Government, not the least of which occurred during the President's visit to Rome.

He seemed to fear weakness on the part of Monsieur Tittoni and the Italian Government, and also the nervousness of politicians and financial authorities in France and consequently he was leaving for Paris on the 8th Instant to see Monsieur Delcassé, and give him all the help in his power towards maintaining a firm and unaggressive attitude.

I have, &c.
EDWIN H. EGERTON.

CHAPTER XVIII.

THE BRITISH "GUARANTEE" TO FRANCE, APRIL-OCTOBER 1905.

[*ED. NOTE.*—The events leading up to the fall of Delcassé are fully described from the German side in *G.P.* XX, II, Chapter 147, and the rumours of a British offer to France *ib.*, Chapter 150. For the contention, sometimes made, that, on the eve of the meeting of the French Ministry on June 6, Delcassé received from England an offer of armed support and an alliance, see Mévil, *De la Paix de Francfort à la Conférence d'Algésiras* (1909), Chapters 4 and 5, and Bourgeois, *Manuel historique de Politique Etrangère,* IV (1926), pp. 495–7. Declarations to the same effect by Delcassé himself and by M. Paléologue in 1922 were published in the *Times* of 16 and 27 March, 1922, and are reprinted in Florent-Matter, *Les vrais Criminels* (1926), pp. 136–141. For the less positive statements of M. Poincaré, see *Les Origines de la Guerre* (1921), pp. 79 and 91, and *Au Service de la France* (1926), I, p. 221.

Several of the documents in this chapter are missing from the F.O. archives. Their text is taken from the archives of the British Embassy at Paris, among which are volumes headed "Communications to French Government," containing notes of communications made by Sir F. Bertie; but these also may not be a complete record.]

No. 89.

Mr. Lister to the Marquess of Lansdowne.

Paris, April 21, 1905.

F.O. France 3708.
Tel. (No. 22.)

D. 7·30 P.M.
R. 10·40 P.M.

Morocco. Political Director of Ministry for Foreign Affairs informs me, with regard to reported negotiations with Germany, that French Government are still waiting.

M. Delcassé repeated to German Ambassador the statement which he had made in [the] Chamber, that if any misunderstandings existed he was prepared to remove them, but so far he has received no reply.

In the meantime, French negotiations in Morocco are going on as before.

He considers agitation in Chamber and Press exaggerated.

[*ED. NOTE.*—Original draft in F.O. 146/3872 identical except for opening words "Directeur Politique informs . . . ." and for "the" in the second paragraph.]

No. 90.

The Marquess of Lansdowne to Sir F. Bertie.

F.O. 146/3871.([1])
Tel. (No. 61.)

Foreign Office, D. 11·25 P.M., *April* 22, 1905.
R. 3 A.M., *April* 23, 1905.

It seems not unlikely that German Government may ask for a port on the Moorish coast.

You are authorised to inform Minister for Foreign Affairs that we should be prepared to join French Government in offering strong opposition to such a proposal

([1]) [Missing from F.O. France 3708.]

and to beg that if question is raised French Government will afford us a full opportunity of conferring with them as to steps which might be taken in order to meet it.

German attitude in this dispute seems to me most unreasonable having regard to M. Delcassé's attitude and we desire to give him all the support we can.

[ED. NOTE.—On April 21, Sir A. Nicolson reported a suggestion from the French Ambassador at Madrid that Sir F. Lascelles should "privately speak to the Emperor in regard to the Morocco difficulty," and this suggestion was forwarded to Sir F. Lascelles by Lord Lansdowne on April 23 (v. supra p. 67, No. 80).

The reply from Sir F. Lascelles was enclosed by Lord Lansdowne in his telegram to Sir F. Bertie given below:

The Marquess of Lansdowne to Sir F. Bertie.

Foreign Office, April 24, 1905.

F.O. 146/3871.
Tel. (No. 66.)

D. 4·30 P.M.
R. 9·30 P.M.

The following from H[is] M[ajesty's] Representative [Sir F. Lascelles] at Berlin April 24. Tel. No. 10.

Your telegram No. 59.

I do not think it advisable for me to approach the Emperor on the subject of Morocco. If His Majesty should mention it to me I should be prepared to express my opinion as I have already done to Under Sec[retar]y of State for Foreign Affairs but a suggestion on my part that the German mission to Fez should be suspended would probably be resented by the Emperor and do more harm than good. I am not likely to have an opportunity to see the Emperor for some considerable time as although it is expected that he will be present at the Reviews of the 1st and 2nd of May he will not take up his residence at Potsdam till towards the end of the month.]

No. 91.

Draft by Sir F. Bertie.

F.O. 146/3861.

Paris, April 24, 1905.

[In the "Communications to French Government from Sir F. Bertie" exists one endorsed as follows:—]

" Draft M. Delcassé, Aide Memoire, Paris 24 April.

" Morocco. H.M. Government promise their support to F[rench] G[overnment] " against possible demand by Germany for a port."

Le Gouvernement de S[a] M[ajesté] B[ritannique] trouve que les procédés de l'Allemagne dans la question du Maroc sont des plus déraisonnables vu l'attitude de M. Delcassé.

En vue de l'attitude adoptée par M. Delcassé la façon d'agir de l'Allemagne paraît au Marquis de Lansdowne des plus déraisonnable et il [le G[ouvernemen]t de S[a] M[ajesté]] désire accorder à Son Excellence tout l'appui en son pouvoir.

Il ne paraît pas improbable que le Gouvernement Impérial Allemand fasse la demande d'un port sur la côte du Maroc.

Je suis autorisé à faire savoir à M. Delcassé que le Gouv[ernemen]t de S[a] M[ajesté] serait prêt à se joindre au Gouv[ernemen]t de la République pour s'opposer fortement à une telle proposition et prier M. Delcassé dans le cas où la question surgirait, de donner au Gouvernement de S[a] M[ajesté] B[ritannique] Anglais toute occasion de conférer discuter concerter avec le G[ouvernemen]t français les mesures qui pourrait [sic] être prises pour aller à l'encontre de cette demande.

[*ED. NOTE.*—Over this is written " to be typewritten of (on) square paper for the Ambassador.'' It is obviously the draft for the interview with M. Delcassé, and is corrected in part by Sir F. Bertie himself. It seems to record the actual communication he proposed to make to M. Delcassé, *v.* pp. 74–5.

The marginal reference to No. 93, below (p. 75) shows that this paper (No. 91) was presented on the 25th in substantially the form in which it here appears. The final text of the communication was given later by Sir F. Bertie in a despatch of 13 January, 1906, as follows :—

" Le Gouvernement de Sa Majesté Britannique trouve que les procédés de l'Allemagne dans la question du Maroc sont des plus déraisonnables vu l'attitude de Monsieur Delcassé, et il désire accorder à Son Excellence tout l'appui en son pouvoir.

" Il ne parait pas impossible que le Gouvernement Allemand fasse la demande d'un port sur la côte du Maroc.

" Le Gouvernement de Sa Majesté Britannique serait prêt à se joindre au Gouvernement de la République pour s'opposer fortement à une telle proposition, et prie Monsieur Delcassé, dans le cas où la question surgirait, de donner au Gouvernement de Sa Majesté Britannique toute occasion de concerter avec le Gouvernement Français les mesures qui pourraient être prises pour aller à l'encontre de cette demande.'' See below p. 175, No. 213.]

No. 92.

Sir F. Bertie to the Marquess of Lansdowne.

F.O. 146/3872.([1])
Tel. (No. 28.) Conf[idential].   *Paris, April 25, 1905.*
(Original draft.)   D. 4·30 P.M.

Your tel[egram] No. 61 of 22nd. M. Delcassé very grateful for support of H[is] M[ajesty's] Gov[ernmen]t. French Government have not heard of any steps by Germany to obtain a port on Moorish coast.

M. Delcassé will telegraph informing French Minister of possibility of attempt to get concession and instructing him to warn Sultan of Morocco against it.

His Excellency promises to communicate with Y[our] L[ordship] if he receives any information and to consult with H[is] M[ajesty's] G[overnment] as to steps to be taken.

(1) [Missing from F.O. France 3708.]   **F. B.**

No. 93.

Sir F. Bertie to the Marquess of Lansdowne.

F.O. 146/3842.([1])   *Paris, April 25, 1905.*
(No. 156.) Conf[idential].   (By post.)

[Sir F. Bertie acknowledges receipt of telegram No. 61 of 23 April([2]) and states he saw M. Delcassé who first discussed question of Sir F. Lascelles approaching the German Emperor, but did not greatly favour it.]([3])

I then asked M. Delcassé whether he had information as to any steps being taken by Germany with the view of obtaining a Port on the Coast of Morocco.

His Excellency answered that he knew that some years ago C[oun]t Hatzfeldt had approached H[is] M[ajesty's] Gov[ernmen]t on the subject, that no doubt the German Government still entertained the desire, but how would they manage to carry it out now?

I asked whether any hint had been received that a Port was what was desired by Germany.

M. Delcassé assured me that he had not been approached in any way on the subject.

I then told H[is] E[xcellency] that I supposed that H[is] M[ajesty']s Gov[ernmen]t must have received reliable information that a Port was the aim of

(1) [Missing from F.O. France 3705. The text is taken from a rough draft in the Embassy archives, and the address and signature are defective.]
(2) [This is date of reception, not of despatch, *v.* p. 72, No. 90.]
(3) [The omitted passage here summarised is of no importance, *cf.* p. 67, No. 80.]

the German Emperor for Y[our] L[ordship] had informed me that it seemed not unlikely that the German Government might ask for a port. You had authorised me to say that in view of M. Delcassé's attitude in the Morocco Question H[is] M[ajesty's] Gov[ernment] considered that the conduct of Germany was most unreasonable, and that they desired to give to His Excellency all the support in their power; that it seemed not improbable that the German Government might ask for a port on the coast of Morocco and that in such case H[is] M[ajesty's] Gov[ernmen]t would be prepared to join the French Gov[ernmen]t in offering strong opposition to such a proposal (pour s'opposer fortement à une telle proposition) and they begged that if the question were raised M. Delcassé would give full opportunity to H[is] M[ajesty's] Gov[ernmen]t to concert with the French Gov[ernmen]t as to the measures which might be taken to meet it (les mesures qui pourraient être prises pour aller à l'encontre de cette demande).

(See Aide-Mémoire left with M. Delcassé, Ap. 25, dated 24th.)

M. Delcassé asked me to inform Y[our] L[ordship] that the French Government were most grateful for the support of H[is] M[ajesty's] Gov[ernmen]t in view of the attitude of Germany. He would at once inform the French Minister at Fez of the possibility of an attempt on the part of the German Government to obtain a port and instruct him to warn the Sultan of Morocco against listening to such a demand.

His Excellency promised to communicate at once with Y[our] L[ordship] if he received any information and to consult with H[is] M[ajesty's] G[overnment] as to the steps which should be taken if such a demand was made on behalf of Germany.

M. Delcassé then asked me how Germany could obtain a Port if France and England opposed it.

My answer was that the Sultan of Morocco might be led to believe that he could rely on material support from Germany in his resistance to French demands for reforms and be induced to make a pledge to Germany of a Port as a pledge of confidence in her. Of course Germany could not really take advantage of such a concession if France and England were determined to prevent it but it was possible that the Emperor thought that bluff might enable him to fulfil his desire.

Monsieur Delcassé seemed to doubt the probability of the Sultan making any such concession to Germany when France was making no demands which would in any way affect the integrity of Morocco.

On my inquiring whether any result had come from the after dinner conversation which the newspapers stated that M. Delcassé had had with the German Ambassador some days ago H[is] E[xcellency] was good enough to send for and to read to me his record (in a despatch to the French Ambassador at Berlin) of that conversation and he told me that down to the present time he had not received any communication as a consequence of his observations to Prince Radolin or of the observations which the French Ambassador had made with M. Delcassé's authority at the Berlin Foreign Office to Dr. Mühlberg. H[is] E[xcellency] informed me that he had forwarded to the French Embassy in London a copy of his despatch for Y[our] L[ordship's] information.([1])

The general feeling in Paris is that the chief object which the German Emperor has had in view in his recent proceedings is to show to the French people that an understanding with England is of little value to them and that they had much better come to an agreement with Germany. To this end " il fait la guerre à l'Angleterre sur le dos de la France " and the French Public realising that the Emperor's wrath is against England for enabling France to carry out her Morocco policy and not against France for taking advantage of her agreement with England feel that if they keep their heads nothing really serious will come of His Majesty's ill temper which they believe is not entirely shared by the German Government and still less so by the German people.

F[RANCIS] B[ERTIE].

([1]) [No trace of this communication has been found.]

No. 94.

The Marquess of Lansdowne to Sir F. Bertie.

F.O. Abyssinia 53.
(No. 307.) Secret.
Sir, Foreign Office, May 17, 1905.

... (¹) Taking this incident as his text, His Excellency went on to dwell with much animation upon the present attitude of the German Government, which was, he said, engaged all over the world in attempting to sow discord between us. The situation which had arisen was regarded by M. Delcassé as not profoundly dangerous, but as sufficiently serious to occasion him much pre-occupation. The German Emperor was, H[is] E[xcellency] thought, now calming down, and the improvement was, he believed, to some extent due to the sound advice given by His Majesty the King to Prince Radolin when they met at Paris. The attitude of the German officials was however most extraordinary. They were absolutely reticent and "wooden-faced" ("font visage de bois") whenever they were spoken to about Morocco.

His Excellency also referred briefly to the reported occupation of Haichow by a German force, as to which I told him that our latest reports from Peking and Berlin suggested the idea that the story was exaggerated and probably had its origin in the presence at that place of a German survey party. I observed that the moral of all these incidents seemed to me to be that our two Governments should continue to treat one another with the most absolute confidence, should keep one another fully informed of everything which came to their knowledge, and should, so far as possible, discuss in advance any contingencies by which they might in the course of events find themselves confronted. As an instance of our readiness to enter into such timely discussions, I reminded H[is] E[xcellency] of the communication which had recently been made to the French Gov[ernmen]t by you at a moment when an idea prevailed that Germany might be on the point of demanding the cession of a Moorish port. His Excellency expressed entire agreement with what I had said, and added that it was necessary to spare no efforts in order to counteract the effect of suggestions sedulously made by German Agents to the effect that Great Britain, with characteristic perfidy, had involved France in this Morocco imbroglio, securing to herself at the same time what she most wanted in Egypt. He spoke in the highest terms of the support which the French Government had received from that of His Majesty during the trying times through which they were passing.

I said that I had heard fears expressed that, in order to put an end to a state of things which could not fail to be highly inconvenient to them, the French Government might be induced to purchase the acquiescence of Germany by concessions of a kind which we were not likely to regard with favour, in other parts of the world. I had myself no such misgivings, and felt convinced that each side might continue to rely upon being treated with absolute frankness by the other. His Excellency expressed his entire concurrence in what I had said.

I am, &c.
LANSDOWNE.

MINUTES.

Here is the report of your conversation with Cambon of the 17th May. It referred to several questions. I have marked the passage as to mutual confidence.—T. H. S.

I suppose this was the origin of the offensive and defensive alliance.—L.(²)

(¹) [The whole despatch relates to a conversation with M. Cambon, the early part of which concerned the Abyssinian railways.]
(²) [The date of these minutes is uncertain. Cp. pp. 79, 81 and 82-3 and for the German side G.P. XXII, pp. 631-2 n.]

No. 95.

The Marquess of Lansdowne to Sir F. Bertie.

F.O. 146/3834.
(No. 344.)

Foreign Office, D. *May* 31, 1905.
R. *June* 3, 1905 (By Bag).

Secretary of State transmits copies of the undermentioned papers.

Foreign Office,
May 31, 1905.

M. Cambon. Private May 24th.	Gratitude of M. Delcassé for for [*sic*] assurance of support of His Majesty's Government in the event of further complications arising out of the Morocco question, &c.
To M. Cambon. May 25.	Repeats opinion verbally expressed that British and French Governments should treat one another with the utmost confidence and discuss together any eventualities likely to arise.

(Endorsed).   2 Enc.
    Recd. June 3.
by bag.
                                F.B.
                                R.L.

Enclosure 1.
Copy.   Privée

Ambassade de France
à Londres
le 24 Mai 1905.

Cher Lord Lansdowne,
    Lors de notre dernier entretien relatif au Maroc vous avez bien voulu me rappeler le memorandum remis à M. Delcassé le 24 Avril dernier par Sir Francis Bertie([1]) et vous avez ajouté que, dès à présent, si les circonstances l'exigeaient, si par exemple nous avions des raisons sérieuses de croire à une aggression injustifiée de la part d'une certaine puissance, le Gouvernement britannique serait tout prêt à se concerter avec le gouvernement français sur les mesures à prendre.
    J'ai fait part à M. Delcassé de cette communication dont il a apprécié l'importance et dont il m'a exprimé sa satisfaction.
                Votre bien dévoué.
                    (sd.)   Paul Cambon.

Enclosure 2 (Copy).
Dear M. Cambon,

Foreign Office, May 25, 1905.

    I am much obliged for your private note of the 24th, in which you repeat to me the statement which you made to M. Delcassé in consequence of our conversation on the 17th instant. I should like if you will allow me to do so to repeat in my own language the substance of my remarks upon that occasion, and I will do so in the words of the note which I had made at the time and communicated to Sir Francis Bertie.([2])
    You will remember that we had been discussing the attitude assumed by the German Gov[ernmen]t in Morocco and in other parts of the world. You expressed the opinion that the situation which had arisen, although not regarded by M. Delcassé as profoundly dangerous was nevertheless sufficiently serious to occasion him much preoccupation.

([1]) [*v. supra* pp. 74–5, No. 93.]
([2]) [The despatch is No. 307 secret of the 17th May, which Sir F. Bertie received by bag on the 20th (see above p. 76, No. 94). There is no record that Sir F. Bertie communicated this to the French Government at the time. He did not always record his communications or even the fact of having made them.]

I observed that the moral of all these incidents seemed to be that the French and British Gov[ernmen]ts should continue to treat one another with the most absolute confidence, that we should keep one another fully informed of everything which came to our knowledge, and so far as possible discuss any contingencies by which we might in the course of events find ourselves confronted, and I cited as showing our readiness to enter into such timely discussion the communication recently made to the French Gov[ernmen]t by Sir F. Bertie at a moment when the idea prevailed that Germany might be about to put pressure on France in order to obtain the cession of a Moorish port.

I do not know that this account differs from that which you have given to M. Delcassé. but I am not sure that I succeeded in making quite clear to you our desire that there should be full and confidential discussion between the two Gov[ernmen]ts, not so much in consequence of some acts of unprovoked aggression on the part of another Power, as in anticipation of any complications to be apprehended during the somewhat anxious period through which we are at present passing.

Yours, &c.

(Sd) LANSDOWNE.

No. 96.

Sir F. Bertie to the Marquess of Lansdowne.

F.O. France 3706.([1])

(No. 207b.)

My Lord,

Paris, D. *June* 10, 1905.

R. *June* 14, 1905.

I had a visit today from Monsieur Delcassé. According to his account his fall was brought about entirely by the intrigues of the German Government who have spent a good deal of money for the purpose. His policy had been to be ready to make commercial concessions to Germany if she were willing to discuss with the French Government the question of Morocco, but not to yield anything politically or territorially. With him the German Government had not been willing to deal. What they required was his head, as they regarded him as the obstacle to their schemes in having negotiated the Anglo-French understanding and in encouraging the idea of an understanding between England and Russia. He would not have moved from the attitude which he had taken up and he would have been careful not to do anything in Morocco which could be considered contrary to the Treaty rights of Germany, for to give advice and furnish military advisers to the Moorish Government could not be twisted into an infringement of any German right. As to a Conference the Spanish Minister for Foreign Affairs had told him that he thought that Spain, France and England, should reply to the Government of Morocco in identic terms declining the proposal. M. Delcassé concurred in that view. He did not believe in an attack by Germany on France if England, Spain and France held together. Italy had disinterested herself as regards Morocco and was bound not to oppose France.

If Monsieur Delcassé left the Government because his colleagues did not approve his views as to the way of dealing with Germany in the Morocco business. it would seem probable that they might be ready to yield something more than commercial advantages.

I have, &c.

FRANCIS BERTIE.

([1]) [A draft of this despatch is in the Embassy Volume, F.O. 146/3842. But in this copy a part of the letter, finally erased by Sir F. Bertie, stated that he had been absent for three days at Dieppe during the crisis of the resignation of M. Delcassé, and so had not seen him until the 10th. In this Embassy copy the following entry is in the margin: "reproduction of a private letter of June 10." Some correspondence between Mr. Balfour and the King on the Delcassé incident is given in Sir Sidney Lee: *King Edward VII* (1927), II. p. 344.]

No. 97.

Sir F. Lascelles to the Marquess of Lansdowne.

F.O. Germany (Prussia) 1617.
(No. 160.)   Most Confidential.   Berlin, D. *June* 12, 1905.
My Lord,   R. *June* 15, 1905.

On the evening of the 10th instant, I had a long conversation with Prince Bülow, whom I had asked to receive me before my departure from Berlin on leave of absence.([1]) His Serene Highness said that he was very glad to see me, as he wished to discuss with me fully the relations between our two countries, which, he regretted to say, were far from being satisfactory. During the South African war great animosity was felt in Germany against England. The people had interested themselves in those wretched Boers ("ces misérables Boers") and had become violently excited. Since the war, however, the ill-feeling towards England had died away, and he could assure me that now nine-tenths of the German people asked for nothing better than to live on friendly terms with England. Now the animosity had crossed the Channel and public opinion in England was as bitter or indeed even more bitter against Germany than German opinion had been against England during the war. He regretted that this state of things should exist and that the English press should continue its hostility against Germany. I was aware of the sensitiveness of the Emperor to English opinion, and hardly a day passed without His Majesty sending him a sheaf of English papers to read.

I said that it was a pity that His Majesty read the English papers at all. Unfortunately His Majesty believed that it was in the power of His Majesty's Government to influence the press, and I had frequently assured His Majesty that this was not the case. I had however not been able to persuade His Majesty of the error of his belief.

Prince Bülow said that it was not only of the press that he had to complain, but that he had reluctantly come to the conclusion that His Majesty's Government themselves were animated by hostility towards Germany. On my expressing my astonishment at this statement and observing that the recent appointment of a German Representative on the Board of the Abyssinian Bank, though a small matter in itself, was a proof of their willingness to meet the wishes of the German Government, Prince Bülow said that he could tell me in the strictest confidence, that information had reached him that shortly before Monsieur Delcassé's fall, England had made an offer to France to enter with her into an offensive and defensive alliance against Germany. France had refused, but the fact that the offer had been made was a proof of the unfriendliness of His Majesty's Government towards Germany.([2])

I replied that I was greatly astonished to hear that such an offer had been made, and I was strongly inclined to doubt the accuracy of His Serene Highness' information. Prince Bülow said that it was true that the information was not official, but it came from a source which made it impossible for him to doubt its accuracy.

Prince Bülow went on to say that he had had a long conversation with Count Bernstorff, who had recently returned from England, and had expressed the opinion that the mutual suspicion which existed in both countries was due to a complete misunderstanding ("un malentendu énorme"). Each seemed to think that the other was about to attack her. Now the idea that Germany wished to attack England would appear ludicrous to any German mind. He might just as well say that he was

([1]) [For Prince Bülow's record of this conversation, see *G.P.* XX, II, pp. 628–630.]

([2]) MARGINAL MINUTE BY KING EDWARD.

How badly informed he is!

E.R.

afraid of receiving my visit because he believed that I should pull a revolver out of my pocket and shoot him.

I replied that personally I had never believed that Germany intended to go to war with England, but that the idea did not seem to me to be any more ridiculous than that England was about to attack Germany.

The conversation then turned on the question of Morocco. Prince Bülow said that although he did not personally care much about a Conference, he hoped the Powers would agree to it as the best means of settling the question which had been raised. He defended the action of Germany on the ground that if the Sultan had accepted the reforms proposed by France, there would have been an end to the commerce of any other nation in Morocco. The country would have practically become a French protectorate, and all the concessions to be granted in the country would be given to French subjects. Germany had asked for no special advantages for herself, and her object was to keep the door open for all Nations.

I said that Your Lordship had been good enough to inform me of your recent conversation with Count Metternich in which; although not declining the Conference, you had stated that you had caused the Sultan of Morocco to be informed that you considered the idea an unpractical one.(¹) Personally I did not think the idea a good one. It did not appear to me likely to lead to much, and there was something illogical in the idea of an independent Oriental Sovereign submitting to a Conference of European Powers the reforms he proposed to grant to his own subjects. If, however, it were to lead to a settlement of the question it might be a good thing. Prince Bülow replied that he had not yet received a definitive reply either from England or France, each of whom seemed, as far as he could judge, to wish to throw the onus of refusal on the other.

Prince Bülow, in answer to my inquiries, said that he hoped that Peace would now soon be made between Russia and Japan. It was a step in the right direction that the two belligerents should have agreed to appoint Representatives to discuss the question, but they had both declined to give the slightest indication of the terms they would be prepared to accept.

I have, &c.

FRANK C. LASCELLES.

(¹) [v. infra pp. 92–3, No. 117.]

No. 98.

Sir F. Lascelles to the Marquess of Lansdowne.

F.O. Germany (Prussia) 1617.
(No. 161.) Most Confidential.   *Berlin,* D. *June* 12, 1905.
My Lord,   R. *June* 15, 1905.

After my interview with Prince Bülow, of which I attempted to give an account in my preceding despatch of this day's date, I called upon Herr von Holstein, whom I had not seen for a considerable time. In referring to the unsatisfactory relations between our two countries, Herr von Holstein said that if any one had told him two years ago that a war between England and Germany was within the bounds of possibility he would have simply laughed, but now things had reached such a point that it could no longer be considered impossible. There seemed to be even influential people in England who were seeking to familiarise public opinion with the possibility of such a war, which could by no possibility bring any advantage to either party.

I repeated a remark which Prince Bülow had just told me had been made by Count Bernstorff, that the strained relations between our two countries were due to a huge misunderstanding. In Germany people seemed to think that England was about to attack, and in England there were people who believed that the German fleet had been built and was always kept in home waters for the sole purpose of attacking England.

Herr von Holstein said it was all very well to bring that forward as a pretext for argument, but I could not surely wish him to believe that any one in England really thought that there was the remotest possibility of Germany making an attack on England. Come, now, did I believe it myself? I replied that I certainly did not believe in the danger of an attack, but the idea was not more absurd than the German fear of being attacked by England.

Herr von Holstein argued that the German fear was much more reasonable. Of course if we were to attack Germany the Emperor would stand up to us, but he would certainly never dream of attacking us himself. If we did not want war, what explanation could be given of the constant attacks in the Press, the utterances of Admirals and Civil Lords of the Admiralty urging the destruction of the German Fleet, and, above all the offer of His Majesty's Government to conclude an offensive and defensive alliance with France against Germany.([1])

I said that Prince Bülow had mentioned this point in his conversation, and that I could scarcely believe that his information was correct. Herr von Holstein replied that although not official, he feared there could be no doubt of its accuracy. I said that I did not understand how an offensive and defensive alliance with us could be of much advantage to France. We should no doubt be able to pick up some German ships and do enormous harm to her commerce but we could not come to France's assistance on land, and I understood that the best military opinion was that Germany would not have much difficulty in defeating France. Herr von Holstein said that he believed that Germany would be victorious, but it would not be an easy matter for the French frontier was strongly fortified and the outer crust of France was stronger than in 1870. I said that I was not inclined to believe in war. France certainly did not desire it, and I could not understand what advantage it would bring to Germany, who did not want any French territory.

Herr von Holstein said that he did not apprehend any immediate danger. The Moroccan Question would not lead to any serious complications. He repeated what Prince Bülow had said as to the necessity of the German action to prevent Morocco from becoming a French Protectorate, and he argued that Germany had acted in a most considerate and conciliatory manner. It would have been open to her to declare that the geographical position of Morocco made that country a matter of interest to all the Great Powers of Europe who could not admit that one of them should obtain exclusive influence there. Instead of doing so Germany had merely put forward her commercial interests. She had asked for no special advantages for herself, and any improvement that might take place in Morocco would be to the advantage not only of Germany, but of all the nations who had commercial interests there. As for the proposed Conference he regarded it as a piece of diplomatic etiquette that the Powers who had acquired certain rights in Morocco in virtue of the Madrid Convention should have their say as to the reforms which would benefit them all. This at all events was a proof that Germany was not pursuing a selfish policy, and that she did not wish for any territorial acquisition, although certain articles in the English press seemed calculated to force her to ask for a port.([2])

I said that the idea of a Conference did not smile upon me. Conferences were apt to accentuate rather than smooth over divergences of opinion. I presumed that Count Tattenbach's Mission to Fez had been successful, and that Germany might consider that

([1]) MARGINAL MINUTE BY KING EDWARD.

This is nearly as absurd as it is false!

E.R.

([2]) MARGINAL MINUTE BY KING EDWARD.

Of course!

E.R.

G

she had safeguarded her commercial interests in Morocco. If, however, the Sultan of Morocco really wished to consult the Powers as to the reforms which he proposed to grant to his own subjects, it seemed to me that he might submit his scheme of reforms to the Representatives at Tangier of those Powers who were chiefly interested.

Herr von Holstein said that he thought that this would come to about the same thing as submitting them to a Conference.

With regard to the prospect of peace between Russia and Japan, Herr von Holstein had nothing to add to what Prince Bülow had told me.

I have, &c.
FRANK C. LASCELLES.

[*ED. NOTE.*—The text of the Madrid Convention is given in *B.F.S.P.*, Vol 71, pp. 639–44.]

No. 99.

The Marquess of Lansdowne to Sir F. Lascelles.

F.O. Germany (Prussia) 1615.
(No. 136.)
Sir,   *Foreign Office, June 16, 1905.*

I have read with the utmost interest your despatches Nos. 160 and 161, Most Confidential, of the 12th instant, and I entirely approve of the language used by your Excellency on the occasions of your interviews with Prince Bülow and Baron Holstein. I trust that it will have the effect of dispelling, at all events to some extent, the illusions under which the German Government appears to labour with regard to the feelings and attitude of His Majesty's Government. Some of the statements made to you by these high officials were of a kind which it was difficult for you to deal with in the absence of information which you did not possess. I therefore thought it advisable to supplement what you had said by a few additional words addressed to the German Ambassador at this Court. I made you aware of my intention, and was glad to find that you were entirely in favour of my giving effect to it. I therefore invited Count Metternich to call upon me this morning, and expressed to him the surprise with which I had read your report of the observations addressed to you by Prince Bülow and Baron Holstein as to the relations at this moment existing between the two countries. These observations were characterized by a tone of apprehension for which there seemed to me to be a total absence of foundation. So far as I was able to follow the argument of these personages, the strained relations which were believed to exist between Great Britain and Germany were due, in the first place, to the attitude of the English press, and, in the second, to the belief that Great Britain and France had been engaged in something like a conspiracy against Germany—a conspiracy which was supposed to have led to the offer by England of an offensive and defensive alliance against Germany, which offer France was said to have refused.

With regard to the attitude of the press, His Excellency who knew this country so well, must, I thought, be well aware that His Majesty's Government was in no way answerable for the language of our newspapers. Some of them were not sparing of their attacks upon His Majesty's Ministers, and I could easily name one or two journals, amongst those by whom Germany had been most hardly judged, which had, at different times, been not less unsparing in their comments upon the manner in which the foreign relations of this country were conducted.

With regard to the alleged offensive and defensive alliance, the offer of which was cited as a proof of our unfriendliness, I could scarcely believe that the assertion was seriously made, or that the story was worth contradicting. If, however, H[is] E[xcellency] thought that a contradiction from me would serve a useful purpose, I was glad to assure him that no offensive and defensive alliance had ever been offered or even discussed on either side.

I gathered that, in addition to these two points, we were regarded as to some extent responsible for the complications which had arisen in Morocco. As to that, I could only say that, so far as I understood the German policy, as explained to you by Baron Holstein, Germany desired to be regarded as the defender of commercial liberty in that country, and repudiated the idea of pursuing a selfish policy in it. If that were so, there seemed to me to be no antagonism between the British and the German policy, nor were either of them inconsistent with that which was openly proclaimed in the Anglo-French Declaration, or with that which, so far as my information went, France was perfectly content to pursue.

His Excellency thanked me for having spoken to him so frankly on the subject. He repeated with some earnestness his complaint of the manner in which an anti-German campaign was being waged in the British press, but he accepted unreservedly my contradiction of the rumour that we had sought to make an offensive and defensive alliance with France against Germany. As for Morocco, he said that the German Government had given the French Government a year to explain their policy, and that they had proposed a European Conference as a convenient way of clearing up the doubts which existed with regard to it. He admitted however that, so far as Morocco was concerned, Germany had no reason to complain of Great Britain, and that there was therefore no reason why we should quarrel about that country. He expressed an earnest desire that the relations between Great Britain and Germany should be improved, and he did not see why such an improvement should be impossible, citing as a case in point the tension which he said had at one moment existed between the United States and Germany—a tension which he thought had now entirely disappeared and made way for feelings of a very cordial description.(¹)

I am, &c.
LANSDOWNE.

(¹) [For Count Metternich's report, see *G.P.* XX, II. pp. 630–634.]

No. 100.

Mr. Lister to the Marquess of Lansdowne.

F.O. France 3707.
(No. 371.)   *Paris,* D. *October* 11, 1905.
My Lord,   R. *October* 13, 1905.

With reference to my despatch No. 369 of the 8th instant,(¹) I have the honour to enclose herein, extracted from to-day's edition of "Le Matin," a further article which has been published by M. Lauzanne in connection with the series which appeared under the heading "the Truth about the Moroccan affair."(²)

M. Lauzanne states that it had not been his intention to add another line to what he had already written but the utterances of the Press, which attributed the articles to the inspiration of M. Delcassé, forced him to explain under what circumstances they had been written.

Two of the articles were ready more than three months ago, and the one concerning the meeting of the cabinet on the 6th of June was written on the evening of the 8th.

They were not published at once in order to avoid causing irritation during the negotiations between M. Rouvier and Germany.

M. Lauzanne declares that he had not consulted M. Delcassé in regard to the articles; that his statement concerning the action of England in the event of an attack

(¹) [Not reproduced.]
(²) [Not reproduced.]

on France is supported by various English newspapers; and concludes by comparing the German Press to a man who purposes to commit a crime and curses the barbarity of the Penal Code.

I have, &c.
REGINALD LISTER.

No. 101.

Sir F. Bertie to the Marquess of Lansdowne.

F.O. France 3707.
(No. 375.)   Paris, D. October 14, 1905.
My Lord,   R. October 16, 1905.

After the Council of Ministers yesterday, a communication was made through the Agence Havas to the Press, to the effect that the accounts which have recently been published in the newspapers in regard to the incidents which occurred at the time of, and especially the details concerning, the Cabinet Council which preceded the resignation of M. Delcassé are incorrect.

An article by M. Stephanne Lauzanne, copy of which is enclosed herein,(¹) appeared in to-day's edition of "Le Matin," upholding the accuracy of his information, and quoting a statement made at Limoges on Sunday by M. Jaurès, to the effect that he had received an identical account from three Ministers.

M. Lauzanne says that the German Press has been clamouring for a denial of the disclosures, which every member of the Government knows to be correct, and that the note which was communicated yesterday to the Press should be regarded not as a denial but merely as an act of complaisance.

The communication has called forth articles in most of the leading newspapers, and has been construed by them as was the letter of M. Delcassé to the editor of the "Figaro," as a proof of the correctness of the opinions which they have respectively expounded on the question.

I have, &c.
FRANCIS BERTIE.

(¹) [Not reproduced.]

No. 102.

Sir F. Lascelles to the Marquess of Lansdowne.

F.O. Germany (Prussia) 1617.
(No. 248.)   Berlin, D. October 15, 1905.
My Lord,   R. October 23, 1905.

I have the honour to transmit to your Lordship herewith translations of extracts from the leading German newspapers on the recent disclosures of the "Matin," regarding the events which preceded and caused the resignation of M. Delcassé from the French Foreign Office.(¹)

The statement concerning Great Britain's supposed offer of armed support to France against Germany has evoked expressions of keen resentment in the press, who are almost unanimous in clamouring for an official denial of the allegations set forth in the "Matin."

So far the "North German Gazette" has restricted itself to a reproduction of the French articles, but I have reason to hope that within the next few days a statement

(¹) [Not reproduced.]

will be published of an official character in its columns to the effect that the Imperial Government are disposed to attach no credence to the aggressive anti-German policy which is being attributed to British and French statesmen.

I have, &c.
FRANK C. LASCELLES.

No. 103.

Sir F. Lascelles to the Marquess of Lansdowne.

F.O. Germany (Prussia) 1617.
(No. 249.)   *Berlin,* D. *October* 16, 1905.
My Lord,   R. *October* 23, 1905.

In my immediately preceding despatch I had the honour to foreshadow an Article in the semi-official "North German Gazette" which would reflect the views held by the Imperial Government concerning the statement in the "Matin" that England had offered armed support to France against Germany. This article, précis of which I have the honour to enclose, has now appeared, and will, I trust, by its reasonable review of the situation, exercise a calming effect on the public mind as well as on the unofficial Press.

I have, &c.
FRANK C. LASCELLES.

Enclosure in No. 103.

Précis of an Article in the "Norddeutsche Allgemeine Zeitung" of October 15, 1905.

After blaming those who were dissatisfied with the Franco-German understanding for causing so great a sensation, the "Norddeutsche" declares that the influential circles in France had nothing to do with the "Revelations" of the "Matin." It proceeds :—

"Reuter's bureau has meanwhile announced, in contradiction to the 'Matin's' assertions, that Germany had been informed by Great Britain that there was never a question of an offer of assistance to France by England, that France never asked for such assistance, nor was it ever offered by England. We are in a position to state that the English Government spontaneously caused a communication of this character to be sent here, and that this communication was accepted on the German side in the same straightforward spirit in which it was given. An incident in the diplomatic relations between England and Germany has not been produced by the assertions of the 'Matin'; but, on the other hand, this is a case of a communication characterized by the English Government as confidential, which, in the view of the London Government, was not intended for publication. We therefore refrain from further discussion of this communication; and the only further statement which we should particularly desire to make is that all assertions according to which the German Government had demanded explanations from the English or from the French Government in regard to the assertions of Paris journals are incorrect. A step of that nature would not, in view of the form in which these assertions were made, have been in accordance with diplomatic courtesy. Nor would it accord with the straightforward sentiments with which we willingly regard the intentions of French and English statesmen. In the larger circles of the German people the incident has been received with tranquillity;

and the 'Tribuna' of Rome is quite correct when it asserts that the announcements by English correspondents of hatred against England in Germany are exaggerations. On the contrary, the German people and press have shown great calmness.''

No. 104.

Sir F. Lascelles to the Marquess of Lansdowne.

F.O. Germany (Prussia) 1617.
(No. 252.)   Confidential.
My Lord,

Berlin, D. October 20, 1905.
R. October 23, 1905.

In an interview with Baron von Richthofen on the 17th instant, I expressed the hope that the excitement in the Press, which had been caused by the revelations in the "Matin," was now beginning to subside, as would no doubt be the case after the publication of the article in the "North German Gazette" of the 15th instant, to which I had the honour to call Your Lordship's attention by my despatch No. 249 of the 16th instant.

I told Baron von Richthofen that I had recently had a conversation with Dr. Rosen, who had expressed the opinion that it would be very desirable that some person in authority in England should take an opportunity of publicly denying the report that England had offered assistance to France in the event of a war breaking out between her and Germany. I said that I saw no necessity for an English Statesman denying a statement which nobody in England believed, and which the German Government, after Your Lordship's conversation with Count Metternich in June last, knew to be false.

Baron von Richthofen said that the German Government had loyally accepted the assurances which Your Lordship had given to Count Metternich in June,([1]) and to which Sir T. Sanderson had referred in a recent conversation with Count Metternich. This fact had now been published by the "North German Gazette," and it would no doubt have the effect of calming the excitement caused by the Delcassé revelations. On my expressing a doubt as to whether Monsieur Delcassé was the author of the revelations in the "Matin," Baron von Richthofen said that it was possible that M. Delcassé may not have been responsible for their publication, but that there could be very little doubt that the information contained in them came from him.

I went on to say that, although I hoped that this particular question might be considered as closed, there still existed in both Countries an amount of mutual suspicion and distrust which was greatly to be regretted, and which was perhaps more difficult to deal with than a definite quarrel, which would admit of explanation. I had conversed with several of my German Friends on the relations between our two Countries. Individually they did not share the belief, which was very general in Germany, that England wished for a war and was prepared to attack her; but when I observed that in my Country a great many people believed that Germany wished to attack England, they merely laughed and wondered how it was possible for any one to entertain so preposterous an idea. Now, the fear that was felt in England as to the intentions of Germany, although I certainly did not share it myself, was no more preposterous or ridiculous than the fear felt in Germany as to the intentions of England. It was evident that a war between the two countries would be a great calamity for both, and I did not see how it could possibly bring advantage to either.

Baron von Richthofen said that he entirely agreed with me. He looked upon a war between our two Countries as entirely out of the question. He admitted the existence of suspicion and distrust on both sides, which he would gladly see removed, and which he hoped would calm down in time, and he considered that it was fortunate

([1]) [*v. supra* pp. 82–3, No. 99.]

that there was no question pending between the two Countries which was likely to produce any serious complication, as the present temper of public opinion on both sides would make it very difficult to come to an arrangement if any serious difference of opinion should arise.

I have, &c.

FRANK C. LASCELLES.

No. 105.

(a.)

WRITTEN OPINION BY LORD SANDERSON.

Extract from a private letter from Lord Sanderson to Harold Temperley.

65, *Wimpole Street*, W. 1,.
August 17, 1922.

Confidential.

. . . . In a little book " A Century of British Foreign Policy " by Gooch and Masterman, published about 1915, there is a passage about p. 62.(¹) Quotations are given from publications by M. Mévil and M. Jaurès, to the effect that in 1905 when the German Government first took an aggressive tone about French projects of reform in Morocco, the British Government promised military assistance to France if she were attacked by Germany, including a landing of an expedition of 120,000 men in Schleswig. The writers come to the conclusion that there can be no doubt that some promise was made, and ask if it is not time that it should be revealed.

I think I am justified in affirming that *no* such promise was made—and that we went no farther than warning the German Government that if Germany attacked France in connexion with the Entente we could not undertake to remain indifferent.

There were no doubt preparations by our military authorities for defending Belgium in case of an attack by Germany on France through Belgian territory, and these preparations must have been known to the French military attaché in London. There was also a good deal of loose talk in naval circles and in some high quarters of a possible expedition to Schleswig in the possible event of war. I do not believe such a measure was ever seriously entertained, and I looked upon the report as put about for the purpose of a warning.

In M. Poincaré's book " Les Origines de la Guerre " there are statements (pp. 72 and 82)(²) that in the spring of 1905 the British Government showed an inclination to supplement the Entente of 1904 by an agreement of the nature of the Franco-Russian Alliance, and that M. Cambon even forwarded to M. Delcassé a written formula proposed by Lord Lansdowne, but there is no record of this in our archives, nor has Lord Lansdowne any recollection of it. All that is to be found is that he and Lord Bertie laid stress in conversation on the need for frank and intimate communication and consultation with a view to harmonious action in opposition to any designs of Germany to acquire a port on the West coast of Morocco. It is possible that M. Cambon may have taken down in writing the phrases used by Lord Lansdowne in this respect. . . . [The remainder of this memo. deals with another point.]

S.

(¹) [p. 62 is correct.]
(²) [These references are to the English edition.]

(b.)

COMMENT BY LORD LANSDOWNE.

The above opinion was submitted by the Editors to Lord Lansdowne, together with all relevant papers. He replied on the 4th April, 1927, " I should have no objection, if you thought fit to do so, to your saying that I had seen Lord Sanderson's opinion, and that my recollection accords with his, and that I have nothing to add to the discussion."

[*ED. NOTE.*—In a letter to Sir E. Grey of March 31, 1906 (Grey MSS., Vol. 40), Sir N. O'Conor quoted some evidence to the effect that the German Ambassador had threatened M. Rouvier in June 1905 with military action in consequence of a belief that a " Convention or Agreement " was about to be signed with Great Britain, and that this led to Delcassé's fall. Sir Edward Grey, in a letter of April 9, described the account as " interesting," and added " There was no Agreement pending between us and France then, so that was a German pretext."]

CHAPTER XIX.
MOROCCO AND THE POWERS, MAY-DECEMBER 1905.(¹)

No. 106.

Mr. Lowther to the Marquess of Lansdowne.

F.O. Morocco 434.
Tel. (No. 54.)

Fez, D. *May* 31, 1905.
R. *June* 3, 1905, 10·30 P.M.

Arrived all well to-day. Very courteous reception on part of officials and public.

Just received a note from Moorish Commissioner stating that he has been requested to invite all Gov[ernmen]ts represented at Tangier to discuss manner of giving effect to reforms suitable to present condition of affairs which Sultan intends to introduce and as to the sources from which the necessary expenditure will be met.

He requests me to inform Y[our] L[ordship] of above and that I may be given authority to attend.

MINUTE BY KING EDWARD.

The Conference seems inevitable and might clear up many things.

E.R.

(¹) [*Cf. G.P.* XX, II, Chs. 147–150, pp. 291–698, and *G.P.* XXI, I, Ch. 151, pp. 1–87.]

No. 107.

The Marquess of Lansdowne to Sir F. Bertie.

F.O. Morocco 434.
(No. 357.)
Sir,

Foreign Office, June 1, 1905.

The French Ambassador called at this Office to-day and said that, according to the reports which had been received from the French Minister at Fez, the Sultan seemed to have been a good deal impressed by Count von Tattenbach's arguments, and was disposed to propose a European conference on the French proposals of reform, basing his arguments in favour of that course on the clause of the Madrid Convention which secured most-favoured-nation treatment to all the Signatory Powers. M. Cambon said that a conference was clearly out of place, and that the French Gov[ernmen]t would be glad to know whether we 'had any news confirmatory of this report as to the Sultan's attitude, and when Mr. Lowther might be expected to arrive at Fez. They hoped that his presence and support might be of great use to M. Saint René-Taillandier.

H[is] E[xcellency] was informed that we had not yet heard of Mr. Lowther's arrival, but that he should be at Fez in the course of the next few days. The telegram from Tangier of yesterday's date,(¹) from which it appeared that the Sultan had not proposed a European conference, but wished to refer the French proposals for military reorganization to a conference of the Representatives at Tangier, was read to H[is] E[xcellency] and he was also informed that we would let him know as soon as Mr. Lowther reached Fez.

I am, &c.
LANSDOWNE.

(¹) [Not reproduced. It reported the issue of instructions by the Sultan for invitations to be sent to representatives of Signatory Powers of the Madrid Convention to attend a conference at Tangier " to discuss question of military reorganization." F.O. Morocco 434.]

No. 108.

The Marquess of Lansdowne to Mr. Lowther.

F.O. Morocco 434.   *Foreign Office, June* 5, 1905.
Tel. (No. 30.)   D. 3 P.M
   Your tel. 54 (of May 31).
   Inform Moorish Gov[ernmen]t that proposal to invoke assistance of all Gov[ernmen]ts having representatives at Tangier to take part in discussion of reforms so urgently needed for improvement of administration, is in our opinion wholly undeserving of encouragement.
   Such a discussion would involve participation of a large number of Powers many of them having no interest worth speaking of in Moorish affairs.
   We could not take part in it, and we desire to dissuade Sultan from pressing upon the Powers a project which we consider most ill-advised and contrary to interests of his country.

No. 109.

The Marquess of Lansdowne to Sir F. Bertie.

F.O. Morocco 434.
(No. 363.)
Sir,   *Foreign Office, June* 5, 1905.
   I took the opportunity of mentioning to the French Ambassador in conversation this morning, the statement contained in Mr. Lowther's telegram No. 54 of the 31st ultimo to the effect that the Moorish Government had suggested that the question of the reforms to be introduced in the administration of the country should be discussed by all the Powers having representatives at Tangier. I said that the proposition seemed to me to be a most ill-advised one, and that H[is] M[ajesty's] G[overnment] did not wish to give it any encouragement. They desired however to learn before pronouncing themselves how it was regarded by the French Government. H[is] E[xcellency] told me that he shared the opinion which I had expressed, and that he earnestly trusted that we should instruct our representative to say that we would have nothing to do with the proposal. I subsequently communicated to H[is] Ex[cellency] the substance of my tel[egram] No. 30 of this day's date to Mr. Lowther.
   During the course of our conversation H[is] Ex[cellency] told me that he had learned privately that the French Ambassador at Washington had spoken to Mr. Taft, who had observed that the U[nited] S[tates'] Government would probably not be favourably disposed towards the idea of a conference. I told H[is] Ex[cellency] that I would take an opportunity of mentioning the subject to the U[nited] S[tates'] Government, who, as one of the Powers having a representative at Tangier, would no doubt be consulted. I should endeavour to convince them that the proposal was unsound and should not be entertained.

                                                             I am, &c.
                                                             LANSDOWNE.

No. 110.

The Marquess of Lansdowne to Sir M. Durand.

F.O. Morocco 434.
(No. 150.)
Sir,   *Foreign Office, June 5, 1905.*

I met Mr. Whitelaw Reid again this morning at Buckingham Palace, and I mentioned to him the proposal contained in Mr. Lowther's telegram No. 54 of the 31st ultimo to the effect that the question of the reforms to be introduced in the administration of Morocco should be discussed by all the Powers having representatives at Tangier. I observed that this proposal concerned the Government of the United States as one of the Powers having a representative at Tangier. It seemed to me to be ill-advised, and I could not conceive a procedure less likely to bring about the salutary reforms which were so much needed in Morocco than a discussion undertaken by ten or a dozen Powers, some of whom had virtually no concern whatever in that country. We should, I said, certainly oppose it. It would be extremely interesting to me to know how it was regarded by the Government of the United States, and I should be grateful for any information with which Mr. Whitelaw Reid might be able to supply me as to this point. His Excellency expressed general concurrence with what I had said, and promised to telegraph the substance of my observations to the Government of the United States.

I am, &c.
LANSDOWNE.

No. 111.

Sir F. Bertie to the Marquess of Lansdowne.

F.O. France 3708.
Tel. (No. 41.) Secret.

Paris, June 6, 1905.
D. 6·8 P.M.
R. 10 P.M.

My immediately preceding telegram.

Prime Minister sent for "Times" correspondent this afternoon, and stated to him that policy of France with regard to Anglo-French understanding would remain exactly the same.

I understand that he is no less than M. Delcassé opposed to Conference.

No. 112.

The Marquess of Lansdowne to Monsieur Cambon.

F.O. Morocco 434.   *Foreign Office, June 6, 1905.*
M. Cambon.([1])

With reference to our conversation of yesterday morning, it may interest you to know the substance of the telegram which I have sent to our representative at Fez. He has been instructed to inform the Moorish Government that, in the opinion of His Majesty's Government, the proposal to invoke the assistance of the Powers who are represented at Tangier to discuss the question of the reforms which are so urgently needed for the improvement of the administration is wholly unworthy of support. A discussion of this nature would involve the participation of a large number of Powers, many of which have no interests worth mentioning in Morocco. The project is one which His Majesty's Government consider most ill-advised, and contrary to the interests

([1]) [This is a draft only, hence the address and signature are incomplete.]

of Morocco. H[is] M[ajesty's] G[overnment] could not take any part in it, and they desire to dissuade the Sultan from pressing it upon the Powers.

Your Excellency will also be interested to hear that late last night I received a telegram from H[is] M[ajesty's] Ambassador at Washington stating that the President has informed the German Ambassador that, so long as the French Government object, the United States Government could not adhere to the proposal for a Conference of the Powers.

L[ANSDOWNE.]

No. 113.

The Marquess of Lansdowne to Sir M. Durand.

F.O. Morocco 434.
(No. 151.)
Sir,   *Foreign Office, June 7, 1905.*

The American Ambassador called at the Foreign Office today for the first time. He was authorised to tell me that the President had informed the German Ambassador at Washington that he did not see how the United States could take part in any Conference as to Morocco unless France acquiesced. The President had made a similar statement to M. Jusserand, but did not desire that publicity should be given to the matter.

I had some conversation with Mr. Whitelaw Reid as to the situation in Morocco and the manner in which it was affected by M. Delcassé's resignation. I gave His Excellency a short account of the purport of my conversation with M. Cambon (see my despatch No. 364 of the 7th inst[ant] to Sir F. Bertie)([1]) and we agreed that in the circumstances it would be better to "mark time" so far as the proposed Conference was concerned.

I am, &c.
LANSDOWNE.

([1]) [This despatch records an interview with M. Cambon on June 7. Lord Lansdowne communicated to M. Cambon the circular handed to him by Count Metternich on the previous evening (*v. infra* p. 92, No. 116) and discussed with him the applicability of Article XVII of the Madrid Convention of 1880.]

No. 114.

Sir F. Bertie to the Marquess of Lansdowne.

Paris, June 8, 1905.

F.O. Morocco 434.   D. 6·15 P.M.
Tel. (No. 43.)   R. 8 P.M.

Morocco. I am informed on excellent authority that at Council of Ministers held last Tuesday M. Delcassé stated his view that French, British, and Spanish Governments should address identic note to the Sultan declining the Conference.

His colleagues did not agree with this view.

No. 115.

Sir M. de Bunsen to the Marquess of Lansdowne.

F.O. Morocco 434.
(No. 50.) Confidential.   *Lisbon, D. June 8, 1905.*
My Lord,   R. *June 11, 1905.*

The Minister for Foreign Affairs informed me yesterday that the German Chargé d'Affaires had just called upon him to say, under instructions from his Government, that Germany had accepted the invitation of the Government of Morocco to take part in an international Conference for the discussion of the affairs of that country.

Senhor Villaça added that he had expressed no opinion as to the reply which it was desirable that Portugal should give to this invitation. He was awaiting, he said, a report from the Portuguese Minister in London, who he hoped would be able to inform him of Your Lordship's views on the question.

I have, &c.
M. DE BUNSEN.

No. 116.

The Marquess of Lansdowne to Mr. Lowther.

F.O. Morocco 434. *Foreign Office, June 8, 1905.*
Tel. (No. 35.) D. 10 P.M.
My Tel[egram] No. 30.

German Ambassador communicated to me yesterday a Circular addressed by his Government to Signatories of Madrid Convention, stating that Germany considers that such a Conference as has been proposed by Moorish Gov[ernmen]t offers the best means for the introduction of the contemplated reforms. The German Gov[ernmen]t rely on Article 17 of the Madrid Convention under which all the Signatory Powers are entitled to most-favoured-nation treatment, and no Power can have preferential position. German Gov[ernmen]t have therefore accepted invitation of Moorish Gov[ernmen]t.

I have told H[is] E[xcellency] that when the Moorish Gov[ernmen]t suggested a discussion of the question of reforms by all the Powers having representatives at Tangier we had instructed you to discourage the proposal as ill adapted to secure the desired object. I added that in view of resignation of French Min[iste]r for For[eign] Affairs it seems desirable to await information respecting attitude of French Gov[ernmen]t before further considering the matter.(¹)

(¹) [For Count Metternich's report, see *G.P.* XX, II, pp. 416–417. His telegram dated June 6 says he communicated the Circular on that day to Lord Lansdowne, as does a despatch from Lord Lansdowne to Mr. Lowther, No. 128 of June 7, *v.* also *infra* No. 117. Count Metternich's letter says, evidently in error, that he got it on the 7th.]

No. 117.

The Marquess of Lansdowne to Sir F. Lascelles.

F.O. Morocco 434.
(No. 131.)
Sir, *Foreign Office, June 8, 1905.*

I asked the German Ambassador to call upon me this evening after the meeting of the Cabinet at which the situation in Morocco had been discussed.

I told His Excellency that I felt sure that he would expect me, now that I had had an opportunity of discussing the matter with my colleagues, to add something to the personal observations which I had made when, on the 6th instant, he communicated to me the German Circular.

I wished, in the first place, to make him aware of a fact which we did not feel justified in withholding from his knowledge. It was this, that we had learned from our Minister, in a telegram dated from Fez and received by us on the 3rd instant,(¹) that the Moorish Government had invited all the Governments represented at Tangier to discuss the manner in which effect might be given to reforms suitable to the present condition of affairs in Morocco. His Majesty's Government had, immediately on

(¹) [*v. supra* p. 88, No. 106.]

receipt of this proposal, desired Mr. Lowther to inform the Moorish Government that in their opinion the proposal was not deserving of encouragement. Such a discussion would involve the participation of a large number of Powers, many of them having no interest worth speaking of in Moorish affairs. The procedure moreover did not seem to us well calculated to attain the object in view, and we had instructed Mr. Lowther to dissuade the Sultan from pressing it upon the Powers.

We now found that the proposal had been taken up by the German Government, and that they supported it by an appeal to the Madrid Convention of 1880. This no doubt somewhat altered the situation, and it was still further modified by M. Delcassé's resignation. We were at present without information as to the attitude of the reconstructed French Government, and we had therefore come to the conclusion that for the moment it would be better that we should reserve our opinion. I added that, so far as the question of reforms was concerned, we remained of opinion that the Conference was not likely to prove an efficacious remedy. Our experience of similar attempts made by a large number of Powers to arrive at an agreement as to schemes of reform was not of a very encouraging kind.

His Excellency said that owing to the singular conduct of the French Government in keeping Germany without information as to her dealings with Morocco, a very complicated position had arisen, from which such a Conference seemed likely to provide a means of escape. He repeated to me that although the German Government had not been able to obtain any definite account of the French programme, it was clear that the French Government was endeavouring to obtain exclusive control of the country. He added that the German Government had no desire to reap a diplomatic triumph at the expense of France or to humiliate her; she could not however afford to be ignored, and her only wish was to maintain the "legal status" of Morocco, which would be impaired by the conduct of the French Government.

I said that I gathered from what His Excellency had told me that the Conference, if it were to meet, would be expected to deal not only with the introduction of reforms, but with the maintenance of the independence and integrity of Morocco, and the preservation of the open door. His Excellency said that this was the case. I asked him whether it was quite clear that what France was doing in Morocco really implied a disregard of these principles or a denial of m[ost]-f[avoured]-n[ation] treatment to other Powers. The acquisition of that influence which a civilised Power naturally exerts over a barbarous one when the two are in close contact must, I thought, always tend to place the civilised Power in a privileged position, but that influence did not seem to me to involve any wrong to others. If the civilised Power took upon itself the white washing of the prisons, the reorganisation of the police or the improvement of roads and railways all the other Powers could scarcely expect to be allowed to do the same. I asked H[is] E[xcellency] whether Germany did not enjoy a privileged position in Shantung. H[is] E[xcellency] denied that Germany was doing in Shantung what France was attempting to do in Morocco. He said that he quite understood that it should be necessary for France to act as "policeman" in the regions adjoining the Algerian frontier, but if the policeman proceeded to lay hands upon the whole country and its administration the other Powers could not be indifferent. It seemed to him that it now rested entirely with France to say whether an amicable settlement of the difficulty should be arrived at, or whether the present situation of uncertainty and unrest should be prolonged. His own impression was that the French Government would come to terms, "if," His Excellency said, "you do not stiffen their backs for them."[1]

I am, &c.
LANSDOWNE.

[1] [For Count Metternich's report, see G.P. XX, II, pp. 422–424.]

No. 118.

Mr. Lowther to the Marquess of Lansdowne.

F.O. Morocco 434.   *Fez, D. June* 9, 1905.
Tel. (No. 60.)   R. *June* 13, 1905.

Your telegram No. 30 of 5th June.([1])

Have communicated your Lordship's reply to Moorish Government. They appear to think that Conference can take place even if Powers principally interested in Morocco decline to take part. Neither French Government nor any other have yet answered.

([1]) [*v. supra* p. 89, No. 108.]

No. 119.

Sir E. Egerton to the Marquess of Lansdowne.

F.O. Morocco 434.   *Rome,* D. *June* 9, 1905.
Tel. (No. 68.)   R.

Your telegram No. 35 to Mr. Lowther, Morocco.([1])

Italian Minister for Foreign Affairs has not yet answered German circular and is awaiting further information.

His attitude is in the main similar to that of Austria but as Italian Government have engagement with France respecting Morocco he has advised French Government to seek conciliatory solution of present difficulty.

([1]) [*v. supra* p. 92, No. 116.]

No. 120.

Sir E. Egerton to the Marquess of Lansdowne.

F.O. Morocco 434.
(No. 99.) Confidential.   *Rome,* D. *June* 10, 1905.
My Lord,   R. *June* 17, 1905.

Yesterday I saw Monsieur Tittoni, and he spoke to me on the subject of Monsieur Delcassé's resignation and Morocco.

I told him of the instructions to Mr. Lowther and that the German circular advocating a Conference had been received by Your Lordship who was of opinion that it was desirable to await information from Paris before considering the matter further.

His Excellency said he had likewise received the German circular which he had not yet answered.

He proposed to take the same line as Austria, which I understand (but not from His Excellency) to mean acceptance, subject to the general assent of other Powers.

On my saying that Italy was not exactly in the same position as Austria, having come to a special agreement with France respecting Morocco, Monsieur Tittoni answered " Yes, and it was on account of that understanding with France that he had telegraphed to Paris to urge the Government of the Republic to do all that is possible to conciliate the Emperor." His Excellency is convinced that it is not Prince Bülow but the Emperor who for some reason which he ignores has started this question.

His Excellency seriously deplores the loss of Monsieur Delcassé and the menacing tone adopted by the German Ambassadors here and elsewhere, repeating that he would not answer the Circular until he was in possession of more information.

I have, &c.
EDWIN H. EGERTON.

No. 121.

Sir E. Egerton to the Marquess of Lansdowne.

F.O. Morocco 434.
(No. 102.)
My Lord,

Rome, D. *June* 13, 1905.
R. *June* 17, 1905.

I asked Monsieur Tittoni today whether he was about to send an answer to the German Circular advocating the Moorish proposal for a Conference.

He said he was on the point of doing so,—consenting to join the Conference if all the Powers, including those interested, decided to do so.

I have, &c.
EDWIN H. EGERTON.

No. 122.

Sir E. Egerton to the Marquess of Lansdowne.

F.O. Italy 906.
(No. 105.)   Most Confidential.
My Lord,

Rome, D. *June* 13, 1905.
R. *June* 17, 1905.

It was the French Ambassador who came to inform me on the 6th instant when I was laid up in bed from a feverish attack that the German Ambassador, Count Monts, had said to Monsieur Tittoni that if the French Minister maintained his threat of military measures against the Sultan of Morocco, a German army would cross the French frontier.

Monsieur Tittoni in surprise seems to have said, in that case France would probably not be alone.

Upon this Count Monts answered, if England joined, the matter would be inconvenient, as it would affect the commerce of Germany, but that on land England would do nothing.

(I should add that later and to another person the Count spoke more seriously of England's power.)

The Minister for Foreign Affairs incredulous telegraphed to Berlin and was informed that there was no ground beyond a newspaper paragraph for the statement that a French ultimatum had been sent.

Monsieur Barrère assured me that Monsieur Tittoni appeared not to have been as much disturbed as he would have expected by this bluster of the German Ambassador and certainly to have had no sympathy with it.

Monsieur Barrère attributes to Count [*sic*] Holstein an evil influence over the Emperor and does not apparently think Count Bülow initiated the present move about Morocco.

A few days later, after the retirement of Monsieur Delcassé, which he attributes mainly to the jealousy of other politicians of the Chamber, Monsieur Barrère assured me that the leaders of French diplomacy, the two Cambons, Jusserand, and himself, were firmly united in sympathy for the policy of their late Chief and considered that there was no call for alarm; the French position was a sound one in harmony with England and others. It was absurd to accuse Delcassé of attempting to isolate Germany; he had simply made the relations of France with all foreign nations better.

I have, &c.
EDWIN H. EGERTON.

No. 123.

Sir C. Hardinge to the Marquess of Lansdowne.

St. Petersburgh, June 14, 1905.

F.O. Morocco 434.   D. 8 p.m.
Tel. (No. 98.)   R. 10 p.m.

Morocco. Y[ou]r Tel: No. 190. Count Lamsdorff told me to-day in answer to my enquiry that the German Amb[assado]r had asked him what reply he proposed to send to invitation of Moorish Gov[ernmen]t to take part in an international conference. He had answered that before giving a reply he wished to know more of the object of conference, and what Powers would take part in it. I gave him the substance of Y[our] L[ordship]'s instr[uctio]ns to Mr. Lowther. He added that Russia had absolutely no interests in Morocco but that as he had heard that France and Spain had refused to take part in it and that Italy and Austria were equally indisposed he did not wish Russia to stand alone with Germany. He intended to wait for text of note of Moorish Gov[ernmen]t before replying to it.

No. 124.

The Marquess of Lansdowne to Sir F. Bertie.

F.O. Morocco 434.
(No. 393.)
Sir,   *Foreign Office, June 16, 1905.*

The French Ambassador asked me to receive him this afternoon.

He told me that he had not yet received any instructions as to the decision of the French Government with regard to the proposed Conference.

He was however able to tell me, but in the strictest confidence, that M. Rouvier and Prince Radolin had again met, and that the latter had intimated that if the French Government would accept the idea of a Conference "in principle" the German Government would be ready to commence a discussion such as M. Rouvier had invited with a view to an understanding which might render the meeting of the Conference unnecessary. M. Rouvier was, as I was aware, entirely favourable to the idea of a discussion, but did not like that of a Conference, even in principle. On the other hand, Prince Radolin had let him infer that if the proposal for a Conference were absolutely negatived, Germany would probably give trouble in Morocco. The Sultan might, *e.g.*, be encouraged to pursue an obstructive policy, incidents might arise, and France might have to choose between a public humiliation and conduct which might provoke a collision between the two Powers. A considerable impression had, His Excellency said, in his opinion been produced on M. Rouvier's mind by Prince Radolin's language.

His Excellency told me that he thought he had better return to Paris to-morrow morning and discuss the situation which had arisen with M. Rouvier, who was new to his work and must obviously find it difficult to gather up the threads of the negotiations which had taken place. His Excellency asked me what I thought.

I said that it seemed to me that His Excellency's return to Paris could only do good. As for our attitude, he was well aware of it. We had refused to take part in a Conference when the Moorish Government had asked us to do so, and we remained of opinion that a Conference was not the best means of procuring reforms. As for Prince Radolin's suggestion, it seemed to me that he wished to put the cart before the horse, and that the first thing to be done was that France, which was suspected by Germany of having designs upon the integrity of Morocco, and upon the commercial rights of other Powers, should be given an opportunity of explaining what her designs really were. The account of them which His Excellency had given me did not, I said, seem to me to point to anything inconsistent with the requirements which

Prince Bülow and other high German officials had put forward in conversation with Sir F. Lascelles.

Until such an exchange of views had taken place I could not see that there was anything to be gained by admitting the theoretical necessity of a Conference, except perhaps to enable Germany, which had brought about M. Delcassé's downfall, to secure a further success. Our attitude must of course depend upon that of the French Government, but if they maintained their refusal, so, most certainly, should we.

I am, &c.
LANSDOWNE.

No. 125.

Sir A. Nicolson to the Marquess of Lansdowne.

F.O. Morocco 434.
Tel. (No. 40.)

Madrid, June 17, 1905.
D. 4 P.M
R. 6·30 P.M.

German Ambassador in speaking to me this morning on the question of Morocco said that he had reason to hope that a solution would be found to the difficulty with France without recourse to a Conference as he understood that Great Britain was opposed to its convocation.

I said that a direct solution between Germany and France would be welcome news and that I was glad there was a possibility of abandoning idea of a conference which to my mind would only confuse and complicate matters.

I informed French Ambassador who has just returned from Paris of above and he will telegraph it to French M[inister for] F[oreign] A[ffairs] as he agrees with me (? that) German Ambassador was not merely expressing his personal views.

No. 126.

The Marquess of Lansdowne to Sir F. Bertie.

F.O. Morocco 434.
(No. 400.)
Sir,

Foreign Office, June 21, 1905.

The French Ambassador, who returned from Paris late last night, called upon me this morning, and brought with him a copy of the reply which the French Government has decided to return to the German proposal for a Conference as to the affairs of Morocco. A copy of this document is attached to this despatch. His Excellency told me that it would be handed to Prince Radolin today.

I learned from His Excellency that Prince Radolin had had no less than three interviews with M. Rouvier, and that the latter had on each occasion dwelt upon the inutility of a Conference. He had however been considerably perturbed by Prince Radolin's insistence. The German representatives at Rome and Madrid had moreover been extremely violent in their language. His Excellency mentioned to me in confidence that the German Emperor had addressed a personal communication on the subject of the Conference to President Roosevelt, who had replied that the United States' Government had no special interests in Morocco, and that they would be guided by the decision of the Powers who possessed such interests, and notably by that of France.

I saw His Excellency again after the Cabinet which met this morning, and told him that I was authorised to inform Count Metternich that, the French Government having communicated to us the answer which they had given to the German Government, we learned therefrom that they did not desire at the outset of the discussion to exclude the idea of a Conference, but were of opinion that France and Germany should begin by a frank exchange of ideas as to the subjects which the German Government desired to refer to such a Conference; that the French Government were convinced that their intentions with regard to Morocco were completely misunderstood; that they had no designs upon the sovereignty of the Sultan or upon the rights of other Powers; and that they believed that there was, in fact, no fundamental difference between the views of the two Governments, that a direct agreement was the best and promptest mode of arriving at a satisfactory result, and that the discussion which M. Rouvier invited might show that there was no occasion for holding a Conference. I should tell Count Metternich that in these circumstances His Majesty's Government would have to withhold their reply to his communication until they knew the result of the communications now passing between the French and German Governments.

I am, &c.

LANSDOWNE.

Enclosure in No. 126.

Memorandum communicated by M. Cambon, June 21, 1905.

Par deux communications adressées l'une à Fez au ministre, l'autre à Tanger au chargé d'affaires de France, le gouvernement de la République a été saisi d'une proposition du gouvernement marocain tendant à la réunion à Tanger d'une conférence composée des ministres des puissances signataires de la convention de Madrid et des délégués du makhzen en vue de s'entretenir : 1° du mode de réformes que S[a] M[ajesté] chérifienne se propose d'introduire dans son empire et qui seraient appropriées à sa situation présente; 2° de la manière de pourvoir aux frais de ces réformes.

Le gouvernement impérial saisi de la même proposition a fait connaître au gouvernement de la République par une note remise le 6 juin 1905 que la conférence lui paraissait être le meille[u]r moyen de préparer ces réformes qui ne pouvaient s'effectuer qu'avec le consentement de toutes les Puissances signataires de la convention de Madrid. Le gouvernement impérial estime que la mise en pratique de ces réformes est subordonnée au respect des articles de la dite convention et notamment de l'article 17 qui, d'après lui, accorderait à chacun des signataires le traitement le plus favorable et interdirait conséquemment l'attribution de tout privilège à l'un quelconque d'entre eux. Cette communication a été complétée par des observations verbales sur lesquelles nous aurons à revenir.

Après nous avoir fait connaître ses vues, le gouvernement impérial sollicite les nôtres dans le même sens et nous demande de nous rendre à la conférence. Cette démarche nous inspire les observations suivantes :—

Les termes de l'adhésion donnée par le gouvernement impérial à la proposition marocaine en modifient le caractère d'une manière assez sensible. Le gouvernement chérifien se borne à demander aux Puissances un conseil relatif à l'exercice de ses droits souverains. Aux yeux du gouvernement impérial, la conférence n'a pas seulement pour objet de préparer des réformes, mais encore de garantir aux Puissances les droits qu'elles tiennent de la convention de 1880. Cette différence entre les propositions du gouvernement chérifien et les vues du gouvernement impérial a amené le gouvernement de la République à se demander en ce qui concerne les réformes, si le meilleur moyen de les réaliser était de les soumettre à une conférence où l'unanimité des Puissances représentées serait nécessaire à la validité d'une décision quelconque, alors que certaines d'entre elles ont au Maroc des intérêts extrêmement faibles; et d'autre part, si l'on ne porterait pas atteinte aux droits souverains du sultan par les conditions restrictives qu'on mettrait à leur exercice. Ces considérations n'ayant pas pu échapper au gouvernement impérial, son adhésion à la conférence semble bien avoir eu pour principal objet la sauvegarde des droits et des intérêts des Puissances, menacés, selon lui, par la situation exclusive ou privilégiée que la France aurait cherché à obtenir au Maroc.

La note remise le 6 juin, et surtout les observations qui l'ont appuyée confirment cette impression, mais elle semble reposer sur un malentendu.

Ce malentendu s'explique par le fait d'ailleurs non contesté que nos propositions au makhzen sont encore inconnues du gouvernement impérial. Quant à nos intentions dont nous sommes très sûrs, il n'en est pas de même, et nous les avons mises plusieurs fois déjà en pleine lumière; nous sommes prêts néanmoins à les exposer à nouveau dans les termes les plus explicites.

Nos propositions au gouvernement chérifien n'ont ni la portée, ni le caractère qui leur a été assigné. Nous n'avons pas tenté d'obtenir du Sultan la direction des affaires intérieures et extérieures de son empire, ni une main mise sur son système militaire.

Nous n'avons nullement cherché à introduire au Maroc un régime analogue à celui qui n'a été d'ailleurs appliqué dans la régence de Tunis qu'avec le consentement de l'Allemagne. L'assimilation faite entre les deux situations n'est pas exacte; mais, à supposer qu'elle le fût, à supposer même que contrairement à notre sentiment la convention de 1880 visât d'autres points que l'exercice du droit de protection, on ne pourrait pas en tirer la conséquence que les intérêts économiques des Puissances seraient appelés à en souffrir.

En effet, les modifications apportées à certaines parties du statut tunisien ont laissé intacts les traités antérieurement signés par le gouvernement beylical. Au Maroc le gouvernement chérifien a souscrit en 1890 des engagements envers l'Allemagne qui donnent au commerce allemand les garanties les plus complètes; il n'est jamais venu à notre pensée que ces engagements puissent n'être pas respectés.

Nos propositions au gouvernement chérifien respectent donc les principes et sauvegardent les intérêts qui ont éveillé les préoccupations du gouvernement impérial. Ni la souveraineté du sultan, ni l'intégrité de son territoire, ni la situation des Puissances telle qu'elle résulte des traités, ne peuvent être altérées.

La France s'est bornée à demander qu'on voulût bien reconnaître que sa situation de pays limitrophe du Maroc, ayant avec lui une grande étendue de frontières communes rend légitime le souci particulier qu'elle prend du maintien de l'ordre dans l'empire, de la bonne administration du pays et de sa prospérité. Les propositions qu'elle a faites n'ont pas d'autre but, et, si ce but est atteint, toutes les Puissances sont appelées à en tirer avantage; la civilisation générale en profitera. En prenant en main cette cause, la France s'est inspirée des intérêts qu'elle regarde comme solidaires de toutes les Puissances civilisées. Les accords qu'elle a déjà conclus avec certaines d'entre elles sont venus de là.

L'un daté du 8 avril 1904 a été signé avec l'Angleterre, il porte expressément que le gouvernement de la République n'a pas l'intention de changer l'état politique du Maroc, le gouvernement impérial en trouvera ci-joint le texte. Un autre est daté du 6 [sic] octobre dernier; il a été signé avec l'Espagne et a été notifié aussitôt au gouvernement impérial par l'ambassadeur de la République à Berlin. Il vise pour les confirmer formellement les déclarations contenues dans le premier.

S'il n'y a pas eu jusqu'ici une entente semblable avec le gouvernement allemand il résulte des déclarations mêmes de ce dernier que ses principes, loin d'être en opposition avec ceux du gouvernement de la République, sont avec eux en parfaite harmonie. Les deux gouvernements ne peuvent différer que sur la meilleure manière d'en assurer l'application. Le gouvernement impérial croit la trouver dans la conférence; un accord direct serait à nos yeux un procédé plus simple et destiné à aboutir à un résultat plus prompt et plus sûr. Le gouvernement impérial ne saurait méconnaître les inconvénients qu'il y aurait pour lui comme pour nous à se rendre à une conférence sans accord préalable, accord qui ne saurait porter atteinte à ceux qui ont été conclus antérieurement et qui, eux-mêmes, n'en ont porté aucune aux principes et aux intérêts auxquels le gouvernement impérial donne sa sollicitude.

Dans l'état actuel des choses, une réponse définitive à la question qui nous a été posée serait encore de notre part insuffisamment éclairée. Le gouvernement de la République est vivement frappé de cette double considération que la conférence pourrait être dangereuse si elle n'est pas précédée d'une entente, et inutile si elle la suit. Mais il ne l'écarte pas de parti pris. Quelles que soient ses préférences il tient compte, dans un haut intérêt de conciliation de celles qui lui ont été exprimées. Il désire seulement savoir quels sont dans la pensée du gouvernement impérial les points précis qui seraient traités à la conférence et les solutions qu'il proposerait d'y apporter. Si la conférence doit avoir lieu cet échange de vues serait évidemment le plus sûr moyen d'assurer le succès de sa tâche et de lui permettre d'y travailler en sécurité. Ce serait aussi le plus propre à seconder efficacemment [*sic*] les efforts sincères des deux cabinets et à amener l'entente que le gouvernement de la République juge désirable au même degré que le gouvernement impérial.

No. 127.

The Marquess of Lansdowne to Sir E. Goschen.

F.O. Morocco 434.
(No. 60.)

Sir,   *Foreign Office, June 21, 1905.*

The Austro-Hungarian Ambassador asked me to-day whether His Majesty's Government had arrived at any decision as to the action which they would take in reference to the proposal of the German Government that an International Conference should be assembled for the purpose of dealing with the situation which has arisen in Morocco.

I told His Excellency that we had reason to know that communications were still passing between the French and German Governments upon this subject; that the French Government was of opinion that the first step to be taken was a frank exchange of ideas between the two Governments as to the subjects which it was desired to refer to such a Conference; that they disclaimed any design upon the sovereignty of the Sultan or upon the rights of other Powers; that they were convinced that their intentions with regard to Morocco were completely misunderstood; and that there was, in fact, no fundamental difference between the views of the two Governments, that a direct agreement appeared to them the best and promptest mode of arriving at a satisfactory result, and that the discussion which M. Rouvier invited might show that there was no occasion for holding a Conference at all. In these circumstances His Majesty's Government considered that they could not with advantage express any opinion as to the propriety of a Conference, and they must therefore withhold their reply to the proposal of the German Government until they learnt the result of the discussion now proceeding between the French and German Governments.

I am, &c.
LANSDOWNE.

No. 128.

Mr. Lowther to the Marquess of Lansdowne.

F.O. Morocco 434.   *Fez, D. June 23, 1905.*
Tel. (No. 71.)   R. *June 27, 1905.*

Moorish Government is getting somewhat anxious about French and German pourparlers. But German Minister has informed them that there is nothing in them but ordinary exchange of courtesies and that Germany will never retract from position she has taken up.

No. 129.

Mr. Wyldbore Smith to the Marquess of Lansdowne.

F.O. Morocco 434.
Tel. Separate.

Tangier, June 24, 1905.
D. 3·40 P.M.
R. 7 P.M.

My Tel[egram] Separate of 3rd June.(¹)

Danish Government have replied that they accept the Sultan's invitation on condition that all the Great Powers interested will also accept.

I have forwarded despatch to Mr. Lowther at Fez.

(¹) [Reports transmission of invitation to Danish Government.]

No. 130.

Mr. Lowther to the Marquess of Lansdowne.

F.O. Morocco 434.
(No. 162.)
My Lord,

Fez, D. June 26, 1905.
R. *July 10, 1905.*

Count Tattenbach yesterday informed the Sultan that all the Powers had now practically decided to attend the Conference at which His Majesty expressed himself as well pleased.

His Majesty's present idea of the probable action of the Conference is somewhat as follows :—

The Conference after considerable discussion will decide that such and such reforms are to be introduced by His Majesty and that the financial question being the principal one, the Powers will also undertake that all their subjects and all the Moorish subjects under foreign protection shall pay taxes. The Moorish Government is to be protected from the aggression of any one Power by a guarantee on the part of some of the Powers represented at the Conference. What benefit the guaranteeing Powers are to obtain for their liability does not enter into His Majesty's calculation nor is their [*sic*] any stipulation to be made in the event of His Majesty not carrying out the reforms which will be proposed by the Conference.

My informant who told me of these views of the Sultan said His Majesty did not seem very clear as to how the payment of the taxes would be enforced, as none of the tribes would, under present circumstances, pay; but seemed to think that His Majesty contemplated the building up of a military force under the supervision of different Powers, His Majesty being as unwilling to be controlled in this one branch by one Power as much as he is in all matters of Reform.

I have, &c.
GERARD LOWTHER.

No. 131.

Mr. Lowther to the Marquess of Lansdowne.

F.O. Morocco 434.
(No. 166.)
My Lord,

Fez, D. June 28, 1905.
R. *July 10, 1905.*

I asked the German Minister today whether he had any news as to the negotiations, which were reported to be proceeding between Paris and Berlin, but His Excellency said he was not kept informed of these negotiations. For his part, he could not believe that they would have any result.

If an arrangement was made between France and Germany as to a limitation of the discussions in the proposed conference, every other Power might likewise claim to insist upon a similar limitation and he felt very strongly that such arrangements could not be made behind the back of the Sultan.

After explaining to me again the position of Germany in the matter in much the same terms as he had used in my conversation with him at Tangier as reported in my despatch No. 78 of April twenty eighth(1) but in more forcible and uncompromising language, he gave me clearly to understand that, what he desired the Conference should do, would be to bring about an amendment of the Anglo-French Convention of April 8th, 1904.

His Excellency said that Germany had no intention of allowing France to assume a Protectorate over this country in any shape or form.

The Declaration of the Government of France contained in Article II to the effect that "it had no intention of altering the political status of the country" might have held good on the 8th of April 1904, but had no binding effect on the following day.

Germany was being excluded from the different parts of the world by preferential tariffs and she desired a field for her activity here.

Turning to the matter of reform, His Excellency said that he was convinced that the Sultan earnestly desired them. The Sultan would not of course under the altered condition of our relations with His Majesty speak to me as openly as he did to him, but he had acquired the conviction that His Majesty was most anxious to introduce these reforms and was only prevented from doing so by the fact that the number of foreign protected subjects was so great that His Majesty could not possibly exact taxation from the few who were not under some foreign Protection. The system of protection, Count Tattenbach said, had been fearfully abused. The Germans themselves had of course held strictly to the Convention of 1880 and had consequently lost much influence in the country, but by the system Foreign Governments had directly obstructed all reforms.

I told Count Tattenbach that I was convinced that no Power desired to encourage this irregular protection and would be quite prepared to see all taxed alike, but they must have some guarantee that these taxes were applied to the purposes for which they were said to be levied, and as long as the Sultan and his Government had the complete and unfettered control of the money it would inevitably be squandered. That reforms in this country could ever come from within was a proposition that I regarded with much misgiving. If he had, as he said, a strong conviction that this could be done, I was equally convinced to the contrary. It was self-evident that the remnant of the Army was completely out of control and the people having now got accustomed to the non-payment of taxes, payment would eventually have to be exacted by force—but for this a previous reorganisation of the Army would be required and this was one of the Reforms to which the Sultan had shown the greatest opposition.

Various other points were discussed between us and it was evident that Count Tattenbach's idea was that the proposals to be put forward at the Conference would include distinct understandings regarding the integrity of the Sultan and his kingdom and an international control of all the administration of the country.

I have, &c.

GERARD LOWTHER.

MINUTE BY KING EDWARD.

In plain English—Germany ousts France fr[om] Morocco and puts herself in her place!

E.R.(2)

(1) [The conversation recorded in this despatch dealt with the grievance of Germany against France at the conclusion of the Anglo-French Convention without communication to her, and with German interests in Morocco.]

(2) [*v.* also Sir Sidney Lee: *King Edward VII* (1927), Vol. II, p. 344.]

No. 132.

(a.)

The Marquess of Lansdowne to Mr. Whitehead.

F.O. Morocco 434.
(No. 150.)
Sir,   *Foreign Office, June 28, 1905.*

The German Ambassador came to see me to-day, and brought with him a copy of the reply given by the German Government on the 24th instant to M. Rouvier's note upon the subject of Morocco. His Excellency asked me whether I had yet seen the document in question, and I told him that the French Ambassador had given me an outline of its contents. The despatch had, His Excellency told me, been communicated to all the Powers Signatories of the Treaty of Madrid of 1880. I asked His Excellency what was his impression as to the present situation. He told me, as his personal opinion, that he regarded it as decidedly more hopeful, although Germany still adhered to her view as to the necessity of a Conference. The tone on each side was however most conciliatory. He was particularly anxious that I should know that at no moment had the German Government desired to fasten a quarrel upon France. He said this because he was aware that an impression to the contrary existed in this country. I said that the language attributed to some of the German representatives had certainly suggested the idea that it was desired to fasten a quarrel upon France. I had noticed with pleasure the considerate tone of the French note, and I was glad to learn from His Excellency that the language of the German Government was not less conciliatory.[1]

I am, &c.

LANSDOWNE.

[1] [For Count Metternich's report, see *G.P.* XX, II, pp. 635–637.]

(b.)

Memorandum communicated by Count Metternich.

(Translation.)

In a Memorandum communicated to the Imperial Government on June 23rd, 1905[1] the Government of the French Republic express the view that the Conference of the Signatory Powers to the Convention of Madrid suggested by His Shereefian Majesty is neither necessary nor advisable in order to carry out the reforms which they have proposed to the Government of Morocco.

In this Memorandum the French Government declare that their object in making these proposals is neither to obtain control of internal and foreign affairs and of the army in Morocco, nor to prejudice the independence of the Sultan and the integrity of his dominions or the treaty rights of other powers. The Imperial Government note these declarations with the more satisfaction that the Government of Morocco view the French proposals in a different light. The Imperial Government further are in complete agreement with the French Government in holding that the object of the proposed reforms must be to secure good Government, the maintenance of order, and the economic prosperity of the country. The other Powers, whose subjects reside in Morocco or maintain commercial relations with that country are equally interested with France in promoting these aims. It would therefore seem natural that the ways and means of attaining this object should be settled by mutual deliberation. Should the French Government, however, as they propose, undertake the accomplishment of this task alone, there is reason to fear that they will be driven more and more by the force of circumstances to take over the administration of the country and that they

[1] [*v. supra* pp. 98–100, *Encl.* in No. 126.]

will thereby gradually acquire a position in Morocco which, according to their own declarations, it is not their purpose to obtain.

The reforms proposed by the French Government with regard to the army, the administration of the interior and the financial system, as communicated to the Imperial Government by the Government of Morocco, would consitute a serious danger to the independence of Morocco. Moreover they do not appear to coincide with the statements contained in the Memorandum that the economic advantages of such reforms would benefit all the Powers to an equal extent; they would rather have the effect of according preferential treatment to the Power entrusted with carrying out the reforms, especially with regard to the granting of concessions. This is also evident from the proposals respecting commercial and financial affairs which, according to a communication from the Government of Morocco, have been put forward by the French Government.

It is not in accordance with the provisions of the Convention of Madrid that one of the Signatory Powers should acquire such a special position. Article 17 of the Convention, under which the right of each Signatory Power to the most favoured nation treatment is guaranteed, is specifically opposed thereto, as under this article preferential treatment is not to be accorded to any Power. The Imperial Government must in this respect maintain their view that the most-favoured-nation treatment is not, as the French Government would seem to assume, exclusively limited to the exercise of the right of protection or to economic interests, but that it refers to all the claims of the Signatory Powers to influence in Morocco. This is clear not only from the text of the Article, which is couched in general terms, but from the circumstances and conditions which led both to the Convention of Madrid and the adoption of the Article referred to.

The consent of the other Powers is therefore necessary before reforms can be carried out in Morocco, at any rate in so far as it may seem advisable to grant special privileges to a single Signatory Power for the purpose. The easiest way of obtaining this consent would be to summon a Conference which, quite apart from the legal considerations involved, would afford a suitable method of arriving at a compromise between the existing political and commercial interests of the Signatory Powers.

The Conference would moreover materially facilitate the task of obtaining the consent of the Sultan to the reforms, which is the first condition for their execution, since the proposals would then have received the sanction of all the Powers concerned. The Memorandum states that France, in consequence of the proximity of Algeria and the extent of the common frontier, is specially called upon to carry out the reforms, and it must be admitted at once that France has a very legitimate interest in securing the maintenance of order in the frontier districts. But on the other hand it cannot be claimed that the other Powers should therefore be excluded from participating in the work of the reforms.

While the reforms agreed upon at a Conference would absolutely guarantee the independence of the Sultan, such a Conference would also correspond with the purposes which inspired the Sultan to issue invitations thereto. The Imperial Government has accepted the invitation for this reason and the character thereof has not been altered by the fact that they reserve to themselves the duty of safeguarding their treaty rights. They do not, as stated in the French Memorandum, regard the reconfirmation of the rights of the Signatory Powers under the Convention of Madrid as the object or even as a principal object of the Conference; but they consider that if these treaty rights are to be limited in order that reforms may be carried out, such limitation can only take place with the unanimous consent of the Powers. In correspondence with this view the Sultan has given it to be understood that his consent to the execution of reforms depends on the unanimous decision of the Signatory Powers.

Before the French Government adopt a decisive attitude in connection with the Morocco Conference, they desire to learn the views of the Imperial Government with regard to the solution of the various separate questions pending in Morocco. To comply with this desire the Imperial Government would be obliged to draw up a complete programme for the Conference and to a certain extent to anticipate its decisions. They regret that they are not in a position to do this both on grounds of form and for practical reasons.

The invitation to the Conference proceeded from the Sultan, who specified as the object thereof the discussion of reforms corresponding with the prevailing conditions in Morocco and the provision of the necessary means for carrying them into effect. It will therefore fall to the Sultan in the first place to communicate details of the programme of the Conference to the Signatory Powers.

It follows accordingly that until it has been definitely decided to summon a Conference it would be useless to enter upon an exchange of views as desired by France; for any understanding arrived at in this way would possess importance only in so far as it received the consent of all the other Signatory Powers, a consent which in the present state of affairs could only be secured at the Conference.

Finally the Imperial Government cannot at this moment make separate proposals with regard to the programme of the Conference, since the questions involved must first be submitted to a searching examination; a further delay in deciding, however, could in itself endanger the summoning of a Conference and therefore the work of reform. The Imperial Government express the hope that the Government of the French Republic will withdraw their objections to a Conference in view of the permanent advantages which the carrying out of reforms would ensure both to Morocco and to the peace of the world.

Berlin, June 24, 1905.

No. 133.

The Marquess of Lansdowne to Mr. Lister.

F.O. France 3704.
(No. 424.)
Sir,   *Foreign Office, June* 28, 1905.

I had another long conversation to-day with the French Ambassador as to the situation in Morocco.

His Excellency repeated to me again that when M. Bihourd handed the French note to Prince Bülow, the latter had observed that "c'était pour lui une grande déception," having regard to the assurances which the German Ambassador had been authorised to give to M. Rouvier. The French Government, Prince Bülow said, seemed determined to disregard the susceptibilities of the Sultan. The German Government, on the other hand, desired to maintain his independence and the integrity of his possessions, although they were fully disposed to reserve the future of the country for France (" à réserver l'avenir pour la France "). M. Bihourd had observed that in his opinion there were several points upon which the two Governments were in agreement, but Prince Bülow took no notice of this observation, merely observing that he thought the situation critical and that the two Governments should be careful not to "linger upon a path which was surrounded by abysses and precipices."

His Excellency went on to say that as Prince Bülow had thus made an appeal to the assurances which Prince Radolin was supposed to have given, it was desirable that I should know what these assurances amounted to. Prince Radolin had had a conversation, which he was careful to describe as a private one, with M. Rouvier, and had given him informally a memorandum containing statements to the following effect :—The German Government expected the French Government to signify its formal acceptance of the Conference. Even if the British Government refused to participate, the Conference might take place, because Great Britain had, so far as Morocco was concerned, abdicated in favour of France. France would certainly be a gainer, because her claims in Morocco would thus receive an European sanction.

Should the Conference not take place, Germany would uphold her opinion as to the independence of the Sultan, although she recognised the right of France to police the regions adjoining her Algerian possessions. Elsewhere however, and notably on the seaboard of the Atlantic, the army and the police of Morocco should be dealt with by different Powers, and in regard to finance there should be no monopoly for the French Bank.

M. Rouvier had, H[is] E[xcellency] said, told Prince Radolin that he had no desire to anticipate the decision at which the Conference might arrive, but he asked that there should be an exchange of views between the two Governments, so that the Conference might be in a position to bring about some useful results. In his view the correspondence which had already taken place furnished the materials for an understanding of the kind which he desired : materials which could be easily put into proper shape for this purpose. As for the Sultan of Morocco, no encroachment was intended on his rights, nor was it desired to prevent him from proposing a programme of reforms should he desire to do so. M. Rouvier did not reject the idea of a Conference, but he pointed out that it was for the German Government to render a Conference possible, and to enable it to take place under conditions which France could accept, and which would guarantee that it would not be held in vain. The French Government was quite prepared, if necessary, to associate the Sultan with the French and German Governments in the preparation of a programme for the Conference.

Prince Radolin thereupon replied that he was ready to ask the German Government for authority to give an official character to his previous declarations, which might be summarised as follows :—

(1.) The sovereignty of the Sultan was to be maintained ;
(2.) The integrity of his possessions was to remain unimpaired ;
(3.) The future of the country was to be reserved for France, and nothing was to be done to the detriment of her position in reference to Morocco (qui pourrait empirer la situation de la France au Maroc) ;
(4.) The régime which might be established as the result of such an international arrangement was to have a temporary character ;
(5.) The German Government would abandon their claim to deal with the question of reforms in the Atlantic regions of Morocco.

Prince Radolin had said that he would suggest these bases to the German Government, and that if they were approved they would, as soon as France had accepted a Conference in principle, be formally adopted by the German Government as the bases upon which the Conference would deliberate.

M. Rouvier had proceeded to suggest to Prince Radolin that, if an agreement were come to on these terms, the representatives of France, Germany and Great Britain should retire simultaneously from Fez. Prince Radolin had raised no objection to this.

There had also, M. Cambon told me, been an interview between M. Bihourd and Baron Richthofen, when the latter expressed his opinion that the conciliatory disposition which had been evinced on each side would probably have the result of bringing about an agreement. Baron Richthofen had said the same thing to the Italian Ambassador.

His Excellency ended by telling me that, in his opinion, the prospect was now much more hopeful, partly because the German Emperor had no doubt found out that his peremptory attitude had created a bad impression throughout the world, and partly because French opinion, which had for a time been very irresolute, was now adopting a more decided tone.

I told His Excellency, in reference to our last conversation that I had ascertained from Lord Cromer that the Grand Mufti of Cairo was in bad health, and was not at all likely to visit Morocco for the purpose of making mischief there. His Excellency thought that it might nevertheless be desirable if he could be induced to postpone his visit. I also said that I had mentioned to my colleagues the information which

His Excellency had given to me with regard to the possibility of a concession being given to a German company for the construction of a port on the Moorish seaboard near the Algerian frontier. In our view much would depend upon the nature of the concession, which might be harmless if it merely involved the construction of a port for the Sultan's convenience by a firm of German contractors. On the other hand, anything like the establishment of a strategic base in these waters by another Power would, in our opinion, be a serious matter. We hoped that any further information which the French Government could obtain would be communicated to us.

His Excellency's demeanour during our conversation struck me as much more hopeful than it had been on previous occasions.

I am, &c.
LANSDOWNE.

No. 134.

Mr. Lister to the Marquess of Lansdowne.

F.O. Morocco 434.
(No. 238.) Very Confidential.   *Paris*, D. *June* 28, 1905.
My Lord,   R. *July* 1, 1905.

I called upon Monsieur Rouvier this afternoon on the occasion of his weekly reception at the Quai d'Orsay and asked him whether he had anything which he wished me to communicate to Your Lordship.

He said that he had nothing special to say; that he reported daily to Monsieur Cambon the progress of the negotiations, and that His Excellency kept Your Lordship fully informed of all that was going on in Paris.

I alluded to the conversation which Monsieur Cambon had with Your Lordship on the 27th instant as reported in your despatch No. 419 of that date,(¹) and Monsieur Rouvier told me that he had modified his opinion with regard to the departure of the French and English representatives from Fez. If a conference were to take place it would be better that they should all three leave together. I had already gathered from a conversation which I had had earlier in the afternoon with the Director [*sic*] Politique that Monsieur Rouvier was inclined to accept a conference, although Monsieur Louis had said that it could only be accepted on condition that nothing " inconnu " (by which I understood him to mean nothing that had not been agreed upon beforehand) should be submitted to it for discussion. I asked Monsieur Rouvier whether he intended to insist upon this condition, but he was not nearly so decided in his opinion as Monsieur Louis. He merely shrugged his shoulders and said that it was impossible to be certain beforehand that nothing " inconnu " would turn up. He considered that under the conditions a conference was perhaps the best way of arriving at a satisfactory solution. The Emperor had made it a point of personal honour : France would go into it with the support of England, Spain, and possibly Italy, whereas Germany would be alone ; Germany was prepared to admit the preponderance of French interests on the Algerian frontier. It was absolutely necessary to arrive at some solution as the present situation was excessively dangerous. So long as the Conference was not accepted, Germany considered that she was entitled to a free hand in Morocco, and she was very very [*sic*] active. She would ask for all sorts of concessions, ports, cables, etc., and were the Sultan to accede to such demands the situation both for France and England would become far more critical. Monsieur Rouvier hinted that once the present diffi- culties had been more or less tided over at the Conference, it would be possible to see that Germany did not get too much in Morocco. There appear to me to be indications that the feeling is growing in France that it is necessary to treat the Morocco question in as

---

(¹) [Not printed. The conversation related to the withdrawal of the British and French representatives from Fez, the expected concession to a German company for the construction of a harbour to the east of the mouth of the Muluya River, and the possibility of a visit by the " Grand Mufti " of Cairo to Morocco. M. Cambon referred also in confidence to the presentation of the French note to Prince Bülow.]

conciliatory a spirit as possible, but that when further demands are made by Germany they should be met by a firm refusal. This opinion can be traced in the writings and utterances of Messieurs Jaurès and Clémenceau and I have heard them [*sic*] expressed by men of very different political opinions. The feeling of resentment against Germany on account of her present action is very strong and the spirit of the "revanche" is reawakening; the French have pulled themselves together wonderfully after their first panic and they now seem prepared to face calmly the contingency of war in the future should the pretensions of Germany continue.

There is I think no doubt that Monsieur Rouvier could at present command a very large majority in the Chamber on any question of Foreign policy, and his efforts to preserve peace by conciliation so far as conciliation can go without loss of dignity, will only enhance his position in the eyes of his countrymen, and assure him their unanimous support in the event of such a policy being rendered impossible.

I mentioned to Monsieur Rouvier that I had heard from private sources that the Emperor had been in a very excited and irritable state of late, and he answered that he feared that the French note could not have improved his temper, although he personally considered that it had been most moderate and courteous. His Majesty had expected a complete climb-down to follow upon the change of direction of the Ministry for Foreign Affairs, but as His Excellency said, there was no reason because he parted with Monsieur Delcassé that he should throw himself "dans les bras de l'Empereur et sur son cou."

There appears little doubt that His Imperial Majesty has been misinformed as to the state of feeling in France. He believed that the French socialists would follow the lead of Monsieur Hervé, whereas MM. Jaurès and Clémenceau, their two most distinguished chiefs, have gone in a diametrically opposite direction. Prince Radolin and Monsieur de Miquel have collected and reported all the stories with regard to the French Army, which they have picked up in the salons and clubs of the Faubourg St Germain, and which are in most cases grossly exaggerated, and Monsieur Delcassé's resignation has not brought about the complete *volte-face* in French foreign policy which the Emperor had been led to expect.

> I have, &c.
> REGINALD LISTER.

No. 135.

Mr. Whitehead to the Marquess of Lansdowne.

F.O. Germany (Prussia) 1617.
(No. 174.) Confidential.   *Berlin, D. June* 28, 1905.
My Lord,   R. *July* 3, 1905.

I had a short conversation with Monsieur Bihourd, the French Ambassador, yesterday, and asked His Excellency whether he could give me some idea of the nature of his interviews with the Imperial Chancellor on the 23rd and 25th instant.

His Excellency replied that both the French Note and the German answer were in very general terms, and that the latter maintained all the German arguments in favour of a Conference. As regards the Chancellor's remarks when handing him the German reply, His Excellency said that Prince Bülow was a fluent speaker but that when one came to recall and note down what he had said very little came out of it. One point however was noticeable, namely that during the whole of the two interviews the Imperial Chancellor had never once mentioned the name of Great Britain ("n'a pas une seule fois prononcé le nom de l'Angleterre").

With regard to the German contention that Article 17 of the Madrid Convention of 1880 assured most favoured nation treatment to the Signatory Powers in all respects and not only in regard to protected persons, Monsieur Bihourd stated that it had occurred to him that this contention could be met by the question why it was considered necessary, in that case, to introduce the most favoured nation clause specially in Article I of the Commercial Treaty between Germany and Morocco of the 1st June, 1890 (State Papers, Vol. 82, p. 968). I did not gather that His Excellency had used this argument in his conversation with Prince Bülow.

I have, &c.
J. B. WHITEHEAD.

No. 136.

Sir A. Nicolson to the Marquess of Lansdowne.

F.O. Spain 2209.
(No. 126.) Confidential.   *Madrid,* D. *June* 29, 1905.
My Lord,   R. *July* 10, 1905.

I have had opportunities of some conversations with Señor Montero Rios and Señor Sanchez Roman, respectively President of the Council and Minister of State, in regard to the future line of policy of the new Spanish Government, and they both assured me that the Government would loyally observe the engagements which preceding Governments had undertaken, and that their desire was to live on good and friendly terms with all Powers. They both stated, in practically identical terms, that while scrupulously observing the above mentioned engagements, Spain, as they expressed it, had not " abnegated her personality," and was free to take any course, in matters outside the Franco-Spanish Agreement, as might be dictated by her interests. Señor Sanchez Roman expanded the above somewhat quaint phrase, by intimating that Spain did not desire to act as a satellite of France in all matters.

Both Señor Montero Rios and Señor Sanchez Roman reiterated more than once that the chief aim of their foreign policy was to be on specially intimate terms with Great Britain, and to strengthen as far as possible the good understanding at present existing. The latter gentleman said that he wished the relations could become "fraternal" and perfectly frank and loyal : but he begged that this desire which was shared to the full by his Sovereign and the Prime Minister should be considered as communicated confidentially.

I reciprocated the friendly feelings they evinced : and enquired whether they had been placed in possession of the substance of an informal conversation which Your Lordship had held with Monsieur de Villaurrutia in London.([1]) Neither of them had cognizance of it, and I therefore sketched in broad outline the tenour of Your Lordship's remarks. I told both the President of the Council and the Minister of State that I made the communication in strict confidence, and with no desire that they should give me an immediate reply. On the contrary I wished merely to acquaint them with the suggestion which had occurred to Your Lordship, and which doubtless they would desire to take into consideration and reflect upon. It was, I remarked, a proposal which might be seriously treated later, and which was I submitted of mutual advantage to both parties. I asked for no expression of opinion at present.

It seemed to me advisable to prepare the ground at this early date, as it will be a proof of the sincerity of our friendly disposition towards Spain and also be evidence of the importance we attach to Spain maintaining intact the possessions she holds outside of the Peninsula. I venture to think that this is a point which should not be neglected in present circumstances. Both Ministers appeared to receive the suggestion in a friendly spirit, but agreed that it was a question which required consideration, and which could be discussed when a solution had been found to more pressing questions.

([1]) [This interview was described in a despatch to Sir A. Nicolson No. 64, Confidential, of June 8, 1905. It related to the possibility of an Anglo-Spanish understanding with reference to Spanish interests in the Mediterranean and elsewhere. It will be published in a chapter upon Mediterranean Agreements in a later volume.]

Señor Sanchez Roman asked whether I did not consider that the proposed Conference on Morocco, if it were held, would not be a mere form. I told His Excellency that, in my personal opinion, little practical result so far as regards an improvement in the condition of Morocco was likely to ensue from an International Assembly. The Sultan was penniless and powerless: and the tribes exceedingly turbulent and independent of authority. An International Assembly could perhaps formulate several admirable proposals for re-establishing order and introducing security for life and property, but I did not quite see in what manner or by what means these proposals were to be carried into execution. It would however be advisable to await the result of the negotiations between France and Germany.

I have, &c.
A. NICOLSON.

No. 137.

The Marquess of Lansdowne to Sir F. Bertie.

F.O. Morocco 435.
(No. 436.) Confidential.
Sir,   *Foreign Office, July 1, 1905.*
The French Ambassador called on me this morning. He told me in strict confidence that there had been a further conversation between M. Rouvier and Prince Radolin, and that the result had been to strengthen the impression that an understanding might be arrived at under which, upon certain pre-arranged bases, a Conference might take place and perhaps have useful results.

M. Rouvier had suggested to His Excellency the following preliminary description, partly derived from his conversations with Prince Radolin, of the bases in question.

Germany would declare that it was not her object in any way to prejudice the ulterior rights reserved for France in Morocco ("L'allemagne ne poursuit aucun but compromettant l'avenir reservé à la France au Maroc") or to act contrary to French interests. The following principles would be laid down :—

1. Maintenance of the sovereignty and independence of the Sultan ;
2. Preservation of the integrity of his possessions ;
3. Maintenance of commercial liberty ;
4. Admission of the necessity of military and financial reforms, the introduction of which would be for the time being regulated and sanctioned by means of an international arrangement of strictly limited duration ;
5. Recognition of the special position belonging to France in Morocco in consequence of the extent of the French frontier and the special relations resulting from the vicinity of the two countries ;
6. The Sultan to be admitted to the councils of France and Germany for the purpose of determining the programme of the Conference.

M. Rouvier thought that if an agreement upon these lines could be arrived at the Missions might be at once recalled from Fez.

H[is] E[xcellency] told me that the description which he had given to me must only be taken as a sketch, and that the actual terms of the agreement would have to be most carefully considered. He would himself like to introduce some mention of the Agreement between Great Britain and France as to Morocco. I told His Excellency that I did not see on the face of the terms which he had suggested anything which I could adversely criticise. In the event of its becoming necessary to tax foreigners for the purpose of carrying out reforms, I did not see how it was possible to avoid some form of discussion with the other Powers, particularly as that view had been strongly held by France two or three years ago. With regard to His Excellency's proposed reference to the Anglo-French Declaration, I thought it might be usefully cited for the purpose of showing that the policy of both France and Great Britain had been in favour of maintaining the independence and integrity of Morocco and preserving commercial equality.

I am, &c.
LANSDOWNE.

No. 138.

Sir A. Nicolson to the Marquess of Lansdowne.

F.O. Spain 2210.
(No. 127.) Confidential.
My Lord,

Madrid, D. *July* 1, 1905.
R. *July* 10, 1905.

Monsieur Cambon, the French Ambassador, returned here yesterday from Paris, and informed me last night that he had had an interview with the new Minister of State, Señor Sanchez Roman, during which the conversation naturally turned to Morocco and to the attitude of Spain in connection with that question.

Monsieur Cambon told me that he had considerable difficulty in comprehending all His Excellency said, owing to the somewhat superficial acquaintance which the latter has with the French language : but that he gathered generally that the Spanish Government would adhere to the engagements to which they were bound under the Franco-Spanish Agreement. Monsieur Cambon stated to me that although the language of Señor Sanchez Roman was satisfactory, so far as it went, on this point, he was under the impression that His Excellency was disinclined to go beyond the strict letter of the Agreement, and that the cordiality of fulfilling the engagements and in acting frankly in accord was not so marked as was the case with His Excellency's immediate predecessor. Señor Sanchez Roman had employed to Monsieur Cambon the same phrase which he had used in his conversation with me to the effect that Spain would not "abnegate her personality," and he understood this to mean that the new Government considered that they had perfect liberty of action in all matters lying outside the strict limits of the Franco-Spanish Agreement. Señor Sanchez Roman, Monsieur Cambon added, had casually mentioned that he had had daily interviews with the German Ambassador, and on being asked to communicate generally the subjects which had been discussed at these interviews, His Excellency had replied that he considered it would be advisable not to mention to one Representative what passed between him and another Representative.

Monsieur Cambon, I could see, was not satisfied with the result of his first interview, and was a little perplexed by the caution and reserve observed by the Minister of State.

I told Monsieur Cambon that the disinclination on the part of Señor Sanchez Roman to be expansive as to what passed between him and the German Ambassador was in a sense a good sign as it showed he was anxious to be discreet and reserved. I added that I had received assurances both from Señor Montero Rios and from the Minister of State that they would loyally act in concert with us, and as they had only recently taken office at a delicate juncture I thought we should, in any case for the present, remain satisfied with these assurances.

As I had been requested by both the above gentlemen not to mention their desire to be on specially intimate terms with Great Britain I said nothing in regard to that point. As to what was passing between the German Ambassador and the Spanish Government I said I had no information, and did not propose to enquire. I think it would be undesirable to exhibit the least anxiety on the subject as I have no reason to fear that either King Alfonso or his Government will be led into any course which may be embarrassing or which may seriously affect the relations of Spain with France or Great Britain. At the same time I told Monsieur Cambon that I understood that the general opinion in Madrid was that Germany had recently scored a diplomatic success, and I doubted not that the German Ambassador would not be disposed to endeavour to modify that opinion.

I would venture to remark that I think that the general feeling among political circles and the Press in Spain might at this moment be summarized as follows :—that there is a disinclination to blindly follow France in questions of an international character, and that Spain should exercise independence in her treatment of foreign affairs; that though the Franco-Spanish Agreement in regard to Morocco is not universally approved, it is considered obligatory to faithfully observe its provisions : and that there is a strong and general desire to remain on the best possible and most intimate terms with Great Britain.

I have, &c.
A. NICOLSON.

No. 139.

The Marquess of Lansdowne to Mr. Lister.

F.O. Morocco 435.
(No. 437.)
Sir, *Foreign Office, July 3, 1905.*

The French Ambassador told me today that M. Rouvier had had another interview with Prince Radolin, and had handed to him a memorandum embodying the bases which His Excellency had described to me on the last occasion when he had spoken to me about Morocco. In conformity with His Excellency's suggestion, words had been added to the effect that amongst the French interests to be recognized by Germany were those arising out of the arrangements into which France had entered with us as to the future of Morocco. The wording of the fourth paragraph had also been amended so as to make it clear that police as well as military reforms were contemplated, and it had also been asserted distinctly that, owing to the special position of France with regard to Morocco, she was concerned in the maintenance of order, not only in those regions which adjoined her possessions, but throughout the whole of the Shereefian territory. Prince Radolin had received the communication of these proposals without any observations.

I am, &c.
LANSDOWNE.

No. 140.

Foreign Office to Manchester Chamber of Commerce.

Sir, *Foreign Office, July 3, 1905.*

I am directed by the Marquess of Lansdowne to acknowledge the receipt of your letter of the 26th ultimo on the subject of the Anglo-French Convention of the 8th April, 1904, and to state that the Board of Directors of the Manchester Chamber of Commerce appear to be under a misapprehension in supposing that an opportunity is likely to be afforded for revising that Agreement. The Declaration in question has been signed by the two Governments, and has already been put into execution, and cannot now be altered.

I am, &c.
E. GORST.

No. 141.

Mr. Lowther to the Marquess of Lansdowne.

F.O. Morocco 422.
(No. 170.) Confidential. *Fez,* D. *July* 3, 1905.
My Lord, R. *July* 12, 1905.

I had some conversation yesterday with my French Colleague as to the possibility of the missions being withdrawn from Fez but he said that in the absence of all instructions he preferred to reserve his opinion.

When the French programme for reforms was first refused by the Moorish Government and the invitation issued to the Conference he had privately informed Monsieur Delcassé that he thought the usefulness of his Mission had ceased for his word no longer carried any weight with the Makhzen.

Then came the fall of Monsieur Delcassé and the whole question entered upon a new stage. He had received a private intimation that the instructions of his Government were on the way, but as they were coming from Paris by a special messenger, Major Gambetta, he could not hope to have them in his hands until the 9th or 10th of this month.

To effect a dignified withdrawal His Excellency was of opinion that three conditions were essential :—

(1.) That the Conference should be abandoned.
(2.) That some arrangement should be come to with Germany.
(3.) That he should be authorized to speak with considerable authority to the Makhzen, for instance that he should place in their hands the complete programme of reform with a very earnest request that they should give it careful attention—"réfléchir sérieusement" was the expression His Excellency used.

His Excellency hoped that the instructions he might receive would sufficiently fulfil these conditions to enable him to make some arrangement for leaving, but they might require some modification or addition.

At the present moment he did not see that any steps could be taken towards withdrawing his Mission.

We agreed that as long as the French and English Missions were here Count Tattenbach would not budge and we also were of opinion that he would probably leave if we both left, though that must depend to a great extent on the effect produced on the Moorish mind by the actual state of the question at that moment.

At present the Makhzen seems to be in rather a despondent and suspicious mood, and not to like the negotiations which are proceeding between Paris and Berlin.

I have, &c.
GERARD LOWTHER.

No. 142.

Mr. Whitehead to the Marquess of Lansdowne.

Berlin, July 4, 1905.
F.O. Germany (Prussia) 1618. D. 7·52 P.M.
Tel. (No. 15.) R. 9·45 P.M.

Morocco. Baron Richthofen told me this evening that he hoped the negotiations between France and Germany would be satisfactorily terminated this week, as nearly all the questions at issue had already been settled.

No. 143.

The Marquess of Lansdowne to Mr. Lister.

F.O. Morocco 435.
(No. 447.)
Sir,   *Foreign Office, July 6, 1905.*

I asked the French Ambassador today whether, as there seemed to be a strong probability of a Conference with regard to the affairs of Morocco, he did not think it might be as well to consider what Powers should be allowed to take part in such a Conference. The German proposal was, I understood, that all the Powers who had signed the Convention of 1880 should take part in it. The original proposal of the Sultan of Morocco, which the Germans professed to support, was, on the other hand, that the matter at issue should be referred to the representatives of the Powers at Tangier. My impression was that Russia had not taken part in the Madrid Convention, but gave her adhesion to it subsequently. I thought we should have to consider carefully how the Conference should be composed : a numerous body of representatives would be for many reasons most inconvenient. On the other hand we ought not to exclude those who were likely to take our view. His Excellency quite agreed, and expressed a decided opinion that Russia and the United States should take part. He thought the Conference should take place at Tangier, and should be given, so far as possible, a local character.

I am, &c.
LANSDOWNE.

No. 144.

Sir A. Nicolson to the Marquess of Lansdowne.

                                                      Madrid, July 7, 1905.
F.O. Morocco 435.   D. 1·40 P.M.
Tel. (No. 50.)   R. 7·35 P.M.

Minister for Foreign Affairs begged me confidentially to ascertain details of the subjects which will be submitted for discussion at the Conference, as Spanish Government are anxious to come to an early understanding with His Majesty's Government in the matter.

I told him that presumably full communications would be made from Paris as soon as discussions with Berlin were terminated, and that I doubted if Conference would meet before the autumn ; but he asked me to communicate with you.

I can see that Spanish Government are nervous lest no opportunity be accorded to them of expressing their views till matters are practically decided between France and Germany, and Great Britain ; and it might be well if I could convey from your Lordship some reassuring message.

He asked me to mention to none of my colleagues that he had spoken on the subject.

No. 145.

The Marquess of Lansdowne to Sir A. Nicolson.

F.O. Morocco 435.
Tel. (No. 49.)   *Foreign Office, July 8, 1905.*

Your tel[egram] No. 50 (of July 7). We shall be careful to avoid committing ourselves without previously consulting Spanish Gov[ernmen]t. Up to the present no list of subjects has been put forward either by France or Germany, although these two

Powers have discussed certain reservations necessitated by the position of the former as the immediate neighbour of Morocco.

Germany you will remember has supported proposal originally made by Sultan, viz : that conference should discuss reforms of local administration and mode of providing for their cost.

No. 146.

Mr. Lister to the Marquess of Lansdowne.

Paris, July 9, 1905.

F.O. France 3708.
Tel. (No. 49.) *En clair.*

D. 9·12 A.M.
R. 1 P.M.

Following communiqué was made to press late last night :—

"Le Prince de Radolin a été reçu aujourd'hui à six heures par M. Rouvier. Le Président du Conseil et l'Ambassadeur d'Allemagne se sont entendus définitivement sur la rédaction des communications à échanger entre les deux Gouvernements. Les communications seront portées probablement à la connaissance du Parlement dès lundi. Elles sanctionnent un accord de vues sur les questions marocaines qui, sauvegardant les intérêts de la France, a amené son adhésion à la Conférence."

No. 147.

Papers communicated by the French Ambassador, July 11, 1905.[1]

F.O. Morocco 435. ———

(a.)

M. Rouvier, Président du Conseil, Ministre des Affaires Étrangères, à son Altesse Sérénissime le Prince Radolin, Ambassadeur d'Allemagne à Paris.

Paris, le 8 Juillet, 1905.

Le Gouvernement de la République s'est convaincu par les conversations qui ont eu lieu entre les représentants des deux pays tant à Paris qu'à Berlin, que le Gouvernement Impérial ne poursuivrait, à la Conférence proposée par le Sultan du Maroc, aucun but qui compromît les légitimes intérêts de la France dans ce pays, ou qui fût contraire aux droits de la France résultant de ses traités ou arrangements et en harmonie avec les principes suivants :—

Souveraineté et indépendance du Sultan ;
Intégrité de son Empire ;
Liberté économique, sans aucune inégalité ;
Utilité de réformes de police et de réformes financières dont l'introduction serait réglée, pour une courte durée, par voie d'accord international ;
Reconnaissance de la situation faite à la France au Maroc par la contiguïté, sur une vaste étendue, de l'Algérie et de l'Empire Chérifien, et par les relations particulières qui en résultent entre les deux pays limitrophes, ainsi que par l'intérêt spécial qui s'ensuit pour la France à ce que l'ordre règne dans l'Empire Chérifien.

En conséquence, le Gouvernement de la République laisse tomber ses objections premières contre la Conférence et accepte de s'y rendre.

[1] [Printed *Documents Diplomatiques, Affaires du Maroc, 1901–5*, (Paris 1905), pp. 251–2.]

(b.)

Le Prince Radolin, Ambassadeur d'Allemagne à Paris, à **M.** *Rouvier, Président du Conseil, Ministre des Affaires Étrangères.*

Paris, le 8 Juillet, 1905.

Le Gouvernement de la République acceptant de se rendre à la conférence proposée par le Sultan du Maroc, le Gouvernement Impérial m'a chargé de Vous confirmer ses déclarations verbales, aux termes desquelles il ne poursuivra à la conférence aucun but qui compromette les légitimes intérêts de la France au Maroc, ou qui soit contraire aux droits de la France résultant de ses traités ou arrangements et en harmonie avec les principes suivants :—

Souveraineté et indépendance du Sultan ;

Intégrité de son Empire ;

Liberté économique, sans aucune inégalité ;

Utilité de réformes de police et de réformes financières dont l'introduction serait réglée pour une courte durée par voie d'accord international ;

Reconnaissance de la situation faite à la France au Maroc par la contiguïté, sur une vaste étendue, de l'Algérie et de l'Empire Chérifien, par les relations particulières qui en résultent entre les deux pays limitrophes, ainsi que par l'intérêt spécial qui s'en suit pour la France à ce que l'ordre règne dans l'empire chérifien.

(c.)

Déclaration.

Le Gouvernement de la République et le Gouvernement Allemand conviennent :

1°. de rappeler à Tanger simultanément leurs missions actuellement à Fez, aussitôt que la conférence se sera réunie ;

2°. de faire donner au Sultan du Maroc des conseils par leurs représentants, d'un commun accord, en vue de la fixation du programme qu'il proposera à la conférence sur les bases indiquées dans les lettres échangées sous la date du 8 Juillet 1905 entre le Président du Conseil, Ministre des Affaires Étrangères, et l'Ambassadeur d'Allemagne à Paris.

Fait à Paris, le 8 Juillet, 1905.

(Signé)   ROUVIER.
           RADOLIN.

No. 148.

Sir A. Nicolson to the Marquess of Lansdowne.

Madrid, July 11, 1905.

F.O. Morocco 435.   D. 1·50 P.M.
Tel. (No. 52.)   R. 6·15 P.M.

French Ambassador has received instructions to communicate to Spanish Government documents which have passed between French Government and German Ambassador as to Conference, and he will do so to-day.

I think it is extremely probable that Minister for Foreign Affairs will ask me what view His Majesty's Government take as to the programme of the Conference being settled at Fez between Sultan, and French, and German Representatives ; and also as to whether His Majesty's Government propose now to reply to note and accept Conference in principle while reserving opinion as to details of programme.

The Journal supposed to reflect views of Spanish Government has an article intimating that Spain and Great Britain are being disregarded and matters being settled without their being consulted. Journal therefore advises Spanish Government to come to an understanding with us. I think that article describes fairly view of Spanish Government.

No. 149.

Mr. Wyldbore Smith to the Marquess of Lansdowne.

Tangier, July 11, 1905.

F.O. Morocco 435.
D. 8·30 P.M.
Tel. Separate.
R. 10 P.M.

Belgian Minister informs me that his Government have accepted Sultan's invitation to attend Conference. This reply will be given to Sultan's Acting Commissioner here tomorrow.

No. 150.

The Marquess of Lansdowne to Sir F. Bertie.

F.O. Morocco 435.
(No. 459 A.)
Sir,
Foreign Office, July 11, 1905.

The French Ambassador informed me today that the French and German Governments had come to an agreement as to the bases on which a Conference for the discussion of the question of reforms in Morocco might be held in compliance with the invitation issued some time ago to that effect by the Sultan. His Excellency left with me three documents, of which copies are attached to this despatch,([1]) containing the text of the correspondence exchanged between the two Governments.

The urgent necessity of the reform of the administration has long been apparent. The domestic condition of the country has for many years past been such as to threaten on the one hand the stability of the Sultan's Government and on the other the interests of all foreigners having business relations with the country. Life and property are insecure, even in the immediate neighbourhood of Tangier, and the resources of the State have been dispersed in fruitless efforts to put down an insurrection mainly due to long-continued mis-government. Within the last few weeks a British subject holding the office of Vice-Consul for two European Powers has been brutally murdered on the outskirts of a Moorish city.

It is therefore clearly to the advantage of all countries interested in the welfare and prosperity of North-West Africa that this state of affairs should be improved. When however the idea of a Conference was first proposed His Majesty's Government had grave doubts whether this method of procedure would be the best calculated to achieve the object in view. The proceedings of a Conference are necessarily of a somewhat dilatory character, and in this case it seemed to H[is] M[ajesty's] Government that they would be rendered more so by the participation of a number of Powers, a large proportion of whom have no interests of importance in Morocco. H[is] M[ajesty's] Government had, moreover, recognised that for geographical reasons France, as the Power whose dominions were conterminous for a great distance with those of Morocco, was in a position of peculiar advantage for furthering the necessary reforms, and although they were fully prepared to admit that the work of amelioration thus undertaken should be carried out in such a manner as to involve no injustice to others, they were strongly of opinion that no Power was better qualified for this important task. Nor would the assumption of this rôle have involved any denial of the rights of other Powers. It was indeed distinctly set forth in the Anglo-French Declaration that there was no intention of altering the political status of Morocco, and that the two Governments were equally attached to the principle of commercial liberty both in Egypt and Morocco.

Any rights which other countries may have to most-favoured-nation treatment in Morocco would not, in the opinion of H[is] M[ajesty's] Government, preclude the

([1]) [*v. supra* pp. 115–6, No. 147.]

possibility of a privileged position being in certain respects accorded to France in her dealings with the Moorish Government. Most-favoured-nation treatment is variously interpreted in different countries. But no Power has, I believe, ever contended that the obligation to give such treatment debars one country from invoking the assistance of another in improving its domestic administration, and it is obvious that such assistance can be most conveniently and effectually given when the Power which affords it is the immediate neighbour of that which receives it, nor was there any desire or intention on the part of France to deprive other Powers of the rights and privileges to which they were justly entitled under Treaty.

The preliminary explanations which have taken place as to the scope and object of the Conference have gone far towards removing the original objections which H[is] M[ajesty's] G[overnment] felt to the proposal. There is now a reasonable hope that its deliberations may lead to useful results, and the Moorish Gov[ernmen]t have accordingly been informed that H[is] M[ajesty's] G[overnment] are willing to accept in principle the proposal to participate in it upon the understanding that they are consulted as to the subjects which are to come under discussion, and as to the time and place of meeting, and that a satisfactory settlement of these points is attained.

I am, &c.
LANSDOWNE.

No. 151.

The Marquess of Lansdowne to Mr. Lowther.

F.O. Morocco 435.   *Foreign Office, July* 12, 1905.
Tel. (No. 42.)   D. 6·40 P.M.

French and German Governments having come to an agreement as to bases on which the Conference may be held, His Majesty's Government consider it desirable, in view of the interests of this country in Morocco to participate. You should therefore inform Moorish Government that, subject to a satisfactory settlement of the programme, as to which we shall have to be consulted, and as to time and place of meeting, His Majesty's Government will be prepared to join.

No. 152.

The Marquess of Lansdowne to Sir F. Bertie.
F.O. Morocco 435.
(No. 463.)
Sir,   *Foreign Office, July* 12, 1905.

The French Ambassador called at this Office yesterday and left the three papers of which copies are attached to this despatch relating to the proposed Conference as to the affairs of Morocco.(¹)

His Excellency came to see me this morning, and told me that after all that had happened M. Rouvier was more convinced than ever of the necessity of maintaining a close understanding with this country. It was, in his view, essential that the two Governments should treat one another with the fullest confidence, and that no further steps should be taken without previous discussion between us. While holding this opinion, M. Rouvier thought it desirable to proceed with caution in dealing with the German Government, and thought we should avoid parading a desire to run counter to them.

(¹) [*v. supra* pp. 115–6. No. 147.]

His Excellency told me privately that the events of the last few weeks had had the effect of opening M. Rouvier's eyes with regard to the policy and intentions of Germany. He had been led to suppose that with M. Delcassé's retirement all traces of German irritation against France would disappear. He had been rudely undeceived, for within six hours of the announcement of M. Delcassé's resignation the German Note had been presented. The subsequent negotiations had added to M. Rouvier's disenchantment. He had found Prince Radolin difficult to deal with, and by no means trustworthy.

I told His Excellency that I was sure he would admit that His Majesty's Government had given the French Government their loyal support throughout these occurrences, and we had no intention of withdrawing it. At the same time I was bound to tell him that the apparent sacrifice of M. Delcassé in the face of German pressure had created an unfavourable impression in this country, and I therefore thought there was a good deal to be said for M. Rouvier's view that it would be as well to avoid any action calculated to bring about fresh complications.

We then had some conversation with regard to other points connected with the Conference. His Excellency said that the French Government had come to the conclusion that upon the whole it had better not take place at Tangier. Tangier would, in the first place, be too much within the influence of Moorish intrigues, in which the German Government was but too likely to participate. In the next place, the climate would be almost unendurable, and the representatives would have to submit to great discomfort. I asked His Excellency what he thought of some place in Spain. He said that Madrid would also be open to objection for climatic reasons, but that he thought the Conference might be held at San Sebastian. I observed that there was a great deal to be said in favour of holding the Conference somewhere in Spain, and that I felt sure that such a decision would be agreeable to the Spanish Government.

I told His Excellency that we should of course expect to be consulted as to the programme, and he at once said that, in his view, it should be submitted to us before any decision was arrived at with regard to it. It would presumably be based upon the original invitation issued to the Powers by the Sultan. It was however a question whether the representatives of the Powers at Tangier should be themselves deputed to take part in the Conference. His Excellency approved my suggestion that I should tell the Spanish Ambassador that the French Government would certainly communicate the draft programme both to Great Britain and Spain before any decision was come to with regard to it.

I am, &c.
LANSDOWNE.

No. 153.

The Marquess of Lansdowne to Sir F. Bertie.

F.O. Morocco 435.
(No. 469.)
Sir,   *Foreign Office, July* 13, 1905.

The French Ambassador told me today that he had received a further despatch from M. Rouvier upon the subject of the Morocco question. M. Rouvier had had an interview with Prince Radolin, who had said that the German Government desired to arrive at an understanding with the French Government as to the programme and objects of the Conference.

M. Rouvier was anxious to act with us in the matter and would communicate to us his ideas as to the programme. He was inclined to limit it so as to confine the deliberations of the Conference to questions of police and finance, taking as a basis the proposals which had already been submitted by M. Saint René Taillandier to the Moorish Government. As soon as M. Rouvier had come to an understanding with us he would consult the Spanish Government, and would then go to the German Government.

I told M. Cambon that I should be glad if he would let me have in writing an outline of the French proposal. As at present advised I saw no objection to limiting it to the points which he had mentioned. I thought the proposals should be as simple and uncontroversial as possible. His Excellency told me that M. Saint René Taillandier had proposed a scheme of military re-organisation involving the appointment of French instructors who were to hold office for two or three years, at the end of which time they would presumably have completed the work of re-organisation. I suggested that the military question should be so far as possible treated as one of police, and His Excellency said that the object of M. Saint René Taillandier's "military" proposals had been merely the maintenance of order.

With regard to the financial proposals, His Excellency said that there were two main points : the establishment of a Banque Marocaine and that of bonded warehouses ("magasins généraux"). As regards the bank, he saw no reason why the participation of other Powers should not be allowed, and the use of the bonded warehouses would be open to everyone. There was therefore no monopoly involved.

I am, &c.
LANSDOWNE.

No. 154.

Sir A. Nicolson to the Marquess of Lansdowne.

Madrid, July 14, 1905.
F.O. Spain 2211.
D. 1·15 P.M.
Tel. (No. 55.)
R. 3·30 P.M.

M[inister] [for] F[oreign] A[ffairs] read to me this morning the instructions which are being sent to Spanish Minister at Tangier. They are similar to those sent to Mr. Lowther.

He told me that he had also read them to French Ambassador who had expressed entire concurrence with them.

No. 155.

Mr. Lowther to the Marquess of Lansdowne.

F.O. Morocco 435.
(No. 188.)
Fez, D. July 19, 1905.
My Lord,
R. *July* 31, 1905.

Two days after the text of the bases of the agreement arrived at between the French and German Governments on the subject of the proposed Moroccan Conference reached here, the Sultan sent for Count Tattenbach and inquired his opinion on it.

As far as I have been able to ascertain the German Minister's language was somewhat as follows :—

Germany has been as good as her word, she promised the Sultan that the Conference should be held although France objected and she has obtained it. It is true that in the exchange of notes there is some general recognition of the preponderating position of France in Morocco, but this need not be taken too seriously. The notes speak of the international approval that is to be given to the reforms to be introduced but in the Conference itself it will be easy to stretch this into a permanent international contr[o]l as regards finance, the army, &c.

The German Minister's language seems to have had a very soothing effect upon the Sultan and to have convinced His Majesty that there is no immediate danger and that he will now be left in his somnolent attitude for some years to come.

In the meantime the French Minister has received no instructions to communicate the text of the arrangement to the Makhzen and has only endeavoured to modify the impressions produced by Count Tattenbach's language by some very guarded and moderate appreciations of the arrangements, which he has communicated in a purely unofficial manner.

I have, &c.
GERARD LOWTHER.

No. 156.

Mr. Lowther to the Marquess of Lansdowne.

F.O. Morocco 422.
(No. 190.) Confidential.   *Fez, D. July* 20, 1905.
My Lord,   R. *July* 31, 1905.

In view of the undertaking given by Germany in Prince Radolin's note of the 8th July to the effect that Germany would not at the Conference pursue a policy contrary to the rights of France resulting from her treaties and arrangements with Morocco, it may be of interest to record that the French Minister has informed me in confidence that before negotiations with the Moorish Government regarding reforms were broken off he had actually obtained from the Minister for Foreign Affairs the acceptance in writing of that Government of the Army Scheme proposed by France.

I have, &c.
GERARD LOWTHER.

No. 157.

M. Paul Cambon to the Marquess of Lansdowne.

F.O. Morocco 435.
Privée.   *Ambassade de France à Londres,*
Cher Lord Lansdowne,   *le* 20 *Juillet* 1905.

Je reçois de M. Rouvier un projet de programme pour la conférence marocaine que je vous envoie. Mon départ pour Edinbourg m'empêche de vous le porter. Si vous l'approuvez vous seriez bien aimable de me le faire savoir en chargeant Gorst ou Barrington d'écrire un mot au C[om]te de Manneville. Si vous désirez causer avec moi j'irai vous voir lundi matin.

Votre bien devoué,
PAUL CAMBON.

Enclosure in No. 157.

Projet de Programme pour la Conférence Marocaine.

A. Organisation de la police hors de la région frontière, c'est à dire hors des districts où elle est réglée par un accord franco-marocain :

I) Création de corps de troupes marocaines pour la police à Tanger, Larache, Rabat et Casablanca.
II) Surveillance et répression de la contrebande des armes par mer.

B. Ré   financières.

Concours financier donné au Maghzen par la création d'une banque d'État avec privilège d'émission, se chargeant des opérations de trésorerie, s'entremettant pour la frappe de la monnaie dont les bénéfices appartiendraient au Maghzen.

La Banque d'État procéderait à l'assainissement de la situation monétaire. Les crédits ouverts au Maghzen seraient employés à l'équipement et à la solde des troupes de police et à certains travaux publics urgents, notamment amélioration des ports et de leurs outillages.

Engagement par le Maghzen de n'aliéner aucun des services publics au profit d'intérêts particuliers.

Principe de l'adjudication sans exception de nationalité pour les travaux publics.(¹)

(¹) [The substance of M. Cambon's letter and its enclosure was sent to Sir F. Bertie as Despatch No. 495 of July 20.]

No. 158.

The Marquess of Lansdowne to Count de Manneville.

F.O. Morocco 435.

Count de Manneville.(¹)   *Foreign Office, July* 21, 1905.

Lord Lansdowne has examined the proposed programme for the Morocco Conference, which the Ambassador sent to him yesterday, and desires me to say that he is prepared to accept it. He presumes that the Spanish Gov[ernmen]t are also being consulted on the subject.

Lord Lansdowne believes that the question of taxation and notably that of foreigners, as to which some regulations were accepted in Nov[ember] 1903 by the Powers represented at Tangier, is not included in the programme, and he would suggest, for the consideration of the French Gov[ernmen]t whether this question might not usefully be added to the subjects for discussion. It is evident that it is one which would, in any case, require the assent of the Powers interested and the Conference would seem to offer a convenient opportunity for arriving at a satisfactory settlement of the matter.

L[ANSDOWNE].

(¹) [This is a draft only, hence the address and signature are incomplete.]

No. 159.

Mr. Wyldbore Smith to the Marquess of Lansdowne.

                                        Tangier, July 21, 1905.

F.O. Morocco 435.   D. 11·20 P.M.

Tel. (Separate.)   R. 8 A.M., *July* 22.

Morocco Conference.

Russian Government have replied to Sultan's invitation that, although they have no interests in Morocco, since the majority of the Powers have accepted invitation to attend Conference, Russian Government will participate therein.

No. 160.

Sir M. Durand to the Marquess of Lansdowne.

F.O. Morocco 435.   *Lenox, July* 22, 1905.

Tel. (No. 80.)   D. 9 P.M.

Your Tel[egram] No. 42 to H[is] M[ajesty's] Rep[resentativ]e at Tangier.(¹)

State Dep[artmen]t informs me that U[nited] S[tates'] Gov[ernmen]t will also take part in Morocco Conference.

(¹) [*v. supra* p. 118, No. 151.]

No. 161.

Mr. Lowther to the Marquess of Lansdowne.

F.O. Morocco 435.   *Fez, D. July 24, 1905.*
Tel. (No. 80.)   R. *July 28*, 1905, 9·45 P.M.
    Minister for Foreign Affairs has expressed to me strong opinion in favour of Conference being held at Tangier, observing that Moorish Government have no cyphers, and that much delay would be caused by its being held elsewhere.

No. 162.

The Marquess of Lansdowne to Mr. Lowther.

F.O. Morocco 435.   *Foreign Office, July 27, 1905.*
Tel. (No. 46.)   D. 6 P.M.
    Conference.
    H[is] M[ajesty's] G[overnment] have approved the programme put forward by French Gov[ernmen]t.
    It is briefly :

> Organization of police outside regions to which existing Franco-Moorish Agreement applies.
> Control of smuggling of arms by sea.
> Institution of a State Bank.
> Non-alienation of any public services in favour of private interests.
> Open tenders for public works without distinction of nationality.

No. 163.

The Marquess of Lansdowne to Mr. Lowther.

F.O. Morocco 435.   *Foreign Office, July 28, 1905.*
Tel. (No. 47.)   D. 7·45 P.M.
    Conference.
    H[is] M[ajesty's] G[overnment] are of opinion that Tangier would not be a suitable place of meeting and you may join your French colleague in making a representation to this effect to the Sultan and suggesting some other place, such as San Sebastian.
    As regards concession of Tangier mole and warehouses to Germans, you may join your French Colleague in a protest against the granting of any concessions or privileges to·foreigners until Conference has had a full opp[ortunit]y of considering this and other allied questions in all their bearings.

No. 164.

Mr. Wyldbore Smith to the Marquess of Lansdowne.

Tangier, July 31, 1905.

F.O. Morocco 435.
Tel. Separate.
   Morocco Conference.

D. 3 P.M.
R. 5 P.M.

American and Portuguese Ministers inform me that unconditional acceptances of their respective Governments to the Sultan's invitation arrived this morning and have been handed over to the Sultan's Acting Commissioner here.

No. 165.

Mr. Lowther to the Marquess of Lansdowne.

F.O. Morocco 435.
(No. 207.)
My Lord,

Fez, D. July 31, 1905.
R. *August* 14, 1905.

No communication has yet been made to the Moorish Government by the French Minister regarding the acceptance by his Government of the invitation to be present at the Conference. The Paris arrangement of July 10th [*sic*] has merely been conveyed in an unofficial form to the Makhzen, whose members are however expecting proposals to be made to them regarding a programme for the deliberation of the Conference. Although quite unprepared with a programme of their own, whatever plan is suggested by the Foreign Ministers will inevitably meet with stout resistance.

From Your Lordship's despatch to Sir F. Bertie No. 463 of July 12th,([1]) I gather that M. Cambon considered that this opposition could in a measure be met by proposing to the Moorish Government a programme based on the original invitation to the Powers, but in that document no mention was made of the nature of the reforms proposed.

"Reforms suitable to the present condition of affairs, which His Majesty intends to introduce into his Empire," are the words used in the note of the Moorish Government. The Sultan and his advisers are constantly complaining of the abuses of protection, a condition of affairs which prevents His Majesty levying taxes, the protected being frequently supported by their Governments in their refusal to pay. His Majesty's aim in the Conference will be merely to obtain the sanction to levy taxes on foreigners and that the matter of reform be left to him. To this taxation there would obviously be no objection provided some reform were obtained. An indication to this effect might perhaps be introduced into the Programme.

It is impossible to exaggerate the difficulties that will present themselves to the Conference in inducing the Moorish Government to accept the smallest reform, as His Majesty will invariably plead the anti-Christian feeling, which he represents himself as being powerless to resist. There are indications that this is already being prepared namely :—

The message conveyed to myself and my colleagues, as reported in my No. 193 of the 24th ultimo,([2]) regarding the alleged anti-Mahomedan action of some foreigners here.

The rumours that the *mot d'ordre* has been issued that it is no longer necessary to treat foreigners with the regard that has been observed during the past few months.

The invitation to the tribes to send Delegates.

All this points clearly to the fact that the Moorish Government intends to have recourse to all possible means of obstruction.

([1]) [*v. supra* pp. 118–9, No. 152.]
([2]) [No. 193 of 25 July, records communication from Ben Sliman Abdelkrim relating to alleged actions of foreigners in entering mosques, &c.]

However limited the programme is to be, one of the most essential points to be proposed will be the police, at least for the coast towns, and such police under foreign control. The right of punishment and the payment of the men must be equally in the hands of foreigners, and to this the Moorish Government would offer a strenuous resistance : first owing to their religious prejudice against any Mahomedan being punished by a European, secondly under the plea that it would be interfering with the authority of His Majesty.

These objections might possibly be overcome by the introduction of a nominal Moorish Chief of equivalent rank to the Foreigner in Command.

Certainly, if the expression used in the Paris Arrangement of July 8th— "résultant de ces traités et arrangements" is to be taken to mean published and unpublished treaties and arrangements, it must considerably limit the scope of the discussions of the Conference.

The important treaties and arrangements which bear on the matter and which form valuable "points d'appui" for France are, as far as I am aware, the following :—

1. The Protocol of Paris, 1901.([1])
2. The Frontier Agreement, 1902.([1])
3. Notes exchanged confining the instruction of the frontier troops to French officers, 1902 or 1903.([1])
    (The text of this I have not seen.)
4. The option for future Loans, contained in Article 33 of the Loan Contract of 1904.([1])
5. The right of certain examination and control of the Customs provided in Article XV of the Loan Contract of 1905.
6. The agreement about the army said by the French Minister to have been accepted by the Moorish Government. (See my despatch No. 190, Confidential, of the 20th ultimo.([2])
    (The text of this I have not seen.)
7. The Command of the Police of Tangier, at present in the hands of a French officer. This was established by an exchange of notes.([1])

With these arrangements to support her and with the presentation of a very moderate programme there may be some hope of a beginning being made towards reform.

I have, &c.
GERARD LOWTHER.

([1]) [Printed, *Documents Diplomatiques, Affaires du Maroc, 1901–5* (Paris 1905), pp. 16–18, pp. 34–8, pp. 44–7, p. 151, pp. 160–2.]
([2]) [*v. supra* p. 121, No. 156.]

No. 166.

The Marquess of Lansdowne to Mr. Whitehead.

F.O. Germany (Prussia) 1615.
(No. 187.)
Sir,   *Foreign Office, August 1, 1905.*
During the course of a desultory conversation with Count Metternich on the 29th ultimo I mentioned to him that I had heard that efforts were being made to obtain for a German firm a concession for the construction of a mole at Tangier. I had also heard that the Sultan was to be offered a German loan upon favourable terms. I asked Count Metternich whether he did not think it would be better that, pending the meeting of the Conference, all the Powers should desist from efforts of this kind. Count Metternich replied that, so far as he was aware, there had never been any reason for which a concession to construct public works in Morocco might not be given to German, or indeed to any other applicants. He could not therefore see why the fact that a

Conference was about to be held should be an obstacle to such an arrangement. I observed that if other Powers were to follow suit, and to insist upon equivalent concessions, a state of things would be produced not very likely to facilitate the deliberations of the Conference.

Count Metternich, during the course of the discussion, let fall that the German Government had obtained a copy of M. S[ain]t René Taillandier's original proposals to the Sultan's Government, which, he said, were of a very far-reaching and exclusive character, and of a kind to justify the German Government in their suspicion that France desired to oust all other Powers from Morocco. I asked Count Metternich whether these proposals did not refer especially to that part of Morocco which was immediately contiguous to the Algerian frontier. His Excellency did not seem to be fully informed upon this point.

I am, &c.
LANSDOWNE.

No. 167.

Mr. Lister to the Marquess of Lansdowne.

F.O. France 3706.
(No. 292.)
My Lord,

Paris, D. August 2, 1905.
R. August 5, 1905.

There is no doubt that the feeling of resentment against the attitude of Count Tattenbach at Fez is steadily increasing in France.

M. Louis spoke of it to me the other day with considerable bitterness, and described it as inexplicable. The "Temps," in a leading article, entitled "Count Tattenbach," severely criticizes his action. It clings to the hope that he has exceeded his instructions and recalls the fact that it was for very similar indiscretions that he was removed from Morocco several years ago. Germany has accused France of wishing to make of Morocco a second Tunis, but France does not intend that Germany shall make a Turkey of her. It is all very well for Germany to go on repeating that she is quite indifferent to Morocco, but it is high time that she should disavow the manœuvres of Count Tattenbach, and give him a further taste of the severity shown him on a former occasion. Several interesting articles in the same strain have also appeared in the "Aurore" from the pen of M. Clémenceau himself, one of which, entitled "no dupery," is particularly outspoken. M. Clémenceau considers that the present activity of Count Tattenbach at Fez is only the forerunner of worse surprises in the future. There is little chance of the Emperor remaining satisfied with his first victory. The situation is critical and M. Clémenceau is of opinion that, while avoiding anything in the nature of a menace, France should give notice that, rather than allow herself to be duped, she will retire from the present negotiations. A few words of warning from M. Rouvier are all that are required, and M. Clémenceau is convinced that if these words were spoken they would have a very calming effect upon Count Tattenbach's attitude.

Copies of the articles from the "Temps" and the "Aurore" are enclosed herewith.(¹)

I have, &c.
REGINALD LISTER.

(¹) [Not reproduced.]

[ED. NOTE.—On the 7th August, a French naval squadron visited Portsmouth; on the 9th King Edward lunched on the French flagship. The French naval representatives were later entertained at Windsor by the King, and at Westminster Hall by both Houses of Parliament. *v.* Sir Sidney Lee: *King Edward VII*, II, (1927), p. 345.]

No. 168.

Sir C. Hardinge to the Marquess of Lansdowne.

F.O. Morocco 435.
Tel. (No. 138.) Secret.

St. Petersburgh, *August* 3, 1905.
D. 8·32 P.M.
R. 9 P.M.

Your telegram No. 294.

French Ambassador informs me most confidentially that he has trustworthy information that, in addition to other subjects, the question of Morocco and Anglo-French relations were discussed at the recent interview between the two Emperors. The German Emperor expressed the opinion that the Anglo-French Arrangement and the Morocco Agreement were aimed against Germany, and he warned the Emperor against any policy combined with England and France tending to isolate Germany.

The Emperor Nicholas agreed that such a policy would be contrary to interests of Russia.

No. 169.

Mr. Cartwright to the Marquess of Lansdowne.

F.O. Morocco 435.
(No. 149.) Confidential.
My Lord,

San Sebastian, D. *August* 8, 1905.
R. *August* 10, 1905.

With reference to my telegrams Nos. 63 and 65 of yesterday and today respectively, I have the honour to inform Your Lordship that yesterday morning I saw Monsieur Cambon, the French Ambassador, by appointment, and His Excellency asked me whether I could see my way to obtaining from the Spanish Government some clear and definite proposal with regard to their wish that the Morocco Conference should be held on Spanish soil.

Monsieur Cambon explained to me that the French Government were desirous to meet, as far as possible, Spanish susceptibilities, but, with regard to the locality of the Conference, if France was to show her good will towards Spain, he must have something tangible to lay before Monsieur Rouvier to show what were the wishes of the Spanish Government on the subject.

I therefore called on Señor Montero Rios, the President of the Council, who received me at once. His Excellency made no secret of the strong desire of the Spanish Government that the Great Powers should consent to let the Conference be held on Spanish soil; he used every possible argument against the choice of Tangier for that purpose, but I found him most reluctant to make any written communication on the subject, I imagine from fear of exposing his Government to a refusal and to enable him to say in the Cortes, if the Conference should finally be held at Tangier, that Spain had only said that she would welcome the Conference in this country if the Powers thought fit to propose to hold it there.

The result of my interview with Señor Montero Rios was that he consented, if Monsieur Cambon would call upon him in the afternoon, to seek with him a formula by which the Spanish Government would officially but verbally suggest that the most suitable country in which to hold the Conference was Spain. His Excellency was indifferent as to the actual city selected for that purpose.

I reported the above to Monsieur Cambon, who called on the President of the Council in the afternoon and, after considerable difficulty, persuaded him to make a written communication to the French Government, in the form of a *Note-verbale*, formally proposing Spain as the country in which to hold the Conference.

Copy of the *Note verbale* was communicated to Herr von Radewitz [*sic*], the German Ambassador, and to myself last night by Señor Ojeda, the Under-Secretary of State for Foreign Affairs, and I have the honour to enclose, herewith, a copy of the same.

I have, &c.

FAIRFAX L. CARTWRIGHT.

Enclosure in No. 169.

Note Verbale.

En tenant compte de ce que :—

(*a.*) La place de Tanger est loin d'offrir toutes les conditions désirables pour garantir la liberté d'action et de discussion dans la Conférence, par suite de l'insubordination et troubles qui règnent dans les proches tribus et de l'impuissance des autorités locales pour remédier à cet état de choses ;

(*b.*) Qu'il est à désirer que la Conférence ait lieu dans un endroit qui soit, d'une part proche à l'empire afin d'assurer au Plénipotentiaire de S[a] M[ajesté] Shérifienne une communication facile et suivie avec son gouvernement et d'autre part que ce même endroit offre aux plénipotentiaires qui auront à assister les commodités nécessaires ainsi que la pleine liberté pour leurs délibérations ;

L'Espagne offre pour le lieu de la Conférence avec un grand plaisir pour sa part aux Puissances, quelqu'une des villes au Levant et au Sud de la Péninsule, par exemple, Cadiz, Malaga, Algeciras. L'expérience justifie, du reste, ce qui précède, car il ne faut pas oublier ce qui est arrivé pour la Conférence de Tanger l'année 1879 en contre-position de celle de Madrid dans l'année 1880. Ce n'est que dans cette dernière qu'il fut possible d'arriver à un accord définitif sur le droit de protection qui n'avait pu être obtenu dans la précédente Conférence, fort vraisemblablement par suite de l'endroit où elle eut lieu.

No. 170.

Mr. Lister to the Marquess of Lansdowne.

F.O. Morocco 435.
(No. 302.)   *Paris, D. August* 15, 1905.
My Lord,   R. *August* 16, 1905.

In the course of conversation this morning, Monsieur Louis said that he was somewhat surprised at the present attitude of the German Government with regard to the Morocco Conference. At the beginning they had clamoured for its immediate meeting, whereas now they appeared far from being in any hurry. They were disinclined to discuss the question of dates. The Emperor, Prince Bülow, Baron Richthofen, and Monsieur de Mühlberg were all absent from Berlin, and the direction of the Foreign Office had been left to Count Pourtalès, German Minister at Munich, who was not *au courant* of all that had passed, and would probably plead ignorance in order to delay taking any decision. Monsieur Louis said that it really looked as though the Germans had realized that they would obtain less than they had originally expected by a conference, and that their interests would have after all been better served by manœuvres, such as those in which Count Tattenbach had proved himself to be such an adept.

The question still continues to be the object of discussion in the whole of the Paris press, and Monsieur Clémenceau in an article to-day entitled " C'est trop," is more outspoken than ever. As his readers know, he has never attached particular importance to Morocco in itself, but he considers that the dignity of France has been seriously compromised by the recent action of Germany, and insists upon the necessity of the French Government taking a strong stand before it is too late.

I have, &c.
REGINALD LISTER.

No. 171.

Mr. Lowther to the Marquess of Lansdowne.

F.O. Morocco 435. *Fez,* D. *August* 19, 1905.
Tel. (No. 85.) R. *August* 22, 1905 (by bag).
Morocco Conference.
My despatch No. 215.
German Minister states that he has replied to his Gov[ernmen]t approving generally program for Conference but stating that proposal for foreign police, owing to question of punishment, will be opposed by Moorish Gov[ernmen]t (see my despatch No. 210),([1]) also that Moorish state bank being against religion of country, an international bank must be substituted. German Min[iste]r now says Moorish Gov[ernmen]t will not offer any serious resistance to program.

([1]) [Not reproduced.]

No. 172.

Mr. Cartwright to the Marquess of Lansdowne.

F.O. Morocco 435.
(No. 154.) Confidential. *San Sebastian,* D. *August* 24, 1905.
My Lord, R. *August* 28, 1905.
I have the honour to inform Your Lordship that this morning I had the opportunity of having some conversation with Monsieur Cambon, the French Ambassador, who has just returned here from Paris. His Excellency told me that on the previous day Herr von Radowitz, the German Ambassador, had called on him to make certain enquiries with regard to the arrangements to be made for the King of Spain's journey through France on his way to Berlin in November next. Monsieur Cambon took this opportunity of enquiring whether the German Ambassador had received any recent instructions from Berlin respecting Morocco. The reply was that for the last three weeks he had not received a single word on the subject from his Government. On this Monsieur Cambon expressed to Herr von Radowitz in very forcible terms the feeling at the French Foreign Office with regard to the recent conduct of Germany in the Morocco Question. Three months ago Germany was in a desperate hurry to solve the difficulties which had arisen in Morocco, no time was to be lost, France was worried to give an immediate reply on the question of the Conference; she had done so, she had met Germany's demands in a conciliatory spirit; the Conference was accepted in principle and the sketch of the subjects proposed to be discussed at it had been sent to Berlin. A change however had come over the scene; Berlin now was mute; the German Government seemed to take no further interest in the meeting of the Conference but meanwhile Count Tattenbach did not cease his activity at Fez. Monsieur Cambon impressed upon Herr von Radowitz that the apparent disloyalty of Germany in this Moroccan question was causing great irritation in France and he must not suppose that the French Government would allow themselves to be duped by Germany's dilatory ways in the present negotiations and if

[15869] K

Count Tattenbach continued to extort concessions from the Sultan of Morocco while France loyally abstained from pressing for any for herself, he warned the German Ambassador that it might become necessary for the Powers mainly interested in Morocco to insist that all concessions recently obtained should be examined by the Conference before they were finally ratified. The present attitude of Germany, concluded Monsieur Cambon, if persisted in could only cause irritation all round and do no good to anyone.

To all this Herr von Radowitz had little to say except that during the summer the Emperor and the Chancellor were away from Berlin and that some delay in the negotiations must inevitably occur.

Later in the day Monsieur Cambon went to see the President of the Council and repeated to him what he had said to Herr von Radowitz. Señor Montero Rios expressed his entire approval of Monsieur Cambon's language and stated that he would speak in the same sense to the German Ambassador at the very first opportunity.

After some moments of silence and hesitation, Monsieur Cambon said to me, the President of the Council suddenly opened out his heart to him and took him into his confidence in a manner which struck him very much taking into consideration the feeling of distrust which still exists in this country against France. Señor Montero Rios said that Spain was at present placed in a very difficult position: she was too weak to do anything by herself and therefore had put herself, and would continue to remain, in line with France and Great Britain on the Morocco Question, but she could not help feeling deeply hurt and depressed at the high-handed and discourteous manner in which she was being treated by Germany who had not even deigned to give any reply to his proposal (mentioned in my Despatch No. 149 of the 8th instant)(1) that the Conference should be held in Spain, a point on which he laid great stress. But there were other matters of even greater importance in which Spanish aspirations and interests were being trampled upon by Germany. It had been generally understood that Tangier and the Northern Coast of Morocco should be more or less in the sphere of Spanish influence, it was there that a large number of Spanish subjects resided and where real Spanish economic interests existed; yet it was just there that German intrigues had succeeded in obtaining a concession for a German Firm for the construction of a mole and the general commercial development of Tangier, and not satisfied with that it now appeared that practically the whole of the state property in the neighbourhood of that place had been mortgaged to a German Bank in return for a loan which was not for national purposes but merely to provide for the Sultan's amusements. Suppose it was decided to introduce an international administration of Tangier and neighbourhood how could the funds be found for this purpose if the State lands there could be claimed as the property of a German Bank? Under all these provocations on the part of Germany Spain had to remain mute. France was the mouthpiece of the three Powers who were working together to save the situation in Morocco and His Excellency expressed an earnest hope that she would not yield all along the line to German pressure and would bear in mind what were the modest but real interests of Spain in Morocco. Señor Montero Rios concluded, so Monsieur Cambon informed me, by bringing down his fist upon the table and saying, "we shall not forget what Germany has done to us on this occasion."

The impression left on Monsieur Cambon's mind is that the Spanish Government though outwardly maintaining a calm demeanour, are at the present moment deeply incensed with the Kaiser's Government.

I have, &c.
FAIRFAX L. CARTWRIGHT.

(1) [v. supra pp. 127-8. No. 169.]

No. 173.

The Marquess of Lansdowne to Mr. Lister.

F.O. Morocco 435.
(No. 585.)

Sir,   *Foreign Office, August 30, 1905.*

With reference to the final paragraph of my despatch No. 546 of the 12th instant[1] on the subject of the Morocco Conference the French Minister called at this Office this afternoon and informed Sir Eldon Gorst of the proposals which the French Ambassador at Madrid is to submit to the Spanish Government with a view to arriving at a preliminary understanding on matters in which Spain is specially interested.

The proposals are as follows :—

Police.—Spain to undertake the police arrangements at Laraiche—perhaps at Tetuan—and on the land frontiers of the Spanish "Présides."

At Tangier Spain to administer the police arrangements of that port, on the condition that a French Inspector General would superintend generally the policing of all four ports.

Contraband by Sea.—The prevention of this contraband to be entrusted to the Spanish and French navies—a Franco-Spanish Division being alternately under the command of an officer of each country.

Participation of Spanish Capital in the State Bank.—The presidency of the Board of Administration to be assigned to France. The number of Spanish members to be proportionate to the amount of Spanish capital which would be superior to that of the other Powers (France excepted).

The circulation of the Spanish peseta in Morocco to be preserved.

Monsieur Geoffray stated that Monsieur Jules Cambon had been instructed to place himself in communication with Mr. Cartwright and that the French Government counted on his cooperation should the necessity arise.

I am, &c.
LANSDOWNE.

(1) [Not printed. The last paragraph dealt with the suggestion of the Spanish Government that the Conference should be held at Algeciras or Malaga, and that Spain should (1) undertake the police arrangements at a number of ports, (2) be entrusted with prevention of introduction of contraband of war, and (3) be allowed a privileged position in the neighbourhood of the Spanish *présides*.]

No. 174.

Papers communicated by M. Geoffray, September 1, 1905.[1]

(a.)

F.O. Morocco 435.

Prince Radolin to M. Rouvier.

Le 25 Août, 1905.

En réponse à la lettre du 1ᵉʳ de ce mois[2] j'ai l'honneur d'informer V[otre] E[xcellence] que c'est avec intérêt que le Gouvernement Impérial a pris connaissance des propositions du Gouvernement français et qu'il les a soumises à un examen minutieux. À la vive satisfaction du Gouvernement Impérial le résultat de cet examen a été que les propositions peuvent être regardées comme une base acceptable pour les délibérations de la Conférence aussi bien en ce qui concerne leur nombre que leur contenu. Particulièrement le Gouvernement Impérial se range à l'avis du Gouvernement français que le programme de la Conférence devrait être sommaire et qu'il devrait s'abstenir d'entrer dans les détails afin de préjuger le moins possible les résolutions de la Conférence.

(1) [Printed *Documents Diplomatiques, Affaires du Maroc, 1901–5*, (Paris 1905), pp. 283–6. 290–3. The date of Prince Radolin's communication is there given as 26 August.]
(2) [*Ib.* pp. 256–60.]

[15869]   K 2

Si le Gouvernement français se réfère à la Note du 6 Juillet en ce qui concerne son concours à l'exécution des réformes à faire, le Gouvernement Impérial se permet de faire remarquer qu'il n'a reçu cette Note qu'au moment lorsque ses dernières propositions au sujet d'échange de Notes franco-allemandes étaient déjà parties. Par conséquent le Gouvernement Impérial n'a pu préciser sa manière de voir au sujet de ces propositions et il en a informé le Gouvernement français. L'accord entre les deux Gouvernements a donc été amené sans se référer à cette Note, et le Gouvernement Impérial espère qu'aussi maintenant une entente puisse se faire sans avoir recours à la dite Note.

Quant aux propositions du Gouvernement français en détail le Gouvernement Impérial se permet d'expliquer sa manière de voir par ce qui suit :—

1°. Le Gouvernement Impérial est d'accord avec le Gouvernement de la République que l'organisation d'une police sure dans les lieux les plus importants du Maroc, proposée sous le § 1 du projet de programme, serait le meilleur moyen pour obtenir la pacification du pays. Pourtant, le choix des endroits ne devrait pas figurer, comme il a été proposé, dans le programme mais, conformément au principe général recommandé par la France, il devrait être réservé à la Conférence pour éviter autant que possible d'entrer en détails.

Le Gouvernement français désire réserver l'organisation de la police dans les districts-frontière à l'arrangement particulier entre la France et le Maroc, cette affaire ayant été traitée depuis 50 ans comme affaire exclusivement franco-marocaine. En tant que le Gouvernement Impérial connaît les arrangements concernant la frontière entre la France et le Maroc, il existe des stipulations sur l'organisation de la police dans les districts-frontière du Maroc, portant que le Maroc est tenu à entretenir à certains endroits des postes de police qui, le cas échéant, doivent concourir avec les postes du côté français. Les postes de police marocains sont sujets à l'influence du Maroc puisque leur organisation et administration ne regarde que le Gouvernement marocain. Il paraît donc tout naturel que l'état des choses ressortant d'une telle organisation de la police frontière soit réservé à un arrangement entre la France et le Maroc.

Si, cependant, il serait question d'organiser l'administration de la police marocaine dans les districts-frontière de la même manière comme cela a été pris en vue pour les autres parties de l'Empire chérifien, il serait à examiner, si une telle organisation n'aurait pas besoin d'une sanction internationale par la Conférence ; et cela d'autant plus, qu'il ne serait peut-être pas sans inconvénient de subvenir à l'entretien de la police-frontière, conformément au programme de la Conférence, (*sub* II, al. 3) par les crédits ouverts au Maghzen, sans que la Conférence participât à la fixation de l'étendue de l'obligation d'entretien.

Il serait naturellement à tenir compte de la situation particulière dans laquelle la France se trouve comme pays limitrophe du Maroc, par la proposition qu'un mandat de la Conférence pour l'organisation de la police de frontière ne pourrait être concédé à aucune autre Puissance qu'à la France. Un tel mandat serait à donner, en ce qui concerne son contenu, dans la même forme comme le mandat pour l'organisation de la police dans les autres parties de l'Empire marocain, et accorderait ainsi à la France une base universellement reconnue pour la sécurité de sa frontière.

2°. Le Gouvernement de la République propose *sub* 1, 2 du projet de programme, comme objet des délibérations : "Surveillance et répression de la contrebande des armes par mer." Elle justifie cette proposition avec la remarque que la surveillance de l'introduction illégale des armes devrait être confiée à des mains plus vigoureuses qu'à celles du Gouvernement chérifien. Le Gouvernement Impérial se rallie également à cette proposition et croit seulement devoir observer que les stipulations de la Conférence, pour être efficaces, devraient viser la contrebande des armes par terre et par mer. Une stipulation restreignant uniquement l'introduction des armes par mer serait à même de repousser la contrebande d'armes à la voie par terre. Le programme de la Conférence aurait, dès lors, à prendre en vue un règlement uniforme de l'introduction des armes par toutes les frontières du pays.

On pourrait tenir compte dans le programme des points mentionnés *sub* 1 et 2 en rayant, dans le titre de la partie 1, les mots "hors de la région frontière, &c."; dans le No. 1 les mots : "à Tanger, Larache, Rabat et Casablanca," et dans le No. 2 les mots : "par mer."

3°. Le Gouvernement Impérial accepte également les réformes financières et commerciales proposées *sub* II et III du projet de programme. Particulièrement il lui paraît comme une idée bien juste que la banque marocaine qui doit être créée doit avoir un caractère international tant par sa direction que par la participation du capital. Pour l'exécution des réformes financières il serait recommandable d'ajouter au programme de la Conférence les délibérations sur un meilleur rendement des impôts et la création de nouveaux revenus particulièrement en ce qui concerne les propriétés foncières.

4°. Le Gouvernement Impérial n'a pas d'autre supplément à proposer au programme de la Conférence. Mais il se réserve sa décision dans le cas où de telles propositions seraient faites d'un autre côté.

5°. Le Gouvernement de la République, jusqu'à présent, ne s'est pas prononcé d'une manière définitive, s'il est d'accord que, conformément à l'invitation du Sultan, la Conférence se réunisse à Tanger. Le Gouvernement Impérial est d'avis qu'il faut maintenir Tanger comme lieu de la Conférence, parce que les questions à résoudre ne peuvent être bien jugées qu'au Maroc même et que pour leur examen il est indispensable de recourir à des personnes connaissant les lieux.

Le Gouvernement Impérial se plaît à espérer que les considérations précitées seront approuvées par le Gouvernement de la République, et que de cette façon l'accord relatif au programme de la Conférence désiré par les deux Gouvernements soit conclu. Dans ce cas le Gouvernement Impérial est tout disposé à donner de suite les instructions nécessaires à son ministre à Fez pour que, d'accord avec le ministre de France, il donne à S[a] M[ajesté] le Sultan des conseils pour le programme de la Conférence.

À la fin de la lettre en date du 1er de ce mois, V[otre] E[xcellence] se référant à deux lettres privées des 29 et 31 juillet a fait des observations relatives au Ministre Comte de Tattenbach parce que celui-ci, par des stipulations avec le Sultan, aurait procuré des avantages particuliers à des entrepreneurs allemands au Maroc.

Comme j'avais l'honneur de le faire remarquer à V[otre] E[xcellence], le Gouvernement Impérial, de même que le Gouvernement de la République, est fermement décidé à ne pas se procurer d'avantages économiques ou autres avant la réunion de la Conférence par des négociations particulières avec le Sultan. En ce qui concerne les détails mentionnés dans vos lettres j'ai l'honneur de me référer aux éclaircissements que j'ai donnés dans l'entre-temps.

(*b.*)

M. Rouvier to Prince Radolin.

Paris, le 30 Août, 1905.

Par sa lettre en date du 25 de ce mois Votre Altesse veut bien me faire connaître les observations que le Gouvernement impérial croit devoir formuler en réponse aux propositions du Gouvernement de la République concernant le programme de la conférence marocaine.

Ces observations portent sur 3 points :—

I°.—*Organisation de la Police.*

Le Gouvernement impérial propose de supprimer du libellé du paragraphe 1ᵉʳ du titre I le membre de phrase "hors de la région frontière, c'est à dire hors des districts où elle est réglée par un accord franco-marocain."

Le Gouvernement impérial ne méconnaît pas que la police de la frontière doive être réservée à un arrangement franco-marocain, mais il envisage l'hypothèse où "il serait question d'organiser la police marocaine dans les districts frontière d'une manière identique à celle qui est prévue pour les autres parties de l'Empire chérifien," et il se demande "si une telle organisation n'aurait pas besoin d'une sanction internationale par la conférence," notamment en raison de l'affectation éventuelle à cette organisation d'une partie des crédits ouverts au Maghzen et dont la conférence doit préciser les moyens de controler l'emploi.

La police sur la frontière franco-marocaine est réglée par des usages traditionnels, des traités et des conventions successifs qui n'ont cessé d'être et doivent rester l'affaire exclusive des deux pays. Les conditions et rapports de voisinage assignent à cette police un rôle spécial, ils en déterminent et justifient le régime, et ne permettent pas de concevoir que ce régime puisse être établi ou modifié autrement que par le seul accord des deux pays voisins.

Les règles que la conférence posera pour l'organisation de la police hors de la région frontière pourront fournir d'utiles indications aux deux pays, s'imposer même à eux par l'autorité qu'elles emprunteront à leur origine, mais elles ne sauraient les lier ni entraver leur liberté d'action dans un domaine tout différent, où l'intérêt international est suffisamment sauvegardé par les principes de l'indépendance du sultan et de l'intégrité de son territoire, auxquels la France a donné mieux que son adhésion, des gages déjà historiques de son attachement.

Nous avons un trop grand intérêt à ce qu'il ne puisse subsister aucun doute sur la manière dont nous envisageons le droit, essentiel à l'égard de la France, que je viens de définir, pour pouvoir accéder à la suppression demandée par le Gouvernement impérial.

Nous accepterions toutefois de substituer à la rédaction proposée la rédaction suivante : "hors de la région frontière où elle est réglée et continuera à l'être par l'entente directe des deux pays voisins."

Sous réserve des observations précédentes le Gouvernement de la République accepte que le choix des endroits où la police sera organisée ne figure pas dans le programme proposé et consent à la radiation des mots "à Tanger, Larache, Rabat et Casablanca."

2°.—*Surveillance de la contrebande des armes.*

Le Gouvernement de la République accepte que les stipulations de la conférence visent la contrebande des armes par terre et par mer, sous réserve que l'application dans la région frontière du règlement ainsi élaboré restera l'affaire exclusive des deux pays.

En ce qui concerne les réformes financières et commerciales le Gouvernement de la République enregistre avec satisfaction l'adhésion du Gouvernement Impérial à ses propositions formulées sous les titres II et III du projet. Les conditions d'organisation et de fonctionnement de la Banque d'État doivent être laissées aux délibérations de la conférence.

Le Gouvernement de la République accepterait d'ajouter au programme de la conférence l'étude d'un meilleur rendement des impôts et de la création de nouveaux revenus, mais sous réserve de n'en point faire une condition des autres réformes.

Le Gouvernement de la République fait ses réserves au sujet de toute proposition complémentaire qui serait produite d'autre part.

En résumé l'accord complet sur le projet de programme ne tient plus désormais entre les deux Gouvernements qu'au maintien dans le paragraphe relatif à l'organisation de la police, de la réserve concernant les droits spéciaux de la France en ce qui concerne la police de la frontière. La suppression de cette réserve ne répondrait pas au sentiment du Gouvernement impérial, puisqu'il reconnaît d'une façon générale les droits qu'elle garantit, et sur l'étendue desquels il lui est d'ailleurs loisible de conserver son interprétation. Rien ne semble donc plus s'opposer à ce que nous prescrivions sans délai à nos deux réprésentants de procéder en commun aux démarches nécessaires pour faire accepter par le Sultan le projet de programme dont ci-joint le texte. Je suis prêt pour ma part dès que je recevrai avis conforme de Votre Altesse, à adresser télégraphiquement à l'agent de la France des instructions en ce sens.

Le Gouvernement de la République se serait volontiers rallié à la réunion de la Conférence à Tanger, proposée par le gouvernement marocain, s'il n'en avait été détourné par les considérations suivantes :—

L'expérience démontre que c'est précisément à Tanger que les questions, de l'ordre de celles qui vont être débattues, ont le moins de chances d'être résolues en raison, tant du milieu, que des influences locales. Les Puissances n'ont pu aboutir à un accord sur les points réglés par la conférence de 1880 que lorsque la discussion, après deux années d'infructueux efforts, en eut été transportée hors du Maroc, sans que cela ait présenté d'ailleurs le moindre inconvénient pour la bonne information des plénipotentiaires.

Les conditions favorables dans lesquelles se sont développées les travaux de la conférence de 1880, auxquels le gouvernement impérial s'est spécialement référé lorsqu'il a proposé la nouvelle conférence, leur heureuse issue, après des prémisses plutôt contraires, nous engagent à recourir de nouveau à une hospitalité que l'Espagne peut revendiquer presque comme une tradition.

Il est manifeste d'autre part que l'état de trouble et d'insécurité de l'empire chérifien, qui s'est, notamment dans la région de Tanger, singulièrement aggravé, constituerait à lui seul une raison suffisante pour que la conférence ne siégeât pas dans cette ville. Les délibérations des représentants des puissances, suivies de plus près et avec plus de curiosité, de passion même par la population indigène, la présence d'éléments de protection que la prudence pourrait commander, risquent de soulever des explosions de fanatisme qui mettent en danger les représentants des puissances et leurs nationaux et ressortissants non seulement à Tanger mais encore dans toute l'étendue de l'empire chérifien.

En conséquence nous proposons pour lieu de réunion de la conférence, Madrid, ou telle ville espagnole qui semblerait mieux convenir par sa proximité plus grande du Maroc.

P.S.—Les questions de la concession du port de Tanger et de l'emprunt auxquelles se réfèrent les derniers paragraphes de la lettre de Votre Altesse ont fait l'objet de plusieurs communications écrites du Gouvernement français, soit à Votre Altesse, soit a la Chancellerie de Berlin par l'entremise de M. Bihourd.

Je suis donc fondé à attendre du Gouvernement impérial une réponse aux propositions formulées dans ma lettre adressée à Votre Altesse en date du 25 Août et dans la note jointe.

L'adhésion donnée par le Gouvernement impérial au principe de l'adjudication en matière de travaux publics me permet de penser qu'il accueillera ma suggestion en ce qui concerne la concession du port de Tanger que le Comte de Tattenbach a conclu presque au même momment [sic] où le gouvernement impérial, saisi de notre projet de programme, en adoptait ce point particulier.

Quant à l'emprunt négocié par les banques allemandes, l'accord aujourd'hui certain entre nous au sujet du programme permettant de considérer la réunion de la conférence comme très prochaine, les raisons que nous avons exposées pour que le Gouvernement impérial s'emploie à faire abandonner cette opération n'en ont que plus de force et nous exprimons la confiance qu'elles prévaudront auprès de lui.

(c.)

Annexe.

Projet de Programme.

I.—*Organisation de la police hors de la région frontière, où elle est réglée et continuera à l'être par l'entente directe des deux pays voisins.*

1.) Création de corps de troupes Marocains pour la police.
2.) Surveillance et répression de la contrebande des armes.

II.—*Réforme financière.*

Concours financier donné au Maghzen par la création d'une banque d'état avec privilège d'émission, se chargeant des opérations de trésorerie, s'entremettant pour la frappe de la monnaie, dont les bénéfices appartiendront au Maghzen.

La banque d'état procéderait à l'assainissement de la situation monétaire.

Les crédits ouverts au Maghzen seraient employés à l'équipement et à la solde des troupes de police et à certains travaux publics urgents, notamment à l'amélioration des ports et de leur outillage.

III.—*Engagement par le Maghzen de n'aliéner aucun des services publics au profit d'intérêts particuliers.*

Principe de l'adjudication, sans acceptation de nationalité pour les travaux publics.

No. 175.

Mr. Cartwright to the Marquess of Lansdowne.

F.O. Spain 2211.
Tel. (No. 70.) Secret.
Morocco Conference.

San Sebastian, September 4, 1905.
D. 2·30 P.M.
R. 7 P.M.

Your despatch to Mr. Lister, No. 585 of 30th August.([1])

In the temporary absence of M. Cambon, French Chargé d'Affaires informs me most confidentially that on 2nd [*sic* 1st] September French Ambassador and President of the Council exchanged letters offering and accepting proposals enumerated in above-mentioned despatch. President of the Council was evidently greatly pleased at French proposals, as M. Cambon first communicated them on the morning of 2nd September and before the evening the written letters were drafted and signed and exchanged.

Only alterations made in proposals as stated in your Lordship's above-mentioned despatch, are :—

1. Police of Tangier to be under French officers for, I understand, fifteen years, after which question is left vague.
2. Police of Casablanca and Rabat to be French.
3. Contraband by sea. Command of naval squadron to be French during first year.

French Chargé d'Affaires not being authorized to communicate above to me, hopes that your Lordship will keep this information secret until M. Cambon communicates it to your Lordship.

([1]) [*v. supra* p. 131, No. 173.]

No. 176.

M. Paul Cambon to the Marquess of Lansdowne.

F.O. Morocco 435.
Personnelle et Confidentielle.

Cher Lord Lansdowne,

Versailles, le 6 Septembre 1905.

Au cours de nos dernières conversations sur les affaires Marocaines je vous ai tenu au courant de nos pourparlers avec le cabinet de Madrid dans le but d'assurer la garantie des intérêts et des droits des deux pays dans l'Empire Cherifien en nous conformant à l'esprit de l'arrangement intervenue le 3 octobre 1904 entre la France et l'Espagne.

Les pourparlers viennent d'aboutir à une entente qui s'est affirmée le 1ᵉʳ Septembre et par une échange de notes entre M. Montero Rios et notre ambassadeur à Madrid et qui porte sur la police des ports, sur la surveillance et la répression de la contrebande d'armes et sur les intérêts divers des deux pays.

M. Rouvier m'a chargé de vous faire connaître confidentiellement les termes de cet accord mais notre absence mutuelle de Londres ne permettant pas cette communication je vous envoie une analyse des dispositions adoptées.

Pour la police des ports il est entendu que les corps de police qui devront être organisés seront formés de troupes indigènes. Les cadres seront Français dans les ports de Rabat et de Casablanca et Espagnols dans les ports de Tetuan et de Larache. Pour Tanger la police sera confiée à un corps Franco-Espagnol commandé par un Français.

Pour la contrebande de guerre sa surveillance et sa répression seront à la charge de la France dans la sphère de la frontière algérienne et à la charge de l'Espagne dans la sphère de ses possessions africaines.

Sur mer la surveillance sera confiée à une division de navires de guerre des deux puissances qui sera commandée alternativement pendant un an par un officier Français et par un officier Espagnol.

Pour les intérêts économiques financiers et autres, il est convenu que différentes entreprises de caractère commercial et industriel pourront être exécutées par des groupes Franco-Espagnols et que les deux Gouvernements en favoriseront la création sur la base de l'égalité des droits des associés dans la proportion du capital engagé, que les Français et les Espagnols ainsi que leurs établissements et écoles jouiront des mêmes droits et privilèges et que les deux Gouvernements emploieront tous les moyens pacifiques en leur pouvoir pour empêcher l'autorité Marocaine de modifier l'état juridique des personnes et les conditions auxquelles seront soumises les marchandises des deux nations. Il est convenu également que la monnaie d'argent Espagnole continuera à être librement introduite au Maroc et conservera sa valeur libératoire.

Les deux Gouvernements sont d'accord sur la nécessité de créer au Maroc un établissement de crédit, sous la dénomination de Banque d'État ou toute autre, dont la Présidence sera réservée à la France. La participation de l'Espagne devra être supérieure à la part de chacune des autres puissances prises séparément, la France exceptée; le personnel Espagnol de l'administration sera proportionnel à la part du capital souscrit par l'Espagne.

La France et l'Espagne se déclarent fermement décidées à marcher complètement d'accord au cours des délibérations de la conférence projetée et s'engagent à se prêter réciproquement le concours pacifique le plus entier sur toutes les questions d'ordre général concernant le Maroc.

Telles sont en résumé les dispositions prises pour concilier des intérêts dont la divergence ne pourrait qu'être préjudiciable à l'ordre public; c'est un pas de plus dans la voie de la solution de la question Marocaine et il faut espérer que nous ne tarderons pas à réaliser les mesures prévues dans ce nouvel accord.

Croyez, je vous prie, cher Lord Lansdowne, à mes sentiments les plus dévoués,

PAUL CAMBON.

No. 177.

Mr. Cartwright to the Marquess of Lansdowne.

San Sebastian, September 7, 1905.

F.O. Morocco 435.
Tel. (No. 72.) Secret.

D. 12·30 P.M.
R. 7 P.M.

Morocco Conference. My telegram No. 70 of 4th September.

M. Cambon, who has returned here, repeated to me this morning communication made to me by French Chargé d'Affaires, adding that letter addressed to him by

President of the Council, after asserting that Spanish Government will remain faithful to Franco-Spanish engagement of last year, concludes with a declaration that at the Conference Spain will give unqualified support to French and British Plenipotentiaries.

M. Cambon thinks this written engagement very important, as he had some doubts as to Spanish attitude at Conference under pressure from Berlin, especially as the King will visit that place probably before Conference meets. M. Cambon begs your Lordship to keep this matter secret, as he is convinced that German Ambassador, who leaves to-day for Germany, knows nothing about it.

No. 178.

Mr. Cartwright to the Marquess of Lansdowne.

F.O. Morocco 435.
Tel. (No. 73.) Confidential.
Morocco Conference.

San Sebastian, September 7, 1905.
D. 12·34 P.M.
R. 5 P.M.

M. Cambon informs me that, in talking to German Amb[assado]r about undesirability of Tangier as place of meeting of Conference, latter confessed that it would be difficult for Germany to defend selection of that place but she would have to do so for form's sake as long as possible.

German Amb[assado]r last night referring to imprisonment of Algerian subject by Moorish Gov[ernmen]t said to me that Germany would be compelled to support French representations at Fez but this did not seem to give H[is] E[xcellency] much pleasure and he considered incident most unfortunate at this moment.

No. 179.

The Marquess of Lansdowne to M. Cambon.

F.O. Morocco 435.
Dear Monsieur Cambon, *Derreen, September 9, 1905.*

I am extremely obliged to you for your confidential letter of the 6th([1]) containing a most interesting summary of the understanding lately arrived at between the French and Spanish Governments upon the subject of Morocco. Pray express to Monsieur Rouvier my best thanks for his thought of imparting this information to His Majesty's Government.

We have, as you know, from the first been extremely anxious that there should be a complete and friendly understanding between France and Spain in regard to the part to be taken by the two Powers respectively in dealing with the Moorish problem. Such an understanding seems now to have been happily arrived at, and its existence will render it possible for the two countries, each of which has a special interest in Morocco, to work together in complete harmony.

The latest reports which reach us suggest the idea that Germany will in all probability, though with reluctance and after resisting so far as she can, eventually abandon her demand that the Conference should meet at Tangier.

Believe me, &c.
LANSDOWNE.

([1]) [*v. supra* pp. 136–7, No. 176.]

No. 180.

Mr. Wyldbore Smith to the Marquess of Lansdowne.

	Tangier, September 12, 1905.
F.O. Morocco 424.	D. 5·15 P.M.
Tel. Separate.	R. 7·45 P.M.

Intertribal fighting continues, though somewhat further from Tangier.

Note circulated by doyen of Corps Diplomatique suggesting that he should make a representation to Cid Torres in their name as to the want of security here has been approved by all the Representatives here except the German Chargé d'Affaires, who, although acknowledging state of insecurity, advocates each Legation acting separately.

No. 181.

The Marquess of Lansdowne to Sir F. Bertie.

F.O. Morocco 435.
(No. 604.) Confidential.
Sir,   *Foreign Office, September* 14, 1905.

I have received a private letter from M. Cambon, dated Versailles, September 6th, in which he informs me that the negotiations between the French and Spanish Gov[ernmen]ts for the purpose of securing the interests and rights of the two countries in the Empire of Morocco in accordance with the spirit of the Franco-Spanish Arrangement of October 3rd, 1904, have resulted in an Agreement which was confirmed on Sept[ember] 1st, by an exchange of notes between M. Montero Rios and the French Ambassador at Madrid.

M. Cambon gives me confidentially, by desire of M. Rouvier, the following analysis of the provisions of the Agreement :—

It is arranged that the force to be organized for policing the ports shall be composed of native troops; the officers and non-commissioned officers to be French at the ports of Rabat and Casablanca, and Spanish at the ports of Tetuan and Laraiche. At Tangier the policing to be entrusted to a Franco-Spanish corps, commanded by a Frenchman.

The control and suppression of the smuggling of arms to be undertaken by France in the sphere of the Algerian frontier and by Spain in the sphere of the Spanish African possessions.

The prevention of smuggling by sea to be entrusted to a division of warships of the two countries commanded by a French and Spanish officer during alternate years.

With regard to economic, financial and other interests, it is agreed that various enterprises of a commercial and industrial character may be carried out by Franco-Spanish groups and that the two Gov[ernmen]ts shall encourage the creation of such groups on the basis of equal rights for shareholders in proportion to the capital invested; that Frenchmen and Spaniards as well as their establishments and schools shall enjoy the same rights and privileges and that the two Gov[ernmen]ts shall employ all peaceful means in their power to prevent the Moorish authorities from modifying the juridical status of individuals or the conditions to which the goods of the two countries are subjected. It is also agreed that Spanish silver money shall continue to be freely introduced into Morocco and that its character as legal tender shall be preserved.

The two Governments are in accord as to the necessity of instituting in Morocco a banking establishment whether under the title of State Bank or under any other name, the Presidency of the Board of Administration to be assigned to France. The Spanish share in this undertaking is to be superior to that of any other single

Power except France. The number of Spanish members of the board to be proportionate to the amount of Spanish capital.

France and Spain declare their firm intention to proceed in complete Agreement during the deliberations of the proposed Conference and undertake to afford each other the most complete peaceful support on all questions of a general nature concerning Morocco.

M. Cambon observes that this Agreement is a fresh step towards the solution of the Moorish question, and expresses the hope that it will not be long before the measures provided for in the new Agreement are realized.

I have requested M. Cambon to express to M. Rouvier my best thanks for his thought of imparting the above information to H[is] M[ajesty's] G[overnment], adding that we had, from the first, as H[is] E[xcellency] knew, been extremely anxious that there should be a complete and friendly understanding between France and Spain in regard to the part to be taken by the two Powers respectively in dealing with the Moorish problem. Such an understanding seems to have been happily reached and its existence would render it possible for the two countries, each of which had a special interest in Morocco, to work together in complete harmony.

I have informed M. Cambon that the latest reports which had reached us suggested the idea that Germany would in all probability, though with reluctance and after resisting as far as she could, eventually abandon her demand that the Conference should meet at Tangier.

I am, &c.
LANSDOWNE.

No. 182.

Sir F. Bertie to the Marquess of Lansdowne.

F.O. France 3707.
(No. 348.)   Paris, D. September 24, 1905.
My Lord,   R. September 27, 1905.

Yesterday, when I had carried out Your Lordship's instructions of the 22nd in regard to the project for a loan for the Cretan Insurgents, I asked the Minister for Foreign Affairs whether any progress was being made in the negotiations with Germany respecting Morocco.

Monsieur Rouvier said that the German Government did not seem to desire a speedy conclusion. It was difficult to judge what the German Government wanted, for almost every day some fresh point was raised.

I have, &c.
FRANCIS BERTIE.

No. 183.

The Marquess of Lansdowne to Sir F. Bertie.

F.O. Morocco 435.
(No. 634.)
Sir,   Foreign Office, September 27, 1905.

The French Minister called upon me this afternoon and gave me the following confidential information as to the progress of the negotiations between France and Germany as to Morocco :—

The Franco German negotiations relating to Morocco have been delayed for some time owing to some difficulties as to the reservations to be inserted in the programme of the Conference with regard to the region adjoining the frontier. The French Government, taking their stand upon the rights which have belonged to them for fifty years (treaty of 1845),([1]) and upon the special position which has been expressly recognized to them by the Agreement of the 8th of July last,([2]) proposed a wording which should place beyond discussion their exclusive right to regulate questions relating to the policing of this region by direct agreement with the Sultan to the exclusion of international intervention in any circumstance and at any time, with the sole reservation that France shall respect her engagements with regard to the independence of the Sultan and the integrity of his territory. Monsieur Rosen refused to accept a formula so explicit : he considered that it was sufficient to reserve to France the rights which she had acquired by treaty or agreement in the region adjoining the frontier, thus leaving open to international interference all matters not regulated by these agreements.

But after an interview with the Minister for Foreign Affairs, the German delegate agreed on the 15th of September to submit to the approval of the Imperial Government a wording sufficiently satisfactory to France. On the 19th September, after a short absence, Monsieur Rouvier learnt that Monsieur Rosen had altered his mind : losing sight of the fact that it was only a question of drawing up a programme, not of coming to final decisions, he now wanted to make an acceptance of the French proposals concerning the region adjoining the frontier conditional upon France entering into an agreement not to ask at the Conference for a mandate to organize alone and without participation the police in the rest of the Moroccan Empire.

Monsieur Rouvier refused to accept a solution which would have altered the basis of the negotiations. It seemed to him that after having recognized that it was not desirable to prejudge in any way the decisions of the Conference, Germany could not without inconsistency make her definitive acceptance of the programme subject to such a condition. He further pointed out to Monsieur Rosen and Prince Radolin that there was no practical necessity for the undertaking they were asking him to give and that as the decisions of the Conference were to be unanimous Germany had a sufficient guarantee against France being entrusted with an exclusive mandate, since she had the right to oppose it and thus to prevent the realization of the French claim.

The persevering efforts made by Prince Radolin and Monsieur Rosen to induce the Minister for Foreign Affairs to take an engagement in some shape or form on this point have led M. Rouvier to believe that they have misunderstood his real intentions. Faithful to the understanding of the 8th July he has never at any moment desired to anticipate the decisions of the Conference; he has only affirmed that he desired as much as the Imperial Government to avoid any flagrant disagreement between France and Germany at the Conference and to co-operate in the work of bringing about at the said Conference those solutions which will best serve the interests and *amour-propre* of the two Powers.

With this object, he has suggested to the representative of Germany the following wording of the draft programme :—

" The two Governments have agreed to propose to the Sultan the following draft programme drawn up in conformity with the principles adopted in the notes exchanged on the 8th July :—

" 1. Organization by means of an international agreement of the police outside the region adjoining the frontier.

" 2. Supervision and suppression by the same means of the traffic in arms.

" 3. Financial reforms.

" (The rest as in the programme of August 30th.)([3]) "

Prince Radolin and Monsieur Rosen promised on the 23rd September to submit the above draft to Prince Bülow to whom it has also been communicated by the French Ambassador in Berlin.

([1]) [Printed, *B.F.S.P.*, Vol. 34, pp. 1286–91.]
([2]) [*v. supra* pp. 115–6, No. 147.]
([3]) [*v. supra* pp. 135–6, No. 174 (c).]

Monsieur Bihourd was directed to point out to the Chancellor that, with a view to conciliation, the Minister for Foreign Affairs had not reproduced in the new draft the wording at first proposed by him : but the German Government will understand that it is not possible to abandon the reservation itself. Monsieur Bihourd has also been directed to inform Prince Bülow that the French Government are anxious that the programme of the Conference should be promptly settled and communicated to the Sultan and to the Powers signatories of the Madrid Convention. They would not refuse any subsequent discussions which the Imperial Government may desire.

It would appear from the language held in private by Monsieur Rosen in Paris that the demand which he made with regard to a renunciation in advance by France of the exclusive mandate which might be offered to her did not form part of his instructions and that he had taken upon himself the initiative in the matter.

An agreement seems to have been reached on the questions of the place of meeting of the Conference, of the loan and of the port of Tangier.

I asked Monsieur Geoffray whether he knew the place of meeting that had been selected. He said that upon this point also it had been impossible to obtain a distinct reply from the German Government. It was however his impression that Algeciras would probably be accepted.

I am, &c.
LANSDOWNE.

No. 184.

The Marquess of Lansdowne to Sir F. Bertie.

F.O. Morocco 435.
(No. 635.)
Sir, *Foreign Office, September* 30, 1905.

The French Minister called here today and communicated, by instructions of his Gov[ernmen]t the text of the draft programme of the Morocco Conference which was signed on the 28th instant by the French Minister for Foreign Affairs and the German Ambassador in Paris. A copy of this document is enclosed. The text is to be submitted to the Sultan of Morocco by the French and German Ministers at Fez.

M. Geoffray at the same time left a *pro-memoriâ*([1]) in which it was stated that the French and German Gov[ernmen]ts had agreed to ask Spain if she would consent to the selection of Algeciras as the seat of the Conference. He was instructed to inform me that the French Minister at Fez has been authorized to communicate to his English colleague the documents recording the Franco-German Agreement as soon as he has received them. M. S[ain]t René Taillandier has been left at liberty to decide whether he should concert with the German Minister and take joint action with him to explain the programme to the Sultan and Count Tattenbach is to receive similar instructions from his Gov[ernmen]t.

It has been agreed between the French and German Gov[ernmen]ts that the two Missions should leave Fez as soon as possible. M. S[ain]t René Taillandier has been authorized not to delay his departure in the improbable event of the Makhzen raising difficulties in regard to the programme.

M. Geoffray further left at this Office a copy of a note agreed upon and signed by M. Révoil and M. de Rosen, which was communicated to the Press. A copy of that document is also transmitted herewith.

I am, &c.
LANSDOWNE.

([1]) [Not reproduced. The remainder of Lord Lansdowne's despatch is a paraphrase of this document.]

Enclosure 1 in No. 184.

Text of Draft Programme. Signed at Paris, September 28, 1905.

Les deux Gouvernements se sont mis d'accord pour proposer au Sultan le projet de programme suivant élaboré en conformité des principes adoptés dans l'échange de lettres du 8 Juillet :—

I.—1°. L'organisation, par voie d'accord international, de la police hors de la région frontière.

2°. Règlement organisant la surveillance et la répression de la contrebande des armes. Dans la région frontière, l'application de ce règlement restera l'affaire exclusive de la France et du Maroc.

II. *Réforme financière.*—Concours financier donné au maghzen par la création d'une banque d'État avec privilège d'émission, se chargeant des opérations de trésorerie, s'entremettant pour la frappe de la monnaie dont les bénéfices appartiendraient au Maghzen.

La banque d'État procéderait à l'assainissement de la situation monétaire.

Les crédits ouverts au Maghzen seraient employés à l'équipement et à la solde des troupes de police et à certains travaux publics urgents, notamment à l'amélioration des ports et de leur outillage.

III. Étude d'un meilleur rendement des impôts et de la création de nouveaux revenus.

IV. Engagement par le Maghzen de n'aliéner aucun des services publics au profit d'intérêts particuliers.

Principe de l'adjudication, sans acception de nationalité, pour les travaux publics.

Fait à Paris, le 28 Septembre, 1905.

(Signé) ROUVIER.
RADOLIN.

Enclosure 2 in No. 184.

A Note signed by M. Révoil and M. de Rosen, and communicated to the Press.

Les négociations entre la France et l'Allemagne concernant le projet de programme de la conférence sur les affaires marocaines viennent d'aboutir.

L'accord s'est fait sur un programme qui comprend—organisation de la police, règlement concernant la surveillance et la répression de la contrebande des armes, réformes financières consistant principalement dans l'institution d'une banque d'État, étude d'un meilleur rendement des impôts et de la création de nouveaux revenus, enfin fixation de certains principes destinés à sauvegarder la liberté économique.

Quant à la région frontière, par une réserve spéciale insérée au projet de programme il est entendu que les questions de police continuent à y être réglées directement et exclusivement entre la France et le Sultan et restent en dehors du programme de la conférence. Dans la même région, l'application du règlement sur la contrebande des armes restera l'affaire exclusive de la France et du Maroc.

Les deux Gouvernements se sont mis d'accord pour demander à l'Espagne si elle accepterait que la ville d'Algéciras fût choisie comme lieu de réunion de la conférence.

En ce qui concerne la question de l'emprunt et du port, elles ont été réglées de la manière suivante :—

Pressé par sa situation financière, le Maghzen s'était adressé à un intermédiaire étranger résidant au Maroc—qui a eu lui-même recours à un groupe de banques allemandes—pour obtenir une avance de courte durée remboursable sur le prochain emprunt ; le Gouvernement Marocain offrait en gage ses biens immobiliers dans les différentes villes de la côte.

Un accord s'est établi entre le groupe des banques allemandes et le consortium des banques françaises, en vue de participer à cette opération qui gardera son caractère d'avance de courte durée, avec gage spécial, et remboursable sur le prochain emprunt ou par les voies et moyens de la banque d'État dont la création figure au programme de la Conférence. L'opération laisse intacte la question du droit de préférence du consortium français.

En ce qui concerne la construction d'un môle dans le port de Tanger, le Gouvernement Marocain avait, par une lettre adressée à la Légation d'Allemagne en date du 26 Mars, demandé à la maison Borgeaud et Reutemann l'établissement de deux plans entre lesquels il choisirait. Comme à la même époque, une C[ompagn]ie française avait été autorisée à étudier les mêmes travaux, il a été entendu qu'on prendrait un délai pour examiner les titres de cette C[ompagn]ie, et que, à moins que la C[ompagn]ie française ne présente des titres identiques à celui de la C[ompagn]ie allemande, celle-ci exécutera les travaux commandés par le Maghzen.

Le projet de programme et la proposition concernant le lieu de la réunion de la conférence vont être soumis, sans délai, par les deux Gouvernements à l'adhésion du Sultan et à celle des puissances signataires de la Convention de Madrid ou y ayant adhéré.

Dès que les propositions concernant le programme et le lieu de la réunion de la conférence auront été soumises au Sultan, les deux Missions quitteront Fez pour retourner à Tanger.

No. 185.

The Marquess of Lansdowne to Mr. Lowther.

F.O. Morocco 436.   *Foreign Office, October* 1, 1905.
Tel. (No. 55.)   D. 1 P.M.

French Minister has communicated agreement come to with Germany as to Conference. It corresponds with the description given in my Tel[egram] No. 54.([1]) Your French Colleague will communicate text to you. He and German Minister are left discretion as to making joint communication to Sultan respecting programme of Conference. The two Missions are to leave Fez as soon as possible.

You may arrange in consultation with your French colleague for leaving at the earliest convenient date.

([1]) [Missing from volume.]

No. 186.

Mr. Lowther to the Marquess of Lansdowne.

F.O. Morocco 436.
(No. 258.)   *Fez, D. October* 22, 1905.
My Lord,   R. *November* 2, 1905.

I had the honour to inform Your Lordship today by telegram that the Moorish Government had sent a favourable reply to the French Minister on the subject of the Programme for the Conference and had acceded to the suggestion that it should be held at Algeciras.

Monsieur Saint René Taillandier has been good enough to communicate to me a translation of the note he has received from the Moorish Government conveying this decision and I have the honour to inclose it herewith.

I have, &c.
GERARD LOWTHER.

Enclosure in No. 186.

Abdelkrim-ben-Sliman to M. Saint-René Taillandier.

(Traduction.)   *Le 23 Chaaban*, 1323 (22 *Octobre*, 1905).

J'ai reçu votre lettre en date du 16 Octobre de l'année courante, à laquelle était annexée copie du programme renfermant les principes des articles sur lesquels porteront les délibérations à la prochaine Conférence internationale; vous m'avez prié de les porter à la connaissance de S[a] M[ajesté] Chérifienne, conformément aux ordres que vous avez reçus à ce sujet de votre Gouvernement respecté; vous avez exprimé l'espoir de voir S[a] M[ajesté] Chérifienne donner son adhésion à la réunion de la Conférence à Algéciras, puisque le Gouvernement Espagnol honoré a consenti à ce qu'elle fût réunie à l'endroit précité, &c.

J'ai porté votre lettre ainsi que le programme à la connaissance de S[a] M[ajesté] Chérifienne, qui m'a ordonné de vous répondre qu'Elle a consenti à accepter que les délibérations portent sur les articles du programme en question à la prochaine Conférence, s'il plaît à Dieu; ensuite, après délibération entre les délégués du Gouvernement Chérifien et les délégués des Puissances amies sur le détail des articles du Programme, ce qui aura fait l'objet d'un accord entre tous les délégués, après que S[a] M[ajesté] Chérifienne aura été consultée, sera mis en exécution.

S[a] M[ajesté] Chérifienne a donné également son adhésion à la réunion de la Conférence à Algéciras, conformément à votre indication amicale.

ABDÉLKRIM-BEN-SLIMAN.

No. 187.

Mr. Lowther to the Marquess of Lansdowne.

F.O. Morocco 436.
(No. 259.) Confidential.   *Fez*, D. *October* 24, 1905.
My Lord,   R. *November* 4, 1905.

With reference to my despatch No. 258 of the 22nd instant,([1]) the following information has reached me regarding the manner in which the programme agreed upon by the French and German Governments was received by the Sultan and his advisers.

When the text was first communicated to the Makhzen unofficially on the 10th instant, His Shereefian Majesty seems to have been plunged into deep depression and ill-humour for some days until the receipt of the official notes containing the programme addressed to the Minister for Foreign Affairs by the French and German Ministers. His Majesty apparently only then realized that any alteration of the Programme was almost impossible and His Majesty's ill-humour seems to have given place to a more violent attitude, indeed so violent that his Minister for Foreign Affairs was compelled to feign illness for two days in order to avoid approaching His Majesty. The German Minister was interviewed daily by the Moorish Ministers and repeated suggestions were made to His Excellency to bring about some modification in the programme more especially in those articles which are distinctly opposed to the personal interests of those members of the Makhzen who thrive upon the present financial system of the Government—such as the engagement by the Makhzen not to pledge any of the public services for the benefit of private interests and the creation of the State Bank.

Eventually the Minister for Foreign Affairs was instructed to send for the German Minister and make a final appeal to him to use his influence to obtain some modification. Count Tattenbach however told His Excellency very distinctly that his Government would listen to no such proposals and that he could not put them forward, but that His Majesty could rely upon German support at the Conference to obtain some valuable

([1]) [Not reproduced.]

alterations. His Majesty then decided to cause the reply to be sent which I enclosed in my despatch No. 258 of the 22nd instant.

I have no doubt that Monsieur Saint René Taillandier's intimation of his decision to leave Fez on a definite day, when he communicated the programme, must have practically convinced the Sultan that there was but a faint hope of obtaining a modification of the programme

I have, &c.
GERARD LOWTHER.

No. 188.

Count Metternich to the Marquess of Lansdowne.

F.O. Morocco 436.
(Translation.)   *German Embassy*, D. *October* 28, 1905.
My Lord,   R. *October* 30, 1905.

In accordance with my instructions and in pursuance of an Agreement with the French Gov[ernmen]t, I have the honour to tr[an]s[mit] to Y[our] E[xcellency] herewith a copy of the Franco-German Convention executed in Paris on the 28th ult[imo]. It contains the programme of a Conference shortly to be summoned by the Sultan of Morocco for the deliberation of measures calculated to effect an improvement in the present state of the Shereefian Empire.

I have been instructed at the same time to enquire from Y[our] E[xcellency] whether the British Gov[ernmen]t, as one of the Signatory Powers of the Convention signed at Madrid on July 3rd, 1880 with regard to the exercise of the right of protection in Morocco, is prepared, upon rec[eip]t of a formal invitation, to participate in the Conference on the basis of the programme, and whether they concur in the proposal of the French and German Gov[ernmen]ts that the Conference should take place in the Spanish town of Algeciras.

I have, &c.
METTERNICH.

Enclosure in No. 188.

Franco-German Convention, dated September 28, 1905.

Les deux gouvernements se sont mis d'accord pour proposer au sultan le projet de programme suivant élaboré en conformité des principes adoptés dans l'échange de lettres du 8 Juillet :—

1.—(1.) Organisation, par voie d'accord international, de la police hors de la région frontière.

(2.) Règlement organisant la surveillance et la répression de la contrebande des armes. Dans la région frontière, l'application de ce règlement restera l'affaire exclusive de la France et du Maroc.

II. *Réforme financière.*—Concours financier donné au Maghzen par la création d'une banque d'État avec privilège d'émission, se chargeant des opérations de trésorerie, s'entremettant pour la frappe de la monnaie dont les bénéfices appartiendraient au Maghzen.

La banque d'État procéderait à l'assainissement de la situation monétaire.

Les crédits ouverts au Maghzen seraient employés à l'équipement et à la solde des troupes de police et à certains travaux publics urgents, notamment à l'amélioration des ports et de leur outillage.

III. Étude d'un meilleur rendement des impôts et de la création de nouveaux revenus.

IV. Engagement par le Maghzen de n'aliéner aucun des services publics au profit d'intérêts particuliers.

Principe de l'adjudication, sans acception de nationalité, pour les travaux publics.

Fait à Paris, le 28 Septembre, 1905.

(Signé)   RADOLIN.
ROUVIER.

No. 189.

Sir A. Nicolson to the Marquess of Lansdowne.

F.O. Morocco 436.
Tel. (No. 88.)

Madrid, November 14, 1905.
D. 8 P.M.
R. 12 midnight.

Morocco Conference.

French and German Chargé d'Affaires have officially requested Spanish Government to issue invitations to the Conference and to arrange with Sultan as to the date of meeting.

Spanish Government have instructed their Representative at Tangier to ask Sultan to fix a date and have requested that H[is] M[ajesty] should officially notify to them his acceptance of programme and of Algeciras.

I have suggested that it would be well that Spanish Government should also inform Sultan that their action is taken at the request of French and German Governments and that it will hasten matters if a specified date be submitted to H[is] M[ajesty].

No. 190.

Mr. Lowther to the Marquess of Lansdowne.

F.O. Morocco 423.
(No. 287.) Confidential.
My Lord,

Tangier, D. December 4, 1905.
R. *December 11, 1905.*

I had to-day a long conversation with Dr. Rosen, the German Minister, on the general subject of German policy in Morocco and also on the work that the Conference at Algeciras was likely to accomplish.

Dr. Rosen said that the entire German policy here was founded on the fact that, as long as the French contemplated a "Guerre de revanche" Germany would not tolerate that Morocco should be made a recruiting field, for they must be prepared for the contingency that had occurred in 1870, namely that the whole of the African army of the French should be thrown against them in the field. France at present showed little disposition to take up arms but circumstances might change, and the French public with vacillating moods might assume a very different attitude.

Dr. Rosen asked me whether it was a fact that the French Minister had actually signed an agreement with the Sultan on the subject of the reorganization of the army. I pleaded ignorance but it seemed to me clear that the information on this subject which I reported to your Lordship in my despatch No. 190 Confidential of the 20th of July,(¹) had probably also reached him. It seems however doubtful whether the document in the hands of the French Government on this subject is of much real value.

(¹) [v. supra p. 121, No. 156.]

Proceeding, Dr. Rosen said that with the intention before them of not allowing France to use Morocco as a recruiting ground it was clear that the German Government would never agree that France should be given a mandate to police all the coast and on this point no concession was possible. He could not quite see the difficulties of the establishment of an international police. He appreciated the objections to which it might give rise in the mind of the Sultan if a gendarmerie of different nationalities was to undertake the police of different coast towns, for such a scheme would carry with it the idea of eventual spheres of influence, but Dr. Rosen seemed to favour a plan by which the police should be organized and controlled by a central body bearing an international character. I asked his Excellency whether as France had been recognized as privileged to police the Algerian Frontier, this would carry with it the duty of suppressing the Pretender, to which he replied that if the Pretender caused disturbances on the frontier it would come within their duties. Having rejoined that as the Pretender was constantly moving about it would be difficult to say when he was or was not within the district to be policed by the French, Dr. Rosen seemed to think this was a matter for the Conference. I may here remark that Dr. Rosen has been credited with the view that the Conference would be called upon to grant to France the mandate to police the frontier, which point was presumably finally disposed of in Paris. The above view is very likely what gave rise to this statement.

Dr. Rosen added that he had every reason to believe that the French Government had been sending assistance to the Pretender but they had no agents in the district where he had been fighting and no reports had reached the German Government on which they could rely. He quite saw the immense difficulty of establishing an efficient gendarmerie not so much in the towns where it would be workable, but to keep open the trade routes, for no Christian officer in detached block-houses on the road would be allowed to live, and to these block-houses must be assigned Moorish officers or non-commissioned officers who, having received instruction under foreign officers and receiving their pay regularly, might become efficient.

I remarked to his Excellency that I presumed that he and M. Révoil had probably come to some understanding on most of the questions touching Morocco. His Excellency said he could assure me that there was no secret arrangement. though on many points they had come to an understanding, and he had every reason to believe that this understanding would be faithfully adhered to at the Conference. Turning to the question of the suppression of contraband the Minister said that this, like the question of gendarmerie, depended much upon the funds at the disposal of those who undertook this onerous duty. Having pointed out to him that the Legations were in a measure to blame for the general and barely-concealed manner in which this trade was carried on, he asked for an explanation, and I pointed out to him that in numerous cases the penalties which foreign officials were able to apply were trivial, and that as they saw Moorish officials conniving at this nefarious practice it often occurred that they shut their eyes to offences of this nature. If a general regulation were to be drawn up and approved by all the Powers, inflicting very severe penalties, some improvement would no doubt be brought about. At present arms and ammunition were openly introduced through the Custom house and when consignments of smuggled goods were detected they were openly put up to auction.

I presumed that the Conference would not [sic] come to a decision that the Custom Houses should be placed under foreign control and this would to a great extent remedy this and other abuses. This innovation and a reliable gendarmerie with perhaps three or four revenue cutters, if the funds permitted of it, would doubtless go far to put a stop to the present state of affairs. Dr. Rosen agreed to the suggestions I put forward but seemed to have no other ideas, but he added that it was evident that his Government were desirous of checking this traffic as they had recently dismissed a German Consular Agent for his complicity in a smuggling affair and fined him twenty pounds. As I had touched upon the question of the introduction of foreigners to control the Custom Houses, I asked Dr. Rosen how far this would be affected by the last French loan contract which gave the French the right to introduce their employés into the Customs.

for purposes of control, a right of which they had however not availed themselves, as at present they merely receive the sums required for the payment of the interest on the loan. The French Government might put forward a claim for monopoly of control in the Customs with as much right as they did for the policing of the frontier. Dr. Rosen seemed disinclined to discuss this point.

With regard to financial reform it seemed to him that some concessions favourable to France might be made, though he did not indicate the direction of such concessions. It would eminently be most desirable that the Hassani money should be regulated, and he was in favour of the establishment of a bank somewhat on the lines of the Imperial Ottoman Bank or of the Imperial Bank of Persia and one or two officials should be introduced from those countries to enable Morocco to benefit by their experience. With regard to the question of the raising of fresh revenues Dr. Rosen said that the French Government seemed very disinclined to encourage this idea, and had in Paris insisted very much upon the wording " étude d'un meilleur rendement et de la création de nouveaux revenus " which seemed to have left the impression on his mind that they would be averse to an increase of the Customs Duties and the establishment of anything of the nature of Government monopolies.

The other points in the programme as adopted in Paris seemed to the German Minister to present no subject for argument as indeed he was convinced that no serious difficulties would arise at the Conference, and while not being sanguine that reforms of a very radical kind would be likely to be the outcome of its deliberations he yet hoped that something might be done to put an end to the present intolerable condition of affairs when the lives of all respectable members of the Christian community were in daily danger at the hands of the unruly population round the gates of Tangier.

Dr. Rosen said that there never was any question of his being present at the Conference. He had asked Prince Bülow not to consider his name as his want of experience of this country would, he considered, be a serious drawback at the meetings of the Conference. M. de Radowitz and Count Tattenbach had been appointed and although the latter had been somewhat severely handled in the French press he was convinced that he had not been guilty of many of the faults attributed to him. At the same time he was of opinion that Count Tattenbach had not taken the Arrangement of the 8th July with sufficient seriousness and he had in some degree overstepped that Arrangement.

I have sent a copy of this despatch to Sir A. Nicolson.

I have, &c.
GERARD LOWTHER.

No. 191.

Sir E. Gorst to Sir F. Bertie.

F.O. Morocco 436.
Private.
My dear Bertie, *Foreign Office, December 13, 1905.*

Sir E. Grey wishes me to send you the enclosed copy of a letter I have received from Nicolson on the subject of the Moorish Conference. It would be obviously desirable that the programme agreed to by the French and German Governments should be communicated to the other Powers represented at the Conference, as it has been to H[is] M[ajesty's] G[overnment], so as to obviate any proposals for enlarging the scope of the discussion. Such communication ought presumably to be made by the French and German Governments together, or at any rate by one of them. Further, the President of the Conference (presumably the Spanish) ought to rule out of order any discussion outside the lines of the programme.

Sir E. Grey would like you to take an opportunity of mentioning these considerations to M. Rouvier.

I am telling Nicolson what I have written to you.

Yours sincerely,
ELDON GORST.

Enclosure in No. 191.

Sir A. Nicolson to Sir E. Gorst.

F.O. Morocco 436.
Private.
My dear Gorst,

British Embassy, Madrid,
December 10, 1905.

There appears to be a little confusion of mind among one or two of the R[ep]r[esentative]s here as to what is to be discussed at the Conference, as the Austrian Ambassador, who is to be a delegate, assured me today that neither Count Goluchowski nor he had knowledge of the programme. He had seen C[oun]t Goluchowski but a fortnight ago. He further intimated that it was not to be taken for granted that subjects outside of the programme should not be discussed : and he saw no reason why he, for instance, should not raise any questions affecting general interests in Morocco. C[oun]t Welsersheimb may be talking off his own bat; but he has spoken I believe in the same sense to the Foreign Minister and to the Russian Ambassador. I do not wish to attach undue importance to these casual conversations, but I presume we intend to keep strictly within the lines of the programme, and not to take part in discussions which may wander outside of it, especially if reference is made to our arrangement with France.

I should like to have official instructions on this point, which I could keep in my pocket and only use in case of necessity. It would be well to be prepared for surprises.

Yours ever.
A. NICOLSON.

No. 192.

Sir A. Nicolson to Sir Edward Grey.

F.O. Morocco 436.
(No. 230.) Confidential.
Sir,

Madrid, D. December 14, 1905.
R. December 23, 1905.

Monsieur de Villaurrutia, formerly Minister for Foreign Affairs, informed me yesterday that Señor Moret had mentioned to him that he had received a visit from the German Chargé d'Affaires who alluded to some reports which had appeared in the newspapers to the effect that the Spanish Government were contemplating appointing Monsieur de Villaurrutia as Spanish Representative at the Algeciras Conference.

The Chargé d'Affaires added that he was authorized to intimate that, should such an appointment be made, it would not be regarded in a friendly light by his Government.

I am not acquainted with the reply which Señor Moret gave to this notification, but he had communicated the fact to Monsieur de Villaurrutia as a reason for not being in a position to offer him the post.

Monsieur de Villaurrutia would have been an admirable selection. He was Secretary to the Madrid Conference in 1880, has served for some time in Tangier, and was Chief of the Section in the Foreign Office which dealt with Moorish Affairs. Moreover he is an excellent linguist.

The German Ambassador during Monsieur de Villaurrutia's short tenure of office as Minister for Foreign Affairs was always strongly opposed to him, as the

German Government considered that he was on too intimate terms with Monsieur Delcassé. Nevertheless it is to be regretted that the Spanish Government are not allowed a free hand in the choice of their Representative.

I have the honour, &c.

A. NICOLSON.

MINUTE BY KING EDWARD.

A case of bullying as usual!

E.R.

No. 193.

Sir Edward Grey to Sir A. Nicolson.

F.O. Morocco 436.

(No. 163.)

Sir, *Foreign Office, December 14, 1905.*

I have to inform Your Excellency that His Majesty The King has been pleased to approve your appointment as the Representative of His Majesty's Government at the Conference on the affairs of Morocco which is shortly to be held at Algeciras.

In accordance with your recommendation your staff will consist of Messrs. Vaughan and St. Aubyn of His Majesty's Embassy at Madrid, and of Mr. Irwin of His Majesty's Legation at Tangier.

Your Excellency is fully conversant with the various matters which will be discussed by the Conference. The programme drawn up by the French and German Governments has, as you are aware, been communicated to and accepted by His Majesty's Government, and your intimate knowledge of Moorish affairs renders it unnecessary for me to give you any detailed instructions for your guidance.

Generally speaking however Your Excellency will, in accordance with Articles II and IX of the Anglo-French Declaration of April 8th, 1904 respecting Egypt and Morocco, cordially support the proposals which your French colleague may bring forward with a view to the improvement of the existing state of affairs, and you should encourage your Spanish colleague to adopt a similar attitude. You should at the same time take care that no measure or arrangement is sanctioned which might impair the rights and privileges secured to Great Britain in that Declaration, more especially in Articles II, IV, V, and VII.

Should any question of this nature appear to you to be likely to arise, you should refer home for instructions.

I am, &c.

EDWARD GREY.

No. 194.

Sir F. Bertie to Sir Edward Grey.

F.O. France 3707.

(No. 461.) *Paris, D. December 15, 1905.*

Sir, *R. December 16, 1905.*

I have the honour to transmit herewith copies of the French Yellow Book just published, respecting the Affairs of Morocco (1901–1905), as well as a Memorandum drawn up by Mr. O'Beirne illustrating certain points connected with the part played by German diplomacy in this question.

I have, &c.

FRANCIS BERTIE.

Enclosure in No. 194.

Memorandum on Yellow Book relative to Morocco (1901–1905).

French Relations with Morocco prior to Anglo-French Agreement.

The correspondence dates from March 1901. Down to March 1904, the month preceding the signature of the Anglo-French Agreement, it relates chiefly to difficulties arising on the Morocco–Algiers frontier. The French Government had frequent cause to complain of aggressions by tribes on the Moorish side of the frontier. In July, 1901, a Protocol was signed in Paris by M. Delcassé and the Moorish Envoy, providing for measures to be taken mutually by the two Governments for policing the border region. After the conclusion of this arrangement the aggressions of Moorish tribesmen continued as before. In 1902 and 1903 there were frequent cases of attacks on French Convoys and Detachments, aggressions against Algerian tribes and murders of French citizens. In August 1903, at the request of the Moorish Authorities, French Military Instructors were furnished to the Moorish garrison at Oujda, in North-Eastern Morocco, near the Algerian frontier. At this time military operations were in progress against the Moorish Pretender, and the French Government gave valuable assistance to the Moorish Government by allowing the passage of arms and of Moorish troops through Algerian territory, and by furnishing artillery and gunners for use at Oujda.

A question not connected with the frontier in which the French Government intervened was the negotiation of a loan of 7,500,000 francs to the Moorish Government by a French Syndicate in 1903. The French Minister for Foreign Affairs used his influence with the French Banks concerned in order to induce them to take up the loan.

Left margin references:
P. 15.
Pp. 31, 61, 64, 71, 72, &c.
M. Taillandier. August 26. P. 104.
Pp. 101, 105.
M. Delcassé to M. Taillandier, January 5, 1903. P. 53.

French Policy in Morocco subsequent to Anglo-French Agreement.

On May 19th, 1904, shortly after the signature of the Anglo-French Agreement, the French Minister at Tangier, M. Taillandier, wrote to the Moorish Minister for Foreign Affairs explaining that it was to the interest of France to preserve the integrity of Morocco and the Sultan's Sovereignty, and dwelling on the need of internal reforms.

On June 16th a French Syndicate concluded an Agreement for a fresh loan of 62,000,000 francs to the Moorish Government, secured on the revenues of all the Moorish ports and intended to pay off all previous loans. Agents representing the Creditors were installed in the different ports to superintend the collection of the Customs Duties, with powers of control over the Moorish officials.

On July 29th the Moorish Government accepted the offer made by the French Minister to lend French officers to organise the military forces at Tangier.

On December 12th M. Taillandier suggested to M. Delcassé the urgency of pressing upon the Moorish Government the necessity of—

(1) establishing order on the frontier;
(2) improving the administration of the seaports;
(3) establishing order in the towns and their neighbourhood, by the organisation of a police force;
(4) creating a Moorish State Bank.

Left margin references:
P. 133.
P. 140.
M. Taillandier, July 29, 1904. P. 160.
P. 177.

On December 15th M. Delcassé sent M. Taillandier instructions in contemplation of his approaching mission to Fez. Among the measures to be recommended to the Moorish Government were the appointment of a certain number of French Officers and men to take service under the Moorish Government in the different Moorish garrisons; the creation of a new Moorish police force, of which the nucleus was to be furnished by the Algerian native police, and which was to be officered by Frenchmen. M. Taillandier was to press for the institution of a State Bank (under the auspices apparently of the French Syndicates which participated in the most recent loan); the

Left margin reference:
P. 178

construction of a carriage road, and the establishment of a telegraph line between Marnia and Oujda, as a preliminary to further works of the same kind.

M. Taillandier commenced negotiations at Fez in February, 1905. In despatches dated March 10th and 18th he gives an account of interviews with the Sultan, at which he pressed for the adoption of the different reforms desired by France. He informed the Sultan that the contiguity of the French possessions placed France in an unique position towards Morocco, so much so that the "Powers particularly interested, after France," had recognised her exclusive right to inspire the necessary reforms. *Pp. 200, 201.*

The Moorish Government having proposed in April 1905 that certain stipulations made by them with regard to the French police reform should be guaranteed by the Powers, M. Taillandier was instructed by M. Delcassé to state that there could be no question of any Power acting as intermediary between the French and the Moorish Governments. *M. Delcassé to M. Taillandier. May 3, 1905. P. 217.*

On April 11th M. Taillandier reported that the Sultan had agreed to the creation of bodies of troops reorganised by French methods at Tangier, Rabat, and another port. Meanwhile the German Emperor had visited Tangier, and the arrival of the German Mission at Fez brought about a complete change in the attitude of the Makhzen. *P. 208.*

On May 27th M. Taillandier received a letter from the Moorish Minister of Foreign Affairs intimating that all reforms would be adjourned until the meeting of an International Conference. *M. Taillandier to M. Delcassé, May 27, 1905 P. 223.*

German Contentions with regard to French Policy in Morocco.

It will be noticed that the correspondence summarised above gives no ground for the German statement (*vide* M. Bihourd's despatch of June 25th, 1905, p. 244) that France had proposed a treaty to the Moorish Government which would have destroyed the Sultan's independence. The French Minister at Tangier, so far as can be gathered from the correspondence, confined himself to impressing on the Moorish Government the special interest which France, as a neighbour, took in the establishment of order in Morocco, and strongly urging the necessary reforms. As regards the other German contention, that France intended to take the affairs of Morocco into her own hands (*vide* M. Rouvier's Circular despatch of June 8th, 1905, page 230), the grounds afforded for it by the correspondence are, substantially, that by undertaking the reform of police and finances in Morocco, France would have a tendency to acquire paramount influence in that country. It was also suggested by the German Ambassador in Paris that the Moorish Pretender had received support from the French Authorities in Algeria (*vide* M. Rouvier's despatch to M. Jonnart, June 21st, 1905, page 239). This was entirely denied by M. Jonnart, and the correspondence shows that the French Government, on the contrary, gave assistance in various ways to the Moorish Government.

Early Attitude of Germany on the Morocco Question.

The earliest reference to Germany in the correspondence occurs in a despatch from M. Delcassé of June 23rd, 1901, reporting a conversation with the German Ambassador in Paris. Prince Radolin referred to newspaper suggestions of a French Protectorate, and M. Delcassé said that if by a Protectorate was meant a special position on the part of France, it was evident that such a position existed. Prince Radolin acquiesced. *P. 18.*

There is no further record of communications with the German Government on the subject of Morocco until March 23rd, 1904, a few days before the conclusion of the Anglo-French agreement, when M. Delcassé had another conversation with the German Ambassador. Prince Radolin having asked whether an agreement was about to be signed between France and England M. Delcassé replied that negociations were in progress, and said that as regarded Morocco France wished to maintain the political and territorial *status quo*, but she had suffered serious detriment from the condition of disorder prevailing in Morocco, and in her own interest she must lend Morocco her aid *M. Delcassé to M. Bihourd, March 27, 1904. P. 142.*

towards the establishment of law and order. In any case the freedom of commerce would be rigorously respected.

M. Delcassé authorised the French Ambassador in Berlin to use similar language, but M. Bihourd reported on April 17th, 1904, that for want of opportunity he had not yet done so.

M. Bihourd to M. Delcassé, April 17, 1904. P. 126.

On April 12th, Prince Bülow speaking in the Reichstag on the subject of the Anglo-French Agreement, said that as regarded Morocco German interests were chiefly commercial, and the German Government had no ground for fearing that they could be disregarded by any Power.

P. 129.

On April 18th, M. Delcassé sent the French Ambassador at Berlin instructions as to the declarations he should make to the German Government on the subject of the

P. 131.

Anglo-French Agreement. M. Bihourd telegraphed on April 27th that he had seen Baron Richthofen, and had stated to him that he appreciated Prince Bülow's recognition in the Reichstag that the Agreement did not threaten German interests.

M. Bihourd to M. Delcassé, October 7, 1904. P. 165.

On October 7th, five months later, M. Bihourd, by instruction of M. Delcassé, communicated to the German Government the Franco-Spanish declaration regarding Morocco of October 6th [sic], and stated in reply to a question asked by Baron Richthofen as to the effect of this arrangement on German commercial interests, that these were fully guaranteed by the Anglo-French Agreement.

Change in Germany's Attitude.

M. de Chérisey to M. Delcassé, February 11, 1905. P. 196.

A complete change in Germany's attitude became apparent in the Spring of 1905. The French Chargé d'Affaires at Tangier reported on February 11th that the German Chargé d'Affaires had informed him that his Government had no knowledge of recent international arrangements regarding Morocco, and did not consider itself bound by them. M. Delcassé thereupon instructed the French Ambassador at Berlin to remind Prince Bülow of the different communications made to the German Government on the

M. Bihourd to M. Delcassé, February 15, 1905. P. 197.

subject. M. Bihourd made this communication to M. de Mühlberg, the German Under-Secretary of State, on February 15th. M. de Mühlberg practically endorsed the German Chargé d'Affaires' statement to the effect that the German Government did not consider itself bound by the Anglo-French Agreement.

P. 202.

On March 22nd M. Bihourd reported that he had heard nothing further from the German Government with regard to his conversation with M. de Mühlberg, and added that the Imperial Government was clearly unwilling to enter into any exchange of views with the French Government on the Morocco question.

M. Delcassé to M. Bihourd, April 14, 1905. P. 211.

On April 14th M. Delcassé had a conversation with Prince Radolin in the course of which he reminded the Prince of the communications made to him and the German Government with regard to the Morocco arrangements and expressed his perfect readiness to dispel the misunderstanding which he thought had arisen between the two Governments. Prince Radolin maintained the greatest reserve.

M. Bihourd to M. Delcassé, April 25, 1905. P. 214.

On April 25th M. Bihourd offered, by M. Delcassé's instructions, to furnish Prince Bülow with the text of M. Delcassé's conversation with Prince Radolin of March 23rd. Prince Bülow declined, saying that he had already received a report of the conversation.

M. Rouvier (Circular despatch), June 8, 1905. P. 230.

On June 8th M. Rouvier (who had meanwhile succeeded M. Delcassé as Minister of Foreign Affairs) transmitted to the French Ambassador at Berlin the text of the first portion of a note left with him by the Secretary of the German Embassy in Paris, arguing in favour of a meeting of a Conference of the Powers. The second portion of this note, which was read by the Secretary of the German Embassy (a copy not being left), referred to the supposed intention of France to take into her hands the management of the internal and foreign affairs of Morocco. M. Rouvier denied that there was any such intention.

M. Rouvier to M. Bihourd, June 11, 1905. P. 232.

On June 10th M. Rouvier had a conversation with Prince Radolin, who pressed for a meeting of a Conference, and said, "If the Conference does not take place, then you have the status quo, and you must know that we are behind Morocco."

On June 16th a further note was presented by the German Ambassador with arguments in favour of a Conference. It stated that the reforms necessary in Morocco should be executed in pursuance of a mandate given by the Powers, and intimated that such mandate should be given to France as far as concerned the frontier regions, but that as regards the regions distant from the frontier, the reorganisation of the army and police should be carried out by different Powers in the different districts. The Morocco State Bank should be founded jointly by the Powers. P. 234.

M. Rouvier, on June 21st, handed a note to the German Ambassador expressing the objections of the French Government to the proposed Conference, and stating its preference for a direct accord with Germany. P. 235.

On June 23rd M. Bihourd had a conversation with Prince Bülow, at which the Chancellor used alarming language as to the results of French hesitation in accepting the proposal for a Conference. The Prince also stated that the Morocco question could not be a cause of war between the two countries, such a conflict could result only from a more general cause. On the other hand he said that the German Government was ready to " reserve the future " for France, and he intimated that if France would agree to the Conference the German Government would adopt an attitude satisfactory to her in the subsequent negotiations. M. Bülow (¹) to M. Rouvier, June 23, 1905. P. 240.

On June 24th a further note was handed by the German Ambassador to M. Rouvier pressing for the Conference. P. 242.

On June 25th Prince Bülow in a conversation with M. Bihourd said that in view of the declaration of the German Emperor, the independence of the Sultan must be proclaimed, and an organisation of the necessary reforms must be attempted by the Powers; but if, as was very possible, the attempt failed, then France might assume the rôle to which she aspired. In the course of this conversation Prince Bülow referred to a supposed treaty proposed by M. Taillandier to the Sultan, which, he said, would have the effect of destroying the independence of Morocco. M. Bihourd to M. Rouvier, June 25, 1905. P. 244.

Assent of France to the Conference.

Early in July, France agreed to the principle of the International Conference. Letters were exchanged on July 8th between M. Rouvier and Prince Radolin, providing for the meeting of the Conference and laying down the following principles as its basis :— P. 250.

(1.) Sovereign Independence of the Sultan.
(2.) Integrity of his Empire.
(3.) Liberty of Commerce.
(4.) Desirability of police and financial reforms, of which the introduction should be regulated " for a short time " by international agreement.
(5.) Recognition of the position in which France was placed as a contiguous Power, and of her special interest in the establishment of order.

On July 9th M. Rouvier informed M. Bihourd that Prince Radolin concurred in his proposed statement to the French Parliament that the Anglo-French Agreement was in no wise affected by the arrangement now come to between the French and German Governments. M. Rouvier added that he had more than once informed Prince Radolin that France would ask the Conference to give her a mandate for the execution of military reforms and that Prince Radolin has raised no objection. M. Rouvier to M. Bihourd, July 9, 1905. P. 249.

Policy pursued by Germany in Morocco.

Some indication respecting the policy pursued by Germany in Morocco may be gathered from the above correspondence. While the German note of June 16th, suggesting organisation of reforms in the different districts by different Powers, might seem to imply a desire on Germany's part to obtain a sphere of influence, Prince

(¹) [This is an error. The document is addressed to M. Rouvier by M. Bihourd.]

Bülow's conversations with the French Ambassador appear to show that the German Government did not attach great importance to the Morocco question itself. Prince Bülow intimated very clearly that, although the German Government was bound, in view of the Emperor's declarations, to insist upon a Conference, on the other hand if the French Government once assented to a Conference, they would find the German Government ready to make very large concessions to their wishes. He made it plain that the Imperial Government was ready to "reserve the future" in Morocco for France, and he also stated that the Morocco question could not be a cause of war between the two countries, though he suggested that there was a more general cause which might lead to conflict (? the desire to isolate Germany). Unless these different assurances were entirely misleading, and intended merely to persuade France to go into a Conference, it would seem that the Chancellor at this time contemplated without any great concern the possibility of France eventually assuming a predominant position in Morocco.

Germany's Complaint that she was not duly informed of Anglo-French Agreement.

As regards Germany's complaint that she had not been notified of the Anglo-French Agreement, the correspondence shows that the omission was mainly one of form, and that M. Delcassé displayed the greatest readiness to communicate with the German Government, as soon as he realized that they considered themselves not to have been duly informed. It is important to note that M. Delcassé, after his conversation of the March 23 1904 with Prince Radolin regarding the impending Anglo-French Agreement, authorised M. Bihourd to hold similar language to the German Government; and although M. Bihourd from lack of opportunity did not act on that authorisation, he did have a conversation with Baron Richthofen on April 27, in which reference was made to the Agreement.

Negotiations subsequent to France's Assent to the Conference.

Programme of the Conference.

P. 253.

On July 20th 1905, M. Rouvier handed a note to the German Ambassador stating that in the opinion of the French Government the Programme of the Conference should cover—

(1.) The organisation of the police outside the frontier region, in which region it was governed by arrangements come to between France and Morocco.

P. 256.

(2.) Financial Reform : By a later note of August 1st M. Rouvier explained in some detail the views of the French Government as to the accomplishment of these and other reforms (including reform in the methods of allotting contracts for public works).

P. 283.

In a note of August 26th the German Ambassador questioned the French claim to reorganise the police in the frontier region.

P. 307.

M. Rouvier to M. Bihourd, September 25, 1905. Pp. 305, 306.

The definitive text of the Programme was ultimately settled during Dr. Rosen's visit to Paris in September. At that time M. Rouvier made a statement to M. Rosen to the effect that, beyond the stipulations of a note (to be signed on behalf of the two Governments) embodying the terms of the Programme, France was bound by no engagements whatever in going into the Conference. This declaration was afterwards handed to Dr. Rosen in writing. The note in question was signed on Sept[ember] 28th, 1905.

P. 307.

German Contract for the Construction of a Pier at Tangier.

M. Taillandier, July 12, 1905. P. 253.

The French Government obtained information in July 1905, that in consequence of strong pressure used by Count Tattenbach the Moorish Government was about to grant a concession to a German firm, for the construction of a pier and for other works in the port of Tangier.

The French Government contended that Count Tattenbach's action was contrary to the spirit of the Agreement between the two countries of July 8th, by which it was intended to refer all questions of rival national interests to the Conference; also that a French firm had prior rights to the concession. Earnest and repeated representations which were made by the French Government met with a very unsatisfactory reception from the German Government. The latter maintained that Count Tattenbach had not negociated for any concessions to German firms, but that the firm in question had obtained certain promises from the Moorish Government prior to the Count's arrival in Fez. It is plain, however, from the correspondence that pressure was used by Count Tattenbach subsequently to July 8th, in order to bring the matter to a final conclusion. The two Governments ultimately agreed to examine the rival claims of the German and French firms concerned. It was found that the German firm had received a letter, dated March 15th, 1905, from the Moorish Government, which contained an implied promise to entrust them with the construction of the proposed pier. On the other hand the French firm could only show that they had been invited by the Moorish Authorities to make surveys and submit plans for the proposed work.

M. Rouvier's note, July 20, 1905. P. 253.
M. Rouvier to Prince Radolin, July 29, 1905. P. 254.
M. Rouvier to Prince Radolin, July 31, 1905. P. 255, &c.
Prince Radolin to M. Rouvier, August 21, 1905. P. 274.
M. Bihourd to M. Rouvier, August 29, 1905. P. 288.
M. Taillandier (already quoted), July 12, 1905. P. 253.
M. de St. Aulaire to M. Rouvier, September 7, 1905. P. 304.
M. de St. Aulaire, October 3, 1905. P. 310.

M. Rouvier accordingly signified to the German Government that the French Government had no objection to the German firm commencing work, but that they made the fullest reserves with regard to the rights of the French Company against the Moorish Government.

M. Rouvier to M. Bihourd, November 24, 1905. P. 319.

Proposed German Loan to the Sultan.

In August, 1905, it came to the knowledge of the French Government that the German Minister in Morocco was negotiating with a view to a fresh loan to be made by a German firm to the Sultan, certain Imperial domains near Tangier and elsewhere being pledged as security. The French Government made repeated protests against this transaction, using practically the same arguments as in the case of the concessions for works in the harbour of Tangier. They contended that it was contrary to the spirit of the arrangement of July 8th, and they pointed out that the French Syndicate which had made the last loan to the Moorish Government had obtained the promise of preferential rights in regard to any future loans. The German Government did not deny that Count Tattenbach had lent his support to the scheme, but they maintained that since the proposed loan did not involve any consideration in the nature of a concession to the German firm, the French Government could not raise any objection to it.

M. Taillandier to M. Rouvier, August 2, 1905. P. 261.
M. Rouvier to M. Bihourd, August 7, 1905. P. 263.
M. Bihourd to M. Rouvier, August 8, 1905. P. 264.
Ditto, August 14, 1905. P. 268.
M. Rouvier to M. Bihourd, August 17, 1905. P. 270.
Ditto, August 21, 1905. P. 273.

The difficulty was eventually settled by the French banks interested in the previous loan being permitted to participate in the proposed transaction; the question of their preferential rights being reserved.

P. 307.

No reference has been made in the above summary to the case of the arrest of the Algerian French citizen named Bouzian El Miliani, which did not give rise to any controversy with the German Government.

HUGH O'BEIRNE.

Dec[ember] 17 [15 ?], 1905.

P.S.—Reference has inadvertently been omitted to an allegation of the German press that M. Taillandier, during his negotiations at Fez, led the Sultan to believe that he had received a mandate from the European Powers. M. Taillandier gave this report an emphatic denial. It will be remembered (see above) that he reported having informed the Sultan that the " Powers particularly interested after France," had

M. Taillandier to M. Delcassé, April 9, 1905. P. 207.

recognised the exclusive right of France to inspire the necessary reforms. It is very likely that this statement was misinterpreted by the Sultan, and taken to imply a mandate from all the Powers.

H. O'B.

No. 195.

Sir F. Bertie to Sir Edward Grey.

F.O. Morocco 436.

(No. 465.) Confidential.   *Paris, D. December 15, 1905.*

Sir,   R. *December 16, 1905.*

I called at the Foreign Office yesterday with the view of carrying out the instructions which I had received from you in Sir Eldon's Gorst's letter of the 13th instant.(¹)

I took with me, in case the President of the Council might be absent, a Memorandum to be communicated to His Excellency, of which I have the honour to transmit to you herewith a copy.

Monsieur Rouvier was at the Chamber and I saw Monsieur Louis, Directeur Politique at the Ministry for Foreign Affairs. I explained to him the object of my visit and I gave the Memorandum to him for the information of the Minister.

Monsieur Louis told me that the information which had reached you from His Majesty's Ambassador at Madrid had also been received at the Quai d'Orsay from the French Ambassador at the Spanish Capital. There was evidently, Monsieur Louis said, a misunderstanding somewhere, for on the 28th of September Monsieur Rouvier had instructed the French Chargé d'Affaires at Vienna to communicate to the Austro-Hungarian Minister for Foreign Affairs the arrangement come to between the French and German Governments, and two days later (viz., September 30) the Chargé d'Affaires reported that he had made the communication and that the Minister for Foreign Affairs had thanked him for it. A like communication had been made to all the Governments to be represented at the Morocco Conference, and by none of them had any exception been taken to the terms of the Franco-German Agreement.

It seemed probable that the Austro-Hungarian Ambassador misunderstood something said to him by Count Goluchowski or that he had not been kept fully informed by the Vienna Foreign Office of the Morocco negotiations.

In consequence of the information from Madrid Monsieur Rouvier telegraphed on the 13th instant to the French Embassy at Vienna directing that the Austro-Hungarian Government should be reminded of the communication made to them at the end of September, and be requested to give instructions to their Delegates at the Conference that the discussions should be confined within the limits of the Programme settled between the French and German Governments.

Monsieur Louis said that he had no doubt that your views as stated in the Memorandum which I had given to him for communication to Monsieur Rouvier, would be much appreciated and fully shared by His Excellency.

Monsieur Louis added that the attitude of the Austro-Hungarian Ambassador at Madrid might possibly be accounted for by the following circumstances. Just before the signature of the Franco-German Agreement of the 28th of September, Monsieur Rouvier had formally stated to Doctor Rosen that outside of the agreement to be signed the French Government took no engagement whatever. The German Government had replied that though bound by their Agreement, they reserved to themselves the faculty of supporting in the Conference any proposals made by another Government which they might consider good. The language of the Austrian Representative at Madrid might possibly be taken as an indication that proposals outside the Franco-German Programme might be put forward by some Government at the instigation of the German Government.

(¹) [*v. supra* pp. 149–50, No. 191.]

You will find in the Yellow Book just published, at page 305, No. 348, the text of the Declaration made by Monsieur Rouvier to Doctor Rosen, referred to by Monsieur Louis. It was also made to the German Ambassador, and it is recorded in a despatch dated September 25 from Monsieur Rouvier to the French Ambassador at Berlin with an instruction to him to hold the same language to Prince de Bülow.

The despatch says :—

"Je crois utile de vous rendre compte d'un entretien que j'ai eu aujourd'hui avec le Docteur Rosen.

"Après lui avoir demandé s'il avait la réponse de son Gouvernement au sujet de la rédaction proposée pour le projet de programme, je lui ai dit :

"'En dehors de la formule qui sera signée par les deux Gouvernements, j'entends n'avoir d'engagement sur aucun point.

"'Je ne puis que renouveler mon affirmation que j'ai, au même degré que le Gouvernement impérial, le désir d'éviter tout désaccord flagrant entre nous à la Conférence et de concourir à y faire prévaloir les solutions qui ménagent le mieux les intérêts et les amours-propres de manière qu'il n'y ait *ni vainqueur ni vaincu*, suivant l'expression même du Prince de Radolin.

"'La garantie pour l'Allemagne réside dans ce fait que, les décisions de la Conférence devant être prises à l'unanimité, il suffirait de son opposition pour que le mandat général ne nous soit pas confié.

"'J'ai chargé le Représentant de la République à Berlin de porter ces explications à la connaissance du Prince de Bülow.'

"Après cet entretien, j'ai fait venir le Prince de Radolin et je lui ai répété textuellement ce que j'avais dit au Docteur Rosen.

"Quand vous verrez le Prince de Bülow, je vous prie de lui tenir le même langage."

A despatch of the next day's date from Monsieur Rouvier to the Ambassador at Berlin states that he had given to Docteur Rosen the declarations in writing, "afin d'éviter toute équivoque et de ne laisser subsister aucun doute sur mon intention de ne prendre par avance aucun engagement à l'égard de l'œuvre de la Conférence."

There is no record in the Yellow Book of the Counter-Declaration made by the German Government. I will endeavour to obtain the text of it at the Quai d'Orsay.

I have, &c.
FRANCIS BERTIE.

Enclosure in No. 195.

Memorandum.

L'Ambassadeur d'Autriche-Hongrie à Madrid, au cours d'une conversation avec l'Ambassadeur d'Angleterre, a déclaré que ni lui ni le Conte Goluchowski n'avait connaissance du programme élaboré pour la Conférence du Maroc ; et a exprimé l'avis, qu'il n'y aurait pas d'objection à ce que la discussion portât sur des sujets non compris dans ce programme tels que des sujets d'intérêt général au Maroc. L'Ambassadeur d'Autriche-Hongrie aurait exprimé les mêmes opinions au Ministre des Affaires Étrangères Espagnol, ainsi qu'à l'Ambassadeur de Russie à Madrid.

Sir Edward Grey est en conséquence d'avis qu'il y aurait intérêt à ce que le programme de la Conférence fût communiqué à toute les Puissances qui y prendront part ; et que le Président de la Conférence qui, comme on est en droit de le présumer, sera le Plénipotentiaire espagnol, eût comme instruction d'écarter de la discussion toute question non comprise dans le programme arrêté entre les Gouvernements français et allemand.

Paris, le 14 Décembre, 1905.

No. 196.

Sir Edward Grey to Sir A. Nicolson.

F.O. Morocco 436.   *Foreign Office, December* 18, 1905.
Tel. (No. 98.)   D. 3·10 P.M.
(Morocco Conference.)
Your telegram No. 102 (of the 17th instant). Last paragraph.(¹)
I concur. Act in concert with French Colleague.

(¹) [The last paragraph of this telegram asked for permission to defer communicating British consent to change of locality to Madrid, over which there had been some misconception, until France and Germany had intimated their views.]

No. 197.

Sir Edward Grey to Sir F. Bertie.

F.O. Morocco 436.
(No. 794.) Very Confidential.
Sir,   *Foreign Office, December* 20. 1905.
The French Ambassador told me today that he had heard that, when the King of Spain was in Berlin, the German Emperor had suggested to him that in the event of a conflict between France and Germany, Spain should, without crossing the frontier, assume an attitude benevolent to Germany by mobilising part of her army towards the Pyrenæan frontier. I said that we had not heard anything of this. His Excellency said that he did not attach too much importance to a rumour of this kind, but that it would be very inconvenient if, in the proceedings of the Conference, Spain was not "bien sûrement avec nous." I replied that Germany was very active at the present time, and that as regards public opinion in London and Berlin there had been some friendly expressions on both sides. I thought it right that, whenever there was a friendly expression on the part of Germany, it should be replied to in sympathetic terms by us; otherwise some colour would be given to the suspicion that the Anglo-French "entente" was directed against Germany, which was not true, but as regards the Conference we had instructed Sir Arthur Nicolson to give the French delegates the fullest support, under the terms of Article IX of the Anglo-French Declaration, and I added, "nous serons bien sûrement avec vous."

I am, &c.
EDWARD GREY.

No. 198.

Sir Edward Grey to Mr. Whitehead.

F.O. Morocco 436.
(No. 330.)
Sir,   *Foreign Office, December* 20, 1905.
The German Ambassador, who had not been able to attend the official reception last week, paid me a visit yesterday. Our conversation was quite informal, as Count Metternich said that he had not had any communication from his Government on the subject of Morocco since the beginning of October, at which time he had been in Berlin and was in that way acquainted with what the views of the Government were.
I said that I had been very glad to notice recently that there had been signs, both in Berlin and in London, that some sections at any rate of public opinion in both places were exhibiting a more friendly feeling towards each other, and that, amongst other things, Count Metternich had himself made a very agreeable speech in London.
Count Metternich said that there had been a strong expression of feeling in Germany during the summer against England, due to the impression that, during this

year, the English Government had been pressing the French further than the French themselves wished to go in opposition to German interests; that they had, in fact, been more French than the French themselves. This, he said, accounted for the feeling which had been displayed in Germany.

I said that there had also been a very unfavourable impression produced here owing to the feeling that Germany, who had taken but little interest in the Morocco Agreement when it was first published, had, as it appeared to us, unexpectedly caused a great deal of trouble with regard to it this year. It had seemed to people here that the object of this might be to disturb the Anglo-French *entente*, and, as the friendship with France was very agreeable to people in England, they naturally resented anything which appeared to them to be an attempt to disturb it. Count Metternich said that we had a perfect right to dispose of our own interests in Morocco and assign them to others if we pleased, but that we had no right to give away the interests of any other country. Germany could not admit that the fact that France had a frontier gave her the privileged position which she claimed in Morocco. Germany was quite prepared to see reforms in Morocco, but they must be reforms on an international basis. He gave as instances of the sort of thing that he meant the Commission of the Public Debt at Constantinople and the proposals with regard to Macedonia. I said that I assumed that these were the sort of things which might be discussed at the Conference, but that, as we had not initiated the Conference, we did not intend to initiate any discussions at the Conference. I could not therefore, before the Conference took place, say what was likely to occur at it. I might say generally that we should go into the Conference with no desire or intention whatever of acting in any way hostile to Germany, but that we were bound to keep in a thorough manner the engagements which we had undertaken to France in the Anglo-French Declarations of April 1904, and until the Conference got to work we could not say how far those engagements would be found reconcilable with German policy. At present, we knew nothing of what the proceedings at the Conference were likely to be except the programme which had been drawn up and agreed upon between Germany and France. I understood Count Metternich to agree that there would be little object in discussing the affairs of Morocco further before the Conference opened.(¹)

I am, &c.
EDWARD GREY.

(¹) [For Count Metternich's report, see *G.P.* XX, II, pp. 685–690. He makes the date of the interview the 18th, not the 19th as Sir Edward Grey says.]

No. 199.

Sir Edward Grey to Sir A. Nicolson.

Tel. Private.(¹)   *Foreign Office, December 20, 1905.*
Your private letter of Dec[ember] 12.

Our policy at the Conference will be to give fullest support to the French delegate, under the terms of Art[icle] 9.(²)

I will endeavour to ascertain at once from the French Gov[ernmen]t what they anticipate will be the demands of the German Gov[ernmen]t and whether they are disposed to make any concessions. We can then consider how far any requests which French might be willing to make would affect our interests.

With regard to your suggestion as to policing of the ports, I should prefer the mixed police force in each port to assigning a port to each Power or to a minor Power; but it is not for us to suggest any concessions.

(¹) [Carnock MSS.]
(²) [*v. Gooch & Temperley*, Vol. II, p. 392.]

No. 200.

Sir Edward Grey to Sir A. Nicolson.

Private.(¹)
Dear Sir Arthur Nicolson,   *December 21, 1905.*

I was very glad to get your letter. The Morocco Conference is going to be difficult if not critical. As far as I can discover the Germans will refuse altogether to concede to France the special position in Morocco, which we have promised France not only to concede to her but to help her by diplomatic methods to obtain.

If she can succeed in getting this with our help it will be a great success for the Anglo-French *Entente;* if she fails the prestige of the *Entente* will suffer and its vitality will be diminished.

Our main object therefore must be to help France to carry her point at the Conference.

In return for this it is essential that we should be in her confidence both before and during the Conference and we are telling the French Gov[ernmen]t this.

The French Ambassador told me yesterday the rumour about Spain, which you will get in the official letter.

Spain may be encouraged by the knowledge that we mean to support France at the Conference and all the influence you have will no doubt be used to keep her thoroughly with us.

If France does begin to talk of concessions to Germany they must be such as do not infringe the conditions of the Anglo-French declarations, which were inserted to protect British interests. It is difficult to say in advance, what we could or could not do about a port: if the point really became vital at the Conference, it would have to adjourn till the Government here could be consulted.

But we can if need be discuss such points as these later on. At present all I gather is that Germany will begin by pressing for all reforms in Morocco to be on an international basis.

Yours very truly,
E. GREY.

(¹) [Carnock MSS.]

No. 201.

Sir Edward Grey to Sir A. Nicolson.

F.O. Morocco 436.   *Foreign Office, December 21, 1905.*
Tel. (No. 99.)   D. 1·30 P.M.

The French Ambassador expressed considerable apprehension in conversation yesterday of attempts that might be made to detach Spain from France. If any signs of this are apparent you should when a good opportunity occurs impress upon Spanish Minister that it is our intention to support France at the Conference and that it would be very undesirable for Spain to allow herself to be separated from us.

No. 202.

Sir A. Nicolson to Sir Edward Grey.

Madrid, December 22, 1905.
F.O. Morocco 436.
D. 1·30 P.M.
Tel. (No. 104.)
R. 4·5 P.M.

Your tel[egram] No. 99.

I took the opportunity this morning at weekly reception of Minister of Foreign Affairs to speak in sense of your above-mentioned telegram. His Excellency said that Spain would act with us but he was not so open and cordial as usual. I, therefore, added that the agreements Spain had made with France and, if I might be permitted to say so, her interests also indicated to my mind the line she should follow.

The French Ambassador here had informed me yesterday that he had already spoken seriously to Minister for Foreign Affairs as to Spain not being led away and he had begged me also to impress on His Excellency that we would act in accord with France.

There is no doubt that Germany during the whole of this year has been making efforts with successive Spanish Governments to detach them from France and us, and these efforts have not been without their effect in some Government circles here.

No. 203.

Sir A. Nicolson to Sir Edward Grey.

F.O. Morocco 436.
(No. 239.)
Madrid, D. December 22, 1905.
Sir,
R. December 26, 1905.

The German Ambassador called on me yesterday, and said that he had travelled from Paris with his French colleague, and was pleased to find that he was animated with the same desire as himself that the proceedings of the Conference should run smoothly and lead to some good results. There was a desire at Berlin that the Conference should meet as soon as possible, and every wish that the questions which were to be discussed should be treated in a friendly and conciliatory spirit. I replied that I was certain that this was also the wish of my Government, and I trusted that the work of the Conference would be rapidly and easily accomplished.

I have, &c.
A. NICOLSON.

No. 204.

Sir F. Bertie to Sir Edward Grey.

F.O. Morocco 436.
(No. 482.) Confidential.
Paris, D. December 22, 1905.
Sir,
R. December 27, 1905.

I went to the Foreign Office today in order to carry out the instructions which you gave me on the 18th and 21st instants.

I told the President of the Council that, as he had probably heard from the French Ambassador in London, the change of Ministry in England would not cause any change in the attitude of His Majesty's Government towards France. You had authorised me to say that they would loyally act up to the engagements taken by their predecessors and they would give to France their unreserved support in the

M 2

Conference on Morocco within the four corners of the Anglo-French Agreement and the programme arranged between the French and German Governments; but in order to enable them to do so effectively, and to put them in a position to act in concert with France, it would be desirable that His Majesty's Government should be made acquainted with the views of the French Government on the matters to be discussed, and as to the concessions, if any, which might be made for the satisfaction of Germany. The German Ambassador in London had made it a matter of reproach to His Majesty's Government that they had in the first instance rejected the suggestion of a Conference whereas the French Government had accepted it; that England had in fact been more French than the French Government, and His Majesty's Government desired to avoid being liable to such an accusation at the Conference.

His Majesty's Government wished to know what instructions M. Rouvier intended to give to the French Delegate, so that analogous directions might be given to the British Delegate so far as they could be consistently with the terms of the Anglo-French Agreement; and it would be necessary that the French and British Delegates should communicate freely and confidentially with each other on all matters in discussion.

I further said to M. Rouvier that he had no doubt noticed the exchange of complimentary messages between groups of persons in Germany and in England. These messages had not been in any way inspired by His Majesty's Government. You desired to be on good terms with Germany, but an improvement in the relations between the British and German Governments would depend on the attitude of the German Government in regard to Morocco and other questions in which England was interested.

M. Rouvier expressed his satisfaction at the assurances which I had given to him in your name. He had not, he said, attached much political importance to the exchange of civilities to which I had referred. He promised that as soon as he had settled the instructions to the French Delegate he would communicate them to His Majesty's Government. They would, he said, be based on the programme arranged with Germany and the statement which he had made in the Chamber on the 16th instant (see Embassy despatch No. 470 of December 17).(¹) Great latitude should, however, he thought be given to the Delegates of England and France so that they might be free to discuss together and deal in concert with any proposals put forward by any of the other delegates.

I asked His Excellency whether he had any information as to what Germany might propose. He replied that he had no idea. He thought that satisfaction might be found for Germany in economic matters such, for instance, as a prolongation of the term of 30 years in regard to equality of Customs duties, taxation, and railway charges, which was agreed on between France and England by the Declaration of April 8, 1904.

I told His Excellency that I had heard in London, but not from an official source, that Germany might propose that the police force should be organised on the model of the Macedonian Gendarmerie, leaving the portion of such force on the Algerian frontier to be officered solely by French officers.

M. Rouvier replied that if it were proposed to divide Morocco into secteurs as had been done with Macedonia, France would most certainly reject such a suggestion. If the attitude of Germany in the Conference prevented any settlement of the question of Morocco, the *status quo* would continue, a condition of things which could not be satisfactory to any of those having interests in Morocco, and would, for want of funds for the institution of reforms, become worse and worse.

I then mentioned to M. Rouvier that, the French Ambassador having expressed to you some apprehension that attempts were being made by Germany to detach Spain from France, you had instructed His Majesty's Ambassador at Madrid that if

(¹) [This despatch, sent by Mr. Grahame in Sir F. Bertie's absence, transmitted copies of the *Journal Officiel* giving a report of M. Rouvier's speech.]

he noticed any tendency on the part of the Spanish Government to allow themselves to be so detached he was to impress on them that His Majesty's Government intended to support France at the Conference and that it would be contrary to the interests of Spain to allow herself to be separated from France and England; that Sir A. Nicolson had spoken in that sense to the Spanish Minister for Foreign Affairs, who had replied that he would act in concert with France and England. The attitude of the Spanish Minister not being, however, as frank and cordial as usual, His Majesty's Ambassador had pressed the view that the Agreements with France and also the interests of Spain plainly indicated to her the line she should take.

M. Rouvier had received this information from the French Ambassador at Madrid and he observed that there was no doubt that the present Spanish Government were not so cordial in their manner towards France as their predecessors, and that it would require the concerted persuasion of the British and French Ambassadors to keep them up to the Spirit of their engagements. If however Señor Montero Rios were appointed Spanish Delegate, he might probably be relied on to act with the British and French Representatives, inasmuch as it was he who signed on behalf of Spain the Franco-Spanish Agreements. If Spain failed to support France she could not expect to obtain the benefits to be derived from the Franco-Spanish Agreements regarding Morocco.

I then asked the President of the Council whether he knew anything as to the line which would be taken by Italy.

His Excellency replied that he could not suppose that Italy would support any German pretensions in Morocco, as if she did so she would naturally forfeit the advantages accorded to her in regard to Tripoli by her Agreement with France.

His Excellency had, he said, received satisfactory assurances from the Austro-Hungarian Government and he did not expect to meet with opposition to French interests from that quarter nor from Belgium.

As to Holland, M. Rouvier had no very precise information. He rather expected that she would be found to act with Germany, but the attitude of a small State would, comparatively speaking, not be of much consequence.

I have, &c.
FRANCIS BERTIE.

No. 205.

Sir A. Nicolson to Sir Edward Grey.

Madrid, December 26, 1905.

F.O. Spain 2211.   D. 12·2 p.m.
Tel. (No. 106.) Secret.   R. 7 p.m.

Spanish Prime Minister told French Ambassador three days ago([1]) that when King of Spain was in Berlin German Emperor proposed to His Majesty that he should revive a secret Agreement made between the late King of Spain and Germany by which the former engaged to furnish military assistance in the event of hostilities with France. King of Spain replied that since his father's days international situation had changed, and in any case he could, as a constitutional Sovereign, come to no such agreement without consulting his Ministers. The question seems then to have been dropped.

([1]) [A fuller account of this conversation is given, *infra*, p. 167, No. 208.]

No. 206.

Sir Edward Grey to Sir E. Egerton.

F.O. Morocco 436.
(No. 201.)

Sir,   *Foreign Office, December* 27, 1905.

The Italian Ambassador asked me about the Morocco Conference today. I told him that it appeared probable that the place of meeting would now be Algeciras and the time about the middle of January. I was unable to say what the course of events at the Conference was likely to be, but we should of course give our support to France under the terms of Article IX of the Anglo-French Declarations.

The Italian Ambassador touched upon the relations between ourselves and Germany. I said that the Anglo-French *entente* had been in no way directed against Germany, and that neither the late Government nor the present Government had the least intention of using it to the disadvantage of Germany, and I knew the French Government had no intention of that kind either. The Ambassador said he knew this was so now, but that M. Delcassé might have had an idea at the back of his head. He hoped there would not be too much hurry in any improvement in the relations between England and Germany which must be of slow growth, and he dwelt upon the number of years which it had taken to prepare public opinion in England and France for the good understanding which now exists between them. I said that more friendly manifestations of opinion between England and Germany could not of course make any progress unless things went smoothly at the Morocco Conference, and that at that Conference the four Powers most directly interested in the Mediterranean were Italy, France, Spain and ourselves. I understood that we had no difficulties with each other with regard to our interests in the Mediterranean, and that we were all now good friends. I hoped we should all come out of the Conference as good friends as we went in. His Excellency said that Italy had not only friendship but also an alliance to be considered. I said I knew that this was so, and until the Conference had actually got to work it was no doubt difficult to be sure what conflict of interests would be apparent.

I am, &c.
EDWARD GREY.

No. 207.

Sir E. Egerton to Sir Edward Grey.

F.O. 371/171.
(No. 214.) Confidential.   *Rome, D. December* 27, 1905.
Sir,   R. *January* 1, 1906.

To-day I called on the Marquis di San Giuliano at the Consulta for the first time.

As he had only just arrived at the Ministry, and as he told me he had not yet read previous correspondence, our conversation was naturally informal, and he agreed to consider it so.

I said there seemed special need at present for " suite " (continuity and steadiness) in international policy, and I alluded to the Morocco Conference, in which England and Italy, I said, were bound by engagements to France; and Abyssinia, respecting which the three Governments appeared on the point of coming to an arrangement.

His Excellency observed that England and Italy were not exactly in the same position, as Italy was bound by the Triple Alliance; to which I replied that a European political combination did not appear to regard special agreements respecting a local question, such as that of Morocco; and that I trusted that Germany would not create any serious question at the Conference.

He said he had not made himself acquainted with the instructions sent by his predecessor to Signor Silvestrelli, as to his attitude in support of the French delegate in the coming Conference; but he in general wished to depart as little as possible from the line traced by Signor Tittoni.

I subsequently reminded His Excellency that His Majesty's delegate would, in accordance with the Anglo-French declaration, give full diplomatic support to his French colleague.

I have, &c.
EDWIN H. EGERTON.

No. 208.

Sir A. Nicolson to Sir Edward Grey.

F.O. 371/171.
(No. 241.) Secret.
Sir,

Madrid, D. December 27, 1905.
R. January 13, 1906.

The French Ambassador, in relating to me a conversation which he had held with Señor Moret, the Spanish Prime Minister, mentioned that the latter had stated that he was most desirous of supporting French policy during the approaching Conference on Moorish affairs, and that the instructions which he purposed to give to the Spanish delegate would, he was sure, be held to be thoroughly satisfactory to the French Government. Señor Moret said that he was pleased to find from a report which the Duke of Almodovar had made to him of some observations which I had made to His Excellency that His Majesty's Government also intended to support France cordially during the Conference, and it was a great satisfaction to him to feel assured that the new Government in Great Britain were desirous that the three countries should work harmoniously together.

Señor Moret added that it would be useless to disguise the fact that Germany had of late been making persistent efforts to detach Spain from France and Great Britain, and to cause her to revolve in the orbit of Berlin. As an instance of this, Señor Moret said he wished to inform M. Cambon very confidentially that during the visit of King Alfonso to Berlin in November last, the German Emperor had spoken to His Majesty of the intimate relations which had existed between the late King Alfonso XII and the German Court, and had intimated that it would be good policy on the part of His Majesty if he were to revive a secret agreement which his father had made, by which Spain had undertaken to furnish military assistance to Germany in certain eventualities.

King Alfonso had replied that when that agreement had been made his father had just re-established the monarchy in Spain and was seeking for support and assistance. Now the monarchy was established and the international situation had completely changed from what prevailed in the days to which the Emperor had alluded. King Alfonso added that he was, moreover, a constitutional sovereign and could not enter into any agreements, secret or other, without previously consulting with, and obtaining the consent of, his constitutional advisers. The question was then dropped.

I have, &c.
A. NICOLSON.

No. 209.

Lord Acton to Sir Edward Grey.

F.O. 371/75.
(No. 57.) Confidential.
Sir,

Berne, D. December 31, 1905.
R. January 5, 1906.

I had a conversation this afternoon with the German Minister on the subject of the relations between Germany and England. His Excellency is, as you are aware, a brother of the German Chancellor.

Herr von Bülow said that he hoped that the advent of the Liberal party to power would be marked by an improvement in the situation. The Liberals were less Chauvinist than their opponents, and he had noted with satisfaction the observations made by the Prime Minister in his recent speech at the Albert Hall in favour of arbitration and of the limitation of armaments.

Germany did not desire war with England. The increase of her navy had the sole object of providing her with a weapon of defence of sufficient efficiency to render a naval attack by France or England an operation of considerable gravity to the assailing force. The aggressive language held by the Navy League had been disavowed by the Government; and the last measure introduced for the further increase of the navy was extremely moderate, for, if carried out at the rate of progress determined upon, it would result in the creation twenty years hence of a German fleet about half the size of the present British navy. Personally Herr von Bülow had always advocated a *rapprochement* with England rather than with Russia. In his opinion it would have been possible on more than one occasion prior to the Boer war to come to terms with Mr. Chamberlain, and to conclude, if not a definite Agreement, at any rate an *entente cordiale*. But the feelings excited by the war had put an end for a time to that potentiality, and the accession of his brother to power had undoubtedly given a Russophil trend to German policy.

Herr von Bülow fully admitted that German public opinion had been in the wrong during the Boer War, not only as regards the intensity of the animosity displayed, but also in respect of German interpretation of the conflict as a struggle between unscrupulous treasure-hunters and a law-abiding peasantry.

Herr von Bülow observed that there was a feeling in Germany that Count Metternich was not the right man to represent Germany in London, as he had not won for himself that position of personal friendship enjoyed by M. de Soveral and Count Mensdorff. No doubt Count Metternich was not an ideal Ambassador to England, but it would be hard to select a better man from among the available candidates. It was well known that Count Seckendorff aspired to the post, but although he would be suitable from a personal point of view, his mental and political equipment would scarcely be equal to the task. A possible choice might be found in Baron Reischach, who was a man of ability and great personal charm, and was also conversant with English public life from his long experience at the Court of the Empress Frederick.

His Excellency then referred to Morocco. No doubt the sudden intervention of Germany had not been dictated by the desire to safeguard German interests in that region. The object had been a higher one. Germany was bound in self-defence to emancipate herself from the isolation with which she was threatened. First Russia, then Italy, and lastly England had been won over by France. The cordon must be broken, and the penultimate defeat of Russia had furnished the propitious moment. The Emperor had hesitated for some time in deference to Prince Bülow's scruples, but it was finally decided to make " a loud splash " and clear the situation. He thought that a *détente* would make itself felt when once the Conference was over.

In his repeated assurances of Germany's friendship, his Excellency went out of his way to remind me that he was, if not the Keeper, at least the confidant of his brother's political conscience.

I have, &c.
ACTON.

CHAPTER XX.

THE ANGLO-FRENCH AND ANGLO-BELGIAN CONVERSATIONS OF JANUARY—APRIL 1906.

[ED. NOTE.—On December 29, 1905, Colonel Repington (Military Correspondent of the *Times*) wrote to Sir E. Grey describing a " confidential talk " with Major Huguet, the French Military Attaché, on the 28th. Major Huguet, he wrote, " confessed that his Embassy felt anxious upon the question of the attitude of the new Government in England. His people, he said, had nothing to complain of, since the speeches of Sir Henry C[ampbell] B[annerman] as well as yours, had produced an excellent effect. It was not a question of sympathies, but rather of acts, and of what the British Government were prepared to do in a situation which presented dangerous aspects. . . . . I hinted that I was inclined to let you know the general purport of this part of our conversation, and to this he raised no objection." To this Sir E. Grey replied in a letter of December 30 : " I am very interested to hear of your conversation with the French Military Attaché. I can only say that I have not receded from anything which Lord Lansdowne said to the French, and have no hesitation in affirming it." (Grey MSS., Volume 71.) Colonel Repington states further that after consulting Lord Esher and Sir George Clarke, Secretary of the Committee of Imperial Défence, he submitted to the French Government through Major Huguet a list of questions with reference to the co-operation of British and French forces in the event of war. The French replies were handed to him on January 12 and discussed by him with Lord Esher and Sir George Clarke on the same day. On January 13th Sir George Clarke saw Sir John Fisher on the subject of Naval plans. . (*The First World War*, 1914–18, (1920), Vol. I, pp. 2–14, *cf.* Sir E. Grey's minute to No. 212, p. 174, below, and Lord Sanderson's letter, pp. 176–7, No. 216 (a).

The documents in this chapter are supplemented by the narratives of Lord Grey, *Twenty-Five Years* (1925), I, Ch. 6; Spender, *Life of Campbell-Bannerman* (1923), II, pp. 248–259; Lord Haldane, *Before the War* (1920), pp. 30–31; *v.* also L. Wolf's *Marquess of Ripon* (1921), II, pp. 221–3. The despatches of January 10, January 15 and January 31, are reproduced here on account of their importance. For some notes on interviews with Major Huguet and other persons in 1905–1906, with extracts from his Diary, see *The Life of General Sir J. M. Grierson* by D. S. MacDiarmid (1923), pp. 213–7. *Cf.* also Winston Churchill : *World Crisis, 1911–4* (1923), p. 32, and reference in Lord Grey's speech of August 3, 1914, *Twenty-Five Years* (1925), II, pp. 295–6, and *Parl. Deb.*, 5th ser., Vol. LXV, pp. 1811–2.

The documents recording the technical discussions then authorised are for the most part missing from the Foreign Office archives. The gaps have been filled as far as possible from the archives of the War Office and Admiralty. The records of the Committee of Imperial Defence contain no reference to them, but Lord Sydenham (Sir George Clarke) has communicated a statement to the Editors (p. 185). His successor, Sir Maurice Hankey, has stated to the Editors that he has found no other information relating to this topic during this period. The references in the Admiralty archives are scanty, the only document directly bearing on it being printed on p. 186. A document from the Grey MSS. is given on p. 203. The War Office archives contain four files covering the years 1906–1912. The first relates to the general authorisation of the negotiations, and all documents of 1906 are reproduced here (see pp. 176–7 and 178–9). The second file is strictly technical in character, dealing with such matters as railway transport, calculations of times required for mobilisation and concentration, etc. The third file contains all the written records of the Anglo-French military conversations. These were however conducted verbally, and the only notes preserved were of a detailed and technical description. The following statement gives a list of these notes :

(1.) " Note sur la composition de l'armée anglaise destinée à opérer sur le continent dans le cas d'une guerre entre la France et l'Allemagne—renseignements demandés par l'état-major général de l'armée anglaise." Signed A. Huguet. Dated January 22, 1906.

(2.) " Note de l'état-major général français en réponse à la note de l'état-major général anglais en date du 22 Janvier 1906." Signed A. Huguet. Dated February 13, 1906.

(3.) " Note de l'état-major général de l'armée anglaise—réponses aux questions posées par l'état-major général français dans sa note du 13 Février 1906." Signed A. Huguet. Dated February 23, 1906.

(4.) " Note sur l'organisation générale du service militaire des chemins de fer en France, en temps de guerre." Signed A. Huguet. Dated May 3, 1906.

(5.) " Projet d'application aux transports et des dispositions règlementaires en France." Signed A. Huguet. Dated May 3, 1906.

(6.) " Note du 4 Mai 1906 de l'E[tat] M[ajor] F[rançais] en réponse à la note de l'E[tat] M[ajor] A[nglais] du 20 Février 1906."

All these documents emanate from the French side; and the Editors have printed the second of the Series in the Appendix (*infra* pp. 438–440) as generally indicative of their character.

The fourth file contains the whole of the correspondence of Colonel Barnardiston and General J. M. Grierson on the subject of the Anglo-Belgian military conversations of January–April 1906. The Belgian side of these negotiations was revealed by the publication in the *Norddeutsche Allgemeine Zeitung* in the autumn of 1914 of General Ducarne's letter to the Belgian Minister of War dated April 10, 1906. This report and other relevant documents were included in the official publication *Collected Diplomatic Documents relating to the outbreak of the European War* (1915), pp. 350–367. The report of General Ducarne was published with comments by Fernand Passelecq in *Le Second Livre Blanc Allemand : Essai critique et notes sur l'Altération officielle des Documents Belges* (Paris 1916). *Cf.* B. Schwertfeger : *Der geistige Kampf um die Verletzung der belgischen Neutralität* (Berlin 1919).

The British records now published seem very full and complete. In a few cases, noted when they occur, a sentence or two is omitted for personal reasons; and certain highly technical tables have been omitted as of no diplomatic or political interest. But the correspondence is printed almost *in toto*, as the Editors were of the opinion that even trivial details might be of real interest or importance.]

No. 210.

(a.)

Sir Edward Grey to Sir F. Bertie.([1])

F.O. 371/70.
(No. 22.)   Very Confidential.
Sir,
                                                  Foreign Office, January 10, 1906.

After informing me this afternoon of the nature of the instructions wh[ich] M. Rouvier was addressing to the French Plenipotentiary at the Conference about to meet at Algeciras on Moorish affairs (as recorded in my immediately preceding despatch)([2]) the French Amb[assado]r went on to say that he had spoken to M. Rouvier on the importance of arriving at an understanding as to the course wh[ich] would be taken by France and Great Britain in the event of the discussions terminating in a rupture between France and Germany. M. Cambon said that he did not believe that the German Emperor desired war, but that H[is] M[ajesty] was pursuing a very dangerous policy. He had succeeded in inciting public opinion and military opinion in Germany, and there was a risk that matters might be brought to a point in which a pacific issue would be difficult. During the previous discussions on the subject of Morocco, Lord Lansdowne had expressed his opinion that the British and French Gov[ernmen]ts should frankly discuss any eventualities that might seem possible, and by his instructions Y[our] Exc[ellenc]y had communicated a memorandum to M. Delcassé to the same effect. It had not been considered necessary at the time to discuss the eventuality of war. But it now seemed desirable that this eventuality should also be considered.

M. Cambon said that he had spoken to this effect to M. Rouvier who agreed in his view. It was not necessary, nor indeed expedient, that there should be any formal alliance, but it was of great importance that the French Gov[ernmen]t should know beforehand whether, in the event of aggression against France by Germany, Great Britain w[oul]d be prepared to render to France armed assistance.

I replied that at the present moment the Prime Minister was out of town, and that the Cabinet were all dispersed seeing after the Elections, that we were not as yet aware of the sentiments of the country as they would be expressed at the polls, and that it was impossible therefore for me in the circumstances to give a reply to H[is] Exc[ellenc]y's question. I could only state as my personal opinion that if France were to be attacked by Germany in consequence of a question arising out of the Agreement wh[ich] our predecessors had recently concluded with the French Gov[ernmen]t public opinion in England would be strongly moved in favour of France.

([1]) [Published by Lord Grey : *Twenty-Five Years* (1925), I, pp. 72–4.]
([2]) [*v. infra* pp. 213–4, No. 233.]

M. Cambon said that he understood this, and that he would repeat his question after the Elections.

I said that what Great Britain earnestly desired was that the Conference sh[oul]d have a pacific issue favourable to France.

H[is] Exc[ellenc]y replied that nothing w[oul]d have a more pacific influence on the Emperor of Germany than the conviction that, if Germany attacked France, she would find England allied against her.

I said that I thought the German Emperor did believe this, but that it was one thing that this opinion sh[oul]d be held in Germany, and another that we should give a positive assurance to France on the subject. There could be no greater mistake than that a Minister sh[oul]d give such an assurance unless he were perfectly certain that it would be fulfilled. I did not believe that any Minister could, in present circumstances, say more than I had done, and however strong the sympathy of Great Britain might be with France in the case of a rupture with Germany, the expression which might be given to it, and the action which might follow, must depend largely upon the circumstances in which the rupture took place.

M. Cambon said that he spoke of aggression on the part of Germany, possibly in consequence of some necessary action on the part of France for the protection of her Algerian frontier or on some other grounds wh[ich] justified such action.

I said that as far as a definite promise went I was not in a position at present to pledge the country to more than neutrality—a benevolent neutrality if such a thing existed.

M. Cambon said that a promise of neutrality did not of course satisfy him, and repeated that he would bring the question to me again at the conclusion of the Elections.

In the meanwhile he thought it advisable that unofficial communications between our Admiralty and War Office and the French Naval and Military Attachés should take place as to what action might advantageously be taken in case the two countries found themselves in alliance in such a war. Some communications had he believed already passed, and might he thought be continued. They did not pledge either Gov[ernmen]t.

I did not dissent from this view.([1])

I am, &c.
EDWARD GREY.

([1]) [This conversation should be compared with that between Sir E. Grey and Count Metternich on January 3, v. despatch from Sir E. Grey to Sir F. Lascelles No. 11 of January 9, *infra* pp. 209–11, No. 229.]

(b.)

Minute by Lord Sanderson.

F.O. 371/70.
Sir E. Grey, *Foreign Office, January* 11, 1906.

I noticed that in your conversation yesterday with the French Ambassador the latter stated that unofficial communications had already passed between our Admiralty and the French Naval Attaché as to the methods in which the two countries might assist one another in case of a joint war against another Power, and that he added that some similar communications had taken place between the Military Authorities and the French Military Attaché, not directly but by intermediaries. I thought this latter remark looked very much as if the conversations which we know that Col. a'Court-Repington has had with the French Military Attaché had been taken by the latter and by the Embassy as being authorized by our General Staff.

I therefore asked General Grierson today whether he had made any inquiries of the kind directly or indirectly.

He told me that he had not done so, but that if there were any probability of his being called upon at short notice to furnish plans for joint operations it would be important that he should obtain information on several points.

I asked him to write a letter to me on the subject which I could send to you for your instructions, and I suggested to him that if he should have an opportunity he should inform the French Military Attaché that he [had] not authorized anybody to communicate on these subjects on his behalf.

I annex his letter just received. Are you disposed to authorize him to commence unofficial communications with the French Military Staff?

Do you think that any similar communications should be commenced with Belgium? They would have presumably to be carried on through our Military Attaché at Brussels. The Belgians would, I suppose, let the Germans know.

S.

Jan. 11, 1906.

MINUTE.

See my note on M. Cambon's memo[randum].—E. G.   [*Infra* p. 174.]

No. 211.

Major-General J. M. Grierson to Lord Sanderson.

F.O. 371/70.   *Winchester House, St. James's Square, S.W.,*
Dear Lord Sanderson,   *January* 11, 1906.

As I told you today in our conversation, I have had no communication with the French Military Attaché on the subject of British military cooperation with France except, to a certain extent, about the 16th or 18th December when I rode with him in the Row (a chance meeting), and he told me of the French fears as to an attack by Germany. He asked me some questions about our war organization, and I referred him to the Army List, which shows it and actually gives the composition on mobilisation of a division which does not exist in peace. He also asked if we had ever considered operations in Belgium, and I said that, as a strategical exercise, I had worked such out last spring. That, to the best of my recollection, was all that passed between us, and I have not seen him since that date.

At the same time I think that, if there is even a chance of our having to give armed assistance on land to France or to take the field on her side in Belgium in consequence of a violation of Belgian territory by the Germans, we should have as soon as possible informal communication between the military authorities of France and/or Belgium and the General Staff. There are a great many points which we must settle before we can make our plans for the despatch of a force to join either the French or the Belgian armies, and these we cannot settle without information which the staffs of these armies alone can give us. Then there are arrangements to be made as to the utilisation of railways, harbours, billets, transport, and supplies, which would be quite different in a friendly country from those we should have to make " on our own " in a hostile country, and these *greatly* influence our establishments and consequently the numbers we can put in the field. All these take a great deal of time, and it is exactly that factor which will be wanting on the outbreak of war. To make our help effective we must come *at once* with every available man. First successes are everything, and if the French could gain those they would " get their tails up " and all would go well.

For all these reasons I urge that, if there is a chance of such operations, informal communication should be opened between the General staffs on both sides, and I see no difficulty in such communication being made on the express understanding that it commits the Government to nothing.

I remain, &c.
J. M. GRIERSON.

No. 212.

Minute by Lord Sanderson.

F.O. 371/70.
Sir E. Grey, *Foreign Office, January* 12, 1906.
I have just received from the French Ambassador the enclosed copy of his letter to M. Rouvier.

S.

Jan. 12, '06.

To be kept in the Dep[artmen]t as a Secret Paper. See Sir E. Grey's note at the end of the memorandum.

S.

Enclosure 1 in No. 212.

M. Paul Cambon to Lord Sanderson.

Albert Gate House, S.W.,
le 11 *Janvier* 1906.

Cher Lord Sanderson,
Voici la copie de la lettre que j'adresse aujourd'hui à M. Rouvier et que je vous ai lue ce matin.

Votre bien affectueusement dévoué,
PAUL CAMBON.

Enclosure 2 in No. 212.

M. Cambon to M. Rouvier.

11 *Janvier* 1906.

Faisant allusion à mes derniers entretiens avec le Marquis de Lansdowne et à la lettre personnelle de Sa Seigneurie du 25 Mai dernier,([1]) j'ai demandé à Sir Edward Grey s'il était disposé à envisager avec moi toutes les éventualités qui pourraient surgir de l'affaire du Maroc. J'ai dit que je ne croyais pas, quant à moi, aux intentions belliqueuses de l'Empereur Guillaume, mais que son attitude et son langage avaient surexcité les esprits dans le monde militaire allemand et qu'il pouvait être entraîné plus vite et plus loin qu'il ne voulait. J'ai en conséquence demandé au Secrétaire d'Etat pour les Affaires Etrangères si, le cas échéant, la France pourrait compter sur l'appui de l'Angleterre et, pour bien préciser les choses, en cas d'aggression de la part du Gouvernement Allemand, l'Angleterre se rangerait du côté de la France et lui prêterait un concours armé.

Sir Edward Grey a répliqué qu'il ne pouvait répondre à ma question sans avoir pris d'abord l'avis du Gouvernement, que tous les Ministres étant absents cette consultation était impossible, que d'ailleurs, par suite de la dissolution du Parlement, le Cabinet se trouvait soumis en ce moment au verdict populaire, que son existence même était en jeu et qu'il ne pouvait adopter une ligne de conduite qu'après s'être assuré des directions de l'opinion publique, en un mot qu'on ne pouvait aborder un sujet aussi important avant les élections.

Sir Edward Grey a ajouté que, d'après son opinion personnelle, les sympathies pour la France étaient telles et l'entente entre les deux pays répondait si bien au sentiment général qu'il ne lui paraissait pas douteux que l'opinion publique se prononcerait très fortement dans le sens d'un appui à la France mais que c'était là

([1]) [*v. supra* p. 77, No. 95, Encl. 2.]

l'expression d'un sentiment personnel et qu'il ne pouvait engager le Gouvernement à aucun degré.

Lord Sanderson, qui assistait à cet entretien, a fait observer que s'il y avait rupture entre l'Allemagne et la France l'attitude du Gouvernement Britannique et les dispositions de l'opinion anglaise dépendraient des causes de cette rupture et que l'appui de l'Angleterre ne serait sans doute donné que si le conflit se rattachait aux accords franco-anglais.

J'ai répondu qu'il allait de soi que toute entente en vue de l'éventualiré [sic] d'une rupture entre l'Allemagne et la France devait être une conséquence de nos accords, que par example la question du Maroc étant l'un des éléments essentiels de ces accords, un conflit sur ce point aurait pour origine notre arrangement de 1904.

Sir Edward Grey a exprimé le desir de voir l'affaire du Maroc se régler pacifiquement. Il importe d'après lui d'observer à la Conference une attitude très mesurée. Je lui ai répondu que telle était notre intention et que tous nos efforts tendraient à empêcher la Conférence d'aboutir à un échec, qu'au surplus l'Empereur Guillaume ne s'était saisi de la question marocaine que comme d'un prétexte, que son vrai mobile avait été l'espoir d'affaiblir l'entente anglo-française et que s'il avait la certitude de la solidité de cette entente il adopterait une autre attitude, que le meilleur moyen d'écarter les chances de conflit était de resserrer notre accord et de donner à l'Allemagne l'impression qu'il était inébranlable.

En terminant, j'ai dit à Sir Edward Grey qu'aussitôt après les élections je lui poserais de nouveau la question à laquelle il n'était pas autorisé à répondre pour le moment.

J'ai ajouté que, si peu fondées qu'elles fussent, les appréhensions de ces derniers temps avaient imposé aux administrations militaires et navales des deux pays le devoir d'étudier certaines mesures et de se communiquer officieusement en dehors des Gouvernements et par des intermédiaires sûrs certains renseignements confidentiels. J'ai exprimé l'avis qu'il convenait de laisser ces communications se continuer et Sir Ed[ward] Grey m'a dit qu'il n'y voyait pas d'inconvénient.

MINUTE.

This agrees with my own record in substance; except that I did not go so far as to approve of the communications by intermediaries referred to at the end : I did not dissent but I reserved my opinion, because I did not know what they were. I do however approve of their being continued in a proper manner i.e. with the cognizance of the official heads of the Admiralty and War Office. In the case of the Admiralty I gather that whatever is being done is known to Sir J. Fisher. I have now spoken to Mr. Haldane as regards the War Office and he is willing that the French Military Attaché should communicate with Gen[eral] Grierson. The communication must be solely provisional and non-committal.

E. G.

13.1.06.

No. 213.

Sir F. Bertie to Sir Edward Grey.

F.O. 371/70.

(No. 30.) Confidential.   Paris, D. January 13, 1906.
Sir,   R. January 18, 1906.

I have had the honour to receive your despatches Nos. 21 and 22,([1]) very confidential, of the 10th instant, in which you record a conversation with the French Ambassador on the subject of the coming conference at Algeciras in the course of which he spoke of the importance of arriving at an understanding as to the course which should be taken by France and Great Britain in the event of the discussions terminating in a rupture between France and Germany. Monsieur Cambon stated that the Marquess of Lansdowne had, during the previous discussions on the subject of Morocco, expressed the opinion that the British and French Governments should frankly discuss any eventualities that might seem possible, and His Excellency informed you that

([1]) [v. pp. 170–1, No. 210 (a), and pp. 218–4, No. 233.]

by His Lordship's instructions I had communicated to Monsieur Delcassé a memorandum to that effect;([2]) that it had not been thought necessary at the time to discuss the eventuality of war, but that it now seemed desirable that this eventuality should also be considered. Monsieur Cambon went on to say that Monsieur Rouvier agreed in this view; that it was not necessary nor indeed expedient that there should be any formal alliance but that it was of great importance that the French Government should know whether in the event of aggression against France by Germany, Great Britain would be prepared to render to France armed assistance. The Ambassador said that there might be aggression by Germany in consequence of some necessary action on the part of France, for the protection of her Algerian frontier or on some other grounds which justified such action.

The instructions to me to which the French Ambassador referred in his conversation with you, were contained in a telegram from Lord Lansdowne dated 23 April (No. 61).([3]) My report of the interview, which I consequently had with the French Minister for Foreign Affairs, is given in my despatch No. 156 Confidential of the 25th of that month.([4]) The memorandum which I left with him said: "Le Gouvernement de Sa Majesté Britannique trouve que les procédés de l'Allemagne dans la question du Maroc sont des plus déraisonnables vu l'attitude de Monsieur Delcassé, et il désire accorder à Son Excellence tout l'appui en son pouvoir.

"Il ne paraît pas impossible que le Gouvernement Allemand fasse la demande d'un port sur la côte du Maroc.

"Le Gouvernement de Sa Majesté Britannique serait prêt à se joindre au Gouvernement de la République pour s'opposer fortement à une telle proposition, et prie Monsieur Delcassé, dans le cas où la question surgirait, de donner au Gouvernement de Sa Majesté Britannique toute occasion de concerter avec le Gouvernement Français les mesures qui pourraient être prises pour aller à l'encontre de cette demande."

The telegram of the 13th instant from His Majesty's Ambassador at Berlin (No. 5)([5]) which was repeated to me from the Foreign Office, and reached here last night, states that Herr von Holstein fears that if the results of the initial discussions at the conference be unfavourable to France, she may, relying on the support of England, attempt to create a "fait accompli" by invading Morocco.

If there be an invasion of Morocco by French troops, it will not, I am convinced, be consequent on the initial discussions at the Conference being unfavourable to France; but as an act of self-defence in order to counteract an inroad from Morocco, either spontaneous on the part of some Moorish tribe, or promoted by persons acting in the interests of Germany with a view to bringing about the situation anticipated by Herr von Holstein and giving to Germany a pretext to consider that France had given her a provocation entitling Germany to resort to extreme measures.

France cannot be expected not to take the measures necessary to repel raids into her Algerian territory, and if Germany should treat such measures as a provocation it could only mean that she was seeking a pretext for War. There is no desire in France for war. Far from it. The French people earnestly wish for peace, but the proceedings of Germany in the question of Morocco and her whole attitude towards France, have created such a condition of distrust and irritation in the French people towards Germany, that their patience is well-nigh exhausted. The feeling in the spring and early summer was one of fear lest France, in the state of her military unpreparedness, might suffer immediate disaster if Germany attacked her. Since then every preparation has been made to resist attack and the French Government, Army and people have become less apprehensive as to what might be the result to France of a war if Germany were the aggressor, for there is a feeling in this country that

([2]) [v. supra p. 73, No. 91.]
([3]) [v. supra pp. 72–3, No. 90. The telegram is dated April 22, but was received on the following day.]
([4]) [v. supra pp. 74–5, No. 93.]
([5]) [v. infra p. 224, No. 241.]

England, for her own sake, would give armed support to France. It is true that the second article of the Anglo-French Declaration respecting Egypt and Morocco only says that His Majesty's Government will not obstruct the action taken by France for the purposes of the conditions of the Declaration, and that the 9th Article only binds Great Britain to afford to France diplomatic support in order to obtain the execution of the clauses of the Declaration; but if diplomatic support failed to remove the opposition made by another Power without political interests in Morocco to France acting within the conditions of the Declaration, it is felt that the natural sequence would be that France should receive from her partner in the Declaration more than the diplomatic support that had proved insufficient for the purposes of the agreement.

The question has now been put to His Majesty's Government whether, in the event of aggression against France by Germany, Great Britain would be prepared to render to France armed assistance.

It is generally held here that Germany will not go to war if she be convinced that England will side with France, but that if she come to the conclusion that England will abstain from giving armed support to France, she will consider the present moment propitious for crushing France as a preliminary to dealing with the problems of Holland, Belgium, Austria and the naval supremacy of England.

I consider it my duty to warn His Majesty's Government that, in the event of the answer to be given to the enquiries of the French Ambassador not assuring to France more than a continuance of diplomatic support, or of neutrality in the event of a war provoked by Germany, there is serious danger of a complete revulsion of feeling on the part of the French Government and of public opinion in France. The Government would consider that they had been deserted and might, in order to avoid the risks of a war without ally, deem it advisable to make great concessions to Germany outside Morocco in order to obtain liberty of action in that country.

Such concessions might not be very great sacrifices for France, but they might well be very detrimental to the interests of the British Empire, for, in the temper in which France would then be, it could not be expected that she would give them much consideration.

In the event of His Majesty's Government later on being prepared to give an assurance such as is desired by the French Government it would of course be necessary to stipulate that the French Government should take His Majesty's Government entirely into their confidence and take no step likely to cause offence to Germany without consultation with them.

I have the honour, &c.

FRANCIS BERTIE.

MINUTES.

Sir E. Grey.

This despatch is marked to go to the King and Prime Minister only. You may perhaps wish that it should be printed with your despatch No. 22, very confidential, and sent to the members of the Cabinet when they return to town at the end of next week.

S.

Jan. 18, '06.

Nothing is to go to the Cabinet, till I have seen the Prime Minister, which I hope to do next week. This despatch and my No. 22 should go to Lord Ripon (who is in London and whom I hope to see on Monday) as well as to the Prime Minister.

They should of course be added to the papers (about which the Private Secretary has instructions) to be prepared and considered as a whole by the Cabinet eventually.

E. G.

No. 214.

Lord Sanderson to Major-General J. M. Grierson.

W.O. Liaison I/1 and F.O. 371/70.

My dear Grierson,   *January* 15, 1906.

I showed your letter of the 11th to Sir E. Grey, and he has spoken to Mr. Haldane on the subject. They agree to your entering into communications with the French

Military Attaché here for the purpose of obtaining such information as you require as to the methods in which military assistance could in case of need be best afforded by us to France and *vice versa.* Such communications must be solely provisional and non-committal.

Sir E. Grey sees no objection to similar enquiries being addressed by our Military Attaché at Brussels to the Belgian Military Authorities as to the manner in which, in case of need, British assistance could be most effectually afforded to Belgium for the defence of her neutrality.

Yours sincerely,
SANDERSON.

(Approved by Sir E. Grey.)

No. 215.

Sir Edward Grey to Sir F. Bertie.(¹)

F.O. 371/70.
(No. 33.)   Very Confidential.

Sir,   *Foreign Office, January* 15, 1906.

I told M. Cambon to-day that I had communicated to the Prime Minister my account of his conversation with me on the 10th instant. I had heard from the Prime Minister that he could not be in London before the 25th of January, and it would therefore not be possible for me to discuss things with him before then, and the members of the Government would not assemble in London before the 29th. I could therefore give no further answer to-day on the question he had addressed to me. He had spoken to me on the 10th of communications passing between the French Naval Attaché and the Admiralty. I understood that these communications had been with Sir John Fisher. If that was so, it was not necessary for me to do any more; but, with regard to the communications between the French Military Attaché and the War Office, I understood from him that these had taken place through an intermediary. I had therefore taken the opportunity of speaking to Mr. Haldane, the Secretary of State for War, who had been taking part in my election contest in Northumberland on Friday, and he had authorised me to say that these communications might proceed between the French Military Attaché and General Grierson direct; but it must be understood that these communications did not commit either Government. M[onsieur] Cambon said that the intermediary in question had been a retired Colonel, the Military Correspondent of the "Times," who, he understood, had been sent from the War Office.

[I am, &c.
E. GREY.]

(Approved by Sir E. Grey.)

(¹) [Published by Lord Grey: *Twenty-Five Years*, (1925), I, p. 76.]

No. 216.

Sir Edward Grey to Sir F. Bertie.

Private.(¹)
My dear Bertie,   *January* 15, 1906.

You will have seen from the official despatch that Cambon has put the great question to me. Diplomatic support we are pledged to give and are giving. A promise in advance committing this country to take part in a Continental war is another matter and a very serious one : it is very difficult for any British Gov[ernmen]t to give an engagement of that kind. It changes the entente into an alliance and alliances, especially continental alliances are not in accordance with our traditions. My opinion is that if France is let in for a war with Germany arising out of our agreement with her

(¹) [Grey MSS., Vol. 10.]

about Morocco, we cannot stand aside, but must take part with France. But a deliberate engagement pledging this country in advance before the actual cause of the war is known or apparent, given in cold blood goes far beyond anything that the late Gov[ernmen]t said or as far as I know contemplated.

If we give any promise of armed assistance it must be conditional. Should the Morocco Conference break up without result we must be held free to suggest to the French possible modifications of the Morocco declarations, or even concessions, which might lead to an agreement with Germany. And France must not take independent action in Morocco, which might lead to war with Germany without keeping us informed and hearing what we have to say. I think too we should have some *quid pro quo* such as a promise that, if we get into war with Germany over any question of our own France will at least remain neutral if she cannot support us, and keep other European Powers neutral.

But all this must remain in the air till the elections are over : all my colleagues are fighting their own or other election contests and I am alone in London and cannot consult them or get them together.

Meanwhile I should like to have your views of the answer which should be given : my own are still in solution and I haven't yet determined what proposal I shall make to the Prime Minister.

As long as our pledge is confined to diplomatic support I regard us as precluded from objecting to any action on the part of France, which comes within the terms of Article II of our Declarations. You will see that I have telegraphed in this sense to Lascelles apropos of his conversation with von Holstein. I should also think it improper for us to suggest concessions to be made by France : that would look like an attempt on our part to back out of an engagement.

But if we are to make further engagements and undertake a possible obligation to fight, the whole terms may have to be revised.

I have heard party politics at home abused as mean and low, but I think better of them now that Moret has told the French that it will facilitate his support of them at the Conference if they will provide money to quiet the Spanish Opposition; and Russia has demanded a loan on improper terms as the price of her support. The mud of Foreign politics is deeper than any I have been in yet. You seem to take it as a matter of course.

E. GREY.

P.S.—As to taking precautions beforehand in case war should come, it appears that Fisher has long ago taken the French Naval attaché in hand and no doubt has all naval plans prepared. I have now got Haldane's consent to General Grierson being in direct communication with the French Military Attaché. But I am told that 80,000 men with good guns is all we can put into the field in Europe to meet first class troops ; that won't save France unless she can save herself. We can protect ourselves of course for we are more supreme at sea than we have ever been.

All this however is sheer precaution. I detest the idea of another war now and so does the whole of this country and so will the new House of Commons.

E. G.

No. 217.

(a.)

Lord Sanderson to Major-General J. M. Grierson.

W.O. Liaison I/2.   Private & Confidential.
My dear Grierson,   *Foreign Office, January 15, 1906.*
Sir E. Grey told the French Ambassador today that he saw no objection to direct communications between our General Staff and the French Military Attaché on

the subject mentioned in our letters, provided it were understood that the whole matter was being studied academically. He said he thought that M. Cambon had said that some inquiries had already been made through an intermediary.

M. Cambon said this had been the case, that a certain Col[onel] Repington, on the retired list, had come on behalf of the War Office to make certain inquiries of the Military Attaché.

Sir E. Grey made no observation, but I should suggest that you should inform the French Military Attaché as soon as possible that Col[onel] Repington is not commissioned to make inquiries on behalf of the War Office or the Foreign Office.

Yours sincerely,
SANDERSON.

[ED. NOTE.—On January 17, Mr. [Lord] Haldane wrote to Sir E. Grey that he had "sent on Sunday full instructions to Neville Lyttleton, so the French Attaché will find Gen[eral] Grierson ready. I made it clear that we were to be in no way committed by the fact of having entered into communication." (Grey MSS., Vol. 63.) On January 19, he wrote again— "Gen[eral] Grierson is in communication with the French Military Attaché confidentially and without prejudice." (Ibid.)]

(b.)

Major-General J. M. Grierson to Lieutenant-Colonel Barnardiston.

Winchester House,
St. James's Square, S.W.,
January 16, 1906.

W.O. Liaison I/3. Secret.
My dear Barnardiston,

I have received a letter from Lord Sanderson in which he authorizes me, in Sir E. Grey's name, to ask you to consult the Belgian military authorities "as to the manner in which, in case of need, British assistance could be most effectually afforded to Belgium for the defence of her neutrality. Such communications must be solely provisional and non-committal." These are his exact words and you must limit yourself strictly to the scope of these instructions. You may tell the Chief of the Staff what we are prepared to put in the field in this case, 4 cavalry brigades, 2 Army Corps, and a division of mounted infantry, and you know from our conversations the general lines on which you should go. The total numbers will be about 105,000 and we shall ferry over to the *French* coast—Calais, Boulogne, Dieppe, & Havre—railing afterwards if necessary to Belgium, and then, when command of the sea is assured, changing our base to Antwerp.

You should show this letter to Sir E. Phipps, and of course keep him acquainted with all you do or hear, but the fewer people that know what you are doing the better.

I remain,
Yours very sincerely,
J. M. GRIERSON.

[ED. NOTE.—The resulting correspondence between Colonel Barnardiston and General Grierson is given together at the end of this chapter, p. 187 *sqq.*]

<hr>

No. 218.

Lieutenant-Colonel Barnardiston to Sir E. C. Phipps.

F.O. 371/9.
Sir,

Brussels, D. January 17, 1906.
R. at F.O., January 26, 1906.

Statements have recently appeared in the press with reference to measures which are reported to have been taken by the military authorities towards a mobilization of the Belgian army.

[15869]

N 2

It is said that the issue of preserved provisions has been stopped, and that Commanding Officers have received instructions concerning the mobilization of their units; also that the men of the 14th and 15th classes of militia have been warned to hold themselves in readiness to join the corps to which they have been posted without delay.

While some of these statements may not be exactly correct, I have good reason to believe that the mobilization arrangements of the army have been thoroughly over-hauled, and that every precaution is being quietly taken to insure a transition of the army from a peace to a war footing at very short notice, should the state of European politics demand it.

It may be worth while, in this connection, to point out that it is not necessary for Belgium to await an actual declaration of war or outbreak of hostilities before mobilizing her army. Her neutral position and obligation to defend her neutrality render this step a precautionary measure which cannot be construed into an unfriendly act, as would be the case with a belligerent Power.

I have, &c.

N. W. BARNARDISTON, *Lieutenant-Colonel,*
Military Attaché.

No. 219.

Sir Edward Grey to Sir F. Bertie.([1])

F.O. 371/70.
(No. 76.)   Secret.
Sir,   *Foreign Office, January* 31, 1906.

The French Ambassador asked me again today whether France would be able to count upon the assistance of England in the event of an attack upon her by Germany.

I said that I had spoken on the subject to the Prime Minister and discussed it with him, and that I had three observations to submit.

In the first place, since the Ambassador had spoken to me a good deal of progress had been made. Our military and naval authorities had been in communication with the French, and I assumed that all preparations were ready, so that, if a crisis arose, no time would have been lost for want of a formal engagement.

In the second place, a week or more before M. Cambon had spoken to me, I had taken an opportunity of expressing to Count Metternich my personal opinion, which I understood Lord Lansdowne had also expressed to him as a personal opinion, that, in the event of an attack upon France by Germany, arising out of our Morocco Agreement, public feeling in England would be so strong that no British Government could remain neutral.([2]) I urged upon M. Cambon that this, which I had reason to know had been correctly reported in Berlin, had produced there the moral effect which M. Cambon had urged upon me as being one of the great securities of peace and the main reason for a formal engagement between England and France with regard to armed co-operation.

In the third place, I pointed out to M. Cambon that at present French policy in Morocco, within the four corners of the Declaration exchanged between us, was absolutely free, that we did not question it, that we suggested no concessions and no alterations in it, that we left France a free hand and gave unreservedly our diplomatic support on which she could count; but that, should our promise extend beyond diplomatic support, and should we take an engagement which might involve us in a war, I was sure my colleagues would say that we must from that time be consulted with regard to French policy in Morocco, and, if need be, be free to press upon the French Government concessions or alterations of their policy which might seem to us desirable to avoid a war.

([1]) [Published by Lord Grey: *Twenty-Five Years*, (1925), I, pp. 78–81.]
([2]) [*v. infra* p. 209, No. 229.]

I asked M. Cambon to weigh these considerations in his mind, and to consider whether the present situation as regards ourselves and France was not so satisfactory that it was unnecessary to alter it by a formal declaration as he desired.

M. Cambon said that in Morocco, if the Conference broke up without favourable result, Germany might place herself behind the Sultan and acquire more and more influence, that trouble might be stirred up on the Algerian frontier, that France might be obliged to take measures to deal with it as she had done before, and that Germany might announce to France, as she had already once done, that an aggression on Morocco would be an attack upon her, and would be replied to accordingly. In such an event war might arise so suddenly that the need for action would be a question not of days, but of minutes, and that if it was necessary for the British Government to consult, and to wait for manifestations of English public opinion, it might be too late to be of use. He eventually repeated his request for some form of assurance which might be given in conversation. I said that an assurance of that kind could be nothing short of a solemn undertaking. It was one which I could not give without submitting it to the Cabinet and getting their authority, and that were I to submit the question to the Cabinet I was sure they would say that this was too serious a matter to be dealt with by a verbal engagement but must be put in writing. As far as their good disposition towards France was concerned, I should have no hesitation in submitting such a question to the present Cabinet. Some of those in the Cabinet who were most attached to peace were those also who were the best friends of France, but though I had no doubt about the good disposition of the Cabinet I did think there would be difficulties in putting such an undertaking in writing. It could not be given unconditionally, and it would be difficult to describe the conditions. It amounted in fact to this : that if any change was made, it must be to change the " entente " into a defensive alliance. That was a great and formal change, and I again submitted to M. Cambon as to whether the force of circumstances bringing England and France together was not stronger than any assurance in words which could be given at this moment. I said that it might be that the pressure of circumstances—the activity of Germany, for instance—might eventually transform the " entente " into a defensive alliance between ourselves and France, but I did not think that the pressure of circumstances was so great as to demonstrate the necessity of such a change yet. I told him also that should such a defensive alliance be formed, it was too serious a matter to be kept secret from Parliament. The Government could conclude it without the assent of Parliament, but it would have to be published afterwards. No British Government could commit the country to such a serious thing and keep the engagement secret.

M. Cambon in summing up what I had said, dwelt upon the fact that I had expressed my personal opinion that, in the event of an attack by Germany upon France, no British Government could remain neutral. I said that I had used this expression to Count Metternich first, and not to him, because, supposing it appeared that I had over-estimated the strength of feeling of my countrymen, there could be no disappointment in Germany, but I could not express so decidedly my personal opinion to France because a personal opinion was not a thing upon which, in so serious a matter, a policy could be founded. In speaking to him, therefore, I must keep well within the mark. Much would depend as to the manner in which war broke out between Germany and France. I did not think people in England would be prepared to fight in order to put France in possession of Morocco. They would say that France should wait for opportunities and be content to take time, and that it was unreasonable to hurry matters to the point of war. But if, on the other hand, it appeared that the war was forced upon France by Germany to break up the Anglo-French " entente," public opinion would undoubtedly be very strong on the side of France. At the same time M. Cambon must remember that England at the present moment would be most reluctant to find herself engaged in a great war, and I hesitated to express a decided opinion as to whether the strong feeling of the Press and of public opinion on the side of France would be strong enough to overcome the great reluctance which existed amongst us now to find ourselves involved in war. I asked M. Cambon however to bear in mind that, if the French Government desired it, it would be possible at any time to re-open the conversation. Events might change, but as things were at present I did not think it was necessary to press the question of a defensive alliance.

M. Cambon said the question was very grave and serious, because the German Emperor had given the French Government to understand that they could not rely upon us, and it was very important to them to feel that they could.

[I am, &c.]

E. G[REY].

MINUTE BY KING EDWARD.

Approved.—E.R.

No. 220.

Memoranda by M. Cambon and Lord Sanderson.

(*a.*)

Memorandum by M. Cambon.

F.O. 371/70.
Private.

31 *Janvier* 1906.

Le Principal Secrétaire d'Etat aux Affaires Etrangères m'a dit qu'il avait entretenu Sir H. Campbell-Bannermann [*sic*] des éventualités que je l'avais prié d'envisager lors de notre dernière entrevue. Sa réponse à la question précise que je lui avais posée le 10 Janvier courant peut se résumer ainsi :

"Jusqu'à présent, il n'y a pas de temps perdu. Nos administrations navale et militaire sont entrées officieusement en communication ; elles échangent leurs renseignements et leurs vues et elles se mettent d'accord pour parer à toutes les éventualités.

"Vous m'avez dit qu'il importait de donner à Berlin l'impression que si la France était l'objet d'une agression à l'occasion de nos accords, si par exemple un conflit s'élevait à propos du Maroc, elle ne resterait pas isolée et que l'Allemagne trouverait l'Angleterre à côté de la France. J'ai fait le nécessaire pour donner cette impression au Gouvernement Allemand. Une semaine avant notre premier entretien, j'ai dit au Comte Metternich que, d'après mon opinion personnelle, si la France était attaquée à l'occasion des affaires marocaines, le sentiment public anglais se prononcerait si fortement que le Gouvernement ne pourrait se dérober à l'obligation de la soutenir par les armes. Lord Lansdowne lui avait déjà fait une déclaration analogue mais, tout en parlant en mon nom personnel, j'ai accentué l'expression de mon opinion et je sais que l'Ambassadeur d'Allemagne l'a transmise à son Gouvernement. L'effet moral que vous désiriez produire a certainement été atteint.

"Est-il nécessaire de faire davantage dès maintenant?

"Nous ne pourrions prendre un engagement tel que celui dont vous parlez sans consulter le Gouvernement. Or, vous savez qu'un certain nombre des membres du Cabinet qui sont les meilleurs amis de la France sont aussi très attachés aux idées pacifiques et qu'ils appréhendent tout ce qui ressemble à une perspective de conflit armé. La modification de caractère de nos accords soulèvera donc une discussion. Nous vous avons promis notre appui diplomatique au Maroc, c'est-à-dire que nous vous avons laissés libres d'y poursuivre telle politique que vous jugerez conforme à vos intérêts, et que nous ne nous sommes pas faits juges de cette politique, mais, le jour où notre appui se transformerait en concours armé, le Gouvernement pourrait demander à être consulté sur des projets qui peuvent l'entraîner dans un conflit et vous n'auriez plus une aussi complète liberté d'action. En outre le Cabinet trouverait une déclaration de concours armé d'une telle importance qu'il ne consentirait pas à lui laisser un caractère purement verbal, il demanderait un échange d'engagements écrits. Nos accords se doubleraient ainsi d'un traité d'alliance défensive, or jamais en Angleterre des arrangements de ce genre n'ont été conclus sans être communiqués au Parlement. L'avis préalable du Parlement n'est pas nécessaire, mais la communication presqu'immédiate après la signature est de règle.

"La situation est-elle si périlleuse que nous soyons tenus de recourir à de tels préparatifs de défense?

"Il ne semble pas qu'en ce moment l'Allemagne ait une attitude plus agressive que dans ces temps derniers, qu'elle soit plus pressante et plus mal disposée. L'opinion anglaise, qui ne croit pas à un péril imminent, ne s'expliquerait pas une mesure prématurée; elle est pacifique et n'admettrait l'adoption d'arrangements en vue d'une guerre que si l'Allemagne manifestait des intentions provocantes. Dans le cas où nous verrions naître le péril, nous pourrions envisager des éventualités qui ne sont pas encore apparentes."

J'ai répondu à Sir Edward Grey que je ne croyais pas plus que lui à un danger immédiat, que le Gouvernement Allemand paraissait assez embarrassé de sa situation à la Conférence d'Algésiras, que les déclarations qu'il avait reçues de Londres avaient dû lui faire une certaine impression et que j'espérais un apaisement plus ou moins prochain, mais qu'il était de notre devoir d'envisager toutes les hypothèses. Si la Conférence aboutit à une rupture ou si, sans se rompre, elle laisse les choses dans un tel état que l'Allemagne ait au Maroc sa liberté d'action, si l'Empereur Guillaume obtient du Sultan des ports sur l'Atlantique ou l'organisation de la police, si, poussé par les agents allemands, le Maghzen encourage les incursions sur notre territoire, si, pour nous protéger, nous sommes obligés de franchir la frontière marocaine, si le Gouvernement de Berlin, réalisant des menaces que je crois vaines, mais qui n'en ont pas moins été formulées, prétend nous interdire l'usage du droit de légitime défense, c'est la guerre. Or les hostilités éclatent aujourd'hui avec une rapidité foudroyante; ce n'est pas une question de semaines, ni même de jours, c'est une question d'heures. Ainsi L'Amirauté Anglaise a l'intention dans le cas d'un conflit avec l'Allemagne de barrer la Manche aux escadres germaniques. Si elle est obligée d'attendre les manifestations de l'opinion anglaise et les delibérations du Cabinet, elle agira trop tard, l'escadre allemande aura passé, c'est une affaire de vingt-quatre heures. Il convient donc d'être d'accord avant le commencement des hostilités:

"Il faut aussi se préoccuper de l'opinion française. Malgré toutes les insinuations venues de Berlin, elle est persuadée que l'Angleterre ne nous abandonnerait pas. Quelle direction prendrait-elle si elle pouvait croire qu'elle ne doit avoir de ce côté aucune certitude?

"D'ailleurs, ai-je ajouté en terminant, Vous m'avez dit que d'après vous l'opinion publique obligerait le Gouvernement à nous soutenir.

"Oui, a répondu Sir Edward Grey, je l'ai déclaré au Comte Metternich avec plus d'assurance et plus de force qu'à vous-même, mais vis-à-vis de vous je répète que c'est une opinion personnelle qui ne saurait engager le Gouvernement. Seulement je laisse la porte ouverte et il est bien entendu que nous reprendrons cette conversation si les circonstances nous y obligent. L'Allemagne ne nous paraît pas en ce moment nourrir des desseins offensifs; le jour où nous aurions des raisons de penser le contraire nous aviserions."

MINUTES.

Conversation between Sir E. Grey and M. Cambon on January 31, 1906.

M. Cambon's version agrees in all material respects with what Sir E. Grey has recorded in the draft despatch to Sir F. Bertie.

I only note the following points in which they slightly differ:—

(A.) The French note alludes to the intention of the British Admiralty in case of a conflict with Germany, to bar the Channel against the German squadrons. This passage does not occur in Sir E. Grey's draft. M. Cambon makes his observation respecting the rapidity of the outbreak of hostilities (which he describes as a question of "hours"—not "minutes," as Sir E. Grey said) in connection with this passage concerning the barring of the Channel.

(B.) The French note contains no allusion to the argument given in the following passage of Sir E. Grey's draft :

"I did not think people in England would be prepared to fight in order to put France in possession of Morocco. They would say that France should wait for opportunities and be content to take time, and that it was unreasonable to hurry matters to the point of war."

Feb. 2.

E. A. C.

I think the purport of M. Cambon's note is accurate.

E. G.

(*b.*)

Memorandum by Lord Sanderson.

F.O. 371/70.   *Foreign Office, February 2, 1906.*

I called on the French Ambassador yesterday afternoon, according to Sir Edward Grey's instructions, in order to hear the account which he had drawn up of his conversation with Sir Edward Grey on the previous day. I took with me a copy, which Sir Edward Grey had given me, of his own account of the conversation.

M. Cambon read to me his summary of what had passed. It differed in form from Sir Edward Grey's account, in that it gave a summary of what had been stated on either side instead of putting these statements in the form of consecutive remarks and answers. It also gave some remarks of detail on the part of M. Cambon in the way of illustration of his arguments, which Sir Edward Grey had omitted. But in substance it corresponded with Sir Edward Grey's own account.

I suggested one small alteration, and then produced Sir Edward Grey's statement. M. Cambon after reading this, said that he should like to make some alterations in his report in order to bring out a remark of Sir Edward Grey's that he had felt less hesitation in giving a decided opinion to the German Ambassador, inasmuch as if it proved to be in any way mistaken, that would not entail any disappointment in Germany; but that he felt the need of being more cautious in expressing personal opinion to the French Ambassador, which, if in any way mistaken, might be the cause of serious disappointment in France. M. Cambon had omitted this remark, and said he wished to insert it. He promised that when he had corrected his memorandum he would send a copy of it to Sir Edward Grey.

I then said that as I was no longer an official, I might speak to him quite freely, and that I wished to make to him one or two observations on my own personal views.

In the first place, in the course of my experience, which was a pretty long one, I knew of no instance of any secret Agreement by the British Government which pledged them further than that if a certain policy agreed upon with another Power were in any way menaced, the two Powers should consult as to the course to be taken. That I thought was the limit to which the Government could properly bind itself without in some way making Parliament aware of the obligations that it was incurring.

And this I think we could do moreover if the French wish it.
E G.

Secondly, it was a maxim which had been impressed upon me by several statesmen of great eminence that it was not wise to bring before a Cabinet the question of the course to be pursued in hypothetical cases which had not arisen. A discussion on the subject invariably gave rise to divergences of opinion on questions of principle, whereas in a concrete case unanimity would very likely be secured. M. Cambon observed that this view was a perfectly just one.

I am glad this point was so well pointed out to M. Cambon.
E. G.

Thirdly, I told him that I thought that if the Cabinet were to give a pledge which would morally bind the country to go to war in certain circumstances, and were not to mention this pledge to Parliament, and if at the expiration of some months the country suddenly found itself pledged to war in consequence of this assurance, the case would be one which would justify impeachment, and which might even result in that course unless at the time the feeling of the country were very strongly in favour of the course to which the Government was pledged.

M. Cambon thanked me for these remarks and said that he had already told me he did not feel apprehensive personally that war between Germany and France was imminent. He thought it more likely that if the Conference at Algeciras did not come to a satisfactory issue, the Germans would endeavour to obtain a dominant position in Morocco, which might eventually lead to trouble.

I said that no doubt the situation would be one which would require great patience and prudence on the part of France, but that the position of France in Morocco was naturally a stronger one than that of Germany, and that I thought in the long run the advantage must be with her.

M. Cambon said that this might be so, but he was a little apprehensive of the Germans getting into favour with the Sultan and obtaining concessions from him in the manner which they had practised so successfully in Turkey.

I said that there was this difference, that commercial development in Morocco was absolutely impossible without reforms, and that the Germans could not really obtain any great advantages there without such reforms being instituted. They could scarcely really undertake them alone, and they certainly could not do so without rendering themselves distasteful to the Sultan.

M. Cambon paid me some compliments, and seemed to me on the whole satisfied with the results of his interview with Sir Edward Grey.

MINUTE BY KING EDWARD.

Approved.—E.R.

No. 221.

(a.)

Written Statement by Lord Sydenham.

[ED. NOTE.—Lord Sydenham of Combe in his volume *My Working Life* [1927], pp. 196–7, contests Lord Grey's statement in *Twenty Five Years* that the proceedings " must have been known to those Ministers who attended the Committee of Imperial Defence." The wording (Vol. I, p. 93) is in fact " must subsequently have become known to." Lord Sydenham has been good enough to afford the Editors the following information :]

July 19, 1927.

The " Conversations " were quite informal in Lord Lansdowne's time. In fact, so far as I know, Colonel Repington acted as go-between. It was *after* Sir H. Campbell-Bannerman's Government was formed that regular communications between the General Staffs were carried on at the instance of Monsieur Cambon and I think that Lord Grey is mistaken in saying in " Twenty Five Years " that all the regular members of the C[ommittee of] I[mperial] D[efence] had all the information. This was not so. In my time the question never came to me officially and I only heard quite informally what was going on. The points which, I think, were settled were :

(1.) That in certain contingencies four divisions *might* be sent to France.
(2.) Railway facilities were studied.
(3.) The position assigned to our contingent in the French battle line was marked on the map.

Whether different arrangements, enabling the C[ommittee of] I[mperial] D[efence] to be cognisant of the negotiations, were made after the end of September [1907] when I left for India I do not know.

[*NOTE.*—The following document from the archives of the Admiralty throws further light on the negotiations, and describes an informal discussion of the type alluded to by Lord Sydenham.

Admiral C. L. Ottley to First Sea Lord.

Secret.   *January* 13, 1906.

First Sea Lord: Submitted.

Another informal meeting was held in the offices of the Secretary of the C[ommittee of] I[mperial] D[efence] yesterday afternoon: Lord Esher, General Sir John French, Sir George Clarke, General Grierson and myself being present.

It was settled between the Military Officers that, in the event of our being forced into war (by a German violation of Belgian Neutrality or otherwise)—our proper course would be to land our Military forces at the nearest French ports, Calais, Boulogne, Dieppe, and Havre—About 100,000 British troops and 42,000 horses would be available for such a purpose within 14 days of the outbreak of war, and *some* British troops would be ferried across each day after the 3rd day—so that the entire British Army might be on French soil on the 14th day.

The process of transporting the troops would be in the nature of a *Ferry* over . . . . .

I submit for consideration that it appears very desirable that the C[ommander] in C[hief] Channel Fleet should be apprized of what is being now thought of . . . . (¹)]

C. L. OTTLEY.

(¹) [The rest of the minute represents Admiral Ottley's own views.]

[*ED. NOTE.*—*v.* further document on the naval negotiations of 16 January, 1906, on. p. 203.]

(*b.*)

Memorandum by Brigadier-General Sir G. N. [Baron] Nicholson.

Action taken by the General Staff since 1906 in preparing a plan for rendering military assistance to France in the event of an unprovoked attack on that Power by Germany.

W.O. Liaison I/6. Secret.   *War Office, November* 6, 1911.

In January 1906, when French and German relations were strained in connexion with Morocco, the General Staff with the approval of the Ministers of State concerned began to consider what steps could be taken to render military assistance to France in the event of an unprovoked attack on that Power by Germany, should His Majesty's Government in such an event decide to render such assistance.

The problem was treated as being of a secret and hypothetical nature, and all that was done at first was to estimate the force which could be made available and the period within which it could be mobilized at the stations where the several units composing the force were quartered. After due consideration, and having taken into account the requirements of home defence, the General Staff were of opinion that our military resources would admit of the formation of an expeditionary force for the purpose in view, consisting of four Divisions and a Cavalry Division. But if the scheme were to be of any value should the occasion arise for carrying it into effect, it was necessary to go further and to collect and formulate information regarding the ports of embarkation and railway transport thereto, transport by sea across the Channel, the ports of disembarkation, and railway transport therefrom to the assumed area of operations.

The consideration of some of these questions obviously involved secret and unofficial communication with one or more members of the French General Staff, and reference was made to the Foreign Office on the subject. In reply Lord Sanderson informed General Grierson, then Director of Military Operations, on the 15th January, 1906, that Sir Edward Grey in concurrence with the Secretary of State for War agreed to communications being entered into with Colonel Huguet, the French Military Attaché, for the purpose of obtaining such information as might be required, it being understood that the communications must be solely provisional and non-committal.

Colonel Huguet was accordingly consulted, and a preliminary scheme was drawn up with the assistance of the Admiralty in regard to the ports of embarkation and disembarkation and the arrangements for sea transport across the Channel. As secrecy was essential, no official letters passed on the subject between the War Office and the **Admiralty.**

Meanwhile the tension between France and Germany began to relax, and hopes were entertained, which were afterwards realized, that the dispute about Morocco might be capable of amicable settlement, at any rate for the time being.

In October, 1906, General Ewart succeeded General Grierson as Director of Military Operations, and found that the original scheme needed revision on account of changes in the organization of the Home Army. Intimation had also been received of certain changes in the French plans of mobilization and concentration, which affected the ports of disembarkation and the railway transport therefrom. A revised scheme was therefore prepared, but before communicating it to Colonel Huguet Sir Neville Lyttelton, then Chief of the General Staff, approached the Foreign Office and on July 26th, 1907, submitted a covering memorandum indicating the action which it was proposed to take. In this memorandum it was clearly laid down that the scheme was not binding on the British Government, but merely showed how the plans made in view of the situation in 1906 would be modified by the changes made in the organization of the Home Army in 1907. The memorandum with a few verbal amendments was approved by Sir Edward Grey, and Colonel Huguet was informed accordingly.

At the same time the Admiralty were unofficially acquainted with the changes in the scheme so far as that Department was concerned, and Lord Fisher, then First Sea Lord, authorized General Ewart to settle details with Sir Charles Ottley, then Director of Naval Intelligence, and the Director of Naval Transport. . . . . [1]

[1] [The remainder of this memorandum deals with later events and will be published in due course.]

(c.)

Correspondence between Major-General J. M. Grierson and Lieutenant-Colonel N. W. Barnardiston. January–April 1906.[1]

[1] [The following extract refers to these negotiations. It is from a preliminary survey preceding the detailed General Report on Belgium for the year 1906. It is enclosed in Sir A. Hardinge's despatch No. 23 of January 31, 1907.—R. February 4, 1907. F.O. 371/9.

Foreign Relations.

8. At the beginning of the year the possibility of a European war as the result of the Morocco complications caused a good deal of anxiety in Belgium, involving as it did the prospect of hostilities between France and Germany, and perhaps a violation of Belgian territory by a German invading force, aiming at turning the flank of France's eastern defences. A frank and confidential exchange of views between the British and Belgian military authorities determined to their mutual satisfaction the action to be adopted by both Governments in such an eventuality; but all danger that such action might be necessary was averted by the settlement at Algeciras, in which the Belgian Delegates participated, like those of the other minor Powers, on the principle of observing strict neutrality as between the rival camps. This was the only passing cloud on an otherwise clear horizon, and throughout the year the relations of Belgium with all her neighbours retained their normally friendly and neutral character. In the debate on the Foreign Affairs Budget in the Senate, M. Edmond Picard, a clever Socialist speaker, who is not, however, taken very seriously, denounced the " Prussian danger " and Pan-Germanist designs on Antwerp, and was answered in the correct diplomatic language which Belgian Ministers are bound to use on such a subject by Count de Smet de Naeyer.]

(1.)

Lieutenant-Colonel N. W. Barnardiston to Major-General J. M. Grierson.

W.O. Liaison IV.   Secret.   *British Legation, Brussels,*
My dear General,   *January* 19, 1906.

In accordance with your instructions I went yesterday to see General Ducarne the Chief of the General Staff, who expressed himself as very happy to learn that such assistance as was outlined might possibly be given. I was careful to explain that all my communications were entirely provisional and non-committal.

He said that before he could talk absolutely freely with me he must inform the War Minister that I had approached him on the subject, and I told him that Sir E. Phipps had also mentioned the matter to the Foreign Minister, but I begged him to bear in mind that as our " pourparlers " were merely between the two General Staffs, were entirely without any engagement of any kind and that it was very desirable they should not be known, that the matter might be mentioned to as few people as possible.

Today Gen[era]l Ducarne called on me and said he had spoken to the War Minister,(1) who was equally gratified at the possibility of support, and had authorized him to discuss matters with me.

As regards the manner in which we can best assist the Belgians, General Ducarne explained the mobilization arrangements to me very fully. I must write these at length later, as this must go by the Bag in a few minutes.

Briefly the Belgian Army will be concentrated in the neighbourhood of Brussels, where it will remain until accurate information is received of the enemy's movements. It will then be in a position to act against the flank of an Army moving on Antwerp, or if that is no longer to be feared to move against the flank of one advancing through Luxemburg. The Liège and Namur garrisons he assured me could hold out for one month; they have absolute confidence in themselves and their armament against anything the Germans can bring against them at the outbreak of hostilities.

The manner in which we can help will depend on the actual dates on which we can get here, and in order to determine this Gen[era]l D[ucarne] has offered to work out a scheme of Railway concentration for us from the ports you mentioned. For this purpose he wants the actual number of men, horses vehicles etc, which our force would consist of, and I have promised to give these on Monday. I can get then the War Establishments and the Wargame. As regards the requisitioning, quartering, etc, in which we wish to be on the same footing as the Belgians he will have to make enquiries. As soon as I get the information from him I think I had better come over and talk it over with you again. In the meantime, I may tell you that Gen[era]l Ducarne tells me they are well-informed on all that is going on over the frontier, and that at present he sees no indications whatever of any abnormal military preparations.

Believe me.

Yours very sincerely.

N. W. BARNARDISTON.

(1) [v. an Editorial Note on p. 203 on this point, in which a statement by the Belgian Government is incorporated.]

(2.)

Lieutenant-Colonel N. W. Barnardiston to Major-General J. M. Grierson.

W.O. Liaison IV. Secret.

My dear General, *Brussels, February 2, 1906.*

I had another interview with General Ducarne on Monday.

He will be glad to have the revised arrangements giving details, and dates of arrival at the various French ports, of the different detachments, so that he can have the Railway arrangements worked out. He fears that sufficient rolling stock for transport of the mounted branches will be difficult to find in France, which would necessitate sending Belgian wagons there. He said that the French wagons are side-loading which might necessitate construction of disembarkation platforms. The Belgian wagons are end-loading and both embarkation and disembarkation are very simple affairs. He thinks therefore that it may be quicker to send the mounted troops by march-route. When he received the detailed information, however, this can be worked out.

I spoke to him on the subject of newspaper correspondents, officers to be attached to Head Quarters of Army Corps, Divisions and Brigades, Gendarmeries and Interpreters. There are no laws in Belgium by which the Press can be restrained, but Gen[era]l Ducarne would consider what Regulations could be framed with regard to correspondents in the field, and how they could be enforced. I don't think there will be any difficulty about this, and I gave him an outline of the practices with regard to issue of passes and the conditions accompanying them, Press censors, etc., which I believe are usual.

I told him that about 28 officers of Field rank (or Senior "Capitaines Commandants" who are generally officers of standing in the Belgian Army) would be required for attachment to the units mentioned above; some 273 gendarmes, mounted and dismounted, including officers and their servants, and about 100 interpreters. As regards the latter Gen[era]l Ducarne said it would be quite impossible to find them among the army, or gendarmerie. The Belgian lower, and lower middle classes, he says, are very indifferent linguists, few being acquainted with English. He thinks that it might be possible to find the men we should want among the civil population belonging to the "Garde Civique," but any enquiries in this direction would have to be made through the Director of the "Garde Civique" at the Ministry of the Interior; General Ducarne does not think it would be advisable to make such enquiries now, and suggests letting the matter stand over for the present.

General Ducarne's information regarding Germany, received, I gathered, about the middle of last week, is to the effect that no changes whatever have taken place in the garrisons in the Rhine Valley between Coblentz and Wesel all of which are at the normal strength. New detraining platforms are being made north of Trèves, on the Trèves–Cologne line. The German population in the Rhine valley are evincing rather a warlike spirit. The French while quite prepared to fight, if driven to it, are not desirous of war.

A book, on the lines of the battle of Dorking by an anonymous writer signing himself "Zeestern" (Gen[era]l D[ucarne] did not tell me the title but promised to try and get me a copy) has been published and created much sensation, 100,000 copies having been sold in a very short space of time. His informant says that the German mobilization will be *startlingly sudden* ("foudroyant") Gen[era]l Ducarne cannot explain how this can take place, but his informant appears to have been insistent on this point, and on the use of the expression "foudroyant."

I hope the table etc. for General Ducarne may arrive by next Bag, also any information you can give him on affairs over this frontier, as I understand I am to go to Copenhagen for the funeral of King Christian, which will take place about the 14th I believe though the actual date is not yet fixed, and I should take this opportunity of paying my farewell visits at Christiania and Stockholm. By the way Gen[era]l Ducarne had no positive information about any increase in sidings etc. at Herbestal.

He says he will not be getting any more information just at present. He complains of being hampered in this respect by want of funds—owing to their position as a neutral state, they have to be most careful, and the Government won't supply secret service money. He gets plenty of information from the Gendarmerie, Douaniers etc. on the frontier, but naturally their radius of observation is limited.

I don't think there is anything more to tell you at present. Many thanks for your letter received yesterday.

Believe me, dear General,
Yours very sincerely,
N. W. BARNARDISTON.

(3.)

Major-General J. M. Grierson to Lieutenant-Colonel N. W. Barnardiston.

W.O. Liaison IV.   *Winchester House, St. James's Square, S.W.,*
My dear Barnardiston,   *February 12, 1906.*
   Things are going on satisfactorily, but slowly. I cannot send you any more precise details before the 15th so you will not be able to do anything more until you return from Copenhagen. . . . .([1])

                                        I remain,
                                             Yours very sincerely,
                                                  J. M. GRIERSON.

([1]) [Alludes to the delay in obtaining the necessary information from Admiralty.]

(4.)

Lieutenant-Colonel N. W. Barnardiston to Major-General J. M. Grierson.

W.O. Liaison IV.   Secret.
My dear General,   *Brussels, February 14, 1906.*
   Thanks for your note of 12th. I have seen General Ducarne again today. He will be glad to have the details of the assembly of our troops at the French ports, especially a Time Table showing exactly what troops will arrive each day and then be ready to be moved on by rail.
   He also asks for coloured drawings of our Field Service uniforms for information of Belgian troops, and enquired whether we had similar ones of the Belgian army. I said yes. He spoke about maps, and I told him we were bringing out a reproduction of the $\frac{1}{160000}$ on a scale of $\frac{1}{100000}$. He offers to give us, on the outbreak of war, 200 copies of the Belgian Staff map at $\frac{1}{40000}$ and the same number of the $\frac{1}{160000}$ if required. They may be useful for Staffs.
   He can give us 30 officers for attachment to higher units and Staffs, and 273 Gendarmes to work with our Military Police. These figures are based on what I gave him. He cannot supply the 100 Interpreters in uniform, and can only suggest civilians being obtained from among the number of Bank Clerks and similar individuals who will be thrown out of employment by the closing of their Establishments on the outbreak of war.

Intelligence.

   I showed the enclosed cutting from "Le Soir" of 4th Feb[ruary].([1]) I had been told there was no abnormal purchase of horses going on in the Condroz district, but General Ducarne says that there is greater activity than usual. He however attributes it to the fact that in a short time a duty on imported horses is to be imposed in Germany, and that dealers are consequently buying all they can now. He assures me that there is an ample supply of horses remaining for Belgian Military requirements.
   He learns that the German garrisons on the Rhine have their normal units, but that a certain number of reservists who are still liable to 30 to 50 days service are being recalled. This was found out accidentally through a Postcard from the German Legation here to an individual informing him that he had to rejoin to complete 42 days training being left by mistake at the house of an officer in the same street. It is confirmed by the Police. Gen[eral] D[ucarne] remarked that recalls of that sort were common during the summer for manœuvres etc, but he thought it singular in mid-winter.
   The French are reported to be reinforcing their garrisons on the N.E. frontier,

([1]) [Not reproduced.]

as they appear to be in possession of information which convinces them that the Germans intend an advance through Belgium. They are however effecting this in a very unusual manner by transferring men from one Regiment to another. For example 100 men are sent from the Yth Reg[imen]t at Dunkirk to the Nth Reg[imen]t at Lille and so on. The General then went on to speak of his plans and how we could help him in this in a general way, as he awaits the further details which you are going to send him to have the scheme worked out carefully.

He took 2 hypotheses :

(*a*.) In the case of a "coup-de-force" by Germany against Antwerp.

200,000 men or 5 Army Corps will be required to invest Antwerp. These can be concentrated opposite the Dutch frontier between Venlo and Aix-la-Chapelle on the 7th day of mobilization. There are two lines of defence which the Belgian Army of 100,000, which will be concentrated, as I have explained before, on the 4th day, could take up.

(1.) An advanced line from about Neerpelt to near Maastricht, on the Campine Canal.

This is liable to have its left flank turned and to be cut off from Antwerp.

(2.) A line roughly between Turnhout and Diest.

This he proposes to occupy. The country lends itself to defence and gives no favourable positions for the hostile artillery.

The advanced line will be occupied, on the 2nd day of mobilization by 2 Cavalry Divisions, with 4 batteries Horse Artillery and 4 companies of cyclists, and probably supported by the remainder of the Carbonnier [*sic*] Reg[imen]t. The Germans cannot reach this line before the 10th day, and the most effective way in which we could assist would be by detraining between Louvain and Aerschot, to support the Belgians on their right flank.

(*b*.) The second supposition is that of a German advance through Belgian Luxembourg against the Upper Meuse. The most northerly road available (see General Ducarne's Memo[randum] Annex C. to Report of Military Commission 1901) is that through Eupen, Verviers, Durbuy, Ciergnon, Revin. An advance through the Ardennes to the S.E. of this line would bring them opposite the French Army of 4 Corps between Mézières and Sedan. They cannot cross the frontier between Eupen and Gouvy probably before the 8th day of mobilization, and they could be at Marche by the 10th—perhaps the 9th. The Belgians will be on and in advance of the Meuse between Liège and Namur.

To be of any use we must have some troops on the Meuse between Namur and Dinant by the 10th day. Even if it were only, say, 2 Divisions and a Cavalry Brigade it would be useful, as the Germans would hardly be able to know accurately what was there, and these troops would of course be quickly followed by others.

Working on the data I gave him, General Ducarne calculated that, using 3 double lines of railway, which are available, 2 Divisions and a Mounted Brigade could be transported to this point in 1½ days. This we should certainly be able to promise. He proposes to work out, when he receives the details and Time Table of the arrival of troops at the French Ports, the transport of the whole force, detraining 1 Army Corps at Namur and on the line Namur–Assesse; 1 Army Corps at Yvoir, and the mounted troops at Fosse. There are 3 double lines of railway available, on each of which 40 trains per day can be run. He calculates that each A[rmy] C[orps] will require 175 trains, and the mounted troops the same number, and that 4 days will be necessary for the operations, plus one day extra for entraining and detraining etc. All necessary vehicles can be supplied by the Belgian railways : the trains will be taken over at the frontier by French or Belgian drivers respectively, as they don't know each others roads.

General Ducarne will be very grateful for any intelligence you can pass on to him.

He expressed much surprise that I should be moved away from here at this time when it was necessary to have some one here thoroughly acquainted with the Belgian army and its capabilities, and with the plans and arrangements we have been discussing. I said we hoped the crisis would be over in a month's time.

Hoping to find some news and some valuable information for General Ducarne on my return from the North,

Believe me, dear General,
Yours very sincerely,
N. W. BARNARDISTON.

(5.)

Major-General J. M. Grierson to Lieutenant-Colonel N. W. Barnardiston.

W.O. Liaison IV.   Secret.   *Winchester House, St. James's Square, S.W.,*
My dear Barnardiston,   *February 27, 1906.*

I waited till today's bag to reply to yours of 14th Feb[ruar]y as you were away when the last bag went.

I cannot yet give the exact details of the dates of arrival of our force at French ports as we keep on constantly polishing it up and improving the scheme, but the enclosed([1]) is the latest "general idea" from which you will see that notable acceleration has been made in the mobilization of the 7th Division. Gen[eral] Ducarne can from it get an idea of the times by which we could reach certain points.

I shall have coloured prints made of our service uniform and badges and send them over to you, but we already know all we want of the Belgian, French and German armies and are getting ready a small vade-mecum.

We should be very glad to get 400 copies of the $\frac{1}{40000}$ and the same number of the $\frac{1}{160000}$ for the use of the staffs, on the outbreak of war. I note what Gen[eral] Ducarne says about attached officers gendarmes, and interpreters. An officer I have travelling about between the Rhine and the frontier reports absolutely no signs of extra military activity.

I hardly think that the Germans would undertake such an eccentric operation as the advance against Antwerp and its investment. The movement through Belgian Luxemburg seems to me a much more probable contingency, and, from the table, you will see that by the 10th day we could have 2 divisions, 1 cav[alr]y brigade, etc., etc., at Namur–Dinant, and that by the 16th day we would probably be complete except perhaps the parks of the 2 A[rmy] C[orps].

I am afraid that no calculations can be made as to the date of arrival of the M[ounted] I[nfantry] Division, as its mobilization entirely depends upon the collection of its cobs which have *all* to be purchased.

Do you really think that the Belgians would fight if the Germans only marched through Luxemburg? I noticed in a recent F[oreign] O[ffice] despatch that the French minister at Brussels has his doubts on this subject. Would they join us in a strong offensive in the direction of Bastogne and are they equipped with sufficient supply columns to keep this up? Railways are few and far between in the Ardennes and the country is very difficult.

You might also try to find out what the Belgians think the attitude of Holland would be and whether a violation of Dutch Limburg would bring all the Dutch forces into action or whether they would protest and withdraw. Also their attitude if we used their waters in making Antwerp our base.

I send you some papers on supply arrangements we have made with the French, which *please return*. Would you please make similar representations as to the supply of our troops to Gen[eral] Ducarne and arrange accordingly with him.

If things are still unsettled by the time your appointment expires, I shall ask to have you kept on along with Yarde-Buller but anyhow he will come over as arranged.

With many thanks for your letter,
I remain,
Yours very sincerely,
J. M. GRIERSON.

([1]) [This table is omitted as being purely technical.]

Lieutenant-Colonel N. W. Barnardiston to Major-General J. M. Grierson.

W.O. Liaison IV.   Secret.

My dear General,   *British Legation, Brussels, March* 3, 1906.

The King of Denmark was not able to receive me till Thursday, but I succeeded in getting away on Thursday evening and arrived here late last night, and found your letter of 27th Feb[ruary] enclosing schedule of Disembarkation Scheme, and papers on supply arrangements, the latter of which I return herewith.

I have not been able to see General Ducarne today, but on Monday I shall take him the Schedule, and will also convey to him the information you were able to send me.

It was *200* copies of each description of Map ($\frac{1}{40000}$ and $\frac{1}{100000}$) which he promised. I hope I did not make a mistake. I will tell him you would be glad of them.

I certainly think the Belgians would fight if the Germans only marched through Luxemburg. That is certainly the feeling in the army, and as Gen[era]l Ducarne said to me, they would consider it a duty owed to the country for the sacrifices made to maintain an army during all these years, to act vigorously against any violater of their neutrality. I believe there are certain people who would counsel sitting still, partly because they think that nothing that Belgium could do would make any difference, and partly because they think a policy of protest merely, would pay them better politically. I will speak again to General Ducarne on this subject.

As regards the action of Holland, her neutrality is hardly likely to be violated except in the case of a direct advance on Antwerp, which is not very probable. It is difficult to say what action the Dutch Government would take under such circumstances, but the Belgian General Staff do not think that, even if the Dutch put their Army in the Field, they could do much against German troops. Their Field Army, as I have pointed out several times, is not sufficiently trained or accustomed to act in large bodies to make it a match for the Germans. With reference to the question of our using their waters, this is a ticklish matter about which no absolute certainty can be made. You will see that I have treated of it in the "Military Resources of Holland" and also in the paper I wrote on Belgian neutrality and the Lower Scheldt question. . . . .

Believe me, dear General,

Yours very sincerely,

N. W. BARNARDISTON.

[*ED. NOTE.*—The last paragraph and the postscript to this letter are omitted, as having no bearing on the negotiations.]

(7.)

Lieutenant-Colonel N. W. Barnardiston to Major-General J. M. Grierson.

W.O. Liaison IV.   Secret.

My dear General,   *Brussels, March* 17, 1906.

I took General Ducarne the Table giving dates of disembarkations of our force at French Ports, and made him generally acquainted with the contents of your letter of 27th Feb[ruary] which enclosed it.

Intelligence.

Besides telling him what you had heard with reference to the state of affairs on the Rhine etc., I mentioned what I had been told about the re-armament of the German Field Artillery, which I mentioned to you in my last letter. He said that it confirmed what he had heard from a retired officer in whom he had great confidence (Monsieur Van Beckhoven, civilian head of the 6th Bureau, 1st General Direction at the War Office, who is occupied in the study of foreign armies and who compiled the very complete and excellent Tables on organization etc. in the " Bulletin de la Presse " here) but which he had not believed. He thinks that the recalling of certain reservists, of which we had already heard, may have been in order to train them in the use of the new gun.

I again brought up the subject of the attitude of Belgium in the event of a violation of her neutrality in connection with which you alluded to the views of the French Minister here. General Ducarne reiterated the intention of the General Staff to take the most vigorous offensive compatible with the safety of their base, Antwerp, and he assured me that the War Minister is entirely in agreement with him on this subject. This is borne out by the statement of the latter in the Senate on the 2nd inst[ant] during the Debate on the Antwerp Defences. M. Wiener had alluded to statements which he asserted to have been made to the effect that in the event of war the army would take refuge in Antwerp. The War Minister immediately interrupted him with "Il ne peut être question de cela!" And the Premier, Count de Smet de Naeyer added "Jamais cela a été dit au parlement Belge!"

The Belgian army would undoubtedly in my opinion, join in a strong offensive against the flank of a German advance through Luxemburg. The only thing which would make them hesitate to commit themselves too far would be the possibility of a German advance against Antwerp from Aix-la-Chapelle or further north. But General Ducarne declared that were he in command, and were 3 or 4 German Divisions heard of at Aix he would go and attack them there. I agree with you in the unlikelihood of such an eccentric advance as that against Antwerp.

Attitude of Holland.

As regards the attitude of the Dutch, I am less confident. In military circles, and in the discussions which take place at the War School there is a strong feeling in favour of vigorous action should Dutch neutrality (for instance in Limburg) be violated by Germany in an advance on Antwerp, or through Belgium. This feeling though might be less strong had Germany already had some initial successes, or if for some reason it appeared that she were going to be victorious in the war. In fact the Dutch are very much afraid of Germany, and this is a factor which has got to be reckoned with. A Dutch General in a high position, with whom I had some conversation last week at the Hague said that while he himself was absolutely convinced of the necessity, in preservation of her own independence, of Holland opposing by force and with all her might any attempt against the independence of Belgium, he was by no means sure that the country would realize the danger. Although the Dutch four Field Divisions are a force which cannot be considered as a " quantité négligeable " still as I have pointed out in my manœuvre and other reports, their period of training is too short and their opportunities of being exercised in large bodies are too few to make them a match in the field for the Germans. This is also the opinion here in Belgium.

The question as to what the Dutch would do in the event of our coming up the Scheldt is also a problem which cannot be answered with any assurance. I have treated this question in the " Military Resources of the Netherlands " p. 121. Here again we have the German bug-bear to reckon with, and I think the Dutch attitude would depend largely on whether they thought the Germans were going to get the better or the worse of the conflict. But they could do nothing. The fortifications on the Lower Scheldt are valueless. Even if the Dutch adopted a hostile attitude towards us, I don't fancy they would do more than protest perhaps with a slight show of naval force to save their face.

Next as to the Supply question dealt with in Q[uarter] M[aster] G[eneral]'s minute etc.

Supply.

There will be no difficulty as regards the supply of wines and spirits for Hospitals. As regards hay the Belgians always live on the country, our troops will be on exactly the same footing as to requisitions etc and the Belgian intendance will operate in fullest co-operation with our own supply services to obtain what is necessary and to indicate sources of supply, contractors etc. Should there be any indication of scarcity in the country, there will be no option but to import it. I think arrangements however could be made later. The same remarks apply to fuel.

With reference to Q[uarter] M[aster] G[eneral]'s reply to C[hief of] G[eneral] S[taff] minute 1 (c). I have already arranged that we shall have the right to requisition, by Royal Decree. Our requisitions therefore will be carried out exactly as prescribed in the " Règlement sur les Prestations militaires " with the assistance, if necessary, of the Belgian officers attached to the force (see my previous letters). The above also answers paragraph 2 of above quoted minute.

As regards 3 (food and water on railway journey). The Belgians cannot arrange for this. No machinery exists here for feeding troops etc on railway journeys as there is no necessity for it, unlike in Germany and France where long journeys have to be undertaken for concentration. These arrangements moreover cannot easily be improvised at short notice. Could not the troops travelling from Calais etc be fed once on the journey through France where arrangements for the purpose already exist, and carry a cooked ration? The journey through Belgian territory will not, I think, occupy more than about four hours.

With reference to admission of stores, supplies, cattle etc free of duty, and the arrangements with respect to payments, and the manner in which they are to be made etc, General Ducarne cannot enter into any negotiations without taking into our confidence certain Government Departments (Finance, Railways, etc). At present only five people in Belgium know of our " pourparlers " viz : himself, myself, H[is] B[ritannic] M[ajesty's] Minister, and the Ministers of War and Foreign affairs. Is it advisable at present to let anyone else into the secret? Could not arrangements of this kind be made when the L[ines] of C[ommunication] Staff arrive? I don't think there will be the least difficulty in the matter, as the Belgian Gov[ernmen]t will be only too ready to assist us in every way.

As regards the arrangements for supply of our force, I communicated them generally to General Ducarne and he will arrange for the interpolation of supply trains as suggested in Q[uarter] M[aster] G[eneral]'s minute.

The Belgian Divisions are amply supplied with transport for supply purposes in the event of a forward movement. The distances from railroads are not excessive and their Divisions only require one train a day each. General Ducarne anticipates no difficulty in this respect.

General Ducarne expressed a wish to see one of the maps at $\frac{1}{100000}$ which we are bringing out. If we give him one, I think we should also give one to Major Gillis the Head of the Map Section, to whom we are indebted for the means of making it, and who is not under General Ducarne's direction.

I think I have now answered all the points raised in your letter. I shall go and see General Ducarne again before closing this in case he has anything to ask or communicate.

Believe me, dear General,
Yours very sincerely,
N. W. BARNARDISTON.

P.S.—My German Colleague here told me that they knew the French were in a very bad way as regards stores etc, when the " tension " occurred last year but that since then the latter had been very active and that their magazines etc were now well supplied.* If this is true it shows a somewhat remarkable forbearance on Germany's part in not attacking France last year. He also denied that there was such a bellicose feeling in the German army, as is generally believed.

*P.P.S.—I have seen General D[ucarne] and told him this, and he says it is confirmed by some remarks of the "Rapporteur" of the French War Budget, in which he hints at the disquieting state of affairs which had existed on the Eastern frontier, in this respect. I shall have General D[ucarne]'s Railway and concentration scheme in a few days now.

N. W. B.

(8.)

Major-General J. M. Grierson to Lieutenant-Colonel N. W. Barnardiston.([1])

W.O. Liaison IV.   *Winchester House, St. James's Square, S.W.,*
My dear Barnardiston,   *March 19, 1906.*
     I received your letter of 16th and the big one by bag this morning. Many thanks for the latter which is quite satisfactory so far as it goes. If only I could get the Admiralty to finish the time tables for over-sea transport there would be nothing more now to be done. I am not however quite happy over the choice of detraining stations at Yvoir and Assesse. I have been to see both and think that it would be difficult to arrange matters at either as the ground is so swamped. Ciney seems to me a much better place than either, and even Dinant is better than Yvoir, but I should think we might almost use Jemelle.
     I have shown your letter of 16th to the C[hief of] G[eneral] S[taff], but he regrets that he cannot make any change. The Treasury would only agree to the monthly extension and that with difficulty, and so there is nothing for it but to make the best of it. I don't think that Yarde-Buller has explained to the Minister exactly what he was told, which was *not* to make his official bow at Brussels, but, after he had settled his house, etc., to go on at once to Scandinavia and take his time over making his bows there. However, this will be settled by the instructions which the F[oreign] O[ffice] is now sending.

Yours very sincerely,
J. M. GRIERSON.

([1]) [Endorsed "Replied 24.3.06."]

(9.)

Lieutenant-Colonel N. W. Barnardiston to Major-General J. M. Grierson.

W.O. Liaison IV. Secret.   *British Legation, Brussels,*
My dear General,   *March 24, 1906.*
     Thanks for your letter of 19th.
     When the scheme for the transport, etc., of our troops is worked out by the General Staff here General Ducarne will let me know, and I can then mention to him (without mentioning you) about the disadvantages as detraining stations of Yvoir and Assesse. But I think that very probably they will be realized, when the scheme is worked out in detail. I know there were some points on which Gen[era]l D[ucarne] was not satisfied with it, and was going to have it altered. But do you not think that failing these points, it would be better to select others at all events not further to the front than they are? Ciney is only about 12 miles from Marche, and Jemelle only about 6, and the Germans could be at Marche by the 10th day, perhaps by the 9th. It seems to me they would be placed too far to the front for safety. Will you let me know what you think about this? Dinant would do all right.

I expect to see Gen[era]l Ducarne next week. He promised to let me know directly the scheme was completed, and we would then discuss it together. The papers look like an agreement at Algeciras being reached very shortly now.

Believe me, dear General,
Yours very sincerely,
N. W. BARNARDISTON.

(10.)

Lieutenant-Colonel N. W. Barnardiston to Major-General J. M. Grierson.

W.O. Liaison IV. Secret.

My dear General, *Brussels, March 30, 1906.*

I enclose translated copies of Tables given me by General Ducarne giving a summary of the Transport of our Troops from French Ports to Belgium under the two suppositions of (*a*) a German advance on Antwerp, and (*b*) Ditto through the Ardennes.(¹) With reference to these it is necessary to give a few explanations in addition to the notes on the Tables themselves. General Ducarne has selected the French lines named as being, according to his information, the most suitable, but it is possible that the French General Staff may think it advisable to make some modifications in them. As regards the journey from Cherbourg it has not been possible to work out an absolutely accurate time table beyond Valenciennes, and General Ducarne has therefore assumed that at least 24 hours must be allowed for the journey, including halts for meals, etc., etc., between those two places. From Valenciennes on through Belgium the Time Tables have been worked out in detail and graphics prepared.

As the hours of arrival of the Transports at the various Ports have not been given, an arbitrary interval of 12 hours, to allow for disembarkation and rest, has been allowed before entraining.

Arrangements will have to be made with the French to supply Engine drivers (and I suppose engines) on the French side of the frontier, who are acquainted with the roads run over.

The detraining stations have been selected so as to ensure the detraining being done under cover of the Belgian Army in its positions, and also to place us in a situation from which we can act most decisively. In the first case this will be roughly in the triangle of Brussels–Aerschot–Louvain, in rear of the right flank of the Belgians who will be in a position between Turnhout and near Diest. Then cavalry, if obliged to retire, will fall back a Brigade on each flank, supported by cyclists and the Carbonnier Reg[imen]t. Should the Germans attack the position we shall be favourably placed to act against their left flank.

In the second case, that of the German advance through the Ardennes, the detraining stations, in the Triangle Namur, Ciney, Dinant, have been selected on the assumption that the Belgian army will be in position S.E. of the Meuse, somewhere between Ciney and Durbuy. If the German advance, or other reasons, should compel them to occupy a position further to the rear, Ciney will not be used, but only stations nearer Namur. The strategical situation in this theatre, with the Belgians on the Meuse between Namur and Liège, ourselves between Namur and Dinant and four French Corps in the vicinity of Mézières, seems to me a very favourable one.

But in both cases, it is most necessary to expedite our disembarkation. You will see by the Tables that on the 10th day of mobilization we can only have in the Field two Divisions, one Cavalry Brigade and a Cav[alry] Reg[imen]t. It has been calculated that on this day the Germans can reach with their main body, in the Ardennes, Marche, and in the Campine the line Turnhout–Diest. Time is of the greatest importance, and Gen[era]l Ducarne begged me to say to you how very desirable

(¹) [Not reproduced. They are purely technical in character.]

he considers it to press on our mobilization and cc ccentration to the utmost. The moral and material effects of a reverse owing to so many of our troops not being at hand at the critical moment would be disastrous and would probably not be retrieved by their belated arrival. It is true that we are working on calculations based on the most unfavourable circumstances for us, but it will not do to assume too much in our favour when we have to deal with an Army as well trained and staffed as the German.

In studying the first hypotheses General Ducarne is considerably perturbed by the position of Maastricht. If the Germans seize it the lines of the Meuse and the Maastricht Canal are at once turned. What will the Dutch do? No one knows. These lines however are only intended to be held by the Cavalry Div[isio]n and the cyclists, so that I do know that the question is a very important one.

I forgot to say that Gen[eral] Ducarne will arrange for all our Camps, etc., and will detail an officer to meet the Head Q[uartermaste]rs of all the larger units on arrival by train and conduct them to their destination.

Intelligence.

I think I told you in one of my earlier letters that the Belgians were well supplied with information from over the border. I find that I was mistaken, and that Gen[eneral] Ducarne's remarks which had led me to that conclusion only applied to that particular time when he had, on his own initiative, an emissary on the Rhine. The information from the Gendarmes and "douaniers" on the frontier is also restricted to a very small area and is less important than I had thought. Beyond this the Belgians have no organized sources of information whatever. On more than one occasion the War Minister has endeavoured to get the assent of the Foreign Department to the initiation of some system of spies, but has always been met with a statement that it would be easy to organize it on the outbreak of war. So far as I can see therefore there will be no means, in this direction of knowing what is going on at Aix-la-Chapelle, Elsenborn, etc., after war has broken out except from rumours which may get across the frontier, and these, for many reasons are extremely unlikely to be reliable. I am afraid I gave Davies a wrong impression on the subject last Sunday. I had no idea that state of affairs was so bad, but I had a long talk with Gen[eral] Ducarne on Tuesday which opened my eyes. So far as I can see the Belgians will know nothing until their frontier has actually been crossed. It is especially during the first week of mobilization that we shall want reliable information from the Rhine and Prussian Wallonia, and if we make ourselves responsible for it we can easily work it from here, with the reservation that I mentioned to Davies on the platform just before he left, i.e., that we must be prepared to deal with an active splendidly organized system of contre-espionage here.

Newspapers.

I have looked into the Belgian constitution and Code and there is no such thing here as a state of siege.* Therefore there are no legal means of muzzling the press, and we shall have to rely on their patriotism not to publish anything which might affect national defence. I think that if this were pointed out to newspaper Editors by a circular they would readily concur even the Socialists. This would be worked through the medium of the "Syndicat de la Presse."

I don't think there is anything more to tell you today. Will you keep me informed of anything which it may be desirable for Gen[era]l Ducarne to know or of any modifications which the French G[eneral] S[taff] may think it advisable to make in the Railway Scheme?

Believe me, dear General,
Yours very sincerely,
N. W. BARNARDISTON.

* Except in the fortified positions in which it may be proclaimed.—[N. W. B.]

(11.)

Lieutenant-Colonel N. W. Barnardiston to Major-General J. M. Grierson.

W.O. Liaison IV.   Secret.   *British Legation, Brussels,*
My dear General,   *March* 31, 1906.

I add this to say that I have just had another talk with General Ducarne who particularly asked me to impress upon you his strong feeling of the paramount importance of hastening our mobilization and the transport of our troops across the Channel. His view is that the Germans doubtless are aware of our intention to support the French and to act in union with the Belgians in defending their neutrality. That, for this reason, they will use *every possible effort* to press on and try to beat us in detail. The whole of our 100,000 men cannot be on the Meuse or near Louvain till the 16th day of mobilization, and as I pointed out in my other letter, by the 10th day, which may be a critical one, we shall only have about 2 Divisions and a Cavalry Brigade available. Supposing their force to be, say 200,000 men, they can easily reinforce their advanced guard to 100,000 and be equal to the strength of the Belgians or ourselves taken separately.

Gen[era]l Ducarne is convinced that the German mobilization will be completed on the 3rd day and that their concentration will commence immediately afterwards and be completed on the frontier by the 7th day. I suppose that our delay is only caused by transport difficulties. Cannot these be overcome so as to reduce the period we require by half? If we could get our force into France by the 10th day it would be an immense gain.

By the way General Ducarne asks that this concentration scheme may be regarded as having emanated from your office, and not from him if and when you communicate it to the French. He thinks it well that no one but ourselves should know that the Belgian G[eneral] S[taff] have had anything to do with the matter. There are spies everywhere, and a knowledge of what he has been doing might place him in a difficult position.

He also asks that what he has told me about intelligence arrangements may be regarded as entirely between ourselves.

Have you heard that the German VIIIth Corps and a Cavalry Division are to be concentrated at Elsenborn for manoeuvres this year?

The Belgians are still ready for immediate mobilization. The Meuse forts are still garrisoned I believe; and I know that no officers are allowed to leave Belgium.

I am assured, from a Belgian source, that the Dutch cannot be relied on to act against a violation of their Limburg territory, and that they will probably withdraw from Maastricht in the event of war. In any case judging from the Dutch character I should fear that any action which they might take would be too late to be of any use.

Believe me, dear General,
Yours very sincerely,
N. W. BARNARDISTON.

(12.)

Lieutenant-Colonel N. W. Barnardiston to Major-General J. M. Grierson

W.O. Liaison IV.   Secret.   *British Legation, Brussels,*
My dear General,   *April* 14, 1906.

I hear from Russell that I may expect to leave here about the middle of May, so I suppose I may conclude that the negotiations on which I have been engaged will be dropped. As a matter of fact, there remains but little to settle now, except matters of detail, and I think we may congratulate ourselves on having arrived at a satisfactory general agreement with the Belgians on a joint line of action, and on our having added very materially to our knowledge of what they are prepared to do.

General Ducarne has been most frank in his relations with me, and has taken the keenest interest in our "pourparlers" and, as you know, the General Staff have also worked hard in the arrangements—though without knowing they were really doing it with a purpose.

Perhaps you will be able later to send some recognition of this, if it can be done quite privately, for, as I mentioned to you in my last letter, in sending the Time-Tables for the Railway Transport, it will not do, even now to let the world know what we have been working at.

I should like to give Gen[eral] Ducarne and Major Gillis, the maps I asked for, if there is no objection.

I hope to bring back with me all my notes etc made during this period, and to hand them over to you, so that there should be no danger, in the future, of there being any "incriminating" documentary evidence of our relations with the Belgian Gen[era]l Staff, in this country.

Believe me, dear General,

Yours very truly,

N. W. BARNARDISTON.

P.S.—I am hard at work now on the "Military Resources of Belgium" and shall do as much as I can to them before leaving.

N. W. B.

(13.)

Major-General J. M. Grierson to Lieutenant-Colonel N. W. Barnardiston.

W.O. Liaison IV.   *Winchester House, St. James's Square, S.W.,*
My dear Barnardiston,   *April* 17, 1906.

Yours of 14th to hand. I am afraid that for the present all chance of our little plans coming off is at an end, though one never knows what the future has in store for us. I don't quite see in what way we can recognize General Ducarne's kindness and cooperation, for an official act can hardly be done privately. What do you suggest?

The maps for him and for Major Gillis have now been received in their proof stage and will be sent, when complete to you.

I think it would be much better that you should deposit all notes etc. here on your return and leave none in Brussels.

Let me know that your ideas are on the above point, and with many thanks for all you have done.

I remain,

Yours very sincerely,

J. M. GRIERSON.

[Endorsed :—" Suggested Private Letter to Du[carne] from C[hief of] G[eneral] S[taff]."]

(14.)

Major-General J. M. Grierson to Lieutenant-Colonel N. W. Barnardiston.

W.O. Liaison IV.   *Winchester House, St. James's Square, S.W.,*
My dear Barnardiston,   *April* 30, 1906.

I have shown yours of 20th to the C[hief of] G[eneral] S[taff] and he has consulted the S[ecretary] of S[tate]. Both think that it would be inadvisable to write a letter, but they wish you to call upon Gen[eral] D[ucarne] and express to him the thanks of both and their highest appreciation of the cordial way in which he has cooperated in the preparation of schemes which might have been of the most extreme importance to both our countries. They also wish to thank him for his personal courtesy and kindness to you.

Would you please do this before you come away?

I remain,

Yours very sincerely,

J. M. GRIERSON.

[ED. NOTE.—The following paragraphs are printed from the detailed General Report on Belgium for the year 1906. (Enclosed in Sir A. Hardinge's despatch No. 56, Confidential, of April 10, 1907. R. April 29, 1907.)

They are given here as indicating the background of these negotiations.

F.O. 371/198.

V.—FOREIGN RELATIONS.

Neutrality of Belgium.

111. The dominant factor in the foreign relations of Belgium is its neutrality. This neutrality is guaranteed by the Treaty of the 19th April, 1839, between the Netherlands, Belgium, the five Great Powers which guaranteed by the earlier Treaty of 1831 the independence of the Belgian State—namely Austria, France, Great Britain, Prussia, and Russia, and the then existing Germanic Confederation, and the VIIth Article of which runs as follows : " La Belgique, dans les limites indiquées aux Articles I, II et IV, formera un Etat Indépendant et perpétuellement neutre. Elle sera tenue d'observer cette même neutralité envers tous les autres Etats." This neutral character had, as has been pointed out above, been provided for in the Treaty of the 15th November, 1831, by which the Great Powers recognized Belgian independence, and practical effect had been given to it by that of the 14th December of the same year, under which nearly all the barrier fortresses along the French frontier of the Netherlands, Menin, Ath, Mons, Philippeville, and Marienbourg, garrisoned in virtue of the Barrier Treaty throughout the Austrian rule of the 18th century mainly or exclusively by Dutch troops, were dismantled; but it was not till 1839 that the adhesion of Holland and of the Germanic body, the price for which was the separation from Belgium of portions of Limburg and Luxemburg, completely regulated the international situation of the kingdom. Experience has demonstrated that diplomatic guarantees of the independence and integrity of small States are only of relative utility, and that such States if they wish to preserve their existence against the ambition of some of their guarantors and the cowardice or corruptibility of others, must protect it not by mere paper defences, but by the vigilant development of their own military resources. Belgium has throughout her recent history fully realized this fact, and the expediency of still further improving and modernizing her military system is one of the burning questions which divide her domestic parties. But, inasmuch as she is precluded from a recourse to arms except for the purpose of repelling an attack on her independence or neutrality, her diplomacy must necessarily reflect, even more so than is the case of most of the minor Powers, the attitude of strict impartiality in her relations with her neighbours imposed on her by her international position. For practical purposes its most important duties are the maintenance of good relations with Belgium's two powerful neighbours on the southwest and east, France and Germany, with the sister kingdom of the Netherlands, and with Great Britain, whose shores face hers, and to whom she has always looked as the natural guardian of her independence. With the rest of the world her diplomatic intercourse has as its main object the promotion of her great and growing commercial interests, but to these four States her affairs in their bearing on her foreign relations are of supreme political importance.

Relations with France.

112. Up to 1870 the great danger to the national existence of Belgium lay undoubtedly in the traditional ambitions of France. The annexation of Flanders and Brabant, attempted by Louis XIV, was accomplished by Napoleon : and the fortresses which the Sovereign of the United Netherlands was required in 1815 to maintain as a Treaty obligation by the Courts of Austria, Prussia, Russia, and Great Britain were situated on the French frontier alone. The July Monarchy was friendly to Belgian independence, partly owing to its own pacific character and partly because of the family connections between the Orleans and Coburg dynasties, and of the fact that the Governments of both countries were disliked by the Northern Powers, and especially by the Emperor Nicholas, on account of their relatively popular character and recent revolutionary origin. The second Empire renewed the older Napoleonic traditions of expansion and aggression; the ethnological fictions dignified by Napoleon III with the title of the principle of nationality enjoined no respect for a kingdom of mixed races held together by a mere community of ancient traditions, and in 1866, after Sadowa, Count Benedetti proposed to Prussia, in return for his master's recognition of her supremacy in Germany, the acquisition by France of

Luxemburg and Belgium. "Il est évident," wrote Napoleon III, "que l'extension de la suprématie de la Prusse au delà du Mein nous sera une occasion toute naturelle, presque obligatoire, de nous emparer de la Belgique." In 1868 a new attempt in this direction was made by the French Emperor. He induced the Eastern Railway of France ("Chemin de Fer de l'Est") to buy the Belgian-Luxemburg Railway, and thus to bring into the French railway system the lines connecting Sedan and Arlon with Liège and Namur, and through those towns with Brussels. The Luxemburg Railway Company was a private concern, but M. Frère-Orban publicly declared that the Belgian State would refuse to sanction or recognize its sale, and, with the help of the British Government, induced France to give up the plan. Two years later the collapse of the French Empire at Sedan put an end to French designs on Belgium.

113. From that time onwards the Belgian Government has been free from any serious anxiety on the side of France, except in so far as the conflict between French ambitions in Africa and the policy of the Sovereign of the Congo has as in 1894 (when M. Hanotaux threatened to blockade Boma and to encourage the revolutionary movement in Belgium unless the Anglo-Congolese Convention of the 12th May were modified), indirectly from time to time affected the good relations between Brussels and Paris. So long as the political situation in Western Europe is dominated by a latent antagonism between France and Germany, strong enough to prevent their co-operation, but not acute enough to produce actual war, Belgium feels secure from the alternative perils of partition between her two powerful neighbours, or invasion by one or the other. If, as has occasionally been conceivable, the Nationalist party were to regain power in France, and were to be induced to substitute a Franco-German for the present Anglo-French entente, or to revive the colonial traditions of M. Ferry and M. Hanotaux, the prospect of a settlement of Franco-German differences at the expense of Belgium would, I think, cause a great deal of alarm here. In reading in our archives the history of the period during which M. Hanotaux directed French foreign affairs, I have been struck by the anxiety betrayed by Belgian statesmen, such as the late Baron Lambermont and even by the King, in their conversations with my predecessors, Sir Francis Plunkett and Sir Edmund Monson, at the hostility of France towards England and at the possibility that it might ripen into war. The fear that any union between France and Germany, especially if directed against England (such as that for instance, unsuccessfully proposed to the French by the German Government on the question of South Africa), might lead to some partition of Belgium has been openly expressed in the Belgian Legislature, of course by private members only: and I think there is little doubt that what most sensible Belgians wish is that the two Western Powers should be united by a friendship sufficiently close to preclude any Franco-German combination against England, and at the same time sufficiently pacific and inoffensive in its character to preclude war between them and Germany. . . . .

Germany.

. . . . 116. Of late years the growing power of Germany has made her, what France formerly was, the supposed aspirant to hegemony in Western and Central Europe, and the avowed desire of the Pan-Germanists to absorb Holland, and at least Flemish Belgium, including Antwerp, has led the Belgians, in common with other small peoples, to regard her expansion with some anxiety. Her commercial activity, especially at Antwerp, where there are now 40,000 Germans settled, and where the foreign trade once monopolized by England has passed mainly into German hands, is believed by many of them to portend future dangers to the maintenance of Belgian independence. The Government are of course very careful to betray no such feeling, and to assume that this activity is, as it professes, entirely commercial, but unofficial Belgians, even men in such important positions as M. Wiener, have expressed themselves to me as uneasy about it. . . . .

. . . . 118. In its commercial and economic aspects the growth of German interests in the Low Countries is in a great measure the result of the immense development of German industry, especially in Westphalia and Rhenish Prussia, during the last twenty years, and of the export of its products through Rotterdam and Antwerp; but this increase of commercial activity has been certainly used by German patriotic expansionists in promoting German political influence. I have been assured that for many years past German clerks from Hamburg, Bremen, and other ports are encouraged and receive financial assistance from German patriotic societies to seek engagements in Belgian business houses in Antwerp, where their industry, linguistic knowledge and thoroughness as workers make them sought after at nominal wages, and, indeed, often for nothing, and are then helped, after mastering the local ropes, to set up small businesses (which soon increase and expand) of their own; that the leading German merchants have greatly strengthened their position by allying themselves matrimonially, as well as commercially, with the great commercial families of Antwerp; and that the Pan-Germanists have systematically encouraged and subsidized the Flemish movement, of which Antwerp is the centre, with its Teutonism and antagonism to France. All this is believed to be deliberately planned with a view to the increase of German political as well as commercial influence, and with the object of rendering Antwerp as completely German a city as Johannesburg under Boer rule was a British one. It is easy to generalize on such a subject and to paint a highly-coloured picture by combining features, each of which taken separately seems insignificant or susceptible of explanation, nor is my own knowledge of Belgium or of Antwerp yet sufficient to enable me to state with any certainty what solid ground exists for all these fears. I can only say that German diplomacy is, so far as I am able to judge here, very anxious to conciliate Belgian opinion and avoid arousing its susceptibilities, and although the Emperor is said to dislike King Leopold, the official relations between the two Governments and Courts, closely connected as are the latter by family ties, are naturally correct and even friendly. It is no doubt probable that, in the event of a fresh war with France, Germany would, if we joined the French, but hardly otherwise, attempt a raid on Antwerp in order not merely to turn the French flank, but to anticipate any action on our part, and with a view to the ultimate retention of northern Belgium if she were victorious over both or over one of her opponents. It is noteworthy that Belgian writers of imaginative works of the Battle of Dorking type seem to assume this as a foregone conclusion. One I picked up at a station last summer described in detail as one of the features of the European war of, I think, 1910, a German invasion of Belgium and the dismal failure to repel it of the Anglo-Belgian forces, whose union was taken for granted. Whether these fears are well or ill-founded, the belief in the German danger is evidently becoming an increasingly rooted conviction in the Belgian mind, and has played an important part in determining the altered attitude observable within the last two years towards Belgium's third continental neighbour, Holland.](¹)

(¹) [For the German views on French, British, and Belgian military plans, v. G.P. XXI, II, Ch. 155, App.]

[ED. NOTE to p. 188, No. 221 (c) (1).—No report has been found in the official or private papers preserved in the Foreign Office of any conversation between Sir Constantine Phipps and the Belgian Minister for Foreign Affairs, nor is there any record of an instruction being sent to him. The references to the negotiations as a whole are very scanty. In addition to Lord Sanderson's letter to General Grierson (supra, p. 177), the only mention the Editors have been able to find is in some private letters from Sir Arthur Hardinge, who succeeded Sir C. Phipps in January 1906. In a letter dated February 8, 1906, Sir Arthur Hardinge wrote : "The Military Attaché has I believe reported fully to the War Office on the exchange of views which he has had with General Ducarne on the common action to be taken in the event of war." Similar references occur in his letters of February 17, and March 15 (Grey MSS., Vol. 3).

The Belgian Government state that Colonel Barnardiston's letter is inconsistent with the account of this conversation given by General Ducarne. He reports that " Barnardiston me répondit que son ministre à Bruxelles en parlerait à notre ministre des Affaires Etrangères " (cf. Passelecq : Le second livre Blanc Allemand, p. 95. In a bundle of rough notes deposited by Colonel Barnardiston in the War Office, there is an account of this interview. There the words used are " I said that Sir C. Phipps had said he would mention the fact guardedly to the Foreign Minister.") They say that it was by the Belgian Minister of War that the Foreign Minister was informed of these conversations (Colonel Barnardiston referred to both Ministers as cognisant of them in his letter of March 17, supra, p. 195), and that their archives contain no reference to any communication having been made on the subject to him by Sir C. Phipps. They point out that it is improbable that Sir C. Phipps would have spoken to the Foreign Minister on so important a matter unless he had received instructions to do so, and that if he had mentioned it, he would have reported the conversation. (This last paragraph is a statement by the Belgian Government, but the passages within round brackets are Editorial additions.)]

[ED. NOTE.—The following document was discovered in the Grey MSS. (Vol. 48) after the volume was in type. It is therefore inserted here, though it should properly have been printed on p. 186.

Sir Edward Grey to Lord Tweedmouth.

Private.
Dear Tweedmouth,   January 16, 1906.
Cambon tells me that the French Naval Attaché has been unofficially and in a non-committal way in communication with Fisher, as to what help we could give in a war between Germany and France. We haven't promised any help, but it is quite right that our Naval and Military Authorities should discuss the question in this way with the French and be prepared to give an answer when they are asked, or rather if they are asked.

Meanwhile the mood of the German Emperor is said to be pacific; the tone of German diplomacy is quiet and not aggressive. Any movement of our ships which could be interpreted as a threat to Germany would be very undesirable at this moment and most unfortunate so long as there is a prospect or even a chance that things may go smoothly at the Morocco Conference which meets to-day. I hope therefore that the Admiralty won't plan any special cruises or visits to Foreign ports or unusual movements of squadrons without consulting the F[oreign] O[ffice] as to the possible political effect.

I assume that the present disposition of the Fleet is satisfactory as regards possibilities between Germany and France; if so the quieter we keep for the present the better.
                                                                                      E. GREY.]

CHAPTER XXI.

THE ALGECIRAS CONFERENCE, JANUARY-APRIL 1906.(¹)

I.—THE PRELIMINARIES.

No. 222.

Mr. Lowther to Sir Edward Grey.

F.O. 371/171.
(No. 309.)   *Tangier,* D. *December* 29, 1905.
Sir,   R. *January* 6, 1906.

I have the honour to report that the following Foreign Ministers here have been appointed to represent their respective countries at the forthcoming Conference at Algeciras(²) :—

M. Malmusi	...	...	...	Italy.
Count Martens Ferrão	...	...	...	Portugal.
Count de Buisseret	...	...	...	Belgium.
Count Koziebrodski	...	...	...	Austria.
Mr. Gummeré	...	...	...	United States.
M. Bacheracht	...	...	...	Russia.

I have, &c.
GERARD LOWTHER.

(¹) [*Cf. Documents Diplomatiques, Affaires du Maroc, Protocoles et Comptes Rendus de la Conférence d'Algésiras* (Paris 1906), and *G.P.* XXI, I, Chs. 151–153; also A. Tardieu: *La Conférence d'Algésiras* (3rd edit. 1909), and J. B. Bishop: *Theodore Roosevelt and his Time* (1920), Vol. I, Chs. XXXVI and XXXVII.]

(²) [The First Italian Delegate was Marquis Visconti Venosta; the First Delegate of Austria-Hungary, Count Welsersheimb; of the United States, Mr. Henry White; and of Russia, Count Cassini.]

No. 223.

Mr. Spring-Rice to Sir Edward Grey.

F.O. 371/171.
(No. 14.)   *St. Petersburgh,* D. *January* 2, 1906.
Sir,   R. *January* 6, 1906.

In the course of a conversation which I had yesterday with the French Minister, M. Boutiron informed me that the Russian Government had instructed Count Cassini, the Russian Ambassador at Madrid, to afford his French colleague his cordial support in the matter of the Morocco Conference. M. Boutiron added that the Imperial Government entirely shared the objections entertained by the French Government to the subdivision of the labours of the Conference among sub-commissioners.

I have, &c.
CECIL SPRING-RICE.

No. 224.

Sir A. Nicolson to Sir Edward Grey.

F.O. 371/171.
Private.

Dear Sir Edward Grey,   *Madrid, January* 2, 1906.

M. Paul Cambon is here on a visit to his brother, and I have had some conversa-·
tions with both of them in regard to the approaching Conference. They have both been
perfectly frank and open with me, and have shown me the telegrams which have
recently arrived from M. Rouvier.   The latter mentioned in one telegram that
M. Révoil had been told to show me his instructions, and to consult fully and freely
with me on all questions concerning the Conference. I mention the above as, so far as
my horizon extends, I think it indicates a sincere desire to conceal nothing from us.

I am afraid you may think me wearisome if I revert once more to the police
question, but as it will be the crux of the Conference, I hope you will allow me to report
what has passed between the MM. Cambon and myself on the subject.

I have told them that, to my mind, it would be most unfortunate if the Conference
were to break down on the police question, and that it would be still more unfortunate
if it were made to appear that France was to blame for the miscarriage.   To speak
quite frankly the situation seemed to me as follows. Germany or possibly the Moorish
delegates would propose that some of the minor Powers should undertake the police
organization : France would object : we should follow suit : no agreement would be
reached, the Conference would break up, and it would be published abroad that
Germany had asked nothing for herself, that she had been actuated by the disinterested
and humane desire that the necessary protection should be accorded to the foreigners
at the ports, and that the task should be entrusted to Powers of whom no one could be
jealous or suspicious ; and that, for her own selfish aims, France had opposed the
proposal, and had thus prolonged an intolerable situation in Morocco, subjecting the
lives and property of foreigners to a continued reign of terror. It was, I submitted,
essential that if the Conference did fail, it should not be on account of the opposition
of France. I thought, however, that I saw a way round the difficulty.

I had had, I said, a conversation with one of the Russian Delegates, who has been
for eight years Russian Minister at Tangier, and he explained to me the following plan.
He considered that when the police question came before the Conference it should be
dealt with entirely and solely as a matter affecting the security and safety of foreigners,
whom the Moorish Authorities were unable to protect. All considerations of a political
character and all reference to " special interests," etc : should not be touched upon in
discussion. A police force was urgently needed. The question was how could it be
best organized, and whence could the necessary organizing materials be drawn?
An international control was, to any one who had lived in Morocco, clearly unworkable
in practice. Officers and above all N.C.O's must be found who were acquainted with the
language and who had experience in dealing with Arabs. In order to properly work the
system, the N.C.O's must be (f the same religion and practically of the same race
as the natives with whom they would be in daily contact : and also the officers and
N.C.O's must be nationals of a country which enjoyed a position in Morocco. No minor
Power could possibly fulfil these requirements : Germany herself did not meet all of
them. It would not be practicable to place Algerian N.C.O's, and these were the only
men who could be of use, under any other officer than a French officer. It was,
therefore, clear that to France alone could fall the task of organizing the police at the
ports. At Tangier and Rabat there was already the nucleus of a French organization ;
and this could be extended to one or two other ports where the insecurity was the
greatest. It might, he continued, be agreed upon that the organization should only be
experimental and for a short period : and this might mollify German opposition.
But to one who looked at the question solely from a practical point of view it was
evident, the Russian Minister said, that France alone could undertake the task.

The above, I said, were the views of the Russian Minister which he had embodied in a memorandum for the information of the Russian Ambassador who is the other Russian delegate. If, I said, Germany and others opposed the Russian plan, the blame of a failure would rest with them and not with France.

The MM. Cambon quite agreed that France must not cause the failure of the Conference; and they considered the plan of the Russian Minister satisfactory, and difficult to combat. They added that they thought that Spain should also be taken into partnership for the police organization. This, I said, would be easy: as she possessed competent officers in her African garrisons and had also a small body of Riff N.C.O's at Ceuta who would do as well as the Algerians.

The MM. Cambon did not think that Germany would accept the Russian proposal: but on her then would fall the onus of breaking up the Conference. They asked me if the Russian Minister would propose his plan at the Conference. I said that I did not know, but they had better speak to him of that point: and it would be well that when the police question came to the fore his proposal should at once be made. They asked if the Russian Minister had communicated his proposal to others. On this I could give them no information.

They asked me, supposing, as they considered probable, that the Conference failed, what did I think would be the consequences? I replied that in my opinion it was quite possible that the Sultan would then apply to Germany to take in hand the military, financial and police administration. They remarked that that would mean war. I said that I did not consider that this would necessarily follow: but I did think that they would have to take up a very firm attitude at Fez, and prevent the Sultan from handing himself over to the Germans. The question would resolve itself into a contest for predominant influence at Fez: but I do not believe in a war arising at this juncture over Morocco. Pray forgive me for writing at such length, but M. Paul Cambon will presumably talk to you on the subject on his return to London.

Yours very truly,
A. NICOLSON.

No. 225.

Sir F. Lascelles to Sir Edward Grey.

F.O. 371/75.
(No. 3.) Confidential.
Sir,

Berlin, D. January 3, 1906.
R. January 6, 1906.

The usual New Year reception of the Ambassadors by the Emperor took place with the customary formalities on the 1st instant. His Majesty shook hands with each Ambassador, and indulged in a short conversation, which struck me on this occasion as being shorter than usual. When it came to my turn, His Majesty shook me warmly by the hand and made some jocular remarks about my having been absent from the dinner which, following a precedent set by my predecessor, I am in the habit of offering at this time of year to the chimney sweeps of Berlin. After explaining that I never attended the dinner in person, and confined myself to the pleasure of paying for it, I said that the King had charged me to convey the most friendly messages to His Majesty. He was evidently gratified and expressed his thanks, adding that he had already that morning exchanged friendly telegrams with the King.

I then said that I hoped that a change for the better had set in as regards the relations between the two countries. His Majesty's manner at once changed. He became serious, and said he doubted whether this was the case. He would like to believe it, but the English press was as bad as ever, and he knew that attempts were being made to influence the press of foreign countries against Germany. On my attempting to protest, His Majesty said with considerable vivacity that he knew that large sums had been spent for this purpose, and what was more, he knew who had paid the money, and this must be stopped. He then passed on to my next neighbour, the Turkish Ambassador, and I had no opportunity of renewing the conversation.

I have, &c.

F. LASCELLES.

MINUTE BY KING EDWARD.

The Emperor's statement regarding large sums of money being spent on the British Press for influencing that of the Press of Foreign Countries against Germany is much to be regretted. H[is] M[ajesty] should be informed by the B[ritish] Ambassador that there is no truth in it.

E.R.

No. 226.

Sir F. Lascelles to Sir Edward Grey.

F.O. 371/75.
(No. 4.) Confidential.   *Berlin, D. January* 3, 1906.
Sir,   ·   *R. January* 6, 1906.

I called yesterday afternoon upon Baron von Richthofen, whom I had not had an earlier opportunity of seeing since my return to Berlin. His Excellency received me with the greatest cordiality, and agreed with me in thinking that a decided improvement had taken place in the relations between the two countries. I said that I had had the advantage of more than one conversation with you, and that I could state that you would gladly see the relations between the two countries placed upon a friendly footing on the understanding that friendship with Germany should not in any way interfere with our friendship for other countries.

Baron von Richthofen said that he quite understood this. No one could expect that we should forego our understanding with France, and the German Government certainly would not ask us to do so. I said that what·we desired was to be good friends with all, and that few things would give us greater pleasure than to see good relations established between Germany and France.

I then alluded to the recent conversations I had had in England with Count Metternich, who had impressed upon me that much would depend upon the attitude which Great Britain would assume at the forthcoming Conference. If this attitude were conciliatory all would be good, but if England were to urge France to resist the moderate demands of Germany, he feared that the relations would become worse than ever. I had replied that in England the fear was entertained that the German demands would be so exaggerated that France would be unable to accept them, and that, in that case, we should be obliged to support France in resisting them.

Baron von Richthofen said that the German demands would certainly not be exorbitant; on the contrary, they would be very moderate, and would be to the advantage of all Powers who had commercial relations with Morocco. They would merely be that the reforms which are to be carried out in Morocco should be placed upon an international, and not upon a one-Power, basis.

I replied that I was not greatly enamoured of the idea of an international basis, and the results of its operation in Turkey, both as regards the Armenian and Macedonian questions, were not such as to render its adoption desirable in any other country. Baron von Richthofen replied that at all events it was better than the one-Power basis, which would exclude all other Powers who might have interests in the country. I said the ideal would be that the reforms to be introduced into Morocco should be placed as far as possible on a Moroccan basis, with as little interference as possible from other Powers. Baron von Richthofen said that that would indeed be the ideal, but that the weakness of the Shereefian Government made it unrealizable.

Baron von Richthofen then referred to the change of Government in England, and expressed his satisfaction at the constitution of the new Cabinet, which contained several known friends of Germany. He felt, therefore, that His Majesty's present Government would be less hostile to Germany than their predecessors.

I denied that His Majesty's late Ministers entertained any hostility to Germany, and I said that I was convinced that there would be no change in the foreign policy of His Majesty's Government.

I then told Baron von Richthofen of the remark which the Emperor had made to me on the previous day, as reported in my preceding despatch, as to the tone of the English press, for which, as he was aware, His Majesty's Government were in no way responsible. His Excellency begged me not to attribute too much importance to a remark of that nature from the Emperor, who, as I was aware, was extremely sensitive to the criticisms of the press. His Excellency added that there certainly had been a great improvement in the tone of some important organs of public opinion in England, and he had great hopes that the movement which had recently been inaugurated by the Chambers of Commerce throughout Germany, in response to the meetings which had been held in England, with a view to bringing about a more friendly feeling between the two countries, might be crowned with success.

I said that I trusted that this might be the case but although I had accepted two invitations to such meetings, and would emulate Count Metternich's example in speaking in favour of a friendly understanding, I was afraid that some time must still elapse before the mutual suspicion and distrust which unfortunately existed in both countries should have entirely disappeared.

I have, &c.
FRANK C. LASCELLES.

No. 227.

Sir A. Nicolson to Sir Edward Grey.

F.O. 371/171.
(No. 6.) Confidential.   *Madrid, D. January* 5, 1906.
Sir,   R. *January* 13, 1906.

The Duke of Almodovar stated to me this morning that he had, of late, been in constant communication with the German Ambassador, an old friend of his, in regard to the Conference, and had requested His Excellency to assist him in his approaching difficult task as President of the Assembly. He had also spoken with the German Ambassador as to the procedure of the Conference, and it seemed to him that it would be best to defer to the later sittings the questions of the suppression of contraband trade and of the police organisation. I observed to the Duke of Almodovar that, in my opinion, it would be wisest to begin with questions which would raise no difference of opinion, and that the contraband trade would be a good subject with which to commence, as we were surely, including the Moorish delegates, all of one mind on that question. His Excellency remarked that I had on one occasion mentioned the advantage of the maritime patrol being exercised by French and Spanish coastguard vessels, and here he feared that Germany would raise objections.

I enquired on what grounds Germany could object to those who had both ports and vessels handy being entrusted with the duty. I presumed Germany did not herself desire to participate in these patrols, as she had neither vessels in the Mediterranean nor ports where the ships could lay, refit, and recoal. His Excellency said that he had understood from M. de Radowitz that his Government would propose that German vessels should take part in the patrol duties.

The Duke of Almodovar then said that Germany would insist on the policing of Mogador being confided to her. I said that, judging from the views expressed in the Cortes and in a portion of the Spanish press, this project would be most unfavourably regarded in Spain, in consequence of the proximity of Mogador to the Canary Islands. I added that we must wait till the Conference met, and till all these questions were examined and discussed : and I then turned to other subjects.

I report these observations of the Duke of Almodovar as they have some significance, both in regard to his tendency to rely on German advice and support, and also with respect to the requests which Germany may advance at the Conference.

I have, &c.
A. NICOLSON.

MINUTES.

The Duke of Almodovar, as President of the Conference, will evidently be in the hands of the German Ambassador.—B. A.

This is important.—E. G.

This would appear to be the first fairly clear intimation that Germany is aiming at a definite point on the West coast. The policing of Mogador would develop before long into something larger. I inquired the other day what had happened since 1884 about the claim of Spain to Santa Cruz di Mar Pequena. My reason was that I suspect a possibility of Spain being induced to part with this claim to Germany. Our position really depends on the opinion of the Defence Committee. I have read what Senor Moret said to Sir A. Nicolson (see his despatch No. 1657(¹) of January 9) and I admit that any arrangement between Spain and Germany on the west coast is difficult, because of the neighbourhood of the Canaries; but an equivalent concession elsewhere is not impossible.—E. G.

(¹) [Nicolson to Grey, No. 9 of January 9, 1906, F.O. 371/171, printed on p. 212 as No. 231. The number given by Sir E. Grey in his minute is that of the F.O. registry.]

No. 228.

Sir Edward Grey to Sir C. Hardinge.

F.O. 371/171.　　　　　　　　　　　　　*Foreign Office, January 8, 1906.*
Tel. (No. 6.)　　　　　　　　　　　　　　　　　　D. 6 P.M.

It might be well to let it be clearly understood before you leave St. Petersburg that our attitude at the Morocco Conference will be to support France fully according to the terms of our agreement with her. It may be desirable that the Emperor should be assured of this.(¹)

(¹) [*Cf.* Sir Sidney Lee : *King Edward VII* (1927), II, p. 361.]

No. 229.

Sir Edward Grey to Sir F. Lascelles.(¹)

F.O. 371/171.
(No. 11.)
Sir,　　　　　　　　　　　　　　　*Foreign Office, January 9, 1906.*

I told the German Ambassador on the 3rd inst[ant] that since we last had a conversation on the subject I had been giving further attention to the question of Morocco, and that I felt uneasy as to the situation. I had noticed that a little time ago Prince Bülow had described the question as "*très mauvaise.*" I had also heard that Lord Lansdowne had said to Count Metternich that, in the event of war between Germany and France, public feeling in England would be such that in his opinion it would be impossible for England to remain neutral.(²) Count Metternich said that Lord Lansdowne said that would be so in the event of an unprovoked attack by Germany on France, and that of course the question of what was unprovoked was one of interpretation.

I said that we did not intend to make trouble at the Morocco Conference. We wanted to avoid trouble between Germany and France, because I really thought that

(¹) [This despatch was published by Lord Grey in *Twenty-Five Years* (1925), I, pp. 82–5, and see his account in his speech of August 3, 1914, *Parl. Deb.*, pp. 1811–2. For Count Metternich's report, see *G.P.* XXI, I, pp. 45–52.]
(²) [*V. supra* p. 180, No. 219.]

[15869]

if there was trouble we should be involved in it. Public feeling here would be exceedingly strong, not from hostility to Germany, but rather because it had been a great relief and satisfaction to the English public to find themselves on good terms with France, and if France got into difficulties arising out of the very document which had been the foundation of the good feeling between us and France, sympathy with the French would be exceedingly strong.

Count Metternich restated again emphatically the German point of view, which was that we and the French had no right to dispose of the interests of a third party in Morocco, however we might deal with our own. I said that we had undertaken distinct engagements to give diplomatic support to France for the purposes of the Agreement—the engagements which were published in Article IX. Count Metternich observed that all we had promised was diplomatic support, and that what Germany resented was that public opinion in England spoke as if armed support had been promised. I said that I could only speak on such a matter as a private individual, my opinion being worth no more than that of Lord Lansdowne speaking in the same way, but the opinion was the same. It was not a question of the policy of the Government; what made a nation most likely to take part in war was not policy or interest, but sentiment, and if the circumstances arose, public feeling in England would be so strong that it would be impossible to be neutral.

Count Metternich said that Germany felt herself too strong a nation and in too strong a position to be overawed by a combination even of two other Great Powers. I said I understood that, but I was speaking frankly now because such a contingency had not arisen, and therefore it was possible now to talk frankly, whereas at a later date, if things became very difficult, he might be much less willing to listen and I might be unable to speak freely. "But," I said, "if things go well at the Morocco Conference, you may be sure of this, that the Anglo-French *entente* will not be used afterwards to prejudice the general interests or the policy of Germany. We desire to see France on good terms with Germany. This is the one thing necessary to complete the comfort of our own friendship with France, and we shall certainly not 'egg on' France at the Conference further than she wishes herself to go." I said this because Count Metternich had told me the other day that he considered that the British Government had been "more French than the French." He said he entirely believed now that we were not more French than the French, and that what I had said represented our real attitude. I said that it really was so, and that our diplomacy was perfectly open and frank. We had gone to a certain point in our engagements with France, from which we could not think of receding. We must keep those engagements, but if the keeping of those engagements proved, at the Conference, to be compatible with Germany's view of her own interests, there would be a sensible amelioration immediately in English public opinion.

We spoke of the tone of the Press both in England and in Germany. Count Metternich complained of a recrudescence of a bad tone in our Press, and its mis-statements. I said that we could not control our Press and that we were not inspiring it, and if I were to say anything in public now to promote a better tone I should at once be told by the Press that this was all very well, but that they must wait till the Morocco Conference took place before they could accept my view. On the other hand, if things went well at the Conference, it would be possible afterwards for any one in my position to speak in a friendly tone with effect.

We had some conversation on the details of the Conference. Count Metternich said that Germany could not content herself simply with guarantees for her economic interests because such guarantees would be worthless if France really had the control of affairs in Morocco. German commerce would then suffer, as foreign commerce had suffered in Tunis and in Madagascar. I said that there were guarantees for the open door in Morocco which did not exist in the cases of Tunis and Madagascar. Count Metternich said that that would not be enough. If French influence was supreme in Morocco, concessions and so forth would be entirely in French hands. I said I understood that there was to be a State Bank for Morocco, and that the French had already agreed to German participation in the Bank, and surely that in itself was a certain guarantee.

Beyond general statements that Germany could not allow France a special position in Morocco, Count Metternich gave me no idea of what the proposals of Germany were likely to be, or of her attitude at the Conference.

I am, &c.
EDWARD GREY.

No. 230.

Sir Edward Grey to Sir F. Lascelles.

F.O. 371/75.
(No. 12.)
Sir,   *Foreign Office, January* 9, 1906.

I have received and read with much interest your despatches Nos. 3 and 4 of the 3rd instant reporting your conversations with the German Emperor and Baron von Richthofen on the subject of the state of relations between this country and Germany.(¹)

Your Excellency's language on both these occasions is approved by H[is] M[ajesty's] Gov[ernmen]t.

With regard to Baron von Richthofen's observation that the demands put forward by Germany at the approaching Conference on Morocco would merely be that the Reforms which are to be carried out in that country should be placed upon an international and not upon a one Power basis, I have to observe that a special position has been conceded by Great Britain to France by Article II of the Declaration of the 8th of April 1904.

That Article states that—

"The Government of the French Republic declare that they have no intention of altering the political status of Morocco.

"His Britannic Majesty's Gov[ernmen]t, for their part, recognize that it appertains to France, more particularly as a Power whose dominions are conterminous for a great distance with those of Morocco, to preserve order in that country, and to provide assistance for the purpose of all administrative, economic, financial, and military reforms which it may require.

"They declare that they will not obstruct the action taken by France for this purpose, provided that such action shall leave intact the rights which Great Britain, in virtue of Treaties, Conventions, and usage, enjoys in Morocco."

It is impossible for H[is] M[ajesty's] Gov[ernmen]t to suggest to France any departure from the attitude prescribed by the terms of this Article. Moreover, by Article IX, "the two Governments agree to afford to one another their diplomatic support, in order to obtain the execution of the clauses of the present Declaration regarding Egypt and Morocco."

This engagement H[is] M[ajesty's] Gov[ernmen]t are bound to fulfil so long as France does not of her own motion propose or consent to some modification of the position conceded to her by Article II.

The details of this and other questions connected with Moorish affairs must now be left to be dealt with by the Conference at Algeciras.

If however Baron von Richthofen should revert to the subject Your Excellency can refer him to the two articles cited above as those which must decide our attitude at the Conference.

(¹) [*v. supra* pp. 206–8, Nos. 225–6.]

[15869]   P 2

As regards the general question of our relations, the attitude and feeling of H[is] M[ajesty's] Gov[ernmen]t are expressed in a conversation which I held with Count Metternich on the 3rd instant, a record of which forms the subject of my despatch to Y[our] E[xcellency] No. 11 of to-day's date.([1])

I am, &c.

EDWARD GREY.

([1]) [*v. supra* pp. 209–10, No. 229.]

No. 231.

Sir A. Nicolson to Sir Edward Grey.

F.O. 371/171.

(No. 9.)   *Madrid*, D. *January* 9, 1906.

Sir,   R. *January* 13, 1906.

I paid a visit to Señor Moret, the Prime Minister, this afternoon to bid him goodbye before I proceeded to Algeciras, and I took the opportunity of mentioning to him that we intended to act cordially with France throughout the Conference; and that I had little doubt that Spain would follow a similar course. It was clear to me, I said, that Spanish interests could be best served by adapting her line of action to that of France. At the same time I sincerely trusted that the proceedings of the Conference would progress smoothly, and that some beneficial results would ensue from its deliberations. It would be most unfortunate if an agreement could not be reached on the questions to be discussed, and personally I should consider it lamentable if the Conference were to fail. I enquired if he could give me any indications as to what proposals Germany was likely to make, as I knew he had had several interviews with the German Ambassador.

Señor Moret assured me most positively of his earnest desire to act cordially with France and Great Britain, and he quite agreed that we had interests in common. In his interviews with the German Ambassador the latter had constantly laid stress on the conciliatory and friendly disposition of the German Government, but he had indicated that in regard to police organisation, the best plan would be to allocate certain sections or districts to several Powers, and had intimated that the Mogador "rayon" would be the most suitable for Germany.

To this, Señor Moret remarked, Spain could never consent, and he trusted that in this she would be supported by Great Britain and France. I replied that the proposal would in time, and probably not a very long time, bear the character of a partition of Morocco; and even apart from these possibilities it would not, in itself, tend to introduce peace and security. I hoped, nevertheless, some means would be found to reconcile conflicting views : and I had great confidence in Marquis Visconti-Venosta being a most useful intermediary to this end.

Señor Moret said that he had welcomed the appointment of Marquis Visconti-Venosta to the post of Italian Representative, but he feared that this police question would be most difficult to solve.

I have, &c.

A. NICOLSON.

No. 232.

Sir E. Egerton to Sir Edward Grey.

F.O. 371/171.

(No. 10.)   Secret and Confidential.   *Rome*, D. *January* 9, 1906.

Sir,   R. *January* 13, 1906.

. . . .([1]) The Marquis Visconti-Venosta, when I dined with him yesterday, dwelt on the delicate position of an Italian delegate at the Conference with the Triple Alliance in Europe and the engagements with France in North Africa.

([1]) [The first part of this despatch is omitted as it deals with purely personal matters.]

(I never allow in conversation here that engagements for special objects in one part of the world can extend to another.)

He trusted the discussions of the Congress would not take a wide range and would not be complicated by subsidiary details.

He had been given to hope that Germany was disposed to be conciliatory and he would do his best that the Conference would end with a "cloture," not a "rupture."

I said that if the result of the Conference were to secure to Germany full commercial advantages for a long period, and a status in the finances of Morocco consonant with the preponderating rights of France and with those of others, the German nation would have no right to be dissatisfied.

He appeared to agree with me that it would be undesirable were Germany to make a stand on the thorny ground of police or any internal administrative question.

Prima facie he preferred a system of separate committees to treat various subjects; but I mentioned that I had heard opinions adverse to such special commissions; when the matters in discussion are few and the numbers of a Conference not large, discussion *in pleno* might be more expeditious, and control easier over the matters discussed.

He asked me about his future colleagues, and I told him that the Duke of Almodovar and Count [sic] Radowitz were charming men, over whom I trusted he would be able to exercise a calming influence.

Today I had a conversation with Monsieur Barrère on the subject of the Conference. He considers the essential point to be the recognition of the special position of France in Morocco.

That being conceded, rights and advantages in accordance with that position may be enjoyed by other Powers.

He even suggested that a certain exceptional position with regard to Morocco might be claimed by Mediterranean Powers. I answered I strongly disagreed; it would be somewhat offensive to Germany. It is useless to lay stress on its false position.

Most people think that the German Emperor and Prince Bülow have made a mistake in blustering about Morocco; it was best to help them out of it.

Monsieur Barrère said that from his experience he thought to have special commissions at Algeciras would be a waste of time.

As for the main question, he considered that the altered tone of the German Government arose from the conviction that the French nation had begun to look things seriously in the face, and to refuse any longer to be bullied.

I said I had heard the same language of French patience being exhausted three months ago when I went through Paris, and did not like it. I believe in this case in the public opinion of the civilized world.

I have, &c.
EDWIN H. EGERTON.

No. 233.

Sir Edward Grey to Sir F. Bertie.

F.O. 371/171.
(No. 21.) **Confidential.**

Sir, *Foreign Office, January 10, 1906.*

The French Amb[assado]r called here this afternoon and stated that he had been at Madrid where he had been in consultation with his brother, the French Ambassador there, and Sir A. Nicolson as to the course to be pursued in the approaching Conference at Algeciras.

[15869] P 3

They had agreed that it was very important that the Conference should not separate without coming to a conclusion, as in that case the German Gov[ernmen]t would consider themselves free to take what action they thought best, and would probably obtain concessions from the Moorish Gov[ernmen]t of a very inconvenient nature. For this reason it was undesirable that the Conference should commence by discussing the arrangements for organization of the police, which was the question on which it would be most difficult to arrive at an agreement. If an attempt were made to bring forward that question it might be met by a statement that, before discussing it, it would be necessary to ascertain what resources were available for the purpose of this and other reforms.

The first question therefore would be that of finance, the creation of a National Bank and the share which the various Powers should have in its capital and management. These questions ought not to present any serious difficulty.

The next question might be that of the prevention of trade in contraband of war. It was clear that the pacification of the country and measures for the preservation of order were scarcely practicable so long as no effective provision was made to prevent the introduction of arms and munitions of war. This question might give rise to some difficulties as the trade was largely carried on in Spanish vessels, but it ought not to present insuperable difficulties.

Lastly would come the question of Police. It was probable that the German Gov[ernmen]t would not themselves make proposals but would induce the Moorish Gov[ernmen]t to bring them forward. It might be expected that one of two alternatives would be proposed, viz., either that the coast should be divided into sections, and that the Police of each section, with the districts lying behind it, should be entrusted to a different Power, or that one of the minor Powers, such as Holland, should be entrusted with the whole organization.

The first of these alternatives would be objectionable as Germany would make use of it to establish herself on the Atlantic Coast.

The second would be ill-advised inasmuch as the Power undertaking the organization of the Police ought to have at its disposal a supply of Mussulmans of Arab race for the purpose.

Neither alternative would be acceptable to France. It would not however be desirable to adopt a purely negative attitude which would make the objecting Powers responsible for a continuance of the present deplorable condition of the country. Some other alternative should therefore be brought forward. The present Russian Minister at Tangier, M. Bacheracht, had made a careful study of the reforms that might be introduced into Morocco, and had devoted part of his attention to the question of police. His recommendations on the subject seemed sound, and might be made the basis of a proposal which might conveniently be brought forward by the Russian Plenipo[tentia]ry at the Conference.

The proposal would be to the effect that the duty of organizing the police should be entrusted to France, who was interested in the first line and had at her disposal all the necessary materials for the force. The susceptibilities of Spain and her interest in the matter on account of her possessions on the Moorish Coast must however be considered and on these grounds she should be associated with France in the task. In order to avoid an appearance of wishing to place the matter too much under the exclusive management of the two Powers it might be proposed that the mandate to France and Spain should be for a short period, say for a year or even six months, at the end of which time they should submit to the Powers the progress that had been made and the arrangements that were contemplated in the future.

M. Cambon said that he had submitted these views to M. Rouvier who had addressed instructions to that effect to M. Révoil. The latter was starting at once for Madrid and would show his instructions to Sir A. Nicolson.

I asked if it was intended that the Conference should merely adjourn and should meet again six months or a year hence to receive a report on the police arrangements.

M. Cambon said that that would scarcely be necessary. The Conference might separate, and it might be provided that the report should be presented to the Powers. He added that if I wished it he would ask M. Rouvier's permission to communicate to me M. Révoil's instructions or a summary of them.

I thanked him, and said that I would be glad if he would do so.

I am, &c.
EDWARD GREY.

No. 234.

Sir Edward Grey to Sir A. Nicolson.

F.O. 371/171.
(No. 5.)
Sir,   *Foreign Office, January 10, 1906.*

The Spanish Amb[assado]r called on me on the 3rd inst[ant] and enquired whether I could give him any news with regard to the Morocco Conference. H[is] E[xcellency] told me that he had reason to think that the Duke of Almodovar felt anxious on the subject.

I told Señor Polo de Bernabé that I had not heard what the German proposals would be; that I assumed that as Germany had desired the Conference she would make proposals. Everything would depend on the nature of these proposals.

Our course, in any event, was clear. We should keep our public engagement to France.

All the four Powers most directly interested in the Mediterranean had made arrangements with each other which were satisfactory to themselves and it was most undesirable that they should allow these arrangements to be disturbed.

The Ambassador said that his Government were determined to keep their engagements, and I remarked that I was convinced that, for all of us, this was not only the honourable but the wise course.

I am, &c.
EDWARD GREY.

[ED. NOTE.—On the 11th January, 1906, the British Government accepted the Spanish invitation to take part in the Algeciras Conference, which was dated the 30th December, 1905.]

No. 235.

Sir F. Lascelles to Sir Edward Grey.

F.O. 371/171.
(No. 13.)
Sir,

Berlin, D. January 10, 1906.
R. January 13, 1906.

I have the honour to transmit herewith two copies of a White Book on the Morocco Conference which has just been laid before the Reichstag by the Imperial Government together with a précis of its contents.

The majority of the papers have given a very favourable reception to this publication, which, they point out, contains only those of the documents bearing on the case, which are necessary to establish in the eyes of the world the justice of Germany's demand that the French proposals with regard to Morocco should be submitted to the Signatory Powers to the Madrid Conference.

[15869]   P 4

I have also the honour to transmit an article from the "Frankfurter Zeitung,"(¹) calling attention to the weakness of the German position at the Conference, and expressing doubts as to whether this will be ameliorated by the publication of the White Book.

I have, &c.
FRANK C. LASCELLES.

(¹) [Not reproduced.]

Enclosure in No. 235.

Précis on German White Book on Morocco Question.

The White Book commences with samples of French and English newspaper articles, which appeared between January and April, 1905, showing the existence in France of a wish to secure a "monopoly" in Morocco, and announcing that the French Minister in Fez had claimed to have a European mandate to introduce reforms in that country.

The first official document, dated the 21st February, 1905, is a despatch from the German Consul Vassel at Fez, reporting an interview with the Sultan, in which His Majesty expressed the intention of affording precisely similar treatment to four Powers, England and Germany on account of their trade, and France and Spain also, on account of their proximity. The Sultan further went on to ask whether the French Minister had received a mandate from all the Powers. This Mr. Vassel at once denied as far as Germany was concerned.

On the 21st April Consul Vassel reports that the Sultan denies the truth of M. Delcassé's statement to the effect that the Moorish Government had desired the French Government to make reform proposals and had promised to accept them, and describes the indignation of the Sultan on learning that the French Government had contradicted the report that their Minister had claimed to have a European mandate. His Majesty's version of his interview with M. Saint-René Taillandier is also given.

On the 15th May Count Tattenbach reports that the Sultan denies having accepted French proposals in principle, as had been stated by M. Delcassé in the Chamber of Deputies after the Emperor's visit to Tangier.

On the 17th May the German Minister reports that the French Minister, on arriving at Fez, had delivered to the Moorish Government a message from M. Delcassé to the effect that the French Government considered it contrary to their interests that their reform proposals should be submitted to the Signatory Powers for their information or discussion. No other Power had a right to intervene in Morocco. The Moorish Government must accept the French proposals, as they were unable to preserve order themselves. The French Government would act as circumstances might dictate, and would carefully watch the course of events in Morocco.

A number of documents also appear on the neglect of the French to bring the Anglo-French Morocco Agreement officially to the notice of the German Government. In these the standpoint is adopted that a formal communication of this Agreement in writing should have been made to the Imperial Government in order that they might make representations if they considered their rights under the Madrid Convention to be infringed. Verbal communications and official publications of the text were merely means of bringing Germany face to face with a *fait accompli*.

On the 7th March Consul Vassel reported on the French reform plans, and on the 30th May a despatch from Count Tattenbach, founded on information supplied by the Maghzen, gives the proposals of the French Government, and characterises them as calculated to undermine the independence of Morocco, whilst he describes the threats with which M. Taillandier urged the Moorish Government to accept them, and their reply to him.

A report dated the 6th June shows that the French proposals were made verbally to the Moorish Government, and that the French Minister refused to put them in writing.

On the 28th May the Moorish Government sent a note to M. Taillandier rejecting his proposals, and suggesting the Conference, although he had tried to prevent the despatch of this note, and had announced that France would take no part in such a Conference, and further that, if such a Conference did meet, the Powers would certainly intrust France with a mandate to carry out the necessary reforms alone.

The broad outlines of German Morocco policy are outlined in the despatch to the Imperial Ambassador in London, dated the 11th April, which was read by Prince Bülow to the Reichstag on the 6th December (see Mr. Whitehead's despatch No. 297 of the 7th December, 1905).([1])

After the Moorish Government had proposed a Conference, Prince Bülow issued a Circular despatch, dated the 5th June, to the principal German Missions abroad in support of this proposal, pointing out that the introduction of reforms was restricted by Article XVII of the Madrid Convention, and that the consent of the Signatory Powers was necessary before any one Power could claim a special position in Morocco.

Despatches to the German Ambassador in Paris of the 12th and 16th June give the German points of view as to the questions to be settled at a Conference, but refusing to discuss the question of reforms until France had accepted the Conference.

M. Rouvier's Memorandum of the 21st June, giving arguments against the Conference, is followed by a reply from Germany, dated the 24th June, pointing out that, if France introduced reforms alone, the force of circumstances would compel her to interfere with the independence of Morocco. These are followed by the French acceptance of the Conference on the 8th July, and the Agreement of the 28th September as to the advice to be given to the Sultan with respect to the programme for the Conference.

The White Book concludes with documents showing the attitude of the Imperial Government in the question of the Tangier mole.

([1]) [Not reproduced. The despatch gives press comments upon Prince Bülow's speech, and encloses a copy of the speech. F.O. Germany (Prussia) 1617.]

No. 236.

Sir M. Durand to Sir Edward Grey.

F.O. 371/171.　　　　　　　　　　　　　　Washington, D. January 11, 1906.
Tel. (No. 1.)　　　　　　　　　　　　　　R. January 12, 1906, 8 A.M.

Secretary of State informed me to-day that his Government regarded Morocco Conference as a matter in which American interests were not concerned to any great extent. The American Delegates have been instructed to stand for the open door, to interfere as little as possible in other matters, to use their influence for peace, and to avoid any action which could tend to weaken Anglo-French entente.

No. 237.

Sir F. Lascelles to Sir Edward Grey.

F.O. 371/171.
(No. 14.) Confidential.　　　　　　　　　　Berlin, D. January 11, 1906.
Sir,　　　　　　　　　　　　　　　　　　R. January 15, 1906.

I called this evening by appointment on Prince Bülow, with whom I had a conversation of more than an hour's duration. The principal subject discussed was the forthcoming Conference at Algeciras. His Serene Highness said that it was the earnest hope of the Emperor, of the whole German People and of himself that the

Conference would settle the Moroccan question in a manner which would be satisfactory to all Parties concerned and which would not leave any feeling of bitterness or rancour which might be the cause of complications later. All the reports which had been spread that Germany demanded an acquisition of territory or a sea port or any special privileges for herself were perfectly untrue. All that she asked for was the open door, equality of opportunity for all the Nations having Commercial relations with Morocco and that no one Nation should be granted a privileged position in these respects. There was only one question which His Serene Highness thought would offer any difficulty. It had been arranged during the negotiations at Paris that the Police on the Algerian Frontier should be entrusted to France. Monsieur Rouvier had admitted that this was a considerable concession for which he was grateful. Dr. Rosen had asked, in return for this concession, for an assurance that France would not put forward at the Conference, a claim to police the rest of Morocco. M. Rouvier had declined to give an assurance in writing as his doing so would have damaged his position with the French Chamber, but he gave a verbal promise that the French Representatives at the Conference should not put forward such a claim. It would certainly have been more satisfactory to the German Government if they had been able to obtain this promise in writing, as in the event of M. Rouvier's fall from Power it would have been possible that his successor might not have felt himself bound to carry it into effect. The German Government had complete confidence in M. Rouvier's word, and knew therefore that the claim would not be put forward by him. But it was just possible that it might be put forward by some other Power, and he asked me most confidentially whether I thought that His Majesty's Government, actuated by their friendship for France, would put forward a claim on her behalf which M. Rouvier would be prevented from doing by the promise he had given.

I replied this was the first time that I had heard the idea mooted, and as I had heard nothing from you on the subject, either in the conversations which I had the advantage of having with you in London, or in the Despatches which I have had the honour of receiving from you, I doubted whether it had been brought to your notice. I should of course telegraph to you at once, but I would refer to the very frank language in which you had clearly explained to Count Metternich the real attitude of His Majesty's Government. We were bound to support France at the Conference and had no intention of avoiding our obligation, but we had no wish to "egg on" France or to be "more French than the French."

Prince Bülow said he had received a full report from Count Metternich of his conversation with you. He was grateful to you for your frankness and thoroughly understood the attitude of His Majesty's Government which was exactly what he always expected it would be. He had always been convinced that England would not abandon France and the German Government would not ask her to do so.

His Serene Highness then explained at considerable length the reasons which would make it impossible for Germany to consent to a mandate being given to France to organize the Police throughout Morocco. All the expert advice he had been able to consult was unanimous on the point that if France were given that power, she would acquire complete control over the whole country and would be in a position to favour her own trade to the detriment of that of other countries. Experience had shown that this had always been the case in French possessions. In no French Colony had German merchants been able to obtain a footing, whereas in English Colonies German and English merchants were competing in the same markets and living on perfectly friendly terms. It was almost certain that trade with Morocco would be largely developed and Germany had no wish to be excluded from her fair share in such development.

Reverting to the question of Police, His Serene Highness said that provided that France was not given an international mandate, he thought that the question might be satisfactorily settled, either by mapping out the Country other than the frontier districts which were to be left to France into zones in which the different Powers might exercise Police Control, or perhaps what would be better, by placing the control of the whole in the hands of some neutral Power, such as Switzerland, Belgium or Sweden who could not be supposed to have any desire of attacking France. He had been interested at receiving a telegram from Monsieur Visconti Venosta stating that he was preparing a scheme ("una combinazione") which he hoped might meet with the approval of the Powers. The Veteran Diplomatist was a man of great resource and it would be interesting to see what his scheme would be. In any case it ought not to be difficult to find some method which might perhaps be adopted for a limited term, and be modified later if found unworkable.

I asked Prince Bülow whether I might gather from what he had said that he desired to get rid of the Moroccan Question altogether. He replied that such was indeed his earnest wish, and he thought that he had good grounds for hoping that the Conference would afford him the opportunity of doing so in a manner honourable to all the parties concerned. He had no wish to inflict a humiliation on France. He naturally did not wish to be humiliated by her, but he earnestly hoped that the relations between Germany and France which had been strained of late might become normal in consequence of a peaceful solution of the Moroccan Question by the Conference. The memories of the war of 1870 still rankled in France and had created a chasm between the two Countries which it would probably take another generation to fill in. It might be too much to hope that the relations between the two Countries should become friendly, but they might become correct and even good, and then he believed that the last obstacle would be removed to the reestablishment of really friendly relations between Germany and England which formerly existed and which in his opinion ought still to exist.

I have, &c.
FRANK C. LASCELLES.

No. 238.

Sir F. Lascelles to Sir Edward Grey.

Berlin, January 12, 1906.
D. 10 A.M.
R. 11·45 A.M.

F.O. 371/171.
Tel. (No. 3.)

Prince Bülow, with whom I had a long conversation last night, expressed his earnest hope that Algeciras Conference would pass off peacefully and in a manner which would be honourable to all parties concerned. There was only one point which might cause any difficulty, viz : the general mandate for the organisation of police. Germany could not consent to its being given to France who would thereby acquire complete control over whole of country. Monsieur Rouvier had given a verbal promise that France would not put forward demand for such a mandate at the Conference. Prince Bülow trusted that H[is] M[ajesty's] G[overnment] did not intend, in order to show their friendship for France, to put forward this claim on her behalf.

I said that I had received no instructions from you on this point which I doubted having been brought to your notice, but that although of course we should support France in the Conference, as you had already explained to German Ambassador, we should not "egg on" France to go further than she wished.

Prince Bülow went on to say that it would be a grievous thing if M. Rouvier, while keeping the letter of his promise, should get some other Power to put forward a claim on her behalf, which would be unacceptable. He hoped, however, there was no danger of this, and the police question might be solved either by creating spheres in which the police should be controlled by different Powers or perhaps by entrusting to some perfectly neutral Power such as Switzerland, Belgium or Sweden task of organizing the force. He understood that M. Visconti-Venosta was preparing a propos. he subject and he hoped that Conference would end without leaving any feeling of bitterness in any quarter. If this could be obtained relations between Germany and France would soon be improved and no obstacle would remain to the establishment of really friendly relations between Germany and England.

The impression left on my mind by this conversation was that Prince Bülow was anxious to get rid of Morocco difficulty in a peaceful manner if this could be done without the appearance of humiliation either to Germany or France.

No. 239.

Communication from M. Geoffray, January 13, 1906.

F.O. 371/171.

M. Rouvier to M. Révoil.

Paris, D. *le* 12 *Janvier,* 1906.
R. *January* 13, 1906.

La déclaration faite par le Gouvernement à la Chambre des Députés, le 16 Décembre dernier, a posé les principes de notre action politique dans la question marocaine. Je n'ai pas besoin de les exposer à nouveau. Mais, au moment où vous allez représenter la France à la Conférence internationale d'Algésiras, il convient, dans l'intérêt même de votre mission, que vous soyez muni d'instructions d'après lesquelles vous puissiez régler votre attitude à la Conférence et qui résument en même temps les vues du Gouvernement sur les points les plus importants du programme soumis aux délibérations des Puissances. Tel est l'objet de la présente dépêche.

En ce qui concerne les préliminaires de la Conférence, vous appuyerez la proposition de déférer la présidence, suivant une tradition constante, au représentant de l'Espagne. Quant au mode de discussion, il paraîtrait fâcheux que la Conférence se constituât en commissions spéciales dont la tendance serait de pousser trop avant dans le détail des diverses réglementations que peuvent comporter les questions portées au programme.

Vous devrez tout d'abord déposer sur le bureau de la Conférence les traités et accords internationaux conclus par la France au sujet du Maroc, à savoir : la déclaration franco-anglaise du 8 Avril, 1904, la déclaration franco-espagnole du 3 Octobre, 1904, les protocoles franco-allemands des 8 Juillet et 28 Septembre, 1905. Cette communication destinée à préciser notre attitude ne saurait d'ailleurs donner lieu à une discussion de principe. Elle ne comprendra pas les arrangements que nous avons passés avec le Gouvernement Chérifien en 1901 et 1902, au sujet de la frontière, ayant été expressément écartées du programme de la Conférence établi d'accord avec l'Allemagne et accepté par tous les autres États qui prendront part à cette réunion internationale.

La principale étude confiée à la Conférence est celle des moyens de remédier à l'affaiblissement du pouvoir Chérifien. Ce but ne peut être atteint que par la suppression des deux causes qui entretiennent l'insécurité du Maroc. L'une est la contrebande des armes. Les Puissances peuvent y couper court par leurs propres moyens, puisqu'elle est le fait de leurs ressortissants. Ce serait la première question à examiner. D'autre part, le Maroc et le Maghzen souffrent de l'absence d'une police régulière. Mais on ne peut constituer cette police sans avoir trouvé d'abord les ressources nécessaires pour la payer. On devrait donc discuter en second lieu la réforme financière et les diverses questions d'ordre économique qui s'y rattachent. L'organisation de la police constituerait ainsi le dernier chapitre du programme de discussion.

En ce qui concerne la répression de la contrebande des armes, vous demanderez qu'elle soit confiée aux deux seules puissances limitrophes du Maroc, la France et l'Espagne.

Parmi les réformes d'ordre financier, la création d'une banque d'État paraît être la plus essentielle. En cette matière nous exposerons à la Conférence les engagements déjà pris par le Maghezen [sic] à notre égard et consignés dans une lettre du Ministre des Finances Marocain (Juin 1904).

D'autre part, une clause du contrat d'emprunt de 1904(¹) réserve aux établissements français, souscripteurs de cet emprunt, un droit de préférence, à conditions égales, pour toute opération de crédit ultérieure. Ces promesses et ces conventions précises ne sauraient être présentées comme portant atteinte au régime de la nation la plus favorisée. Elles se justifient par l'importance de nos capitaux, de notre commerce, de nos colonies au Maroc, et spécialement par ce fait que 67 millions sur 72 qui constituent la dette étrangère du Maroc ont été prêtés par le marché français. La statistique du trafic nous attribue 30 %, à l'Angleterre 40 %, à l'Allemagne seulement 10 % du mouvement général, et si nous fusionnons nos intérêts avec les intérêts anglais et espagnols, ce groupement représente 80 % de l'activité économique du pays. Bien que cette situation de fait nous paraisse devoir déterminer la combinaison des capitaux qui entreront dans les futures institutions financières du Maroc, nous n'irons point à l'extrême de ce que nous considérons comme nos droits. Les administrateurs seraient pris suivant la même proportion dans les différentes nationalités. La présidence reviendrait à la France et la banque serait constituée sous le régime légal français.

Je crois inutile de démontrer que nos prétentions ne vont point à l'encontre du régime dit '' de la nation la plus favorisée '' et de l'article 17 de la Convention de Madrid, non plus que du système de '' la porte ouverte.'' Cette clause et cette doctrine ne sauraient être invoquées dans une matière telle que l'organisation d'une banque d'État, alors surtout que celle-ci sera constituée par des capitaux internationaux.

L'accord du 28 Septembre a défini dans ses grandes lignes le programme de la banque. Vous vous y référerez.

D'autre part on devrait augmenter les ressources actuelles du Maghzen, tout à la fois en assurant le contrôle rigoureux des douanes et en réprimant la contrebande. Ces mesures seraient heureusement complétées par l'assainissement de la circulation monétaire et la stabilité de l'Hassani à un cours normal, opérations qui s'imposeraient tout d'abord à la banque et qu'elle serait seule en état d'accomplir. Ce serait au contraire se méprendre sur la solution des difficultés financières dont souffre le Maroc que de la chercher dans un relèvement général des droits de douane. En cette matière on devrait bien plutôt conseiller une meilleure spécification qu'une augmentation uniforme des tarifs.

D'une façon générale c'est sur le programme économique que nous sommes disposés à accorder les satisfactions les plus complètes. Mais vous éviterez de donner votre acquiescement définitif aux solutions de cet ordre jusqu'à ce que vous ayez pu vous assurer que les plénipotentiaires n'entendent pas faire prévaloir de solutions inacceptables relativement à l'organisation de la police.

Vous savez d'ailleurs, que nous sommes acquis au principe de la liberté économique sans aucune inégalité. Nous l'avons inséré dans tous nos accords concernant le Maroc. Vous y adhérerez de nouveau et de la manière la plus complète devant la Conférence, comme je l'ai fait dans ma déclaration du 16 Décembre à la Chambre. Vous devrez d'autre part maintenir intégralement les règles posées sous le No. 4 dans le programme de la Conférence : '' engagement par le Maghzen de n'aliéner aucun des services publics au profit d'intérêts particuliers ; principe de l'adjudication sans exception de nationalité pour les travaux publics,'' toutes les grandes entreprises devant demeurer marocaines et l'exécution en être confiée par l'effet de la libre concurrence aux traitants, de quelque nationalité que ce soit, qui offriront les meilleures conditions.

En ce qui concerne la police, vous marquerez qu'il ne s'agit pas de réorganiser l'armée marocaine, qui doit rester sous l'autorité exclusive du Sultan et pour laquelle il suffit de maintenir les missions existantes.

Le moment venu vous spécifierez les droits définitivement acquis par nous (sans

(¹) [Cf. Documents Diplomatiques, Affaires du Maroc, 1901–5, (Paris 1905), pp. 141–52.]

qu'on puisse les retenir comme limitant nos prétentions) à Tanger, Oudjda, Rabat et même Casablanca, où la mission a déjà été confiée à des instructeurs français.

A notre point de vue, deux observations dominent toute la question de la police :—1°. la police frontière est en dehors du programme de la Conférence : celle-ci ne peut dès lors s'en occuper en quelque manière que ce soit; 2°. nous ne pouvons, en ce qui touche la région non frontière, nous prêter à une organisation de la police qui porterait atteinte à notre situation spéciale et aggraverait les difficultés de la question marocaine en perpétuant les rivalités présentes ou en en faisant naître de nouvelles : c'est à quoi paraîtrait devoir aboutir fatalement l'internationalisation de la police.

Nous considérons que la France, comme puissance musulmane et comme puissance limitrophe, est qualifiée pour obtenir le mandat d'exercer la police dans l'Empire Chérifien. Nous sommes prêts à la partager avec l'Espagne que les mêmes raisons désignent pour remplir ce rôle conjointement avec nous. La réforme de la police nous semble d'ailleurs devoir être limitée aux villes de la côte et comporter un recrutement de gendarmes marocains avec des cadres mixtes.

Vous devrez donc vous attacher à faire écarter toute solution qui tendrait soit à partager le mandat de police entre plusieurs Puissances, soit à en investir une petite Puissance, soit même à en confier l'exécution à des officiers de Puissances neutres. Le premier système qui sectionnerait le Maroc en zones d'influence pouvant conduire au partage de ce pays, encouragerait des prétentions rivales qui risqueraient à chaque instant de provoquer des complications dangereuses. Quant aux deux autres combinaisons, elles paraissent impraticables, et l'expérience faite en Macédoine de l'emploi d'Officiers appartenant à une petite Puissance, montre qu'on n'en peut attendre aucun résultat efficace.

Au cas où à cet égard les propositions conformes à nos désirs se heurteraient devant la Conférence à une opposition irréductible nous considérerions que, les questions économiques étant réglées selon nos vues, un accord pour le maintien du *statu quo* en ce qui concerne la police serait une solution acceptable, si cet accord réservait nos droits et impliquait la renonciation des autres contractants à toute action tendant à rouvrir la question auprès du Sultan sans entente préalable avec nous.

En résumé et aux termes mêmes des assurances qui nous ont été maintes fois répétées au cours des négociations, nul ne saurait attendre de nous une adhésion à aucune solution qui serait de nature à compromettre l'avenir de nos intérêts nationaux. Sous cette condition, vous marquerez, en toute occasion, notre sincère désir de respecter les droits des autres pays, d'ouvrir libéralement le Maroc à la libre concurrence des intérêts commerciaux, et vous affirmerez en même temps notre volonté de ne faire valoir nos droits et nos intérêts propres qu'avec les garanties les plus formelles données aux droits souverains du Sultan, à l'indépendance et aux traditions constitutives de son Empire.

ROUVIER.

No. 240.

Sir F. Lascelles to Sir Edward Grey.

F.O. 371/171.

(No. 17.) Confidential.   *Berlin, D. January 13, 1906.*
Sir,   R. *January 15, 1906.*

Herr von Holstein who has recently returned to his duties asked me to call at the Ministry for Foreign Affairs yesterday evening. He said that there could be no doubt that the French desired to obtain a general mandate for the organization of the Police in Morocco. Indeed a suggestion had been made to the German Ambassador in Paris that Germany should herself propose this solution. The suggestion was unofficial but evidently inspired. Germany so far from proposing such a measure, would strenuously oppose it if it should be brought forward by any other Power. The danger which he foresaw was that France, dissatisfied with the results of the Conference, and relying on the support of England in any thing she might do, might seek to create a *fait accompli* by invading Morocco. The Sultan would appeal to the Emperor and war would be the result. What would then be the attitude of His Majesty's Government? Would they consider that a French invasion of Morocco constituted an unprovoked attack by Germany on France? On my observing that the danger seemed to me a very remote one, Herr von Holstein said that France recently had been ostentatiously preparing for war. They had purchased large quantities of chemicals in Germany and had ordered an inordinate amount of barbed wire to surround their fortresses. This he believed was chiefly bluff, and he thought that the danger to which he had alluded would be averted if His Majesty's Government could see their way to giving the French a hint, that with every wish to support them, it was doubtful whether in the event of their invading Morocco, public opinion in England would allow them to do so by force of arms. The French were a prudent people and if there were the slightest doubt that the full support of England would not under all circumstances be given them, he was convinced that they would not attempt the invasion of Morocco.

In the long discussion which followed Herr von Holstein said that Germany could not consent to any provisional arrangement which would give the control of the Police to France even for a limited time. The Police was the administration and its control by France would create a French Protectorate. The Emperor less than a year ago had stated that he looked upon the Sultan as an Independent Sovereign, and could scarcely be expected now to agree to his being put under French Protection.

I replied that this seemed to me to be the weak point in the German case. They had proclaimed the Sultan as an independent Sovereign and at the same time had invoked the Convention of Madrid which in itself was an infringement of his Sovereign rights, and were now about to urge the introduction of reforms which, by being placed under International Control would still further diminish them. This was not logical. Would it be possible to place the reforms on a Moroccan rather than on an International basis—that is to say that the Conference should decide what reforms are required, and the Sultan should be called upon to introduce them? Count Tattenbach to whom I had mentioned this idea in conversation said that the Sultan was personally well disposed towards the reforms, but that his Government would probably raise difficulties as to their introduction.

Herr von Holstein, to whom the idea seemed a new one, said that he thought it might provide a solution of the difficulty. Had I worked out any details? Was the idea approved by His Majesty's Government? Would the British Representative at the Conference be instructed to propose it? To these questions I replied that it was only an idea which had crossed my mind in conversation with Count Tattenbach to whom I had expressed the opinion that the results of the operation of the International system at Constantinople, both as regards the Armenian and Macedonian questions, were not such as to render its extension desirable to other Countries. I presumed that it would be necessary for the Sultan to apply for foreign assistance both as regards the organisation of the Police and the finance of his Country.

Herr von Holstein said that the last unofficial suggestion which the German Government had received from France was to the effect that the labours of the Conference should be directed to maintain the *status quo*, to suggest some provisional arrangement as to the Police to guard against the danger of the susceptibilities of any Power being aroused if the suggestions of its Delegates should be rejected, and with this view to suggest that the British Delegates should be instructed that they should consult with the Powers most interested by which Herr von Holstein presumed that France and Germany were meant, before submitting any definite proposal to the Conference. These points he thought might be met if it were possible to place the matter on a Moroccan rather than an International basis. He would give his best attention to the idea which at first blush seemed to him to offer a possible solution of the difficulty in which the members of the Conference would find themselves placed.

I have, &c.

F. C. LASCELLES.

MINUTES.

The proposal which the French government favour with regard to the police does not according to our information extend further than the police of the ports. The police of the interior would remain under the Sultan.—S.

The police are on a " Moroccan " basis now and there can be no reform without in substance altering that basis. But it is possible that " Moroccan " may be a useful adjective at the Conference.—E. G.

<hr>

No. 241.

Sir F. Lascelles to Sir Edward Grey.

F.O. 371/171.
Tel. (No. 5.)
Conference.

Berlin, *January* 13, 1906.
D. 10·40 A.M.
R. 12 *noon*.

Herr von Holstein fears that, if results of Conference are unfavourable to France, she may, relying on support of England, attempt to create a *fait accompli* by invading Morocco. He is convinced that this danger would be averted if H[is] M[ajesty's] G[overnment] could give a hint to France that in such a contingency there is some doubt as to whether public opinion in England would admit of the support of France by force of arms.(¹)

Full report by messenger to-day.(²)

(¹) [*v. infra* No. 242.]
(²) [*v. supra* pp. 222–3, No. 240.]

<hr>

No. 242.

Sir F. Bertie to Sir Edward Grey.

F.O. 371/171.
Tel. (No. 4.)

Paris, *January* 14, 1906.
D. 1·37 A.M.
R. 8 A.M.

Sir F. Lascelles tel[egram] No. 5. Jan[uary] 13.
Morocco.

I am convinced that the French Gov[ernmen]t desire to avoid war and that in the contingency contemplated by Baron Holstein they will not provoke war by invading Morocco in order to produce a *fait accompli*. Any communication to the French Gov[ernmen]t by H[is] M[ajesty's] Gov[ernmen]t such as the Baron suggests would shake the confidence of the French Gov[ernmen]t in H[is] M[ajesty's] present Gov[ernmen]t resulting from their assurances as to policy of England (and) might lead France either to make concessions to Germany in Morocco injurious to us or bring her out of Morocco by concessions elsewhere detrimental to our interests but not greatly to those of France.

(See L[or]d Lansdowne's telegram No. 61 April 22(¹) and my desp[atch] 156 April 25 last.(²))

If any communication is to be made to French Gov[ernmen]t I recommend that it should be limited to a friendly warning that the German Gov[ernmen]t impute to them a design of invading Morocco in the event of initial discussions in the Conference being unfavourable to France, a design which we are convinced that they do not entertain.

(¹) [*v. supra* pp. 72–3, No. 90.]
(²) [*v. supra* pp. 74–5, No. 93.]

No. 243.

Sir Edward Grey to Sir F. Lascelles.

F.O. 371/171.   *Foreign Office, January 15, 1906.*
Tel. (No. 4.)(¹)   D. 1·15 P.M.
    Your telegram No. 5. I hope the result of Morocco conference will prevent the
contingency, which Herr von Holstein contemplates, from arising. Should it however
be otherwise we cannot deprecate any action on the part of France which comes within
the terms of the Anglo-French declarations of April 1904. Herr von Holstein should
know this.

(¹) [Repeated to Paris (No. 8) and Madrid (No. 6.)]

No. 244.

Sir Edward Grey to Sir F. Bertie.

F.O. 371/171.
(No. 32.)
Sir,   *Foreign Office, January 15, 1906.*
    Speaking to me this afternoon with regard to the procedure at the Algeciras
Conference, Monsieur Cambon said that he had noticed that the instructions given to
the French Plenipotentiary, which he had communicated to me on the 13th instant,(¹)
contemplated dealing with the question of contraband first, but he did not think this
desirable because it led so easily to the question of police, which was to be reserved
until the end. He had mentioned this point to M. Rouvier, who had replied that the
instructions would now be altered so that the economic questions should be those which
were first dealt with at the Conference. I told M. Cambon that I had had a telegram
from Sir Arthur Nicolson giving an account of what had passed between him and
M. Révoil respecting the opening of the Conference, and I gave M. Cambon a
memorandum giving the substance and result of this. Copy of this paper is enclosed
herewith. I also told M. Cambon that I had heard from Berlin that the German idea
was that the police should be organised either in separate "secteurs" in Morocco
controlled by different Powers, or that they should be entrusted to a neutral Power
such as the Swiss, the Belgians or the Swedes, and that a rumour reached me from
Berlin that the Marquis Visconti Venosta was preparing a proposal of this kind.
M. Cambon said that he could not think that the Marquis Visconti Venosta was likely
to be a partisan of Germany, because he was a man who had views of his own. I said
that I did not suppose that he was going to act as a partisan of Germany, but that it was
always possible for someone to suggest to him that he might play the part of pacificator
or intermediary, which was a fine but also a dangerous one, and I thought therefore
that the French Government ought to know of the report which had reached me.
    M. Cambon in the course of this conversation again said that he was sure there
would be no trouble with Germany if Germany was quite convinced that England and
France would keep together. He attributed previous difficulties to Germany having
been doubtful of this. I said that Germany had at any rate no reason to doubt this at
present.

                                                              I am, &c.
                                                       EDWARD GREY.

MINUTE BY KING EDWARD.

Approved.—E.R.

(¹) [*v. supra* pp. 220–2, No. 239.]

Enclosure in No. 244.

Memorandum respecting Morocco Conference communicated to M. Cambon,
January 15, 1906.

F.O. 371/171.

The French Representative at the forthcoming Conference at Algeciras has told Sir A. Nicolson that he proposes, at the opening of the Conference, to lay before it the Anglo-French and Franco-Spanish Agreements of 1904 respecting Morocco, and to announce that on their basis the French Government desire to obtain the adhesion of the Conference to the principles of the " open door " and of the independence and integrity of the Sultan and of Morocco.

Sir A. Nicolson told M. Révoil that he would cordially support the proposed declaration, but that he strongly deprecated the communication of the Agreements on the ground that such a procedure would lead to a discussion of those instruments which could not be admitted by the signatory Powers.

M. Révoil concurred in this view.

With regard to the right of France to police the Moorish-Algerian frontier, Sir A. Nicolson recommended and M. Révoil agreed that in the event of any allusions being made on the subject, the French representative should confine himself to stating that the policing of the frontier was a right acquired by France some sixty years ago, and that it was a matter which solely concerned France and Morocco.

Sir A. Nicolson apprehends that if M. Révoil consented to argue the matter, it might lead to an embarrassing discussion of a subject which France desired to exclude from the purview of the Conference.

It should appear that the Anglo-French and Franco-Spanish Agreements of 1904 were rather intended to give a formal sanction to a *de facto* state of affairs than to create a new situation.

Foreign Office,
January 15, 1906.

No. 245.

Sir F. Bertie to Sir Edward Grey.

F.O. 371/171.
(No. 29.)
Sir,

Paris, D. *January 16, 1906.*
R. *January 17, 1906.*

I have the honour to transmit to you herewith a copy of notes by Sir Charles Hardinge of a conversation which he had yesterday with the French Minister for Foreign Affairs.

I have, &c.
FRANCIS BERTIE.

Enclosure in No. 245.

Notes of a Conversation between Sir C. Hardinge and M. Rouvier on the Subject
of the Morocco Conference.

The statement which had reached M. Rouvier as coming from Prince Bülow, that he had given privately a promise that he would not raise the question of a mandate for the organization of the police in Morocco was absolutely untrue, and he adheres to the declaration made to Dr. Rosen on the 25th of September, to the effect : " En dehors de la formule qui sera signée par les deux Gouvernements, j'entends n'avoir d'engagement sur aucun point." (See Yellow Book, p. 305.)

The aim of the French Government will be to obtain first a solution of Art[icle]s II, III, and IV of the programme of September 28 which are all of an economic nature, and which M. Rouvier thinks should not raise any serious difficulties with Germany. If these questions are dealt with satisfactorily on the basis proposed in the programme, Germany will find herself absolutely excluded from obtaining an independent footing in Morocco which must be prevented at all costs. For this reason France will absolutely decline to accept any proposal for the organization of the police by "Secteurs," or for handing it over to a Minor Power, which might be under the influence of Germany and which would be wanting in the necessary means and prestige to make it a success. When the question of the police is finally raised by the Russian(?) Delegate the only alternatives which would be acceptable to France are :—

1. A joint Mandate to France and Spain;
2. A Mandate to France, Spain, and a third Power to study and elaborate a scheme for submission to the Powers; or
3. The continuation of the *status quo* with the right of the French to supervise the police organization on the Algerian frontier, a right which has never been in question since the commencement of the negotiations.

If the French Government fail to obtain control of the police, they will not consider that a sufficient reason to draw the sword, but they will strenuously resist any attempt on the part of Germany to obtain a footing in Morocco and especially the proposal for police organization by "Secteurs."

M. Rouvier appeared perfectly satisfied with the attitude of H[is] M[ajesty's] Government and I impressed upon him the necessity in the interests both of France and England of thorough frankness with H[is] M[ajesty's] Government during the Conference at Algeciras. He replied that he fully realized the importance of complete unanimity between the two Governments as the surest means of keeping Spain and Italy in line with France and England in the Morocco question.

C. H.

Paris, January 15, 1906.

II.—THE CONFERENCE.

No. 246.

Sir A. Nicolson to Sir Edward Grey.

Gibraltar, *January 17, 1906.*

F.O. 371/171.
Tel. (No. 4.)

D. 11·15 A.M.
R. 2·45 P.M.

Conference. First meeting was held yesterday. Spanish Minister for Foreign Affairs elected President, and Secretaries, &c., appointed.

President, in opening speech, laid down principles of independence and integrity of Sultan and his dominions and of "open door."

French Representative expressed his adherence to above principles, and moved their adoption by the Conference. This motion was seconded by German Representative and accepted.

It was agreed that first subject for discussion would be the suppression of contraband, and President suggested that those who wished to submit proposals should do so in writing, and they would be circulated. A day would be fixed later for their discussion.

Although question has importance for us, I do not propose to submit proposals in writing, but to confine myself to an endeavour to bring others into harmony with our views and interests, especially as regards right of search.

No. 247.

Sir A. Nicolson to Sir Edward Grey.

F.O. 371/171.

(No. 1.) Conference.   *Algeciras,* D. *January* 17, 1906.

Sir,   R. *January* 27, 1906.

Monsieur Révoil, the French delegate at the Conference arrived in Madrid on the 12th instant, and called upon me in the afternoon previous to my departure for Gibraltar.

He expressed a desire to speak to me on some matters pertaining to the Conference, and especially in regard to a statement which he wished to make to the Assembly immediately on its convocation. I understood that he had discussed the question both with Monsieur Rouvier and with Monsieur Paul Cambon; and he intimated his intention to lay on the table of the Conference the Anglo-French and Franco-Spanish Agreements of 1904, the Notes exchanged between the French Government and the German Ambassador at Paris on July 8, 1905, as well as the Note signed by himself and Dr. Rosen on September 28, 1905. He proposed to declare to the Conference that on the basis of the above documents France would be animated, during the proceedings, by the principles of the independence and integrity of the Sultan and of his dominions, and of equality of treatment in commercial matters or in other words, the "open door." He enquired of me whether I would be disposed to support the declaration.

I told Monsieur Révoil that I would cordially associate myself with the terms of his proposed statement; but that I most strongly deprecated laying the Anglo-French and Franco-Spanish Agreements on the table. He observed that he proposed to do so merely with the view of affording some reason for the statement he would make. I replied that it would be easy to make the statement simply as a general declaration of the main principles by which he desired that both the Conference and himself should be guided : but that once the Agreements were communicated to the meeting there was nothing to prevent any member from examining, analysing, and discussing them, and I frankly told him that I could not be a party to such a proceeding. Moreover, I had always understood that any discussion or allusion to the Agreements was to be carefully avoided : and I thought that my Government were under a similar impression. Monsieur Révoil was good enough to say that he appreciated the force of my argument, and that he would, consequently, merely make his declaration and abstain from laying any documents on the table.

M. Révoil then said that it was possible that the German Representatives would raise, in some form or another, the right of France to police the frontier districts : and he showed me the notes, which covered two or three sheets of paper, which he had jotted down to serve as the basis of an argument which he proposed to develop before the Conference. I told M. Révoil that this was a matter which concerned France and not myself, but I trusted that he would permit me to suggest that any lengthy argument would be unpropitious. To my mind the position of France in the matter of the frontier police was an impregnable one. I had observed that the German press, and I believed the German negotiators also, spoke of the exercise by France of the policing of the frontier as a concession which had been made to her, and for which possibly she should make concessions elsewhere. I had understood that France repudiated this view, and had asserted to my mind with perfect justice, that her duties and privileges in that respect were acquired rights under Treaties and Conventions dating back for some sixty years, and that the questions affecting the frontier were matters solely between her and the Sultan. No one could contest with any reason that view, and if I were in his place I should be content to take my stand on that ground, and decline to enter into any discussion. Were he to develop a lengthy argument in support of the above view he would, I fear, find himself embarked on a prolonged discussion, and thereby weaken considerably his position. After some conversation M. Révoil said that he agreed with me : and explained that he had prepared his notes with a view of convincing the ignorant of the strength of France's position on the subject. If I thought explanations were unnecessary or likely to lead to discussion, he would willingly abstain from giving them.

M. Révoil expressed the conviction that we would work cordially together during the Conference, and he wished to assure me that he would take no step without previous consultation with me, and would always treat me with unreserved confidence. I fully reciprocated these sentiments, and said that I would throughout the Conference be perfectly frank and open with him and would support him to the best of my ability.

I have, &c.
A. NICOLSON.

No. 248.

Sir A. Nicolson to Sir Edward Grey.

F.O. 371/171.
(No. 3.) Conference.
Sir,

Algeciras, D. *January* 18, 1906.
R. *January* 27, 1906.

The Conference met for the first time on the 16th instant, and before the sitting was opened, the German Representative, M. de Radowitz, proposed the election of the Duke of Almodovar as President. This motion was agreed to unanimously, and the gentlemen who are to act as Secretaries for the Conference were then chosen.

As soon as the sitting was opened, the Duke of Almodovar read a statement of which I have the honour to enclose a copy,(¹) and on its termination the French Representative, M. Révoil, rose to announce that France would, in treating the questions inscribed on the programme, be guided by the principles of the sovereign independence of the Sultan, the integrity of his dominions, and the equality of treatment in commercial and industrial matters, and he moved that the Conference should declare its adhesion to these principles. This motion was seconded by M. de Radowitz, and carried unanimously. I will forward the text of the declaration of the French and German Representatives as soon as I have received the *procès-verbaux* of the meeting.

The Duke of Almodovar then proposed that the first question which should be discussed by the Conference should be that of the suppression of contraband trade, and he said that those who had any proposals to make on this subject should formulate them in writing, and communicate them to the Secretaries who would cause them to be printed and circulated. When this had been done he would inform us of the date of the next meeting.

I enquired of the President whether this procedure would exclude the faculty of making verbal proposals during the discussions; and I also suggested that it would be well to fix a date before which the written proposals should be delivered, so as not unduly to postpone our next meeting.

I was informed in reply that any Representative would be at liberty to make any suggestions or proposals which might occur to him during the discussions: but that it would be preferable to leave open the date of the next meeting.

After some minor matters were disposed of, the meeting adjourned.

I have, &c.
A. NICOLSON.

(¹) [Not reproduced.]

[15869] Q 3

No. 249.

Sir A. Nicolson to Sir Edward Grey.

F.O. 371/171.
(No. 5.)   Conference.   *Algeciras,* D. *January* 19, 1906.
Sir,   R. *January* 27, 1906.

Marquis Visconti Venosta called on me this morning, and we had a conversation on Moorish Affairs generally and the prospects of the Conference in particular. His Excellency said that he was perplexed to find an issue from the dilemma which had been created by the diametrically opposite and apparently irreconcilable views of France and Germany in regard to the police question. If both parties remained on their present respective standpoints, a compromise seemed impossible of attainment. He said that he had had a short conversation with M. Rouvier on the subject, but the latter had remarked that if a solution could not be found the matter had better be left alone altogether. M. Visconti Venosta observed that this method did not appear to him desirable or as a satisfactory result of the labours of the Conference.

I told His Excellency that I had turned over the question in my mind for some time past, but that I had not hitherto had a detailed conversation with M. Révoil on the subject. My instructions were to support France cordially, and I intended to do so throughout the Conference, but the suggestion, which I had heard previously, to leave the police question alone had caused me some dismay. I considered that the police question, or in other words the protection to be afforded to foreigners living in the coast towns, was the most urgent and the most important of all the subjects before the Conference. To my mind a serious moral responsibility, apart from every other consideration, was imposed on all of us to enable our compatriots, as far as possible, to live in peace and security, and that I should leave the Conference with a heavy heart if nothing had been done to remedy the perfectly intolerable situation which at present existed.

I thought it more than probable that, whatever might be the results of the Conference, there would be a recrudescence of the feeling against the foreigners in Morocco, and their security would be still more in danger than it was at present. Respect for the European had long since vanished from the mind of the native, and any neglect on the part of united Europe to afford the most elementary protection to their subjects seemed to me likely to render the position of our compatriots exceedingly critical.

I thought such considerations must have some weight with the German Representatives, and if it were explained to them how urgent were the needs, they would surely not refuse to seek for some immediate remedy. The police organization, to my mind must be entrusted to those nations who could supply at once efficient and well qualified material for the purpose. Officers and non-commissioned officers were required who had knowledge of the people and of the language, and such could only be furnished by France and Spain. If a mandate accorded to those two Powers was likely to arouse misgivings and jealousy, the mandate might be for a very limited period, for twelve or even six months. By the end of that period the situation in Morocco might improve, and even if it did not, the officers, if capable men, could have organized a police force which might continue to operate under trained Moorish kaïds, provided always the pay of the men, their rations, and general well being were supervised by the consular body in each coast town. Surely such a modest proposal could not meet with serious opposition on the part of any member of the Conference?

At the same time I repeated that I had not gone fully into the question with M. Révoil, and whatever his Government and he decided I would loyally follow, as I was working hand in hand with them, and the above were merely my personal views.

Marquis Visconti Venosta replied that he thought the project was a reasonable one, but he did not know if Germany would accept even it. It would be disastrous if the Conference were to break up without having accomplished some good work and without being able to show some practical results however modest. He did not think war would ensue in consequence of a failure, but an extremely delicate and embarrassing situation would undoubtedly be produced.

I have, &c.
A. NICOLSON

No. 250.

Sir A. Nicolson to Sir Edward Grey.

Gibraltar, January 21, 1906.

F.O. 371/171.
Tel. (No. 11.) Secret.

D. 6·55 P.M.
R. 9 P.M.

United States' Representative spoke to me on 20th January as to German views on police question, and said he was in a position to assure me as a fact that in no circumstances and under no conditions, however strict or limited, would the Germans agree to police being under French and Spanish alone.

If, on the other hand, France would make concessions in regard to police, Germany would make large concessions to her in bank and finance questions; but Germany, before yielding to France on latter points, must have distinct assurances that on police question France would make concessions satisfactory to Germany. I told United States' Representative that I would convey to my French colleague what he had told me, but that he must understand that my position with, and obligations to, French colleague precluded me from suggesting any concessions.

I subsequently spoke to my French colleague, who said he had just received a similar communication from Italian Representative. He was ready to consider matter, but the Germans must be more precise and clear, first, as to the concessions they were prepared to make to France in financial questions, and, secondly, state what concessions they required as to police question.

There must be no misunderstanding on these points, and he told me privately that France had so many reasons to distrust German promises that he thought if an arrangement proved possible, that France must endeavour to obtain the guarantee of some third party, he mentioned the United States, that Germany would fulfil her promises, and not allow the arrangement to be upset by the Sultan.

I also saw Italian Representative, who will sound German Representatives, and endeavour to elicit their precise views. At the same time he thought that eventually it would be better that the two parties should meet together and discuss matter between themselves. He was not much in favour of intermediaries. I think that there is a glimmer of hope that some compromise may be arrived at.

No. 251.

Sir A. Nicolson to Sir Edward Grey.

F.O. 371/171.
Private.
Dear Sir Edward,

Algeciras, January 21, 1906.

My despatches will, I trust, give the necessary information as to the Conference proceedings up to the present date, and so I will confine myself to the question on which hangs the fate of the Conference, and in regard to which I sent you a secret telegram.

M[a]r[qui]s Visconti Venosta and Mr. Henry White were evidently authorised by M. de Radowitz to speak respectively to M. Révoil and myself. Mr. White said to me that for no considerations whatever nor under any conditions would Germany agree to leaving the police organisation to be dealt with by France and Spain alone. Germany feels she has engaged herself too deeply in this question to abandon her

Q 4

position : but in order to induce France to yield on the point she would be ready to make her "large concessions" on the Bank and finance questions. If France maintains an unyielding attitude, then the Conference will fall through.

I told Mr. White that I would faithfully repeat to M. Révoil what he had said, but he must understand that I could not play the part of the "honest broker." I would act as a channel of communication but not as a mediator : that latter part must be left to those who had made no engagements with France.

I saw M. Révoil, and repeated to him textually what had been intimated to me. He said that M[a]r[qui]s Visconti Venosta had just made him a similar communication. He wished to tell me frankly that past negotiations with Germany had made his Gov[ernmen]t and himself exceedingly cautious in regard to German promises. The Germans always required positive engagements from the French side, and offered in return only vague promises on their side. There was no doubt that the Germans would not, in any circumstances, allow France and Spain alone to deal with the police : and they required that France should abandon the idea. What did they offer in return? Nothing but vague promises of "large" concessions on the finance question. He must have, and he had so told M[a]r[qui]s Visconti Venosta and he begged me to repeat it to Mr. White, some clearer exposition. Let the Germans say with full details how far they were prepared to go in regard to finance Concessions, and what they desired to be effected in regard to the police question. Did they want to exclude France from all participation in police duties, and entrust them to minor Powers alone, or did they wish to associate other Powers with France or what?

Moreover, he said, but this was for my private guidance, what guarantees had France that Germany, while herself giving concessions on finance matters, would not allow the Sultan to refuse his consent to them? It was in this regard important to remember the order in which the questions before the Conference were to be discussed. 1. Finance, &c. 2. Police. Now Germany required, as a preliminary, that France should give an engagement that she would meet the views of Germany in regard to the police *before* the discussions on the Bank and finance questions commenced. Germany, when these discussions were entered upon, would have in her pocket France's engagement as to the police : and would be quite secure on that point, and also quite sure that neither the Sultan nor any Power would raise objections to distributing police duties among several Powers with or without the participation of France. But on the finance question could the same security be felt? Supposing that Germany acted quite loyally, gave the required concessions, and assented to, and induced the other Powers to assent, to France having a predominant position in finance matters. Was it quite beyond doubt that the Sultan would also agree to this? The Conference might do so, but its conclusions would have to be sent for ratification to Fez. The police question would in the meanwhile be discussed, and France's concessions be approved, and then might arrive a refusal from the Sultan to agree to the financial arrangement. France would then have conceded everything, and have obtained nothing.

To obviate this he thought it might be necessary, assuming that an arrangement were arrived at with Germany, to obtain the guarantee of a third Power, possibly the United States, that Germany would carry out all her engagements, and that she would insist on the Sultan and all the Powers giving their consent to what was proposed.

I subsequently saw M[a]r[qui]s Visconti Venosta, who said that he had not been made acquainted with the concessions Germany was prepared to make on the finance questions, nor with what would satisfy her in regard to the police question. He only knew what would not satisfy her on the latter point. He would like to see MM. de Radowitz and Révoil brought together to discuss matters, as he had no great faith in delicate negotiations being carried on through intermediaries.

I may add that M. Révoil said that he would be willing to associate Italy with France and Spain in the police. But would Italy accept? and would this satisfy Germany?

My own opinion is that if I were France I would be quite ready to surrender the police duties to anyone for a limited period provided I had predominant control over the Bank and finance matters. I should have far more influence by holding the purse strings than I should have if I were cooped up with a few police in a coast town. But this I did not mention to M. Révoil.

Y[ours] very truly,

A NICOLSON.

No. 252.

Mr. Cartwright to Sir Edward Grey.

F.O. 371/171.   *Madrid,* D. *January* 22, 1906, 8 P.M.
Tel. (No. 5.)   R. *January* 23, 1906, 8 A.M.
    Morocco.

By pressing Acting Minister for Foreign Affairs([1]) this morning to ascertain whether German Government had made any overtures to Spanish Government before opening of Conference, I obtained the following information :—

German Government are aware of contents of Secret Agreement signed on 2nd September at San Sebastian between late President of the Council and M. Cambon. See my telegram No. 70 of 4th September last.([2]) German Ambassador here assumes that as France in above Agreement makes no allusion to policing the west coast ports, she has purposely left matter open to be able, if necessary, to allow Germany to undertake that duty.

German Ambassador has hinted that, if Germany found too strong an opposition at the Conference to allow her to undertake the policing of the west coast, she would then not be unwilling to withdraw her claim in favour of Spain, leaving to Spain the policing of coast west of Spanish possessions, and to France that of the east coast and the Algerian frontier, the question of the interior police being left open.

Acting Minister for Foreign Affairs said that such an offer, if made to Spain, required very careful consideration, as well from a political as from a financial point of view. Spain, of course, could do nothing without the approval of France, but he thought that both His Majesty's Government and France might prefer to see Spain policing west coast than Germany.

The above was told me in strict confidence, but I thought it right to communicate substance to French Ambassador.

My impression is that the idea is not unpleasing to Spanish Government.
    (Sent to Sir A. Nicolson.)

         ([1]) [Señor de Ojeda.]
         ([2]) [*v. supra* p. 136, No. 175.]

No. 253.

Mr. Cartwright to Sir Edward Grey.

Madrid, January 23, 1906.

D. 12·25 P.M.

F.O. 371/171.
Tel. (No. 7.)   Confidential.   R. 9 P.M.

    M. Cambon informs me that rumours having reached French Government that Germany had an idea of possibly proposing neutralisation of Morocco at Conference, French Minister for Foreign Affairs had telegraphed to him that idea was absolutely unacceptable to France, as at first claim France might have [to] enforce against Morocco trouble would arise.

In accordance with his instructions, M. Cambon sounded Spanish President of the Council on the subject, and found him as opposed to idea of neutralization as French Minister for Foreign Affairs. President of the Council asserted that any Spanish Government who accepted neutralization would be stoned by people, as neutralization meant for Spain the giving up of historical traditions and annihilation of her aspirations. In his opinion, a small but civilized Power could be neutralized but not a barbarian one.

Spanish Delegate has been instructed accordingly.

(Sent to Sir A. Nicolson.)

[*ED. NOTE.*—King Edward sent a conciliatory letter to the Emperor William II on January 23, 1906. It is printed in *G.P.* XXI, I, pp. 108–9, and also partially in Sir Sidney Lee: *King Edward VII* (1927), II, p. 525, with the Emperor's reply.]

No. 254.

Sir A. Nicolson to Sir Edward Grey.

Algeciras, January 24, 1906.

F.O. 371/171.
Tel. (No. 13.) Secret.

D. 11·10 A.M.
R. 1·40 P.M.

The question of French and German representatives' meeting privately to discuss matter is becoming a little complicated as from information which has reached French representative (group undecypherable) it would appear that the German Gov[ernmen]t consider that France should take initiative. Moreover German Gov[ernmen]t are apparently opposed to any third party intervening in the matter and desire that France should declare before the Conference her views on police and finance questions.

I may add that beyond verbal and indirect statements of the German representative here no indication has, I believe, been given by German Gov[ernmen]t that in return for concessions by France on police question Germany would make her large concessions in finance matters.

In these circumstances French representative considers, and I venture to think rightly so, that he must proceed with great caution. He is consulting with his Gov[ernmen]t.

No. 255.

Sir F. Lascelles to Sir Edward Grey.

Berlin, January 25, 1906.

F.O. 371/171.
Tel. (No. 10.)

D. 10·5 A.M.
R. 12 *noon.*

Your telegram No. 6(¹) Conference.

Prince Bülow dined with me last night and I communicated to him the substance of Sir A. Nicolson's telegram No. 13 of yesterday. He thoroughly approved of the idea that the French and German representatives should meet and discuss matter. He had no objection to intervention of a third party nor had he any wish that France should declare before the Conference her views on police and finance questions. He could not express an opinion as to the financial concessions which Germany might make to France in return for concessions by France on the police question, as he did not yet know what line Herr von Radowitz had taken up on that question. He had great hope of a satisfactory solution and so far from objecting to intervention of any third Power, he would be glad of their assistance in discussing privately beforehand any definite proposals to be finally laid before the Conference.(²)

(¹) [Repeating Sir A. Nicolson's No. 13, *supra* No. 254.]
(²) [For Prince Bülow's report, see *G.P.* XXI, I, pp. 106–108.]

No. 256.

Sir A. Nicolson to Sir Edward Grey.

Algeciras, *January* 25, 1906.

F.O. 371/171.
D. 2·55 P.M.
Tel. (No. 16.) Confidential.
R. 6·15 P.M.
Police question.

French Delegate has informed me, and it was confirmed to me in substance by the United States' Representative that the German Government have suggested to the United States' Government following three alternative solutions of the police question :—

1. Several Powers to organize in separate districts; each with a port on the Atlantic.
2. A small Power to be entrusted with whole of police organisation. Germany would far prefer Switzerland, but mentioned also Holland or Sweden, and expressly excluded Belgium as being too French in sympathies.
3. Sultan to organize police with the aid of volunteer officers. These latter to be chosen by three of the small Powers.

United States' Government, I understand, declined to entertain first proposal, but seemed disposed to consider other two, with a leaning to the third, as they consider that it would be well to have as little foreign participation as possible.

French (Representative) added that he hears that German Representative has indicated a fourth solution, namely, police to be intrusted to France and Spain, with the addition of a fourth (*sic*) Power, possibly Italy.

I am inclined to doubt whether this last solution is an authorized one. None of the first three solutions would, I believe, be acceptable to France, and they do not seem to me to be practical or adequately to meet situation.

French Representative is to have a private conversation with German Representative to-day, and may elicit some further information. He asked me if he should accept proposal of German Representative for a private conversation, and I strongly recommended that he should, so as to avoid any ground for German Representative saying hereafter that his overture for private and unofficial intercourse had met with no response.

It is to be observed that in none of solutions is any mention made of Spain alone policing the west coast ports.

MINUTES.

We shall have to wait for an expression of the views of the French Government before taking up any definite attitude in respect of the German proposals.

The plan of bringing in Italy raises the interesting question how far that country is tied, as regards Morocco, by the understanding arrived [at] with France in 1900. We have never been informed of the exact purport of that understanding, which was negotiated by the Marquis Visconti Venosta, and which was the outcome of the Anglo-French agreement respecting the delimitation of the respective spheres of interest in Africa after the Fashoda incident. But from a published interview with M. Delcassé reported in the Italian press in 1902, it is clear that Morocco as well as Tripoli formed the subject of the Franco-Italian understanding. (See Lord Currie's despatch No. 3a of Jan. 4, 1902.(¹))

M. Rouvier recently expressed his expectation that the Marquis Visconti-Venosta would act "according to the spirit of that arrangement." (See Sir F. Bertie's despatch No. 20 of Jan. 10, 1906.(²))

E. A. C. Jan. 26.
E. G.

(¹) [This document will be published in a later volume, where the subject of Mediterranean policy is treated.]
(²) [Not reproduced.]

No. 257.

Sir A. Nicolson to Sir Edward Grey.

Algeciras, January 26, 1906.

F.O. 371/171.
Tel. (No. 17.) Confidential.

D. 11·35 A.M.
R. 3 P.M.

French Representative had a private conversation with German representative yesterday morning at the suggestion of latter. From the account which the former gave me of conversation it would not appear that the German Rep[resentati]ve gave much indication of his views on the financial or police questions. He, however, suggested that French and German expert advisers as well as Count Tattenbach should meet together to endeavour to arrive at some understanding as to the constitution and attributes of the State Bank. To this French representative willingly agreed.

German Rep[resentati]ve then enquired what were French views in regard to police question. To this French Rep[resentati]ve replied that he thought they were fairly well known and asked what were German views. To this he obtained no definite reply but German Rep[resentati]ve proposed that they should meet again.

During conversation, German Rep[resentati]ve intimated that Doctor Rosen had understood M. Rouvier did not desire to ask the Conference for a general mandate for the police, but the French Rep[resentati]ve rectified this impression of Dr. Rosen, and stated that he kept his hands perfectly free on this point.

Perhaps a second interview may elicit some further information from German representative as to German views on police.

No. 258.

Mr. Cartwright to Sir Edward Grey.

Madrid, January 26, 1906.

F.O. 371/171.
Tel. (No. 9.) Confidential.

D. 12·30 P.M.
R. 4·30 P.M.

Morocco.

M. Cambon saw President of the Council yesterday and, without making actual reference to communication made to me by Acting M[inister] [for] F[oreign] A[ffairs], as reported in my telegram No. 5 of January 22,([1]) warned him against yielding to possible German offers. M. Cambon obtained verbal assurances that Spanish Gov[ernmen]t would not allow themselves to be seduced by any offers which Germany might make and would remain faithful to her engagements with France. He also asserted that, in his opinion, Spain would lose in the long run if she now broke loose from France and G[reat] Britain.

Sent to Sir A. Nicolson.

([1]) [*v. supra* p. 233, No. 252.]

No. 259.

Sir A. Nicolson to Sir Edward Grey.

F.O. 371/171.
(No. 11.) Conference. Confidential.

Sir,

Algeciras, D. *January* 26, 1906.
R. *February* 3, 1906.

The German Representative, M. de Radowitz, conveyed through two channels to M. Révoil his desire to have some private and friendly conversations in regard to the principal questions which will soon occupy the attention of the Conference, namely those relating to the institution of a State Bank and to the organization of the police.

M. Révoil was willing to agree to the proposal but he wished to ascertain in the first place whether M. de Radowitz was prepared to state frankly what were the desiderata of his Government in regard to the above two questions. Hitherto he had been given clearly to understand to what the German Government would not agree in respect to the organization of the police, and he had been informed that if France would make concessions on that point, she would receive ample satisfaction from Germany in respect to the financial questions and the institution of a State Bank. He was also told that his concessions on the police question were to be preliminary to any which Germany might make on the other points. He told the intermediaries between M. de Radowitz and himself that if he could obtain some enlightenment preparatory to an interview he thought it would be of advantage. Neither of the intermediaries were able to give him information as to the precise views of the German Representative beyond the assertion that Germany would not consent to the police being organized by France alone, or by France and Spain together.

In these circumstances, the prospects of an interview seemed a little dubious; but renewed requests from M. de Radowitz reached M. Révoil, and I strongly recommended him to meet the wishes of his German colleague. I told M. Révoil that I thought that every effort should be made to prevent the Conference from terminating in a failure; and that it was most desirable that it should not hereafter be said that overtures had been made by M. de Radowitz for a friendly and private conversation, and that they had met with no response from the French side.

M. Révoil, therefore, arranged to meet M. de Radowitz, and the interview took place the day before yesterday. [sic] After an exchange of friendly assurances, M. de Radowitz alluded to the institution of a State Bank, and expressed the opinion that it might be found possible to come to an understanding on that point. He suggested that the financial expert of the French mission should meet Count Tattenbach and the German financial expert, and that these three gentlemen should exchange views and endeavour to arrive at an understanding. To this proposal M. Révoil willingly agreed: and I believe the first meeting is to take place to-morrow.

M. de Radowitz then approached the police question. He remarked in the first place that France had already secured the organization of the police on the Algerian frontier which was within the sphere of her interests. M. Révoil pointed out that the sphere of French interests was not limited to the frontier districts, but that she had important and vital interests throughout the whole of Morocco. The policing of the Algerian frontier was a matter which had been settled many years ago between the French Government and that of Morocco and did not come within discussion. M. de Radowitz then observed that Dr. Rosen had carried away the impression from some interviews which he had had with M. Rouvier that the latter did not intend to ask the Conference for a mandate to organize the police in Morocco. M. Révoil replied that it was difficult to give the denial to an impression, but he could assure M. de Radowitz, and there were documents in the Yellow Book to support the fact, that M. Rouvier had given no engagement whatever as to what he would or would not ask the Conference outside of the programme on which France and Germany had come to an agreement.

M. de Radowitz then enquired of M. Révoil what were the views of France as to the police. M. Révoil said that he thought the French views were sufficiently well known but that he was anxious to ascertain those of Germany on that difficult question. To this question M. de Radowitz gave no reply, but said that he hoped on another occasion to be able to discuss that matter also with M. Révoil.

The interview, which had been perfectly friendly throughout, then terminated.

M. Révoil presumes that after that the two financial experts and Count Tattenbach have discussed financial matters, M. de Radowitz will suggest another meeting which of course he will attend.

But he is much perplexed as to how to treat the police question when he again meets M. de Radowitz. He, and the two gentlemen who acted originally as intermediaries, are quite without information as to what really are the precise views of

Germany in the matter. Berlin appears to be using different language on that subject at Washington, Madrid, and at Algeciras. Numerous projects float about the air, some with an official stamp, others less authentic : while M. de Radowitz and Count Tattenbach deliver themselves of contradictory utterances to their various interlocutors here. He doubts if M. de Radowitz will be really explicit with him : and he is puzzled how to deal with the subject.

I have ventured to tell him that in view of the cloud of dust which hangs over the real intentions of Germany it seems to me that the best course would be to be perfectly frank and open. I should be inclined to lay my cards on the table, and state what France desires and expects : and then enquire what Germany has to say. M. de Radowitz would, I thought, then be forced to be explicit on his side : or if he were not, then at any rate France could assert with justice that she had acted loyally and frankly, and could not be reproached with not having given to the other side every possible opportunity of explaining and defining her attitude.

I have, &c.

A. NICOLSON.

No. 260.

Sir A. Nicolson to Sir Edward Grey.

F.O. 371/171.
(No. 12.) Conference. Confidential.   *Algeciras*, D. *January* 26, 1906.
Sir,   R. *February* 3, 1906.

Marquis Visconti Venosta was good enough to call upon me this morning, and he informed me that the United States Representative had read to him a long telegram which he had received from Washington, reporting a communication which had been made by the German Government to that of the United States, putting forward three alternative solutions of the police question.

I told the Italian Representative that I had also received information on this matter : and that the three solutions were : 1. That the police organization should be entrusted to several Powers, each with a separate district and with a port on the Atlantic. 2. That the police organization should be entrusted to one small Power alone. Germany would far prefer that this Power should be Switzerland : but would not object to a Scandinavian Power or Holland. She, however, expressly excluded Belgium as being too French in her sympathies. 3. That the Sultan himself should organize the police with the aid of volunteer officers, such officers to be selected by three of the small Powers.

Marquis Visconti Venosta said that these were, in fact, the proposals : but he had already been shown them by the German Ambassador at Rome more than a fortnight ago. He was under the impression that they formed what might be called the original programme of Germany, and that they had been superseded by other proposals. He, therefore, did not understand their somewhat belated appearance at Washington, unless the German Government had recurred to them, and that they now represented the " derniers mots " of Germany. In that case a solution would be difficult to find as they were clearly inacceptable.

He had been much exercised, he said, to find a common ground between the two parties on which a compromise might be effected, and the task was rendered doubly difficult by the mystery, and indeed confusion, with which Germany had enshrouded her real views and wishes. He attached, he added, little importance to casual remarks dropped after dinner, but he had been struck by one which Count Tattenbach had recently made to him to the effect that a solution might be found by entrusting the police organization to France and Spain with a third Power, possibly Italy.

I remarked that, to my mind, such a solution would be admirable : in fact so satisfactory did it seem to me that I hesitated to delude myself with the hope that it would be proposed. I did not know how the French Government would view it, but I had some reason to believe that M. Révoil would recommend it; and if it opened the prospect of an amicable solution of the problem it seemed probable that all other Powers would concur. I asked him whether Italy would consent. Marquis Visconti Venosta said that he would have to wait for the French and German Representatives to make the proposal to him, and that then he would lose no time in telegraphing to his Government. He did not, however, appear to have much hope that the idea would ever take a more definite shape.

Marquis Visconti Venosta spoke also about the proposed State Bank: and he feared that here it might be found difficult to reconcile conflicting views.

I again expressed my earnest desire that no means should be neglected which would assist towards a peaceful and amicable termination of the Conference; but I stated that I was not so hopeful of such a happy eventuality as I had been a few days ago.

I have, &c.
A. NICOLSON.

No. 261.

Sir Edward Grey to Sir A. Nicolson.

F.O. 371/171.
Tel. (No. 9.)

Foreign Office, January 27, 1906.
D. 3 P.M.

You will of course inform us of any proposed increase of customs duties in establishment of a Bank that we may consider how British trade is likely to be affected before giving final assent.

No. 262.

Sir A. Nicolson to Sir Edward Grey.

Gibraltar, January 27, 1906.
D. 7·5 P.M.
R. 10·10 P.M.

F.O. 371/171.
Tel. (No. 19.) Confidential.

German Representative intimated to Spanish Minister for Foreign Affairs last night that a possible combination for the police would be France, Spain, Italy and Germany. He also informed Minister for Foreign Affairs that Germany desired to obtain footing in Morocco. To the United States representative he has suggested[1] Italy alone should organize police. United States representative has informed his Government that the three solutions communicated by German Embassy to Washington appear to him to be impracticable and insufficient.

French and German experts and Count Tattenbach are to meet tomorrow to discuss Bank question; and French Representative will have later another private conversation with German Colleague on the police question. French Representative is much perplexed by the numerous and contradictory proposals which German Government or their Representatives continually putting forward at different capitals and here.

[1] [See, on this point, correction in Sir A. Nicolson's telegram No. 21, *infra*, p. 240, No. 263.]

No. 263.

Sir A. Nicolson to Sir Edward Grey.

F.O. 371/171.
Tel. (No. 21.)

Gibraltar, January 28, 1906.
D. 1 P.M.
R. 5 P.M.

My telegram No. 19.

I should like to correct one passage in above-mentioned telegram. It was United States' Representative who suggested to the German Representative that Italy alone should be intrusted with police, and the latter replied that such a solution would be very welcome to Germany.

No. 264.

Sir Edward Grey to Sir F. Lascelles.([1])

F.O. 371/76.
(No. 53.)
Sir,

Foreign Office, January 31, 1906.

The German Ambassador spoke to me a week ago about an interview with Sir Frederick Maurice which had been published in the French papers. I told His Excellency to-day that I had, in consequence of his reference to it, read the interview and very much disapproved of it, but no doubt he had now got the explanation which had been published in the "Times." I said it had occurred to me that some of the information which constantly reached me here in connection with the German Army, their unusual purchases of material for war, and so forth, might account for the way in which Sir Frederick Maurice and others discussed the eventuality of war, but I said that I regarded all information of this kind as indicating on the part of Germany not preparations for war, but precautions, which, in view of the state of feeling which existed six months ago, it was quite natural that Germany should take, and which were not the least inconsistent with the pacific intentions which Count Metternich had assured me were hers. "Preparations" I used in the sense of an intention to attack; "precautions," on the other hand, indicated only the intention to defend.

Count Metternich said that France also, according to the statements which Sir Charles Dilke and others had made, had been strengthening her position very much. I said I had no doubt it was true, and that also, in view of the state of feeling which had existed a few months ago, was a perfectly natural precaution for her to take; but I could assure him that as long as I remained at the Foreign Office, or indeed as long as the present Government remained in office, whatever we countenanced would be purely precautions in the sense in which I had used the word, and not aggressive preparations.

I am, &c.
EDWARD GREY.

MINUTE BY KING EDWARD.

App[*rove*]*d.—E.R*

([1]) [Published by Lord Grey: *Twenty-Five Years* (1925) I, p. 90.]

No. 265.

Sir A. Nicolson to Sir Edward Grey.

Gibraltar, *February* 4, 1906.

F.O. 371/172.   D. 12·20 P.M.
Tel. (No. 29.)   R. 7 P.M.

Count Tattenbach paid me a long visit yesterday evening.

Following is a summary of most important (and) significant portions of the conversation :—

His object was evidently either to try to detach me from my French colleague, or to induce me to urge latter to make concessions to the satisfaction of Germany.

He told me that commercial interests of Germany and England were endangered by French predominance in Morocco, and that it would be well if I joined forces with German Delegates to secure full guarantees for open door. He observed that situation had completely changed since Conference had been agreed upon, and that now *vis-à-vis* to France I was exactly in the same position as the other Delegates. He continued that if I urged my French colleague to make all required concessions on police question, my words would be decisive; while if I declined to say those words, I should be practically encouraging my French colleague to resist; and he hinted that if the Conference fell through a great deal of the responsibility would fall on me.

I replied that I had not the least fear that British commercial interests were in any danger, and that he knew that ample guarantees were being offered and would be given as to open door. For me, situation had in no wise changed since the Conference opened, and I was not at all in the same position *vis-à-vis* to France as the other Delegates; that we had special engagements with France which both my Government and myself intended to observe loyally and honourably. It was not for me to urge concessions on my French colleague; it would be most disloyal were I to do so, while I would certainly not encourage him to resist.

I said my French colleague had shown throughout the Conference the most conciliatory disposition and the greatest moderation, and that I intended to stand firmly by him. I added that if an agreement could be reached no one would be better pleased than my Government and myself, and that I had continually expressed, both to my French colleague and to others, my earnest hope that Conference would terminate in a satisfactory and peaceful manner. But it was for France and Germany to devise means for arriving at a satisfactory agreement.

MINUTE.

Fallodon, Christon Bank, Northumberland.

This language should be approved if it has not yet been done. We regard our interests in Morocco as being economic and as being secured by our agreement; if the Germans also regard their interests as economic they should state why the economic guarantees in our agreement with France are not sufficient and suggest in what way they could be strengthened.

E. G.

MINUTE BY KING EDWARD.

[ED. NOTE.—Sir A. Nicolson's Despatch No. 24 of February 4, 1906, expanding this telegram was minuted by King Edward as follows :]

The language held by Sir A. Nicolson to Count Tattenbach is admirable—but the latter will no doubt induce his Gov[ernmen]t to believe that the cause of failure of the Conference is due to British obstinacy.

E.R.(¹)

(¹) [Quoted in Sir Sidney Lee : *King Edward VII* (1927), II, p. 361, *v.* also the King's letter to the Emperor William II of February 5, 1907, *ib.* II, pp. 527–8.]

No. 266.

Sir A. Nicolson to Sir Edward Grey.

F.O. 371/172.
Tel. (No. 30.)

Gibraltar, February 4, 1906.
D. 12·20 P.M.
R. 7 P.M.

M. Révoil and M. de Radowitz had a conversation on police question yesterday evening, and latter had nothing to propose beyond throwing out a hint that possibly Moorish Government might organize a police with European officers selected by them. Conversation led to no results.

Count Tattenbach was more outspoken to me on same subject. He said that Germany would never accept France alone or France and Spain alone. I told him that case was urgent, and that those two countries were the only ones with properly qualified elements to organize a police. They would work under strictly limited conditions and within circumscribed areas. I asked him what alternative he had to propose. He said that small Powers should undertake organisation, but that it would be better to have no police at all. I am afraid prospects of settlement are not very hopeful, and outlook is unsatisfactory.

No. 267.

Sir A. Nicolson to Sir Edward Grey.

F.O. 371/172.
(No. 26.) Conference.
Sir,

Algeciras, D. *February 4, 1906.*
R. *February 10, 1906.*

Count Tattenbach broached to me yesterday evening the question of the police organization in Morocco in a perfectly frank manner. In the course of conversation, he stated that this question had been made the most prominent one in Berlin, and that the Emperor took a special interest in it. He enquired what my views were.

I told him that, as we were speaking in a friendly and unofficial manner, I should not hesitate to state frankly what my own personal views were. I gave him a sketch of the condition of affairs on the other side of the Straits, and of the intolerable situation which existed at Tangier and of which I had had comparatively recent and direct experience. The information which I had received lately was to the effect that the situation had become worse than when I left Tangier little more than a year ago. It was then clear that the case was an urgent one, to which we were all bound to apply as speedy a remedy as possible. I knew of only two countries who had the properly qualified elements at hand to meet the difficulty with the necessary promptitude, and they were France and Spain. If considered desirable their action might be exclusively limited to the coast towns and their mandate accorded for a limited period. I could not see what objection could be raised to such a modest proposal, which circumstances so urgently demanded.

Count Tattenbach at first demurred to my statement as to the condition of Morocco, which he contended was not worse than it had been for the past thirty years, and indeed asserted that the safety of Europeans was more secure than in some parts of London and Berlin. He believed indeed that the organization of police would rather aggravate than ameliorate the situation, and that Europeans would be in the same position as the Spaniards at Ceuta and Melilla, and not able to move a step outside the walls of the town without incurring the risk of being shot down. Germany moreover could never agree to France and Spain being solely entrusted with the organization of the police.

I disagreed entirely with his arguments as to the condition of Morocco, adducing self evident proofs in contradiction of them; and I asked him what were his reasons against a strictly limited mandate being accorded to the above mentioned countries.

I said I wished to examine the question from the purely practical standpoint of the safety to be accorded to Europeans, without bringing any political considerations into the matter.

Count Tattenbach said that he had no reason to give me beyond the fact that Germany would not agree to the dual organization. I observed that this would be a difficult attitude to assume before the Conference, and I ventured to think a difficult one to justify. Had he any other combination to propose? He replied that the organization might be entrusted to the smaller Powers : but I pointed out that this was not a practical proposal.

Count Tattenbach said that even my own colony at Tangier had protested against the French undertaking the police at that town. I assured him that he was mistaken. The great grievance of my colony in my time had been not that the French had done too much, but that they had done little or nothing towards safe-guarding the security of the Tangier inhabitants.

Our conversation was prolonged for some time on this question, but to little purpose; and I finally said that I trusted that M. Révoil and M. Radowitz would be able to devise some solution satisfactory to both parties.

I have, &c.
A. NICOLSON.

<hr>

No. 268.

Sir A. Nicolson to Sir Edward Grey.

F.O. 371/172.
Private.
Dear Sir Edward,   *Algeciras, February 5, 1906.*

I am sending some despatches by this bag reporting, I hope not too lengthily, my conversation with Count Tattenbach. M. Révoil thinks that the Germans are exceedingly embarrassed; and that they are desirous of showing to Berlin that it is hopeless to effect a scission between France and G[rea]t Britain, and that, therefore, it would be better to meet French wishes in regard to the police question. I am not so confident as he is; and I am inclined to think that the Germans foresee the possibility of a breakdown of the Conference, and wish to shift the responsibility for the failure on other shoulders than their own. I often reflect whether they desire that the Conference should succeed, unless of course they are assured that they will wring from France all that they require. They are aware that France has stiffened herself, and though ready to go to great lengths that she will not travel all the way they desire. So far as Moorish affairs in themselves are concerned, Germany could easily profit by having a perfectly free hand at Fez; and I dare say she feels confident that no serious complication would immediately ensue in Europe.

C[oun]t Tattenbach spoke quite easily as to a possible breakdown. He sneered at the Conference being able to effect anything serious towards improving Morocco, which to a great extent is quite true, and he thought that a State Bank, police, &c. could easily be dropped : but if they were to be adopted he was evidently determined that the share France should take in them should not be greater than that of others. He knows quite well that France will not accept such solutions. He spontaneously assured me most positively that Germany required neither a port nor a footing in Morocco and said that he would be ready to give me this in writing. I thanked him and said that his word was sufficient.

To my representations that everyone should do his best towards bringing the Conference to a happy conclusion, he assented, but not warmly, remarking that a failure would certainly produce a state of "malaise" in Europe. He is a rasping, disagreeable man, not straightforward or truthful and evidently has to exercise much effort to control his temper. M. Révoil complains that M. de Radowitz is too elusive to treat with, and that he cannot bring him to the point. This M. Révoil attributes to the fact that the Germans do not really know what they want. I tell him that I have little doubt that they do know : but unfortunately they keep it to themselves. With the permission of M. Révoil, I have informed both the Italian and United States delegates (Marquis Visconti Venosta and Mr. White) of what passed between Count Tattenbach and myself.

We must now await some fresh overtures from the German group; and I hope they will be forthcoming, as very shortly the Conference will reach the delicate questions which have hitherto only be[en] discussed in private.

Y[ou]rs very truly,
A. NICOLSON.

MINUTE BY KING EDWARD.

The success of the Conference seems more than doubtful.

E.R.

No. 269.

Sir A. Nicolson to Sir Edward Grey.

F.O. 371/172.   *Algeciras, February 6, 1906.*
Tel. (No. 31.)   R. 3·35 P.M.
Police question.

German first delegate called on U[nited] S[tates'] delegate yesterday and said that it was clear that France would not go further than to divide police organisation between herself and Spain. U[nited] S[tates] delegate replied that he was convinced that such was the case and that it would be useless to treat on any other basis. German delegate asked if it would be possible to induce France to associate a third Power in the duty. To this U[nited] S[tates'] delegate replied that he did not believe she would. She might possibly accept a third Power to act in some measure as a controller or inspector [? but not] to take an active part in police organisation in the way of furnishing officers, etc : but he added that above were merely his personal views and that he had not spoken to French delegate on the subject. German delegate complained that he had received no news from Berlin for two days.

U[nited] S[tates'] delegate has the impression that German delegate is prepared to yield and that their failure to induce us to put pressure on France has had a great effect. At the same time both he and Russian delegate think that German Gov[ernmen]t have not been thoroughly well informed by their delegates as to exact position of affairs here; and Russian delegate will ask his Gov[ernmen]t to place that of Germany in full possession of the facts.

No. 270.

Sir A. Nicolson to Sir Edward Grey.

F.O. 371/172.   *Algeciras, February 6, 1906.*
Tel. (No. 32.)   R. 3·45 P.M.

Spanish M[inister] [for] F[oreign] A[ffairs] told me yesterday evening that the German delegates had been sounding him as to whether Spain would not undertake the police organization, and had specially mentioned that they would like to see her at Casablanca and Mogador. M[inister] [for] F[oreign] A[ffairs] gave evasive reply as he assures me that he is determined to act in the closest harmony and in fullest co-operation with France. He thinks that German delegates are much perplexed and troubled and that they are anxiously awaiting instructions from Berlin.

No. 271.

Sir A. Nicolson to Sir Edward Grey.

F.O. 371/172.
Tel. (No. 33.)

Algeciras, February 7, 1906.
R. 3·35 P.M.

Police question.

The first German delegate spoke to Marquess di Visconti-Venosta the day before yesterday on the above subject and the latter remarked that in his opinion France would not abandon her position but would claim that the police organization should be entrusted to her and Spain. The German delegate did not reject nor did he accept idea but discussed question as to the form in which authority of the Sultan could be retained over the organisation.

Marquess di Visconti-Venosta in common with all of us who are acquainted with pourparlers considers that possibly the German delegates themselves may be willing to concede the French demands but that all depends on what Berlin may decide, and as to the views of the German Gov[ernmen]t we are without information.

Count Tattenbach who was very positive in his conversation with me on February 3([1]) as to Germany's never accepting the dual organisation had now greatly modified his opposition.

([1]) [*v. supra* p. 242, No. 266.]

No. 272.

Mr. Spring-Rice to Sir Edward Grey.

F.O. 371/172.
(No. 112.)
Sir,

St. Petersburgh, D. February 7, 1906.
R. *February* 19, 1906.

I have the honour to state that I asked Count Lamsdorff to-day whether he had received any news from the Morocco Conference. He said that he had just heard from Count Cassini that a proposal had been made for entrusting Spain and France with the organization of the Gendarmerie, and that this proposal had been agreed to by all the representatives except the German, who had accepted it *ad referendum.*

He expressed the opinion that this solution was satisfactory and asked me what view His Majesty's Government took of it. I said that I had no instructions on the subject but that I imagined that if the French Government approved of it, His Majesty's Government would certainly support it. Our action in the Conference was guided by the terms of the Anglo-French declaration, Clause II of which recognized the right of France " comme Puissance limitrophe de veiller à la tranquillité dans ce pays, et de lui prêter son assistance pour toutes les réformes administratives, économiques, financières et militaires dont il a besoin." I added that I had been informed that some attempts had been made here to throw doubts on the earnestness and good faith of Great Britain in regard to her obligations towards France. Count Lamsdorff at once replied that he had never himself had any doubts on the subject and that Count Cassini's reports bore witness to the zeal with which Sir Arthur Nicolson had supported his French colleague. Speaking with considerable earnestness, he expressed the hope that a solution would be arrived at and that an end would be put to the state of tension from which Europe suffered at present. It would be a disgraceful thing, he said, if Europe should be plunged into war in consequence of a question arising out of the condition of affairs in Morocco. I observed that this was not the real question from which the difficulty arose. The real question was whether or no the Powers of Europe were to be free to choose their own friends and follow their own policy. It was not Morocco that was in question except so far as Morocco was the subject of an agreement between England and France which was, (as we maintained, quite falsely) interpreted as a threat to Germany. Count Lamsdorff maintained that nothing could be further from the thoughts of the Russian Government than an aggressive policy in Europe, and that, from the standpoint of the interests of peace, he had warmly welcomed the conclusion of that understanding. The

[15869]

B 3

agreement was published while he was in Darmstadt with the Emperor : he had at once asked the Emperor's instructions, and, in conformity with His Majesty's desire, he had during his visit to Paris made a public declaration as to the satisfaction with which the Russian Government had received the news. "Les amis de nos amis," he had said, "sont nos amis."

I said that I well remembered the declaration which had made a deep impression in England all the more so as it could not be attributed to any aggressive design. Since the time of Alexander the First the traditions of Russian diplomacy had been bound up with the maintenance of the European equilibrium, and we had every confidence that those traditions would be strictly followed if the balance of power should be threatened.

Count Lamsdorff replied that we need have no doubts on that score, and that it was a source of satisfaction to him that as England and Russia had acted together in Crete and Turkey, for the preservation of order, and the protection of the oppressed, so they were also, at Algeciras, working side by side for the maintenance of peace.

I have, &c.
CECIL SPRING-RICE.

No. 273.

Mr. Spring-Rice to Sir Edward Grey.

St. Petersburgh, February 8, 1906.
D. 3·10 P.M.
R. 4·40 P.M.

F.O. 371/172.
Tel. (No. 26.)
  Morocco.

Count Lamsdorff hears from Russian Representative that a solution has been found as to the gendarmerie, which it is proposed to place under control of France and Spain, a proposal which Germany has accepted *ad referendum*. He expressed his satisfaction and asked views of H[is] M[ajesty's] Gov[ernmen]t.

No. 274.

Sir Edward Grey to Mr. Spring-Rice.

F.O. 371/172.
Tel. (No. 38.)   *Foreign Office, February 8, 1906.*
  Your tel. No. 26.
  Morocco Conference. Police.

You may inform C[oun]t Lamsdorff that H[is] M[ajesty's] G[overnment] would agree to any solution which is acceptable to France.

No. 275.

Sir A. Nicolson to Sir Edward. Grey.

F.O. 371/172.
(No. 35.) Conference. Confidential.   *Algeciras, D. February 11, 1906.*
Sir,   R. *February 17, 1906.*

The past week has, I regret to say, brought the French and German Representatives no nearer together in regard to a satisfactory solution of the police question : and indeed there are indications that the Conference will very possibly separate without having reached any agreement on the above subject. As I have mentioned in previous despatches the question of affording protection to foreigners in the coast towns is the most urgent and perhaps the most important of all the subjects submitted to the Conference, and a failure to solve that question would render the Conference abortive.

Since the conversation which took place between M. Révoil and M. de Radowitz on the 3rd instant, the latter has, I understand, been in frequent communication with his Government, but he does not appear to have been furnished with instructions which would enable him to reopen the discussions with his French colleague. On the other hand I am informed that the German Government have addressed them-selves to two Governments, which I may now state very confidentially are those of the United States and of Italy, requesting them to instruct their delegates to support M. de Radowitz in urging upon M. Révoil to agree to a solution by which the Sultan should undertake the organization of the police with the aid of officers either selected from the smaller Powers or from all the Powers in general. The United States' Representative, Mr. White, on the matter being mentioned to him, declined to act in the manner suggested unless specially authorized by his Government : and he remarked that he had already informed his Government that any such proposal was unworkable and unpractical. His Government have subsequently expressed their concurrence with his views.

M. de Radowitz has not yet evinced any desire to reopen communications with M. Révoil, being probably of opinion that it would be useless to suggest as a solution a project which he knows would be refused.

Mr. White, with the view of bringing the two immediately interested parties to an agreement if possible, and anxious that there should be no misunderstanding as to the nature of the French demands, suggested to his Government that they should take measures for bringing these latter to the knowledge of the German Emperor. There have been so many misrepresentations in the Press and in other quarters as to the character of the French views that it was possible some misconception might exist in regard to them in the highest quarters at Berlin.

Simply stated all that France demands is the following. In order to provide some security for the safety of foreigners in the coast towns, she with Spain would be willing to place at the disposal of the Moorish Government for a period of three years certain instructors, officers and non-commissioned officers, who would organize some small bodies of native police, and who would also be authorized to supervise the punctual and sufficient payment of the men. The police forces should be strictly limited to the coast towns.

The United States Government, I understand, are quite ready to undertake that these demands, in their moderate and practical form, should reach the German Emperor; and they are being telegraphed in consequence to Washington today for transmission to their high destination.

Should they be accepted, the Conference would reach a satisfactory termination without much further delay. Should they be refused I am afraid that it will have to be dissolved having failed in its task.

I have, &c.
A. NICOLSON.

No. 276.

Sir A. Nicolson to Sir Edward Grey.

F.O. 371/172.   *Algeciras, February 12, 1906.*
Tel. (No. 43.) Most Confidential.   R. 2 P.M.

There is an impression here that German Emperor and his Gov[ernmen]t have some misconceptions as to French demands as to police and consider that they are more extensive than they are in reality.

U[nited] S[tates'] Representative has told me in strict confidence, and he begs that it may not be mentioned, that, at desire of his Gov[ernmen]t, he has telegraphed to Washington substance of French demands which are as follows :—

To place at disposal of Moorish Gov[ernmen]t French and Spanish instructors to organise native police force simply in coast towns for a period of three years. These instructors to be authorised to see that payment of police is regularly paid.

U[nited].S[tates'] Gov[ernmen]t have said that they will take care that these demands are communicated to German Emperor.

German representative says that he has not yet received instructions which enable him to reopen conversations as to police with French representative, but French expert intends to communicate today to Count Tattenbach a draft project as to State Bank, so presumably discussions on this question will continue. The general impression here is that an agreement as to police will not be found.

No. 277.

Sir N. O'Conor to Sir Edward Grey.

F.O. 371/91.
(No. 86.)　Confidential.　　　　　　　　*Constantinople,* D. *February* 12, 1906.
Sir,　　　　　　　　　　　　　　　　　　R. *February* 19, 1906.

In my Despatch No. 293 Confidential, of 1st May last([1]) I had the honour to report to the Marquess of Lansdowne the information which had reached me of the attempt made by Germany to induce the Sultan to send a mission to Morocco with a view to creating closer relations between the two Moslem States; even at that time the Sultan showed some reluctance to comply with the German Emperor's suggestion, and His Majesty has since definitely declined to do so.

When that decision was taken, I was not in a position to enlighten Lord Lansdowne as to the reasons which had actuated the Sultan, but it has since come to my knowledge from a trustworthy source that secret emissaries were actually sent from here to Morocco, but that their proceedings and the intrigues which they endeavoured to set on foot aroused the suspicions of the Emperor of Morocco and that His Sherifian Majesty showed that he was disposed neither to send a formal mission to Constantinople nor to receive one thence.

It is also reported to me from the same confidential source that the Sultan wrote to Abdul Aziz saying that the German Emperor was the great friend and Protector of Islam, and that His Sherifian Majesty would do well to follow his counsel and advice. These facts have perhaps at present little more than an academic interest, but it is nevertheless instructive to note that the German Emperor is prepared, in certain eventualities, to endeavour to make use of the influence in the Islamic world which the Sultan possesses as Caliph of the faithful and which he alone among the occupants of the Ottoman throne has succeeded in making an attribute of the Sultanate of Roum.

I have, &c.
N. R. O'CONOR.

([1]) [Not reproduced.]

No. 278.

Sir Edward Grey to Sir Arthur Nicolson.

Private.([1])
Dear Sir Arthur Nicolson,　　　　　　　*Foreign Office, February* 12, 1906.

I am afraid the result of the Conference is likely to be no better than you anticipate. It seems to be recognised however that we have acted up to the letter

([1]) [Carnock MSS.]

and in the spirit of the Anglo-French engagements; and this is very greatly due to you. I think our attitude could not have been better represented and emphasised at the Conference and I am grateful for what you have done on the stage and behind the scenes, and for the way in which it has been done.

I wish I could make any useful suggestion, but my impression is that the Germans do not want the Conference to arrive at any solution, which is acceptable to France on the lines of our *Entente* with her. Such a favourable issue would be regarded as a diplomatic defeat of Germany. Were it otherwise it is obvious that she would agree to the ports being policed by France and Spain under the authority of the Sultan and would concentrate herself on economic guarantees for the open door—50 years instead of 30 and so forth.

Assuming that the Conference separates, *re infecta,* France apprehends that Germany will by separate action at Fez change the situation in Morocco to the disadvantage of France. I doubt Germany being very active in this way; I think she is a little Morocco sick; but in any case time may be on the side of France; for the recovery of Russia will change the situation in Europe to the advantage of France; and it is the situation in Europe that will in the long run decide the position of France and Germany respectively in Morocco.

I am in hopes that when Russia recovers we may get and keep on good terms with her; if so this also will count on the side of France.

Yours very truly,
E. GREY.

If the Conference is to break up France must not be manœuvred into the position of appearing to be to blame. If she is obliged to table proposals as to police, they should be provisional such as M. Cambon outlined to me after his return from seeing you. The idea I think was then that France and Spain might be requested to draw up a plan pending the production of which the Conference should disperse, adjourned *sine die.*

E. G.

No. 279.

Sir A. Nicolson to Sir Edward Grey.

F.O. 371/172.   *Algeciras, February* 13, 1906.
Tel. (No. 45.)   Very Confidential.   R. 3·50 P.M.

French representative has given me very confidentially following information which he received from Paris this morning.

French Ambassador at St. Petersburg has been informed by Count Lamsdorff that, in reply to suggestions made by Russian Amb[assado]r at Berlin that police should be entrusted to France and Spain, Prince Bülow had stated that Germany would not accept above solution but that she would be prepared to settle police question in one of the following ways :—

1. That the Sultan should select instructors from amongst small Powers and that these instructors should be under the control of the diplomatic body at Tangier.
2. That districts should be assigned to different Powers.
3. That a mercenary army of Europeans should be recruited from amongst small Powers.

If no agreement were reached then Prince Bülow said there was no other course but to revert to *status quo* based on **Madrid Convention of 1880.**

French Ambassador at St. Petersburg observed that none of the above solutions would be accepted by France.

Count Lamsdorff enquired of French Amb[assado]r whether the Russian suggestion at Berlin could not be supported by a similar intervention on the part of Great Britain, the U[nited] S[tates] and Italy.

French Ambassador (sic) here asked me to speak to Italian and U[nited] S[tates] representatives and to recommend above course to H[is] M[ajesty's] G[overnmen]t. I told him that I was most anxious to do all that I could to support him and to facilitate a solution, but that after my refusal to German delegate to put any pressure on my French colleague I felt a little difficulty in suggesting to my American and Italian colleagues to recommend pressure being put on Germany. I would far prefer, I added, that question of British intervention should be considered in London or Paris between our two Gov[ernmen]ts. He quite saw my difficulty and said he would move his Gov[ernmen]t to suggest that M. Cambon should speak to you.

He is to see German representative as latter says he has now received his instructions as to police question.

No. 280.

Sir Edward Grey to Sir F. Bertie.

F.O. 371/172.
(No. 99.)
Sir,   *Foreign Office, February* 13, 1906.

The French Ambassador called at this Office to-day and, in the course of a conversation which he had with Sir Charles Hardinge, alluded to the statements made during the last few days by the German News agencies and Press with regard to the intentions and attitude of France at the Algeciras Conference.

In accordance with instructions received from his Gov[ernmen]t, M. Cambon made a communication to the following effect :

It is quite untrue that M. Révoil endeavoured to reverse the order of discussion as adopted by the Conference and to place the question of the police before that of the Bank. It was at the express request of the German Delegate, M. de Radowitz, that the French Delegate agreed to take part, in a semi-official and private interview, in an exchange of views with regard to the Bank and Police. It is also untrue that M. Rouvier withdrew his claim on behalf of France to a general mandate for the police of Morocco in exchange for a recognition of the right to control the police on the Algerian frontier. The French Gov[ernmen]t have never allowed their right to police the frontier, which is theirs in virtue of longstanding agreements with the Sultan, to be called in question. They could not, therefore, think of making their previous rights matter for exchange.

Furthermore M. Rouvier's declarations were published in the Yellow Book and were not disputed by the German Gov[ernmen]t.

As regards the general mandate for the police, M. Rouvier considers it important that the false construction put by the German Press on the expression "mandat général" should not gain credence. The Yellow book contains conclusive proof that we did not at any moment propose to organize a police force outside the coast towns. The proposals of the French Gov[ernmen]t were in the first instance confined to 4 ports, Tangier, Laraiche, Rabat and Casablanca, with the reservation that, if it were subsequently recognized as necessary to organize a police force in other towns, France should be charged with the task. Mention of Fez is, it is true, made in the Yellow Book (No. 265). But in asking for French co-operation at Fez, as at Ujda, in conformity with previous agreements with France, the Sultan did not contemplate organizing a police force, in the strict sense of the words, there, but putting troops there in a position to resist the Pretender.

No doubt could arise as to the meaning of the words " mandat général," of which use was made for want of a more precise expression to indicate the task of organizing the native police in the coast towns. This mandate was general only in the sense that no analogous mandate was entrusted to any other country at any point on Moorish territory. With regard to the mandate with which the French Gov[ernmen]t would, as is well known, be satisfied now in a spirit of conciliation, it would be no longer in any respect a general one, for they are prepared to share the task of carrying it into effect with Spain, after coming to an agreement that that Power should do so in the localities mutually agreed upon.

The French Gov[ernmen]t have declared that this police force would have as its principal task—and, if necessary, they could, doubtless, say for its sole task—the security of foreigners.

The German newspapers profess, without however making any attempt to prove it, that the effect of such an organization would be to assure to France in matters economic a preponderating position which would infringe the principle of the open door. It is difficult to understand how the presence of a few French and Algerian officers and non-commissioned officers at the head of a few hundred Moorish police could have such a result, when the principle of economic equality and liberty has been accepted by France without reserve. If however the guarantees with which this principle has already been surrounded appeared insufficient in view of the mandate for the police which it is proposed to entrust to France and Spain, the French Gov[ernmen]t would be quite prepared to give fresh guarantees if the Conference considered them desirable in this connection.

The French Gov[ernmen]t will thus again demonstrate their sincere desire to see the Conference arrive at a solution which would satisfy all the Powers.

I am, &c.
EDWARD GREY.

No. 281.

Sir Edward Grey to Sir A. Nicolson.

F.O. 371/172.
(No. 10.)
Sir,   *Foreign Office, February* 13, 1906.

I approve the language which you used in reply to Count Tattenbach, as reported in your despatch No. 26 of the 4th of February.([1]) Count Tattenbach seems to have desired that you should put yourself in the position of urging France to yield to the German view. This would have been entirely out of accord with the spirit of the *entente*, and a departure from the letter of our Agreement with France. With reference to Count Tattenbach's remark that you were practically urging your French colleague to resist, and appeared to desire to " egg on " the French in an indirect way, I have to observe that the support you have given to France has been entirely within the limits of the Declarations exchanged between us and France on the subject of Morocco, which are known to the German Government and to which Count Tattenbach must have known that it was our intention to adhere loyally. But apart from these Declarations by which we are bound, it appears to me that the German attitude is not a reasonable one. France is ready to respect the sovereignty of the Sultan and the independence of Morocco. There remain two objects which we desire to see secured. One is the maintenance of order, more especially in the ports; and from the point of view of common sense it is clear that the best way to secure this is to entrust to France and Spain—the only two Powers who have suitable personnel and experience—the organization of the police at the ports. Our second object is to safeguard our economic interests by securing the open door. This we consider has been done by our Agreement with France; but if Germany's interests be,

([1]) [*v. supra* pp. 242–3, No. 267.]

as was at one time declared, economic interests, I am surprised that the Conference has proceeded so far without her making any proposals for stronger guarantees of an economic nature if she considers that those which already exist are not sufficient. I gather from the reports which I have had from you that were Germany to accept an organization of the police at the ports such as I have described, and were she to limit her demands to securing economic guarantees, there would be little difficulty in securing a unanimous agreement of the Conference and one which would be acceptable to France. I consider therefore that Count Tattenbach's remark tending to throw upon you or upon the policy of H[is] M[ajesty's] G[overnment] the blame for obstructing the Conference is entirely unwarranted.

I am, &c.
EDWARD GREY.

MINUTE BY KING EDWARD.

Approved.—E.R.

No. 282.

Sir F. Bertie to Sir Edward Grey.

F.O. 371/70.
(No. 67.)   *Paris, D. February 13, 1906.*
Sir,   *R. February 14, 1906.*

I have the honour to transmit herewith the accompanying despatch which I have received from Captain F. Morgan, Naval Attaché at this Embassy, on the subject of his visit to Toulon, and the feeling actually prevailing in French naval circles.

I have, &c.
FRANCIS BERTIE.

Enclosure in No. 282.

Captain Morgan to Sir F. Bertie.

(Very Confidential.)
Sir,   *Paris, February 11, 1906.*

.... ([1]) *British support to France in the event of Germany forcing a War on the latter Power.*—I can say without any hesitation whatever that the feeling amongst the officers at Toulon is that Great Britain intends to support France throughout over the Moroccan affair, not only by backing up her diplomacy, but by fighting for her, if by some unhappy chance the turn of events result in a war breaking out between her and Germany. One officer who was talking to me about the matter said "Great Britain will fight as hard for us now as she did against us a hundred years ago."

I quote this to show what must be the general feeling amongst the officers, as naturally they talk these things over. The officer in question was not a Flag officer, but a Capitaine de Frégate.

.... Referring to my remarks at the beginning of this Report, on the subject of the part Great Britain would play in the event of France being forced into war with Germany, I forgot to say that I have been much struck with the persistency in which most of the officers and others who have mentioned the subject to me have endeavoured to impress me with the fact that not only do they assume that we are prepared to join France in such a war, because they rely on our support throughout the Moroccan affair, but because they say it is to our interests to do so. Many have proceeded to explain why. These reasons I refrain from entering into, being hardly, I fancy, within the radius of action of a Naval Attaché; they are, however, easy of inference.

I have, &c.
FRED. MORGAN,
Captain R.N. and Naval Attaché.

([1]) [The omitted parts of this despatch are technical in character.]

No. 283.

Mr. Spring-Rice to Sir Edward Grey.

F.O. 371/172.
(No. 123.) Confidential.   St. Petersburgh, D. February 13, 1906.
Extract.   R. February 19, 1906.

I understand that both Count Lamsdorff and Count Witte have expressed themselves in the strongest manner as to their desire for a peaceful settlement, satisfactory
to France. The latter is especially anxious for such a settlement as he is convinced
that it is a necessary preliminary to that financial aid which is hourly becoming more
necessary to Russia. At the same time the main factor in the situation here—that is,
the Emperor's personal disposition—is shrouded in mystery and the diplomatic
negotiations between the Foreign Minister and the French Ambassador throw little light
on the private communications which are known to be passing between the Russian and
the German Emperors.

No. 284.

Sir A. Nicolson to Sir Edward Grey.([1])

F.O. 371/172.   Algeciras, February 14, 1906.
Tel. (No. 47.) Most Confidential.   R. 2·45 P.M.

German representative communicated to French representative German proposals
as to police. The former explained that his communication was private and meant
simply as a basis for discussion and that his Gov[ernmen]t were anxious to arrive at an
understanding.

Proposal is as follows :—

That the Conference request Sultan to undertake organization (? of a) police force
to be established in certain specified localities.

That this force should be organized and commanded by foreign officers who should
be freely selected by the Sultan. The necessary funds would be placed at the disposal
of the Sultan by the future State bank. The diplomatic body at Tangier would exercise
a control over execution of police organization and a superior foreign officer to be
selected from amongst the minor Powers should be entrusted with inspection and should
report to the diplomatic body at Tangier.

The project is to be an experimental one for a period of three to five years.

French representative told the German representative that he took act of the above
communication which was left with him in writing and would refer it to his
Gov[ernmen]t for their instructions.

My French colleague says that he has suggested to his Gov[ernmen]t that it
would be advisable to take no action for the moment on the suggestion of Count
Lamsdorff, that Great Britain, the U[nited] S[tates] and Italy should recommend to
German Gov[ernmen]t to agree to France and Spain being entrusted with police
organization.

He does not think that his Gov[ernmen]t will accept German proposal as it stands
but has hopes that it is not the last word of Germany and that the latter may be inclined
to consent that Sultan's choice of officers should be limited to France and Spain.

([1]) [For a fuller account, v. infra pp. 256–8, No. 287.]

No. 285.

Sir Edward Grey to Sir F. Lascelles.

F.O. 371/172.
(No. 67.)
Sir,
                                        Foreign Office, February 14, 1906.

I observed to Count Metternich today that I regretted that so little progress had been made at the Morocco Conference.([1]) Count Metternich said that progress had been made with some points, such as Moorish taxation, but that no doubt a difference of opinion with regard to the police remained, the German view being that the police should be organised under the Sultan of Morocco with officers drawn from Minor Powers, the police as a whole to be directed by one officer appointed by the Diplomatic Body at Tangier. I said that in our view, from the point of view of common sense, apart altogether from any engagements that we might have towards France, the only Powers who were qualified as regards personnel and experience to organise the police at the ports effectively were France and Spain. France had agreed to respect the sovereignty of the Sultan and the integrity of Morocco. Our British interests were two. In the first place the maintenance of order, which was essential to trade; and for this purpose we considered that the organisation of the police at the ports should be entrusted to France and Spain as the most effective way of securing this object. Our second interest was that there should be economic guarantees for the open door; and this we considered we had obtained, at any rate for a considerable number of years, under the Declarations which we had exchanged with France. I had heard it suggested that our representative at the Conference had gone too far in supporting France and encouraging her to make demands. On the contrary, we had kept well within the limits of the Declarations we had exchanged with France, and it appeared to me that the French attitude had been most moderate and reasonable.

Count Metternich said that the object of the German Government had originally been, and still was, to prevent France from getting a monopoly or a paramount interest in Morocco, and that for her to have the control of the police would give her this. I replied that the organisation of the police at the ports could not really endanger the economic interests of other Powers, and even in this organisation France would be associated with Spain. Besides this there was the question of the establishment of the State Bank, which had something to do with economic interests, and that France had shown herself, as I understood, quite ready to discuss in a conciliatory spirit.

Count Metternich would not accept the view that the organisation of the police at the ports could be entrusted to France without prejudice to the economic interests of other Powers. He said it was only the beginning from which France would proceed to acquire a predominant position in Morocco, which would be inconsistent with equal rights and opportunities for others.

I said there was evidently a difference of view between us. I could only hope that as the tone of the discussions at the Conference remained friendly, and the Conference was still proceeding, some better result might be hoped for there. Count Metternich said that with regard to the tone in which the discussions had been carried on, though he admitted that it had been quite friendly at the Conference, there had lately been a marked outburst of impatience in the French press, which he attributed to official instigation either on the part of M. Révoil or some official source in Paris, and which he took to mean that France wished the Conference to break up without result. I said that the impression produced upon me had been that M. Révoil had acted with the greatest moderation and patience, and that that had been the policy of his Government, but it had to be borne in mind that France had a great deal at stake in Morocco. As a neighbouring Power she was politically very much affected by what went on in Morocco. She had had the greatest share of the trade in Morocco, and owing to the unsettled state of the country, which had diminished the trade on the Algerian frontier, French

([1]) [For Count Metternich's report, see *G.P.* XXI, I, pp. 164–166.]

trade had lately suffered more than British trade or than that of any other country. It was therefore natural that the French press should show a certain anxiety and impatience, but I was firmly convinced that the French Government, simply because their interest in securing a settled condition of things in Morocco was so great, both politically and economically, desired a favourable result from the Conference.

Count Metternich said that Germany considered she had already made a great concession to France by recognising that it belonged to France to police the Algerian frontier. Should the Conference break up without any result because France had been unwilling to meet Germany on other points, Germany would regard the concession respecting the Algerian frontier as not having been made. His Government considered that the organisation of the police should be, as already stated, under the Sultan, with officers of Minor Powers, controlled by one officer appointed by the Diplomatists at Tangier, or else that Morocco should be divided into sections, the policing of which should be entrusted to separate Powers. I said that this seemed to me to be working on the Macedonian model, which was not a hopeful one; and I observed that of all the other Powers at the Conference I did not think one, except Germany, had raised any independent objection to the police at the ports being entrusted to France and Spain. Count Metternich said neither had they objected to the internationalisation of the police at the ports. I said I did not think they could have had any love for internationalisation, which I thought they must all feel would lead to confusion; but I asked, as the other Powers did not object to the police being entrusted to France and Spain, why should Germany raise objection to it, seeing that her trade interests were analogous to the trade interests of the other Powers, being at any rate much nearer to those of the other Powers than they were to those of France and Great Britain, which were much the largest of all? If, therefore, the Powers other than France and Great Britain did not think their trade interests would be endangered by the police at the ports being entrusted to France and Spain, why should Germany object? To this Count Metternich said that a great export trade was more necessary for Germany than it was for such countries as Spain or Italy. Morocco, he believed, had great possibilities and a great future. It was one of the few places still left open, and Germany, looking forward to the expansion of her own trade, could not see the prospect sacrificed.

I said I was sorry that Germany attached so much importance to political influence in Morocco and so little to economic guarantees. Our view was that we could safely concede political influence to France where we had no political ambitions, and accept in return economic guarantees for our trade. It appeared to me that a real difference of view existed between us on this point, but that as the discussion was still proceeding at Algeciras I was not without hope that it might yet be reconciled. We did not appear however to be able to make any progress at present.

Should an opportunity arise you may use similar language at Berlin, but I do not think any good would be done at this moment by making a special communication.

I am, &c.
EDWARD GREY.

MINUTE BY KING EDWARD.

Approved.—E.R.

No. 286.

Sir Edward Grey to Sir F. Bertie.

F.O. 371/172.
(No. 98.)
Sir,   *Foreign Office, February 15, 1906.*

Monsieur Cambon came to see me today and asked me whether I was informed of the German proposal for the organisation of the police in Morocco, which he briefly described to me. He then said that Prince Radolin had been to M. Rouvier and had asked M. Rouvier to discuss the Moroccan question with him. M. Rouvier had replied that Germany having laid down the principle that the Moroccan question could not be settled between the Powers separately, but must be discussed at a general Conference, it was impossible for him (M. Rouvier), after having accepted the Conference, to entertain separate discussion.

M. Cambon said that his view was that the French should stand on the ground which they had occupied, namely that the organisation of the police should be entrusted to France and Spain; but, he said, it would be desirable for the sake of concession, or to give this a chance of being accepted, that something should be added on the suggestion of another Power. The first suggestion should be that the Sultan of Morocco should be asked to take the initiative in the organisation of the police, on the condition that he did so within a short limit of time. Should he not act within this limit of time it would then be for France and Spain to take the initiative. It should also be a condition that the Sultan of Morocco should address himself to France and Spain. It might further be proposed that a French inspector, or two inspectors, one French and one Spanish, should be appointed, who should be charged with the duty of reporting to the Diplomatic Corps at Tangier respecting the police. This organisation of the police would be for the ports alone, not for other parts of Morocco, and its functions would be limited to the protection of foreigners only. All these points, M. Cambon thought, might be accepted by France, but they must be proposed by some other Power. England clearly could not make these proposals because she was too much engaged in the matter and suspected of *parti pris*. Italy and the United States were the two Powers one of whom might most probably make this suggestion. M. Cambon was afraid that President Roosevelt, owing to the objection taken in the Senate to his having sent a Plenipotentiary to Morocco at all might be reluctant to instruct Mr. White to take upon himself the responsibility of making these proposals, but it was possible that they might be made by the Marquis Visconti Venosta. M. Cambon asked me my opinion, and I said I agreed to these proposals and should be quite ready to support them, and that in my opinion it was important that the Conference should not be allowed to separate without these proposals having been clearly made as those which France would be prepared to accept. In this way it would appear that any blame for the failure of the Conference did not rest upon France.

I am, &c.
EDWARD GREY.

MINUTE BY KING EDWARD.
Approved.—E.R.

No. 287.

Sir A. Nicolson to Sir Edward Grey.

F.O. 371/173.
(No. 37.) Conference. Most Confidential. *Algeciras,* D. *February* 15, 1906.
Sir, R. *February* 24, 1906.

During the past few days a certain advance has been made in the negotiations regarding the question of the future police organization in Morocco, but I am afraid not in a direction which is likely to lead to a satisfactory conclusion.

Although I have had the honour to telegraph to you some intimations of the views of the German Government on the police question which were communicated by Prince Bülow to the Russian Ambassador at Berlin, and although I have also mentioned the proposed intervention of third parties, I would wish to limit this despatch to a report of what has passed here, as I am afraid that otherwise the matter might be presented to you in a somewhat confused form.

On the 13th instant M. de Radowitz paid a visit to M. Révoil and stated that, by instructions from his Government, he was now in a position to communicate privately to him a proposal for the settlement of the police question, which he begged M. Révoil not to consider as a "proposition ferme," but as serving as a basis for discussion. M. de Radowitz added that his Government earnestly desired that an agreement should be reached on the above question, and to avoid all possibility of a misunderstanding he had consigned the proposal to writing which he would be happy to leave with M. Révoil on the termination of their interview.

M. de Radowitz then read a declaration, the substance of which was as follows :—

That the Conference should request the Sultan to undertake the organization of a police force which should be established in certain specified localities, and which should be commanded and organized by foreign officers who should be freely selected by the Sultan. The funds which would be required for the establishment of this police force would be placed by the future State Bank at the disposal of the Sultan. The Diplomatic Body at Tangier would exercise a control over the execution of the police organization, and a superior foreign officer to be selected from among the minor Powers would be entrusted with the duty of inspecting the police force and would report to the Diplomatic Body at Tangier. The above project was to be an experimental one and would be put into execution for a period of from three to five years.

M. Révoil replied that he would take act of the communication which M. de Radowitz had been good enough to make to him, and that he would consult with his Government before giving a reply.

I called on M. Révoil yesterday afternoon, the 14th instant, and found him and his expert adviser M. Regnault engaged in drafting several telegrams to the French Minister for Foreign Affairs, giving their views as to the nature of the reply which should be made to the German communication. It appears that M. Rouvier was desirous of ascertaining the opinion of M. Révoil before sending him final instructions. M. Révoil told me that he was in some perplexity as to the character of the reply which he should suggest to his Government. He sketched verbally the terms of a reply which he had under consideration, but I must frankly state that it was so involved and so puzzling that I was unable to gather it's full sense. It neither refused, nor did it accept, the proposal of the German Government, but left the matter quite open, intimating that perhaps M. de Radowitz might be able to discover some formula which might lead to further negotiation. He asked me what I thought of it.

I told M. Révoil that it seemed to me to be very vague, and it might I feared lead to further misunderstandings of which, of late, we had had already so many. I did not myself see what object could be gained by giving a vague answer; suspicions might be aroused, and a wrong interpretation might be given to it. The German proposal was perfectly clear and had been given in writing, and it seemed to me it would, in these delicate matters, be prudent to be equally clear, especially as the German Government were already well acquainted with the views of the French Government.

M. Révoil said that he entirely agreed with me, and he had only put the question to me in order to dispel a doubt which had arisen in his mind. He therefore, in conjunction with M. Regnault, drew up a draft reply which he said he would telegraph to his Government at once.

The reply was to the effect that the French Government agreed that the Conference should request the Sultan to undertake the organization of a police force in certain specified localities; and that the State Bank should supply the requisite funds, and that the scheme should be for a limited period. The French Government desired that the Sultan should select French and Spanish officers to assist in the organization of, and to command, the police force; and they would be ready to examine the question of surveillance over the organization when an agreement had been reached as to the nationality of the officers.

I saw M. Révoil this morning, when he told me that he felt convinced that the German Government would never agree to any proposal as to the police question which would be acceptable to the Government and public opinion in France. He did not see how any satisfactory issue could possibly be found, and he had little confidence, in view of the present attitude of the German Government, in the success of any well meant efforts of third parties to bring about an understanding. He remarked with some bitterness on the absence of good faith which had characterized the action of the German Government and of their Representatives throughout the whole of the negotiations both before and during the Conference, and he observed that he knew that having pinned France down in Morocco Germany would not be inclined to set her free except on impossible conditions. To a remark I made that in the unfortunate event of the Conference having to disperse without having come to an agreement, it might be possible for direct negotiations to lead to a more satisfactory result, M. Révoil replied that he knew what would be the character of any direct agreement, as every point in it would be directed against Great Britain and inspired by a desire to disturb or overthrow the existing Anglo-French understanding.

It was the first time that I found M. Révoil so despondent, and, if I may say so, so ready to look disagreeable facts frankly in the face, as hitherto he has always buoyed himself up with a sanguine optimism that Germany would eventually agree to the police organization being arranged in accordance with the wishes of France.

I have, &c.

A. NICOLSON.

No. 288.

Sir Edward Grey to Sir A. Nicolson.

Private.(¹)

Dear Sir Arthur Nicolson, *Foreign Office, February 15, 1906.*

The German proposal now appears to be that the police should be organized under the Sultan of Morocco by officers taken from a neutral minor Power with one head officer chosen by the Corps diplomatique at Tangier.

In the last resort it might be worth while for the French to consider, whether they should not themselves propose that this should be accepted subject to the condition that the head officer should be a Frenchman selected by the French Government.

We could not press this upon the French. I am afraid we could not suggest it to them without their thinking that it meant a change of attitude on our part, which would not be the case—and they could not put it forward without being prepared to stand by it, if the Germans closed with it.

But if the Germans rejected it the mere fact of France having proposed it would throw on the Germans still more the blame for the failure of the Conference.

If the proposal were accepted I do not think it would work well—in a year or two the French and everybody would be tired of it, but by that time the European situation might be more favourable; the Powers rather than have another conference might agree separately to French and Spanish officers being substituted for the minor Power, and Germany either because her prestige was no longer in evidence, apropos of Morocco, or because the position of France in Europe was stronger might give way.

These are considerations, which it may be worth while suggesting to the French, and *to them only* but only as a last resort at the last moment.

What I want to ask is whether you think this could be suggested at all in such a way that the French would take it in good part from us? and if so whether you could do it to M. Révoil or whether I had better do it to M. Cambon here?

Yours very truly,

E. GREY.

(¹) [Carnock MSS.]

No. 289.

Sir A. Nicolson to Sir Edward Grey.

F.O. 371/172.   *Algeciras, February 16, 1906.*
Tel. (No. 51.) Confidential.   R. 2·50 P.M.

French representative discussed with U[nited] S[tates'] representative and myself the procedure to be followed next week, when it will be impossible to defer any longer the presentation of State-bank and police questions before the Conference. He said that German delegates were, he believed, desirous that the latter question should be left over and that Conference should sign protocols dealing with those questions upon which an agreement had been reached.

Both he and the U[nited] S[tates'] representative, and I agreed with them, were strongly of opinion that police question could not be dropped; and in fact U[nited] S[tates'] representative said he would request authority of his Gov[ernmen]t to leave Conference if the most important part of the program were abandoned. Moreover no agreement has yet been reached on the bank question which should come up for discussion on Monday. We feel that we can no longer with propriety ask the Conference to mark time as it will have sat five weeks next week. Moreover the continued delay is aggravating rather than improving the general situation.

We think it best to let matters take their course and not impede business, and although a discussion on the above questions in Conference is to be regretted still, if no agreement can in the meantime be arrived at, the public discussion will have to be faced.

No. 290.

Sir A. Nicolson to Sir Edward Grey.

F.O. 371/173.   *Algeciras,* D. *February 16, 1906.*
(No. 39.) Conference. Confidential.   R. *February 24, 1906.*
Sir,

M. Révoil informed me yesterday that Prince Radolin had, within the last two or three days, asked M. Rouvier whether His Excellency would not be disposed to transfer to Paris the private negotiations which were taking place at Algeciras between the French and German Representatives in regard to the police question. M. Rouvier had stated positively that he could not possibly fall in with this suggestion. He explained to Prince Radolin that Germany had induced France to go to Algeciras to discuss with the Representatives of the Powers, signatories of the Madrid Convention, certain questions laid down in a programme, and among these questions was that relative to the organization of a police force in Morocco. It would, therefore, be impossible to take this question out of the hands of the Conference, and he must leave the matter to be discussed at Algeciras and not at Paris. M. Rouvier appears to have taken the opportunity of expressing to Prince Radolin his surprise that the German Government apparently still supported the fiction that the French Government had taken an engagement not to ask the Conference for a mandate for the police organization. He drew the attention of Prince Radolin to the statement which he had made both verbally and in writing both to him and to Dr. Rosen, and which had been officially communicated to Berlin, to the effect that he had taken no engagement on any point outside of the programme to which the two Governments had agreed. These statements were made on September 25 and 26, of last year, and no exception had been taken at the time by the German Government, nor had any remark been made when they were published in the Yellow Book.

[15869]   s 2

He subsequently embodied the substance of his remarks in an aide-mémoire, which he communicated to Prince Radolin.

I have, &c.
A. NICOLSON

No. 291.

Sir A. Nicolson to Sir Edward Grey.

F.O. 371/173.
(No. 40.) Conference. Confidential. *Algeciras,* D. *February* 16, 1906.
Sir, R. *February* 24, 1906.

M. Révoil showed me yesterday a telegram which he had received from M. Rouvier in which His Excellency expressed some doubts whether it was advisable to continue the private pourparlers in regard to the police question, and he suggested that perhaps the Representatives of France, Germany, Great Britain, Spain, Russia, Italy, the United States and Austria-Hungary should meet informally, and endeavour to find an acceptable solution on the abovementioned subject.

I told M. Révoil that I thought it was a suggestion which required some reflection, and we arranged to meet in the evening in the rooms of the United States' Representative.

We met again in Mr. White's apartment, and after some conversation we agreed that the proposal, though it undoubtedly presented some advantages, was in our opinion open to greater objections. In the first place it seemed to us extremely doubtful if Germany would consent, as she had always contended that all Powers had an equal status and equal rights at the Conference, a proposition which in many respects is a sound one. She would probably regard the convocation of the eight Great Powers as establishing a kind of inner Conference : while at the same time it would in all likelihood mortify those Powers who were excluded, and incline them to believe that we merely considered them as being convoked to Algeciras for the purpose of registering the decisions of the Great Powers. Moreover if the private pourparlers between the French and German Representatives were to lead to no results, we doubted if the meeting of the other Representatives would assist towards a solution.

The United States' Representative, Mr. Henry White, added that he would naturally have to consult his Government before giving his adhesion to the project, and he frankly stated that he would not be able to recommend its acceptance to them.

M. Révoil said that he would inform M. Rouvier of our views, and as M. Rouvier's telegram had crossed one which he had sent submitting the reply which he proposed to give to the last communication which M. de Radowitz had made to him on the police question, he thought it probable that the French Government would not be disposed to press the matter further.

I have, &c.
A. NICOLSON.

No. 292.

Sir A. Nicolson to Sir Edward Grey.

F.O. 371/173.
(No. 43.) Conference. *Algeciras,* D. *February* 17, 1906.
Sir, R. *February* 24, 1906.

I have the honour to transmit, herewith, copy of the proposal regarding the organization of a police force in Morocco which was handed by M. de Radowitz to M. Révoil on the 13th instant, and also copy of the reply which the latter gave to his German colleague yesterday evening.

Until a reply is received from Berlin in respect to the latter communication it would be idle to speculate as to whether it will be regarded as furnishing a basis for further discussion.

Both M. de Radowitz and Count Tattenbach in desultory conversations with other Representatives have given the latter to understand that, in their view, the door for further negotiation is still open and that the French communication is conciliatory in substance.

I have, &c.
A. NICOLSON.

Enclosure 1 in No. 292.

German Proposal as to Police.

Il serait à proposer que la Conférence demandât au Sultan de se charger de l'organisation de la police. Il aura le devoir d'entretenir, dans des places déterminés, une troupe de police laquelle serait formée et commandée par des officiers étrangers choisis librement par le Sultan. Les fonds nécessaires pour l'entretien de la troupe seraient mis à la disposition du Sultan par la nouvelle Banque d'État. Le Corps Diplomatique à Tanger aura à exercer le contrôle de l'exécution de cette organisation. Un officier supérieur étranger appartenant à l'une des Puissances secondaires pourrait être chargé de l'inspection et en rendre compte au Corps Diplomatique à Tanger.

Toute cette institution serait faite à titre d'essai pour une durée de trois à cinq ans.

Le 13 Février, 1906.

Enclosure 2 in No. 292.

French Reply to German Proposal.

Il n'y a pas d'opposition à l'organisation de la police par le Sultan dans les ports, ni au paiement des troupes et des officiers par la Banque d'État, ni à la courte durée de cette institution, mais sous la condition que les officiers étrangers choisis par S[a] M[ajesté] Chérifienne soit des officiers français et espagnols.

Le point de la proposition allemande relatif à une surveillance de l'exécution de cette organisation pourrait être examiné si la question de la nationalité des officiers avait été résolue comme il est indiqué ci-dessus.

Le 16 Février, 1906.

No. 293.

Sir E. Grey to Sir A. Nicolson.

F.O. 371/172.   *Foreign Office, February* 19, 1906.
Tel. (No. 18.)   D. 3·20 P.M.
  Your telegram No. 52.(¹)
  It would be quite inequitable, when raising duties, to favour particular countries to the exclusion of Great Britain who holds the largest share in the trade of Morocco, and you should accordingly insist on the increase being applied all round.

(¹) [This telegram, from Sir A. Nicolson of February 19, refers to the question of a sur-tax and to the possible opposition to the British proposal that the sur-tax should be 2½ per cent. *ad valorem* for all imports.]

No. 294.

Mr. Cartwright to Sir Edward Grey.

F.O. 371/172.
Tel. (No. 17.) Confidential.
Conference.

Madrid, February 19, 1906.
D. 5·10 P.M.
R. 9·30 P.M.

M. Cambon would be glad to have views of Sir A. Nicolson on the following point, which he does not personally refer to French Delegate for (? fear of) appearing to wish to interfere in the details of the Conference :—

M. Cambon is of opinion that should Germany and France not come to an agreement on the police question, it will be very necessary that an immediate vote be taken in the Conference when Russia brings forward her proposal on the point. Should this be done, M. Cambon thinks that the Powers would (? agree) to Russian proposal and give France a moral victory.

If Germany succeeds in delaying the vote by bringing forward one counter-proposal after another, she will appear to the general public to be making concession (? s) all the time, and, if finally she proposes to give Spain police of ports on west coast, M. Cambon fears that Spain out of delicacy would abstain from voting, and United States may consider proposal reasonable, but (? out of) consideration for France also abstain from voting. Should this happen, the small Powers may group themselves behind United States and therefore not vote, leaving Germany, Austria, and Morocco and probably Italy, to oppose France, Great Britain, and Russia, and probably Portugal. It will not, then, be difficult for Germany to make out that her concessions had met with real support of European public opinion, and that France was in reality isolated on police question. From a French point of view this would be a most regrettable termination to the Conference.

This question of tactics (? ought) to be pursued when the police question comes on for discussion. M. Cambon (? thinks it) should be carefully considered, and he would be glad to have Sir A. Nicolson's views, confidentially, on the subject.

Sent to Sir A. Nicolson.

No. 295.

Sir Edward Grey to Sir E. Egerton.([1])

F.O. 371/172.
Tel. (No. 25.)

Foreign Office, February 19, 1906.
D. 8 P.M.

Your cypher letter rec[eive]d to-day.

Your telegram reporting German complaints of attitude of Spanish Delegate.

German Government are bringing similar pressure to bear at Madrid. In our opinion French attitude both with regard to State Bank and Police at Moroccan ports has been so moderate and practical that though anxious to see friendly solution we must continue to support it. You should let it be known that this is our view. It does not appear that proposals as to Bank or Police, which would be made or accepted by France are objected to on their merits by any Power except Germany.

E. G.

([1]) [Also *mutatis mutandis* to Mr. Cartwright.]

No. 296.

Sir Edward Grey to Sir F. Lascelles.

F.O. 371/172.
(No. 75.)
Sir, *Foreign Office, February* 19, 1906.

The German Ambassador asked to see me today, and showed me the instructions which had been sent to M. de Radowitz with regard to the police question, which are the same as those recorded by Sir Arthur Nicolson. He showed me also the text of the French reply, in which the French expressed themselves willing that the Sultan should be entrusted with the organisation of the police provided that he employed French and Spanish officers, that the arrangement should be regarded as provisional, and that they would be willing to discuss the question of some inspection being exercised by the Diplomatic Corps at Tangier. Count Metternich translated to me from the German the drift, at any rate, of the German reply to these proposals, which was that they entirely rejected the idea of the officers of the police being French and Spanish on the ground that this would destroy the international character of the police, that the French and Spanish officers would work in the interests of their own countries, and look upon their task from a national and not from an international point of view.

I said that this appeared to be a complete deadlock, for which I was exceedingly sorry. Was it really possible that the German Government considered that to entrust to France and Spain the organisation of the police, not in the interior of Morocco but at the ports only, and with functions limited to the protection of foreigners, would destroy the chances of equal trade opportunities in Morocco? Count Metternich said that if the police were to have such slight influence, why did France attach so much importance to the question? I said, in the first place, in the interests of good order: that France and Spain alone had the personnel and experience necessary to organize the police; and in the next place, no doubt France did object to anything like the internationalisation of Morocco; her political interests were so much bound up with the country; she had suffered already in trade, and political disorder was always liable to spread to her own possessions; and we therefore took the view that what was important to us was not to dispute the political influence of France but to secure direct economic guarantees. If Germany did not think the economic guarantees we had secured were enough, why did not she ask for others which were longer in time or more explicit in terms? I understood that the other Powers at the Conference did not object on their merits to the proposals which would be acceptable to France, and if the Conference failed because Germany objected it would postpone the day when it would be possible to improve the relations between England and Germany.

Count Metternich said that, if England was to use the French *entente* always to side with France against Germany, of course Germany would come to look on England as her enemy. I said there had been no question of always siding with France against Germany. Since the *entente* was framed there had been one point of difference—the subject of Morocco—which happened to be one of the very subjects covered by a definite agreement between England and France. We considered the French proposals, looking to her position in Morocco, as being exceedingly moderate and reasonable, and it was absolutely impossible for us not to support her when her action kept so well within the limits of the actual Agreement between us. I could again assure him that, were the Morocco difficulty satisfactorily settled, it was our desire to show that the *entente* was not to be used in a sense hostile to Germany.

Speaking of what might happen if the Conference broke up as a failure, Count Metternich said that Germany did not desire to have war with France. I said I thought it was much too soon to talk of anything so serious as war. I could only say again that in such an event public feeling in England would be so strong that the British Government would be involved in it, and that that was why I was so anxious to find a possible solution.

[15869]   s 4

Count Metternich spoke a good deal about the press, arguing that British attacks upon Germany were more violent than German upon England, and saying that the series of friendly demonstrations in Germany by Chambers of Commerce and so forth lately were meeting with no response in England. I said that I thought it was the Morocco Conference which stood in the way. People in England might not be taking much interest in the particular points raised at the Conference, but they had felt generally that relations were difficult between Germany and France on a matter in which we had engagements to France, and that naturally kept things in suspense. I said I was sure that either I or the Prime Minister, or any one in a prominent position, could speak with considerable effect in moderating the tone of the press and of public feeling in England if we had a favourable opportunity. Were the Algeciras Conference to result in a favourable solution and agreement, there would be such an opportunity, and I should have been delighted to make use of it; but if the Conference broke up without result, and the feeling of *malaise* still remained, it would be impossible for me, however much I desired it, to speak with effect in affecting public opinion in England favourably.([1])

I am, &c.
EDWARD GREY.

([1]) [For Count Metternich's report, see *G.P.* XXI, I, pp. 179–181.]

No. 297.

Sir Edward Grey to Mr. Spring-Rice.

F.O. 371/172.
(No. 93.)

Sir,   *Foreign Office, February 20, 1906.*

The Russian Chargé d'Affaires came to ask me today what was the position at Algeciras and what I thought of it, that he might inform his Government.

I told him that matters had arrived at a deadlock; that the Germans had refused point-blank the last suggestions made by the French on the subject of the police; and that, assuming that both Germany and France had spoken their last word, of which one could never be quite sure until the end, the Conference would break up without result and without any agreement being reached. I said that I should regret this result very much, but that I could not help it. Our interests in Morocco were two. First, the preservation of order, which could only be effectively carried out by entrusting the organisation of the police at the ports to France and Spain, the only two Powers who had the personnel and experience on the spot necessary. The German idea of the internationalisation of the police would be sure to result in difficulties and would not be effective; neither in Macedonia nor in Crete had the results of this system been satisfactory. I pointed out that France was quite willing that the police should be organised under the Sultan, the arrangement to be provisional, limited to the ports, and the functions of the police limited to the protection of foreigners. Our other interest in Morocco was equal opportunities for trade. As regards this we had direct guarantees in our Agreement with France, but it was open to Germany, if she thought our guarantees not good enough, to ask for direct economic guarantees of a more explicit kind. This she had not cared to do. In my opinion, therefore, the attitude of France had been conciliatory and practical, and if the Conference broke up without result it would not be on France that the blame or responsibility would rest.

M. Sazonow asked me what I thought would follow the break-up of the Conference. Would there be war? I said I could not think that war would follow the break-up of the Conference. For Germany to attack France simply because no agreement had been arrived at at the Conference would be a thing too outrageous to conceive. I could not suppose that that was possible, but what I did fear was, that Morocco being in a very disturbed state, either France or Germany might take separate action in

Morocco which might make difficulties between them. If Morocco was a strong and independent country, the break-up of the Conference would not necessarily have any result whatever, but Morocco being in such a disturbed condition, one could not tell what might happen there after the Conference was over.

I assured M. Sazonow that we should continue till the end of the Conference to give our diplomatic support to the French attitude there, as we had done all through. The attitude of the French had been so conciliatory, reasonable and moderate that it had made it very easy for us to give them the support which we had promised. I was most anxious to see France and Germany arrive at an agreement about Morocco, especially because it was a subject on which we had our own Agreement with France, and we would do anything we could to bring about peace between Germany and France which could be done without giving France away or sacrificing her interests.

M. Sazonow alluded to certain preparations in France and to the naval strength which Great Britain had at present in the North Sea as reasons which he hoped would deter Germany from any idea of war. Indeed, he said that it appeared that, should Germany go to war as the result of the Conference at Algeciras, she would have against her the moral opinion of the whole of Europe; and generally he seemed to take the view that German action was responsible for all the present difficulty and uneasiness.

I am, &c.
EDWARD GREY.

No. 298.

Sir A. Nicolson to Sir Edward Grey.

F.O. 371/173.
(No. 46.) Conference.
Sir,

Algeciras, D. *February* 20, 1906.
R. *February* 26, 1906.

I have the honour to transmit, herewith, copies of the German and French projects for the institution of a State Bank in Morocco, which were laid before the Conference today.(¹) These projects will be discussed at a meeting to be held on the 22nd instant.

I would beg leave to point out that the two projects differ both in character and in the details. The German project wishes apparently to invest the Bank with an official character and to associate the Powers either directly or through their Representatives at Tangier with the creation and the administration of the Bank. The French project on the other hand desires to restrict the action of the Bank within it's [*sic*] proper sphere, and I venture to think that the statement of the French Representative, of which I beg leave to transmit a summary,(¹) explains this point of view far more clearly than I can pretend to do.

With respect to the details, I would beg leave to point out that the German project desires that the "siège social" of the Bank should be at Tangier, while the French scheme wishes to place the Bank under French law subject to the jurisdictions of the several countries. By this it is intended that in cases where the Bank is prosecutor the defendant should be tried by his consular tribunal in accordance with the laws of his country, while when the Bank is defendant it should be tried by French law, in first instance by the French consular tribunal, with appeal to a superior court in France. The German project, on the other hand, wishes that in cases where the Bank is prosecutor the defendant should be tried by his consular tribunal, but not in accordance with the laws of his country, but by the Egyptian codes : and when the Bank is defendant it should be tried, without appeal, by a court composed of the "Presidents of the Foreign Consular Tribunals." To those who are

(¹) [Not reproduced.]

acquainted with the Consular Tribunals in Morocco this suggestion seems a singularly unpractical one, and also one by which justice would be strangely administered. To be debarred the right of appeal constitutes a further and I venture to submit a fatal objection.

The proposal in the German project that the Diplomatic Body at Tangier should form a " Conseil de Surveillance " over the Bank, has justly caused surprise. It would be no disrespect to the Diplomatic Body to say that it's [*sic*] members are hardly competent to perform the functions with which the German Delegation desires to invest them, apart from other objections of a more general character.

For the composition of the Conseil d'Administration the two projects suggest different proposals; and the German project does not allude to the rights of the French consortium which is practically the sole creditor of Morocco. It is worthy of remark that the German project (Articles XII and XIII) appears to ignore the position acquired by the French undertakers of the loan to the Sultan of Morocco : and to be oblivious of the fact that, if the French contract is not taken into consideration, two rival and clashing administrations will be established, the State Bank with its attributions and powers, and the French consortium, with it's droits de préférence as regards loans and coinage and its lien on 60 per cent. of the Moorish Customs. Allusion is made to this contradiction in the statement of my French colleague.

I have ventured to draw your attention to a few differences in the two projects which it may be difficult to reconcile, and it is possible that closer study by greater experts than myself may discover other points on which there is a divergence of conception.

I have not the " Acte de Concession " of the Ottoman Bank to which reference is made in five articles in the German project, and so I am unable to express any opinion on these points.

I have, &c.
A. NICOLSON.

No. 299.

Memorandum by Sir Edward Grey.

MOROCCO.

Private.([1])   *February* 20, 1906.

The German Ambassador asked to see me yesterday for the purpose of telling me that his Government had met the last proposal of the French about police in Morocco with a point blank refusal.

If the Conference breaks up without result the situation will be very dangerous. Germany will endeavour to establish her influence in Morocco at the expense of France. France to counteract this or even simply to protect herself and a neighbour from the state of disturbance, which is now chronic in Morocco, will be driven to take action in Morocco, which Germany may make a *casus belli.*

If there is war between France and Germany it will be very difficult for us to keep out of it. The *Entente* and still more the constant and emphatic demonstrations of affection (official, naval, political, commercial, Municipal and in the Press), have created in France a belief that we should support her in war. The last report from our naval attaché at Toulon said that all the French officers took this for granted, if the war was between France and Germany about Morocco. If this expectation is disappointed the French will never forgive us.

There would also I think be a general feeling in every country that we had behaved meanly and left France in the lurch. The United States would despise us, Russia would not think it worth while to make a friendly arrangement with us about Asia, Japan would prepare to re-insure herself elsewhere, we should be left without a friend and without the power of making a friend and Germany would take some pleasure, after what has passed, in exploiting the whole situation to our disadvantage, very likely by stirring up trouble through the Sultan of Turkey in Egypt. As a minor matter the position of any Foreign Secretary here, who had made it an object to maintain the *entente* with France, would become intolerable.

On the other hand the prospect of a European War and of our being involved in it is horrible.

I propose therefore, if unpleasant symptoms develop after the Conference is over, to tell the French Ambassador that a great effort and if need be some sacrifice should in our opinion be made to avoid war. To do this we should have to find out what compensation Germany would ask or accept as the price of her recognition of the French claims in Morocco. There is also a point about Egypt, which might be worked in on our behalf. I should myself be in favour of allowing Germany a port or coaling station, if that would ensure peace; but it would be necessary to consult the Admiralty about this, and to find out whether the French would entertain the idea, and if so what port?

The real objection to the course proposed is that the French may think it pusillanimous and a poor result of the *Entente.* I should have to risk this. I hope the French would recognise that in a war with Germany our liabilities would be much less than theirs. We should risk little or nothing on land, and at sea we might shut the German fleet up in Kiel and keep it there without losing a ship or a man or even firing a shot. The French would have a life and death struggle and that expenditure of blood and treasure with a doubtful issue. They ought therefore not to think it pusillanimous on our part to wish to avoid a war in which our danger was so much less than theirs.

I have also a further point in view. The door is being kept open by us for a *rapprochement* with Russia; there is at least a prospect that when Russia is re-established we shall find ourselves on good terms with her. An *entente* between Russia, France and ourselves would be absolutely secure. If it is necessary to check Germany it could then be done. The present is the most unfavourable moment for attempting to check her. Is it not a grave mistake, if there must be a quarrel with Germany for France or ourselves to let Germany choose the moment, which best suits her.

There is a possibility that war may come before these suggestions of mine can be developed in diplomacy. If so it will only be because Germany has made up her mind that she wants war and intends to have it anyhow, which I do not believe is the case. But I think we ought in our own minds to face the question now, whether we can keep out of war, if war breaks out between France and Germany. The more I review the situation the more it appears to me that we cannot, without losing our good name and our friends and wrecking our policy and position in the world.

NOTES BY SIR C. HARDINGE.

If France takes action in Morocco to protect herself which Germany might resent it is not certain that Germany would declare war and attack France in Europe since such action would at once present a "casus foederis" and bring Russia into line with France. If however it is understood by Germany that England is absolutely "solidaire" with France as far as the Moroccan question is concerned, without any limitations as to whether action by France in Morocco is aggressive or not, such knowledge would almost certainly deter Germany from provoking a conflict by which Germany must lose her entire mercantile marine and almost her whole foreign trade.

If France is left in the lurch an agreement or alliance between France, Germany and Russia in the near future is certain. This has been twice proposed during the last six years and is the Kaiser's ideal, France and Russia becoming satellites within the German system. There are many politicians in Russia in favour of such a scheme amongst them being Count Witte. These are in favour of the French alliance for purely economic reasons and of an *entente* with Germany from fear of her hostility.

If, as a result of the failure of the Conference, compensation is offered to Germany for her recognition of the French position in Morocco with the view of avoiding an almost certain war in the near future, it seems to me that our demand about Egypt should be kept entirely in the background and not be dependent on our assent to any agreement between France and Germany, since it would be interpreted in France as a self-seeking action on our part by which we would secure greater advantages in Egypt than those which we have already obtained from our agreement with France on Egypt and Morocco and from which the French Gov[ernmen]t have so far profited little.

C. H.

Feb. 23.

No. 300.

Sir A. Nicolson to Sir Edward Grey.

F.O. 371/172.
Tel. (No. 61.)

Algeciras, February 21, 1906.
R. 3·5 P.M.

Mr. Cartwright's telegram No. 17.([1])

I have sent him following reply :—

"Pray tell M. Cambon, with my best regards that he may rely on all precautions being taken at the Conference to throw the responsibility of the probable rupture on the proper shoulders. The refusal of Germany to agree to last proposals of France as to police and also her sudden change of attitude on the bank question will, I think, leave little doubt in the minds of the Conference that France is not to blame for the consequences."

([1]) [*v. supra* p. 262, No. 294.]

No. 301.

Mr. Cartwright to Sir Edward Grey.

F.O. 371/172.
Tel. (No. 19.) Confidential.
Conference.

Madrid, February 21, 1906.
D. 7·40 P.M.
R. *February* 22, 8 A.M.

This morning M. Cambon read to me a long telegram just received from French Delegate. It stated that President of the Conference seemed inclined to offer Spanish mediation to arrange understanding between France and Germany. He seemed to consider step a dangerous one, and as likely to lead to Spain being put in an equivocal position as regards her engagements to France. M. Cambon begged me to impress upon Spanish Government necessity for France, Great Britain, and Spain standing firmly together on the bank and police questions.

Before seeing Acting Minister for Foreign Affairs, I called (? on German) Chargé d'Affaires, and found him fairly hopeful. He thought both sides might yield a little, but he did not allude to Spanish mediation; he said it was absolutely necessary for Germany to take every precaution to keep Morocco open to her trade and enterprise, especially as now her Colonies were proving useless, and commercial difficulties were arising with United States.

I then saw Acting Minister for Foreign Affairs, and told him how necessary it was at this moment that Spain, France, and Great Britain should show a common front at the Conference. He replied that Spanish Government were of the same opinion, and held to their engagement, but being host of the Conference, President of the Conference had thought that Spain should make a supreme effort to prevent Conference failing altogether. Spanish Government approved Duke's idea, but left to his judgment proper moment and method for carrying it out.

I pointed out danger of this course, and that it might end in Germany making the world believe that she had succeeded in drawing Spain on to her side. Acting Minister for Foreign Affairs replied that he trusted to the Duke's judgment to prevent this.

With regard to French bank proposals, I understand that Spanish Government are anxious as to the effect of the currency reform introduced into the scheme. They fear that gold standard as proposed may drive out Spanish silver. I have informed M. Cambon of this feeling.

(Strictly Private and Secret.)

French Delegate informs M. Cambon that Second Spanish Delegate expects to be named Ambassador at Berlin, and that German Government, knowing this, are using threat to refuse to receive him unless he uses his influence with Duke in a sense favourable to Germany.

Acting Minister for Foreign Affairs in an outburst of frankness said to me to-day that he hated France and French influence in Morocco, and that he had no confidence in and personal dislike for French Ambassador, giving me his reasons, but as Minister for Foreign Affairs he would act faithfully in accordance with Spain's engagements, although he disliked them. M. Cambon has told me that he can get nothing but strictly official replies from Acting Minister for Foreign Affairs. This is a most unfortunate state of things at the present moment.

(Sent to Sir A. Nicolson.)

No. 302.

Sir Edward Grey to Sir A. Nicolson.

F.O. 371/172.   *Foreign Office, February 22, 1906.*
Tel. (No. 20.)   D. 7·30 P.M.

Mr. Cartwright's telegram No. 19.

It seems to me most desirable that if Spain makes any proposal at the conference, it should only be with the cognizance and approval of the French Delegate.

No. 303.

Mr. Spring-Rice to Sir Edward Grey.

                                     St. Petersburgh, February 22, 1906.
F.O. 371/172.   D. 11·50 A.M.
Tel. (No. 40.)   R. 2·45 P.M.

Morocco.

In view of latest news from Conference Count Lamsdorff suggests that representations should be made at Berlin pressing German Government to accept last French proposal, which seems to him to meet all reasonable objections.

I understand that he spoke very strongly to one of the Ambassadors as to the aggressive character of German policy as shown at the Conference and as to the necessity of the public opinion of Europe making itself felt at Berlin.

No. 304.

Sir Edward Grey to Mr. Spring-Rice.

F.O. 371/172.   *Foreign Office, February* 22, 1906.
Tel. (No. 44.)   D. 7·30 P.M.

Your tel[egram] No. 40.

Morocco.

The German Ambassador communicated to me on the 19th inst. the German reply rejecting entirely the French proposals.

I impressed upon H[is] E[xcellency] the deplorable effect which would be produced by the failure of the Conference owing to the rejection of the French proposals which seemed to us and to the other Powers at the Conference practical, moderate and reasonable.

Since we are bound by our treaty engagements to support France in Morocco any representations which we might volunteer at Berlin are not likely to be effective.

You should tell all this to C[oun]t Lamsdorff and say how valuable we consider any pressure that the R[ussian] Gov[ernmen]t are able to bring to bear at Berlin in order to obtain the acceptance by Germany of the French proposals.

No. 305.

Mr. Cartwright to Sir Edward Grey.

                              Madrid, February 22, 1906.
F.O. 371/172.   D. 5·20 P.M.
Tel. (No. 21.)   Confidential.   R. 7 P.M.

Conference. My telegram No. 19 of yesterday.([1])

Not satisfied with assurance given to me by Acting Minister for Foreign Affairs as to attitude of Spanish Government at Algeciras, I saw President of the Council last night, and pointed out to him how dangerous it was for Spain to mediate between France and Germany unless latter had given assurances that she would meet French demands in a really conciliatory spirit. President of the Council expressed himself (group undecypherable) France as to results of mediation, which was entirely idea of Duke Almodovar, but Spanish Government, for political reasons, could not refuse to attempt to conciliate differences at a Conference held on Spanish soil.

What he feared was that German Delegation would take a vote on some minor point, and unanimity not having been obtained, would declare that this barred further discussion on that part of the programme.

I replied that it would be fatal if the Duke allowed himself to be swayed by Germany in matters of procedure at Conference, and that I must insist if Great Britain, France, or Russia demanded that Conference should put on record views of the Powers on projects proposed, the President of the Conference([2]) shall not oppose himself to this, but shall vote in support of such projects as they merely embodied the principles agreed to by France and Spain at San Sebastian last September. If Duke wavered, nothing could prevent world from believing that Spanish Government was also wavering in their intention of honestly adhering to their engagements.

President of the Council seemed struck by this, and he assured me that Spain would strictly adhere to its engagements, and that he would at once telegraph to Duke to be very careful as to what steps he took, and in no way to compromise Spanish Government.

I inquired of President of the Council whether King had any personal views on these questions. He replied that His Majesty was very strongly in favour of Spain

([1]) [v. *supra* pp. 268–9, No. 301.]
([2]) [The original decypher read : " proposed by the President of the Conference," but was altered to the above by Mr. F. A. Campbell.]

remaining in close friendship with England and France; in fact, on this point he was most decided.

(Sent to Sir A. Nicolson.)

No. 306.

Sir A. Nicolson to Sir Edward Grey.

F.O. 371/172.
Tel. (No. 65.)

Algeciras, February 23, 1906.
R. 2·45 P.M.

Mr. Cartwright's telegram of yesterday.

I think it was desirable and perhaps necessary to give President of Conference to understand that he should abstain from endeavouring to mediate and I admit some reason for a little uneasiness as to attitude of Spanish delegates. At the same time I am of opinion that they are now acting quite loyally and I know that my French colleague shares my views and has so informed his Gov[ernmen]t.

In these circumstances it would, I respectfully submit, be advisable to send some comforting message to the Spanish Gov[ernmen]t to the effect that H[is] M[ajesty's] Gov[ernmen]t appreciate the manner in which they intend to fulfil their engagements. My French Colleague had agreed to submit a similar recommendation to his Gov[ernmen]t. I have every hope that my French colleague and myself will be able to arrange with the Duke a procedure in conformity with our views : and if he were aware that our Gov[ernmen]ts appreciate his attitude it would be of great assistance to us.

No. 307.

Sir Edward Grey to Mr. Cartwright.

F.O. 371/172.
Tel. (No. 10.)

Foreign Office, February 23, 1906.
D. 7·30 P.M.

Your tel[egram] No. 22.(¹)

H[is] M[ajesty's] G[overnment] highly appreciate the manner in which Spain is fulfilling her engagements. They are convinced that the continuance of the loyal attitude of president of conference will have most beneficial results. You should take an opportunity of expressing our satisfaction to Spanish Government if your French colleague is similarly instructed.

(¹) [Telegram No. 22, dated February 22, reported a statement by the Acting Minister for Foreign Affairs corroborating the last paragraph of No. 305, *supra*, pp. 270–1.]

No. 308.

Mr. Spring-Rice to Sir Edward Grey.

F.O. 371/173.
Tel. (No. 42.)

St. Petersburgh, February 24, 1906.
D. 11·11 A.M.
R. 11·45 A.M.

Morocco.

Emperor received French Ambassador on Feb[ruary] 21, and expressed warm sympathy with France, promising to do all in his power to facilitate a solution. French Ambassador says that there was no sign of His Majesty being under German influence. He saw Count Lamsdorff this afternoon and told him that recent refusal of French proposal about police and still more a sudden presentation of a new and impossible demand about Bank showed that Germany intended to make a settlement impossible. Count Lamsdorff agreed, and said that Russian Ambassador at Berlin had by the Emperor's instructions presented the French case in the strongest terms but without success. C[oun]t Lamsdorff expressed the opinion that the difficulty of the situation was that amour-propre of German Emperor was deeply engaged, and that only course now open was to bring to bear opinion of civilised world in order to induce Emperor to accept the almost unanimous decision of Representatives at the Conference. Russia, he said, had done what she could : England was bound by a Convention which she has declared her determination to maintain and her further representations would carry no weight. He threw out the suggestion that the President of the United States might usefully intervene.

Austrian Ambassador called on Count Lamsdorff later and spoke strongly as to the danger of allowing the continuance of present situation.

I will see Count Lamsdorff tomorrow and deliver your message.

MINUTES.

It would be foolish to expect that, if Germany has deliberately accepted a line of policy which she considers in her best interest, she may be persuaded to abandon it on " the opinion of the civilized world " being brought to bear upon the Emperor. The only consideration that would influence her in the desired direction, would be the apprehension of the other powers taking some action to make the German position difficult. But there is not at present danger of such a thing happening : Russia is powerless, France is avowedly not prepared to assert her claims by force, Great Britain, even if she desired, could not move without a French initiative; Austria and Italy and Spain do not count; the United States will not interfere. Therefore Germany feels quite secure in pursuing her own path. Either she will wring concessions out of France at the conference, or she will resume her " liberty of action " at Fez. What the latter may lead to, can be vaguely foreseen.

There is one possibility which it would be well to be on our guard against even now : Supposing a German subject gets murdered or kidnapped in Morocco? Is there not a danger of a second Kiaochau incident? If Germany were to demand and seize a port in Morocco in such circumstances, or obtain a lease, it would be done suddenly, and we ought to be prepared, and know what we should then want to do. It might be possible to object on the ground of the guaranteed integrity of Morocco. But a mere protest would of course not be enough. Co-operation with France would of course be essential. Meanwhile, could we not try to insinuate to the Sultan the obvious dangers of German ambitions? We could urge him to be on his guard against German concessions, and warn him of what happened at Kiaochau. The opportunity might also be taken to tell the Sultan that it was Germany who urged the Sultan of Turkey to send emissaries to Morocco. Mr. Lowther might perhaps be given some means to " influence " important personages.

E. A. C.
Feb. 24.

This is worthy of consideration. We might warn Mr. Lowther to be ready to use these arguments with the Sultan.

E. B.

It is somewhat premature. We must wait to see the outcome of the Conference. C[oun]t Lamsdorff's suggestion of the intervention of the U[nited] S[tates] is, according to Sir A. Nicolson's private letter of the 18th, about to be realised.

C. H.

We cannot stir in Morocco, while the Conference is sitting, but the eventualities referred [to] must not be forgotten.

E. G.

No. 309.

Sir E. Goschen to Sir Edward Grey.

Vienna, February 24, 1906.

F.O. 371/173.
Tel. (No. 2.)

D. 7 P.M.
R. 10 P.M.

Morocco Conference.

Count Goluchowski who seems much depressed by bad outlook at Algeciras has (? told) French Ambassador that in case no agreement is arrived at he is in favour of suspension and not dissolution of Conference.

French Ambassador though apparently not much in favour of such an arrangement said that he presumed that his Exc[ellenc]y would instruct Austrian Representatives to propose suspension under above circumstances. Count Goluchowski said he was discussing matter with Italy and United States and that if supported by them he should do so but not otherwise.

(Repeated to Algeciras No. 27, February 25.)

No. 310.

Mr. Cartwright to Sir Edward Grey.

Madrid, February 24, 1906.

F.O. 371/173.
Tel. (No. 25.) Conference. Confidential.

D. 7·30 P.M.
R. 10 P.M.

Your tel[egram] No. 10.(¹)

M. Cambon having received similar instructions we have today conveyed the thanks of our respective Gov[ernmen]ts to Spanish Gov[ernmen]t for their attitude.

Acting M[inister] [for] F[oreign] A[ffairs] informs me that President of the Council has today sent another telegram to President of the Conference to use his influence without unnecessarily wounding German feelings to arrange that before Conference breaks up a record sh[oul]d be obtained by a vote of the views of the Powers on the more important points in dispute, and that he is to remember that Spain is to remain in line with France and Great Britain.

(Sent to Sir A. Nicolson.)

(¹) [v. supra p. 271, No. 307.]

No. 311.

Mr. Spring-Rice to Sir Edward Grey.

St. Petersburgh, February 24, 1906.

F.O. 371/173.
Tel. (No. 43.)

D. 8 P.M.
R. 11 P.M.

I saw Count Lamsdorff today.

He thanked you for your communication which he quite understood. He had just received a tel[egram] from Russian Ambassador at Berlin which held out little hope that further representations there would be attended with success. He had stated clearly to the German Ambassador, in answer to his contention that Germany was acting in the interests of Europe, that he considered the powers of Europe the best judges of their own interests, and that Germany could not speak for them without their authority.

[15869]

T

He told me that if the Representatives of the Powers at the Conference which met in deference to the wishes of Germany declared themselves satisfied with French proposals he did not believe it possible for Germany on her own motion to break up the Conference. If she did so, her aggressive policy would be plain to the whole world.

He was afraid however that the approaching French Elections might result in a strong nationalist movement (?) to force France into war. He was sure of the Prime Minister but not of the people.

He considered the situation dangerous and had no proposal to make except that the Representatives at the Conference might show a united front which would give Germany an excuse for yielding to wishes of Europe subject to revision after a term of years and reserving her rights.

No. 312.

Sir A. Nicolson to Sir Edward Grey.

F.O. 371/173.

(No. 52.) Conference. Confidential. *Algeciras*, D. *February* 25, 1906.

Sir, R. *March* 3, 1906.

I have had several conversations with M. Révoil in regard to the best procedure to follow with respect to the possible breakdown of the Conference,([1]) as there are two points which we venture to think should be kept clearly and constantly in view—

1st. that the rupture should not occur over the Bank Question; and 2nd. that the responsibility for the rupture should not fall on France and Great Britain.

The first point should, if I may say so, be treated as a question of tactics. It is clear to both my French colleague and myself that unless the German Delegates change their attitude no agreement will be reached on the Bank Question, and it is equally clear to us that the German delegates will endeavour by all the means at their disposal to prevent the Police question being brought before the Conference until that body has discussed in a plenary Sitting the Bank question when the impossibility of an agreement will be made manifest, and perhaps an effort made to adjourn or dissolve the Conference on that point. Both my French colleague and myself desire to avoid this eventuality. The Bank question is not so simple as that of the Police, and it would be difficult for the general public to understand why an agreement had not been arrived at over what would appear to it as merely technical financial details. Moreover, the Police question has been brought prominently before the public : it is a simple one and easily understood by the "man in the street"; it's urgency is apparent : the moderation and conciliatory disposition of France can be most clearly manifested; the right of France with Spain to undertake the policing of the ports and her especial qualifications for this duty can be shown to be indisputable, while the attitude of Germany on this question can be exhibited in striking contrast to that of France.

We are, therefore, strongly of opinion that, before the Bank question emerges from the Drafting Committee, the Police question should be brought forward, and the Conference made fully acquainted with the question in all it's [*sic*] bearings, and an opportunity afforded to the French delegate, and to those who support him, to state their case in an open and public manner. To enable us to effect this we shall have to invoke the assistance of the President of the Conference, and the Duke of Almodovar has readily promised us to give us all the aid in his power.

At the present moment we stand in this position. No date has been fixed for our next sitting, but the Duke of Almodovar at the close of the meeting of yesterday stated that, though he did not mention a day for our reassembling, he would be ready to convoke a meeting on any day desired by any member of the Conference to discuss any question on the programme.

([1]) [Comments of King Edward at this stage are quoted in Sir Sidney Lee : *King Edward VII* (1927), II, p. 362.]

M. Révoil and myself, therefore submitted to our Governments a suggestion that on the 27th or 28th instant we should request His Excellency to call together the Conference on March 1st to discuss the Police question : and we are of opinion that we should then enter fully into this matter so far as we can, and if possible test the sense of the Conference on the subject. The Sitting will have to be in General Committee in accordance with the precedents hitherto observed, but, once the question has been thoroughly discussed at a General Committee, it will not be difficult to bring it rapidly before a plenary sitting so as to avoid its being transferred to the Drafting Committee, there being no necessity for such a reference, as both in its principles and details the question is an exceedingly simple one.

It is, therefore, desirable to consider what I have mentioned as Point No. 2 namely to ensure that the responsibility of a rupture should not fall on France and Great Britain. I have no doubt that the declaration which my French colleague will make on the occasion will demonstrate very clearly that France has done her utmost to go to the furthest limits of conciliation; and I have also no doubt that others will be able to show that France and Spain alone possess the necessary qualified elements for meeting an urgent need.

Such evidence will have much weight : at least I have every reason to hope that it will. But though we are both aware that the general feeling of the Conference is with the French view of the case, still we are in some doubts whether all our colleagues, when the moment arrives, will be disposed to give a frank expression of their views and a public adhesion to the French project. We count upon Spain, Russia, and Portugal being ready to record their votes in favour of the French project; which would make five in all. On the other side we calculate that Germany would secure the votes of Austria-Hungary and Morocco; but we fear that the others, viz., the United States, Italy, Holland, Sweden and Belgium may be disposed to abstain. The United States Representative is, I know, personally in favour of the French view; but considerations of home politics, such as the relations between the President and the Senate, and the desire of the American public not to take a decided line in differences between two European Powers, may force him to maintain silence. Italy is a member of the Triple Alliance, and may hesitate to record a vote diametrically ópposed to the wishes and opinions of her two allies. The three smaller Powers for various reasons may also consider it more prudent to abstain from recording their opinions.

It is in view of this difficulty that M. Révoil and myself are considering what proposals we can submit to our Governments to bring clearly into relief the undoubted disposition of the majority of the Conference to favour the French in preference to the German project as to the organization of the police. We have not yet discovered a course of procedure which we could venture to recommend to our Governments but before this despatch reaches your hands I have hopes that we shall have been in a position to submit certain recommendations.

I have, &c.
A. NICOLSON.

No. 313.

Sir A. Nicolson to Sir Edward Grey.

F.O. 371/173.
Tel. (No. 71.) **Confidential.**

Algeciras, February 26, 1906.
R. 12·45 P.M.

Mr. Spring-Rice's telegram No. 43.(¹)

I have doubts if we shall obtain an open expression on the part of some Powers that they are in favour of the French proposal as to police. I am quite sure that all, with the exception of Germany and Morocco, consider France's proposals are reasonable, moderate and practical; but I fear that some will hesitate to say so openly

(¹) [v. supra pp. 273-4, No. 311.]

[15869]

T 2

or wish to appear as taking side of France against Germany. My French colleague and myself are endeavouring to find some form for a platonic declaration on the part of doubtful powers of their sentiments which should not wound the feelings of Germany, be too explicit and yet sufficiently clear to give evidence of their disposition. It is not easy to find but I hope to be able to telegraph a form to you today or at latest tomorrow for your opinion.

<hr>

No. 314.

Sir A. Nicolson to Sir Edward Grey.

F.O. 371/173.
Tel. (No. 72.)

Algeciras, February 26, 1906.
R. 12·20 P.M.

The Portuguese representative has informed me that his Gov[ernmen]t have instructed him to follow Gr[eat] Britain in any course we may adopt at the Conference when police question is discussed : (from ?) all he tells me, he is quite ready to enforce his support by giving a vote for the French proposal if I so desire. I have thanked him and said that in all probability I may have to call upon him for an open expression of his opinion.

<hr>

No. 315.

Sir A. Nicolson to Sir Edward Grey.

F.O. 371/173.
Tel. (No. 73.)

Algeciras, February 26, 1906.
R. 4 A.M.

Following is the reply which the French delegate has been instructed to make to the last communication of the German representative in regard to police. The reply will be handed in today.

Reply begins :—

"The principle of equality for all in economical matters to which reference is made in German proposal has been accepted by us without reserve. We are convinced that this principle was in no wise endangered by the proposal which we made in regard to the organisation of the police. But if the Conference should be of opinion that so far as regards equality of treatment in economical matters it would be useful to have further guarantees, we will not refuse to examine the question. It is for the Conference to decide on a solution in conformity with the agreement of July 8."(1)

Reply ends.

(1) [*v. supra* pp. 115–6, No. 147.]

<hr>

No. 316.

Sir Edward Grey to Sir E. Goschen.

F.O. 371/173.
(No. 17.)
Sir,

Foreign Office, February 26, 1906.

The Austrian Chargé d'Affaires asked me today about the Conference at Algeciras, and whether the prospects were not a little better. He said he hoped that Baron de Courcel might have brought some favourable news from Berlin. I said that I was afraid there was not any real improvement. As regards what had passed between Baron de Courcel and the German Government at Berlin, I did not know what had happened, but I was afraid that if there had been any very favourable result I should have heard of it by this time.

The Austrian Chargé d'Affaires said that he hoped I did not anticipate any imminent danger if the Conference broke up without result. I said no, nothing imminent; but undoubtedly, with the disturbance continuing in Morocco, a state of general uneasiness would continue through Europe; and I impressed upon him how impossible it was to improve the relations between England and Germany as long as there was this dispute between Germany and France about a matter on which we had an Agreement with France which was publicly known to the whole world, and which had been the very beginning of our friendship with France. If that difficulty were out of the way, the whole political sky in Europe would be cleared, and the tone of the British press and of British public opinion towards Germany would be sensibly improved.

The Austrian Chargé d'Affaires asked me whether I did not think that commercial competition would still continue to have a bad effect on the relations between Germany and England. I said No, that commercial competition did not affect the political relations and did not have a political effect on public opinion in England. I then urged upon him how unfortunate it was that Germany could not see her way to accept the organization of the police in Morocco by France and Spain as a starting point in the negotiations. They were the only two Powers who had the personnel and the experience necessary. International police would mean an international muddle. If Germany would accept this one point—the organization of the police—it would be possible for her or for other Powers who had apprehensions to ask for safeguards and limitations, such as that the police should be restricted to the ports; that their functions should be confined to the protection of foreigners, and perhaps, some other conditions of the same kind. They could further ask for more explicit guarantees with regard to equality of trade than were contained in the Anglo-French Agreement, if these were considered necessary. But as long as objection was taken to entrusting France and Spain with the police it was impossible for any progress to be made.

I am, &c.
EDWARD GREY.

MINUTE BY KING EDWARD.

Approved.—E.R.

No. 317.

Sir A. Nicolson to Sir Edward Grey.

F.O. 371/173.
(No. 53.) Conference.   *Algeciras,* D. *February* 26, 1906.
Sir,   R. *March* 3, 1906.

I have the honour to transmit, herewith, copy of the reply which the French delegate has been instructed to make to the last communication of the German Representative in regard to the question of organizing a police force in Morocco.

M. Révoil intends to hand in the reply to M. de Radowitz this morning.

I have, &c.
A. NICOLSON.

Enclosure in No. 317.

Reply of French Delegate to German Representative's Note respecting Police Organization in Morocco.

Le principe de l'égalité pour tous en matière économique auquel se réfère la proposition allemande a été accepté par nous sans aucune réserve. Nous sommes convaincus que rien n'y saurait porter atteinte dans la proposition que nous avons formulée pour l'organisation de la police. Mais si la Conférence reconnaît au point de vue d'une égalité de traitement économique l'utilité de nouvelles garanties nous ne nous refuserons pas de les examiner. C'est à la Conférence qu'il appartient, conformément à l'accord du 8 Juillet, de déterminer la solution.

Le 26 Février, 1906.

No. 318.

Mr. Spring-Rice to Sir Edward Grey.

F.O. 371/173.
Tel. (No. 47.)
Morocco.

St. Petersburgh, February 28, 1906.
D. 10·50 A.M.
R. 11·30 A.M.

Count Lamsdorff's idea is to find formula which Germany can accept with reserves and subject to revision after a term of years. French Ambassador is sceptical, but thinks that the idea should be encouraged. He hopes that no step may be taken which would have the effect of withdrawing the matter from the cognizance of Europe assembled in Conference—for instance, arbitration or (group undecypherable) Hague Convention—until the Conference has had the opportunity of expressing an opinion.

Emperor is prepared as a last resource to intervene personally but the Russian Gov[ernmen]t are unwilling to expose His Majesty to a rebuff which the present attitude of the German Gov[ernmen]t makes probable.

American and Austrian Ambassadors have been in communication as to the steps to be taken.

Former is prepared if asked by this Government to report on state of affairs to the President. It is believed here that the result of steps taken by the Austrian Gov[ernmen]t at Berlin has discouraged them from recommending the intervention of the Emperor of Austria.

No. 319.

Sir Edward Grey to Sir F. Bertie.

F.O. 371/173.(¹)
Tel. (No. 21.) Confidential.

Foreign Office, February 28, 1906.
D. 6 P.M.

I learn privately from French Ambassador that the proposal made to Baron de Courcel by Prince Bülow was to the effect that at each of a certain number of ports there should be officers of four or five nationalities working together to reorganize the police and that, to show that Germany recognized France's special position in Morocco, she would agree to the police at one of these ports being entirely French.

French government have not paid serious attention to this proposal, regarding it as a trap to enable Germany to demand a port for herself elsewhere on the pretext that this would be merely a set off against the port placed under exclusively French domination.

(¹) [Also to Sir A. Nicolson, No. 34.]

No. 320.

Mr. Spring-Rice to Sir Edward Grey.

F.O. 371/173.
(No. 154.) Confidential.
Sir,

St. Petersburgh, D. February 28, 1906.
R. March 5, 1906.

I have the honour to state that I attended Count Lamsdorff's diplomatic reception on the 21st instant. His Excellency informed me that the German

Ambassador had communicated to him the refusal of his Government to accede to the last French proposals with regard to the Morocco police explaining at the same time that Germany was acting in the interests of all the powers whose commerce would certainly suffer by any such exclusive concessions as were claimed by the French. Herr von Schoen added that Monsieur Rouvier had promised that France would not ask for the control of the police and had also given a pledge that it should be under international control.

Count Lamsdorff had stated in reply that No. 348 of the French Yellow Book contained an explicit statement drawn up by Monsieur Rouvier that he had taken no pledge of any sort over and above the formula to be signed by the two Governments and that No. 350 contained the formula in question which pledged France to propose to the Sultan, not a police under international control, but "organisation par voie d'accord international, de la police hors la région frontière" that is, France was merely pledged to propose a system of police to be approved of by the Powers assembled at the Conference.

With regard to the contention that Germany in opposing the French proposal was in reality acting in the interest of all the Powers, he had observed to Herr von Schoen that the Powers were surely the best judges of their own interests and they had, in the persons of their representatives at the Conference, declared that their interests were sufficiently safeguarded.

Count Lamsdorff then proceeded to speak with somewhat unwonted animation of the difficult position in which Europe was placed by the action of Germany. His impression was that German officials themselves were convinced that the Government was going too far but that they were deterred by the fear of consequences from expressing their opinion. The fact was that the whole matter resolved itself into a question of the *amour propre* of the Emperor who felt that his personal honour was engaged : and for this the whole world had to suffer. He hoped however that it would be possible for Europe to make its voice heard and for this reason he was anxious that the case might be strongly represented at Berlin. . . . .([1])

In my speaking subsequently to Monsieur Bompard of Count Lamsdorff's language, His Excellency remarked that he seemed to have changed his point of view as to the representations in Berlin.

I gather that he had good reasons for doing so. The instructions to the Russian Ambassador at Berlin were to leave no doubts in Prince Bülow's mind that if Germany broke up the Conference Russia would regard her as the aggressor. The answer given was not of a nature to encourage further communications.

The Emperor of Austria, or Count Goluchowski, has also, as I understand, taken measures to recommend moderation, but with equally little success.

Under these circumstances the Russian Government is unwilling to recommend the Emperor to take himself any decisive step, although I understand from Monsieur Bompard that His Majesty is prepared, as a last resource, to make a personal appeal to the German Emperor.

So far as I am informed the correspondence between the Emperors on the subject of Morocco has been limited to general expressions of a mutual desire for the maintenance of peace; but has contained no definite suggestions as to how that object is to be attained. . . . .([2])

I have, &c.
CECIL SPRING-RICE.

([1]) [Passage omitted here describes an interview with the French Ambassador on February 23, who informed Mr. Spring-Rice of the substance of his conversations with the Emperor and with Count Lamsdorff. The interview had already been reported by telegram, *v. supra* pp. 271-2, No. 308.]

([2]) [Passage omitted here gives further views by M. Bompard, and those of M. Hartwig.]

No. 321.
Sir F. Lascelles to Sir Edward Grey.

F.O. 371/173.

(No. 68.)   Confidential.   *Berlin, D. March 1, 1906.*

Sir,   R. *March 5, 1906.*

With reference to my preceding Despatch of this day's date,(¹) I have the honour to report that General Swaine consulted me as to the advisability of his seeking an interview with Baron von Holstein with whom he was on friendly terms during his residence at Berlin as His Majesty's Military Attaché. I strongly recommended him to do so, and I have now the honour to inclose the copy of a memorandum which General Swaine has drawn up of the conversation which he had with His Excellency this morning.

There is nothing very new in Herr von Holstein's remarks, but it is interesting to note that, in spite of the Emperor's remarks on Count Metternich's report of his conversation with Lord Rothschild that he would not give way on the question of Police, His Excellency saw hopes of the Conference ending satisfactorily, and that even if that should not be the case, he did not believe that war would be the result.

I have, &c.

FRANK C. LASCELLES.

Enclosure in No. 321.
Memorandum by General Swaine.

I was this morning received by Baron Holstein at the Foreign Office. He is a very old friend of mine, and delights in instructing me in the way in which our policy should run and our Foreign Office act.

His Excellency began by making some reference to His Majesty The King and by his manner I feared it might be of a nature to which I would rather not listen and therefore arrested him by saying: "We are in England very proud of our King. He has greatly raised the prestige of our Country, and his influence for good has been acknowledged everywhere." Baron Holstein at once replied, "Yes I think you have every reason to be proud."

He then took the Conference at Algeciras in hand. He was violent against Monsieur Delcassé and the senior French Plenipotentiary. It was the latter he maintained who directed not alone the Cabinet in Paris in this question, but also the French press; and he regretted that Sir A. Nicolson's instructions were to blindly support the French instead of forming together with his American, Austrian, and Italian Colleagues a Court of Arbitration to try and find some means of satisfying both sides.

Baron Holstein showed me a despatch from Count Metternich reporting a conversation His Excellency had had with Lord Rothschild and in the margin of which the Emperor had made some pencil remarks to the purport that he was determined to hold out on the police question—"darin stehe ich fest" were the German words.

The Baron thought he saw hopes of the Conference ending satisfactorily; but should it not—even if Germany found herself standing absolutely alone—this would not mean war. He was quite convinced that France would not attack Germany, and the latter Power would certainly not attack France. Germany was much pained at being treated, at the time of the settling of the Anglo-French Convention as "une quantité négligeable" and no great Power would consent to be so treated.

During the whole conversation there was a vein of bitterness in the Baron's manner. It was like a microbe trying surreptitiously to sting. But this is Baron Holstein's way always.

He was much astonished when he heard that I had not been invited to the wedding festivities, especially as it came on the top of his having the moment before said, "It is very necessary that the two Monarchs should be good friends and should not say anything to irritate the other." I replied that the mistake was fully

(¹) [Not reproduced.]

explained away and that we were all on the best of terms, but I added that His Majesty The King had specially selected me to carry out this mission as he believed I was a *persona grata* at Court here. If therefore an Olive Branch was needed I was that Branch and that The King had thereby shown that he was anxious to be on good terms with his nephew. I then left.

L. V. SWAINE, M.G.

March 1, 1906.

No. 322.

Sir F. Bertie to Sir Edward Grey.

F.O. 371/173.
(No. 91.) Confidential.

Paris, D. March 2, 1906.
R. March 3, 1906.

Sir,
    I have the honour to transmit, herewith, copy of a memorandum by Sir Maurice de Bunsen giving an account of a conversation which he had with M. Rouvier yesterday in reference to the Morocco Question.

I have, &c.
FRANCIS BERTIE.

Enclosure in No. 322.

Memorandum by Sir Maurice de Bunsen.

I have just seen M. Rouvier. He spoke very openly and left me under the impression that he will go very far to prevent the Conference ending in failure. Though he did not think war would be the consequence of such failure, Europe would be kept on tenterhooks and the financial operations which are so necessary to set up Russia again, to enable her to take her place in the councils of Europe, would be impossible. He had just heard that gold was much needed in London, to send to Japan. A period of rest was therefore essential. He had noted a slight "détente" in the German press, and did not think the attitude of Germany at this moment was an uncompromising one. M. Révoil had been instructed to reply to the Germans that, as they considered that a Franco-Spanish Police in Morocco was incompatible with absolute commercial equality, France would willingly consent to the Conference being charged with the task of devising any fresh guarantees that might be necessary to secure such commercial equality. He hoped the Conference would be induced to pronounce on this question. But failing an agreement in this way, he was quite disposed to consider seriously a Spanish proposition, made not long ago, that there should be a purely Moroccan Police, without European Officers. Such a force, if regularly paid by the State Bank would anyhow be a great improvement on the present state of things. But his readiness to accept this idea, if need be, had not yet been mentioned to Spain, and he hoped something better might yet be obtained.
    The last German proposals, following on Baron de Courcel's visit to Berlin, did not afford a basis of discussion.

MAURICE DE BUNSEN.

Paris, March 1, 1906.

MINUTES.

M. Rouvier's plan of falling back in the last resort on a purely Moorish police without European officers is that advanced by M. Leroy Beaulieu in his admirable articles in the *Economiste Français* of February 17 and February 24. If not brought forward too late, it might yet succeed in averting a break-down of the discussions on the police question. In that case all would depend on Germany's attitude in the bank question, a contingency strongly disliked by Sir A. Nicolson, as explained in his despatch No. 52 (7548).([1]) For this and other reasons it might be well to give him early notice of the intentions of the French Government.

([1]) [v. supra pp. 274–5, No. 312.]

Qu : Telegraph to Algeciras.

"From a conversation which French prime minister had with Sir M. de Bunsen on March 1 it appears likely that France will in the last resort agree to a Spanish proposal for a purely Moorish police, without European officers, · with pay guaranteed by the state bank."

E. A. C.

Mch. 3.

This is very much what M. Leroy Beaulieu proposes—only he objects to the state bank.

E. B.

Rather than let the Conference fail and a state of unrest supervene in Europe for an indefinite period, such a proposal would, I believe, be by far the most advantageous from a French point of view provided that it is subject to revision, say, after two years. It is a foregone conclusion that a Moorish police force would prove a grotesque fiasco, but in two years time Russia will probably be strong again and France will then be able to press her views more effectually without having in the meantime given Germany a foothold in Morocco. Such an arrangement will not be very useful for the protection of our fellow subjects in Morocco, but we must risk that for the sake of the "entente."

C. H.

I agree and have already spoken to M. Cambon in this sense generally.

E. G.

Tel. sent to Sir A. Nicolson, No. 42, Mch. 5.(¹)

(¹) [*v. infra* p. 285, *Ed. Note.*]

No. 323.

Sir A. Nicolson to Sir Edward Grey.

F.O. 371/173.   *Algeciras, March 3,* 1906.
Tel. (No. 78.)   R. 10 P.M.

There was a plenary sitting on the Bank question today. It was not found possible to come to an agreement on three questions, which were in consequence reserved.

At the end of the sitting the President asked us to meet again on Monday and I inquired what would be the order of the day. I said it was clear that we should not be in a position on Monday to (dispose of?) a subject wh[ich] had been under examination during two weeks either before the Conference or in the drafting Committee and on wh[ich] no definite agreement had been reached. Probably also some members would require instructions.

In accordance therefore with precedents I proposed that we should leave on one side for the moment the reserved questions and proceed with the next subject on the programme viz : the police which we could take on Monday in General Committee.

The German Delegates objected but on a vote being taken my proposal was accepted by all with the exception of Germany, Austria-Hungary and Morocco.

No. 324.

Sir A. Nicolson to Sir Edward Grey.

F.O. 371/173.   *Algeciras, March 3,* 1906.
Tel. (No. 79.)   R. 10 P.M.

My immediately preceding tel[egram].

I think that it is probable that after our Monday sitting it may be decided to devote Wednesday to a discussion on all reserved questions, namely those of bank, police, control, customs, special caisse and expropriation. The disagreement will then be manifested. My French colleague and myself much regret that a failure of the Conference seems inevitable and we are anxious that if Conference breaks up, the form of rupture should be as inoffensive as possible. We have considered whether it would be feasible to draw up a protocol which would ease the dispersal of delegates and bring into relief the points on which an agreement has been reached and also render failure as little abrupt and final as possible but we are of opinion that it is most difficult to devise protocol giving effect to the above views which would at the same time be acceptable to Germans.

We therefore think that under the circumstances it would be better, if an agreement proves to be absolutely impossible, that the sittings should be suspended and that we should leave Algeciras and refer to our respective Gov[ernmen]ts.

I should be most grateful for your views.

No. 325.

Sir E. Egerton to Sir Edward Grey.

F.O. 371/173.　　　　　　　　　　　　　*Rome,* D. *March* 3, 1906.
Tel. (No. 24.)　　　　　　　　　　　R. *March* 4, 1906, 9 A.M.

Morocco Conference.

French Ambassador learns that German pressure on the King and Government of Italy during past week has been very strong.

The German contention is that fact of entering the Conference frees Italy from previous engagement to France about Morocco.

Italian Gov[ernmen]t weak and irresolute.

No. 326.

Sir A. Nicolson to Sir Edward Grey.

F.O. 371/173.
(No. 61.)　Conference.　　　　　　*Algeciras,* D. *March* 3, 1906.
Sir,　　　　　　　　　　　　　　　R. *March* 10, 1906.

At the close of the plenary sitting this morning, the President of the Conference said that he proposed that we should reassemble on Monday next, and on my enquiring what would be the order of the day, His Excellency replied that he must leave that to the Conference to decide. I thereupon observed that there were several questions still undecided in the Bank project which we had been discussing, and that as probably some members would desire to be furnished with instructions on certain points, it would be better to sit in General Committee on Monday and examine the next subject on the programme which was that of the police organization. I pointed out that we had already occupied considerable time in discussing the Bank project, and that before Monday it was not likely that any fresh light would be thrown on the points at issue. In order not to suspend sittings we could very well follow the precedents we had already established in other cases, and while leaving the Bank project on one side for the moment proceed to examine the police question.

The French delegate remarked that we had devoted one plenary sitting and two or three Committee sittings, besides four sittings of the Drafting Committee to the Bank project, and that therefore he should vote for the police question being examined on Monday.

The German delegates objected, and would have preferred to finish the discussion on the disputed questions in the Bank project, apparently even if we had to suspend our sittings for some days. In these circumstances I asked the President to be good enough to take the sense of the Conference on my proposal. France, Spain, Italy,

Portugal, Russia, and Holland voted with me. The delegates of the United States, Belgium and Sweden said they would adopt the views of the majority; while Germany, Austria-Hungary and Morocco desired to postpone the discussion on the police organization until that on the Bank had finally terminated. My motion was accordingly declared carried.

I have, &c.
A. NICOLSON.

No. 327.

Sir F. Bertie to Sir Edward Grey.

Private.([1])
My dear Grey,   *Paris, March 5,* 1906.

The King received at dinner yesterday the President of the Republic and Madame Fallières, the President of the Council and Madame Rouvier, Baron de Courcel and some Gentlemen and Ladies of Society personal friends of His Majesty.([2])

After dinner the King had some private conversation with M. Rouvier and with the concurrence of the Minister Baron de Courcel was later on invited to join in the discussion which ensued on the subject of the Algeciras Conference, the offers of concessions to German exigencies made by France and the attitude of the German Emperor and his Government.

M. Rouvier gave a detailed description of the negotiations and said that, so far as the Bank question was concerned, the French Government would be ready to make further concessions if by such means they could come to an Agreement with Germany on the whole of the subjects in discussion at the Conference, but they could not give way any further in regard to the Police of the Ports.

His Majesty told M. Rouvier that He and His Government considered that the conduct of the French Government had been most conciliatory and He asked Baron de Courcel whether he had brought from Berlin any actual proposals from the German Government. The Baron admitted that he had not been commissioned with official proposals but he enlarged on the necessity for finding some compromise to satisfy Germany and avoiding a rupture of the negotiations by the closing of the Conference without result, for that position would be very dangerous to the peace of Europe.

The King told M. Rouvier that He hoped that the French Government did not attach any credit to the reports industriously propagated by Parties interested in separating France from England that His Majesty's Government desired to bring about a war between France and Germany and that England was not a Country to be relied on in an emergency.

M. Rouvier assured His Majesty that the French had every confidence in His Government and attached no importance to insinuations made against the policy of the British Government.

Later on the conversation was continued by the President of the Republic and M. Rouvier with the King and without Baron de Courcel but what was said as to the policy of the French Government and their feelings in regard to England and His Majesty's Government was to the same effect as what M. Rouvier had previously stated to the King.

What I have stated above is the description given to me by the King of his conversations of last night.

I have shown it to His Majesty and with the insertion made "later on," in regard to Baron de Courcel, by His Majesty's desire he says that the record is quite correct.

Yours sincerely,
FRANCIS BERTIE.

([1]) [Grey MSS., Vol. 10.]
([2]) [*Cf.* Sir Sidney Lee : *King Edward VII* (1927), II, p. 510. The visit was incognito. It is there noted that M. Delcassé was invited to lunch by the King.]

[*ED. NOTE.*—On March 5, Sir Edward Grey sent the following telegram to Sir A. Nicolson:

Sir Edward Grey to Sir A. Nicolson.

F.O. 371/173.   *Foreign Office, March 5, 1906.*
Tel. (No. 42.)   D. 2·50 P.M.

Police. M. Rouvier told Sir M. de Bunsen on the 1st that he was disposed to consider seriously a Spanish proposal that there should be a purely Moroccan police without European officers, to be paid by the State Bank, but he had not mentioned this to Spain, hoping that something better might be obtained.

Has your French colleague mentioned this to you?]

No. 328.

Sir A. Nicolson to Sir Edward Grey.

F.O. 371/173.   *Algeciras, March 7, 1906.*
Tel. (No. 87.)   R. 2·45 P.M.

Bank.

Private negotiations for an arrangement on the above question through intermediaries have led to no result. My French colleague tells me that he will now abandon them and leave matter to the Conference.

No. 329.

Sir Edward Grey to Sir M. de Bunsen.

F.O. 371/173.
Tel. (No. 15.)   *Foreign Office, March 7, 1906.*

Y[our] tel[egram] No. 32.(¹)

You can assure Spanish Gov[ernmen]t that there is no question of our pursuing any other policy than that of adhering strictly to our engagements towards France in Morocco and that H[is] M[ajesty's] G[overnment] have confidence that the Spanish Gov[ernmen]t will do the same. Questions affecting the future *status quo* in the event of the failure of the Conference will require careful consideration between the three Powers.

Please repeat above to Sir A. Nicolson.

(¹) [Sir M. de Bunsen's telegram No. 32 of March 6, D. 3·30 P.M., R. 5·45 P.M., reports a conversation with Señor de Ojeda, Acting Minister for Foreign Affairs, at which the latter had said that " Spanish Government would continue to maintain loyally her engagement to France so long as England and France pulled together."]

No. 330.

Sir A. Nicolson to Sir Edward Grey.

F.O. 371/173.
(No. 62.) **Conference.**   *Algeciras,* D. *March 7, 1906.*
Sir,   R. *March 13, 1906.*

The Conference held a general Committee meeting on the 5th instant to discuss the question of organizing a police force in the coast towns of Morocco. M. de Bacheracht, the second Russian delegate, who has been Russian Minister in Tangier during the past eight years, read a paper of which I have the honour to enclose a copy.(¹) M. de Bacheracht examined the question simply from the point of view of affording the necessary security to foreigners resident in the ports of Morocco, and he disclaimed all idea of allowing political considerations to influence the treatment of the subject. He drew attention to the feebleness of the Moorish Government and to the avowed powerlessness of the native authorities to guarantee the safety of Europeans; and he dwelt at some length on the inefficacy of any international and collective administration.

(¹) [Not reproduced.]

His local experience enabled him to speak with authority on both of the above points, and I am of opinion that his arguments against entrusting the police organization either to the Moorish authorities or to an international body are unanswerable. His conclusions were to the effect that, in order to secure the establishment of an efficient police force, the duty should be entrusted to France and Spain.

M. de Radowitz read a short document, of which I also beg leave to transmit a copy, in which he laid down the principle that, as all the Powers were equally interested in the organization of the police, they should be called upon to take part in it.

M. Révoil gave a short exposition in support of his view that France and Spain were alone in a position to efficiently and promptly assist the Sultan in organizing a police force. He stated that it was an admitted fact that Morocco was incapable of undertaking the duty with her own resources, and he considered that the internationalization of the police would cause the greatest inconvenience in practice. A copy of M. Révoil's statement is enclosed herewith.

The second Spanish delegate, M. Perez Caballero, also read a declaration which was in general conformity with the views expressed by the French and Russian Representatives. I beg leave to forward a copy of his statement.([1])

On the termination of these proceedings I expressed my entire concurrence with the views of the French, Russian, and Spanish delegates, as they seemed to me to offer the only practical solution of the question.

The Portuguese delegate said that he desired to associate himself with the remarks which I had made.

No opinion was expressed by any other delegate.

Some conversation ensued as to what should be our procedure in connection with the Police question, and I had hoped that we should have been able to continue our discussion today in a general Committee meeting : but Marquis Visconti Venosta expressed a desire that the discussion on the Bank question should be resumed on the 8th instant, and this was eventually agreed to, on the understanding that, as soon as the Bank discussion was concluded, the Conference should resolve itself into General Committee on the Police question.

I regret that so long an adjournment was accepted by the Conference, as there is no reason why both today and yesterday should pass without any sitting at all, and I was surprised that a motion for the adjournment till the 8th instant was proposed and passed. As I have on more than one occasion endeavoured to expedite our business, without much success I must admit, I did not think it advisable to press the matter once more, especially as I observed a fairly general desire to allow a few more days to elapse before returning to the Police question.

I have, &c.
A. NICOLSON.

([1]) [Not reproduced.]

[Enclosure 1 not reproduced.]

Enclosure 2 in No. 330.

Declaration by the German Delegate respecting the Police Question.

L'une des bases pour les travaux de ce Congrès est le principe de la liberté économique dans le Maroc, sans aucune inégalité.

Or, cette liberté économique et le développement des intérêts commerciaux au Maroc dépendent, en premier lieu, du maintien de l'ordre et de la sécurité dans l'Empire Chérifien.

Le Sultan du Maroc, dans l'exercice de sa souveraineté, aura à prendre les mesures nécessaires pour la garantie de la sécurité des personnes et des biens des étrangers. La nécessité s'impose aux Puissances Signataires de lui venir en aide par l'organisation d'une troupe de police suffisante, à établir dans les places déterminées.

Les Puissances Signataires, étant également intéressées à cette organisation, devront être appelées à y prendre part.

Enclosure 3 in No. 330.

Declaration by the French Delegate respecting the Police Question.

La France n'a jamais conçu une organisation de la police qui ne respectât pas l'indépendance et la souveraineté du Sultan. Pour ne rappeler que les négociations qui ont eu lieu à l'occasion de la fixation du programme de la Conférence, nous avons posé spontanément le principe que les corps de police seraient placés sous l'autorité Chérifienne.

Il est reconnu toutefois que quelle que soit sa bonne volonté, le Maghzen est actuellement hors d'état d'organiser lui-même et par ses seuls moyens ses corps de police et d'assurer leur entretien et leur fonctionnement régulier et utile.

Il faut donc que le Maroc y soit aidé. Si nous nous plaçons au point de vue pratique, on reconnaîtra que la France et avec elle l'Espagne, sont seules aptes à fournir cette aide avec promptitude et efficacité. Elles seules peuvent mettre sans délai au service du Maghzen des instructeurs parlant la langue et connaissant les mœurs du pays, ayant déjà l'expérience des troupes indigènes semblables à celles qu'on veut créer. Elles seules sont en état de fournir, avec les officiers nécessaires, des sous-officiers musulmans.

Il est bien entendu que la désignation de ces officiers doit être soumise à l'agrément du Sultan, que les corps de police resteront placés sous le commandement des autorités chérifiennes, que le rôle des officiers se bornera à prêter à ces autorités les concours technique pour l'exercice du commandement et le maintien de la discipline. Ils pourvoieront à l'instruction des troupes, surveilleront leur bonne administration et contrôleront le paiement régulier de la solde. On a fait très justement ressortir l'importance de ce dernier point.

L'expérience que la Conférence vient de prendre de la situation du Maroc démontre qu'il faut limiter l'organisation de cette police aux besoins les plus immédiats, au premier rang des quels figure la sécurité dans les ports ouverts au commerce et dans leur banlieue.

Il suffira d'effectifs réduits et à première vue il semble que quatre ou cinq cents hommes dans un ou deux ports principaux, cent cinquante à deux cents dans les autres, peuvent suffire. On arriverait ainsi pour l'ensemble des huits ports à un total approximatif de deux mille à deux mille cinq cents hommes, sous la direction de seize officiers environ, avec une moyenne de quatre sous-officiers par port.

Cette organisation s'inspirerait d'ailleurs des principes déjà acceptés par le Maghzen quand la question a été traitée à Fez.

Dans ces proportions, avec ce mandat limité et pour une courte durée, il est impossible de découvrir quelle atteinte une semblable organisation pourrait porter à l'indépendance du Sultan et à la libre concurrence économique des étrangers.

L'internationalisation de la police n'ajouterait aucune garantie et aurait les plus grands inconvénients pratiques.

D'ailleurs les Gouvernements, d'une part, et, sur place, le Corps Diplomatique et les Consuls, si vigilants pour tout ce qui concerne leur colonies, ne seront-ils pas toujours en mesure de s'assurer que cette organisation n'est pas détournée de son but et ne lèse aucun des intérêts de leur nationaux?

C'est dans cet esprit que nous acceptons la réforme ainsi conçue. Elle assurera le résultat pratique qu'on souhaite atteindre le plus promptement possible et elle tient compte en même temps des légitimes intérêts de la France, en tant que Puissance musulmane dans l'Afrique du nord et de l'intérêt spécial qui s'ensuit pour elle à ce que l'ordre règne dans l'Empire Chérifien.

Le 5 Mars, 1906.

[Enclosure 4 not reproduced.]

No. 331.

Sir A. Nicolson to Sir Edward Grey.

F.O. 371/173.
Tel. (No. 88.)
    Police.

Algeciras, March 8, 1906.
R. 3·30 P.M.

The German delegate informed President of the Conference yesterday that he would be ready to accept French and Spanish officers at seven ports, if a superior officer as inspector, to be selected from a minor Power, were placed in charge of the police at the eighth port. The Duke, I understand, told him that such proposals must be submitted to the Conference; and as it is announced that the Moorish delegates intend to present a police project at to-day's sitting it will probably be found to contain above proposals.

The Russian representative spoke seriously to German delegate yesterday morning as to necessity of terminating the pending questions without further delay, and he hinted that Conference might disperse if the German delegation continued to preserve absolute silence as to their views on police question. This warning probably caused the German delegate to make the above communication to the President of the Conference.

My French colleague tells me that German Amb[assado]r at Paris made a fresh overture to French M[inister] [for] F[oreign] A[ffairs] that police question should be discussed between Paris and Berlin but latter replied that question must be examined at the Conference and at the Conference alone.

[*ED. NOTE.*—Sir A. Nicolson's telegram No. 89 of March 8, D. 3·45 P.M., R. 6·30 P.M., reported the Austro-Hungarian project described more fully *infra* p. 291, Encl. 3 in No. 334.]

No. 332.

Sir A. Nicolson to Sir Edward Grey.

F.O. 371/173.
Tel. (No. 90.) Confidential.
    Police.

Algeciras, March 9, 1906.
R. 3 P.M.

I find that members of the Conference, with the exception of French and Spanish, are unanimous in favour of Austrian proposal. My French colleague tells me that French public opinion would certainly not accept establishment of Swiss or Dutch officers in a Moorish port. He says that it would be possible to accept an inspector who would be entrusted with inspection duties and with right of reporting to the Powers, perhaps through doyen of diplomatic body, but that it would be impossible to go further and he evidently wishes to insist on all eight ports being given to France and Spain. I have doubts whether Germans would agree to such a solution; and it would be most unfortunate if we three were left isolated from the rest of the Conference and that latter should break up in such circumstances. I have explained this to my French colleague and have suggested whether he could not devise some bargain by which the eighth port could be left to France and Spain on condition of France making a concession on State bank. He thinks this might be effected but wishes to reflect on the matter. He is of course much hampered by change of Gov[ernmen]t at this moment.

No. 333.
Sir Edward Grey to Sir F. Bertie.

F.O. 371/173.   *Foreign Office, March 9, 1906.*
Tel. (No. **31**.)   (By Post.)

I expressed to M. Cambon today the opinion that the Austrian proposal as to police in Moroccan ports represented a real concession on the part of Germany and had brought an agreement so near that it would not do to let the Conference break up now without a settlement. I told him Sir A. Nicolson's opinion as expressed in his telegrams Nos. 89 and 90. You should express the same to M. Rouvier.

No. 334.
Sir A. Nicolson to Sir Edward Grey.

F.O. 371/174.
(No. 65.) Conference.   *Algeciras,* D. *March 9, 1906.*
Sir,   R. *March 19, 1906.*

At the general Committee meeting on the 8th instant, the question of organizing a police force for the Moorish ports was again brought forward for discussion.

I have the honour to transmit, in duplicate, copies of the documents and declarations which were laid before the Conference in connection with the above subject. They are :—

1. The French project for the organization of a police force.
2. The " exposé des vues " of the Austro-Hungarian delegation.
3. The Austro-Hungarian project for the organization of a police force.
4. A declaration read by M. von Radowitz.

These several documents and declarations mark undoubtedly a considerable advance towards an agreement; and I trust that at the sitting which is to be held to-morrow it will be possible to find some common ground for an understanding.

I have, &c.
A. NICOLSON.

Enclosure 1 in No. 334.

Projet déposé par la Délégation française concernant l'organisation d'une Police au Maroc.

La Conférence appelée par S[a] M[ajesté] le Sultan à se prononcer sur les mesures nécessaires pour garantir la sécurité des personnes et des biens des étrangers, déclare que les dispositions à prendre sont les suivantes :—

Une troupe de police chérifienne dont les effectifs et les cadres inférieurs seront recrutés parmi les musulmans marocains et placés sous l'autorité de commandants marocains sera organisée dans les huit ports ouverts au commerce.

Pour venir en aide au Sultan dans l'organisation de cette police, des officiers et sous-officiers instructeurs seront mis à sa disposition par les Gouvernements Français et Espagnol qui soumettront leur désignation et leur affectation à son agrément.

Ces instructeurs seront chargés, pour une durée de trois années, d'assurer l'instruction et la discipline des Corps de Police marocaine et devront, en particulier, surveiller leur bonne administration et contrôler le paiement régulier de la solde. Ils prêteront aux autorités investies du commandement de ces Corps de Police leur concours technique pour l'exercice de ce commandement.

L'effectif total des troupes de police ne devra pas dépasser 2,500 hommes, ni être inférieur à 2,000. Il sera réparti, suivant l'importance des ports, par groupes variant de 150 à 500 hommes. Le nombre des officiers instructeurs sera de 16 au maximum; celui des sous-officiers de 32.

Les fonds nécessaires à l'entretien et au paiement de la solde des troupes de police et de leurs instructeurs seront avancés au Trésor Chérifien par la Banque d'État.

7 *Mars*, 1906.

Enclosure 2 in No. 334.

Exposé des vues de la Délégation austro-hongroise, lu par Son Excellence M. le Comte de Welsersheimb à la séance de Comité du 8 Mars 1906.

En soumettant ce projet à l'appréciation de la Conférence, je demande la permission d'exposer en quelques mots les points de vue qui m'ont guidé dans la recherche d'une formule qui pût servir de base à nos délibérations.

Au début, la question qui nous occupe se présentait sous cette forme :

La France, si je suis bien renseigné, réclamait *pour elle seule* le mandat de l'organisation de la police au Maroc.

L'Allemagne s'opposait à cette demande; elle insistait sur la nécessité de donner à l'organisation de la police un caractère international, c'est-à-dire elle demandait que *toutes les Puissances* représentées à la Conférence eussent le droit d'y participer.

Aujourd'hui, la situation n'est plus la même.

Des concessions ont été faites de part et d'autre. La France s'est déclaré[e] prête à associer l'Espagne à l'œuvre dont il s'agit.

L'Allemagne paraît vouloir consentir à restreindre dans une certaine mesure [*sic*], le nombre des nationalités qui seraient appelées à fournir les instructeurs.

On peut donc constater qu'un certain rapprochement s'est déjà produit.

Cependant ces concessions mutuelles n'ont pas suffi pour établir un accord.

Faut-il pour cela abandonner l'espoir de pouvoir y arriver?

Je ne le crois pas, et voici sur quoi cet espoir est fondé :—

Je crois pouvoir entrevoir la possibilité que l'Allemagne, sans être obligée à sacrifier aucun des principes fondamentaux dont la Conférence doit s'inspirer, pourrait accepter une réduction ultérieure du nombre des nationalités qui auraient à participer à l'organisation de la police. Nous avons entendu à la dernière séance de Comité la déclaration de M. le premier Délégué d'Allemagne qui terminait en disant que son Gouvernement était prêt à discuter toute combinaison qui rentrait dans le cadre des principes généraux qui formaient la base des travaux de la Conférence. Ces paroles me semblent indiquer clairement que la possibilité d'un rapprochement ultérieur du côté de l'Allemagne n'est pas complètement exclue à la condition toutefois que d'autre part, les garanties nécessaires soient données pour la sauvegarde des intérêts communs à tous les pays représentés à la Conférence.

En ce qui concerne le point de vue de la France nous savons par la réponse qu'elle a donné[e] à la dernière proposition allemande que, au point de vue du principe de l'égalité de traitement en matière économique, antérieurement reconnu par elle, si la Conférence reconnaît l'utilité de nouvelles garanties, elle ne se refusera pas à les examiner.

Dans la séance du 5, S[on] E[xcellence] M. Révoil a ajouté que, d'ailleurs, les Gouvernements, d'une part, et sur place le Corps diplomatique et les consuls, si vigilants pour tout ce qui concerne leurs colonies, seraient toujours en mesure de s'assurer que cette organisation n'est pas détournée de son but et ne lèse aucun des intérêts de leurs nationaux.

Tant la réponse du Gouvernement français que les paroles de M. le Délégué de France semblent prouver que la France serait prête à accepter un contrôle destiné à surveiller le fonctionnement de l'organisation policière.

C'est donc sur ce terrain que je crois qu'il sera possible d'arriver à un accord et c'est dans cet ordre d'idées que j'ai tâché de faire entrer dans mon projet les éléments qui me paraissent indispensables pour trouver la solution à laquelle nous désirons aboutir.

Enclosure 3 in No. 334.

Projet déposé par la Délégation d'Autriche-Hongrie concernant l'organisation d'une Police au Maroc.

I. Le Sultan aura le commandement suprême de la troupe de police.

II. Le Sultan chargera des officiers français de l'organisation de la troupe de police à Tanger, Saffi, Rabat et Tétouan.

III. Le Sultan chargera des officiers espagnols de l'organisation de la troupe de police à Mogador, Larache et Mazagan.

IV. Le Sultan nommera, en outre, un officier supérieur en rang, qui sera chargé de l'organisation de la troupe de police à Casablanca, et qui, en même temps, fera fonction d'inspecteur général de toutes les troupes de police. Le Sultan le choisira librement parmi les officiers que lui présentera, au nombre de trois, et avec l'assentiment des Puissances signataires, ou le Gouvernement de la Suisse ou celui des Pays-Bas.

V. Les cadres de la troupe de police seront marocains.

VI. L'administration et notamment la paie de la troupe s'effectuera par les employés européens, moyennant des fonds qui seront mis à leur disposition par la Banque d'État.

VII. L'inspecteur général rendra compte de ses fonctions au Corps diplomatique à Tanger, qui aura à contrôler l'exécution de l'organisation policière.

VIII. Cette organisation sera institué[e] à titre d'essai pour la durée de 5 ans.

8 *Mars*, 1906.

Enclosure 4 in No. 334.

Déclaration lue par S[on] E[xcellence] M. de Radowitz, premier Délégué d'Allemagne, à la séance de Comité du 8 mars 1906.

Nous sommes d'accord avec les opinions énoncées dans la dernière séance du Comité et prouvant la nécessité de l'organisation, au Maroc, d'une police placée sous l'autorité souveraine de S[a] M[ajesté] Chérifienne. Nous apprécions les raisons qui recommandent d'avoir recours, pour une participation efficace dans cette organisation, à des officiers choisis en France et en Espagne. Mais nous ne saurions admettre qu'une pareille coopération fût limitée à ces deux nations, sans autre contrôle ni garantie de surveillance internationale.

Il est évident que dans un pays dans l'état de culture du Maroc, l'exercice de la seule force réelle capable de maintenir l'ordre et de garantir la sécurité publique donnerait aux deux Puissances qui en auraient le privilège exclusif une position exceptionnelle laquelle se ferait sentir sur le terrain des intérêts matériels et porterait atteinte au principe de la liberté économique pour tous. Il serait, en effet, à prévoir que le Maroc tomberait dans une dépendance de ces deux États dont résulterait une inégalité de situation inacceptable pour les autres nations.

Les intérêts de l'Europe au Maroc demandent des garanties plus fortes. Protéger et développer ces intérêts communs par une action commune, tel est le principe pratiqué avec succès en d'autres circonstances internationales. Il suffit de rappeler les résultats obtenus en Macédoine et en Chine par les efforts collectifs des Puissances.

Nous demandons donc pour l'organisation de la police marocaine une coopération étrangère qui assure à toutes les nations intéressées l'égalité du traitement économique et la politique de la porte ouverte.

Nous examinerons chaque proposition faite dans ce sens, avec le plus vif désir de voir la Conférence aboutir à une entente en cette importante matière.

No. 335.

Sir Edward Grey to Sir A. Nicolson.

F.O. 371/173.   Foreign Office, March 10, 1906.
Tel. (No. 48.)   D. 1 P.M.

Your telegram No. 91.([1])

I entirely agree with your opinion; it does not seem to us that any real sacrifice of principle can be involved in accepting the Austrian proposal subject to modifications of detail. Germany has conceded the substance and it would be a great pity, if France sacrificed the substance to the shadow.

([1]) [Sir A. Nicolson's telegram No. 91 of March 9, D. 3·30 P.M., R. 6 P.M., reports negotiations with German delegate through the Italian and United States' Representatives. It ends " I am assisting my French colleague as much as I can, but I am still of opinion that it is unfortunate that he does not see his way to accept with some slight modifications the Austrian proposal."]

No. 336.

Sir F. Bertie to Sir Edward Grey.

F.O. 371/173.   Paris, D. March 10, 1906, 11·45 P.M.
Tel. (No. 17.) Confidential.   R. March 11, 1906, 7·30 A.M.

Morocco. Your tel[egram] No. 31 of yesterday.([1]) I saw M. Rouvier at 6 this evening. The repetitions of Vienna tel[egram] No. 4 of 9th of Sir A. Nicolson's tel[egram]([2]) No. 91 (No date given) and of your tel[egram] in reply thereto reached me after my interview with M. Rouvier.([3])

He says that French Gov[ernmen]t will adopt Austrian scheme with some modifications and that his impression from what he hears on good authority is that Germany will accept them and the Conference will not close without result. The principal modifications which the French Gov[ernmen]t will propose are the police instructors at Casa Blanca to be, like at the other seven ports, French or Spanish.

Distribution of ports to French or Spanish instructors to be a matter for agreement between French and Spanish Gov[ernmen]ts. The Inspector General to be a subject of neutral state and to have powers of inspection at all eight ports without right to command or give orders to French and Spanish instructors, and to make his reports to the Sultan of Morocco and not to the diplomatic body at Tangier. M. Rouvier says that a police at Casa Blanca organized by subject of neutral state such as Holland or Switzerland would be incompetent to maintain order for the Moors would have no respect for the subject of such a state. He further says that distribution of ports in Austrian scheme has been arranged by Germany in a manner calculated to cause friction between France and Spain.

Secret. M. Rouvier objects to a Dutchman as Inspector General as likely to be too much under German influence; he would accept a Swiss but he would prefer a Dane.

([1]) [v. supra p. 289, No. 333.]
([2]) [Not reproduced.]
([3]) [v. supra No. 335 and note.]

No. 337.

Sir A. Nicolson to Sir Edward Grey.

F.O. 371/174.
(No. 67.) Conference.   Algeciras, D. March 10, 1906.
Sir,   R. March 19, 1906.

At the meeting of the Conference this morning, in general committee, the Austro-Hungarian project for the police organization was brought forward. My

French colleague had asked me whether I would be willing to say a few words pointing out the inconvenience which would result if the proposed Inspector were at the same time to be himself entrusted with the command of a police force at one of the ports. I told M. Révoil that I should be quite ready to do so, but that I should couch my remarks in a friendly and conversational tone, as I was most unwilling to formulate a distinct proposal or to take any step which might in any way disturb the harmony which was at last exhibiting itself among the members of the Conference.

I, therefore, at this morning's sitting said that I should be grateful for some enlightenment as to one point in the Austro-Hungarian project which related to the position of the Inspector. I observed that I merely wished to lay before my Austro-Hungarian colleague one or two considerations which might perhaps be worthy of some attention by the Drafting Committee to whom I understood both the French and Austro-Hungarian projects were to be referred on the termination of our sitting. It appeared to me that the proposed Inspector would enjoy greater authority and more liberty of action, and at the same time be placed in a better position towards the Moorish authorities, if he were independent of, and above, all connection with the working-out of the details. An Inspector-General was, I believed, usually reserved for the sole duties of inspection, as for instance a Cavalry Inspector General would not be given the command of a Cavalry Brigade. It seemed to me that the Inspector could have his Headquarters at Tangier, and make his official inspection tours from time to time with his aides-de-camp and escort, and thus enhance his prestige and authority in the eyes of the Moorish authorities. On the other hand, were he to be placed on the same level as the other commandants, and were, as was quite possible, his own contingent of police found to be not so efficient nor so well organized as others, his authority would thereby suffer. Moreover, he would be unable to inspect his own contingent, and this might cause an inconvenient exception. It was in view of my desire to strengthen the position of the Inspector that I ventured to make the above suggestions, which I again repeated were merely suggestions thrown out for the consideration of the Drafting Committee.

Count Welsersheimb and the Conference took my remarks in very good part, the former stating that he had feared the Inspector would be too idle were he to merely have inspection duties to perform. No decision was arrived at, and indeed I did not wish that the matter should go further, and the question was consequently dropped, my French colleague remarking that he thought my observations should be considered and that the proposal to accord the command of a contingent to the Inspector was not viewed favourably by him. He added that he appreciated highly the conciliatory disposition shown by the Austro-Hungarian delegate in his proposal and also the desire for an agreement satisfactory to all parties which had been manifested by M. de Radowitz at an earlier part of the sitting when the latter had expressed the adherence of his Government to the proposal of Count Welsersheimb.

The police question was then referred to the Drafting Committee.

The Moorish delegates at this sitting presented replies from the Sultan as to the increase of customs duties, the right of acquisition of real property by foreigners and also some remarks on the police question. I will forward copies of these replies as soon as I receive translations.

The sitting was particularly friendly and harmonious, and there were clear signs of a disposition on the part of the German delegates and of others to come to an amicable arrangement with as little delay as possible.

I have, &c.
A. NICOLSON.

No. 338.

Sir A. Nicolson to Sir Edward Grey.

F.O. 371/174.
(No. 68.)   Conference.   Confidential.   *Algeciras*, D. *March* 10, 1906.
Sir,   R. *March* 19, 1906.

With the presentation of the Austro-Hungarian project in regard to the police organization in the coast towns of Morocco the situation is completely changed here. Up to the 8th instant there was undoubtedly a general feeling in the Conference that Germany had adopted an unyielding, and if I may be permitted to say so, a sullen attitude in regard to the claims and wishes of France, who had won all sympathies by her conciliatory, frank and open demeanour.

It was then a cause for surprise and for great relief when Count Welsersheimb proposed that the police at seven out of the eight ports should be entrusted to France and Spain, and that the force at the eighth port should be placed under a Swiss or Dutch Instructor who should also act as Inspector of the whole organization. It was known that Count Welsersheimb would not make a proposal which would be unwelcome to Germany, and it was recognised on all sides that the latter had made a great concession which all expected would doubtless be accepted by France and Spain.

It was clear to me that if the two latter countries were to regard with coldness or disfavour the Austro-Hungarian proposal they would meet with no sympathy from the other members of the Conference, and I found that even so staunch an ally and friend as Count Cassini was of opinion that terms should be made on the basis of the new proposal.

On the other hand I found that M. Révoil and the Duc de Almodovar, while recognising that a great advance towards an agreement had been made, felt that their respective Governments and public opinion would not permit them to accept a proposal to place the police organization of one port in the hands of officers of a third Power. They considered that on this point they could not yield.

I pointed out to M. Révoil, and on another occasion to the Duc de Almodovar, that practically the whole of the Conference was of one mind that the proposal of Count Welsersheimb was a satisfactory settlement of the difficulty. I did not, I remarked, wish in any way to influence him in what he might think proper to recommend to his Government, but I considered that I ought to lay frankly before him the fact that while a few days ago he had the majority of the Conference with him, the feeling would undoubtedly now be in a contrary sense were he to make no concessions on his part. I would, I said, support him to the best of my ability in whatever course he might take, but I must tell him that in the event of the Conference ending in failure we should be placed in an exceedingly false position with all the public feeling of Europe against us.

M. Révoil said that he had received telegrams which gave him to believe that Germany had not said her last word, and he asked me to see Marquis Visconti Venosta and Mr. White and request them to sound M. de Radowitz whether his Government would not give way a little more. I undertook the mission, and Marquis Visconti Venosta willingly agreed to speak to M. de Radowitz though he was quite sure that the latter had received instructions which admitted of no further concessions. Marquis Visconti Venosta later informed me that, as he had anticipated, M. de Radowitz had stated that his instructions were clear and precise to the effect that the German Government had gone to the extremest limit of concession.

I conveyed the reply to M. Révoil : but I found him still indisposed to believe that M. de Radowitz might not yet be induced to consent to an inspector being appointed who should be entrusted solely with Inspection duties, and that the police at the eighth port should be left to France, or France and Spain conjointly. I suggested that possibly he might make a compromise by ceding something in the way of the allotment of the capital of the Bank if the German delegates would yield in regard to the eighth port; and he told me after reflection that he would be ready to make a bargain of the above description : and that perhaps I might suggest it to Mr. White. I carried out M. Révoil's wishes, and Mr. White was good enough to speak to Count Tattenbach on the subject, but with no result.

The above is a short summary of several conversations and negotiations which have been passing during the past two days : and which will doubtless continue for some little time longer.

At M. Révoil's request, I am to see M. de Radowitz this evening and I will report as to the results of my interview in a subsequent despatch.

I have, &c.

A. NICOLSON.

No. 339.

Sir A. Nicolson to Sir Edward Grey.(¹)

F.O. 371/173. *Algeciras, March 11, 1906.*
Tel. (No. 94.) Confidential. R. 3·45 P.M.

At the request of my French colleague I called on First German Delegate last evening, and said that I fully recognized the concession Germany had made on the police question; that a great step had been thereby made towards agreement; that my Government, and also that of France, were most anxious that the Conference should terminate in a satisfactory manner, but that I wished to tell him that one obstacle existed; and that was the difficulty my French colleague felt in accepting the proposal that the Inspector should act also as instructor at one port. I added that French susceptibilities on this point appeared to be most sensitive, and I inquired whether he would be inclined to suggest to his Government to make one more step and be content with the inspection alone being intrusted to the third Power.

German Delegate replied that he could assure me that he had had the greatest difficulty in persuading his Government to go as far as they had gone, and he gave me his word of honour that his instructions were perfectly precise and positive that the establishment of the inspector at a port as instructor was a *sine qua non* condition. It would be quite useless for him to refer again to them on the subject, and in perfect frankness and honesty he must impress on me that the last words had been spoken.

I conveyed this reply to my French colleague, and I told him that I was perfectly sure that the German Delegate was speaking with all truth and sincerity. I added that he must face the situation as it stood, and that there could be no question of breaking down the Conference on that point, and at a moment when a favourable end was so nearly reached.

He was greatly disappointed, and said that his Government could not accept such a solution. I said that he must put the facts clearly before them. After reflection he said that he could suggest to his Government that the Swiss, together with the French and Spanish, should police Tangier, the Swiss officer acting as Inspector also (the French will not hear of the Dutch). I said that this might prove to be an acceptable compromise, though I did not know if the Germans would accept it.

I told President of Conference of my interview with the German Delegate, and curiously enough he made the same suggestion as to Tangier as my French colleague. I told both of them that I would not refer again to the German Delegate till replies had been received to the suggestion from their Governments, when I would be happy to act again as intermediary.

I think M. Cambon may speak to you on the subject.

(¹) [For fuller report, *v. infra* pp. 297–8, No. 341.]

No. 340.

Sir F. Bertie to Sir Edward Grey.

F.O. 371/173.
(No. 104.) Confidential.
Sir,

Paris, D. *March* 11, 1906.
R. *March* 13, 1906.

I obtained an appointment to see M. Rouvier yesterday evening in order to carry out the instructions which I had had the honour to receive from you in the morning (telegram No. 31 March 9).([1])

His Excellency said that the Austrian scheme for the policing of the ports of Morocco was an acceptable basis; but there were some objectionable features in it which required to be eliminated. France had shown the greatest possible moderation and conciliation. It was now for Germany to display like qualities, for there had not been much of them on her part down to the present time. The Austrian scheme was of course a German project and the distribution of seven of the ports between French and Spanish Police Instructors had been ably arranged in a manner to cause friction between France and Spain. The question of what ports should be policed with French Instructors and which ones should have Spanish Instructors was a matter which ought to be settled by arrangement between the French and Spanish Governments. The Austro-German scheme allotted Casa Blanca to a Dutch or Swiss Inspector who, in addition to exercising a supervision of the police at the seven other ports was to organise the Casa Blanca police force. There was no reason why the police at Casa Blanca should be on a different footing to the police of the other Ports. The French Government objected to the Inspector General being a subject of one of the Minor States, but as a concession to Germany they would consent; but they would not agree to a Dutchman holding the appointment. They would prefer a Dane to a Swiss but they would waive their preference if absolutely necessary to bring about an agreement. They held that the Inspector should have powers of inspection at all the eight Ports, but no authority of command or organisation over the police or their instructors at any of them. The Inspector should be appointed by the Sultan of Morocco and make his reports to His Majesty, and not to the Diplomatic Body at Tangier, which was not competent to decide questions of Police organisation.

M. Rouvier considers that a police force organized by the subjects of a Minor State would be incompetent to maintain order at Casa Blanca for the Moors forming the force would have no respect for Instructors from a small State.

M. Rouvier's objection to a Dutchman as Inspector is that a person of that nationality would probably be under German influence, and his preference for a Dane is grounded on the belief that an Inspector of that nationality would be amenable to Russian and French and English influence. If, however, a great point were made by Germany of a Swiss holding the appointment the French Government would consent.

I told M. Rouvier that Sir Arthur Nicolson had reported to you that he doubted Germany giving way further than concurrence in the Austrian scheme and that having regard to the favourable view taken of it by the majority of the Representatives at Algeciras it would be most unfortunate that the conference should be broken up on such an issue as now separated the French and German Governments, and you had instructed me to inform His Excellency, as you had stated to M. Cambon, that, in your opinion, the Austrian proposal was a real concession on the part of Germany and had brought an agreement so near that it would not do to' let the conference come to an end without a settlement.

M. Rouvier expressed the opinion that the conference would not close without result, for he had good reason to believe that Germany would end by accepting the modifications in the Police scheme desired by France. His Excellency rather demurred to the supposition that the conference was so favourably impressed by the Austrian scheme. He said that France still counted on her side Spain, England, Russia,

([1]) [*v. supra* p. 289, No. 333.]

Portugal, and others had only been gained over by the German Delegates having persuaded them that Germany would make no further concessions.

As M. Rouvier will probably be out of office in a few days it is natural that he should strongly object to make further concessions to Germany and so incur reproaches in the Chamber from his successor and odium in the country.

The repetitions of Sir E. Goschen's telegram No. 4 of the 9th,(¹) of Sir A. Nicolson's telegram No. 91,(²) without date, and of your telegram to him in reply thereto reached me after I had returned to the Embassy from my visit to M. Rouvier.

I have, &c.
FRANCIS BERTIE.

(¹) [Not reproduced.]
(²) [v. supra p. 292, Note.]

No. 341.

Sir A. Nicolson to Sir Edward Grey.

F.O. 371/174.
(No. 69.) Conference. Confidential.   *Algeciras*, D. *March* 11, 1906.
Sir,   R. *March* 19, 1906.

At the request of M. Révoil I called on M. de Radowitz last evening, and said that I had come on an errand, and I hoped that he would let me speak frankly and as an old friend of over thirty years' standing.

I said that in the first place I cordially recognised the extent and nature of the concessions which his Government had made in adhering to the Austro-Hungarian proposal as to the police, and that I was convinced that these concessions had been made with a sincere desire to come to a satisfactory agreement.

It was indisputable that a very great step had been taken towards enabling the Conference to end happily, and that with these preliminary remarks I must now fulfil my errand.

He was as well aware as I was of the difficult position in which M. Révoil and indeed the French Government were placed in the question of the police organization. I did not wish to go into details, but he would doubtless take into consideration the extreme sensitiveness of French public opinion, and the importance which was attached in France to matters affecting the *amour propre* of the nation. M. Révoil, as he would have remarked, was not opposed to much which was contained in the Austro-Hungarian proposal, and he had openly acknowledged the conciliatory and friendly disposition which had dictated the proposal, as well as the courteous and amicable manner in which the German delegation had expressed their adherence to the project. M. Révoil felt, however, that there was one obstacle in the way of his subscribing to the proposal of Count Welsersheimb, and that was the establishment of the inspector in an Atlantic port as an instructor of a police contingent. I was authorized to enquire whether he would be disposed to recommend to his Government to take one more step towards a complete settlement of the question, and consent to the third Power being entrusted with inspection duties only, leaving to France and Spain the executive functions at all the eight ports.

M. de Radowitz said that he could assure me that he had had the greatest difficulty in persuading his Government to go so far as they had gone, and that he had indeed personally risked much by his pertinacity. He begged me to believe that there was no wish to " bluff," and that his Government were sincerely anxious to reach an agreement which should be honourable and satisfactory to all parties. But he could give me his word of honour as a gentleman that the instructions which he had received were emphatic and positive, and that they represented the very last concession which his Government were able to make. He had a great esteem for M. Révoil and he fully recognised his difficult position, but it would be unfair to M. Révoil if he did not state with all possible frankness that it would be absolutely useless for him to endeavour to modify in any way the decision of his Government.

He did not mean to say that some slight modification might not be introduced into the details of the proposal of Count Welsersheimb, but the German Government would never depart from the standpoint that the inspector should, beyond his duties of inspection, have under his instruction the police force at one of the ports.

I conveyed to M. Révoil the reply which I had received from M. de Radowitz, and I added that I was convinced that the latter had spoken in all sincerity and that it would be useless to endeavour to induce the German Government to reconsider their decision. I again impressed on M. Révoil that we must face the facts, and, however disagreeable they might seem to him, he should weigh well and seriously the very grave consequences which would ensue were his Government to reject the Austro-Hungarian project and thereby cause the failure of the Conference.

M. Révoil was much dejected by the reply which I brought to him, and for some time remained silent. I told him that I would be ready to assist him in any way that I could, and I placed my services entirely at his disposal; but it would be well if he were to lay the situation squarely before his Government and await their instructions.

He said that his Government would not, and could not, accept the proposal of placing a port under the charge of a third Power, it was illogical and impracticable : and was introducing the wedge of internationalization. He said with much bitterness that the Germans had internationalised the finances, and they now intended to introduce the principle throughout Morocco. France would leave the Conference having yielded everything and gained nothing.

After some cogitation he said that an idea had occurred to him. He would propose to his Government, but with not much hope of success, that the Swiss inspector with an officer or two should, in cooperation with French and Spanish officers, organize a police force at Tangier to be composed of foot and horsemen and some gunners. Each nation could undertake the instruction of one branch, and the Swiss superior officer could undertake the inspection of the other coast towns. At Casablanca French and Spanish instructors could be placed together.

He asked me to telegraph the above suggestion to my Government, and he would lose no time in submitting it to Paris. I replied that the idea might offer the basis for a compromise but that I did not know if M. de Radowitz could accept it.

With M. Révoil's consent I then called on the Duc de Almodovar, and communicated to him the substance of what had passed. He said that he was not at all surprised at the reply which I had received from M. de Radowitz, as he was aware that Germany had said her last word. He had thought over the question as to whether a compromise was possible, and to my surprise mentioned what was practically the same solution as that which M. Révoil had just suggested.

I said that perhaps he would consult with his Government on the subject, and whenever he or M. Révoil desired to utilize me as an intermediary with M. de Radowitz I should be at their service.

I have, &c.
A. NICOLSON.

No. 342.

Sir A. Nicolson to Sir Edward Grey.

F.O. 371/173.   *Gibraltar, March 12, 1906.*
Tel. (No. 96.) Confidential.   R. 1·30 P.M.

My French colleague explained to me yesterday that though he objected to the Austrian proposal in regard to the inspector having also a police contingent under his care as impracticable and illogical, and as driving in the wedge of internationalisation, his chief concern was that the outcry which would be raised against it in France might be utilised to weaken the Anglo-French understanding. He was afraid that our warnings as to breaking up the conference on what seemed to us a minor point might transpire, and at the approaching elections the nationalists and others might declaim against an understanding from which G[rea]t Britain had derived all advantages and France nothing. He did not for a moment question our perfect loyalty or wish to minimise the constant support we had given the French but he hoped that I would submit the above to you.

I said that I would do so, but I must repeat to him what I had already impressed on him : namely, that we had now the opinion of the majority of the conference against us, even that of Russia : and that a failure of the conference would produce the most serious consequences. I would always support him, but I had given warnings as a friend should, and this was all that my Government had done. He said that he was far from desiring to make any reproaches but he wished to indicate the risk of a change of feeling in France. He asked if a word could not be said to German Ambassador in London.

He is still under the impression that Germany will yield and says that he is convinced that his Government will not.

My French colleague is much depressed and a little unstrung : and I would venture to suggest that it would be of more importance to hear what the Government in Paris and also M. Cambon may say.

MINUTES.

I think there is point in M. Revoil's warning, and we ought to be most careful, on the eve of a general election in France, not to appear as the prime movers in persuading France to accept an arrangement which will certainly meet with strong opposition in France and which, it must be admitted, offers no really satisfactory or even very practical solution.

All that, I think, we ought to do is to point out to the French government the necessity of choosing between two alternatives : either the acceptance of the German (so-called Austrian) proposals on the police and presumably also those on the bank question, or no arrangement at all. It is for the French government to decide which of these alternatives they consider more advantageous to French policy in Morocco. Great Britain should declare herself ready to give her stipulated support whichever choice is made, and, if the second (negative) alternative be adopted, to come to a mutual understanding as to the attitude and measures to be adopted.

At the same time we can urge that in our opinion the situation if there were no agreement, would be more difficult to deal with successfully than the first.

It will be of doubtful use to make any further suggestion to the German Ambassador here.

If we are anxious to make a last effort, I can only suggest our endeavouring to put the French case as strongly as possible before President Rooseveldt and asking him whether he could make a communication at Berlin. Such a move would however come more properly from the French government themselves. Perhaps France and Great Britain could approach the President together?

E. A. C.
Mch. 12.

Approve Sir A. Nicolson's language. I doubt if anything can be done beyond a word from Sir E. Grey to M. Cambon.

E. B.

I have already had my conversation with M. Cambon.

E. G.

No. 343.

Sir Edward Grey to Sir A. Nicolson.

F.O. 371/173.   *Foreign Office, March 12,* 1906.
Tel. (No. 51.)   D. 12·30 P.M.

I gather from Mr. Lowther's report that there is considerable risk of Sultan's making serious difficulties in accepting reforms to be recommended by conference. Risk would be increased if one or the other of the powers were directly or indirectly to encourage Sultan to resist. To meet this difficulty, I would suggest that final act of conference should contain stipulation by which all the treaty powers engage to use their influence with the Sultan in order to obtain his acceptance of scheme of reform. You should consult your French Colleague as to the desirability of inserting a clause in this sense.

No. 344.

Sir Edward Grey to Sir A. Nicolson.

F.O. 371/173.   *Foreign Office, March* 12, 1906.
Tel. (No. 52.)   D. 4·30 P.M.

M. Cambon has explained strong French objection to giving any port to a third Power and French preference for the Swiss inspector at Tangier instead. I told him that you would support your French colleague in this if put forward as an alternative, but that if it failed I thought the French should accept the Swiss at Casa Blanca rather than let the Conference break up. Casa Blanca was only a minor port; if Swiss police failed there it would not matter in practice and would be an illustration of need for putting French or Spanish everywhere. I was sure that opinion here and impartial opinion everywhere regarded Germany as having given way on seven eighths of the question; she had in order to save a little prestige reserved this one small point, which could not in practice endanger French interests, for it would not bring in Germany, who apparently asks nothing for herself.

No. 345.

Sir A. Nicolson to Sir Edward Grey.

F.O. 371/173.   *Algeciras, March* 13, 1906.
Tel. (No. 98.)   R. 2·45 P.M.

As no agreement was reached in the drafting committee on the principal points of the bank and police questions it has been considered prudent not to hold a sitting of the Conference for two or three days.

The president of the conference asked my opinion as to postponing sitting for to-day and I said that it would be better to do so in order to avoid the present disagreement being accentuated in official meeting.

The situation is now so delicate here that a false step might precipitate matters.

The German first delegate called on me yesterday and said that he had telegraphed to his Gov[ernmen]t, as a suggestion, that the proposed inspector should be established at Tangier and not have charge of the police at a port and that he had received a reply that morning stating that such a suggestion was unacceptable and that no further modification could be made in former instructions. He repeated to me that Germany had really said her last word and he assured me most positively that there was no desire to "bluff."

I asked him to deal quite frankly with me and to tell me without any reserve if I must take this reply as the final word, and that no other combination or compromise was possible. He replied that such was the case: and that I might so inform my French colleague.

He added for my own private information that the Emperor had made a great effort to go so far in the way of concession as had been done, and that he really thought that some consideration should be shown by the French Gov[ernmen]t for H[is] M[ajesty's] desire to arrange the matter in as acceptable a form as possible.

From a conversation the German delegate had with the president of the conference the latter gathered that if the French persistently maintain their refusal to agree to the point at issue there was the danger that the German Emperor might withdraw his delegates from the Conference.

I should like to sum up the situation as it presents itself to me here as follows :—

1. French delegate and apparently his Gov[ernmen]t also are still of opinion that Germany will yield on point at issue. I think that there is little doubt that Germany will not yield.
2. That Germany is determined not to allow all the police to be under France and Spain, but to introduce the principle of internationalisation in as modified a form as possible : and that to effect this she must insist on a third power having charge of the police at one port.
3. That France will not accept the principle of internationalisation in any form whatever.
4. That if the two parties cannot agree, the conference must end in failure : and that as matters now stand the responsibility for a failure would in the opinion of the majority of the conference fall rather on France than on Germany.
5. That if France yielded on point at issue, she might obtain her way in the disputed questions in connexion with the state bank.

No. 346.

Sir A. Nicolson to Sir Edward Grey.

F.O. 371/173.   *Algeciras, March* 13, 1906.
Tel. (No. 99.)   R. 2·45 P.M.

Your telegram No. 51.([1])

My French colleague and myself have spoken together on more than one occasion as to the necessity of binding all the Powers to use their influence with the Sultan to obtain his consent to the reforms adopted by the Conference; and we proposed, when the moment arrived, to submit a draft article to our Gov[ernmen]ts which would meet the case. We also thought that it would be well if the Italian Minister or doyen of the diplomatic body should proceed to Fez and obtain, in name of Powers, the adhesion of the Sultan to the decisions of the Conference. These proposals we were holding back until there was a prospect of Conference coming to an agreement. I will speak again to my French colleague.

German first delegate observed to me yesterday that he was sure Sultan would accept all reforms on which Conference was in accord.

([1]) [*v. supra* pp. 299–300, No. 343.]

No. 347.

Sir Edward Grey to Sir F. Lascelles.([1])

F.O. 371/173.   *Foreign Office, March* 13, 1906.
Tel. (No. 15.)   D. 5·30 P.M.

The German Ambassador has urged upon me that the Austrian proposal at Algeciras represents a great concession on the part of Germany and should be accepted. I have cordially recognised the advance made but have urged that Germany should not spoil matters by making a vital question of having neutral police at Casa Blanca. (The Ambassador held out no hopes that Germany would give way on this.)

([1]) [Also to Sir F. Bertie (No. 38) and Sir A. Nicolson (No. 53). The last sentence was omitted from telegram to Sir F. Lascelles.]

No. 348.

Sir Edward Grey to Sir F. Lascelles.([1])

F.O. 371/173.
(No. 95.)
Sir,   *Foreign Office, March* 13, 1906.

Count Metternich read to me to-day the purport of a communication from his Government to the effect that the German Government had thought, last Saturday, that an agreement had been reached at Algeciras, owing to the great concession which they had made. But since then a change had taken place and now, in spite of the fact that all the delegates there, including Sir A. Nicolson, had expressed to Herr von Radowitz the opinion that the French ought to concede the small points still outstanding, it appeared that the French would not give way.

I said I did not think Sir A. Nicolson had said the French ought to accept the Austrian proposal unconditionally. But I recognised that the advance which Germany made had produced a very favourable impression, and speaking for myself personally I said I shared this impression and had been convinced that Germany now desired an agreement at the Conference and had taken a real step of her own to make such an agreement possible. There was, however, the difficulty about establishing Swiss police or police of a third Power at Casa Blanca, and I hoped that Germany, having gone so far as to concede that the police should be French or Spanish at seven of the ports, would not consider it vital that there should not be French or Spanish police at a small place like Casa Blanca, the more so as I understood that in principle the question of having a general Inspector of neutral nationality had been conceded.

Count Metternich said that unless the Inspector had some police of his own, as he would have at Casa Blanca, he would be too much in the air, and that it was necessary for him, in order to have influence, to have the knowledge and experience he would gain from having some police under his immediate control.

I said, on the contrary, it appeared to me that there was something worse than being in the air, and that was being in a hole. If the Inspector had police under his control at Casa Blanca, he would have to make his headquarters in that small place, and he would be hampered in travelling about, as it was intended he should do, by his local responsibilities.

Count Metternich did not take this view, and I could only again urge that I hoped the German Government would not consider the question of Casa Blanca a vital point, in view of the fact that there were other questions such as that of the Bank and of the Inspector under discussion, and would not allow the point about Casa Blanca to prevent an agreement being reached.

Count Metternich said he might urge with equal force that, after the large concession the German Government had made, so small a point should not be held against them.

I told him that I thought these details could not be discussed at length here. The impression I wished to leave upon him was that we had been impressed by the desire of the German Government to reach an agreement : for the last few weeks there had been a dead-lock; now it was only a hitch, and I hoped the German Government would not make a vital matter of the small points still outstanding.([2])

I am, &c.
E[DWARD] G[REY].

([1]) [Also to Sir F. Bertie (No. 159).]
([2]) [For Count Metternich's report, see *G.P.* XXI, I, pp. 282–4, *cf.* A. Tardieu : *La Conférence d'Algésiras*, p. 318, which suggests that Sir E. Grey took a strong line over Casablanca.]

No. 349.

Sir A. Nicolson to Sir Edward Grey.

F.O. 371/174.   *Algeciras, March* 14, 1906.
Tel. (No. 101.) Confidential.   R. 3·9 P.M.

My French colleague read to me a telegram he sent last evening to his Government.

He stated clearly to them that France must either accept German terms or break up the Conference, and that he was of opinion that the former course should be taken, but on the following conditions :—

1. That Swiss Inspector should not have control or command over French or Spanish officers.
2. That Inspector should report to Sultan and not to Diplomatic Body. If matter is pressed, it might be agreed that he should also report to Swiss Government for communication to foreign Ministers.
3. That Inspector should be appointed by Swiss Government and his appointment confirmed by Sultan.
4. That the Swiss police contingent at Casa Blanca should be inspected by senior French and Spanish instructor alternatively.
5. That the distribution of the French and Spanish instructors among the several ports should be left to French and Spanish Governments to settle in agreement with the Sultan.
6. That agreement of France to German terms should also be made dependent on agreement on the bank question, and also on Germany's assenting to a clause in final Protocol of Conference, that the *status quo ante* of those at present in Sultan's service should be respected. This latter condition is to preclude Germany from sending a military Mission to Fez.

As to bank, France would be ready to make some abatement in her claims as to allotment of capital, but not quite down to the level of what Germany requires.

My French colleague suggests to his Government that they should communicate with you, and he proposes that if they agree with his suggestions, that I should open up private negotiations on their behalf with First German Delegate.

Would you have any objection to my doing so when the moment arrives? I have already broken the ice with the German Delegate, and I venture to think that our mediation might be of future benefit.

My French colleague thinks that if his conditions are accepted by Germany, France can then agree to German terms, but otherwise not.

No. 350.

Sir Edward Grey to Sir F. Bertie.

F.O. 371/173.   *Foreign Office, March* 14, 1906.
Tel. (No. 40.)   D. 12·15 P.M.

In view of published instructions to M. Révoil I gather that French Government think it impossible to concede police at Casa Blanca if this is really so we shall of course support them. You should inform French Government and I will tell M. Cambon today.

No. 351.

Sir Edward Grey to Sir A. Nicolson.([1])

F.O. 371/173.
Tel. (No. 54.)   *Foreign Office, March* 14, 1906.

Count Metternich represented to me that all delegates including yourself had expressed opinion to Radowitz that France ought to give way on the outstanding points. I replied that you could not have said that France ought to accept the Austrian proposal unconditionally. There is danger that the French may resent our pressing them about Casa Blanca and if so we must in last resort support them in resisting.([2])

([1]) [Repeated to Paris, No. 39, and to Berlin, No. 16.]
([2]) [Sir A. Nicolson replied in telegram No. 102 of March 15, R. 3·0 P.M. " I most certainly did not say or imply to German delegate that France should give way on any outstanding point. I confined myself to what I have reported in my telegrams."]

No. 352.

Sir Edward Grey to Sir F. Bertie.

F.O. 371/173.
(No. 161.)
Sir,   *Foreign Office, March* 14, 1906.

I asked Mons. Cambon to come to see me to-day, and told him that I had noticed in the papers that the instructions from M. Rouvier to M. Révoil had been published, and that they contained a very categorical instruction to resist the establishment of neutral police at any port whatever. I gather from this that the French Government had made up their mind that under no circumstances could they agree to Casa Blanca being entrusted to the police of a third power. If this was so I wished to tell M. Cambon, in view of what I had said a day or two ago, and to prevent any misunderstanding, that we should of course continue our support at the Conference to the French attitude.

M. Cambon told me that he had reported me the other day to Paris as having expressed myself to the effect that, though I thought the Conference should not be allowed to break up on such a small point as that of Casa Blanca and I hoped the French would be able to concede that point in the last resort rather than break up the Conference, yet I would support whatever solution they might put forward.

I said that was quite accurate, and I had only wished to see him to-day because these instructions to M. Révoil had appeared in the papers. I wished to make sure that there was no misunderstanding as to our continuing to give our support to the French at the Conference.

M. Cambon said he had no information as to these instructions, and he assumed that they were unauthorised and gave only the purport or a summary, and not the text.

                                                    I am, &c.
                                                    EDWARD GREY.

No. 353.

Sir Edward Grey to Sir F. Bertie.

Private.([1])
My dear Bertie,   *House of Commons, March* 15, 1906.

. . . I think the French made a great mistake in not closing at once with the German concession at Algeciras : they could have made it appear to be a diplomatic

([1]) [Grey MSS., Vol. **10**.]

victory for themselves. It was so regarded by everybody outside France at the time. Now of course it is too late. Had the Conference broken up before the Austrian proposal as to the police was made, Germany would have been to blame; public opinion in Europe and (what is more important) public opinion in England would have looked upon her as a tiresome bully. *Now* if there is a break up, people will say that France is unreasonable and did not know how to take her advantage when she had it. You can see that even the "Times" correspondent at Algeciras thinks France ought not to break off on such a wretched point as Casa Blanca, which I believe is a useless hole. However, if she does, we shall back her up. . . .

Yours sincerely,
E. GREY.

No. 354.

Sir Charles Hardinge to Sir A. Nicolson.

Private.([1])

My dear Nico, *Foreign Office, March* 15, 1906.

Best congratulations on your G.C.M.G. which you have thoroughly earned. Such I am glad to say is the universal opinion.

Many thanks for your letter respecting Révoil. It threw an interesting light on his character and helped one to understand better the various changes in his attitude. I sent it on to the King as he reads all private letters on foreign affairs with great zest.

What an opportunity the French lost in not accepting as a great triumph the Austrian proposal and proclaiming a great diplomatic victory over Germany! I am surprised that such quick people as the French missed such a chance. Now they have placed Germany in the position of having shown a conciliatory disposition and of being able at the same time to offer some justification, however small, for breaking up the Conference. If the Conference breaks up over such an absurd point as the Casablança proposal *we* shall be in a disagreeable position, as I remember well your opinion that the French position will not be difficult for Germany to undermine in Morocco and we shall then be exposed to any violent action which the French may take to retrieve their losses and shall find ourselves compelled to support France in a war against Germany. If the Conference is broken off I shall not like the outlook. I felt very strong about telling Cambon that in our opinion the Austrian proposal should be accepted rather than allow the Conference to fall through and I knew that Metternich's statement to Grey that *all* the Delegates, you included, had expressed an opinion that France ought to give way was false and I was opposed to sending you our tel. No. 54,([2]) as I knew that you could have done no such thing and that you know our policy just as well as we know it here. However it was worth your disclaimer which arrived today. What is now going to happen seems very difficult to foresee but I still hope and believe that a compromise will in the end be arrived at.

By the bye, Cambon mentioned to me as the French counter-proposal an idea that the Swiss Inspector should command one of the three arms at Tangier and the French and Spanish the two others. I was surprised at his alluding to three arms and asked what he meant. He said infantry cavalry and artillery(!). That surprised me very much as who has ever heard of police with artillery? I told him he had better keep that idea dark as the Germans had already said that the French intended to get hold of the Moorish army. I also pointed out that as the French object to the Austrian proposal as internationalising Morocco, they would by the French proposal have a splendid example of internationalisation at Tangier, the chief port, and the inspector would obviously have the chief command.

I do not think this had occurred to him.

([1]) [Carnock MSS.]
([2]) [*v. supra* p. 304, No. 351.]

I forwarded to Sidney Greville your telegram about seeing the King. I expect you will probably just have time to see him as I do not think he joins the yacht at Marseilles till the 2nd. It looks as though I shall not see you until my return from the Mediterranean.

No time for more,
Yours ever,
CHARLES HARDINGE.

No. 355.

Sir F. Bertie to Sir Edward Grey.

Tel. Private.(¹)   *Paris, March* 15, 1906.

M. Crozier, French Minister at Copenhagen, has been to see Lister evidently with the approval of M. Bourgeois with whom he had a long interview yesterday.

The following is the substance of what he said.

Several influential and competent members of the French Parliament have in the course of last two or three days endeavoured to persuade Bourgeois that the policy of England under the present government will be to withdraw from taking any part in continental politics and to adopt the policy of isolation which they say would be favoured by Sir Henry Campbell-Bannerman as a follower of Mr. Gladstone, they maintain that the advice given to French Delegate at Algeciras by Nicolson is a first indication of their intention to withdraw as soon as possible from supporting French policy. M. Crozier says that M. Bourgeois being unacquainted with details of recent events is in a very anxious state and does not know whether to believe what these people say or not.

Since Crozier's interview with Bourgeois yesterday afternoon latter will have received message which I communicated to Political Director in consequence of your telegram No. 40 of yesterday.

(¹) [Grey MSS., Vol. 10.]

No. 356.

Sir F. Bertie to Sir Edward Grey.

Paris, March 15, 1906.
D. 7·50 P.M.

Tel. Private and Secret.(¹)   R. 10 P.M.

M. Clemenceau has been to see me this evening. He says that H[is] M[ajesty's] Gov[ernmen]t were suspected in Council of Ministers of having made an arrangement with Germany behind the back of France and it was thought that Sir A. Nicolson's advice to Monsieur Révoil about Casablanca was a proof of it. He (Monsieur Clemenceau) had been at first the only one to combat the supposition which he said he was sure was a mistaken one. He thought that Sir A. Nicolson's advice about Casablanca was merely a clumsiness (maladresse) and he was very glad to find that his conviction that England was not going to desert France was not [*sic*] proved to be true by your message of yesterday evening which was received after Ministerial Council.

I gathered from what he said about the German Emperor and his Gov[ernmen]t and this position of France that the French Gov[ernmen]t will propose compromise about Casablanca.

(¹) [Grey MSS., Vol. 10.]

No. 357.

Sir Edward Grey to Sir F. Bertie.

Foreign Office, March 15, 1906.

Tel. Private.(¹)　　　　　　　　　　　　　　　　　D. 11·30 P.M.

Your private telegrams of today. M. Crozier should be told that there has never been any question here of discontinuing our support of France. We have given it throughout at Algeciras and in every capital in Europe where required and shall continue this so long as the French wish it and trust us. Cordial cooperation with France in all parts of the world remains a cardinal point of British policy and in some respects we have carried it further than the late Government here were required to do.

Any advice Nicolson has given to Révoil has been on the understanding that this support would be continued, and if he has given advice freely it has been because of his complete confidence that this was understood by his French colleague. The same is true of my conversations with Cambon and I know that he has reported them to Paris in that sense.

The Prime Minister has been cognizant of all I have said and has cordially approved of it. He has more than once spoken in public with deliberate and emphatic approval of the *Entente*, notably at the Albert Hall in December.

You may speak in this sense if necessary to M. Bourgeois. M. Etienne should know it too. It is appropriate that his misgiving should have found expression to you in the very place, where it possibly had its origin.

E. G.

(¹) [Grey MSS., Vol. 10.]

No. 358.

Sir F. Bertie to Sir Edward Grey.

Paris, March 16, 1906.

F.O. 371/174.(¹)　　　　　　　　　　　　　　　　　　D. 8·30 P.M.

Tel. Private.　　　　　　　　　　　　　　　　　　　R. 11·15 P.M.

I have seen and explained to Min[iste]r for F[oreign] A[ffairs], M. Clemenceau, and M. Etienne policy of H[is] M[ajesty's] Gov[ernmen]t as explained in your Tel[egram] private of today (March 15).

They are quite re-assured. What alarmed French Ministers was that when M[onsieur] Révoil telegraphed Sir A. Nicolson's opinion in regard to Casa Blanca he said that he supposed that it re-produced the views of H[is] M[ajesty's] Gov[ernmen]t and the reports from the French Ambassador in London indicated a tendency on the part of H[is] M[ajesty's] Gov[ernmen]t to regard Austro-German proposals as being great concessions on part of German Gov[ernmen]t which in the opinion of the French Gov[ernmen]t they certainly were not. On the top of this came reports indulgently [industriously?] propagated by persons working in German interests that England was about to come to an arrangement with her and leave France in the lurch. M. Clemenceau says he did not believe these reports and so informed his colleagues who were inclined to be influenced by representations of many influential persons, members of Parliament, that England was not to be trusted.

Min[iste]r for F[oreign] A[ffairs] had told me today privately and confidentially that the Austro-Hungarian Ambassador called on him yesterday and asked him unofficially but no doubt under instruction from his Gov[ernmen]t whether some means might not be contrived to get out of present *impasse* about the Casa Blanca police.

Min[iste]r for F[oreign] A[ffairs] told him France could not accept Austro-German proposal on that point.

(¹) [Also in Grey MSS., Vol. 10.]

Ambassador then enquired whether some compromise could not be made by which Germany would be compensated in Bank question for a concession in regard to Casa Blanca police.

Min[iste]r for F[oreign] A[ffairs] replied that if the Austro-Hungarian Gov[ernmen]t would suggest scheme for a compromise French Gov[ernmen]t would consider it.

Min[iste]r for F[oreign] A[ffairs] is hopeful that Austro-Hungarian Gov[ernmen]t will make some proposal which the French Gov[ernmen]t can accept.

No. 359.

Sir A. Nicolson to Sir Edward Grey.([1])

F.O. 371/174.   *Algeciras, March* 17, 1906.
Tel.   (No. 104.)   R. 3 P.M.

The sitting of the Conference which was to have been held to-day has been postponed in hopes that the communications which are passing between Berlin and one or two other Governments may offer a chance of a solution being found to pending questions.

First German delegate asked me again yesterday whether I had any news to give him as to the police question. I replied in the negative but added that French were firm in their refusal to admit a third Power in the police organisation and that G[rea]t Britain would support them in their refusal. He then said that he believed that France accepted in principle the appointment of an inspector with simple inspection duties, as otherwise the Conference must end in a failure. I replied that the French delegate had admitted in principle the appointment of an inspector. He added that he had not the vaguest idea as to what view Berlin would take in regard to an inspector alone being appointed, and expressed the hope that I would counsel wisdom to my French colleague. I said that I had no counsels to give but only support which I would accord.

The tone of the German delegate was much modified in comparison with what it was on last occasion, and he by no means gave me to understand that Berlin had said her last word.

Most Confidential. The United States' Government object on their own account to establishment of a third power in charge of the police at a port, as they consider it implies in a certain sense sphere of influence and partition of country. I believe that the United States' delegate intends to let German delegate know this.

([1]) [For a fuller account, *v. infra* pp. 310–11, No. 362.]

No. 360.

Sir Edward Grey to Sir F. Bertie.

F.O. 371/174.
(No. 171.)
Sir,   *Foreign Office, March* 17, 1906.

M. Cambon called at the Foreign Office this morning and read to Sir C. Hardinge a telegram which he had received from M. Bourgeois, recounting a conversation which he had had with Count Khevenhüller, the Austro-Hungarian Ambassador respecting the present position of the negotiations at Algeciras.

2. Count Khevenhüller asked whether the French Government had quite decided to reject that part of the recent Austrian proposal which related to the organisation of a neutral police at Casablanca, and whether they entertained objections to the suggested appointment of an inspector of a third nationality. Upon M. Bourgeois

replying that the French Government could not possibly permit the installation in any Moorish port of a police force which was neither French nor Spanish, but that they would accept the appointment of an inspector on certain conditions, such as that the inspector should make his report to the Sultan and not to the Corps Diplomatique, Count Khevenhüller asked whether it would be possible, in order to prevent the failure of the conference, for the French Government to make concessions on the Bank question, in order to satisfy the *amour-propre* of Germany.

3. M. Bourgeois replied that there was a difference between the questions of the police and the State Bank, in that the former was a political question which had been carefully considered by M. Rouvier, with whose views as to the impossibility of making any concession in the matter of the ports he entirely agreed, but that the organization of the bank was an economic question which he had not yet had time to study, and upon which he did not wish to express any opinion. Count Khevenhüller asked whether, after M. Bourgeois had had time to consider the question, he would be ready to discuss it with him, and to this M. Bourgeois agreed. The Ambassador offered that the Austro-Hungarian Delegate at Algeciras might be authorized to put forward any proposal which might prove acceptable, presumably to Germany as well as to France.

4. M. Cambon considers that the important point in this conversation is the indication given that the German Government are ready not to press for the establishment of a neutral police force at Casablanca.

I am, &c.
EDWARD GREY.

No. 361.

Sir F. Bertie to Sir Edward Grey.(¹)

F.O. 371/174.
(No. 119.) Confidential.
Sir,

Paris, D. *March* 17, 1906.
R. *March* 21, 1906.

. . . . At the same time reports were being spread in Parliamentary circles here that England was likely to come to some arrangement with Germany or perhaps had already done so. I know that some members of the new Government were disposed to think that there might be truth in this insinuation and for the following reason: on the 25th of April last I had by direction of the Secretary of State, spoken to M. Delcassé on the subject of a desire attributed to Germany to obtain a port on the coast of Morocco (see my despatch No. 156 confidential, of the 25th of April)(²) and I had said that if the German Government asked for a port, His Majesty's Government would be prepared to join the French Government in offering strong opposition to such a proposal (pour s'opposer fortement à une telle proposition) and they begged that if the question were raised M. Delcassé would give full opportunity to His Majesty's Government to concert with the French Government as to the measures which might be taken to meet it (les mesures qui pourraient être prises pour aller à l'encontre de cette demande).

The advice given to the French Government that they should in the last resort accept the Austro-German proposal for the police of Casa Blanca rather than break up the Conference was regarded as inconsistent with the communication to M. Delcassé which I have quoted, for it is thought here that Casa Blanca might be converted into a useful port, and in German hands would be a danger to France and the establishment at that port of a police force under a Swiss Inspector and Swiss Instructors would be a step towards its occupation in some form by Germany at the first

(¹) [The full text of this despatch is printed in Lord Grey: *Twenty-Five Years* (1925) I, pp. 105–110.]
(²) [*v. supra* pp. 74–5, No. 93.]

[15869]

convenient opportunity, and that it is with such a view that the German Government have persisted in the stipulation that it should not be policed by a force under French or Spanish instructors.

It is unfortunate that Frenchmen of education and position should be found ready to believe imputations against England of bad faith, but the hereditary distrust of our country which has for so long been a characteristic of the French Race has been ably worked on by persons acting in the interest of Germany in order to create discord between France and England.

I have, &c.
FRANCIS BERTIE.

No. 362.

Sir A. Nicolson to Sir Edward Grey.

F.O. 371/174.
(No. 78.) Conference. Confidential.   *Algeciras,* D. *March* 17, 1906.
Sir,   R. *March* 24, 1906.

It had been intended that the Conference should meet to-day in plenary sitting, but yesterday it was considered advisable to postpone the meeting in the hope that before the next convocation some understanding might be found on the conflicting views in regard to the police question.

Renewed efforts are being made by one or two disinterested Powers to induce the German Government to abandon their desire to establish a third Power in charge of the police at one of the eight ports, and from information which has reached the Representatives of those Powers it would seem that their endeavours may be attended with success. In these circumstances it is well to have patience, and to defer the convocation of the Conference, until the results of the mediation to which I have referred above are known.

I met M. de Radowitz yesterday afternoon, and he enquired of me whether I had any news to give him as to fresh developments in the question affecting the police. I told him that none had reached me, but that I was sure that the French would remain firm in their refusal to admit a third Power at Casablanca, and that my Government would support them in their refusal. M. de Radowitz said that he perfectly understood the attitude of Great Britain, but that if the French Government refused to accept an Inspector General the breakdown of the Conference was inevitable. He hoped that he was right in assuming that no objection would be raised to the appointment of an Inspector. I replied that if I remembered rightly the French delegate had already expressed his adherence in principle to the appointment of that functionary. M. de Radowitz said that he had not the vaguest idea as to what his Government might decide upon with respect to the establishment of a third Power at a Moorish port. He presumed that they would let him know shortly. In the meantime he trusted that I would give my French colleague " des conseils de sagesse." I replied that it was hardly my place to give him " conseils," but that I was always prepared to accord him support.

This conversation with M. de Radowitz gave me the impression that he was now aware that his Government were not immovable on the question of placing a third Power in a Moorish port. He has also spoken to the Marquis Visconti Venosta in a similar tone, and the latter is also of opinion that the way is being prepared for a further concession on the part of Germany, a concession, which, as my Italian colleague remarked, is as unexpected as it is welcome.

I should like, in fairness to M. de Radowitz, to repeat that when he conversed with me on the 10th and again on the 12th instant I am convinced that he was then speaking in all sincerity when he asserted that his Government had no further concessions to make. His Government have apparently since those dates considered it desirable and opportune to take the further step which I sincerely trust may lead to a complete agreement.

I have, &c.
A. NICOLSON.

No. 363.

Sir A. Nicolson to Sir E. Grey.

Algeciras, March 18, 1906.
D. noon.
R. 3 P.M.

F.O. 371/174.
Tel. (No. 106.)

Austrian delegate told both U[nited] S[tates'] Rep[resentative] and myself yesterday that he was still awaiting reply of French delegate to the Austrian proposal as to the police. We conveyed this intimation to our French Colleague who said that French Min[ister] for F[oreign] A[ffairs] had already given a reply to Austrian Ambassador in Paris : but that he would be ready to repeat it to Austrian delegate. It was to the effect that—

(i) France must insist on only French and Spanish Instructors being in all the French ports,

(ii) that the question of distributing these officers amongst the ports must be settled between the French and Spanish Governments and Sultan, and not by the Conference,

(iii) that the French Gov[ernmen]t would be ready to discuss the proposal as to an Inspector and the attributes with which he would be invested.

My Austrian colleague told me that he doubted if Germany would accept this, as she then would have practically ceded everything. He has telegraphed to his Government the communication from French delegate; but it will only confirm what they will have already heard from Paris.

No. 364.

Sir A. Nicolson to Sir Edward Grey.

Algeciras, March 18, 1906.
D. 1·50 P.M.
R. 4 P.M.

F.O. 371/174.
Tel. (No. 107.) Confidential.

German second delegate mentioned to me this morning that perhaps his Gov[ernmen]t might not be indisposed to make a further concession allowing French or Spanish instructors in place of those of a neutral Power to be established at the eight ports : but that his Gov[ernmen]t would require some compensation for this Concession. After consulting with my French Colleague I saw German first delegate and asked him if he could tell me what compensation was required. He told me that he was awaiting instructions from his Gov[ernmen]t on that point and would let me know as soon as he received them. He added that his Gov[ernmen]t were in a conciliatory mood and that I could so inform my French colleague.

I imagine that the compensation has reference to the bank question and to the allotment of capital.

German first delegate said that he was still waiting for a reply from French delegate to German proposal for a compromise on the bank question. I told him I would mention this to my French Colleague : but that I did not think that the French would close negotiations with regard to bank till an understanding was reached on the police question.

I have hopes that the two parties are gradually moving towards each other but they are both so extremely cautious in their advance.

No. 365.

Sir A. Nicolson to Sir Edward Grey.

F.O. 371/174.   *Algeciras, March* 19, 1906.
Tel. (No. 108.)   Most Confidential.   R. 3·30 P.M.

My United States Colleague has shown me a telegram from his Government which states that Germany still holds to the Austrian proposal and they then give full text of a note addressed to the German Ambassador at Washington. The U[nited] S[tates'] Government state in the note that they perfectly [?](¹) approve of the Austrian proposal. They consider that no one Power ought to acquire such a control over the territory of Morocco as to justify belief that she might ultimately come to regard and treat that territory as her own to the exclusion of others. This view of international right was interposed against a claim of France to organise police through the agency of her officers alone. This claim France abandoned and offered to police the ports conjointly with Spain as mandatories of Europe. Austria proposed to give France four ports, Spain three and another to a third Power : and to this proposal U[nited] S[tates] Government objects as giving spheres of influence and foreshadowing partition of Morocco. It was, the note observes, proposed that an officer of a third Power, acting on behalf of all Powers, should secure the general inspection for the purpose of keeping the Powers advised as to whether their agents, France and Spain, were observing the limits and performing the duties of their agency. This arrangement seemed to the U[nited] S[tates] to accomplish the desired purpose. The U[nited] S[tates] Government consider that to distribute ports to separate and single Powers is wrong in principle and destructive of the declared purpose both of Germany and of the U[nited] S[tates]. If the U[nited] S[tates] had sufficient interests in Morocco, they would object seriously ; but they will accept whatever arrangement the European Powers represented at Algeciras agree upon. If the agreement is upon the Austrian proposal or upon any modification of it which includes the principle of the distribution of the ports, the U[nited] S[tates] Government will regret what they deem to be the failure of the true principle to which they have given their adherence.

Above are extracts hastily taken down from a lengthy note. I find a little difficulty in following the reasoning, but shortly put, U[nited] S[tates] Government apparently desire that France and Spain should act as agents of Europe aⱼ so far as I can gather, conjointly, at each port and with a very strict inspection.

France would, I think, object to an inspection carried out on lines proposed, which practically places their officers under control of officer of third Power. The inspection French have in view is one rather over the Moorish authorities to ensure that the latter do not hamper the work of French and Spanish instructors. Any dual organisation at the ports would certainly fail.

U[nited] S[tates] Delegate earnestly begs that nothing be said to French Ambassador or to anyone else unless copy of note is communicated by his Government or their Representatives to the several Powers for their information.

(¹) [The wording here seems to be defective, *cf.* Enclosure in No. 367, *infra* p. 313. Sir E. Grey has written " ? German " over " U.S. " in the third line; but the despatch following (No. 367) makes it more probable that " perfectly approve " is an error.]

No. 366.

Sir A. Nicolson to Sir Edward Grey.

Algeciras, March 19, 1906.

F.O. 371/174.
Tel. (No. 109.) Confidential.

D. 12·15 P.M.
R. 8·30 P.M.

My immediately preceding telegram.

United States' delegate has kindly given me a copy of American note. On careful perusal the reasoning is quite clear and the view of the U[nited] S[tates'] Government is evidently to place French and Spanish instructors at each port conjointly with a strict surveillance over them.

I should think that German Government will accept this proposal but it is doubtful if it would be agreeable to French. In practice I fear that it would not be a success. I am sending you a copy of the note.(¹)

(¹) [Sir E. Grey replied on March 20 (telegram No. 59) expressing regret that new proposals should be made at a time when satisfactory modifications of those of Austria-Hungary seemed probable.]

No. 367.

Sir A. Nicolson to Sir Edward Grey.

F.O. 371/174.
(No. 79.) Conference. Confidential.
Sir,

Algeciras, D. March 19, 1906.
R. March 26, 1906.

I have the honour to transmit, herewith, a copy of the Note which Mr. Secretary Root has addressed to the German Ambassador at Washington in regard to the police organization in Morocco, and which Mr. Henry White has been good enough to give me for my confidential information.

On the first hasty perusal of the document, I was not very clear as to whether the United States Government desired or not to distribute the police charge of the ports between France and Spain, but a second reading makes it, I think, evident that the purpose of the Note is that France and Spain conjointly should be established at each port. I very much doubt if such an arrangement would be workable in practice, and I fear that it would lead to constant friction and confusion.

I have, &c.
A. NICOLSON.

Enclosure in No. 367.

Note communicated by Mr. Root to German Ambassador.

It may be useful for me to restate in writing the answer of the United States, already given to you orally, to the questions which you have asked regarding our course upon the proposal made by Austria on the 8th instant in the Algeciras Conference :—

We do not approve that proposal. We regard it as an essential departure from the principle declared by Germany and adhered to by the United States that all commercial Powers are entitled to have the door of equal commercial opportunity in Morocco kept open, and the corollary to that principle, that no one Power ought to acquire such a control over the territory of Morocco as to justify the belief that she might ultimately come to regard and treat that territory as her own to the exclusion of others. This view of international right was interposed against the claim of France to organize the police in Morocco ports through the agency of her officers alone. France has yielded to this view of international right to the extent of offering to become, jointly with Spain, the mandatory of all the Powers, for the purpose of at once maintaining order and preserving equal commercial opportunities for all of them. It was further proposed that an officer of a third Power, acting in behalf of all the

Powers, should have secured general inspection for the purpose of keeping the Powers advised whether their agents, France and Spain, were observing the limits and performing the duties of their agency. This arrangement seemed to us to accomplish the desired purpose. It seemed, with two mandatories jointly charged, no individual claim of possession or control was likely to grow up; that, with the constant reminder of the general litigants involved in the inspectorship, the duties of the agency were not likely to be forgotten; and it seemed that the proximity of France and Spain to Morocco and their special interests in having order maintained in that territory made it reasonable that they should be selected as the mandatories rather than any other Powers.

The Austrian Proposal offers an alternative to the arrangement which I have described. It is that the eight Morocco ports shall be distributed. That in four the police shall be organized by the French, in three the police shall be organized by the Spanish, and that in the eighth port the police shall be organized by the Swiss or Dutch. This seems to us to provide for a potential partition of the territory in violation of the principle upon which we have agreed with Germany. From our point of view, all the reasons which existed against leaving to France the control of all the ports, exist against leaving to France the control of some, to Spain the control of some, and to Switzerland, either in its own interest or in the interest of any other Power, the control of one. The very fact of division of the ports implies existence of a special right on the part of the three countries in the ports assigned to them respectively. The immediate effect can only be the creation of three separate spheres of influence with inferior right and opportunity on the part of all other Powers, and that nations to whom these spheres are assigned may expect, in the ordinary course of events, to enter complete control.

We do not care whether the inspector, if there shall be one, is Italian or Swiss. We do not care whether he reports to his own Government or to the Diplomatic corps in Tangier or communicates the information obtained to the Powers in any other way. We consider that the distribution of ports to separate single Powers is wrong in principle and destructive of the declared purpose of both Germany and the United States. If we had sufficient interest in Morocco to make it worth our while we should seriously object, on our own account, to the adoption of any such arrangement. We have not, however, any such substantial interest in Morocco as to lead us to take that course. Our chief wish is to be of service in promoting a peaceable settlement of the controversy which brought the Conference together. Under the guidance of that wish we shall accept whatever arrangement the European Powers represented at Algeciras agree upon. If the agreement is upon Austrian proposal, or upon any modification of it which includes the principle of distribution of ports, we shall regret what we deem to be the failure of the true principle to which we have given our adherence. We still hope that there may be no such result.

Washington, March 17, 1906.

No. 368.

Sir A. Nicolson to Sir Edward Grey.

F.O. 371/174.　　　　　　　　　　　　　　　　　　　*Algeciras, March 21, 1906.*
Tel. (No. 111.)　　　　　　　　　　　　　　　　　　　R. 2·45 P.M.

Your telegram No. 59.([1])

Austrians had, I think, abandoned their original proposal before information had arrived as to view of U[nited] S[tates'] Government. The Austrians were contemplating, I am told, a new proposal to give four ports to France and Spain and leaving other four ports to the Sultan to organise: but when German Government were

([1]) [*v. supra* p. 313, *note to* No. 366.]

acquainted with views of U[nited] S[tates'] Government, they at once communicated with Vienna and suggested that the new Austrian proposal should follow lines advocated at Washington.

The Austrian delegate has announced that in a day or two he will be prepared to present the fresh proposal.

No. 369.

Sir A. Nicolson to Sir Edward Grey.

F.O. 371/174.   *Algeciras, March* 21, 1906.
Tel.   (No. 113.)   R. 3 P.M.

Russian delegate has informed me that he has been instructed to deny to French delegate and to others that Russian Government contemplated separating from France in regard to third Power in Atlantic port. Russian Government intended to support French views on that subject as on others.

German delegate had circulated same report as to opinion of Russian delegate in regard to Austrian proposal as he did with regard to mine.

No. 370.

Sir A. Nicolson to Sir Edward Grey.

F.O. 371/174.   *Algeciras, March* 21, 1906.
Tel.   (No. 115.)   R. 1·15 P.M.

United States delegate has shown me a tel[egram] from his Gov[ernmen]t communicating a tel[egram] from German Emperor. His Majesty says that he approves the fundamental principle of the American proposal as to the co-operation of French and Spanish officers to be about equally divided at each port. H[is] M[ajesty] adds that his Gov[ernmen]t would support a proposal based on this mixed system with an Inspector-General. The telegram concludes as follows. ''The immediate removal of all misunderstanding is of far more importance to Germany than the whole Morocco affair.''

No. 371.

Sir Edward Grey to Sir E. Goschen.

F.O. 371/174.
(No. 24.)
Sir,   *Foreign Office, March* 21, 1906.

Count Mensdorff asked me to-day whether I had any news from Algeciras.

I said I was afraid there were too many peacemakers at work. The United States had now made a new suggestion about which I did not yet know the views of any other Government, but it seemed to me to be an unworkable proposal which introduced an unfortunate complication. I had hoped that the Austrian Government were going to propose some modification of their original proposal, and I hoped now that they would not put anything forward without having ascertained whether it would be acceptable to France and Spain.

Count Mensdorff sounded me as to whether there was no hope of neutral police being accepted at Casa Blanca, and I said that there was no hope whatever of that, and if that particular point was insisted on it would break up the Conference.

Count Mensdorff said he believed that a neutral inspector was accepted in principle, which I understood also to be the case.

I am, &c.
EDWARD GREY.

No. 372.

Sir Edward Grey to Sir M. de Bunsen.

F.O. 371/174.
(No. 39.)
Sir,
                                                    Foreign Office, March 21, 1906.

The Spanish Chargé d'Affaires came on purpose to tell me to-day that his Government objected strongly to the proposal of the United States, which would mean French police and French instructors at Tetuan.

I said that I regarded the proposal of the United States as having introduced a most unfortunate complication, and as being in itself quite unworkable. I did not yet know the views of the French Government, but I had assumed that the proposal would be unacceptable both to France and to Spain, and if this were so we would of course continue to support them. I said, however, that we must all three continue to act together as we had been doing. My view had been that the allocation of ports between France and Spain should be settled by themselves and this was why I assumed the United States' proposal would be unacceptable to them.

I am, &c.
EDWARD GREY.

No. 373.

Mr. Spring-Rice to Sir Edward Grey.

F.O. 371/174.
(No. 234.)
Sir,
                                    St. Petersburgh, D. *March* 21, 1906.
                                                    R. *April* 9, 1906.

With reference to my despatch No. 197 of the 17th instant([1]) on the subject of Morocco, I have the honour to inform you that Count Lamsdorff told me today that he had learned that a rumour had been spread in Paris to the effect that Russia was in favour of the Austrian proposal and thought that France ought to yield—in fact a rumour precisely similar to that spread with regard to England.

He had consequently instructed Count Cassini to inform the other delegates that the Russian Government categorically denied the rumour to the effect that Russia had advised France to accept the Austrian proposal or was in favour of the organization of the police of Casablanca by a third Power.

Count Lamsdorff added that he had always been ready to do his utmost to promote a peaceful solution of the questions in dispute but that the Russian Government had never deviated for a moment from her policy of supporting her ally.

He expressed himself strongly on the subject of the rumours which appeared to have been spread simultaneously in Paris and St. Petersburg with regard to the supposed disinclination of the Russian and British Governments to afford France their support in view of the last proposal which had been made with regard to the police. The object was manifest and was in his view very regrettable.

([1]) [Not reproduced. It encloses a copy of a note communicated to Count Lamsdorff on the 17th with reference to British support to France in the affair of Casablanca, *cf. supra*, p. 304, No. 351 and *note*.]

In conclusion, he observed that the points of divergence between the French and German views were now of such slight consequence—for the Germans had announced their intention not to insist on the separate organization of the Casablanca police—that it seemed to him almost inconceivable that the Conference should be unable to come to an arrangement on the subject—if it failed to do so it would be a disgrace to Europe.

I have, &c.
CECIL SPRING-RICE.

No. 374.

Sir Edward Grey to Sir M. Durand.

F.O. 371/174.
Tel. (No. 23.)   *Foreign Office, March 22, 1906.*

United States Chargé d'Affaires has communicated a telegram saying that arrangement for a mandate for Police control at Moroccan Ports to France and Spain jointly with an Inspector General of another country would be accepted by Germany and asking our influence in its favour. If this means that France and Spain, who are to do the work, are to arrange with each other how the police are to be distributed I think it would provide basis for a settlement. But if on the contrary it is to be insisted that French and Spanish police are to be mixed in dual organization at each port I fear this would not be accepted and would be quite unworkable. You should explain this to Mr. Root and keep your French colleague informed. We in common with United States are most anxious to see the Conference end in agreement but everything depends upon the point I have explained and I trust influence of the President, which has been so beneficially exercised, will be able to arrange it satisfactorily.

No. 375.

Sir F. Bertie to Sir Edward Grey.

F.O. 371/174.   *Paris, D. March 22, 1906.*
Tel. (No. 32.)   R. *March 23, 1906, 8 A.M.*

Morocco : 22nd March.

1. Your telegram No. 43 of 21st, and my telegram No. 30 of 21st.([1])

2. I have seen Minister for Foreign Affairs again this evening. What he says is as follows :—

3. On Russian Ambassador at Berlin making communication to German Government from Russian Government that Russia supported, and would continue to support, France in Algeciras Conference, Count von Bülow stated, and authorized him to inform Russian Government that Germany would give up Austrian proposal regarding policing of Casa Blanca, but would expect compensation for this in question of allotment of capital in matter of bank. This information was conveyed to French Government by Russian Ambassador in Paris. German Emperor had, however, so it appears, communicated with President of United States, independently of Count von Bülow, and persuaded President to undertake to propose instructors of mixed nationality, French and Spanish, for all eight ports.

4. Minister for Foreign Affairs has instructed French Ambassador in London to ask you to instruct His Majesty's Ambassador at Washington to act with French Ambassador there in requesting President Roosevelt not to put forward such a scheme, as it would not be acceptable to France and Spain and would cause friction and be unworkable.

([1]) [Not reproduced. They relate to the views of Spain and France as to the proposal of the United States.]

5. If it should be too late to stop proposal, the French Ambassador and Minister for Foreign Affairs hopes that also British Ambassador should ask President of United States not to press consideration of scheme by the Conference until France, England, Spain, and Russia have all had time to consider and propose a compromise. French Delegate is instructed that meanwhile he is to adhere to proposal which he last made under instructions from French Government.

6. The compromise which French Delegate has recommended, and which French Government are considering, is as follows: The police forces at Tangier and at Casa Blanca to be 500 at each of those ports. At the other six ports to be less.

7. At each port where the force is 500 or over the instructors to be of mixed nationality, French and Spanish, probably each nationality taking one-half of force. At the other ports the instructors to be French or Spanish, according as may be arranged between French and Spanish Governments.

8. M. Cambon will probably have made to you to-day communication to above effect. French Minister for Foreign Affairs hopes you will consent to make the suggested representation at Washington.

No. 376.

Sir A. Nicolson to Sir Edward Grey.

F.O. 371/174.   Algeciras, March 23, 1906.
Tel.   (No. 117.)   R. 12·45 P.M.

German second delegate called on me yesterday and I asked him how matters stood in regard to the police question. He said that an Austrian project was in preparation but had been held over owing to a communication from Washington making suggestions of another nature, and which the German Emperor viewed favourably. I said that if he referred to the mixed system it would be unworkable in practice. He replied that if he were the French delegate he would not hesitate to accept it, and then enquired if my Government had expressed any views. I said that the Governments of France and Spain were opposed to the mixed system and that we should certainly support them in their opposition. I added that I hoped that no proposal of the character he indicated would be presented to the Conference.

No. 377.

Sir Edward Grey to Sir M. Durand.

F.O. 371/174.   Foreign Office, March 23, 1906.
Tel.   (No. 24.)   D. 1·30 P.M.

My tel[egram] No. 23.(¹)
You may support your French colleague in any action, which he wishes to take.

(¹) [v. supra p. 317, No. 374.]

No. 378.

Sir Edward Grey to Sir E. Goschen.

F.O. 371/174.
(No. 25.)
Sir,   Foreign Office, March 23, 1906.

The Austrian Ambassador tells me confidentially that Count Goluchowski has given instructions to modify the Austrian proposal by eliminating the part about Casa Blanca, but proposing in return for this that the French should make some concession with regard to the proportion of shares in the bank. The Corps Diplomatique at

Tangier would have supervision over the Police, but they would act only through an executive officer who would be the Inspector and would be chosen from a minor Power. Count Goluchowski expressed the hope that this proposal would be accepted by France.

I asked whether it would be accepted by Germany, but Count Mensdorff could not tell me whether Germany had yet accepted it. He said, however, that the proposal of the United States with regard to a mixed police at each port would, in the view of the Austrian Government, only cause further delay and would not form part of their new proposal.

I said that I could not say whether the French Government could accept the amended Austrian proposal or not, but that as the special provision about Casa Blanca had been the insuperable difficulty I thought that the fact of its being eliminated would enable the new proposal to form a basis for discussion.

I am, &c.
EDWARD GREY.

No. 379.

Sir A. Nicolson to Sir Edward Grey.

F.O. 371/174.
(No. 84.) Conference. Confidential.   *Algeciras,* D. *March 23, 1906.*
Sir,   R. *March 31, 1906.*

Count Welsersheimb, the Austro-Hungarian delegate, spoke to me yesterday in regard to the police question, and I enquired of him if he could tell me how matters stood with respect to his project. He said that the desire of his Government was to find some solution to the existing difficulties which would be agreeable to all parties, and that, as it was clear that France would not agree to the establishment of a third Power at Casablanca, and as it was believed that Germany would not insist on that point, a project had been prepared by his Government which would leave the policing of all the ports to France and Spain, but which would also provide for the appointment of an Inspector General invested with considerable powers and with sufficient authority to exercise a close and effective superintendence.

This project had been communicated to Berlin; but the German Government had not, hitherto, explicitly declared that they would accept it, but had contented themselves with conveying their thanks for the endeavours which the Austro-Hungarian Government were making to further a settlement.

Count Welsersheimb further explained that Count Goluchowski considered that as Germany had made such large concessions on the police question it was fair that she should receive some satisfaction on that of the Bank; and he was, therefore, to link the two questions together, and to endeavour to procure from M. Révoil some substantial abatement in the demands of France in respect to the allotment of the Bank capital.

The views or suggestions reported from Washington had, he said, introduced some confusion into the above plan, and he was unaware what effect they might produce on the intentions of his Government. He would, however, until otherwise instructed, continue to prosecute the programme which he had to fulfil. He would at the same time be glad to know whether the American suggestions found favour with France and Spain, and also with ourselves.

Both M. Révoil and myself were anxious that Count Welsersheimb should not be induced to present a project based on the mixed system and dual organization, and as I was afraid that instructions to do so might arrive at any moment, and as I also was aware that you had informed Count Mensdorff in London that it would be unfortunate if a new project were presented which would be unacceptable to France and Spain, I took the opportunity of telling Count Welsersheimb that I knew that Spain, and I had every reason to believe that France also, objected strongly to the dual organization, and that, of course, we should support France in her objections. I said I would prefer if he heard from M. Révoil's own lips the views of the French Government on the subject, and I therefore brought the two delegates together at my house.

M. Révoil stated to the Austrian delegate the reasons which prevented his Government from accepting the dual organization, and Count Welsersheimb thereupon said that he would at once telegraph to his Government that Great Britain, France and Spain would be unable to agree to a proposal based on the mixed system.

Count Welsersheimb and M. Révoil then discussed the question of the concessions which France might be prepared to make upon the Bank question, but, as their views were divergent is is hardly necessary that I should report them in detail.

There were two points which Count Welsersheimb wished to impress on M. Révoil and myself. The first was that his Government considered that the most important feature of the police scheme should be the investment of the Inspector General with large powers and efficient authority; while the German Government attached chief importance to the distribution of the ports among the French and Spanish officers being decided by the Conference and not left to the Sultan and the two directly interested Governments to arrange among themselves.

At the time of writing this despatch I do not know what project Count Welsersheimb will eventually present: but I think that the situation as it presents itself today may be summed up as follows. I leave aside the American views, as it is by no means evident in what form they may be presented or whether they will be embodied in a project, Austrian, German, or other.

1. The German delegates have not really officially abandoned the "Casablanca" scheme. They have let it be understood that they have allowed it to lapse; but no more than that. It seems to me that they are awaiting what may emerge from Washington, and in the meantime are allowing the Austro-Hungarian Government to discuss projects and compromises without expressing any definite opinion in regard to them.
2. The Austro-Hungarian Government are keenly desirous of finding a common ground of understanding, but are hampered by the reserve of Berlin, and by the difficulty of obtaining from France such concessions on the Bank as may satisfy Germany.
3. The French are willing to make certain concessions, or more correctly, are disposed to make certain abatements in their demands, on the Bank question, but not to the extent which Count Welsersheimb desires. They are willing to agree that the Inspector General should be invested with considerable powers and authority, but are unwilling that he should be an organ of the Diplomatic Body, or that the latter should have the faculty of interfering in the details of the police organization. They are also opposed to the Conference deciding as to how the ports are to be distributed as they consider that such distribution would be effected in a sense contrary to the secret agreements between France and Spain.

I have, &c.
A. NICOLSON.

No. 380.

Sir M. Durand to Sir Edward Grey.

F.O. 371/174.
Tel. (No. 16.)
Morocco.

Washington, March 24, 1906.
R. 10 P.M.

My immediately preceding telegram.

Secretary of State informs me that he sent last night to Mr. White following telegram :—

"Your No. 31. We care nothing whether the actual administrative exigencies necessitate in some ports, as they doubtless will in Tangier for instance, the employment of both French and Spanish officers, whilst at other points either French or Spanish officers may be employed, or at one time French and at another time Spanish, provided that both countries accept a joint responsibility for every port.

"All this distribution of officers can and should be settled as a matter of detail between the two mandatory Powers which undertake the preservation of order, and provided that it is understood that mandate is joint and not several and the responsibility is universal and not local or distributive. The inspector who on behalf of all the Powers enquires into execution of mandate will be wholly unaffected in the performance of his duty by any consideration as to which particular Power at any particular time happens to have its officers at a particular point."

No. 381.
Sir M. Durand to Sir Edward Grey.

F.O. 371/174.　　　　　　　　　　　　*Washington, March* 24, 1906.
Tel. (No. 17.)　　　　　　　　　　　　R. 9 P.M.

Confidential. My tel[egram] No. 15.(¹)

My impression after seeing French Ambassador and Secretary of State is that U[nited] S[tates'] Gov[ernmen]t consider us as opposed to Germany and possibly inclined to push France too far. Neither President nor Secretary of State have discussed Morocco Conference with me and I have asked no questions till yesterday: but I know that President used to think us unduly suspicious of Germany if not unduly hostile.

(¹) [Not reproduced. It reports action taken upon Sir E. Grey's telegram No. 24, *supra* p. 318, No. 377. The French Ambassador did not desire him to use any pressure at present.]

No. 382.
Sir A. Nicolson to Sir Edward Grey.

F.O. 371/174.　　　　　　　　　*Algeciras,* D. *March* 26, 1906, 10·10 P.M.
Tel. (No. 120.)　　　　　　　　　　R. *March* 27, 1906, 7 A.M.

The Conference held a plenary sitting this morning on the police question. We discussed a project drawn up by the Drafting Committee, and to which the Austrian Delegate presented some amendments.

The chief points in our discussion were the following :—

1. The German Delegate formally announced that the German Government agreed to all the eight ports being left to French and Spanish instructors.
2. Austrian Delegate presented an amendment, leaving to the Conference to decide at which ports the French and Spanish instructors should be placed respectively, while the French still maintain that this question should be left to the two Governments to settle with the Moorish Government.
3. Austrian Delegate proposed that the Diplomatic Body at Tangier should control the police organization; and German Delegate announced that his Government considered this to be a *sine qua non* condition, and unless it was conceded he intimated that the German Delegates would leave Conference.

The instructions of the French Delegate are strict on his not yielding on this point.

I have consulted with him, and have said that he should refer once more to his Government on the point.

Both of us are to meet Italian, Spanish, Russian and United States' Delegates privately this evening and endeavour to find a formula which will bridge over this difficulty. I have hopes we shall do so.

German First Delegate impressed on me that the success or failure of the Conference depended on settlement of the above point.

No. 383.

Sir A. Nicolson to Sir Edward Grey.

F.O. 371/174.
(No. 85.)   Conference.   *Algeciras*, D. *March* 27, 1906.
Sir,   R. *April* 7, 1906.

A plenary sitting was held yesterday morning of the Conference, to discuss a police project drawn up in the Drafting Committee, but as it had not obtained the assent of all the members of that Committee, several articles were reserved as will be seen from the enclosed copy of the scheme.

When Article II came forward for discussion, M. de Radowitz announced that he agreed, on behalf of his Government, to French and Spanish instructors being appointed at all the eight ports, and this statement, therefore, disposed of the question of a third Power being entrusted with the instruction of the police at Casablanca. There was some conversation as to the wording of the second paragraph of Article II and the Drafting Committee was requested to amend it. Article III was referred back to the Drafting Committee for redrafting, but the amendments which were desired were of an unimportant character. The same course was taken with regard to Article IV. Article V was adopted.

On the discussion being opened on Article VI, the Austro-Hungarian delegate, Count Welsersheimb, presented two amendments, which will be found in the enclosed paper, entitled Article VI and Article VII (additionnel).

In regard to this latter additional Article, I pointed out that we were dealing with a Moorish police force, placed under the sovereign authority of the Sultan, and that if the Diplomatic Body were to exercise control over it we should be superimposing a foreign authority over that of His Sherifian Majesty; and, moreover, that it would in practice be difficult for the foreign Representatives to supervise the working of the police force in the coast towns.   M. Révoil supported me in my observations; while the German delegate announced that the control by the Diplomatic Body constituted in the view of his Government a principal and cardinal point of any police project, and that they would find it most difficult to continue the discussion of a project of which it did not form part.   The tone of M. de Radowitz was very decided, and left on us all the impression that unless satisfaction were given to the German Government on the subject the break-down of the Conference would be imminent. The matter was passed over for the moment by the amendments being both referred to the Drafting Committee.

The remaining Articles and the two amendments proposed by Count Welsersheimb were then examined by the Conference and were also referred to the Drafting Committee.

I have, &c.
A. NICOLSON.

Enclosure 1 in No. 383.

Project proposed by Drafting Committee respecting Moroccan Police Question.

La Conférence, appelée par S[a] M[ajesté] le Sultan à se prononcer sur les mesures nécessaires pour organiser la police sur des bases nouvelles, déclare que les dispositions à prendre sont les suivantes :—

Article 1.   La Police sera placée sous l'autorité souveraine de S[a] M[ajesté] le Sultan.   Elle sera recrutée par le Maghzen parmi les musulmans marocains, commandée par des Caïds marocains et répartie dans les huit ports ouverts au commerce.

Art. II. Pour venir en aide au Sultan dans l'organisation de cette Police, des officiers et sous-officiers instructeurs français, des officiers et sous-officiers instructeurs espagnols seront mis à sa disposition par leurs Gouvernements respectifs qui soumettront leur désignation et leur affectation à l'agrément de S[a] M[ajesté] Chérifienne.   Un contrat passé entre le Maghzen et les instructeurs, en conformité du règlement prévu à l'article 3, déterminera les conditions de leur engagement et fixera leur solde qui ne pourra pas être inférieure au double de la solde correspondante au grade de chaque officier ou sous-officier. Il leur sera alloué, en outre, une indemnité de résidence variable suivant les localités. Des logements convenables seront mis à leur disposition par le Maghzen qui fournira également les montures et les fourrages nécessaires.

Les Gouvernements auxquels ressortissent les instructeurs se réservent cependant le droit de les rappeler et de les remplacer par d'autres, agréés et engagés dans les mêmes conditions.—(Réservé.)

Art. III. Ces officiers et sous-officiers prêteront pour une durée de cinq années leur concours à l'organisation des Corps de police chérifiens. Ils assureront l'instruction et la discipline conformément au règlement à prendre sur la matière; ils veilleront également à ce que les hommes enrôlés possèdent l'aptitude au service militaire. D'une façon générale, ils devront surveiller l'administration des troupes et contrôler le paiement de la solde qui sera effectué par l'amin, assisté de l'officier instructeur comptable. Ils prêteront aux autorités marocaines, investies du commandement de ces corps, leur concours technique pour l'exercice de ce commandement.

Les dispositions réglementaires propres à assurer le recrutement, la discipline et l'administration des Corps de police seront arrêtées d'un commun accord entre le Ministre de la Guerre chérifien ou son délégué, l'inspecteur, l'instructeur français et l'instructeur espagnol les plus élevés en grade.

Le règlement devra être soumis au Corps diplomatique à Tanger qui formulera son avis dans le délai d'un mois. Passé ce délai, le règlement sera mis en application.—(Réservé.)

Art. IV. L'effectif total des troupes de police ne devra pas dépasser 2,500 hommes ni être inférieur à 2,000. Une garnison de 500 à 600 hommes sera placée à Tanger; de 300 à 500 hommes à Casablanca et à Rabat; le reste de l'effectif sera réparti suivant les besoins par groupes qui ne seront pas inférieurs à 150 hommes. Le nombre des officiers français et espagnols sera de 16 à 20; celui des sous-officiers français et espagnols de 30 à 40.—(Réservé.)

Art. V. Les fonds, nécessaires à l'entretien et au paiement de la solde des troupes et des officiers et sous-officiers instructeurs seront avancés au Trésor chérifien par la Banque, dans les limites du budget annuel attribué à la police, qui ne devra pas dépasser deux million $\frac{1}{2}$ de francs pour un effectif de 2,500 hommes.

Art. VI. Le fonctionnement de la police sera, pendant la même période de cinq années, l'objet d'une inspection qui sera confiée à un officier supérieur de l'armée suisse ou néerlandaise dont le choix sera proposé à l'agrément de S[a] M[ajesté] le Sultan par le Gouvernement fédéral suisse ou néerlandais.

L'inspecteur, sans intervenir dans le commandement ou l'instruction, se rendra compte des résultats obtenus par la police chérifienne au point de vue du maintien de l'ordre et de la sécurité dans les localités où cette police sera installée. Il établira tous les ans, ou plus fréquemment s'il le juge nécessaire, un rapport à ce sujet. Ce rapport, ainsi que toute communication relative à la mission de l'inspecteur, sera adressé au Représentant du Sultan à Tanger et transmis en copie au Corps diplomatique.—(Réservé.)

Art. VII. En cas de réclamation dont le Corps diplomatique serait saisi par la Légation intéressée, le Corps diplomatique pourra demander au Représentant du Sultan à Tanger de faire procéder à une enquête par l'inspecteur, qui devra établir un rapport. Ce rapport sera transmis au Représentant du Sultan à Tanger et communiqué au Corps diplomatique.—(Réservé.)

Art. VIII. L'inspecteur, dont la résidence sera fixée à Tanger, recevra un traitement annuel de 25,000 fr. Il lui sera alloué, en outre, une indemnité de 5,000 fr. pour frais de tournées. Le Maghzen mettra à sa disposition une maison convenable et pourvoira à l'entretien de ses chevaux.

Art. IX. Les conditions matérielles de son engagement et de son installation, prévues à l'art[icle] VIII, feront l'objet d'un contrat passé entre lui et le Maghzen.

Enclosure 2 in No. 383.

Amendments to Drafting Committee's Project proposed by Austro-Hungarian Delegation.

Article VI. Le fonctionnement de la police fera pendant la même période de 5 années l'objet d'une inspection générale, qui sera confiée par S[a] M[ajesté] Chérifienne à un officier supérieur de l'armée helvétique ou néerlandaise.

S[a] M[ajesté] le Sultan le choisira librement parmi les officiers que Lui présentera, au nombre de trois et avec l'assentiment des Puissances signataires, ou le Gouvernement de la Suisse ou celui des Pays-Bas. Il aura sa résidence à Tanger.

L'inspecteur-général, sans intervenir directement dans le commandement ou l'instruction, se rendra compte des résultats obtenus par la Police Chérifienne au point de vue du maintien de l'ordre et de la sécurité dans les localités où cette police sera installée.

Dans l'exercice de ses fonctions il visitera, au moins une fois par an, chacune des 8 places où les corps de police seront établis. Sur le résultat de ces visites d'inspection annuelles il adressera, par entremise du doyen du Corps Diplomatique à Tanger, un rapport à S[a] M[ajesté] le Sultan.

En dehors de ces rapports réguliers il pourra, s'il le juge nécessaire, adresser, par la même voie, au Gouvernement Chérifien des rapports spéciaux sur toute question concernant le fonctionnement de la Police.

Art. VII (Additionnel). Le contrôle du fonctionnement de la Police sera exercé par le Corps Diplomatique à Tanger. A cet effet l'inspecteur-général lui prêtera son concours.

Art. VIII (amendement à l'Article VII). En cas de réclamation à l'égard du fonctionnement de la Police, la Légation intéressée pourra en saisir le Corps Diplomatique qui, après avoir provoqué une enquête par l'Inspecteur-général, donnera à l'affaire la suite qu'elle comportera.

Art. . . . (Additionnel). Des officiers français seront chargés de l'organisation et de l'instruction de la troupe de Police à . . . .

Des officiers espagnols seront chargés de l'organisation et de l'instruction de la troupe de Police à . . . .

No. 384.

Sir A. Nicolson to Sir Edward Grey.

F.O. 371/174.
(No. 86.) Conference. Confidential.   *Algeciras*, D. *March* 27, 1906.
Sir,   R. *April* 7, 1906.

I had the honour to report in my despatch No. 85 of to-day's date the proceedings of the plenary sitting of the Conference which was held yesterday.

Immediately after the sitting M. de Radowitz took me on one side, and said that he wished to impress on me the fact that it had cost his Government much effort to give way on the point of placing a third Power in charge of the police at Casablanca, and that his Government were immovable on the question that the Diplomatic Body should supervise the manner in which the police forces exercised their functions. He had, he said, made as categorical a statement as possible before the Conference, and he could assure me that the success of the Conference depended upon the adherence of France to the German point of view. He begged me to communicate what he had said to my French colleague.

I saw M. Révoil as soon as we had returned home, and repeated to him what M. de Radowitz had said to me. He replied that his instructions were strict in requiring him to resist any intervention of the Diplomatic Body in the police functions, and he was perplexed as to how to deal with the situation created by the German statement, which he recognized was sufficiently precise and categorical. We discussed the matter for some time, and M. Révoil eventually suggested that it might be well if the Spanish, Russian, Italian, and United States' first delegates were to meet us both privately, and endeavour to devise some formula which would satisfy the German views, and at the same time render it easier for him to refer the question to his Government. The wording of the Austrian article as it stood was very crude, and it would be useless for him to submit it to his Government in its existing form.

The abovementioned delegates, M. Révoil and myself, consequently met yesterday evening, and after a lengthy discussion we agreed upon the wording of an article in the following terms :—

"Les rapports et communications faits au Makhzen par l'Inspecteur au sujet de sa mission seront en même temps remis en copie au Doyen du Corps Diplomatique afin que le Corps Diplomatique soit mis à même de constater que la Police chérifienne fonctionne conformément aux décisions prises par la Conférence et de surveiller si elle garantit d'une manière efficace et conforme aux traités la sécurité des personnes et des biens des ressortissants ainsi que celle des transactions commerciales."

Mr. Henry White undertook to submit the above article to M. de Radowitz, as being the outcome of conversations which he had had with several other delegates, but as in no way being a proposal from M. Révoil himself.

This morning Mr. White was in a position to inform us that the German delegates approved of the article as being in conformity with their views; and M. Révoil will now telegraph to his Government in the hope that they will accept it, and thus solve a difficulty which at one moment appeared to be a little threatening.

I have, &c.
A. NICOLSON.

No. 385.

Sir M. de Bunsen to Sir Edward Grey.

F.O. 371/174.
(No. 57.) *Madrid, D. March 27, 1906.*
Sir, R. *April 2, 1906.*

I have had the honour to receive your Despatch No. 39 (9795) of the 21st instant,([1]) informing me that the Spanish Chargé d'Affaires had expressed to you the strong objections entertained by his Government to the proposal of the United States for the policing of the several ports of Morocco under French and Spanish instructors jointly.

It is evident that any proposed settlement conflicting with the Spanish ideal of securing for the coast line from Ceuta eastwards the same exclusive right of supervision as France has claimed and probably secured in respect of the portion of Morocco adjoining her Algerian frontier, was bound to be resisted by this Government.

An Article in to-day's "Liberal" urges that, if indeed the Conference should result in the establishment of an all-Spanish zone along the coast in question, no effort should be spared to develop the resources of Ceuta, Melilla, and Alhucemas, to connect Ceuta by a good road with Tetuan, and to turn Tetuan into a great centre for the spreading of Spanish civilization throughout Northern Morocco.

The American scheme, by introducing a French element into Tetuan, seemed likely to dispel this dream of Spanish expansion.

([1]) [*v. supra* p. 316, No. 372. The reference number in brackets is that of the original F.O. file.]

West of Ceuta, however, the aspect of the question presents itself in rather a different light to Spanish eyes. Though, no doubt, a dual Franco-Spanish police in each of the open ports from Tangier westwards might easily give rise to friction between the French and Spanish officers, Señor Moret, President of the Council, assured me, in the course of conversation, on the 23rd instant, that he would greatly prefer that France should be associated with Spain in the policing of Tangier, rather than that Spain should undertake this responsible task singlehanded. His Excellency told me that the Marquis del Muni, Spanish Ambassador at Paris, shared his views on this point, and his hopes that a modification of the American proposal, limiting its operation to Tangier and one other port, might be accepted by the Conference.

In reply to a question I told Señor Moret that you had not viewed the American proposal as a whole with favour, and that I thought there was a good deal to be said against it even in a modified form, though no doubt, if the French Government now accepted it with modifications, you would reconsider the matter.

His Excellency had been led by the Marquis del Muni to think that Monsieur Bourgeois might accept the scheme in its latest form.

I had the honour to report the upshot of Señor Moret's remarks in my Telegram No. 39 of the 23rd instant.[1]

I have, &c.
MAURICE DE BUNSEN.

[1] [Not reproduced.]

No. 386.

Sir A. Nicolson to Sir Edward Grey.

F.O. 371/174.
(No. 87.) Conference.
Sir,

Algeciras, D. *March* 28, 1906.
R. *April* 7, 1906.

Previous to the meeting of the Conference yesterday evening M. Révoil called upon me and asked if I would undertake to propose at the sitting that the Inspector General should be of Swiss and not of Dutch nationality. He said that it would be a little awkward were he to make the proposal, and he trusted that I would be willing to do so. As I was aware that the French Government attached importance to the Inspector being of Swiss in preference to Dutch nationality, and as I knew you would wish me to assist my French colleague whenever he applied for my aid I consented to meet his wishes, though I confess that the duty was not a pleasing one to me.

I saw M. de Testa, the Dutch delegate, before the Conference met, and I explained to him the proposal which I contemplated submitting to the Conference, expressing at the same time the hope that he would not misunderstand my motives, as I was simply actuated by the desire to suggest a nationality which had the least material or political interest in Morocco. M. de Testa received my observations in very good part, and stated that his Government did not particularly desire that a Dutch officer should be appointed, as they thought that the duties would be difficult and delicate, and would expose the Government of the Inspector to the assumption of a certain responsibility.

The first paragraph of Article VI of the Project relating to the police runs as follows :—

"Le fonctionnement de la police sera, pendant la même période de cinq années, l'objet d'une inspection générale, qui sera confiée par S[a] M[ajesté] Chérifienne à un officier supérieur de l'armée néerlandaise ou suisse dont le choix sera proposé à son agrément par le Gouvernement néerlandais ou fédéral suisse."

When the discussion of this article commenced I stated that I wished to submit a proposal to the Conference which caused me a little embarrassment as it touched upon a somewhat delicate question. I had, however, such entire confidence in the friendly feelings of my Dutch colleague that I felt sure he would not misunderstand my motives in making it. No one, I added, appreciated more highly than myself the excellent qualities of Dutch officers, and no one could have greater confidence than myself in their zeal and devotion to their duties. But in regard to the appointment of an Inspector General it was, in my humble opinion, desirable to seek him in a country which was the most completely detached from an interest in Moorish affairs. Switzerland was not represented in Morocco, and had no commercial or shipping interests in that country. Her citizens were under the protection not of one but of three Powers, viz., the United States, Germany, and France : and moreover she was not a signatory of the Madrid Convention. In regard to her relations with Morocco she therefore enjoyed an unique position, and it would be impossible to find a country whose disinterestedness was more evident and undeniable. I therefore thought that Switzerland was admirably placed to furnish an officer to fulfil the difficult and delicate duties of an Inspector General, and it was well known that she possessed many capable and intelligent officers. I, therefore, proposed that we should ask our respective Governments to be good enough, when the time arrived, to communicate with the Federal Government and beg them to select a superior and competent officer to fulfil the duties of Inspector-General of the Police in Morocco.

M. Révoil associated himself fully with the observations which I had made, and also expressed himself in flattering terms in regard to Dutch officers and the Dutch Government.

M. de Testa thanked both my French colleague and myself for our friendly expressions for which he was sincerely grateful, and observed that his Government had expressed no desire to select an officer and that he would communicate to them what had passed.

M. de Radowitz observed that it would be best to leave to the Sultan the choice of the nationality of the officer, whether he was to be of Swiss or of Dutch nationality : and I pointed out that this would place the Sultan in a very embarrassing position, as he had scarcely the means of forming a judgment in the matter. M. de Radowitz said that in any case he must refer to his Government before expressing a decided opinion on my proposal.

M. de Radowitz told me after the meeting that his Government wished that the Inspector should be of Dutch nationality : but I said that I hoped they would make no difficulty on this point at the present stage of the proceedings. Mr. Henry White observed to him that the general sense of the Conference was in favour of the Inspector being of Swiss nationality.

I do not anticipate that the question will give rise to any difficulty.

I have, &c.
A. NICOLSON.

No. 387.

Sir F. Bertie to Sir Edward Grey.

F.O. 371/174.
(No. 139.)
Sir,

Paris, D. *March* 31, 1906.
R. *April* 2, 1906.

I transmit to you herewith an article from the "Temps" of this evening,(¹) which sums up the situation in which a settlement at Algeciras will leave France and Germany.

The steps which led up to the acceptance of the conference are enumerated, the sudden change from the optimistic tone of Prince Bülow's speeches to the Emperor's appearance at Tangier; the obstinate refusal to treat with M. Delcassé between the April 13 and June 6, 1905; the determined opposition made to M. Rouvier's offers of negotiation without going into a Conference; the unjustifiable

(¹) [Not reproduced.]

proceedings of Count Tattenbach at Fez, and, finally, the perpetual disputes and aggressive "bluff" on the part of the German Delegates at Algeciras, who for two months kept declaring a solution inadmissible which in the third month they accepted. These proceedings, the article declares, have made a great impression on French opinion. "Quand on sort d'une maladie d'un an, la convalescence ne peut être immédiate. La confiance que la France avait marquée à l'Allemagne au mois de Juin 1905, a été mise à une rude épreuve. Il faut lui laisser le temps de renaître et lui en fournir les motifs."

At the same time the article advocates that the sponge should be passed over the hostility which showed itself in the course of the diplomatic struggle which has just ended; the task of French Diplomacy is to restore to Franco-German relations that normal and correct character the absence of which during the last year has been so marked.

The article concludes by quoting some remarks of Prince Bülow made four years ago :—

"L'Europe est une maison où nous sommes les uns et les autres installés, suivant l'heure et le lieu, plus ou moins commodément. Mais notre intérêt commun est d'y affermir notre établissement est [sic] de consolider l'édifice qui nous offre à tous un abri."

This should be the object the article says of French and German statesmen in the period following upon the close of the Algeciras Conference.

The articles in the "Temps" on the Moroccan question are known to reflect the views held at the Quai d'Orsay, and the feeling of relief at the prospect of an arrangement at Algeciras by which neither party can be said to be either "vainqueur ou vaincu," and by which an irritating question loses its acute phase has been generally noticeable in the press utterances of the past few days.

I have, &c.
FRANCIS BERTIE.

No. 388.

Sir A. Nicolson to Sir Edward Grey.

F.O. 371/174.
Tel. (No. 134.)

Algeciras, April 1, 1906.
D. 5·50 P.M.
R. 10 P.M.

We terminated all questions at yesterday's sitting of Conference, and this week will be devoted to drawing up Articles of Convention, which we hope to sign on Saturday.

I am sending by post copies of Regulations regarding public works, formulas of Bank censors, and control of customs, which I agreed to, as there was not time to obtain your sanction. Two last questions were originated by me, and I hope you will approve. I will mention at next sitting question of slavery, and I will support United States' Delegate in question of Jews.

Would you like me to telegraph text of principal Articles of Convention as they are drawn up, or would you trust to me to see they are satisfactory?

Matters are being hastily pushed on in order to sign before Holy Week. I would have preferred more time, but I think I am alone in this desire, and it may be prudent to conclude matter as soon as possible.

No. 389.

Sir Edward Grey to Sir A. Nicolson.

F.O. 371/174.
Tel. (No. 70.)   *Foreign Office, April 2, 1906.*
   Your telegram No. 134.
   I share your regret at the haste with which the final work of drafting and revision is apparently being proceeded with, and earnestly hope that the wish to save a few days extra labour will not lead to the adoption of stipulations insufficiently considered. I rely on your counteracting any such tendency as far as you properly can.
   If you are satisfied that convention clearly safeguards British interests, more particularly as regards those questions of commercial importance which have formed the subject of my special instructions, I leave the matter with confidence in your hands.
   You need not telegraph the text of the Treaty.

No. 390.

Sir Edward Grey to Sir A. Nicolson.

F.O. 371/174.   *Foreign Office, April 2, 1906.*
Tel. (No. 71.)   D. 9 P.M.
   On behalf of H[is] M[ajesty's] Government I congratulate you on the approaching conclusion of the Conference. We feel it is greatly owing to the ability and tact with which you have handled delicate questions, that an agreement has been reached and we highly appreciate the wise and consistent way, in which you have fulfilled our engagements.

No. 391.

Sir Edward Grey to Sir F. Bertie.

F.O. 371/174.
(No. 195.)
Sir,   *Foreign Office, April 2, 1906.*
   M. Cambon took occasion to-day to thank me very cordially for the support which we had given France during the Conference, and he expressed his warm appreciation of the way in which Sir Arthur Nicolson had given it.
   I replied that it had been a pleasure to us to be able to give this support to France, and that I was delighted to think that the proceedings of the Conference had resulted in strengthening the Entente.

                                                          I am, &c.
                                                          EDWARD GREY.

No. 392.

Sir A. Nicolson to Sir Edward Grey.

                                                   Algeciras, April 3, 1906.
F.O. 371/174.   D. 11·15 A.M.
Tel. (No. 138)   R. 2·45 P.M.
   We had the last sitting of the Conference yesterday with the exception of the final one for signing general act, which will probably take place on Saturday.

The Conference wishes the Italian Minister as doyen of the Diplomatic Body to proceed to Fez to procure in the name of the Powers the adhesion of the Sultan to the general act. We think that this would be the best course.

I submitted suggestions that the Conference should express hope that slavery would be gradually abolished and that public sale of slaves should be prohibited and also that the measures taken for the improvement of prisons should be continued. I supported United States Delegate as to Sultan's taking the good treatment of Jews under his care. The Conference has now finished its labours.

No. 393.

Sir A. Nicolson to Sir Edward Grey.

F.O. 371/90.
Tel. (No. 144.) *En Clair.*

Algeciras, *April* 3, 1906.
D. 7·20 P.M.
R. 10·30 P.M.

Your telegram No. 72.([1])

I submitted a resolution to the Conference yesterday that the Delegates should communicate to the Sultan an expression of their earnest hope that His Shereefian Majesty would take into consideration the question of slavery in his Empire and would adopt such measures as he might deem suitable, with a view to limiting, and gradually abolishing the system of slavery, and especially with a view to prohibiting the public sale of slaves in the towns of his Empire.

With the exception of the Moorish Delegates, who stated that the question was not included in the programme, all the Delegates cordially adopted my motion, and it was resolved to make the suggested communication to the Sultan.

([1]) [Not reproduced.]

No. 394.

Sir A. Nicolson to Sir Edward Grey.

F.O. 371/91.
Tel. (No. 145.)

Algeciras, *April* 3, 1906.
D. 7·20 P.M.
R. 10 P.M.

I omitted to mention that at yesterday's sitting the President of the Conference, without specifically asking us to express an opinion, stated that the Spanish Government desired to see a railway constructed from the north to the south of Morocco and in connection with the Europe–Africa system, and which should shorten the route to the South American States. I am not quite clear as to the route, but the Belgian Delegate was the only one who expressed his approval of this comprehensive project, the rest maintaining silence.

III.—THE AFTERMATH.

No. 395.

Sir F. Bertie to Sir Edward Grey.

F.O. 371/174.
(No. 145.)
Sir,

Paris, D. *April* 4, 1906.
R. *April* 5, 1906.

I saw the Minister for Foreign Affairs today and he told me that he had instructed the French Ambassador, and he requested me to convey to you the grateful thanks of himself and the French Government for the cordial and valuable support and cooperation rendered to them by His Majesty's Government during the discussions by the Algeciras Conference of the questions relating to Morocco which had been referred to it.

M. Bourgeois said that, considering the position in which the Morocco question stood when the Conference assembled he thought that the results arrived at were as satisfactory as could well be expected.

I have, &c.
FRANCIS BERTIE.

No. 396.

Sir Edward Grey to Sir F. Bertie.

F.O. 371/174.
(No. 198.)
Sir, *Foreign Office, April 4, 1906.*

The French Ambassador came this afternoon to say that he had been instructed by Monsieur Bourgeois to make a communication, which he read to me, thanking us very cordially for the support which we had given to France during the Conference, especially the help which Sir Arthur Nicolson had given, and expressing great appreciation for the co-operation which had resulted from the Entente.

I shall be glad if you will take an opportunity of thanking Monsieur Bourgeois for this communication, saying how much I appreciate the terms in which it was made; that it has been very satisfactory to us that we worked so cordially together; and that we are very glad to think that co-operation has had the result of strengthening still further the good relations between the two Countries.

I am, &c.
EDWARD GREY.

MINUTE BY KING EDWARD.

Approved.—E.R.

No. 397.

Sir M. de Bunsen to Sir Edward Grey.

F.O. 371/174.
(No. 63.) Confidential. *Madrid, D. April 4, 1906.*
Sir, R. *April 7, 1906.*

General satisfaction is expressed at Madrid at the manner in which Spain has emerged from the Algeciras Conference. The Press claims for her a diplomatic success, one of the leading papers going so far as to say that the position which she has secured in the North of Morocco should afford a new opening for her energies, replacing to a considerable extent her lost Colonies.

Señor de Ojeda, Acting Minister for Foreign Affairs, takes rather a less complacent view of the situation. Though he thinks that some increase has been gained in Spanish prestige, owing to the intervention of England, which has induced France to agree to a fair partition of influence with Spain, he does not seem to look forward to any marked development of the Spanish possessions in Morocco, or to any great improvement in the general situation in that country. The Conference, he considers, has rendered a great service by securing, at least for the present, the peace of Europe. But Germany has asserted a right of intervention in Morocco, the exercise of which is not unlikely to prove some day intolerable to France. If a conflict is to be avoided, there must be no weakening of the understanding between France and England.

This, Señor de Ojeda informed me a few days ago, was his general view of the results of the Conference. Touching on the joint policing of Casablanca and Tangier by French and Spanish officers, as arranged by the Conference, he said that he did not share the President of the Council's approval of this plan, which seemed to him likely to cause frequent friction between the officers of the two countries. He repeated what he has said to me before as to the extreme dislike entertained by the Spanish element in Morocco for the French element, and the difficulty of harmonious cooperation between them.

In interviews with representatives of the Press Señor Moret has declared his complete satisfaction with the work accomplished at Algeciras. In conversation with myself, he does not conceal that, in his view, Germany has secured a good share of the objects she was contending for, and he thinks that some day she will probably endeavour to tempt France into compliance with German schemes elsewhere by offering to leave her alone in Morocco.

The French Ambassador informs me that Señor Moret is in agreement with him as to the advisability of reasserting the existing Agreements between France, England, and Spain concerning Morocco by some public announcement.

I have, &c.
M. DE BUNSEN.

No. 398.([1])

Sir F. Lascelles to Sir Edward Grey.

F.O. 371/77.
(No. 100.) Confidential.
Sir,

Berlin, D. *April* 5, 1906.
R. *April* 9, 1906.

Last night on my return to Berlin from Neu Strelitz I received a private Note from Herr von Holstein, stating that he had sent in his resignation on the previous

([1]) [The following despatch from Sir F. Lascelles of October 23, 1907, supplements the above :

Sir F. Lascelles to Sir Edward Grey.

F.O. Germany 371/263.
(No. 471.) Confidential.
Sir,

Berlin, D. *October* 23, 1907.
R. *October* 28, 1907.

The name of the "Zukunft" and of its editor Herr Maximilian Harden figured very prominently in connection with the disclosures relating to the dismissal from Court of the Eulenburg Clique and Herr Harden has again been so fortunate as to secure another advertisement for his magazine by means of a letter addressed to him by Herr von Holstein, who till lately was so prominent a figure at the Foreign Office.

In an article dealing with the recent changes in the Government and diplomatic service, Herr Harden defended Herr von Holstein from the charges which had been brought against him in connection with German policy in Morocco. Herr von Holstein therefore took the opportunity in thanking Herr Harden for his defence to complain that the Foreign Office had done nothing on his behalf, and that he was therefore compelled to himself correct the series of misstatements concerning his action which had appeared in the press and elsewhere. He begins by denying his statement that his retirement was caused by a difference of opinion with Herr von Tschirschky as to German policy in Morocco, and points out that neither the Secretary of State for Foreign Affairs nor any other Foreign Office official can decide upon important questions of foreign policy without the concurrence of the Chancellor. Prince Bülow, says Herr von Holstein, maintained personal control during the whole course of the Morocco negotiations. Up to the end of February 1906 when Herr von Holstein's connection with Morocco came to an end, all important instructions issued through him were not only signed by Prince Bülow, but had also been discussed in detail with him. Herr von Holstein was in the habit of calling upon the Chancellor, when he was in Berlin, every week, and the time occupied in these discussions was as a rule between one and two hours. He describes these interviews in these words, "It need scarcely be said that the Imperial Chancellor, as a skilful debater in addition to being my superior, always asserted his view, fully, but with the utmost courtesy, and on every occasion I brought away with me from these interviews the conviction that I agreed with the Chancellor's projects." The last interview that took place in which the two Statesmen found themselves in agreement was on February 26 night, and that before leaving the room which he had occupied for 20 years he would like to have a conversation with me, if it suited my convenience to call upon him between 1 and 2 o'clock on the following day.

I went at the appointed time and found Herr von Holstein in a state of great agitation, as he had just heard of the seizure by which Prince Bülow had been attacked in the Reichstag.

He said that he had asked me to call upon him in order to speak to me about his resignation which was now definitive. On two previous occasions he had offered his resignation, on account of his disapproval of the manner in which the business of the Press Bureau was conducted, but was induced to withdraw it at the urgent request of Prince Bülow, who had assured him of his support. I had no doubt seen the recent attacks on him in the press, one of which had been directly inspired by a high Official in the diplomatic service. This alone would not have induced him to resign, but he had received information which he could not doubt that the Emperor had been assured that the British Government regarded him as the one obstacle to the establishment of friendly relations between England and Germany.

I said that he astonished me very greatly. I had always understood that he desired a friendly understanding between our two countries, although we might have had considerable differences of opinion on certain points and perhaps on the methods of bringing it about, but I never doubted the sincerity of his wish for the maintenance of Peace between our two countries.

---

or 27 and after the change of front which took place on March 12 Herr von Holstein ceased to take any part in the affairs of Morocco. "These being the facts of the case," says he, "I am justified in describing the statement that at any stage of the Morocco question whatsoever I adopted measures other than those approved by the Chancellor or followed an aim other than the one laid down by him as a pure invention and a total falsehood."

Turning then to the suggestion that has been put forward that Herr von Tschirschky was not in agreement with the official policy in Morocco, he states that he has in his possession a private letter from Herr von Tschirschky, written when that gentleman was Prussian Minister to Hamburg at the time of the resignation of M. Delcassé, in which he states that he entirely approves of the line of policy pursued by Germany in the Morocco question. Herr von Holstein's letter concludes by denying the statement that his retirement was not serious. He addressed a letter to Prince Bülow on April 2, 1906 a duplicate of which was sent to the Secretary of State for Foreign Affairs on April 3. In his letter to the Chancellor, he said that his resignation " would be better for his own dignity and for Prince Bülow's peace."

Such is the explanation which Herr von Holstein thinks proper to make public regarding the severance of his connection with the Foreign Office last year. There is very wide divergence of opinion as to the reasons why this letter should have been published. Does it mean that Herr von Holstein wishes to attack Prince Bülow or is it a defence of Prince Bülow?

During last summer I was informed on authority which admitted of no doubt that Herr von Holstein and Prince Bülow were on the best of terms possible, and were in the habit of meeting frequently at the Chancellor's house; it was also reported that Herr von Holstein was on the worst possible terms with the Foreign Office officials, and the doors of the Ministry for Foreign Affairs were always closed to him—it is indeed reported that Herr von Holstein complained that in the absence of Prince Bülow he was entirely without information as to what was passing in the Foreign Office. If then the relations between Prince Bülow and Herr von Holstein were so friendly as lately as this summer, and if the letter in the " Zukunft " is intended to embarrass the Chancellor, the obvious inference is that a serious quarrel has taken place between them. If such a quarrel has taken place it is, to say the least of it, peculiar that no hint thereof should have transpired. Another surmise is that Herr von Holstein's letter is directed against the Emperor. It is known that the latter was largely instrumental in obtaining Herr von Holstein's resignation. Herr von Holstein states that he always came away from his interviews with the Chancellor in agreement with Prince Bülow's intentions, and it was not till the change of policy which commenced on March 12 that he ceased to agree with the Government. Does it mean that Herr von Holstein retired from the direction of German policy in Morocco on account of the line which the Emperor compelled the Chancellor to adopt? Lastly there is the conjecture that the letter was merely written in order to give Prince Bülow a fresh chance of asserting his authority and of answering Herr von Holstein's letter by a speech explaining his conduct of Foreign Affairs past and present in the Reichstag.

I have, &c.
FRANK C. LASCELLES.]

Herr von Holstein said that he was inclined to believe that the information given to the Emperor had been invented, but His Majesty seemed to believe it, and would probably have dismissed him before long. There could be no doubt that the Emperor desired a friendly understanding with England. So far his attempts to bring one about had not been successful, and he required a scape-goat which he had now found.

I said I understood that in the position which Herr von Holstein held, it was only natural that he should have made some enemies, who were jealous of the influence he possessed. To this he replied that his influence had been very greatly exaggerated. It was true that he was consulted on all important matters of foreign policy, but he was in the position of a man whose advice was sometimes taken, sometimes rejected, and sometimes partly taken. His influence therefore could not be considered as very great, but such as it was, it had no doubt created jealousies which had been employed with great effect against him. He was now 69 years old. His eyesight was failing. He had done his work, at least, his work was now finished, and in any case it could not have continued much longer, but it was hard that he should be misrepresented as an obstacle to a friendly understanding with England, when the cardinal point of his policy had been that a war between the two countries would be the greatest calamity which could happen to either. It would be a satisfaction to him, in his retirement, if he could think that his Sovereign should some day know that he had been misrepresented, and he would be gratified, if the opportunity should arise, that I should tell His Majesty that in my opinion he ought not to be considered as an enemy of England.

I have, &c.
FRANK C. LASCELLES.

MINUTES.

Herr von Holstein has not, I think, been a friend of this country. That is of course quite a different thing from saying that he desired to have a war against us. No power wants a war. The great object is to get what is desired, without a war. Germany in particular is not likely to bring about a war with England for some time, or in fact unless and until she feels confident, that is, humanly speaking, certain, she can beat us decisively. The time for that is not yet, as Herr von Holstein and all responsible Germans now realize. There was however a time not long ago, when the opinion prevailed in Germany that England was played out and done for, not likely to hold her own in the world. That opinion was, I believe, to some extent, shared by Bismarck and by his immediate disciples, of whom Herr von Holstein was one of the most faithful. This opinion was largely based on the success with which Bismarck "squeezed" England in the interest of German policy. When the process of squeezing at last became less prolific of results and it was found that England still had some life in her, German opinion about England was as it were "désorientée." There was a succession of disillusionments. It had not been expected that we should emerge unscathed out of the South African war; the first and the second treaties of alliance with Japan were both great surprises to the German Foreign Office; and lastly the conclusion of the understanding with France quite upset their calcuations and falsified their confident expectations. These had been nourished, not the least, by Herr von Holstein, and it is not unjust he should now pay the penalty for having persistently failed to appreciate the position which England really occupies in the world—(so long as she is strong).

There is some grim humour in the fact—if it is a fact—that Herr von Holstein's fall is brought about by his own Press Bureau, that pet institution of Bismarckian policy.

Meanwhile his resignation does not appear as yet to have been accepted. There is many a slip . . . . .([1])

E. A. C.

April 9.

Herr v. Holstein is modest with regard to the influence he exercised but members of the German Embassy here have always assured me that no matter who was foreign minister at Berlin, the policy was invariably his.

E. B.
E. G.

([1]) [Thus in original.]

No. 399.

Sir E. Goschen to Sir Edward Grey.

F.O. 371/174.
(No. 33.) Confidential.   *Vienna,* D. *April* 6, 1906.
Sir,   R. *April* 9, 1906.

I have the honour to report that the following communiqué has been published in the Vienna press with regard to the part played by Count Welsersheimb, the Austro-Hungarian Delegate, at the Conference at Algeciras.

"By command of the Emperor, the Minister for Foreign Affairs, Count Goluchowski, has conveyed to the first Delegate of Austria-Hungary at the Algeciras Conference, His Excellency Count Welsersheimb, the great satisfaction and recognition of His Majesty the Emperor and King at the tactful and sagacious manner in which he brought the mediation to a successful issue, and at the same time has expressed His Majesty's thanks for the untiring exertions of His Excellency to which the success finally attained is due."

Count Goluchowski is naturally delighted at the fact that the Austro-Hungarian proposals have been recognised on all sides as having formed the basis of the understanding between France and Germany with regard to the Moroccan Police and State Pank Questions.

At his last diplomatic reception he told me that he was greatly pleased that Austria-Hungary had been able successfully to play the part so clearly marked out for her by her alliance with Germany and her friendly relations with France, and he congratulated himself that, aided by the spirit of mutual forbearance which had been shown by the Representatives at the Conference of these two Powers, he and his colleagues had been the means of clearing the ground for a satisfactory solution of the most delicate questions before the Conference.

His Excellency repudiated the suggestion put forward in many quarters that the Austro-Hungarian proposals were of German origin. The German Government had certainly been consulted before the proposals had been submitted to the Conference, but that had been only natural as it would have been useless to bring them forward without some knowledge as to how far they would prove acceptable as a basis of negotiation.

The numerous concessions which Germany had been called upon to make were surely proof enough that she had had no hand in framing the proposals.

There is indeed every justification for Count Goluchowski's elation, for, setting aside the fact that the understanding reached at the Conference removes a great cause of anxiety, it is quite clear that the general chorus of approbation of the action of Austria-Hungary which has reached the Press from French and German sources, has been most useful to the Monarchy in general and the Minister for Foreign Affairs in particular. It has given a very necessary and timely fillip to Austrian prestige, it has strengthened Count Goluchowski's position very considerably, and I do not think it is too much to say that the feeling of satisfaction felt by the country with regard to the prominent part played by its Government at a momentous European crisis will go far towards facilitating the settlement of the internal troubles which are at present causing so much uneasiness throughout the Empire.

I have, &c.
W. E. GOSCHEN.

No. 400.

Sir E. Goschen to Sir Edward Grey.

F.O. 371/175.
(No. 43.)   *Vienna,* D. *April* 14, 1906.
Sir,   R. *April* 17, 1906.

I have the honour to report that the Emperor of Germany [*sic*] has addressed a telegram to Count Goluchowski, of which the following is a translation :—

" At this moment when, with the consent of your August Sovereign, I am sending to Count Welsersheimb the Grand Cross of my Order of the Red Eagle in recognition of his successful efforts at Algeciras, I feel compelled to offer to you from the bottom of my heart my sincere thanks for the unswerving support you gave to my Representative at the Conference, an act indeed worthy of a true ally. As our second in this encounter you rendered the most brilliant service and in similar circumstances you can always count on a similar service from me."

This morning the semi-official " Fremden Blatt " published a leading article (of which I enclose a translation by Mr. Seymour)(¹) expressing the pleasure which must be felt throughout the Empire at the warm and generous language in which the Emperor of Germany has recorded his gratitude for the action of Austria-Hungary at the Conference, and hailing with delight this fresh proof of the firmness of the Alliance between the two countries.

The unofficial Press, however, and public opinion, as far as it can be now judged, does not appear to be carried away with enthusiasm for the message, and, from what I hear, there appears to be in many quarters a feeling that the telegram might with advantage have been worded differently and less emphasis placed on the idea that Austria-Hungary acted solely in Germany's interests.

Public opinion here has been happy in the idea that the Austro-Hungarian Government were generally recognized as having taken the initiative in finding a solution of the delicate questions before the Conference satisfactory to and in the interests of both France and Germany. Now there is an uneasy feeling that by the Emperor's telegram their Government has been held up to the world as blind followers of their powerful ally.

Amongst the journals which have written in this strain the " Zeit," a rather independent daily paper, takes the most depressing view of the telegram.

It says, in the course of a long article :

" Turn this telegram which way you will it does not please us. It does not please Austrian public opinion, and we can hardly think that it is quite agreeable even to its recipient.

" Even if we had no particularly burning interests of our own to represent at the Morocco Conference, there was all the less reason for us to look after those of another nation before the eyes of the whole world. And this—even if it had so far remained unknown—is officially proved to have been the case by this sensational telegram. What though, as in the present case, this other State was our ally? The Triple Alliance was not engaged in the Conference at Algeciras, or else Monsieur Guicciardini, who manages the Foreign Affairs of Italy, would have sent the same instructions to the Italian Representative as Count Goluchowski sent to Count Welsersheimb who has now been decorated with the Cross of the Red Eagle. Italy, however, took her own line without regard to Germany or the Triple Alliance, just as three years ago, she found the Triple Alliance no obstacle to the establishment of good relations with France. Bülow then coined the word ' Extra-tour,' which he found to be quite in keeping with the treaty duties of

(¹) [Not reproduced.]

Italy. We had therefore no more a duty to fulfil with regard to the Alliance than had Italy.''(¹)

I have, &c.
W. E. GOSCHEN.

(¹) [*Cf.* H. Wickham Steed : *Through Thirty Years* (1924), **I**, pp. 234–5.]

No. 401.

Mr. Lowther to Sir Edward Grey.

F.O. 371/175.
(No. 67.) Confidential.
Sir,

Tangier, D. *April* 17, 1906.
R. *April* 28, 1906.

Now that the Conference at Algeciras has terminated its labours it may not be without interest to examine the first impressions produced on the Moorish Government and people by the decisions arrived at, though these impressions are necessarily but of a very general nature. There can be but little doubt that the manner of procedure adopted at the Conference came as a surprise to the Moorish Government. They regarded the Conference as a sort of tribunal before which France, at their instance, was to be arraigned, Germany acting as the prosecuting counsel. In its note of invitation and subsequently the Moorish Government suggested that His Shereefian Majesty wished to introduce certain reforms and only invited the advice of the Powers as to the manner of carrying these out. That quite a different procedure was adopted no doubt caused a painful impression. They now complain that nothing has been accomplished which in any way improves the position of His Majesty and that the interests of foreign commerce alone have been taken into consideration and that their control over the expenditure has been interfered with. They maintain that, far from strengthening the Sultan's authority and independence, the Conference has alienated from His Majesty the port districts from which His Majesty latterly received the most regular revenues, and that these have practically been handed over to the Foreign Ministers at Tangier. The Pretender has shaken the authority of His Majesty in a large number of provinces. Many of the other provinces in the South which used to be obedient and tax paying have now fallen into a mutinous and non tax paying condition, and, without any army, or any money to maintain an army, the Makhzen cannot again reduce these provinces to obedience. The ports and their immediate districts alone remain to the Sultan as a financial asset and now His Majesty finds the port receipts taken up almost wholly for interest on loans and for port improvements, and by the police scheme the rule over the ports is in a great measure to pass from the Sultan to the Ministers at Tangier. The prospect is presented to the Makhzen of certain improvements in the ports which, however useful to foreign traders, does [*sic*] not open the vista of any serious or general benefit to the country and its Sovereign. Again—if these are only the first steps—there arises the prospect of province after province behind the ports lapsing as time goes on permanently and irretrievably from the Sultan to the Powers.

Such is the general impression left on the Moorish mind by the skeleton programme drawn up by the Representatives of the Powers at Algeciras, nor can that mind see that when the regulations for carrying out that programme have been framed by the Ministers here their position will in any way be improved.

They fully realize that they were deceived by the promises made to them by Count Tattenbach at Fez, and that the support given them by Germany at the Conference fell far short of what they were led to anticipate last summer.

With regard to the acceptance by the Sultan of the Acte Général of the Conference the Viziers appear to be as usual divided. The Grand Vizier, the Minister for Foreign Affairs and the Minister of War have expressed themselves in favour of accepting, while the less serious but more grasping Viziers urge opposition. The

Makhzen still appears to imagine that M. Malmusi, the Italian Minister, is going to Fez to further argue the matter treated of, but it will no doubt be gradually borne in upon His Majesty that M. Malmusi's Mission is of a very different nature, and there can be little doubt that His Majesty will accept the inevitable, and cause the Acte Général to be signed, although there is already some inclination on the part of His Majesty and his advisers, as there was last summer, to say that He cannot adhere to decisions of which his people do not approve, and that the Notables, who are still assembled at Fez, must first be consulted. It is however most unlikely that they will be taken into account, and it is obvious that no "public opinion" on the subject exists, the general public in Morocco never having heard of the Conference, and those who have are entirely unable to appreciate the nature of the subjects under discussion.

I have, &c.
GERARD LOWTHER.

No. 402.

Mr. Lowther to Sir Edward Grey.

F.O. 371/175.
(No. 74.)   Confidential.   *Tangier*, D. *April* 22, 1906.
Sir,   R. *April* 28, 1906.

The substance of a conversation which took place a few days ago between the Moorish Minister for Foreign Affairs and the French Vice Consul at Fez who has just reached there from Algeciras has been communicated to me in a confidential manner. Ben Sliman began by stating that he regarded the outlook after the decisions of the Conference as simply hopeless. If the Makhzen assented to the Conference's decisions there was an end to the Moorish Government, as a Government. The ports were thereby practically handed over for ever to the Powers. These were of importance to Europeans and of a certain financial value to the Sultan although they were but a small part of the country and their populations a mere handful of those of the Sultan's subjects, who, in normal times, had acknowledged His Majesty's rule, and paid taxes. But the decisions of the Conference Ben Sliman considered, in practice if not in theory, left the Sultan no means or hopes of doing anything to reestablish order and restore prosperity to the vast mass of his people, to whose needs at large the proposed reforms were totally inadequate and he was deeply disappointed with them.

His Excellency would therefore infinitely have preferred the reforms to have been so framed that the Powers would have exercised some kind of direction, assistance and advice at the Court itself, the influence of which would have been, in course of time, felt throughout the country to the great advantage of all concerned. As it was, the Makhzen seemed to be left in as impotent and ridiculous a position as ever in the eyes of its subjects. Ben Sliman seemed to have no very clear idea, however, as yet, about what answer the Court would make to the Conference's decisions, but admitted that the Tazzi and Ben Aish groups would urge the Sultan with all the weight of their influence to withhold his consent to the reforms in question and in any case to negotiate further over them; and who could tell whose views would prevail with the Sultan?

The above expression of opinion coincides in a great measure with the general view that I have reported in my despatch No. 67 of the 17th instant([1]) as being those held by the Makhzen.

At this distance I fear that it is difficult to form a very accurate opinion as to how far Ben Sliman was expressing his honest convictions or how far he was speaking "Pour la galerie." I nevertheless feel convinced that however great may be the disappointment of Ben Sliman at the result of the Conference, he will, in spite of the

---

([1]) [See preceding document.]

timidity that characterises him where the Sultan is concerned, advise His Majesty to accept the inevitable and recommend him to adhere to the Acte Général.

I have, &c

GERARD LOWTHER.

No. 403.

Sir Edward Grey to Mr. Lowther.

F.O. 371/91.
(No. 55.)
Sir, *Foreign Office, May* 17, 1906.

I transmit to you herewith a copy of a despatch received from the Delegate of His Majesty's Government at the Conference of Algeciras,* from which you will observe that that assembly decided to refer to the Diplomatic Body at Tangier the question of regulating the liquor traffic in Morocco.

His Majesty's Government attach great importance to this matter. They have had considerable experience in the enforcement of measures aimed at the restriction of the consumption of spirituous liquors in those of their African territories which fall within the liquor zone established by the Brussels Act of 1890. I inclose, for your information, a copy of Article XCI of that Act,† the provisions of which apply to regions where, owing to religious beliefs and other reasons, the native population does not habitually consume distilled liquors. Such is, no doubt, the case in Morocco, whose population profess the Mahometan religion. His Majesty's Government are therefore of opinion that the provisions of Article XCI could, with advantage, be applied in Morocco. The main features of the system contemplated therein are (1) the prohibition of the local manufacture of spirituous liquors; (2) the prohibition of the sale of such liquors to natives, and (3) the laying down of the conditions under which alone limited quantities may be imported for the exclusive use of the non-native population.

There should, I think, be no difficulty in arriving at an understanding with the Moorish Government on the one hand and the Treaty Powers on the other, for the enactment of legislation on the above basis, and the more stringent supervision of an improved customs service stipulated for by the Algeciras Act will no doubt facilitate its enforcement. It may be of advantage, in discussing the matter with your foreign colleagues, to have before you the text of Regulations enacted for the same purpose, and under similar conditions in British territories. I accordingly transmit a copy of "The East Africa Liquor Ordinance, 1902,"‡ which may afford you useful guidance in the matter. I should, however, observe that sections 9–12 of that ordinance dealing with local distillation were subsequently repealed as not being in strict accordance with the Brussels Act, and that the provisions of an amending ordinance of 1903 (of which a copy is also inclosed)§ were substituted for them.

I am, &c.

EDWARD GREY.

* Sir A. Nicolson, No. 94, March 30, 1906 [not reproduced].
† Article XCI of Brussels Convention, 1890 [not reproduced, *v. B.F.S.P.*, Vol. 82, p. 76].
‡ East Africa Protectorate Ordinance, No. 27, 1902 [not reproduced].
§ East Africa Protectorate Ordinance, No. 12, 1903 [not reproduced].

[*ED. NOTE.*—The above notes, with the exception of words in square brackets, are entered on the copy of this document in the *Confidential Print.*]

No. 404.

F.O. 371/78. *Sir F. Lascelles to Sir Edward Grey.*

(No. 141.) Confidential.   *Berlin,* D. *May* 17, 1906.

Sir,   R. *May* 21, 1906.

On the evening of the 13th instant, I received a note informing me that Prince Bülow would be glad to see me if I called upon him on the following day. His Serene Highness has apparently entirely recovered from his recent illness and beyond a little want of colour in his cheeks, shows no traces of the severe attack from which he has suffered. There was certainly no sign of weakness either in his voice or movements during an interview which lasted for almost an hour.

He said that he had been greatly touched by the kind sympathy which had been expressed during his illness. The King had had the extreme kindness to telegraph to Princess Bülow, which was an attention which he would never forget, and he begged me to convey to you the expression of his warmest thanks for the sympathy you had expressed on behalf of His Majesty's Government and he also begged that his feeling of gratitude might be conveyed to Lord Fitzmaurice for the considerate mention of him in his Lordship's speech in the House of Lords.

Prince Bülow alluded to the Algeciras Conference, and said that both Herr von Radowitz and Count Tattenbach had spoken in terms of praise of the tact and courtesy with which Sir Arthur Nicolson had performed his duties. He thoroughly understood that His Majesty's Government could not do otherwise than give their cordial support to France at the Conference, and your conversations with Count Metternich, and the language you had instructed me to hold here, had been such as to leave no doubt in his mind on this point, and it was therefore all the more satisfactory to him to tell me that the manner in which Sir Arthur Nicolson had performed his task, had secured for him the personal appreciation of his German colleagues. He could say much the same of his old friend M. Visconti Venosta, who in supporting the French demands avoided arousing the susceptibilities of his German colleagues. In fact, he thought he might say that the successful result of the Conference was largely due to the friendly tact of these two gentlemen, which had had the effect of moderating the excessive demands of France, which had they been insisted on would have led to a break-up of the Conference.

His Serene Highness then referred to the difference which had arisen between His Majesty's Government and the Sultan with regard to the Turco-Egyptian frontier. He had never doubted that the question would be amicably settled, and the advice which he had offered to the Sultan both through the Turkish Ambassador here and the German Ambassador at Constantinople was that His Majesty should consent to the English demands, as certainly he would not obtain the support of any other Power in resisting them. There was, therefore, no ground for the suspicion which apparently had existed in England that Germany had encouraged the Sultan to resist. He had instructed Count Metternich to assure you that this was not the case.

I replied that you had done me the honour to send me an account of your conversation with Count Metternich in which you had explained that you had not supposed that Germany had encouraged the Sultan in this particular instance, but that you had thought it possible that, in view of the strong support which Germany had on other occasions afforded the Sultan, as, for instance, in the Macedonian question, His Majesty may have been led to believe that he might presume too far. This question fortunately had now been settled, and as far as I was aware there was no other question pending which was likely to lead to a difference of opinion between our two countries.

Prince Bülow said that this was so, and he was looking forward to a peaceful summer. . . . .([1])

I have, &c.

FRANK LASCELLES.

([1]) [The remainder of the report of this conversation is omitted as it deals with other subjects].

MINUTES.

Prince Bülow's statements must be read with some caution.

I understand the relations between Marquis Visconti-Venosta and the German delegates were not so cordial as is now made out.

As regards Sir A. Nicolson I have heard from an absolutely reliable source that the German Foreign Office bitterly complained of his persistent endeavours to egg on the French to oppose German proposals and views on every possible occasion.

If the opposition of the German government to participation in the Russian loan had really been based on purely economic grounds it is fairly certain that Messrs. Mendelssohn would not have been allowed to carry on the negotiations with M. de Witte until, at the 11th hour, and to the great surprise of all the Berlin bankers, the imperial prohibition was issued.

The fact, however, that Prince Bülow now tries to make out how pleased he is with us, may be taken as evidence of Germany's desire to stand well with us. The policy of showing a firm front and asserting British rights has once again been successful in inducing other countries to treat us properly.

E. A. C.

May 21.

We must accept P[rin]ce Bülow's statements as an earnest of good will. I understand that the Emperor has lately expressed himself in the most friendly way about England.

E. B.

P[rin]ce Bülow's tribute to Sir A. Nicolson is satisfactory.

C. H.
E. G.

MINUTE BY KING EDWARD.

A very interesting and satisfactory conversation between Prince Bülow and Sir F. Lascelles.

E.R.

No. 405.

Memorandum communicated by M. Geoffray, August 31, 1906.([1])

F.O. 371/175.

ARTICLE III.	*Observations.*
Le Sultan voudrait qu'on lui accordât le droit de substituer ou de transférer les instructeurs d'un port à un autre. Son interprétation de l'article est que l'Espagne et la France n'auront pas d'autorité supérieure à celle des autres Puissances.	En acceptant que le Sultan puisse déplacer les instructeurs on annihilerait leur action et on créerait des conflits incessants avec le Maghzen. Même en ce qui concerne les missions militaires de Fez, qui sont pourtant à son entière disposition et sur lesquelles il exerce, sans réglementation précise, une action directe, le Sultan n'a jamais émis pareille prétention. Les pouvoirs des inspecteurs ont une origine internationale et nous devons nous exposer [opposer] énergiquement à la concession que suggère M. Gullon (faculté pour le Maghzen de déplacer certains instructeurs en cas d'urgence sans toutefois l'autoriser à modifier les règlements de police que doivent élaborer la France et l'Espagne).
	M. Regnault pense qu'en ce qui concerne l'interprétation donnée à cet article, en vue d'établir que la France et l'Espagne n'auront pas d'autorité supérieure

([1]) [This memorandum was left at the Foreign Office by M. Geoffray on the 31st August. A copy was sent by Sir E. Grey to Mr. White (Tangier). See minute by Sir E. Barrington, *infra* p. 343.]

à celle des autres Puissances, il faut en chercher l'origine dans un des derniers projets élaborés à Algésiras par les Autrichiens. M. de Welsersheimb avait essayé d'abord de faire spécifier que le fait pour l'Espagne et la France de nommer les instructeurs devait éviter de porter atteinte à la souveraineté du Sultan et au principe de la porte ouverte garanti par les Puissances. Une autre proposition se bornait à établir que ce fait ne saurait conférer à l'un des deux pays des droits supérieurs à celui des autres Puissances dans les villes où seraient installés les instructeurs. M. Révoil ayant vivement relevé ces propositions comme offensantes elles ne furent même pas discutées à la Conférence. Ce serait les faire renaitre [*sic*] à Tanger que de transmettre la note marocaine au Corps Diplomatique de cette ville.

Article IV.

Le Maghzen voudrait que les instructeurs soient des européens ayant la connaissance de la langue arabe et non des naturalisés. Les ordres seraient donnés en arabe. Au bout de cinq ans des officiers marocains remplaceraient les instructeurs étrangers.

Si le Maghzen entend par là que nous n'emploierons pas comme instructeurs des "marocains naturalisés français," il sera aisé de lui donner satisfaction ; s'il entend au contraire exclure les " Algériens naturalisés ou non," cette prétention irait contre les déclarations que nous avons faites à Algésiras où nous avons toujours appuyé nos droits à la police sur les aptitudes des cadres musulmans que nous fournirait l'Algérie. Dans notre pensée les emplois subalternes d'instructeurs doivent être offerts à des Algériens.

Article IX.

L'inspecteur-général ne pourra enquêter qu'à la suite de réclamations concernant des questions de police.

Article XVIII.

Le commerce des armes de chasse et de luxe dans l'intérieur du Maroc serait réservé aux Marocains.

L'Acte d'Algésiras n'autorise le commerce des armes de luxe et de chasse qu'à Tanger et en outre dans une zône qui reste à fixer par le Maghzen d'accord avec le Corps Diplomatique. La Conférence n'ayant pas admis que l'autorisation de vendre des armes à l'intérieur puisse être accordée, la question posée par le Maghzen est donc sans intérêt pratique. En outre la solution qu'il préconise serait contraire à la liberté de commerce reconnue aux étrangers par les traités et la Conférence.

Article XXXV.

Il devra être expliqué clairement et en arabe que les intérêts ne devront être payés par le Sultan que pour la somme effective retirée par lui de la banque jusqu'à concurrence des deux tiers du capital initial.

Article LXVII.

La Conférence avait émis le vœu que les droits sur les céréales fussent réduits. Le Maghzen a répondu qu'à son grand regret diverses raisons s'opposaient à cette mesure.

Article XCVII.

Le Maghzen voudrait que le Comité des Douanes fût supprimé au bout de trois ans; s'il n'avait pas alors terminé son œuvre le Maghzen proposerait alors un nouveau terme suffisant pour la réorganisation du service douanier.

Observations.

Il va de soi que le Maghzen ne payera d'intérêts que pour les sommes effectivement prêtées. Le règlement à venir sur les rapports de la banque avec l'État marocain lui donnera sur ce point entière satisfaction.

La conférence a proposé une durée de trois ans comme limite aux pouvoirs des membres du Comité permanent des douanes. Mais elle n'entendait pas mettre fin à une institution qui devra subsister tant que les douanes ne fonctionneront pas régulièrement.

MINUTES.

The French Minister on behalf of M. Cambon comm[unicate]d to-day the accompanying mem[orandum] containing the comments of the French Gov[ernmen]t on the interpretation placed by the Sultan of Morocco on certain Articles of the Algeciras Act. Sir E. Grey had referred to them in a recent conversation with M. Cambon who thought it w[oul]d be convenient that we should be in possession of the views of the French Gov[ernmen]t which might be comm[unicate]d to our minister at Tangier, in the event of the matter referred to coming up for discussion there. I thanked M. Geoffray. E. B. August 31, 1906.

Send to Tangier with instructions to support the French objections in concert with French representative at Tangier if matter is raised there. E. G. [v. Sir E. Grey to Mr. White, No. 102, Confidential of September 6, 1906. F.O. 371/175.]

No. 406.
Sir Edward Grey to Lord Acton.

F.O. 371/175.
Tel. (No. 43.)

Foreign Office, September 3, 1906.
D. 5·30 P.M.

Your tel[egram] No. 85 (of Aug[ust] 31).(¹)
Moorish interpretations received from Spanish Embassy on Aug[ust] 31st.
You should concert with your French Colleague and make a communication in similar terms to Spanish Gov[ernmen]t.

(¹) [Not reproduced. It relates to a conversation with M. Jules Cambon in which the latter described an interview with Señor Gullon, the Spanish Minister of State. He had informed him of the French rejection of the Sultan's demands " in their entirety."]

No. 407.
Lord Acton to Sir Edward Grey.

F.O. 371/175.
(No. 166.)
Sir,

San Sebastian, D. September 18, 1906.
R. *September* 26, 1906.

With reference to my telegram No. 88 of the 4th instant(¹) I have the honour to report that I was informed last night by the Russian Ambassador that Monsieur Isvolsky

(¹) [Not reproduced.]

had stated to the Spanish Ambassador at St. Petersburg that the Russian Government reject categorically the demands put forward by the Sultan of· Morocco in respect of certain articles of the Algeciras Act.

I have, &c.
ACTON.

No. 408.

Sir A. Nicolson to Sir Edward Grey.

F.O. 371/129.
(No. 741.)   *St. Petersburgh,* D. *November* 6, 1906.
Sir,   R. *November* 12, 1906.
Baron d'Aehrenthal called on me today, and informed me that he was to present his letters of recall tomorrow, and would return to Vienna on the 12th instant. He intended to stay a day or two in Berlin to see Prince Bülow.

He mentioned to me that on taking up office he had found that Count Goluchowski had promised to publish a Red Book on the Algeciras Conference, and that he had consulted Berlin with regard to what documents should be published. He had received a request that no reports which dealt with the interchange of views between the Governments at Vienna and Berlin should be made public, and he had also understood from Count Mensdorff that you would prefer that as little as possible should be printed so as not to revive polemics which had already passed out of the public mind. He, therefore, intended to publish a Red Book of a most innocent character, and which would contain little or nothing of interest. . . . .([1])

I have, &c.
A. NICOLSON.

([1]) [The rest of this despatch deals with other subjects.]

No. 409.

Sir M. de Bunsen to Sir Edward Grey.

F.O. 371/285.
(No. 59.)   Confidential.   *Madrid,* D. *March* 18, 1907.
Sir,   R. *March* 25, 1907.
Monsieur Tardieu's article in the last issue of the " Revue des deux mondes " has provoked a good deal of comment in Madrid. While there is a general agreement, with individual exceptions, that his account of the proceedings at the Algeciras Conference is substantially accurate, most of my colleagues hold that its appearance at the present time could serve no useful purpose and that, though stating the French case, it was probably not inspired by the French Government.

The Russian Ambassador informs me that, immediately on the appearance of the article Monsieur de Radowitz, German Ambassador, came to see him and inveighed in an excited manner against its tone and contents, describing the latter as a tissue of falsehoods. Monsieur de Radowitz was evidently nettled by the manner in which the origin of the legend as to the abandonment of France by the majority of the Powers and the accession of the latter to the German side is traced in the Article to himself. Comte Cassini tells me that, in a subsequent interview, he found his German colleague much less combative and disposed to consider that a magazine article was not worthy of serious notice.

Whatever may be the explanation of this change of tone on the part of the German Ambassador, I learn from Monsieur Jules Cambon, who finally left Madrid yesterday, that Monsieur de Radowitz also showed a good deal of agitation in speaking to him on the subject a fortnight ago. Monsieur Cambon pointed out to him that there were prominent pressmen in Germany who sometimes indited articles full of unfriendly allusions to France. He added, however, that he was quite prepared to admit that the article was inopportune and that he regretted its appearance on the eve of his departure to take up his new post at Berlin. His Excellency recommended to his Government that similar language should be held in Paris in the event of the matter being mentioned by the German Ambassador.

Monsieur Cambon considers, however, that the Article gives a very accurate account of what passed at Algeciras.

His Excellency received quite an ovation at the railway station on leaving. All the principal Spanish Ministers and Court officials, besides the Diplomatic body and leading members of Madrid society were present to see him off, and I only heard expressions of regret at his departure. The prospect of possibly a long interval before Monsieur Révoil's arrival is certainly unfortunate.

I have, &c.
MAURICE DE BUNSEN.

No. 410.

Mr. G. Lowther to Sir Edward Grey.

F.O. 371/283.
(No. 99.) Confidential.

Tangier, D. *April* 15, 1907.
R. *April* 27, 1907.

Sir,

Monsieur Guiot, the Representative of the French Bondholders and of the Consortium of the French Banks, and a member of the Comité Spécial of the State Bank of Morocco, informed me today that several meetings of the Bank were to be held in the course of the next month in Paris.

Hadj Dris Benjelun, the Moorish Representative, to whom I referred in my despatch No. 30 of the 8th of February,([1]) is now here and has no intention of proceeding to Paris. To the surprise of Monsieur Guiot and those concerned, this Moorish Official has designated the French Representative in Paris to take his place and if necessary vote for him.

Monsieur Guiot is unable to explain this decision which is entirely contrary to what was anticipated.

I have, &c
GERARD LOWTHER.

([1]) [Not reproduced.]

No. 411.

Mr. G. Lowther to Sir Edward Grey.

F.O. 371/284.
(No. 100.)

Tangier, D. *April* 15, 1907.
R. *April* 27, 1907.

Sir,

I took an opportunity today at a Plenary Meeting of the Foreign Representatives and of the Moorish Delegates to inquire of the latter whether no decision had been arrived at concerning the putting into force the Articles of the Act of Algeciras dealing with Coasting Trade, Custom-House Reform, and the Exportation of Cattle, as I had understood that it had been stated at Fez that the Sultan's Decree had been issued to that effect, and 3½ months had now passed since the Act of Algeciras had been ratified by His Shereefian Majesty.

The Moorish Delegates replied that this Decree had actually been issued, but was accompanied by an instruction to the Sultan's Representatives here to draw up Regulations governing these matters, that this had now been done, and had been returned to Fez for approval.

As a year has elapsed since the Act of Algeciras was signed which would have given ample time for the drawing up of the required regulation, I fear this delay must be regarded as fresh evidence, if any were required, of a disinclination on the part of the Moorish Government to put the Act of Algeciras into force.

I have, &c

GERARD LOWTHER.

No. 412.

Mr. G. Lowther to Sir Edward Grey.

F.O. 371/281.
(No. 5.)
Sir,

Tangier, D. January 5, 1907.
R. January 12, 1907.

In obedience to the instructions contained in your Circular despatch of the 9th April, 1906,([1]) I have the honour to transmit my Report of the events of interest in this country during the year 1906.

I have, &c.

GERARD LOWTHER.

Enclosure in No. 412.

Report by Mr. G. Lowther for the Year 1906.

Views on approaching Algeciras Conference.

The year 1906 opened in Morocco with its native and foreign population holding various views as to the approaching Conference, called ostensibly to bring about reforms in this country. The Makhzen, while declaring that they were earnestly desirous of seeing the introduction of reforms, sincerely hoped that none would be brought about, and had full confidence that the Powers would never be able to agree. The Moorish public in general neither knew of nor, in cases where they did, cared about the Conference. The foreign inhabitants shared with a few Diplomatic Representatives the impression that some good might come to the country, and that a check might be put on the rapacity of the Makhzen by the reforms introduced at Algeciras. The more shrewd held a strong conviction that the Conference was not called for the object of helping Morocco or her people, but rather with the view of clearing the cloudy political horizon in Europe, and that the introduction of any real reforms could only with the greatest difficulty be accomplished under international control, and so would probably not be introduced at all.

Loans.

2. The financial condition of the country was certainly not flourishing. The French loan of 62,000,000 fr. made in 1904 was said to be exhausted. The German "temporary advance" of 500,000*l.* of 1905, which had given rise to so much discussion as being in contravention of the French priority right secured to them under the Loan Contract of June 1904, was half consumed, and the properties to be offered by the Moorish Government as security had not yet been designated. . . .

Algeciras Convention.

. . . . 5. The " Acte Général " of the Algeciras Conference was signed at that place by all the Delegates, except the Moorish, the stipulation being inserted that M. Malmusi, the Italian Minister, and doyen of the Diplomatic Body here, should proceed to Fez and present the instrument to His Majesty for acceptance. The general tenour of the Articles of the Convention were [*sic*] soon known at Fez, and, wise counsels prevailing, it was given out that the Sultan would place no obstacle in the way of signing. This view was, however, soon modified, the Sultan being represented as stating that he would require time to study the Act more carefully, and suggesting that a stipulation should be introduced to the effect that foreign assistance should be dispensed with as soon as in His Majesty's opinion it was no longer required; that the Convention in certain parts should not be applied until the country was more in a condition to assimilate such radical changes.

([1]) [This is the circular which inaugurated the series of Annual Reports required from this date from every British embassy, *v. supra* p. x.]

M. Malmusi left for Fez on the 24th May. Throughout the country the Convention was received with doubt and suspicion, it being a mystery to the large majority. They attributed the disasters that had come upon the country to the rebellion of Bu Hamara, the Pretender, and to the support he was supposed to have received from the French. The formation of the police was objected to by the Kaïds, with whom it might come into conflict. The nationality of the instructors was a matter of indifference to them. . . . . The Oomana (civil officials) merely wondered whether the customs receipts were likely to be augmented, and whether there would still be an opening for enriching themselves, but the idea of an assembly of Christians to advise on the affairs of the faithful was naturally distasteful. Their vanity was wounded and their avarice alarmed. The functions of the State Bank were quite beyond their comprehension. But the general idea, both amongst military and civilian employés, was that the Makhzen would be ingenious enough to discover some plan by which the stipulations of the Convention would be avoided. Kismet was, however, as usual, the key to the general feeling. M. Malmusi did not waste much time at Fez in discussing the "Acte Général." Some attempt was made to induce him to lay the matter before the Notables, and a good deal of opposition was shown for some days by a certain section of the Makhzen, headed by the Tazzi group; but M. Malmusi showed much firmness, and, the Sultan's "Dahir" accepting, the Convention was signed on the 18th June. A note addressed by Ben Sliman to M. Malmusi followed, expressing the hope that the Powers would show leniency in the application of the reforms, and leave them entirely to the Sultan at the end of five years, and a document was handed to M. Malmusi embodying His Majesty's interpretation of certain Articles of the Act. This document was eventually handed to the Spanish Government, who communicated it to the Powers, but no reply has, up to the present time, been made to the Sultan. . . . .

. . . . 22. The year may be said to have been an unfavourable one generally for Conclusion. Morocco. The Sultan's authority, already on the decline, was still further weakened. The Pretender continued to give trouble, and the constant dispatch of small forces to cope with him was a drain on the ill-filled coffers of the Exchequer. The Governors of the south were out of hand, and in the north Raisuli's power and authority assumed almost alarming proportions. Small loans were made to the Makhzen which provided for immediate wants, but the general decay continued, and there is little indication of the advent of either energetic or honest men to put an end to the "slump."

The customs receipts showed a decrease, and robbery on the part of Customs officials became more general than before. The French have certainly added to their unpopularity, if that were possible, and there have been more acts of aggression against them than against other foreigners, and satisfaction has only in rare cases been obtained. On the other hand, the German star is for the moment in the ascendent, and the advice of the German Minister is freely given, although not so freely acted upon, the Moorish Government, as is their custom, preferring a policy of delay and procrastination to anything definite. The year 1907 may be one of great changes for this country, but too much must not be expected, and although the Makhzen may encourage the introduction of certain reforms that may bring grist to their mill, those that appear to offer no direct or immediate advantage will be stoutly resisted.

[ED. NOTE.—An article by Mr. Lucien Wolf, signed "Diplomaticus," appeared in the *Pall Mall Gazette* of 6 March, 1906, under the title "The German Grievance." The following note by Mr. [Sir] W. Tyrrell appears to be a commentary upon it.

Note by Mr. Tyrrell on German Policy in Morocco, 1906.(¹)

In his paper which has now appeared in the "Pall Mall Gazette" on Count Bernstorff's recommendation, M. Wolff [sic] tries to prove (1) that, if the Anglo-French Agreement of 1904 had been communicated to the German Government, all difficulties would have been amicably settled by a few strokes of the pen; (2) that "the whole of the alleged grievance of the German Government on this point," i.e., the non-communication of the Agreement, "is a myth." These two propositions contradict each other and are somewhat difficult to reconcile. The weight of evidence inclines to support the latter view, and we cannot do better than quote Prince Bülow on the subject.

On April 12, 1904, a few days after the publication of the Anglo-French Agreement, Count Bülow informed the Reichstag that Germany had " no cause to apprehend that the Agreement between Great Britain and France was levelled against any individual Power. It seemed to be an attempt to eliminate the points between France and Great Britain by means of an amicable understanding. From the point of view of German interests, they had nothing to complain of, for they did not wish to see strained relations between Great Britain and France, if only for the reason that such a state of affairs would imperil the peace of the world." As regards the main feature of the Agreement—Morocco—Germany had a substantial economic interest in that country. Therefore it was " essentially to their interest that peace and order should reign in Morocco, and they had no ground to fear that their economic interests would be disregarded or injured by any other Power." This appreciation of the Agreement contains no hint as to Germany's wanting " assurances " or " compensation " for wounded feelings or injured interests. She welcomes the Agreement as a further guarantee of the peace so essential for the development of her economic interests in Morocco. Public opinion in Germany, as summed up by Sir Frank Lascelles, whose opinion should carry weight as a competent witness, received the Agreement on the whole quietly, though many were surprised and disappointed; surprised, because they never expected England and France would make up their differences; disappointed, because Germany would no longer be in a position to play off one country against the other. There was no feeling that, because France and England had concluded an arrangement for settling their outstanding differences at nobody else's expense, therefore Germany was entitled to compensation either on the score of wounded feelings or of injured interests. Anyhow, the attitude of the German Government was that the Agreement did not affect in any way German interests, furnishing as it did an additional pledge of peace.

It was not until the Spring of 1905 that the German Emperor paid his now historical visit to Tangier, which created a new situation in Europe. In reply to an interpellation in the Reichstag by Herr Bebel, who accused the Government of a change in their policy, Count Bülow made the following statement on March 29, 1905 : " The Emperor declared to the King of Spain exactly a year ago that Germany sought no territorial advantages in Morocco. . . . .([2])

" Independently, however, of this visit, and independently of the territorial question, there is the question whether we have got to protect German commercial interests in Morocco. That we certainly have. . . . . German commercial interests in Morocco are, as is well known, very considerable, and it is our duty to see that they continue to receive equal consideration with those of all other Powers.

" Now Herr Bebel has declared that our policy towards Morocco has changed. I must first draw Herr Bebel's attention to the fact that the language and attitude of the diplomatist and the politician is directed in accordance with circumstances. I choose according to my own judgment the moment which I consider suitable for the protection of our interests. . . . . But in so far as attempts are being made to alter the legal status of Morocco, or to control the open door in connection with the commercial development of the country, we must also take greater care than before that our commercial interests remain unendangered."

It is perfectly open to a statesman to choose his own time for giving effect to his policy— but to execute the " volte face " implied by this statement is quite a different matter. It means a reversal of the policy which Count Bülow announced 11 months ago Germany intended to pursue with regard to this Agreement.

The reason for such a change is to be found, according to the German official version, in the interpretation which the French Government placed upon the Agreements which they had concluded with England, Spain and Italy, which she claimed gave her an European mandate in the settlement of Moorish affairs : in other words, Germany became convinced that she was face to face with an attempt to " Tunisify " Morocco, and she was therefore entitled to take the necessary steps to safeguard not only her own interests, but also those of the other Powers who were parties to the Madrid Convention of 1880.

The latter claim of Germany may be disposed of by stating that the " other Powers " were the best judges of their interests, and not one of them shared the German alarm. German interests were amply safeguarded by the Madrid Convention and by the German treaty with Morocco of 1890, and it was open to Germany to protect her rights as soon as she saw any· attempt made by France to disregard them. To what attempts on the part of France can Germany point? She replies by quoting the alleged instructions sent to the French Minister at Fez during the winter of 1904/05, which she declares constituted an attempt at the " Tunisification " of Morocco. A careful perusal of the French Yellow Book and the German White Book fails to establish this point. The French Government have repeatedly denied this charge, and the French Minister at Fez equally denies having put forward any demands which could be interpreted as a claim to act as the " mandataire " of Europe. The Germans in their White Book base their contention on the communications made by the Sultan and the Moorish officials to the German Consul and Minister to the effect that France had claimed such a mandate.

([2]) [Thus in original.]

Beyond those statements no evidence is produced in support of such a charge, and we are expected to accept statements as evidence which are made by the parties who are adepts at the favourite oriental game of playing off one European Power against another by the dissemination of false reports. It is a trick with which we are more than familiar at Constantinople, Tehran and Peking, and which is sometimes in favour in some very European capitals. The German White Book opens with extracts from newspapers in support of the German theory. One of the extracts is taken from "The Times" of March 20, 1905, and is to the effect that, whether intentionally or not, the French Minister had given the Sultan to understand that he not only represented France, but virtually the whole of Europe. Since the appearance of this quotation in the German White Book, the "Times" Correspondent at Tangier has publicly stated that the information was supplied to him by the German Consul at Fez. But assuming the German contention to be proved, in what way is the charge of "Tunisification" proved? Germany had treaty rights in Tunis which she voluntarily renounced in favour of France for good reasons of her own, some of which are given in the second volume of the Granville correspondence. In Morocco, it was impossible for France to disregard German rights without Germany's consent. German treaty rights remained intact in spite of the Anglo-French and Franco-Spanish Agreements, and they remained equally untouched by whatever communications passed between the French and Moorish governments, or by whatever promises the former might have obtained from the latter by pressure or persuasion. The German view is that she was entitled to safeguard her economic future in Morocco. Was this future endangered by the recognition on the part of England and Spain of France's special position in Morocco, to which she was historically and geographically entitled? Not in Count Bülow's opinion when he made his statement in the Reichstag of April 12, 1904. Could any verbal or written communications which passed at Fez in any way affect Germany's or anyone else's treaty rights? Assuming again that Germany was right in her alarm with regard to her commercial future in Morocco, she had an opportunity at the Conference to bring forward the grounds for her apprehensions and propose measures for the protection of her interests. So far, however, she has done neither. Inside and outside the Conference, Germany has strongly disclaimed any desire for political or territorial compensation in connection with the Morocco question. Her delegate at Algeciras has offered to state this assurance in writing, and we are justified in asking what were her reasons for raising the Moorish question in the somewhat acute form in which she raised it last Spring. What was the object of obtaining the dismissal of M. Delcassé, the acceptance by France of the Conference, and of the long drawn out negotiations of last summer which ended in the preliminary Agreement of October 1905 [sic], and enabled Prince Bülow to announce that at the forthcoming Conference there would be neither "vainqueurs" nor "vaincus." If Germany's object is not commercial, it is but fair to assume that it is political and, in view of her repeated declarations on the subject, it is also but fair to assume that her political aims are not to be realised in Morocco. All the information at present in our possession points to the conclusion stated that the Germans were completely taken by surprise when they discovered that France and England had been able to settle their outstanding differences without extravagant concessions on either side, that they then jumped to the opposite conclusion and read more into the Agreement than it contained, that they finally determined to probe the extent and vitality of the Agreement. How far the Germans think that they have succeeded in this policy remains to be seen. These speculations are submitted with a view to showing that no amount of communications with or to Berlin would have succeeded in dissipating the suspicions or apprehensions of the Germans that the Anglo-French Agreement contained a "point" against Germany except by their own investigations. It is to be hoped and expected that when they have satisfied themselves that the Agreement is as innocent as it looks—and the severe examination to which they have submitted it ought by now to have convinced them of their previous errors—they will revert to Prince Bülow's original view of it, as stated on April 12, 1904.]

[ED: NOTE.—A. & P. (1906), CXXXVI, (Cd. 3087), pp. 331–388 publishes with a covering letter by Sir A. Nicolson of April 7, 1906, the text of the Acte Général of the Conference, signed on that date, with annexed and related papers. It was presented to Parliament in July 1906. The Acte was ratified by the Sultan of Morocco on June 18, and the deposit of ratifications took place at Madrid, December 31, 1906, v. B.F.S.P., Vol. XCIX of 1905–6 (1910), p. 141, pp. 169–71, p. 1006.]

CHAPTER XXII.
FRANCE AND GERMANY AFTER ALGECIRAS.

No. 413.

Mr. Tower to Sir Edward Grey.

F.O. 371/76.
(No. 14.)   *Munich, D. January 24, 1906.*
Sir,   R. *January 29, 1906.*

Since I took up my post at Munich no subject has interested me so much as the manner in which the Imperialistic idea—the broad idea of Empire as contradistinguished from the narrower standpoint of the individual States—is being fostered throughout South Germany. The educational methods adopted by the extreme partisans of Imperialism at the present day in their writings and speeches have achieved much towards effecting a unification of German national sentiment, and I propose in this despatch to attempt to follow the trend of the movement by quoting the words of leading extremists, and by giving a few instances which have come under my own notice in Munich.

It is the fashion in German political circles to ridicule the extravagant pretensions of the so-called Pan-German Union ('' Alldeutscher Verband ''), but it is nevertheless certain that this organization has played a part, and a not inconsiderable part, in recent German history and, through the German Navy League ('' Flottenverein ''), with which it is now closely connected, is to-day doing much to create a desire for German maritime expansion, for a war fleet and mercantile marine, for colonies beyond the sea and for coaling stations.

In various lectures, speeches, &c., of prominent Pan-Germans it has of recent years been stated that it is not only to the sixty millions of Germans in the German Empire that the Pan-German Union looks, but also to the twenty millions in other lands, of which ten millions are in Austria-Hungary, two millions in Switzerland, and eight millions in Holland. Beyond even these they look to the eight million Germans scattered over other countries.

It is an interesting speculation whether, in the event of a dismemberment of Austria-Hungary on the demise of the Emperor Francis Joseph, any movement towards uniting to the German Empire the German-speaking population of the Dual Monarchy is likely to be successful. Not only would the increase of available conscripts be welcomed by the German Empire, but the possibility of an outlet on the Mediterranean being one day his must tempt a Ruler determined on making his country a first class sea-Power. Unreasonable as it may seem, there exist extreme Pan-Germans who look to Trieste as the future outlet. Should Hungary cease to form part of the Dual Monarchy, it may well be that the separatist infection would spread, and a determined effort might then be expected from the Pan-Germans to join hands with the German-speaking communities in Austria. Even were Tyrol and Styria ultimately to be convinced of the advantage of being incorporated in the German Empire—and to anticipate this requires some effort of imagination—there remains the strong disinclination in North Germany, notably Prussia, to permit a Roman Catholic majority in the Empire. This would be the case if the German-Austrian provinces were admitted. Since Prince Bismarck's '' Kulturkampf '' the Particularist sentiment in the South German States has rather tended towards Anti-Prussianism, and the fact is stronger when one reflects on the encouragement lent to Particularism by the Centre or Ultramontane party in Bavaria.

It is sufficient for my present purpose to point to the desire of the Pan-German party towards union of Germans in general, of which those in Austria are merely an incident.

The chief aims of the Pan-German Union have been declared to be as follows :—

" A closer union of the High and the Low Germans, as well as the German inhabitants of the European Continent exclusive of the Scandinavians but inclusive of the High and Low German emigrants to foreign countries. Further, a common economic organization throughout Central Europe, of which the Germans form the common population . . . . The elevation of Germanism into Pan-Germanism is the necessary step in the evolution which has by successive stages witnessed the Brandenburg and Prussian States, the Zollverein, the North German Confederation, and, lastly, the German Empire." (" Alldeutsche Blaetter,"* No. 24, 1899, p. 193.)

The Union aims at a revival of German nationalism and patriotism all over the world ; at the preservation of German thought, ideals, and customs, both in Europe and across the sea ; at a compact union of Germans in all lands.

To carry out this programme the Union begins by claiming all German-speaking peoples as of German kith and kin. It aspires to the ultimate inclusion of the German-speaking cantons of Switzerland, of the Baltic provinces of Russia, of parts of Belgium and Luxemburg, and, most important of all, of Holland, with her littoral and her Colonies.

From the mass of publications of this Union I take a few instances of the methods employed in the last few years to disseminate their ideas throughout the various States of the Empire.

Boer War.

On January 7, 1896, the Pan-German Union addressed a letter to the Imperial Chancellor, Prince Hohenlohe, urging that " the German Government should lend its powerful support to the South African Republic against Great Britain."

On January 8, 1896, the President of the Union, Dr. Ernest Hasse, wrote to Dr. Leyds, who was then in Berlin, stating that " all good Germans were at one with His Majesty the Emperor in congratulating the Boers on their decisive victory over English officials and soldiers who have, in contravention of the law of nations, broken like robbers into the territory of a nation kindred to Germany and enjoying her friendship." (" Alldeutsche Blaetter," 1896, No. 3, pp. 9 and 10.)

At a meeting of the Pan-German Union at Leipzig on June 8–10, 1897, a resolution was unanimously carried to the effect that " the presumptuous claim of Great Britain to assume the paramount power in South Africa . . . . must be resisted." (" Alldeutsche Blaetter," 1897, No. 25, p. 123.)

Throughout the entire war the Pan-German Union continued to express to the Boers its wishes for the success of their arms, and at the same time to urge the Imperial authorities to lend active support to the South African Republic.

Anglo-German Relations.

In the light of the present improvement in the relations between the United Kingdom and Germany, it is interesting to see what views have been put forward by the pan-Germans on the possibility of friendship between the two countries.

At a Meeting of the Pan-German Union at Dresden in 1899, Dr. Bassenge spoke in the following sense :—

" England is only a half-German Great Power. German efforts to cultivate England's friendship show the greatest ignorance of the present condition of affairs. History teaches that irrefutably, for whenever England has been allied to the Germans it has certainly not been out of love for the Germans. . . . .(¹) It is clear that we can expect no friendship from England, and it comes to this, that over the whole world

---

* The " Alldeutsche Blätter " is the weekly publication of the Pan-German Union. This periodical is published in Berlin, but most of the pamphlets of the Union appear to be issued by the publisher Lehmann, of Munich. [R. T.]

(¹) [Thus in original.]

German and English interests actually clash." ("Flugschriften des Alldeutschen Verbandes," Heft 9, Lehmann, Munich, 1899.)

Rhodes Scholarships.

On the 25th May, 1902, a Resolution proposed by Lieutenant Lehmann (Göttingen) was adopted by the meeting of the Pan-German Union at Eisenach, as follows :—

"A portion of the German students have already acted rightly in declining the arrogant legacy of a (*sic*) Cecil Rhodes. We do not doubt that the rest of the German students will also emphatically reject the gift 'borne by Greeks' which has been made by a Briton fighting Germanism even beyond the grave." ("Alldeutsche Blaetter," Nos. 15 and 22, Lehmann, Munich, 1902.)

Increase of the German Fleet.

Since the year 1895 the Pan-German Union has identified itself with the agitation for increasing the German fleet. Support was given to the movement by the Emperor William on October 18, 1899, at Hamburg, "a dire necessity for us is a strong German fleet," words which have been used as an appeal to the German people, and repeated on many subsequent occasions.

At a lecture delivered at a Meeting of the Pan-German Union at Hamburg in 1899, Dr. Adolf Lehr, a member of the Reichstag, stated that, though it might prove impossible for the German fleet to equal the British in strength, yet such was unnecessary, as they would never have the whole British fleet against them at the same time. "Our fleet must be strong enough to be able to encounter on the high seas such portion of the British fleet as may be opposed to them." ("Flugschriften des Alldeutschen Verbandes," Heft 10, Lehmann, Munich, 1899.)

Customs union with Holland.

The subject of much of the Pan-German literature is the hope eventually to control the mouth of the Rhine, and for this reason the desire is constantly expressed of one day including Holland within the German Zollverein. The hopes of the Pan-German Union were expressed by Dr. Hasse, whom I have before quoted, in a pamphlet entitled "German World-policy" (Lehmann, Munich, 1897), as follows :—

"The present German Zollverein covers an area of 542,070 square kilometres, with over fifty-two million inhabitants, and a foreign trade of 7,670 million marks. An extension over Belgium and Holland, Switzerland, as well as Austria-Hungary with Bosnia and Herzegovina would cover an area of 1,322,238 square kilometres, with more than 108 million inhabitants. . . . . The inclusion of Roumania would add the entire Danube to the basins of the Rhine, Elbe, and Oder. The mid-European Zollverein would thus be assured on the North Sea, on the Baltic, on the Adriatic, and the Black Sea, and geographically a territory with the most favourable opportunities for trade would be offered."

The Far East.

On October 9, 1895, the Pan-German Union addressed the Imperial Chancellor on the subject of German aspirations in the Far East, consequent upon the Peace of Shimonoseki and the combined interference of Germany, France, and Russia.

The Union urged that "Germany should in the interest of the Empire take energetic steps, without regard for the ill-will of other nations, to acquire a strong and safe possession—either a harbour or a group of islands—in Chinese waters." As a suitable acquisition, they designated the harbour of Amoy or the Islands of the Chusan Archipelago. ("Alldeutsche Blaetter," 1895, p. 189.)

It will be remembered that it was in 1898 that Kiaochow was leased from China by Germany.

A party professing Pan-Germanism ("Pangermanismus") is still further advanced in its ideas than the Pan-German Union, which professes "Alldeutschtum." This more advanced party follow the dictates of such writers as Houston Stewart Chamberlain and would embrace even Scandinavians and Anglo-Saxondom in the German fold.

Morocco.

A series of publications of the Pan-German Union have lately appeared. The first of these is a brochure entitled "Morocco Lost? a Cry of Warning at the eleventh hour," by Herr Class, of Mayence, a member of the Pan-German Union. (Lehmann, Munich, 1905.) This pamphlet begins by stating that the German Empire has the first claim to Morocco, and proceeds to say "One or two harbours on the coast of Morocco will not suffice for us, we must have the entire Atlantic coast, as we cannot develop our interests unless we are independent of other Powers possessing rights on the littoral. . . . : West Morocco offers to Germany the last chance of obtaining possession, peaceably and without conflict with European Great Powers, of lands which are more adapted than any of the existing German Colonies or Protectorates for German expansion."

This pamphlet was followed by another, also from the Pan-German Union, entitled, "Why we need Morocco."

Having given the above extracts from writings of Pan-Germans I venture to append a few very recent instances of the manner in which the Bavarian is being to-day educated in matters Imperial.

Morocco.

On January 3, 1906, a lecture was given in Munich by Dr. Grothe on "Morocco and German interests in that country." After describing in minute detail the action of the principal Germans who have been in Morocco, and pointing to the effect produced by the Emperor's visit to Tangier, of which photographs were shown on a screen, the lecturer proceeded to give geographical and topographical information about the west coast of Morocco, particularly Rabat and Dar-el-Baida.

The impression left on the audience, doubtless intentionally, though not expressed in so many words, was that Germany was justified in looking for compensation in return for all she had done for Morocco in the past. The enthusiasm of the large audience on this occasion was a remarkable testimony to the popularity of the subject.

Increase of the Fleet.

1. On the 14th instant I attended a popular lecture in Munich, by Professor Dr. Grube, entitled "The Germans and the Sea." The lecturer demonstrated how German foreign trade had grown by leaps and bounds. In relation to British foreign trade it had thirty years back stood at one-tenth of the volume; a little later it had reached one-eighth, and now stood at one-fifth of the total volume of British foreign commerce. If the present German activity be maintained, said the lecturer, German trade would soon equal its British rival. It was specially the duty of every patriotic German at the present time to reflect upon the immense disparity of German foreign trade and the mileage of telegraphic cables in German hands. It was both detrimental and humiliating to be obliged to trust to British Cable Companies, with the feeling that in time of war, the use of them would be denied to Germans.

The other point on which he laid stress was the imperative need for German coaling stations. "These must be acquired whenever and wherever a favourable opportunity offers."

2. On the 18th instant a meeting took place at Nuremberg to celebrate the 35th Anniversary of the foundation of the German Empire. A speech was made by Dr. Gerhardt, of Berlin, on the Imperial proposals for increasing the fleet. He

described the necessity of German military and naval strength in the interests of the economic condition of the German people, and interest in which no division of parties existed. The following Resolution was put to the Meeting and carried unanimously :—

" The present serious political situation, the exposed position of Germany, and the powerful armaments of other countries, imperatively oblige us to maintain an adequately strong fleet in addition to our reliable and well-prepared army. Such a fleet is necessary for the undisturbed development of the German Empire and for the protection of its interests both at home and abroad. We therefore request the Federal Council to execute with rapidity the projected construction of our ships, and particularly to replace the old vessels with greater speed."

3. At a meeting of the German Navy League in Munich on the 18th instant, a lecture was delivered by Professor A. Stauffer, entitled " Why must Germany be both a Land and a Sea Power?" The lecturer said that the British rated a Power by the measure of her men-of-war, and that, further, German foreign trade, which now amounted to seventy per cent. of its total commerce, was insufficiently protected by the ships which represented the German fleet. After saying that Germany entertained no offensive intentions, and that the object was merely to make sure that any Power attacking Germany would run a serious risk by so doing, he stated that the chief object to be arrived at was to obtain in time of danger a position of supremacy in the North Sea for the German fleet, " as only by that means can we assure the protection of our trade and our colonies." Dr. Stauffer ridiculed the idea that Germany was not able to afford to pay for the increase in her fleet. The example of Japan, a far poorer country than Germany, has shown what can be accomplished in the way of providing a fleet.

He gave the following illustration of the powerlessness of a diplomatic Representative when unsupported by a fleet :—

During the negotiations between Prussia and Japan in 1859 for a Commercial Treaty the Prussian Representative Count Eulenburg suffered various slights at the hands of the Japanese to the extent of actual discourtesy. He took upon himself to threaten the Japanese with the necessity of " Prussia taking other and more drastic measures," but at the same time admitted to his chief at Berlin, " What measures I am sure I don't know myself."[*]

4. At a meeting organized by the Pan-German Union on the 22nd instant at Munich, an address was delivered by Lieutenant General von Liebert, formerly Governor of German East Africa. He pointed to the historical development of nations in consequence of their efficiency and strength at sea and called upon his hearers to sink their Particularist financial objections in view of the necessity of forcing the hand of the Reichstag towards a quicker and more extensive construction of ships. A Resolution was unanimously carried in that sense, and the proceedings terminated by cheers for the German Emperor.

Lastly, I would mention a book called " Seestern, 1906," published at Leipzig, of which 75 thousand copies are already in circulation. It is of the class of the " Battle of Dorking," and describes an imaginary war between Germany and the Franco-British allies in 1907. The author is said to be an officer in the Imperial navy.

I have, &c.

REGINALD TOWER.

P.S.—I have sent a copy of this despatch to Sir F. Lascelles at Berlin.

R. T.

[*] This is published in the papers of the von Schleinitz family, 1905. [R. T.]

MINUTES.

There can be no doubt as to the immense popularity of the Pan-German movement and of the agitation carried on by the German Navy League. Both these organisations are inspired by bitter and often scurrilous hostility to Great Britain. It is of course true that the Pan-German aspirations to dominion over the Low Countries and over the Adriatic are openly disavowed by all responsible people in Germany. But it would be foolish to doubt that if and when a favourable opportunity occurred for realizing such political aspirations in whole or in part, the opportunity would be seized by the German Government with all its wonted energy.

It is well to remember that Prince Bismarck and all his officials never tired of assuring G[rea]t Britain right up to 1884 that the agitation in favour of acquiring German colonies was a movement of a handful of unimportant and misguided faddists. Yet shortly afterwards we had the disagreeable incident of Angra Pequena, and the still more offensive proceedings of the German Gov[ernmen]t in the Cameroons, at St. Lucia Bay, and in New Guinea, from which period, indeed, dates the present anti-English agitation in Germany. January 29.

E. A. C.

Thanks for interesting despatch.

E. B.
E. G.

MINUTE BY KING EDWARD.

A most interesting and carefully written despatch. It is not pleasant reading!

E.R.

No. 414.

Mr. Lister to Sir Edward Grey.

F.O. 371/72.
(No. 221.)
Sir,

Paris, D. May 21, 1906.
R. May 23, 1906.

I saw the Minister for Foreign Affairs this afternoon, and, in accordance with the instructions which you gave me in the course of our conversations of the 17th and 18th instant, I told him that you had desired me to assure him of your great satisfaction at the consolidation of the *Entente* between our two countries : you had already through M. Cambon and Sir Francis Bertie expressed to him your grateful appreciation of the services rendered by France to His Majesty's Government in the Akaba question, but you wished to avail yourself of the opportunity afforded by my return to Paris, to repeat the assurances already given.

M. Bourgeois said that he was much touched at the messages which you had sent him, and asked me to convey to you his most cordial thanks.

As the tone of our conversation was very friendly and unofficial, I ventured to mention that you had alluded in conversation with me to the visit of the German Mayors to England, and had expressed the hope that it would not arouse any suspicion or resentment in France, the reception given to them was an act of mere courtesy, and M. Bourgeois might rest assured that His Majesty's Government would never make any political move in matters which could possibly affect French interests, without previously informing the French Government of their intention.

M. Bourgeois said that you need have no anxiety on the score of the reception given to the German Municipal Authorities. The French Government perfectly understood it and had not given it a second thought. He was glad however of the opportunity afforded by our conversation to say that in his opinion both countries must be mutually prepared to understand and admit not only acts of courtesy towards a third Power, but also negotiations of a political character into which one or other might be obliged to enter. It was the desire of England and France alike to show clearly that the understanding which united them was not directed against any third Power and this could best be done by making it evident to the world that their confidence in one another was such as to leave them free in their dealings with other nations. Thanks to the cordiality of the relations existing between the two countries, any negotiations in which one or other might engage with a third party could be frankly discussed, and in this happy state of things it seemed to him impossible that any misunderstanding should ever arise between them. Even on points with regard to which they might hold different opinions, he felt convinced that a solution could always be arrived at by

2 A 2

means of frank discussion as between two friends who were absolutely loyal one to the other, though their views might not always be identical.

Before going in to see M. Bourgeois I had a few moments' conversation with the Directeur Politique. M. Louis asked me whether I had any message for M. Bourgeois with regard to Abyssinia and told me that on Saturday M. Cambon had made a proposal to Sir Charles Hardinge that France and England should at once sign an agreement with regard to the main outlines of the Ethiopian Railway Scheme. M. Bourgeois also alluded to this proposal and said he was anxiously awaiting your reply to it. He considered such an agreement between the two Powers most important, as not only would it convince King Menelek that France and England were really united in the matter but it would also diminish the danger from possible German intrigues. He thought it best for the moment to leave Italy out of the question : the railway did not directly concern her, and her attitude throughout the negotiations had been, to say the least of it, enigmatic. His interview with Signor Tittoni on the latter's passage through Paris had inspired him with no confidence and he should feel much relieved when an agreement such as M. Cambon had proposed had been actually signed by France and England.

I said that, from what I knew of your conversation with M. Cambon, you held the opinion that the present situation of uncertainty was fraught with considerable danger both as regarded Menelek and Germany.

M. Bourgeois talked to me a little about M. Isvolsky, whom he had met several times *en intimité* when the latter was in Paris last month. He said he had been much struck by the friendliness of his feelings for England and by his desire for some sort of *entente* between the two nations—a desire which M. Bourgeois believed to be quite genuine, for at that moment M. Isvolsky could hardly have anticipated that he would so shortly be called upon to direct Russian foreign policy.

M. Bourgeois spoke on a variety of subjects, but before I left he impressed upon me once more the great importance which he attached to the frank discussion of all political questions affecting our two countries, which would not only render all misunderstanding impossible, but also greatly increase our respective freedom of action *vis-à-vis* to third Powers.

I have, &c.
REGINALD LISTER.

<hr>

No. 415.

Sir F. Lascelles to Sir Edward Grey.

F.O. 371/78.
(No. 150.) Confidential.
Sir,

Berlin, D. May 24, 1906.
R. May 28, 1906.

The funeral of Her Royal Highness the Princess Frederick Charles of Prussia took place on the 19th instant at the Church of Nicolskoi near Potsdam in the presence of the Emperor and Empress, Prince and Princess Frederick Leopold, the Duke and Duchess and Princess Patricia of Connaught, the Grand Duke of Oldenburg, the Grand Duke and Grand Duchess of Mecklenburg Strelitz, the Duke of Anhalt, the Crown Prince, Prince Henry of Prussia, and other German Princes.

At the conclusion of the service, at which, in obedience to The King's commands, I had the honour of representing His Majesty, the Emperor honoured me with a short conversation. His Majesty was in the best of health and spirits and deigned to be jocose. On my expressing my satisfaction at seeing him looking so well, he said, "Yes I am very well as I always am when I come back from the Provinces, where I have assured myself that I am quite prepared to deal with your friends across the frontier if they should attempt to attack me at your instigation." Seeing that His Majesty was speaking in jest, I remarked that the contingency was a very remote one to which His Majesty replied, "Yes I think so too." I then told him that I hoped that His Majesty was satisfied with the reception which the German Burgomasters had met with in England, which I trusted would be duly appreciated in Germany. The Emperor replied that it was a pity that these friendly demonstrations had not taken place sooner, but "Better late than never," and he hoped that friendly speeches would be followed by friendly deeds. Then, assuming a more serious tone, His Majesty said that perhaps Mr. Haldane who, he believed had studied at Heidelberg, might like to come over to Germany to see something of German Military organization.

The Duke of Connaught has been good enough to tell me that the Emperor made a similar remark to him about Mr. Haldane, which, although not amounting to an invitation, left the impression that His Majesty's Secretary of State for War would be welcome if he visited Germany. The Duke of Connaught also told me that he had had a most satisfactory conversation with the Emperor and would be able to make a very favourable report to The King on His Royal Highness' return to England. On my taking leave of Their Royal Highnesses at the Railway station, the Duchess of Connaught told me that both the Emperor and Empress had been very kind.

I have, &c.

FRANK C. LASCELLES.

No. 416.

Sir F. Lascelles to Sir Edward Grey.

F.O. 371/78.
(No. 151.) Confidential.
Sir,

Berlin, D. *May* 24, 1906.
R. *May* 28, 1906.

With reference to my preceding Despatch of this day's date, I have the honour to report that on the 22nd instant, I had an opportunity of repeating to Herr von Tschirschky the conversation which I had the honour of having with the Emperor on the 19th instant. I said it was no easy matter, in reporting the language held by His Majesty to convey a correct impression of His Majesty's meaning. In the present instance I had no doubt that the Emperor was joking when he alluded to the possibility of his being attacked by France at the instigation of England. I was too well acquainted with His Majesty's manner to think that he intended me to take his words seriously. The same remark would apply to His Majesty's observations with regard to the reception of the German Burgomasters in England, which taken literally would have seemed ungracious. The general impression which His Majesty's conversation left upon me was that His Majesty desired to be friendly and this impression had been confirmed by what the Duke of Connaught had been good enough to tell me of the satisfactory conversation he had had with His Majesty.

Herr von Tschirschky said that the impression I had formed was the correct one. The Emperor certainly desired Friendship with England, and it was fortunate that I was sufficiently acquainted with His Majesty to understand what he meant. Herr von Tschirschky said he was very glad I had alluded to the visit of the German Burgomasters to England. The reception they had met with, and the honour which the King had shown them by receiving them had created a profound impression throughout Germany and would he hoped go far to remove the want of understanding which existed among the people in both countries. He had had a long conversation on this subject with Prince Bülow who had expressed his satisfaction at the cordiality of the reception which he hoped would now lead to the establishment of a friendly understanding between the two Governments.

I have, &c.

FRANK C. LASCELLES.

2 A 3

MINUTES.

All this talking about an "understanding" between the two countries has an air of unreality. We have come to an understanding with France, and there may be one with Russia. But the essential thing in both cases is a common ground of action or negotiation. There were actual differences to be adjusted with France; an understanding with Russia would presumably mean a removal of similar differences.

But with Germany we have no differences whatever. An understanding which does not consist in the removal of differences can only mean a plan of cooperation in political transactions, whether offensive, defensive, or for the maintenance of neutrality. It is difficult to see on what point such cooperation between England and Germany is at this moment appropriate; but it is quite certain that any proposals in such a direction would be impartially considered here from the point of view of British interests.

Past history has shown us that a friendly Germany has usually been a Germany asking for something, by way of proving our friendship. It will be prudent to be prepared for proposals for an understanding being made to us by Germany on similar lines. May 28.

E. A. C.

Lord Lansdowne frequently spoke in the above sense to C[ount] Metternich.

E. B.
C. H.

All that is necessary is for the Germans to realize that they have got nothing to complain of.

E. G.

No. 417.

Sir Edward Grey to Sir F. Lascelles.

F.O. 371/78.
(No. 149.)

Sir, *Foreign Office, June 7, 1906.*

The German Chargé d'Affaires, who is going on leave, told me that there were two subjects on which he would like to ask my opinion before he went, in case he should be consulted about them at home.

The first was whether the King would be willing to meet the Emperor.

I said that I could not speak directly with authority as to what the King's wishes might be in this respect. But I knew that he had been willing to meet the Emperor in the Mediterranean in the Spring, and a meeting would have taken place then if the Emperor had gone to the Mediterranean. The King would, I supposed, go to Marienbad as usual later in the Summer, and I had no doubt that that would be a good opportunity for him to meet the Emperor if it was dèsired.

Herr von Stumm said the second subject was whether the British Government would change its attitude with regard to measures for dealing with anarchists.

I said that I did not remember what the attitude of the previous Government had been. . . . .

[I am, &c.
EDWARD GREY.]

MINUTE BY KING EDWARD.

App[rove]d.—E.R.

No. 418.

Minutes by Mr. Eyre Crowe and Sir E. Grey.(¹)

F.O. 371/75. *Foreign Office, June 9, 1906.*

These extracts are of interest because they bear traces of direct inspiration by the German Government. From no other source could the writer in the "Grenzboten"

(¹) [These minutes arose from articles in the *Morning Post* and *Times* of June 9, 1906, concerning the Bagdad Railway.]

have obtained the information respecting the Anglo-Russian negotiations, which I have
marked. And the conclusion of the article as quoted in the Times, certainly represents
an important current of opinion in influential German circles. The view is that
Germany requires the assent of Great Britain to certain political plans (of expansion,
conquest, acquisition of coaling stations; interference in small neutral states, etc.).
That assent Germany strives in vain to get by (friendly) asking! If however Germany
is strong enough to make England think twice before interfering between Germany
and the objects of her policy, then England will find it worth while to make up to
Germany and seek her friendship. In fact, good relations are to be obtained with
England only by the establishment of German hegemony.

The above views are largely held in German naval circles and are constantly
placed before the emperor. That is why their appearance in the Grenzboten article is
significant.

I annex a leading article from the "Morning Post" merely because it seems
to me to put the question at issue in an admirable way.

E. A. C.

June 9.

C. H.

Interesting.

E. B.

There is a good deal to think about in all this. The Germans do not realize that
England has always drifted or deliberately gone into opposition to any Power which
establishes a hegemony in Europe.

I observe that the Germans keep on saying that Russian interests in the Bagdad
R[ailwa]y must be antagonistic to ours and try to prove it by saying that we must
have the sole control of the Southern end. It was dislike of having the Bagdad
R[ailwa]y driven as a wedge between England and Russia that killed the idea of
our co-operating, when it was proposed some time ago. The German writers therefore
either do not want our co-operation or do not see that they are likely to prevent it,
if any attention is paid to what they say on this point.

E. G.

No. 419.

*Minutes by Mr. Eyre Crowe, Sir Eric Barrington, Sir Charles Hardinge and
Sir E. Grey.*(¹)

F.O. 371/78.   *Foreign Office, June 26, 1906.*

This article quoted from the Cologne Gazette, one of the principal inspired organs
in Germany, is significant.

We have it on the authority of Herr von Tschirschky himself that the object of
German policy is to prevent or smash an understanding between England and France,
and it cannot be doubted that advantage will be taken of any incident likely to prove
serviceable for this purpose.

It is a great pity that the otherwise harmless visit of German pressmen should lead
to demonstrations which lend themselves to the tortuous uses familiar to the press-
bureau of the German Foreign Office, and that English public men should, in their
not unnatural ignorance of the ways of German policy, allow themselves to be
exploited by a set of irresponsible busibodies inspired partly by the same ignorance
and partly by less respectable motives.

(¹) [These minutes arose from an extract from the *Cologne Gazette* printed in the *Times* of
June 26, reproduced on p. 360.]

In the interest of our understanding with France it may become necessary to take some steps to counteract the impression which the sudden and indiscriminate fraternization with the very men who have for years poured out the venom of their hatred of England in their papers, and who are equally rabid and hectoring in dealing with France, cannot but tend to produce in Paris.

If this fraternizing were really likely to lead to improved relations between England and Germany, something might be said for it. But in the minds of all those who really know and understand Germany, it is not at all calculated to effect this object. The German press does not influence the German government. On the contrary the German government influences the press. The way to maintain good relations with Germany is to be ever courteous and correct, but reserved, and firm in the defence of British interests, and to object and remonstrate invariably when Germany offends. Everyone who knows the mind of German officials will admit that such an attitude wins their respect. Firmness and punctiliousness are their own ideals and they readily recognise them in others. We were never so badly treated by Germany as in the years when we were always making concessions in order to "gain their real friendship and goodwill." They are essentially people whom it does not pay to "run after."

E. A. C.

June 26.

I am afraid that it is true that the French are nervous, but Ministers past or present have constantly declared that our alliance with France is not incompatible with a desire for the friendship of other countries, and if we secure the latter, the French ought not to mind.

E. B.

The Secretary of State intends to set this right by a statement in the House of Commons on our policy and the pivot on which it turns.

C. H.

There is nothing more in what has been said about Germany lately in this country than a gratification of the desire to gush, which is very strong just now. And it is as difficult to restrain gushing as it is to restrain tears, when people desire to cry.

E. G.

THE TIMES.

THE VISIT OF GERMAN JOURNALISTS.

(From our own Correspondent.)

Berlin, June 24.

In an article on the visit of German journalists to England the *Cologne Gazette* observes that "the importance of those circles which have hitherto joined in welcoming the German guests ought not to be under-estimated, and that it is increased by the fact that prominent members of the Government participated in the reception with great friendliness and unmistakable cordiality." It is worse than unfortunate that in these circumstances the report of the dinner in the Whitehall Rooms which is published by the Rhenish journal should conclude as follows :— "Even those observers who have hitherto been somewhat sceptical departed with the conviction that this pleasant personal intercourse is beginning to exercise a very beneficial effect calculated to compose many differences. If any one is still doubtful he can find confirmation in the uneasiness of our French neighbours which is already beginning to be noticed here."

No. 420.

Sir Edward Grey to Sir F. Bertie.([1])

F.O. 371/75.
(No. 364.)
Sir,   *Foreign Office, July 9, 1906.*

The French Minister told me to-day that Prince Radolin had been to see M. Bourgeois and had said to him that an *Entente* was proceeding between Germany and England. Prince Radolin wished the French Government to know that this *Entente* was in no way intended to impair the relations between France and England, and he hoped, therefore, it would not be disagreeable to France. M. Bourgeois had asked whether Prince Radolin had been instructed by the German Government to make this communication, and had been answered in the affirmative.

The French Minister showed me a note of the conversation which M. Bourgeois had sent him, in which it appeared that Prince Radolin had not actually spoken of an *Entente*, but only of a *Rapprochement*.

M. Bourgeois had replied that, as regards relations between England and Germany, that it was something with which it was not for the French Government to interfere, and that, on the general question of understandings which were intended to make for peace, M. Bourgeois was of course a friend of peace, and favourably disposed to anything which would promote it.

M. Bourgeois had, however, been surprised at receiving a communication of this kind in such a formal way, and had instructed the French Minister to tell me about it.

I said I was equally surprised that such a communication should have been made by the German Ambassador at Paris on the instruction of the German Government. As a matter of fact, there was nothing in the nature of an *Entente* between the two countries, nor was there anything out of which an *Entente* might be made. At present, there was nothing to discuss between the two Governments, except the trouble on the German South-West African frontier, an insignificant boundary question in some other part of Africa, and the German Concession in Madeira, as to which I had some time ago explained to the German Ambassador why we opposed it. In fact, I regarded the relations between England and Germany as being now normal, and I saw no reason for saying anything about them.

It would, I thought, be inconvenient for France that we should be on bad terms with Germany, just as it would be inconvenient for us that France should be on bad terms with Germany, for if we were called on to take sides, we must take sides with France as at Algeciras. As long, however, as Germany kept quiet, there was no reason for trouble, and things would go on quietly.

The French Minister asked me whether I thought Prince Radolin's communication was connected with the visit of the King to Germany.

I said the King was going to pass through Germany on his way to Marienbad, and as the German Emperor was a near relation, the King could not go through the Emperor's country every year without seeing him. But I did not think this could have been the reason for Prince Radolin's communication. All I could suggest was that a great deal of attention had been paid to us from Germany of late. We had received visits from German Burgomasters, German Artists, and, lastly, German Editors. Many people had attended meetings at which the visitors had been received, and they made very friendly speeches. But, as Germany seemed to be forcing the pace so much, some things had been said in conversation during the German Editors' visit to the effect that, if Germany wished any good to come of her being civil to us, she must show some corresponding civility in Paris. I also called the French Minister's

([1]) [This despatch was published by Lord Grey: *Twenty-Five Years* (1925) I, pp. 113–115, *cp. G.P.* XXI, II, pp. 437–440. On the 27th June the German Government instructed Prince Radolin, their Ambassador at Paris, that he should use the word " détente " of Anglo-German relations.]

attention to what I had said in Parliament to the effect that our good relations with France must not be impaired, and any developments in our foreign policy must be such as not to prejudice them. I did not meet the German Editors when they were here. But it was very likely that things of this kind had been said by others who had met them. These things had probably been reported to the German Embassy here and thence to Berlin, and Prince Radolin's communication might be an outcome of them. Otherwise, I could throw no light whatever on this communication.

The only thing of which the Germans had complained for some time past had been the tone of the English press. We had always answered this complaint by pointing out that the German press was at least as bad. There had lately been a tendency on the part of the press of both Countries to write in a better tone about each other, or to leave each other alone, and that was the only thing that had so far happened in the form of a *Rapprochement*.

There was nothing new proceeding between the two Governments.

I think it is desirable that you should explain this in conversation to M. Bourgeois, and should assure him that we have said nothing hitherto to him about our relations with Germany because there is nothing to tell, and my statement in Parliament was intended to convey that civilities and hospitality, which are promoted here by independent persons in no way connected with the Government, do not imply any present or future change of policy.

I am, &c.
EDWARD GREY.

MINUTE BY KING EDWARD.
App[rove]d.—E.R.

No. 421.

Sir F. Bertie to Sir Edward Grey.

F.O. 371/75.
(No. 278.)
Sir,

Paris, D. *July* 12, 1906.
R. *July* 13, 1906.

I had the honour to receive by the post this morning your despatch No. 364 of the 9th instant on the subject of a communication made to M. Bourgeois by the German Ambassador, under instructions from Berlin, relative to a *rapprochement* between England and Germany.

I called this evening on M. Bourgeois at the Ministry for Foreign Affairs and carried out the directions given in your despatch.

His Excellency told me that he had been very much surprised at Prince Radolin's communication, and had wondered at the time and was still meditating, why it was made. If it was with the intention of sowing distrust of England it had certainly failed. The Ambassador had said that an Article in the "Times" had recently stated, with reference to the visit of German journalists to England, that the condition of an understanding with England would be that Germany must be loyal and friendly not only towards England but also towards France, and that being the case, it was thought desirable to make the communication to the French Government.

M. Bourgeois said that he had observed to the German Ambassador that ever since he had been Minister for Foreign Affairs, he had worked for peace and he would rejoice at anything that promoted that cause, though the relations between England and Germany were not a matter in which the French Government had any reason to put themselves forward.

M. Bourgeois requested me to thank you for the statement which I had made to him on your behalf and to inform you that he had thought it well to let you know of the communication made by Prince Radolin, but that he had felt sure that had there really been a question of important negotiations between the German and British

Governments you would have kept the French Government acquainted with them in the same way as they would have kept His Majesty's Government informed of any negotiations which might be entered into by the French Government and interest His Majesty's Government; the essence of the good understanding between England and France being a free and intimate exchange of ideas on all questions affecting the interests of the two countries and peoples.

The Article which Prince Radolin would appear to have had in mind was published in the "Times" of the 7th instant.

I have, &c.
FRANCIS BERTIE.

No. 422.

Sir Edward Grey to Sir F. Lascelles.

F.O. 371/75.
(No. 196.)
Sir,   *Foreign Office, July 31, 1906.*

In the course of conversation with Count Metternich to-day, I said that though it was not my desire to take any official cognizance of views which he had not expressed to me direct, yet I knew that he had recently met friends of mine to whom he had expressed himself as being dissatisfied with the progress of the relations between England and Germany, and as they had reported his views to me very fully, and I understood with his consent, I did not like to appear ignorant of what had passed.

Count Metternich said that there seemed to be sensitiveness in France which would not allow that it was possible for England to be good friends with Germany at the same time as with France. This was a great mistake. The fear that Germany might attack France was purely imaginary. No one inside or outside the German Government had any such idea. France had, in the course of her history, made aggressive wars. But Germany had contended solely for her own unity, and had never made a war of aggression.

At this point, we had a little conversation about the action of Count Bismarck in 1870.

But I said I did not wish to raise questions of history and that, at the present moment, I was quite sure that France did not desire war with Germany, nor did we, and the intentions of both of us were quite pacific. It must be admitted, however, that during last year and up to the time of the close of the Algeciras Conference there had been friction between Germany and France in which we had been involved, and which had impaired cordial relations. Since the Conference, I considered that our relations with Germany had become normal. We had settled the boundary question in the region of Lake Victoria, in connection with which I had already expressed my satisfaction that the negotiations had gone so smoothly at Berlin. In South-West Africa, where the British Colonial Authorities had had a great deal of trouble and inconvenience arising out of the war in the German Colony, our attitude had been most friendly. There had been three violations of our frontier. But so far from these having led to any friction, I had taken advantage of the fact that the German expression of regret for one of these violations had been frank and prompt to turn it to friendly account by an answer in the House of Commons. In addition to this, we had entertained the German Burgomasters and the German Editors, and the King was going to meet the Emperor. It was true that this meeting was understood to be a purely family affair, still it could not take place unless our relations were normal. And yet it was only three months since the close of the Algeciras Conference. Surely this was a great deal to have happened in so short a time in the way of improvement. What more could be expected?

Count Metternich said that, at the time of M. Delcassé, there had been an idea, at any rate on the part of France, to form a "ring" against Germany. The Anglo-French *Entente* remained, and there was now expressed a desire for friendship with Russia. Germany did not see why she should not be included in this ring, instead of being kept outside of it. If she were included in it, all would go well and peace would be assured. But if she were not included in it, she would undoubtedly attempt to break through it.

I said that what was going on between Russia and us was very easily explicable. I had told the Russian Government at the beginning that the one thing we desired was security on the Indian frontier. We were a rich Country, and could afford to spend a good deal more on our army and navy than we were spending. But we did not wish to do so. On the contrary, we wished to reduce our present expenditure, much of which we considered to be wasteful and burdensome. But we could not reduce our army expenditure unless we were sure of repose on the Indian frontier. And we considered that an arrangement between Russia and ourselves would be of mutual advantage to both, by saving wasteful expenditure on both sides.

At present, we were discussing the subject of Thibet with Russia. That certainly was not making a ring against Germany. We might, in time, go on to discuss other questions; and when we came to one in which German interest was concerned, we should not try to settle it without going to Germany and trying to make an agreement with her.

Count Metternich accepted all this, but he observed that the tone of our Press was very different with regard to Russia and Germany. There was a friendliness and desire to be on good terms with Russia which was not expressed in the case of Germany.

I said that the motive for this was, in my opinion, the fact that people here were conscious of the great advantage of removing the old causes of friction between Russia and us. It was not sentimental friendship, but the practical results of an understanding with Russia that we valued.

Count Metternich said that the Press were constantly referring to the remark made in a speech of mine some time ago, that friendship with France was a keystone of our policy, and interpreting it as meaning that friendship with France made friendship with Germany impossible.

I said that speech had been made at a time when there was undoubtedly great friction between France and Germany, and when, to adapt a well-known phrase, one could not be a good second on the duelling ground if one constantly took up the position of an impartial umpire.

Count Metternich said he wished it to be clearly understood that Germany did not desire to impair our friendship with France, and saw no reason why that friendship should prevent friendship with Germany.

I said that was a matter which depended upon Germany's policy. In my opinion, relations with Germany had very greatly improved; they were now normal; and if they were to improve still further, time was all that was required, provided of course that things went quietly and no new cause of trouble arose.

If that were so, Count Metternich said, then it would be necessary to wait. And I said that if things went quietly, there could be no harm in waiting.([1])

I am, &c.

EDWARD GREY.

([1]) [For Count Metternich's record, see *G.P.* XXI, II, pp. 441–448.]

MINUTE BY KING EDWARD.

App[*rove*]*d.—E.R.*

No. 423.

Sir F. Lascelles to Sir Edward Grey.

F.O. 371/78.
(No. 237.) Confidential.
Sir,

Berlin, D. *August* 2, 1906.
R. *August* 7, 1906.

In the interview which I had this morning with Dr. von Mühlberg, the conversation turned upon the approaching meeting of the King and the Emperor at Friedrichshof. His Excellency asked me whether I had noticed a statement which had appeared in the North German Gazette last night to the effect that the Emperor would spend some days with his sister at Friedrichshof, where the King of England would also arrive. I replied that the statement was in complete accordance with the facts. The Emperor was to pay a visit to his sister, and the King would take the opportunity of his passage through Germany to meet the Emperor in Her Royal Highness' house. The meeting would be of a purely private character and I understood there would be no official reception.

Dr. von Mühlberg then told me most confidentially that the Emperor, in recent conversations, had expressed his earnest desire not merely that the relations between the two countries should be improved but that a thoroughly friendly understanding should be established between them, and that His Majesty hoped that it might be possible to convince public opinion in England that the German Fleet, which would be completed according to the Programme, was not to be considered as a menace to the maritime Power of England.

I thanked Dr. von Mühlberg for what he had said, and reminded him that Herr von Holstein, before leaving office, had spoken to me in this sense, and had attributed the necessity of his resignation partly to the fact that his personality was the principal obstacle to the realisation of His Majesty's wish. I did not believe that this was the case, but however glad I should be to see a friendly understanding established between our two Countries, I was strongly of opinion that the time had not yet come for any steps to be taken in that direction. In spite of the undoubted improvement which had taken place in the sentiments of the two people, there was still an amount of suspicion on both sides which would probably be increased if either Government made any definite proposal for a closer understanding.

Dr. von Mühlberg said that he entirely agreed with me that nothing should be done, at all events for the present. The suspicion to which I had alluded unfortunately existed and was especially strong in German naval circles, in which the belief was really entertained that Germany was in danger of being attacked by England. I replied that I had been informed that this was the case, although it was difficult to understand how such a fear could have been seriously entertained. I asked myself what possible advantage either country could hope to obtain by going to war with the other.

I have, &c.
FRANK C. LASCELLES.

No. 424.

Sir F. Lascelles to Sir Edward Grey.

F.O. 371/77.
(No. 255.) Confidential.
Sir,

Homburg, D. *August* 16, 1906.
R. *August* 20, 1906.

In the course of conversation with the Emperor last night I happened to mention the name of Herr von Holstein, and I was astonished at the outburst of indignation which his name elicited. His Majesty said that Herr von Holstein was a most dangerous man. He had, no doubt, great ability, but the influence he exercised over the German Foreign Office was a pernicious one. During Baron von Richthofen's tenure of office as Secretary of State Herr von Holstein exercised very great power. Count Bülow frequently quoted him as an authority and even Foreign Ambassadors (His Majesty cited Count Lanza and M. de Szögyényi) referred in their conversations with His Majesty to Herr von Holstein's opinion; this His Majesty considered to be most irregular. His reading of history had taught him to mistrust irresponsible advisers, and he was determined that there should not be a Stockmar or a Moritz Esterhazy in the German Foreign Office. He had therefore insisted that Herr von Holstein should be placed in a position of responsibility, and on his refusing to accept it, had told Count Bülow that he must decline to hear Herr von Holstein's name mentioned or his opinions quoted.

His Majesty attributed the breakdown in Prince Bülow's health in a great measure to Herr von Holstein, who deliberately inflicted on the Chancellor a vast amount of work of which the Foreign Office ought to have relieved him. Had Herr von Holstein had his way, the Algeciras Conference would certainly have broken down, and His Majesty himself had been obliged to intervene strenuously to prevent instructions being sent to the German Representatives which would at once have brought the Conference to an end. Such a state of things was intolerable, more especially in a State like Germany where the Sovereign was looked upon as the Authority which conducted the affairs of State, and where it was inadmissible that any official should possess Power without at the same time bearing the responsibility which such Power entailed.

After making due allowance for the exaggeration of expression in which His Majesty habitually indulges when interested in any subject, it is evident that the idea that Herr von Holstein had been made the scape-goat for the recent failure of German Diplomacy is not without foundation, perhaps even to a greater extent than his undoubted influence over the German Foreign Office would justify.

I have, &c.
FRANK C. LASCELLES.

No. 425.

F.O. 371/76.([1]) *Sir C. Hardinge to Sir Edward Grey.*
Private.
My dear Sir Edward, *August* 16, 1906.

I am on my way home and am writing these few lines to give you an account of all that took place at Cronberg.

I joined the King at Frankfort Station at 8 o'clock yesterday morning and we reached Cronberg about an hour later. The Emperor and Prince and Princess Frederick Charles were at the station to meet the King. After the usual greetings and presentations to the King and Emperor we went off to the Castle. The day was spent quietly the only distraction being a drive through Homburg to an old Roman fort at Saalburg which the Emperor is restoring at great cost and with some stretch of the imagination to what he believes was its original condition. Anyhow it is one of his special hobbies.

After dinner Tchirsky [*sic*] came up to me and said that the King had asked him to talk to me about the relations between the two countries as I was thoroughly conversant with his and your views on the subject.

I told Tchirsky that you had explained your views at some length quite recently to Count Metternich and that if the conversation had been fully reported there would be practically nothing for me to add. He replied that he had received a report from Metternich but that he still wished to talk the matter over. The conversation lasted for some time. He expressed himself as quite satisfied with the actual situation of affairs although he was still anxious as to the attitude of the French who seemed to imagine that the hand of Germany was to be found in any difficulty that arose whether in China, Tunis or the hinterland of Tripoli. To quote an example an article had appeared in a French magazine only a few days ago written by a French General Langlois, an officer of distinction, in which Germany was accused of sinister designs

([1]) [Typed copy only in the volume. There is no date of receipt, but the typed copy was circulated in the Foreign Office on September 11. The original is among the Grey MSS., Vol. 53, and the text given here has been checked by this, *cf.* Sir Sidney Lee : *King Edward VII* (1927), II, pp. 528–31, which quotes a letter of Sir C. Hardinge of August 19, *cf.* H. Wickham Steed : *Through Thirty Years* (1924), I, pp. 235–6.]

on the independence of Belgium and Holland. All such ideas were without the slightest foundation and German policy was directed solely towards commercial development abroad and economic development at home. Those who believed that the Emperor had warlike intentions at any time were grossly deceived since both His Majesty and the German Government fully realised that no war would be popular in Germany except in defence of some vital interest, and that unless the war was popular it would be difficult to carry it on. He impressed upon me that the two countries have many interests in common, especially commercial interests bound up with the maintenance of the open door in semi-civilised countries. It was in this direction that he would like to see cooperation between the two countries, but where England could under present circumstances render assistance to Germany and to the peace of the world would be by endeavouring to remove or to diminish the distrust felt in France towards Germany.

To this latter statement, I replied that the distrust in France was not unnatural; that after the removal of M. Delcassé, French public opinion, which had hoped for a " détente " in their relations with Germany, had received a rude shock on seeing that the same policy of browbeating was being pursued, and this had created a suspicion that the desire for an armed conflict was the motive. Any danger of this kind had fortunately been removed by the result of the Conference at Algeciras but it would naturally require some little time to pass to allow this impression to wear off. As regards our own relations with Germany I used practically the same language as you used to Metternich and I emphasised the necessity of time to maintain and develop the improvement which had taken place during the past four months, care being taken to avoid raising incidents likely to cause suspicion and above all things to avoid fireworks of every description.

On Tchirsky discussing the various reasons for the distrust which had grown up since the days of the Kruger telegram and the S[outh] African war I took the opportunity of mentioning that I had heard military people remark that the presence of 15,000 troops in German S[outh] Africa was hardly necessary to capture only 250 rebels, and although H[is] M[ajesty's] Gov[ernmen]t felt no alarm on the subject it was useless to conceal the fact that the same military people thought that the troops were being kept there with some ulterior motive. Tchirsky at once replied that he was glad that I had mentioned this suspicion which he assured me was quite unfounded. The German Gov[ernmen]t were very anxious to withdraw their troops who were suffering terribly and dying like flies. It had been necessary to employ no less than 8,000 men on the line of communications in order to make sure of provisions and stores reaching the front but he told me that I might assure you that they intend to withdraw 5,000 men during this autumn and 2,000 more during the winter.

On Tchirsky alluding to the unfriendly attitude of the British press I made him admit that there had been a considerable improvement in that respect, and I added that considering that the bulk of the press in England was more or less associated with the views of the Opposition it would be absurd to attach undue importance to its opinions. I assured him also that the improvement would be maintained provided that there were no more surprises and no attempt made to injure our relations with France or to thwart our negotiations with Russia. Friendship with Germany would be and is perfectly compatible with a French "entente" and an agreement with Russia on outstanding questions such as Thibet, Afghanistan and Persia, where Germany has no political interests, while in such questions as the Bagdad R[ailwa]y which you had fully recognised recently in the House of Commons as a German enterprise, you would not hesitate to consult the German Gov[ernmen]t if there should be any connection between it and the questions under discussion between us and the Russian Gov[ernmen]t.

Tchirsky said that he had been very satisfied with the answers and statements which you had made on different occasions in Parliament in connection with the Bagdad R[ailwa]y, that he quite understood the necessity for us of settling questions in dispute with Russia and that Germany had no political interests of any kind in Central Asia or the Persian Gulf, her interests being purely commercial. He said that he was very pleased to have had an opportunity of discussing these questions with me and he begged me as an old friend, if any cause for such distrust or suspicion should arise, to let him know of it informally through Stumm and that he would do his best to remove it.

On my mentioning that Metternich is somewhat inclined to take a gloomy view of Anglo-German relations he said that he had fully realised his lugubrious nature.

Almost immediately after my conversation with Tchirsky I was sent for by the Emperor and I had rather over an hour's conversation with His Majesty.

The Emperor began by saying that in his opinion the approaching Hague Conference was great nonsense and that it would be much better if the questions to be discussed were settled by direct negotiation between the Gov[ernmen]ts concerned without consulting the small Powers who had neither trade nor other interests involved, and that if Germany and England held out the date of the Conference could be indefinitely postponed. I replied that even were we so disposed it would be rather late in the day to adopt such a policy since we had already expressed our opinion on the programme to be discussed and, if no objections were raised to our views, it would be difficult now to back out of it without laying ourselves open to a charge of bad faith. Moreover the late war had shown that with a view to restricting as much as possible the causes and area of conflict it is very necessary to arrive at an understanding on such questions as what constitutes contraband of war, the right of sinking ships and under what circumstances &c. It would also be interesting to know the views of Europe on the subject of the reduction of armaments.

All questions affecting naval warfare would, His Majesty replied, be much better settled after a preliminary exchange of views between the countries with the greatest commercial interests, and he begged that I would suggest to you that our and the German naval Authorities should be instructed to discuss together various naval questions so as to arrive if possible at an agreement before the Conference meets. Once an agreement had been arrived at it would not be difficult to impose it on other Powers. By this means it would be possible to avoid any undesirable conflict of opinion between England and Germany at the Conference, and even if it was found impossible to reconcile the naval interests of the two countries no harm would have been done by a preliminary discussion. I said that I certainly would mention to you his suggestion, but that at present its realisation would be premature since H[is] M[ajesty's] Gov[ernmen]t had not yet formally decided upon the line which they themselves will adopt on many questions still under discussion in London. I added that I thought it not unlikely that H[is] M[ajesty's] Gov[ernmen]t might, before the meeting of the Conference, take steps to ascertain the views of other Powers but that so far nothing had been settled.

The Emperor then turned to the question of disarmament and remarked that when people talk of the reduction of military forces Germans only smile. The German nation had not forgotten the peace of Tilsit, and ever since they had been firmly resolved to exist by the strength of their right arm, and for this they had built up their overwhelming army of the present day. In any war with France Germany would be able to place in the field three million more men than France and would crush France by sheer weight of numbers. As for Russia it would be a long time before the Russian army could be reorganised. Germany, owing to her position between two great military Powers was compelled to maintain a powerful military organisation, and he thanked God that such was the case. For the last hundred years the idea of military service had become so ingrained in the people that it is now regarded almost as a disgrace not to have served in the army, and every year he received thousands of letters from the parents of young men rejected owing to some physical defect imploring him to take their sons into the army. Moreover it was a delusion to think that military service interfered with the commerce of the country. Merchants and shopkeepers take military service into account and prefer to take into their employment the ex-soldiers whom they regard as superior in every way to the ordinary civilian young man.

The Emperor, after his exposition of the advantages of militarism (of which I have only given a short summary) expressed his pleasure at seeing the King in Germany and at the improvement in the relations between the two countries. He said that he did not wish to raise the question of the Algeciras Conference, but he would like to inform me that when he paid his visit to Tangier last year he received the warmest possible reception from the British and Spanish Colonies in that city who welcomed him as their deliverer from French oppression. He added that an important Representative of the English Colony had paid a visit to a member of his suite and had bitterly complained of the manner in which the French had overridden British rights and interests, treating the country as though it was theirs by right of conquest, and that although complaints had been frequently addressed by the British colony to the Foreign Office their letters had remained unanswered.

I remarked that what His Majesty told me was very interesting, but that it was the first time I had heard of it.

His Majesty then dwelt upon the attitude of the French, remarking that the French nation is a bundle of nerves, and a female race not a male race like the Anglo-Saxons and Teutons. The underlying idea of their policy is that of the "revanche" but they are unable to obtain it for themselves. It was for this reason that they had made an alliance with Russia and later an "entente" with England, but that they are disappointed with the latter as not coming up to their expectations since they have realised, as he himself had done, the intense desire of England for peace. He expressed his conviction that the French people, apart from the Nationalists and followers of M. Delcassé, are equally desirous of peace, and that this is a great safeguard for the future.

I reminded the Emperor of his statement that the German army could crush the French army by sheer weight of numbers and suggested that the explanation of their nervousness and of their alliance with Russia and "entente" with England might be found in this fact which must be as well known to them as to His Majesty. The Emperor replied by assuring me of his most peaceful intentions, and that the question of war with France during last winter had never been seriously contemplated although he was well aware of the fears entertained in France as to his alleged intentions, which were absolutely without foundation. His sole aim and policy were to find commercial outlets for the ever-increasing and superabundant population of Germany.

His Majesty then enlarged at some length on the steps he had taken before obtaining the lease of Kiao-Chao and on how he had conveyed an inquiry to Lord Salisbury as to where he might find an outlet in foreign lands for German enterprise without conflicting with existing British rights. Having received no answer he repeated his inquiry and received a reply to the effect that Lord Salisbury would see him d——d first. Afterwards he approached the Emperor of Russia and settled upon the lease of Kiao-Chao where German trade and enterprise were now prospering in a marvellous manner the new railway already paying 5% interest to the share-holders. The Chinese flag, he said, still floats and the administration is Chinese but the enterprise is German and associated with the principle of the maintenance of the "open door." The day, he said, may come when the Chinese will want to send there a garrison and then he would be glad to reduce the number of German troops.

The Emperor complained that English Secretaries of State never visited Berlin and that it was desirable that they and Germans of note should know each other; also that people of London society seldom come to Germany although they frequented greatly Paris and Rome. I could hardly tell His Majesty that the attractions of Berlin compare unfavourably with those of Paris and Rome, but I mentioned the fact that Mr. Brodrick had been to Berlin two or three years ago and that Mr. Haldane proposed to visit Berlin very shortly. The Emperor expressed great pleasure at the prospect of Mr. Haldane's visit, remarking that the King had spoken of him as one of the cleverest men in England.

[15869]　　　　　　　　　　　　　　　　　　　　　2 B

The rest of His Majesty's conversation dealt chiefly with Russia and the position of the Emperor, as to which he expressed himself in a despondent strain. The mutinous attitude of the troops and the threatening financial situation are, in H[is] M[ajesty]'s opinion, the most serious factors of the present crisis.

Altogether I should say that the King's visit to Cronberg had been an unqualified success. The Emperor was in the best possible spirits, seemed very pleased to see his Uncle again, and no tiresome question nor discordant note was raised. As regards the political attitude of the Emperor and Tchirsky I was struck by their evident desire to be on friendly terms with us, and by the fact that they now seem at last to realise that friendly relations with us cannot be at the expense of our " entente " with France, but that if they are to exist at all they must be co-existent with our " entente." I took every opportunity of rubbing this in.

The King left this morning for Marienbad and I took leave of His Majesty at Rudelheim and returned home.

Yours very sincerely,
CHARLES HARDINGE.

P.S.—I should mention that on taking leave of the Emperor at the railway station His Majesty reminded me of his readiness to discuss questions of naval warfare before the meeting of the Conference, to which I replied that I would not fail to submit his suggestion to you.

C. H.

No. 426.

Mr. Cartwright to Sir Edward Grey.

F.O. 371/78.
(No. 103.) Confidential.   *Munich, D. August* 20, 1906.
Sir,   R. *August* 23, 1906.

I have the honour to report that the South German Press, like that in other parts of this country, has not abstained from writing a great deal on the subject of the meeting between the King and the Emperor at Cronberg, but, in doing so, it has occupied itself rather with personalities and incidents of the visit than with the political meaning of the same. As far as I am able to observe, I note a general absence of articles offensive and hostile to England, but, at the same time, I fail to note any sincere indication of a feeling of friendship for her. It would almost seem as if the order had been given from Berlin to the Press to show great reserve in commenting on the Royal interview, hence a coldness in the articles dealing with this subject which leave upon the mind the impression that the public is intended to be taught that the meeting between the two Sovereigns, by improving their personal relations, will react favourably on the official relations between the two Governments, but too much is not to be expected from this; if good comes out of the Cronberg meeting for Germany, so much the better; if it does not, it is of little consequence.

It would lead to little good if I were to report to you in detail the substance of all press articles which I have read on this subject, but I think it may be well to call your attention to a very soberly written article in the " Frankfort Gazette." The writer of this article states that the German press on this occasion has acted with great tact, but, nevertheless, it has failed in giving satisfaction to the British organs of public opinion, who complain that the German temperament is at times—without reason—too enthusiastic, and at other times too cold. If there has been coolness on the present occasion, it is due to the fact that the German public desires to wait and see for themselves how the British Government are going to act after the Royal interview. The writer asserts that this attitude is not the result of any anti-English sentiment, but on the contrary that Germany is entirely in favour of a better understanding with England; and he states that a better feeling can be noted since the change of Government in Great Britain, but so much resentment has been accumulated on both sides that it cannot be expected that there should be suddenly a genuine and enthusiastic show of friendship. Germany does not ignore that her attitude is being carefully watched over the water, and therefore it is incumbent on the German public to be very careful as to how they express their sentiments and the only thing to do is to wait patiently until a sensible policy is begun by both Governments which will lead to a better understanding, an understanding which the "Frankfort Gazette" approves of as in the interests of general peace.

A step towards a better understanding has been attained by the Cronberg interview, which was the result of many difficulties overcome and for that reason it may be looked upon as a good sign in this direction. What was impossible last year has been effected now. The importance of the meeting cannot be denied in the opinion of the "Frankfort Gazette," on account of the great personalities of the two Sovereigns, who undoubtedly have an important influence on the foreign policy of their countries. It attributes the erratic and somewhat changeable foreign policy of the Empire to the peculiarly impulsive and romantic temperament of the Emperor, and it draws attention to the importance of appreciating, in dealing with public affairs, the cool and determined character of King Edward, whose tenacity of purpose, especially in foreign affairs, makes him a dangerous antagonist. The misunderstanding between the two countries is in great part due to the difference of temperament of their Sovereigns, for in England the changeable character of German foreign policy is attributed by the public to duplicity, whereas the tenacity of purpose of Great Britain makes the Germans fear that they will be worsted by their neighbours if they are not careful and this renders them suspicious and gives rise to numerous articles in the press entitled "Perfidious Albion."

In conclusion the "Frankfort Gazette" asserts that the Anglo-French Agreement has not caused any real anxiety in Berlin and that Prince Bismarck was always in favour of a good understanding between these two Powers, and that France has therefore got no ground of complaint because of the meeting of the Kaiser and the King.

As far as I am able to ascertain there seems to be an impression among the general public that the differences which may exist between Germany and England in different quarters of the globe are not of a nature which renders their settlement impossible. They are not of first rate political importance and it would amount to nothing less than a crime if two great nations should go to war over them. Even the Agreement of 1904 between Great Britain and France which on its first publication produced an outburst of spleen and disappointment in this country, is now viewed with more calmness, almost with indifference, and this seems to be due to the firm conviction of the German nation that their army is invincible and will always inspire a wholesome terror to the French, therefore according to public opinion here the Anglo-French Agreement has in no way improved the Continental position of France, nor has it in any way paralysed the hands of Germany who can still bring pressure to bear upon her neighbour as easily as heretofore when circumstances may require it.

As a serious cause of estrangement between Great Britain and Germany there is in the opinion of many persons that nightmare of a possible understanding between Great Britain and Russia. To far-sighted people here, however, the dangers of such an understanding are not very serious. For them many years must elapse before a new Russia can be evolved out of the present chaos, and they hope that when a Russian Government is formed strong enough to exert an important influence on European Continental politics, a grouping of the Powers will be formed different from the one at present in existence by which the security of Germany will be assured.

There remains, however, one question which, if I may be allowed to express an opinion, lies at the root of the present differences which exist between Great Britain and Germany and which seems to me to be almost incapable of adjustment, and that is the German desire to acquire sea power. Two years ago Count Tattenbach said to me, in a moment of irritation over the Madeira Sanatorium question that, in whatever part of the world German energy and enterprise attempted to obtain a foothold, his compatriots immediately found the way barred by England and in the

2 B ?

majority of cases German interests had to yield to those of Great Britain because Germany was not at present in a position to dispute with her rival the sovereignty of the seas. This feeling of impotency, though not often expressed in official circles, has sunk deeply into the hearts of the German people and it has been ably encouraged by the Navy League and other such like patriotic associations. I am not prepared to assert, however, that there does not exist in this country a considerable section of the public which disapproves of the acquisition of Colonies which will never pay for the expense of their administration, and which Baron Stumm—now Councillor to the German Embassy in London—once described to me as " our miserable and useless possessions "; but that does not mean that the Kaiser has not got the support of the mass of the nation for his policy of increasing as rapidly as possible the naval forces of the Empire. That fleet is not primarily destined to enter into a struggle of destruction with the British Navy. Its destiny it is hoped will be for another purpose. Like all nations with an increasing population and a vast commerce, the German people have indulged in dreams,—dreams which have come to nothing in China and Africa, but which may prove more satisfactory in South America, where with luck it is hoped German influence may some day become predominant.

To establish a real friendship between Great Britain and Germany founded on a solid basis, not merely a truce between antagonists, it will be necessary for Great Britain to abdicate, at least in part, her sovereignty over the seas, and allow Germany to enjoy a fair share of it, a right which she considers she has a claim to,—in other words, Great Britain will have to admit Germany into partnership with her in the matter of sea power, and that means our benevolent neutrality the day when a collision takes place between the fleets of Germany and those of the United States.

I do not believe any one is so sanguine here as to imagine that such an arrangement is possible between the two countries,—therefore no real friendship can exist between them, and Germany will continue to find her aspirations thwarted at every turn by Great Britain. The calm and dignity generally shown by the Press in commenting on the meeting of the two Sovereigns at Cronberg must not be taken as a sign of a real desire on the part of Germany to enter on the path of genuine reconciliation with Great Britain. To do so would be to delude oneself. No real change has occurred in Germany since last year except in appearance. Official influences no doubt have exerted themselves to bring about a lull in Press attacks upon England, nevertheless the shipbuilding programme is not diminished but pushed ahead with energy and the truce in the newspaper war between the two countries is only intended to gain time until the day is reached when Germany has perfected her naval forces and she is in a position to speak with a louder voice at sea. It is not war with England that is then expected to occur but rather the conclusion of a friendly agreement with her, for Great Britain, it is hoped, will then bow to events and recognize " le fait accompli."

I have, &c.

FAIRFAX L. CARTWRIGHT.

No. 427.

Sir Edward Grey to Sir F. Lascelles.

F.O. 371/78.   *Foreign Office, August 30, 1906.*
Tel. (No. 51.)   D. 4·50 P.M.

Paris tel[egram] No. 76.([1])

Please also inform Mr. Haldane that substance of his telegram of Aug[ust] 29([2]) was communicated to M. Cambon by Sir E. Grey the same night.

([1]) [Sir F. Bertie telegraphed on August 30, D. 1·32 P.M., R. 3·0 P.M., that M. Bourgeois had asked him to call Sir E. Grey's attention to the probable effect upon French public opinion of Mr. Haldane's presence at any ceremony which could be regarded as in commemoration of the battle of Sedan.]

([2]) [The substance of this telegram is indicated in the next document, p. 373, No. 428.]

No. 428.

Sir Edward Grey to Sir F. Bertie.

F.O. 371/78.   *Foreign Office, August 30, 1906.*
Tel. (No. 176.) Urgent.   D. 5 P.M.

Your tel[egram] No. 76 has been repeated to Secretary of State for Foreign Affairs who wrote a letter to M. Cambon yesterday as follows :—

"I have just had a telegram from Marienbad in which Mr. Haldane says he has made inquiry at the Embassy at Berlin and is informed that the review and dinner to which he has been invited have no connection with commemoration of Sedan wh[ich] is to take place on the 31st and at which Mr. Haldane will not be present."

(BARRINGTON.)

No. 429.

Lord Granville to Sir Edward Grey.

F.O. 371/78.   *Berlin,* D. *August 30, 1906, 11·45* P.M.
Tel. (No. 34.)   R. *August 31, 1906, 7·30* A.M.

Your telegrams Nos. 50(^{1}) and 51 of to-day.

Following from Mr. Haldane :—

I have ascertained from most reliable source that the parade and dinner have no kind of connection with Sedan.

Victory always celebrated on 2nd September, this year, owing to Sunday, on 31st August, on which day I have no invitation whatever.

I consider it would have a most deplorable effect if I were to give up attending the dinner or parade, and Sir F. Lascelles agreed with me most strongly in this opinion last night.

Safest course would seem to be to rely on explicit statements, confirmed again to-night, which it would be almost an insult to appear to disbelieve.

MINUTES.

We have done all we could short of preventing Mr. Haldane from going to Berlin at all, and there is really no ground for complaint on the part of the French.

E. B.

Sir E. Grey's instructions rec[eive]d this morning have been tel[egraphe]d to Sir F. Bertie, 12·15 P.M.

[E. B.]
E. G.

(^{1}) [Not reproduced.]

No. 430.

Sir Edward Grey to Sir F. Bertie.

F.O. 371/78.   *Foreign Office, August 31, 1906.*
Tel. (No. 180.) Urgent.   D. 1 P.M.

Berlin Telegram No. 34.

You should explain to M[inister] [for] F[oreign] A[ffairs] that visit of Mr. Haldane to Berlin is for purpose of studying German army in connection with reorganisation of British Army. While there it was impossible for him not to accept any invitation at all, but he will avoid the function which is commemorative of Sedan. Significance of date was not know[n] to him when he left England.

No. 431.

Sir F. Lascelles to Sir Edward Grey.

Berlin, August 31, 1906.

F.O. 371/78.   D. 3·46 P.M.
Tel. (No. 35.)   R. 5·18 P.M.

Mr. Haldane's visit to Berlin.

At Mr. Haldane's request, Lord Granville called on French Ambassador this morning, and explained fully Mr. Haldane's grounds for believing that dinner and parade have nothing to do with Sedan, and the reasons for his opinion that throwing them over now would be far worse for the relations between the three countries than risk of adverse comments by French press. French Ambassador insisted that there was no doubt that the parade and dinner were in commemoration of Sedan, and remarked that the French Military Attaché invariably absented himself from Germany during these days.

His Excellency therefore considered that it was very unfortunate that Mr. Haldane should have accepted the invitation, though he quite realized that it was in complete innocence of any intention to offend, and in ignorance of connection with Sedan. At the same time his Excellency agreed that it was now too late, and that it would be undesirable to refuse at the last moment.

Lord Granville said that Mr. Haldane would like to call and make his acquaintance and ask whether his Excellency thought a visit to the French Embassy, which would be certainly reported, would perhaps counterbalance the bad impression in France. French Ambassador was inclined to think this a good plan, but would prefer to telegraph to Paris first.

At Lord Granville's request his Excellency promised to state in his telegram his view that it was impossible for Mr. Haldane now to refuse, even on the plea of illness, &c.

Lord Granville did not gather French authorities had any additional grounds for their belief in the connection of Sedan, and there would not appear to be any adequate reason for disbelieving the statements made to Mr. Haldane by the officers attached to him.

MINUTES.

There seems nothing more to be done. It is evident that Mr. Haldane could not get out of it now. We shall see how the Germans take advantage of it, and how much their recent expressions of friendliness and of a desire for better relations are worth.

G. S. S.
E. B.
E. G.

No. 432.

Mr. C. Spring-Rice to Sir Edward Grey.

F.O. 371/73.
Private.   *Foreign Office, August 31, 1906.*

I had a long conversation today with the French Ambassador on whom I called in order to ask for a letter of introduction to the French Minister in Tehran. I explained how useful it had been to me in St. Pet[ersbur]g to receive the advice and assistance of M. Bompard and I hoped that my French colleague in Persia would offer similar help especially in my dealings with the Russian Legation. He gave me a letter written in the most friendly terms, which I will present on my arrival at Tehran. The conversation then turned to the general question of Anglo-French relations and especially to Mr. Haldane's visit. He said that he had known Mr. Haldane for a long time—in fact since his own arrival in London. He appreciated thoroughly his genuine admiration for the Germany which he knew. Personally M. Cambon thought that the real Germany—or Prussia—was a very different thing to the Germany of students and philosophers. But like Napoleon III, Mr. Haldane was no doubt impressed by the romantic and intellectual side of German life. This was natural and praiseworthy and implied no hostility to France. M. Cambon also said that he had a profound confidence in the King, Government and people of England and especially in yourself. He could not believe for an instant that we cherished the intention of "using our entente with France to get better terms for ourselves with Germany," as was said. But he could not help remembering that such things *were* said and that the press both in Germany and France was used with extraordinary adroitness in order to alienate France and England. Whatever we believed ourselves, it was our duty to avoid, as far as was reasonably possible, providing material to the adroit managers of the press campaign with which Morocco had made the world familiar.

The facts however were such that they could easily afford material for such a press campaign. The meeting of the Emperor and the King followed closely by the mission of Haldane to Marienbad and his official visit to Berlin during that September week which was anxiously regarded as the Sedan anniversary—which the French military attaché avoided and which the Spanish King had recently refused to attend, even at the risk of giving offence of a serious nature. All this was "material" of a pronounced character.

He repeated that he did not for a moment suspect Mr. Haldane of any desire to strike out a policy of his own, inconsistent with the formal and official policy of his government, or even of personal sympathies differing from those of the British nation. Nor did he or the French Government suspect the good faith of our Government. But legends take long to die: the legend in France was "perfide Albion" and it would be foolish to ignore this fact, or the existence of the determined and well conducted manoeuvres of the inspired and subsidized press.

For himself he could only make the observation—of an objective character— that nothing in the Emperor's recent language gave a solid ground for hope that the policy of Germany in Morocco would change in a sense friendly to France. If German policy then continued to be as heretofore unfriendly to France—it was unnecessary to allude to the conclusions which would be drawn if England made friendly overtures to Germany with a view to a closer cooperation.

The conversation was of an entirely personal and friendly character and arose out of my request for his assistance in obtaining a personal recommendation to my French colleague. It had nothing of the nature of an official communication or of a complaint. Tyrrell to whom I spoke of his language thought that you might be glad to hear what he said.

I may add that he had on his table de la Gorce's history of Napoleon III. It contains Vol. VI and VII, very full details as to the politeness lavished by the Prussian Military authorities on French officials, &c., in the years 1868–69. He alluded to this.

[C. SPRING-RICE.]

No. 433.

Sir F. Lascelles to Sir Edward Grey.

Berlin, September 1, 1906.
D. 1·50 P.M.
R. 2·45 P.M.

F.O. 371/78.
Tel. (No. 36.)

My telegram No. 35 of yesterday.

French Ambassador called on Lord Granville this morning and stated that he had received an answer from Paris agreeing that it was impossible now for Mr. Haldane to upset the arrangements, and approving of proposal that Mr. Haldane should call on H[is] E[xcellency] to-day. French M[inister] [for] F[oreign] A[ffairs] added that

[15869]

2 B 4

H[is] M[ajesty's] Gov[ernmen]t had promised, if adverse comments appeared in French press, to publish distinct statement of facts of the case.

Lord Granville pointed out to H[is] E[xcellency] fact of no comments having yet appeared in the German press which could be taken up in France, but the Ambassador feared they might still come or the Germans might be hoping for a commencement of attack from the French press when they could declare their innocence.

No. 434.

Sir F. Lascelles to Sir Edward Grey.

F.O. 371/78.
Tel. (No. 37.)

Berlin, September 1, 1906.
D. 4·52 P.M.
R. 6·20 P.M.

My telegram No. 36 of to-day.

Mr. Haldane, accompanied by Lord Granville, called on French Ambassador at 3 o'clock.

French Ambassador remarked, in the course of conversation, that one must never exaggerate things, and gave Mr. Haldane the impression of being slightly ashamed of the whole affair. All the Military Attachés, excepting the French but including both Russians, were present at the parade this morning.

MINUTES.

This is more satisfactory.

G. S. S.

Sent to S. of S. Sept. 1.

E. B.
C. H.
E. G.

No. 435.

Diary of Mr. Haldane's Visit to Germany.(¹)

F.O. 371/76.

(This document consists of the second part of a diary sent by Mr. Haldane to the King by His Majesty's desire, with the exception of that part of his conversation with M. Tchirsky [*sic*] which relates to The Hague Conference.)

Secret.

Berlin, September 2, 1906.

The narrative which I sent on Saturday morning to Your Majesty extended to Friday evening. Next day several things happened. The French Government were so uneasy about my being present at the parade on Saturday that I took care to go only at some distance from the Emperor. I wore plain clothes, and drove among various civilian guests of His Majesty, including a number of ladies. But the Russian Military Attaché was so convinced that the parade had nothing to do with Sedan that he went to a prominent position. As we had conjectured, there was no more reference to "Sedan-tag" than to "Jena-tag"! Indeed, it became clear that such celebration as there had been of Sedan had taken place, not on the 1st September, but on the 31st August, the real day (the 2nd) being a Sunday.

I thought it well to call on the French Ambassador in the afternoon and explain all this to him. He was cordial, and said there was nothing at all in the affair—that

(¹) [The explanatory sentence at the head of this document is taken from a printed copy of the diary bound up with the original in F.O. 371/76. It seems to imply that the last section of the diary (pp. 380–1) was not sent to H.M. King Edward. Lord Haldane has informed the Editors that there was a first part to the diary; but this has not been found in the Foreign Office Archives or in the King's Library at Windsor. Lord Haldane stated further : " The whole was written by King Edward's desire for himself in my own handwriting, and was sent to him by special messenger to Marienbad. His instructions were that I was to write freely and omit nothing." (Lord Haldane to G. P. Gooch, July 8, 1927.) Lord Haldane has described his visit in *Before the War* (1920), Ch. II, *cf.* Sir Sidney Lee : *King Edward VII* (1927), II, p. 531.]

a mountain had been made out of a mole-hill, that his Government agreed that I could not get out of going, and that he himself was of opinion that the best relations between England and Germany meant improved relations between France and Germany, and that Your Majesty's visit had had a good effect. Lord Granville and I, at his request, sent an intimation to Reuter to the effect that I had called on the French Ambassador. He said his Government had asked for this.

I return to the parade. It took place at 8 in the morning, and I was there early. Notwithstanding my somewhat retired position, the Emperor galloped up, and I had an interview with him standing in the carriage. He was in excellent spirits and humour. "A splendid machine I have in this army, Mr. Haldane; now, isn't it so? And what could I do without it, situated as I am between the Russians and the French? But the French are your allies, so I beg pardon." I said that were I in his Majesty's place I should feel very comfortable with this machine, and that for my own part I enjoyed much more being behind it than I should had I to be in front of it. He laughed, and then talked of the organization of his War Office, which I had been inspecting the day before, and of the technical points in it. I had got a pretty good hold of the business side of this organization, and His Majesty was interested not the less because he had never gone very deeply into it himself. For, as he said, his teacher was General Bronsart von Schellendorff, who wrote about the Staff side of the war organization—not about the "intendantur"—which I had been inquiring into, with a view to improvements at home. Fortunately, I had read Bronsart von Schellendorff's book twice through, and also that of Clausewitz, on which it was founded, and His Majesty continued the conversation until he had to go, saying that it was odd that an English civilian should have read the things that only German and Japanese soldiers read. . . . .([1])

In the afternoon a message from the Emperor arrived, with a present of various military atlases and tables which His Majesty thought would interest me, and I was bidden, along with Colonel Ellison, to dine at the Schloss. Before dinner Prince von Bülow called. I was out, but later met him at the Schloss, and had an excellent conversation with him. He began by alluding to the good effects produced by the meeting at Cronberg, and said that the Emperor and he were thoroughly aware of the desire of Your Majesty and your Government to maintain the new relations with France in their integrity, that in the best German opinion this was no obstacle to building up close relations with Germany also. I said that this was our view also, and the only danger was trying to force everything at once. Too great haste was to be deprecated. He said that he entirely agreed, and quoted Prince Bismarck, who had laid it down that you cannot make a flower grow any sooner by putting fire to heat it. I said that none the less frequent and cordial interchanges of view were very important, and that even the smallest matters were not to be neglected. He alluded to my personal intimacy with Count Metternich with pleasure. I begged him if there were any small matters which were too minute to take up officially, but which seemed unsatisfactory, to let me know of them in a private capacity through Count Metternich. This I did because I had discovered some soreness at restrictions which had been placed on the attendance of foreign military officers in England at manœuvres, and I had found out that there had been slight reprisals. I did not refer to these, but said that I had Your Majesty's instructions to give any assistance to German officers who were sent by the German Government to study. I said that while our Army was small compared with theirs, it had had great experience in the conduct of small expeditions, and that there was a good deal that was worth seeing.

This brought Prince von Bülow to the question of the Navy. He said that it was natural that with the increase of German commerce Germany should wish to increase her fleet—from a sea-police point of view—but that they had neither the wish nor, having regard to the strain their great Army put on their resources, the power to build against us. I said that the best opinion in England fully understood this

([1]) [A sentence is omitted here as being of a purely personal character.]

attitude and that we did not in the least misinterpret recent progress, nor would he misinterpret our resolve to maintain, for purely defensive purposes, our Navy at a two-Power standard. Some day, I said, there might be rivalry somewhere, but I thought we might assume that if it ever happened it would not be for a great many years, and that our policy as a nation was at present strongly for Free Trade, so that the more Germany exported to Britain and British possessions the more we exported in exchange to them. He expressed himself pleased that I should say this, and said that he was confident that a couple of years' interchange of friendly communications in this spirit would produce a great development, and perhaps lead to the most pleasant relations for both of us with other Powers also. The conversation was both pleasant and interesting. I had seen Sir Edward Grey on my way to Marienbad, and knew what he thought I might properly say.

After dinner I had an audience of the Emperor. He was most cordial, and spoke with pleasure of my interest in German literature. His Generals had told him that I knew the details of the development from after the battle of Jena of the economic and constitutional history better than they did, and this gave him pleasure. He had given instructions, hearing that I had been investigating the military organization with an interest that had not often been shown, that everything was to be shown to me. His sons, like himself, were keen soldiers. I said that it was in the blood, and that we in England were proud of His Majesty as being an Englishman as well as a German. He then said that he had been often misunderstood in England; that he had even made suggestions for the improvement of the Militia some years ago with keen desire to be of use, but that he feared no one had read them. By good fortune I was able to say with absolute truth that two months ago I had heard of the Emperor's suggestions from the Duke of Connaught; that I had obtained the original paper, prepared by His Majesty's General Staff, and with his own pencil writing on it; that I had the plan proposed under investigation at this very time. His Majesty expressed himself as greatly pleased at this, and said that there was, he thought, yet another paper of his, about the operations in South Africa in 1900, though probably not so useful. The conversation then passed to the career of Frederick the Great.

I had also a conversation with the Empress, to whom I gave Your Majesty's message of affectionate regard. Her Majesty was very friendly.

After dinner the whole party went to the opera, where a stage box was assigned to Colonel Ellison and me and our two German officers. The Royal family occupied the Royal box. Sunday was spent quietly in making calls. On Monday I went, by arrangement, to the house in the Tiergarten of the Great General Staff. After an hour and a-half explanations from General v[on] Gründel [sic], who had been detailed to show its organization, I returned the call of the Chief of the General Staff, v[on] Moltke. We had half-an-hour's talk. He spoke with warm approval of our new organization of the English army into six great divisions instead of army corps, and said that their view was that this was what we should always have done in England, in order to make an army capable of easy transport with our fleet to distant theatres of war. Just as the army was the great thing with Germany so the fleet was with us, and they did not take " als [?] uebel "[1] that we should lay stress on keeping absolute command of the sea. They would do the same were they us. They must increase their fleet as a sea-police for their commerce, but the burden of expenditure would be too great for them if they were to try to rival ours, and also do what was more important for them—keep their great army up. This was essential to them, and he thought they could defeat both France and Russia if attacked. But, small as our army was, they had profited by studying it. Nothing finer in recent military history had been displayed than the organization of Kitchener's Nile expedition. The Germans had had troubles in South-West Africa because their soldiers were not trained like ours for the conduct of distant expeditions, where self-reliance and initiative were even more important than scientific preparation. Our management of lines of communication with our base, too,

[1] [sic, es übel?]

in China, was very fine. *Per contra*, we could have studied their organization with profit before our South African war. A war with England would be for them, as for us also, a fearful calamity, because it could not be short, whichever won, and would mean slow exhaustion while America—a very real danger this in his opinion—helped herself to the trade of both of us. Therefore it should not be contemplated.

On arriving back at the hotel I found a telegram from the Emperor bidding me to lunch with him. I was in time to go. He and the Empress, the War Minister, v[on] Einem, and four members of the Household were there. I sat next the Empress. After luncheon the Emperor took me away into his private room, and I had an hour-and-a-half's conversation. He was cordial, and talked sometimes in English and sometimes in German. He spoke of the French *entente*. He said that it would be wrong to infer that he had any critical thought about our *entente* with France. On the contrary, he believed that it might even facilitate good relations between France and Germany. He wished for these good relations, and was taking steps through gentlemen of high position in France to obtain them. Not one inch more of French territory would he ever covet. Alsace and Lorraine had originally been German and now even the least German of the two, Lorraine, because it preferred a Monarchy to a Republic, was welcoming him enthusiastically whenever he went there. That he should have gone to Fez [Tangier] where both English and French welcomed him, was quite natural. He had desired no quarrel, and the whole fault was Delcassé's, who had wanted to pick a quarrel and bring England into it. I told His Majesty that if he would allow me to speak my mind freely I would do so. His Majesty assented, and I said to him that his attitude had caused great uneasiness throughout England, and that this, and not any notion of forming a tripartite alliance of France, Russia and England against him, was the reason of the feeling there had been. As for our *entente* we had some time since difficulties with France over Newfoundland and Egypt, and we had made a good business arrangement (" gutes Geschäft ") about these complicated matters, and had simply carried out our word to France. He said that he had no criticism to make on this, excepting that if we had only told him early there would have been no misunderstanding. Things were better now, but we had not always been pleasant to him and ready to meet him. He had asked Lord Salisbury to give him a coaling station, had been curtly refused, and had therefore asked the Emperor of Russia for Kiaou-chow. His army was for defence, not for offence. As to Russia, he had no Himalayas between him and Russia—more was the pity. Now, what about our two-Power standard! (All this was said with earnestness, but in a friendly way, His Majesty laying his finger on my shoulder as he spoke. Sometimes the conversation was in German, but oftener in English.) I said that our fleet was like His Majesty's army. It was of the " Wesen " of the nation, and the two-Power standard, while it might be rigid and so awkward, was a way of expressing a deep national tradition, sacred as the Gospel, and a Liberal Government would hold to it as firmly as a Conservative. Both countries were increasing in wealth, we, like Germany, very rapidly, and, if Germany built, we must build. But I added, there was an excellent opportunity for co-operation in other things. The present Liberal Government was Free Trade to the marrow of its bones, and would not encourage colonial preferences against other nations beyond what could be avoided. We did not believe in them, and our creed was to increase our imports in order to increase our exports. There was a great opening for international Free Trade development, which would smooth other relations. The Emperor said he quite agreed. He was convinced that Free Trade was the true policy for Germany also. But Germany could not go so quick here as England could. I said that I had read Frederick List's great book defending a Protective policy for Germany, and knew that military and geographical considerations affected matters for that country. His Majesty remarked that Chamberlain's policy had caused him anxiety. Chamberlain was unfriendly to Germany. He had spoken slightingly of the German army, and when he (the Emperor) had tried at Sandringham to get on with him, he had found it difficult. I said that many of my countrymen had lived all their days in an island and were more apt to misunderstand Germany than those who had lived much there. Possibly this was so with Mr. Chamberlain. After all, perhaps Mr. Chamberlain thought we might some day have a real conflict over our trade. I myself thought it not likely, but did not disguise from myself that it was at least possible. But I saw no reason to dwell on what might well be wholly avoided with a little care on both sides. The undeveloped markets of the world were enormous, and we wanted no more of the surface of the globe than we had got. The Emperor said what he wanted was not territory but trade expansion. He quoted Goethe to the effect that if a nation wanted anything it must concentrate and act from within the sphere of its concentration. I said that the line of policy adopted by His Majesty would, if thoroughly followed out result in much good. There was a rivalry that was not only legitimate but beneficial. The Germans had got away from us over 50 millions per annum of chemical trade merely by better science and organization. "That," said the Emperor, "I delight to think, because it is legitimate and to the credit of my people." I agreed, and said that similarly we had taken away the best of the world's ship-building. Each nation had something to learn. The Emperor then passed to The Hague Conference, trusting that disarmament would not be proposed. If so, he could not go in. I observed that the word disarmament was unfortunately chosen. "The best testimony," said His Majesty, " to my earnest desire for peace, is that I have had no war, though I should have if I had not earnestly striven to avoid it."

Throughout the conversation, which was long and animated, His Majesty was most cordial and agreeable. He expressed his wish that more English Ministers would come to Berlin, and more of those of the Royal Family whom he had made officers of his regiments. He mentioned His Royal Highness the Prince of Wales and Prince Christian, as two whom he should be glad to see in Germany. The Cronberg visit had however, been a great pleasure to him.

I left the Palace at 3·30 having gone there at 1.

At 4·15 on Monday the 3rd I returned the call of Herr von Tchirsky, who had invited me to dine, and had an hour's talk with him.([2]) He struck me as frank and candid. I explained that my business in Berlin was merely with War Office matters, and ever as regards these quite unofficial, but he wanted to talk. He said there had been much tendency to misinterpret in both countries, but that things were much better. I might take it that our precision about the *entente* with France and our desire to rest firmly on the arrangement we had made, was understood in Germany, and that it was realized that we were not likely to be able to build up anything with Germany which did not rest on this basis. But he thought, and the Emperor agreed, that the *entente* was no hindrance to all that was necessary between Germany and England—which was not an alliance, but a thoroughly good business understanding. Some day we might come into conflict if care was not taken; but, if care was taken, there was no need of it. I said that I believed this to be Sir E. Grey's view also, and that he was anxious to communicate with the German Government beforehand whenever there was a chance of German interests being touched. His Excellency then said he wanted to speak to me unofficially about The Hague Conference. The Emperor had taken alarm at the word disarmament, and would not enter the Conference if this was to be discussed. Germany might, on the other hand, well enter a Conference to record and emphasise the improvement all round in international relations, the desirability of further developing this improvement, and the hope that with this improvement the growth of armaments would cease. I said that I would report this; that the difficulty I saw was that we as a Government were pledged to something that seemed more definite, and we had actually done something. He smiled and said, "You yourself, Excellency!" I said, "Yes, both in naval and military matters we had actually done something, and our people wished us to do more." He said with earnestness that he hoped no vote would be taken—Germany

could not alter the proportion of her Army to her population, for this rested on a
fundamental law. The fleet programme was, moreover, fixed, and the Emperor would
never consent to what for him would be theatrical. For Germany to stand alone
would be to put herself in a hole, and it would be a friendly act if we could devise
some way out. I said America would certainly propose something, which went a
good way. He did not like the initiative coming from America. The United States
had no sympathy with European military and naval difficulties. He said could we
not ourselves get the assent beforehand of the Powers to such a general resolution
as we had been speaking of. To this he thought he could get the assent of the
Emperor. Of detailed business there was enough for the Conference to discuss. I
said I saw difficulties which even the friendliest spirit might find it difficult to get over
with the movement on foot among the various peoples at this time, but that I would
faithfully report what his Excellency had said. He passed to general topics. He was
emphatic in his assurance that what Germany wanted was increase of commercial
development. Let us nations among ourselves avoid pin pricks, and leave each other
free to breath[e] the air. He said he thought we might have opportunities of helping
him to get the French into an easier mood. They were very difficult and suspicious,
and it was hard to transact business with them. They made trouble over small points.

R. B. H.

MINUTES.

As the Emperor during his conversation with Mr. Haldane alluded to certain incidents
connected with foreign politics of the last few years I have thought it useful to have some
minutes prepared in the Dep[artmen]t(³) giving what we regard to be the true version of the
incidents in question and which you may perhaps like to show to Mr. Haldane. I also add a
very useful mem[orandu]m prepared by my Private Secretary Mr. Montgomery.

Sep. 15, 1906.   C. H.

This is very useful I have read the minutes to Mr. Haldane today.

Sep. 16, 1906.   E. G.

With regard to the German Emperor's statement that he had asked Lord Salisbury to give
him a coaling station, has been curtly refused, and had therefore asked the Emperor of Russia for
Kiao-chou, Sir F. Lascelles in his despatch No. 38 v. conf[identia]l of February 2, 1898,(⁴) reported
that during a conversation with H[is] M[ajesty] on the previous day, the Emperor, in referring
to Kiao-chou, said he would tell me exactly what had taken place.

After the murder of the German missionaries in China, H[is] M[ajesty] had addressed
himself directly to the Emperor of Russia who had given his consent to the proposals which
H[is] M[ajesty] had laid before him. When, however, the German ships went to Kiao-chou,
Count Mouravieff, who was probably not aware that the consent of the Emperor of Russia had
been given, protested strongly and used language which seriously alarmed the Ministry for Foreign
Affairs in Berlin. He tried to maintain that the occupation of Kiao-chou was a violation of the
Cassini Convention.* H[is] M[ajesty], however, declined to be moved by Count Mouravieff's
bluster which he knew was not authorized by the Emperor of Russia. He therefore gave the
necessary instructions to Baron von Rotenhan who was temporarily in charge of the Ministry for
Foreign Affairs and at the same time ascertained from the Chinese Government that the Cassini
Convention which Count Mouravieff had more than once invoked, had no existence in fact.

In order to obtain any further information which might be forthcoming on the subject,
Lord Sanderson has been consulted. His reply is annexed.

[B. A.]

Confidential.
My dear Tyrrell,   *September* 13, 1906.
Your letter has been forwarded to me in Scotland and I reply at once so far as my memory
serves me.
When the Germans occupied Kiao-chou, the Russian Government began to protest. The
German Government at once replied that the proposed measure had been mentioned some time

(³) [Not reproduced.]
(⁴) [v. *Gooch & Temperley*, Vol. I, pp. 4–5, No. 4.]
* This was alleged to have been concluded by C[ount] Cassini, Russian Min[iste]r at Peking,
at the close of the war between China and Japan, and conceded *inter alia* certain special privileges
to Russia as a response to the loyal aid given by Russia in the retrocession of Liaotung and its
dependencies.   [B. A.]

before by the German Emperor to the Emperor of Russia, who had given his consent. The Russian Gov[ernmen]t replied that they were not aware of any such pledge on the part of the Tsar. The German Gov[ernmen]t however persisted and gave the date. The matter was submitted to the Tsar, who then recollected that in a conversation after dinner the Emperor William had told him that Germany would have to proceed to the occupation of a Chinese port in order to secure satisfaction for the murder of some German missionaries, and that he hoped Russia would not oppose her action. The Emperor of Russia had therefore said that he saw no objection to the proceeding so far as Russia was concerned, and could not oppose it.([5])

The conversation was of a general character and the Tsar's recollection of it was vague, but he considered himself bound by his word and directed that the Russian protest should be dropped.

I cannot remember whether Kiao-chou was supposed to have been specially mentioned—or whether the Tsar made some proviso that the port occupied should be south of the Gulf of Pechili.

I think the essential facts could be found in the Despatches from Berlin, Petersburg and Copenhagen, but it is quite possible that Alan Johnstone may have furnished details in a private letter. My recollection is that there was something to the effect that the conversation occurred while the two Monarchs were smoking cigars and taking a cup of coffee after dinner.

The Russian Gov[ernmen]t made a stipulation before the next meeting of the two Emperors that *no* business should be discussed between them without previous notice.

I cannot too earnestly warn Mr. Haldane to take the most careful note of any remarks the Emperor may have addressed to him, especially if they can in any way be interpreted as suggestions or enquiries. His Majesty has a way of dropping such remarks casually and then bursting out several months afterwards with a complaint that his question has not been answered, or that his warning or invitation has been entirely disregarded—I could cite several instances, but that is probably unnecessary.

I shall be back in London in the middle of next week, and will look in, and answer any further questions.

Yours ever,
SANDERSON.

Foreign Office.

The story I heard in Russia was that the 2 Emperors were playing tennis when in the intervals of the game the German Emperor turned round to the Russian Emperor and said " I am afraid we shall have to occupy a Chinese port to get satisfaction for the murder of the missionaries. It will be a very tiresome undertaking, will it not? " The Russian Emperor agreed vaguely and forgot all about it till he woke up one morning to find Kiao-chao occupied by the Germans and they asserted that his specific consent was obtained!

The next time the two Emperors met the Russians stipulated that there should be no political conversations à deux, the German Emperor did his best to steal a march on them and took the Russian for a tête-à-tête drive during which he tried to discuss politics but the Russian maintained an obstinate silence for 2 hours until the drive was over!

O.([6])

There are one or two remarks made by the Emperor to Mr. Haldane, in addition to those referred to in the Minutes prepared by the Department, which seem to call for some comment :—

(1.) " That he should have gone to Tangier, where both English and French welcomed him, was quite natural. He had desired no quarrel and the whole fault was Delcassé's who had wanted to pick a quarrel and bring England into it." And later on, in reply to some remarks of Mr. Haldane to the effect that in our action with regard to Morocco we had simply carried out our word to France: " He said that he had no criticism to make on this, excepting that if we had only told him early there would have been no misunderstanding." The Germans had on more than one occasion told us that they took no great interest in Morocco, notably in 1901; in a Memorandum communicated by Count Metternich on Sep[tember] 3 in reply to a paper, containing a series of notes on various questions, which was handed to the German Emperor by the King on the occasion of their meeting in that year.([7])

The words of that part of the Memo[randum] communicated by C[oun]t Metternich which referred to Morocco were : " In Morocco we follow a policy of reserve. The Morocco question by itself is not sufficiently important for us to justify a policy by which Germany might incur the risk of serious international complications."

In face of declarations such as this, was it strange that we thought it unnecessary to consult with Germany before coming to an arrangement respecting Morocco, or that we attributed ulterior motives to the Emperor's visit to Tangier and his subsequent action with regard to Morocco?

([5]) [*v.* on this *Gooch & Temperley*, Vol. I, p. 1, Ed. Note.]

([6]) [This minute is by Lord Onslow. It is undated, but must be of a date after 23 October, 1911, when he succeeded to the title.]

([7]) [*v. Gooch & Temperley*, Vol. II, pp. 92–6, No. 104.]

(2.) '' Things were better now, but we had not always been pleasant to him and ready to meet him.'' It seems fair to take the latter part of this sentence as referring, to some extent at any rate, to the abortive negotiations for an understanding in 1901. We entered into those negotiations in a perfectly open and '' pleasant '' spirit; it was not till we found how wide the German mouth was opened that we held back. It was the Germans who would not meet us, not we them; they laid down the lines of an agreement which was too far-reaching and refused to deal with us on any other terms. Their suggestions practically amounted to a proposal that we should join the Triple Alliance. In the course of a long conversation with Lord Lansdowne on Dec[ember] 19, 1901 (v. desp[atch] to Berlin 393 of that date, annexed for reference)([8]) Count Metternich said : '' The agreement between these two groups (i.e., the Triple Alliance on the one hand and Great Britain and her Colonies and dependencies on the other) would be to the effect that if either group were to find itself attacked by another Power, and that Power were to be 'joined by another Power or Powers both groups should make common cause against the aggressors.''

Count Hatzfeldt had at an earlier stage of the negotiations been equally explicit. In Lord Lansdowne's desp[atch] to Berlin No. 193A of May 24, 1901, he writes '' Was I, then,'' I said, '' to understand that the proposal was simply that we should join the Triple Alliance? Count Hatzfeldt answered in the affirmative.''([9]) In reply to a suggestion on the part of Lord Lansdowne that, assuming that we could not accept the German proposal as it stood, the two countries should arrive at an understanding with regard to particular questions of interest to both, Count Metternich '' unhesitatingly replied that no such minor proposal was likely to find favour with the German Government. It was a case of ' the whole or none.' ''

(3.) '' Mr. Chamberlain was unfriendly to Germany.'' Owing to the animus felt and freely expressed in Germany against Mr. Chamberlain on account of his connection with the Boer War and owing to the erroneous reports of the speech in which he was supposed to have spoken slightingly of the German army (this question is dealt with more fully in the Department's Minute) the Emperor and most of his countrymen have long since lost sight of the fact that Mr. Chamberlain, in his speech at Leicester in November 1899, was the first—and probably the only—British Cabinet Minister to publicly advocate an alliance with Germany. This speech was made soon after Mr. Chamberlain had met the Emperor at Windsor, where he had been led by His Majesty to believe that a public utterance of this nature would meet with a friendly response in German official quarters. The reception with which his advances met in Germany both from the Government and from the Press, was so cold that it may legitimately be described as a distinct rebuff.

C. H. M.

September 14, 1906.

[ED. NOTE.—An unsigned note attached to the above minutes refers to the existence of the secret file in the Foreign Office from which several papers relating to the Anglo-German negotiations of 1901 were printed in Gooch & Temperley, Vol. II (Chapter X, pp. 60–88). It refers also to a paper of 1910 (No. 21148 of June 13, 1910). This paper is a long minute by Sir Eyre Crowe arising from a question asked in the House of Commons by Mr. Gibson Bowles (Parl. Deb., 5th Ser., Vol. XVII, p. 888).

HOUSE OF COMMONS, 8TH JUNE, 1910.

MR. GIBSON BOWLES asked the Secretary of State for Foreign Affairs whether there is any record in the Foreign Office of any overtures either in 1899 or in 1901 between Great Britain and Germany for the accession of Great Britain to the Triple Alliance between Germany, Austria and Italy, or are there any papers relating thereto; were any overtures begun in January, 1901, and broken off in March, 1901, for any understanding with Germany, or any joint action with Germany; and is there any correspondence that he can lay upon the Table for the information of Parliament?

SIR E. GREY : I cannot answer questions of this kind about relations between Great Britain and other Powers ten years ago.

Minute by Mr. Eyre Crowe [May 20, 1910].

This is an embarrassing question. It is no doubt based on the passages from the book just published by the notorious Rudolf Martin—(a former high official in the Prussian Ministry of Finance, who was some years ago made to resign owing to repeated indiscretions on his part)—which were quoted in the '' Standard '' of May 5. (Annexed hereto.)([10]) I have obtained a copy of the book.

Mr. Martin asserts, in the course of a general attack on Prince Bülow's policy, that Mr. Chamberlain, on behalf of Great Britain, offered in 1889 [sic] to divide Morocco with Germany,

([8]) [Printed in Gooch & Temperley, Vol. II, pp. 80–3.]
([9]) [ib. Vol. II, pp. 64–5.]
([10]) [Not reproduced.]

as a preliminary to a general " entente " with that Power; and that in 1901, during the Emperor's visit to England on the occasion of Queen Victoria's funeral, Mr. Chamberlain made a formal proposal that England should join the triple alliance by a treaty " to be ratified by parliament," the " casus fœderis " to arise when either party was attacked " from two sides." Prince Bülow is then severely criticized for neglecting this magnificent offer, without reference to the Emperor.

These are phantastic perversions of events which have hitherto been treated as profound secrets. The real facts are these:

In November 1889 [? 1899] Mr. Chamberlain at the direct suggestion of Prince Bülow, ventilated in a public speech the idea of an alliance between England and the United States on the one hand, and the triple alliance on the other. Owing to the Boer war, public opinion in Germany was at the time violently anti-British, and Mr. Chamberlain's speech met with a very hostile reception in the German press. Whether influenced by this or by other causes, Prince Bülow did not hesitate to throw Mr. Chamberlain over in the most marked manner, the German semi-official and inspired press pouring abuse and ridicule on the proposal, which was treated as if it had been an impertinence.

According to Mr. Martin, it was the affair of the " Bundesrath " and the controversy arising out of it, which for the time put an end to the negotiations respecting Morocco and an Anglo-German understanding. They are stated to have been resumed by Mr. Chamberlain in January 1901 and continued by Lord Lansdowne until March of that year. What really happened was this:

On March 18, 1901, the German Chargé d'Affaires, Baron Eckardstein, speaking, as he declared, unofficially, but clearly with full authority, sounded Lord Lansdowne in conversation as to the conclusion of a defensive alliance between England and Germany. The conversations were fitfully continued, partly with Baron Eckardstein, and partly with the Ambassador, Count Hatzfeldt, during the course of the year. The German proposals, on gradually taking more precise shape, eventually emerged as an invitation to England to " join the triple alliance." It was admitted to follow from such an arrangement " that each of the allies would have a right to claim a voice in guiding and controlling the external policy of the others."

Lord Lansdowne throughout the discussions confined himself to criticizing and pointing out objections, without however rejecting definitely the German overtures. The Germans very carefully, even markedly, abstained from ever putting anything in writing. Count Hatzfeldt fell seriously ill in June 1901, the subject then dropped, and Baron Eckardstein declared " that Count Hatzfeldt was regarded by the German government as having pushed matters rather too far and too fast, and that, for a time at all events, it was not thought advisable that the negotiations should be continued." In the late summer however Baron Eckardstein suggested renewing the discussion. It was just at the end of the parliamentary session, and Lord Lansdowne explained that the arrival of the summer holidays made it impracticable to lay before the cabinet proposals " upon so momentous a question."

When Lord Lansdowne reverted to the subject with the new German Ambassador, Count Metternich, in December 1901 the latter declared his gov[ernmen]t had been under the impression that " our failure to reopen the discussions indicated a desire to drop the question altogether and it was assumed that some event had happened which had led us to close the question." On being assured that this was not the case Count Metternich went on to say that the present moment was not favourable for further pursuing the question and that moreover an opportunity so favourable as that which presented itself last summer might not again occur.

I have narrated these events in some detail in order to show that although there is a substratum of truth in Mr. Martin's statements they are so grossly inaccurate and distorted that they convey a completely erroneous impression. . . . .(¹¹)]

(¹¹) [The remainder of this minute discusses in detail the reply to be given to Mr. Gibson Bowles. The final wording is given above, p. 383.]

No. 436.

Sir F. Lascelles to Sir Edward Grey.

F.O. 371/79.
(No. 273.) Confidential.   Berlin, D. September 2, 1906.
Sir,   R. September 10, 1906.

On the evening of the 28th Ultimo I arrived at Berlin in order to be present at the Royal Christening on the following day, to which I had the honour of being invited. Shortly after my arrival I received a visit from Prince Radolin who had come from Paris for the same purpose.

Prince Radolin expressed his pleasure at the recent meeting of the King and the Emperor, which had passed off in so satisfactory a manner, and which he could tell me had given great pleasure to the Emperor, as he believed it had also to the King. I assured him that that was the case, and that His Majesty had expressed himself as completely satisfied with the visit to Friedrichshof.

Prince Radolin having referred to the friendly relations which existed between him and Sir Francis and between Princess Radolin and Lady Feodora Bertie, I told him that rather more than a year ago a report had reached me that a serious misunderstanding had occurred between him and Sir Francis, and that no less a person than Herr von Holstein had expressed the opinion that, in private life, the incident must inevitably have led to a duel. Prince Radolin replied that he was at a loss to understand how the report had arisen. He had always been on friendly terms with Sir Francis, and there never had been the slightest question of any offence having been offered or taken. It was true that at the time when the German Government was pressing for a Conference on the Morocco Question, Sir Francis Bertie had expressed his opinion somewhat freely on the subject, but both the Italian and the Austro-Hungarian Ambassadors in Paris, in their conversations with Prince Radolin, had not concealed their disapproval of the action of the German Government, though perhaps in a more diplomatic form.

Prince Radolin went on to say that the three Ambassadors were perfectly right in the view they took of the question. It would have been perfectly easy, after Monsieur Delcassé's fall, for the German Government to have come to a satisfactory arrangement with the French Government by direct negotiation through the ordinary diplomatic channel. Instead of this, the German Government not only insisted on the Conference, but also sent Doctor Rosen, whom he described as a tactless individual, with fresh demands which could only increase the irritation in France and the suspicion as to the ulterior aims of Germany. The result of the Conference was certainly not satisfactory to Germany. She had found herself in a position of almost complete isolation, and the understanding between England and France had been greatly strengthened.

Prince Radolin was in hopes that, now that the relations between Germany and England had become better, it might be possible to bring about an improvement in the relations betwen Germany and France. Unfortunately the Authorities in the German Foreign Office were under the impression that any *rapprochement* between England and Germany would be resented in France and would render an improvement in the relations between Germany and France more difficult. He was convinced that this was not the case, and that the great majority of French statesmen were perfectly well aware that as long as the relations between England and Germany were in a strained condition it was hopeless to expect anything in the nature of a better understanding betwen France and Germany. It was for this reason that he had been so glad to hear that the meeting between the King and the Emperor had been of so satisfactory a nature, as he felt that, as the tension between the two Sovereigns had now been allayed, the principal obstacle to the establishment of correct if not indeed friendly relations between France and Germany had now been removed.

I have, &c.
FRANK C. LASCELLES.

No. 437.

Sir F. Bertie to Sir Edward Grey.

F.O. 371/79.
(No. 338.)
Sir,

Paris, D. September 6, 1906.
R. September 8, 1906.

The "Times" of yesterday gives a summary and the important points of an article which is to appear in the September number of the "Deutsche Revue."

The article which has evidently been inspired by very high if not by the highest authority in Germany, and probably by both, discusses the recent interview at

2 c

Friedrichshof between Their Majesties the King and the German Emperor, the relations between England and Germany, those between England and France and the attitude of France as regards Germany and a *rapprochement* between the British and German Governments.

The Article states that :—

(*a*.) A pacific policy in France could not but desire the relations between England and Germany to assume a friendly character. An Anglo-German understanding therefore offers for France the best possible guarantee of peace, for no one in Germany thinks of an aggressive war against France, which even in the event of victory would offer to Germany no advantages. The ambitions attributed to Germany in the French Press being imaginary the reason for the anxiety shown by French Diplomacy to prevent the *rapprochement* between Germany and England cannot be the preservation of peace. It must be the hope of British support in case of war, and of a war which France intends to bring about, the Delcassé traditions continuing to be the policy of French Diplomacy, viz., to hem in Germany diplomatically with the help of England, Russia, and other States so closely that the ultimate and inevitable attempt of Germany to break through the circle should end by her defeat diplomatic and military.

(*b*.) The Article, after referring to the view taken in France that England will hold unswervingly under every Cabinet to the *entente* with France, and stating that the present Cabinet contains several Germanophil Ministers, chief amongst them the War Minister and the Lord Chancellor, and setting forth what it considers to be your view in regard to the *entente* and a reconciliation with Russia, and negotiations with Germany in questions affecting the "Nearer East," states that the kernel of Anglo-German relations therefore lies herein, that you shall not identify yourself with the French interpretations, viz the Delcassé Policy—that is to say the isolation of Germany —but shall meet her with confidence.

(*c*.) The question, the Article says, may be summed up as follows :—

"Will the Anglo-French Group close up still more closely as a counterpoise to Germany, which is the object of French Diplomacy, or, conscious that it is not strong enough, especially in view of the temporary elimination of Russia and of the actual dispositions of her policy, will it now strive to expand the understanding to Germany, which, it must be understood, should not be taken to mean the accession of Germany to the policy of the Western Powers? Since the meeting at Friedrichshof we may be justified in assuming that we are travelling, though slowly and step by step, to a period of *rapprochement*. Germany could argue with some force, and let us hope not without success, that a peaceful policy for Great Britain can alone consist in holding out the hand to Germany, and that peace would thereby be much more effectively secured than by Congresses and Disarmament Proposals. The relations between England and France would not be thereby imperilled, since England has irrevocably declared that the *entente* with France is a permanent basis of her policy. No doubt could exist on that point in France, even if England were to woo Germany openly and without constraint. As for the possibility of a Franco-German *rapprochement*—that is to say, of more friendly relations of France to Germany—false hopes and baseless fears would appear still to stand in its way, and an open relationship of friendliness on the part of England towards Germany might materially help to remove them. The policy of *ententes* outside of Germany and against Germany is uncertain in execution and not without danger in its consequences. This policy of counterpoises will persist however as long as England, out of fear of displeasing Paris, continues to treat with coolness the honourable approaches of Germany; Germany is thereby necessarily compelled to remain on her guard. Towards Germany England has only the choice between either the policy, which might easily become disastrous, of an Anglo-French counterpoise, or that of including Germany within the circle of her friendships. These logical conclusions can hardly fail to have carried weight at Friedrichshof and in the British Foreign Office. Substantial results will only naturally mature slowly."

(*d.*) As to the question of German Naval Expansion and the comments made on it in the English Press, the Article emphasizes the necessity for England of accepting the situation as follows :—

"England must reconcile herself to the thought of seeing the German Fleet occupy alongside of the British Fleet a position commanding and imposing respect on the sea. . . . .(¹) A year ago the belief did exist in Germany that our relations with England were in a stage analogous to the relations of Prussia and Austria before 1866, and that in all probability a cordial understanding would have to be preceded by a sharp encounter. The estrangement which rendered such a belief possible, though it may not have justified it, is past. Both nations may feel confident that it will be possible to arrive at a cordial agreement without any previous armed conflict."

For convenience of reference I have marked with distinguishing letters the various portions of the above-recited Article which relate to different parts of the questions therein dealt with, and I have the honour to submit for your consideration the following comments on the Article, which I believe represent the views held on the several points raised in it by responsible persons in France.

(*a.*) Contrary to the view put forward by the "Deutsche Revue," the policy of France is one of peace and she desires the relations between England and Germany to be of a nature to obviate a recourse to arms between those two countries; for she feels that, whether her engagements bound her to become a party to such a war or not, she would inevitably be dragged into it either by being attacked by Germany or in defence of her vital interests.

The French do not at all believe that no one in Germany thinks of an aggressive war against France; on the contrary they have the conviction that had it not been that England and France held together in the question of Morocco France would have been either humiliated or attacked by Germany.

The German Government gave out that it was M. Delcassé personally who was the obstacle to good relations between Germany and France. M. Rouvier, who had no experience of foreign affairs, sacrificed M. Delcassé, and took his post as Minister for Foreign Affairs, but he soon realized that the stumbling block was not his late colleague but the good understanding which that Minister had negotiated with England, and that the policy of the German Government was to impress on France the disadvantage of friendship with England and the benefits to be expected from an agreement with Germany.

Inasmuch as the ambitions attributed to Germany in the French Press are in great part those announced by prominent German writers and speakers, and that many of them are very natural for patriotic Germans to feel, French opinion does not consider them to be imaginary on the part of the French Press. Provided that a *rapprochement* between Germany and England has only for its aim the removal of any outstanding Diplomatic Difficulties between the two countries and tends therefore to the preservation of peace, no objection will be felt in France, for no party in the country desires to bring about a war with Germany in reliance on British support.

I do not believe that the Delcassé traditions which the Revue alleges to continue to be the policy of French Diplomacy was to hem in Germany diplomatically with the help of England, Russia and other States so closely that the ultimate and inevitable attempt of Germany to break through the circle should end by her defeat diplomatic and military. M. Delcassé was alarmed at the growing strength and dictatorial attitude of Germany and the aim of his policy was by coming to terms with England to prevent an Anglo-German agreement to the detriment of French interests, which he knew to be the desire of the German Emperor and his government, and conse-

(¹) [Thus in original.]

quently through improved relations or an understanding with England to render France less liable to attack by Germany.

(b.) There is no doubt that German agents, with the view of creating distrust against England, have propagated the theory that there is a tendency on the part of some of His Majesty's advisers to favour an understanding with Germany rather than one with France, and this may account for the nervous sensitiveness shown by M. Bourgeois in regard to the possibility of Mr. Haldane, in the course of his visit to Germany, accepting an invitation to attend ceremonies which might be connected with the celebration of the great French defeat six and thirty years ago. I do not think that M. Bourgeois personally is suspicious of any intention on the part of His Majesty's Government to depart from the spirit of the understanding between the British and French Governments, viz. to consult confidentially and freely and act together so far as possible in all questions affecting the interests of England and France, but he has to count with others who are not sure of the stability of British policy, and to remember that the Nationalist party and many Royalists were formerly in favour of an understanding with Germany and that an agitation for such a policy might easily be started again if the French public were led to suspect that His Majesty's Government contemplated an agreement with Germany, not only on specific questions actually at issue, but on general policy.

(c.) The Revue refers to the possibility of more friendly relations between France and Germany through open relationship of friendliness on the part of England towards Germany and lays stress on the view that the policy of *ententes* outside of Germany and against Germany is uncertain in execution and not without danger in its consequences.

The suggestion that England should act the part indicated would certainly entail a great danger to the existing relations between her and France, for it would be taken as an attempt to persuade the mouse to make friends with the cat and be regarded as covering some secret designs arranged with Germany.

It appears to me that our policy as regards relations between France and Germany should be not to create friction as was Prince Bismarck's practice in regard to the relations between France and England; but to do nothing to facilitate an understanding between Germany and France; for it is difficult to conceive how an understanding of any real importance between these two countries could be satisfactory to Germany without being detrimental to our interests.

(d.) With regard to the necessity for England emphasized by the Revue to accept German naval expansion and to reconcile herself to seeing the German fleet occupy alongside the British fleet a position commanding and imposing respect on the sea, opinion in France is that the reductions in English naval expenditure will not lead to any diminution in German naval preparations to contest the naval supremacy of England in the north of Europe whenever a suitable opportunity may occur, and that it is incumbent upon France and that it will be necessary for England not to relax in their determination to keep up the existing relative strength of their naval forces in proportion to the increases in the German fleet.

I have, &c.

FRANCIS BERTIE.

No. 438.

Sir F. Lascelles to Sir Edward Grey.

F.O. 371/78.
(No. 279.) Confidential. *Berlin, D. September 14, 1906.*
Sir, R. *September 17, 1906.*

On the 11th instant, Herr von Tschirschky's usual reception day, I called upon His Excellency whom I had not had an opportunity of seeing since the meeting of the King and Emperor at Friedrichshof. Herr von Tschirschky expressed his satisfaction at the success of the King's visit, and said that the Emperor had been much pleased at his friendly intercourse with the King, and at the conversations he had had with His Majesty.

I said that the King fully reciprocated these sentiments. His Majesty had charged me to report to you that he was fully satisfied with his visit and to add that the Emperor had been very kind.

I went on to say that I understood that although the King and the Emperor had conversed in a most friendly manner on a variety of subjects, the relations between England and Germany had not been referred to in their conversations. Fortunately there was no question pending between the two Countries of sufficient importance to create a serious difference of opinion, and I was not without hope that the improvement in the personal relations between the two Sovereigns might eventually lead to a better understanding between the two Countries, but for this more time would be necessary, and, in my opinion it would be advisable to avoid any exaggerated expression of the effect produced by the conversations of the two Sovereigns which would tend to revive the mutual suspicion which still existed in certain quarters but which I hoped was in process of being allayed.

Herr von Tschirschky said he quite agreed with me. It was a great thing that the meeting between the two Sovereigns, which would have been an impossibility a year ago, had passed off so satisfactorily. It would no doubt produce an effect in both Countries which he hoped would eventually lead to a better understanding, which, however, could only be brought about by time and by a renewal of confidence.

Herr von Tschirschky referred to Mr. Haldane's recent visit to Berlin which had given great pleasure to the Emperor, and which he hoped would not be without effect. He also said that it had given him great pleasure to renew at Friedrichshof his acquaintance with Sir Charles Hardinge whom he had learnt to appreciate in St. Petersburg.

Herr von Tschirschky told me that he was about to leave Berlin on a six weeks' leave of absence, and that until Herr von Mühlberg's return the Ministry for Foreign Affairs would be under the charge of Count Pourtalès, the Prussian Minister at Munich.

I have, &c.

FRANK C. LASCELLES.

No. 439.

Minutes by Sir C. Hardinge and Sir E. Grey.([1])

F.O. 371/74.   *Foreign Office, September* 18, 1906.

It was obvious that the special facilities and favours granted to Sir John French at the French manœuvres would be interpreted as proofs of the existence of an alliance or military convention which is not the case, although discussions took place last spring between the naval and military Auth[oritie]s of the two countries as to joint action in case of war. The present elastic situation is more satisfactory for us although the fact that we are not bound hand and foot to the French makes the latter nervous and suspicious.

C. H.

There is much to be said on both sides. The difficulty of making an alliance with France now is that Germany might attack France at once, while Russia is helpless, fearing lest when Russia recovered she (Germany) should be crushed by a new Triple

([1]) [These minutes arose from an article in the *Kölnische Zeitung*, headed " An Anglo-French Military Convention? "]

[15869]   2 c 3

Alliance against her.   She might make an alliance between us and France a pretext for doing this as her only chance of securing her future.

E. G.

No. 440.

Sir F. Lascelles to Sir Edward Grey.

F.O. 371/79.
(No. 288.)   Very Confidential.   *Berlin,* D. *September* 21, 1906.
Sir,   R. *September* 24, 1906.

With reference to my preceding Despatch of this day's date,([1]) I have the honour to report that during my recent visit to Coburg I had two long conversations with The German Emperor.   His Majesty said that he had received great pleasure from the Duke of Connaught's attendance at the Manœuvres, and he believed that His Royal Highness and the Officers who accompanied him had been much impressed by what they had seen of the German Army.   He believed that His Royal Highness had always during the last thirty years been present at the Manœuvres when they took place in Silesia and it had been a great satisfaction to confer the rank of Field-Marshal upon His Royal Highness.   I said that the Duke of Connaught, who had recently done me the honour to stay at His Majesty's Embassy at Berlin, had not only greatly appreciated the honour which His Majesty had conferred upon him, but had been deeply touched by the kind and even affectionate terms in which His Majesty had notified the appointment.   His Royal Highness had shown me His Majesty's letter and called my special attention to its very friendly language. The Emperor also alluded to the pleasure which his conversations with Mr. Haldane had given him and repeated what he had frequently said to me before, that he wished that more English Statesmen would visit Berlin and see things for themselves. I ventured to remind His Majesty that some years ago Lord Curzon, who at that time was Under Secretary of State for Foreign Affairs, had been greatly disappointed at not being received by His Majesty when he visited Berlin.   His Majesty replied that he remembered that Mr. George Curzon, as he was then, had asked for an audience during the last days of Holy Week when it was impossible for him to grant audiences.

In discussing the situation in Russia, His Majesty said that it was impossible to foresee what would take place.   There seemed to be no men capable of dealing with the existing state of things.   Disorders were continually taking place.   Murders were constantly committed and something very like anarchy prevailed.   He doubted whether General Trepow's death, which seems to have been a natural one, entailed any real loss on the Country.   It was impossible to believe anything which appeared in the newspapers, and in Russia itself no one seemed to know what to expect.   As a proof of the effect which sensational and inaccurate statements (His Majesty employed somewhat stronger expressions) could produce, His Majesty said that he had recently received a Telegram from some Professors and Students at Kieff, protesting against his having received Mr. Witte during his recent stay at Homburg.   There was not a word of truth in the report.   He had not received Mr. Witte, and had had no intention of doing so.

With regard to France, The Emperor said that it was his earnest wish to establish good relations with that country.   " And here," said His Majesty, " you could help me if you chose.   All you would have to do would be to tell the French to be decently civil to me.   They will certainly do what you tell them, and things could easily be brought on to a better footing.   If on the other hand you keep on telling them that they can always count upon your support against me, the situation may become dangerous.   They are constantly making small difficulties."   His Majesty waxed eloquent over the Dreyfus case which was a terrible exposure of the state of morality in France.   No less than four Ministers of War had deliberately committed perjury, and a campaign of calumny had been carried on which was a disgrace to any civilized

---

([1]) [Not reproduced.]

Country. On my observing that Monsieur Bihourd was about to resign his post, His Majesty said that he had not heard of his intention to do so, but his departure would leave His Majesty perfectly indifferent. He had no objection to Monsieur Bihourd personally but what he would like to see in the shape of a French Ambassador in Berlin would be a gentleman who could form a correct opinion of what took place in Germany and had sufficient weight with his Government to make them believe what he said. Monsieur Bihourd was evidently wanting in the first qualification, and His Majesty admitted that he felt considerable irritation in reading Monsieur Bihourd's published Despatches in which he spoke of the existence of a war party, not only in military circles but in His Majesty's immediate *entourage*. "There never was such nonsense," exclaimed His Majesty; "My *entourage* entirely share my opinions and are as peacefully inclined as I am myself."

Perhaps the most interesting part of the Emperor's conversation was his allusion to the state of affairs in the Balkan Peninsula and to the personality of the Prince of Bulgaria, who was in the room at the time. Prince Ferdinand, whom His Majesty described as the cleverest and most unscrupulous of the Princes who reigned in Europe, had attempted to have a political conversation with His Majesty, who had cut him short by saying that any difficulties he might have with the Sultan were entirely his own fault for not keeping his people in order and preventing them from crossing the frontier into Macedonia, and murdering and pillaging the people there. The Prince was a very ambitious man and hoped to make himself King or Emperor of the Balkans. If he ever succeeded, which however was not probable, the foolish Russians would discover that he had been working all along for himself and not for them. On my asking whether His Majesty thought that the Prince would be tempted to move in the event of the death or serious illness of the Sultan, he replied that it was quite possible. In such a case there might be confusion at Constantinople, which the Prince might think would give him his opportunity. His Majesty however did not believe in the dissolution of the Turkish Empire, which had been so much talked of at any time during the last 200 years. He was also glad to believe that the Sultan had recovered from his indisposition which had not been so severe as had been made out. No doubt complications might arise if the Sultan were to die, and he thought that the Powers had made a mistake in weakening the authority of the Sultan by introducing Reforms into his dominions. In His Majesty's opinion the wiser course would have been for the Powers to have increased the authority of the Sultan who alone was in a position to maintain order in so turbulent a country as Macedonia. There was however another danger which His Majesty believed to be a real one, viz. : the possibility of an understanding between the Prince of Bulgaria, the Prince of Montenegro who was very nearly as clever and quite as unscrupulous as His Royal Highness, and the King of Servia. The position of the King of Servia was a very precarious one, and he could offer no resistance to an attack by Bulgaria and Montenegro. It was well known that the King of Italy desired to extend his Kingdom to the other side of the Adriatic, and he was on intimate terms with several of the Albanian Chiefs who might be willing to assist him. This of course would bring Austria into the Field, and for his own part he would be glad to assist her against Italian encroachments, but then there was the question of Hungary who, if separated from Austria, would probably gravitate towards a powerful Balkan State. On my expressing a doubt whether the Hungarians would wish to exchange their connection with Austria for the domination of a Slav State, The Emperor said that the Hungarians had no money and could not stand alone. If therefore they were separated from Austria they would inevitably have to turn to some other State. I was astonished to hear the very unfavourable terms in which The Emperor spoke of the King of Italy. He openly professed to be a socialist and prided himself on the fact that he was the only Sovereign in Europe who could afford to be so. He had excessively ambitious views but no great authority in his own country and his administration left much to be desired. As for the Italian Ministers, it was impossible to believe a word they said. Last year before going to Naples, His Majesty had instructed his Ambassador in Rome to enquire whether there was any truth in the report that the President of the French Republic was about to pay a visit to the King of Italy, as in that case His Majesty would keep out of the way. Monsieur Tittoni had assured Count Monts that there was absolutely no foundation for the report. His Majesty therefore went to Naples, and the following week Monsieur Loubet was in Rome. His Majesty thereupon insisted that Monsieur Tittoni should pay an official visit to Count Monts and formally express his regret at having deceived him, and this had been done.

The Emperor also alluded to the question of the Regency of Brunswick which had become vacant by the death of Prince Albrecht of Prussia. His Majesty said that it was a matter which did not concern him and with which he would certainly not interfere, unless of course an attempt should be made to reinstate the Duke of Cumberland or to appoint his Son as Regent. To this His Majesty would most strongly object. The Duke of Cumberland had always treated him with the greatest rudeness, although he thought himself entitled to some thanks for having given back to him the private fortune of the King of Hanover which had been confiscated after the war of 1866, and restored to him the Castle of Herrenhausen. His Majesty did not forget that he had Guelph Blood in his veins, but he sincerely hoped that no Guelph would ever again sit on a German throne. They had frequently shown an Anti-German tendency. In old days they had joined the Popes against the Empire, in 1866 they joined Austria against Prussia, and what was perhaps more unpardonable than all, the late King of Hanover in 1870 had attempted to raise a Hanoverian Legion to fight on the side of France. The Duke of Cumberland did not even think it necessary to send a Telegram of condolence to His Majesty on the death of the late Regent. His Majesty regretted the attitude which the Duke of Cumberland had adopted as he would gladly have extended the hospitality of the Berlin Court to His Royal Highness' Daughters, who were charming Ladies. He thought that the best solution of the Regency question would be the selection of one of the late Regent's Sons as his Father's successor, but this was a matter for the Brunswickers to decide for themselves.

The Emperor made an allusion to his recent speech at Breslau which had called forth so many unfavourable criticisms in the German Press. He said that he had been glad to see that the English and French Press had pointed out that His Majesty was right and that the Germans as a nation had very little to complain of. It was a new experience to me to hear His Majesty express any satisfaction at anything that appeared in the English Press, and I took the opportunity of saying that a change seemed recently to have come over the German Press. There were many papers which freely criticized the action of the Government to a much greater extent than formerly, and on the whole the Press seemed to be becoming more independent. His Majesty said that this was undoubtedly the case, but then it should be remembered that since the Hanoverian money had been given back to the Duke of Cumberland the Government had no longer at its disposal the "reptile fund" with which Bismarck used to so lavishly subsidize the Press.

I have attempted in this Despatch to report as faithfully as I am able the language which The Emperor held to me in the course of two conversations, each of which lasted for upwards of an hour. His Majesty's manner throughout was marked by great cordiality and amiability. He spoke very freely and openly, and his remarks were accompanied by that full measure of exaggeration which invariably characterizes His Majesty's conversation.

I have, &c.
FRANK C. LASCELLES.

MINUTES.

An interesting and varied conversation.

C. H.

Yes. What the French want is some evidence that Germany has ceased to oppose them in Morocco. After their attempt to be civil to Germany last year by discarding Delcassé they cannot be expected to make advances again till it is clear that German policy has changed.

E. G.

No. 441.

Sir F. Bertie to Sir Edward Grey.

F.O. 371/74.
(No. 407.)   *Paris,* D. *October* 27, 1906.
Sir,   R. *October* 29, 1906.

M. Pichon called on me yesterday to pay the customary visit on taking office as Minister for Foreign Affairs.

His Excellency authorized me to assure you that the change of Government in France would in no way affect the foreign policy of the Country. It would continue to be friendship and intimate relations with England and alliance with Russia, and the French Government earnestly trusted that an understanding would be come to between His Majesty's Government and the Russian Government on the various questions at issue between them.

I have, &c.
FRANCIS BERTIE.

No. 442.

Sir Edward Grey to Sir F. Bertie.

F.O. 371/74.
(No. 620.)
Sir,   *Foreign Office, November* 8, 1906.

M. Cambon told me to-day that the new French Government were desirous not only of maintaining, but of drawing closer the cordial relations between the two Countries, and in France they were all of one opinion on the subject. He thought that, here, there was a party which was inclined to orient its policy rather towards Germany.

I replied that there were people who thought it possible to be on equally good terms with Germany and with France, but they were quiet just now, because there was no occasion for a quarrel with Germany. If a subject like the Algeciras Conference was to arise again, France might depend upon it that our support would be just as strong and our attitude as firm as it had been before. We shared entirely the feeling of the French Gov[ernmen]t as to our relations.

M. Cambon said that Germany was now disposed to adopt a smoother tone towards France, and the view of his Government was that the French should be equally polite. But there was nothing of importance that required discussion between the two Countries.

I said that that was exactly our position with regard to Germany, and there was nothing stirring in the political relations between us. We were sometimes embarrassed by rather too many invitations to pay visits, which it would be discourteous to refuse, but there was nothing political in them.

M. Cambon went on to say that the French and Spanish police at Tangier were very much needed, but could not be arranged until the Bank was in a position to supply funds. The police could not, probably, be instituted before March, and meanwhile France and Spain were arranging to send warships, and, if necessary would disembark a force to maintain order.

I said I was very glad to hear this, as it would enable me to give a reply to any enquiries made with reference to the protection of our interests, and to say that the two Powers to whom it particularly belonged to preserve order at Tangier were taking measures to secure it.

M. Cambon told me that Menelek's health was better.

I said that, of course, in the event of danger in Abyssinia, all the Legations, including the Russian and German, would have to act together for self-protection, but

I expected Sir John Harrington home soon, and should then hear more about the situation. In the meantime, I heard from Rome that the Italian Representative was trying to remove any objections Menelek might have to the tripartite Agreement, and that in any case Signor Tittoni would sign by the middle of the month.

I told M. Cambon that M. Isvolsky had reported himself as being very pleased with his visit to Berlin, and had told us that there was no danger of outside interference with our negotiations about Persia.

I also took the opportunity of telling M. Cambon that we were asking the Russian Government whether they were taking steps to ascertain what would be a convenient date for the next Hague Conference. May or June would suit us, but we would consider favourably any other date which might be preferred by other Powers. We still desired that the question of reduction or limitation of armaments should be discussed. But we recognised that if there was to be any direct result at the Conference, it could only be arrived at by general agreement. We realised that France could neither reduce nor limit her armaments unless Germany was prepared to take effective action in the same direction.

M. Cambon referred to the German Emperor's dislike to having the question discussed at all, even to the extent of abstaining from the Conference altogether if such a question were brought up.

I said that Germany would be taking a very grave responsibility if she went as far as that. If that were the actual decision of the German Emperor, it ought to be stated publicly.

I am, &c.
EDWARD GREY.

MINUTE BY KING EDWARD.
App[rove]d.—E.R.

No. 443.

Sir F. Bertie to Sir Edward Grey.

F.O. 371/74.
(No. 463.)   *Paris, D. November 21, 1906.*
Sir,   *R. November 22, 1906.*

The policy of the Government was yesterday challenged in the Senate by a "Nationalist" Senator, M. Gaudin de Villaine, who subjected the President of the Council to a certain amount of "heckling." He declared that M. Clemenceau's statesmanship consisted of war on the Roman Catholics at home and of an "English Policy" abroad. On Monsieur Clemenceau retorting that, as to the latter point, it was impossible to answer anything so vague, M. Gaudin de Villaine interrupted him saying :—

"Is there a military convention between France and England? Yes or No." I have the honour to transmit to you herewith, extracted from the "Journal Officiel" M. Clemenceau's reply, in which he said that he had only been at the head of the Ministry for three weeks, but that among the documents laid before him by the Minister for Foreign Affairs concerning such agreements, for instance, as those on the subject of Morocco he had not seen anything of the sort. He protested against questions of that kind being addressed to him, and added that there might be occasions when a Government conscious of its responsibilities ought not to give any reply to them and that it was not right that anything should be said from that Tribune which might "décourager des amitiés" or "rompre des accords." It is stated in the

"Matin" that his replies to M. Gaudin de Villaine were very cavalier in tone and he concluded with the ironical phrase "J'ai bien l'honneur de vous saluer."

The Senate expressed their confidence in the Government by 213 votes to 32.

I have, &c.

FRANCIS BERTIE.

No. 444.

Minutes by Mr. E. Crowe, Sir Charles Hardinge and Sir E. Grey.(¹)

F.O. 371/74.   *Foreign Office, November* 24, 1906.

The article tries to justify M. Clemenceau's cryptic utterance respecting the alleged Anglo-French military convention, by urging that it is not fair or wise to discuss whether, on certain contingencies arising, the two countries might not be led to extend their political cooperation by entering into an agreement for assistance of another kind.

This is no doubt a sensible view, but the curious thing is that M. Clemenceau was asked not whether he intended to conclude a military convention, but whether one had already been concluded. To this question the "Temps" argument is no answer at all.

It remains to be seen whether the question will be taken up in Germany.

E. A. C.

Nov. 24.

Hardly worth sending to Berlin.

E. B.

M. Cambon alluded to this incident yesterday and I pointed out to him that it would be awkward if a similar question were put in Parliament. There is no doubt that the German Gov[ernmen]t are very anxious for a denial of the existence of a military Convention which many Germans (such as C[oun]t Reventlow who states in an article sent home from Munich that such a Convention almost undoubtedly exists) believe to have been concluded. In view of the fact that Conferences took place last spring to concert joint measures of action and that no Convention actually exists it would, I thought, have been best if M. Clemenceau had given a "démenti."

M. Cambon was not quite of the same opinion as he regards the myth of the existence of a Convention as a deterrent to Germany.

C. H.

It would have been difficult for M. Clemenceau to deny the existence of a convention without giving the impression that such a Convention was not desired. I shall endeavour to avoid a public denial, if I am asked a question.

E. G.

(¹) [These minutes arose from a despatch from Sir F. Bertie (No. 465 of November 22, 1906), enclosing an article in the *Temps* of the same date, entitled "Notre Politique extérieure."]

No. 445.

Extract from General Report on Spain for 1906.([1])

F.O. 371/336.   *Madrid, April 27, 1907.*

49. On the termination of the Conference, the Spanish press generally expressed satisfaction with the manner in which Spain had emerged from the ordeal; but both Señor Moret and Señor Ojeda thought that Germany had secured a good share of the objects for which she was contending, and that the situation in Morocco had not much improved. In reality little interest is taken by the country at large in what goes on in Morocco. It is only when some crisis occurs, such as that which originated in the German Emperor's visit to Tangier in March 1905, that Spanish statesmen are compelled to come forward and demand for Spain a preferential position in the regions adjoining her possessions. The acute period having passed, Spain relapses again into indifference. An attempt has been made by the institution of a Morocco Society to promote the policy of Spanish penetration into the interior of Morocco; but after a much advertized meeting in Madrid little has been heard of its doings. Some provision, however, has been made in the Budget of 1907 for improved harbour works at Ceuta and Melilla. It is also provided in the Commercial Treaty of 1906 between Spain and Switzerland that Spain reserves the right to apply a special régime of favour to imports from Morocco, which is not to be extended to Switzerland, and therefore not to other nations enjoying most-favoured-nation treatment in Spain.

Naval demonstration at Tangier. 50. It required much pressure, assisted by British advice at Madrid, to induce Spain to take the more determined step of combining with France in making a naval demonstration at Tangier in December 1906. The objects of the measure were to bring about a state of tranquillity in the much disturbed region of Tangier and its neighbourhood; to impress the Sultan with the necessity of taking measures for the removal of Raisuli; and, above all, to assert the principle that, in the event of armed intervention becoming necessary to restore order, either before or after the constitution of the new police force, this duty appertained to France and Spain, on the invitation of the foreign Representatives at Tangier. In the execution of this policy, the Spanish men-of-war "Pelayo" and the "Princesa de Asturias" combined with the "Charlemagne" and other French vessels under Admiral Touchard to keep a mixed landing force afloat in the Bay of Tangier for use in case of emergency. No landing, however, was necessary, and in January 1907 an identic note announced to the Powers that, the ends of the demonstration having in large part been secured, the vessels would be withdrawn.

51. Discussions took place both in the Senate and in the Chamber of Deputies on the subject of Morocco, in connection with the Bill which was introduced in the former House on the 10th December, 1906, providing authority for the ratification of the General Act of Algeciras. The Bill became law on emerging from the Lower House on the 12th December. The debate to which it gave rise included many speeches by former Ministers of State, some of whom asserted that the position of Spain had been better before than after the Conference, and that the naval demonstration was a very dangerous adventure, on which Spain had imprudently embarked at the dictation of France, without any clear idea of its possible developments. Señor Perez Caballero made several good speeches, pointing out the advantages gained by the Conference, and especially the great one that the position of Spain in Morocco was now recognized by all the Powers that signed the General Act, and not by France and England alone. It was, however, no doubt with a great sense of relief that Spain was able to withdraw her landing force from the waters of Tangier without having had occasion to use it ashore.

52. Once again public opinion has gone to sleep, so far as Morocco is concerned, and the measures which are being concerted to set the new police on foot excite very little interest outside the Spanish Foreign Office. It can, indeed, hardly be said

([1]) [Enclosure in despatch No. 78 from Sir M. de Bunsen.]

that the action of Spain in the field of foreign affairs is determined by any consistent line of policy accepted by her statesmen. In Morocco her policy is founded on the forlorn hope that her Settlements on the north coast may prove the starting point for an expansion of Spanish influence into the interior. In general she is actuated by a fear of the power of France, leading her at one time to seek the alliance and protection of that country and at another to look for support in other quarters. There is no present indication of any intention on her part to break away from the "bloc" of the Western Powers, but it is evident that her fidelity to this connection will be severely tested if the Church quarrel in France should prove incapable of a peaceful settlement. Spain is profoundly Catholic, if not profoundly religious, and co-operation with an aggressively secular State will not be easy. It is feared that France might be led to encourage a breach between Spain and the Vatican. This would produce a dangerous situation, for little more is required to kindle the flames of another Carlist war.

53. Spain, conscious of her weakness, looks forward with dread to any struggle between two or more great European countries. In such a contingency her aim would be to preserve her territory from becoming once more the battle-field of the nations. While war between France and England appeared to be the greatest impending danger, Spain was well aware that the Balearic Islands, and possibly the Canaries, would almost inevitably fall into the hands of one of the combatants. This cause of disturbance having happily been removed for the present, she feels more secure than she did in the past. But she watches with apprehension the possibilities of a conflict arising in some other part of Europe, and affecting, as it almost certainly would, the Mediterranean Powers. *Spanish policy in the event of a European war.*

54. With Germany her relations at present are not intimate. Germany is believed to resent the attitude of Spain at Algeciras, and she has not abandoned her endeavour to detach Spain from the French connection. She is extending her commercial penetration into Spain, notwithstanding the failure to conclude a Commercial Treaty. *Relations with Germany.*

APPENDIX A.

F.O. 371/257.   *Memorandum by Mr. Eyre Crowe.*

Memorandum on the Present State of British Relations with France and Germany.

(8882.*) Secret.   *Foreign Office, January 1, 1907.*
The Anglo-French Agreement of the 8th April, 1904, was the outcome of the honest and ardent desire, freely expressed among all classes and parties of the two countries, that an earnest effort should be made to compose, as far as possible, the many differences which had been a source of perpetual friction between them. In England, the wish for improved relations with France was primarily but a fresh manifestation of the general tendency of British Governments to take advantage of every opportunity to approach more closely to the ideal condition of living in honourable peace with all other States.
There were two difficulties: It was necessary, in the first instance, that the French Government should realise the benefit which France would derive from a policy of give and take, involving perhaps, from her point of view, some immediate sacrifice, but resulting in the banishment of all occasions for quarrels with a powerful neighbour. It was, secondly, indispensable, if French statesmen were to carry with them the public opinion of their own country, without which they would be powerless to act, that the suspiciousness of English designs and intentions, with which years of hostile feelings and active political rivalry had poisoned the French mind, should give place to confidence in the straightforwardness and loyalty of British Governments not only in meeting present engagements, but also in dealing with any future points of

difference, in a conciliatory and neighbourly spirit. It was natural to believe that the growth of such confidence could not be quickly forced, but that it might slowly emerge by a process of gradual evolution. That it declared itself with unexpected rapidity and unmistakable emphasis was without doubt due, in the first place, to the initiative and tactful perseverance of the King, warmly recognised and applauded on both sides of the Channel. The French nation having come to look upon the King as personally attached to their country, saw in His Majesty's words and actions a guarantee that the adjustment of political differences might well prepare the way for bringing about a genuine and lasting friendship, to be built up on community of interests and aspirations.

The conviction that the removal of causes of friction, apart from having an independent value of its own, as making directly for peace, would also confer on the Governments of both countries greater freedom in regulating their general foreign relations, can hardly be supposed to have been absent from the mind of the British and French negotiators. Whenever the Government of a country is confronted with external difficulties by the opposition of another State on a question of national rights or claims, the probable attitude of third Powers in regard to the point in dispute must always be a matter of anxious concern. The likelihood of other Powers actively taking sides in a quarrel which does not touch them directly may reasonably be expected, and, indeed, is shown by experience, very much to depend, quite apart from the merits of the dispute, on the general trend of relations existing between the several parties. It is impossible to over-estimate the importance in such a connection of the existence of a firmly established and broadly based system of friendly intercourse with those Powers whose position would enable them to throw a heavy weight into the balance of strength on the other side. If a country could be imagined whose foreign relations were so favourably disposed that, in the defence of its legitimate interests, it could always count upon the sympathy of its most powerful neighbours, such a country would never—or at least not so long as the national armaments were maintained at the proper standard of efficiency—need to entertain those fears and misgivings which, under the actual conditions of dominant international jealousies and rivalries, only too often compel the abandonment of a just cause as the only alternative to the more serious evil and risk of giving suspicious and unfriendly neighbours a welcome opportunity for aggression or hostile and humiliating interference. If both France. and England were acutely conscious that, in the contingency of either of them being involved in a quarrel with this or that Power, an Anglo-French understanding would at least remove one serious danger inherent in such a situation, patriotic self-interest would, on this ground alone, justify and encourage any attempt to settle outstanding differences, if and so far as they were found capable of settlement without jeopardising vital interests.

It was creditable to M. Delcassé's sagacity and public spirit that he decided to grasp the hand which the British Government held out to him. The attempt has been made to represent this decision as mainly if not solely influenced by the desire to strengthen the hands of France in a struggle with Germany, since, as a result of the impending collapse of the Russian power in the Japanese war, she was incurring the danger of finding herself alone face to face with her great enemy. This criticism, even if it does not go so far as wrongly to ascribe to the *Entente* an originally offensive character directed against Germany, will be seen, on a comparison of dates, to be founded in error. The war with Japan, which Russia herself did not believe to be imminent before it had actually begun, broke out in February 1904. It is true that the Anglo-French Agreements were signed two months later. But no one, certainly not the French Government, then anticipated the complete overthrow of Russia in the Far East, nor the disastrous reaction of defeat on the internal situation in the Czar's European dominions. In fact, the two chief criticisms directed against M. Delcassé's general policy in his own country were, first, that he would not believe those who foreshadowed a coming war between Russia and Japan, and, secondly, that when the war had broken out, he remained almost to the last confident of Russia's ultimate success. Moreover, the negotiations which ultimately issued in the Agreements of the 8th April, 1904, were opened as far back as the early summer of 1903, when few would have ventured to prophesy that Russia was shortly to be brought to her knees by Japan. If one might go so far as to believe that the bare possibility of such a defeat may have begun to occupy the mind of M. Delcassé in the early spring of 1904, and that this reflection may have contributed to convincing him of the wisdom of persevering with the English negotiation, it would yet remain impossible to assert with truth that his primary object in entering upon that negotiation was to seek in a fresh quarter the general political support of which the temporary eclipse of Russia was threatening to deprive his country. But even if the weakening of the Franco-Russian alliance had been the principal and avowed reason why France sought an understanding with England, this would not justify the charge that the conclusion of such understanding constituted a provocation and deliberate menace to Germany. No one has ever seriously ascribed to the Franco-Russian alliance the character of a combination conceived in a spirit of bellicose aggression. That the association of so peace-loving a nation as England with France and Russia, or still less that the substitution of England for Russia in the association with France, would have the effect of turning an admittedly defensive organisation into an offensive alliance aimed directly at Germany cannot have been the honest belief of any competent student of contemporary history. Yet this accusation was actually made against M. Delcassé and, incidentally, against Lord Lansdowne in 1905. That, however, was at the time when the position of France appeared sufficiently weakened to expect that she could be insulted with impunity, when the battle of Mukden had made manifest the final defeat of France's ally, when internal disorders began to undermine Russia's whole position as a Power that must be reckoned with, and when the Anglo-French *Entente* was not credited with having as yet taken deep root in the popular imaginations of the two peoples so long politically estranged. No sound of alarm was heard, no such vindictive criticism of M. Delcassé's policy was even whispered, in 1904, at the moment when the Agreement was published, immediately after its signature. Then, although the world was somewhat taken by surprise, the Agreement was received by all foreign Governments without apparent misgiving, and even with signs of relief and satisfaction. At Berlin the Imperial Chancellor, in the course of an important debate in the Reichstag, formally declared that Germany could have no objection to the policy embodied in the *Entente*, and that, in regard more particularly to the stipulations respecting Morocco, she had no reason to fear that her interests would be ignored.

The history of the events that ensued, culminating in the Algeciras Conference, revealed to all the world how little Prince Bülow's declaration corresponded to the real feelings animating the German Government. Those events do not require to be more than briefly recalled. They are fresh in the public memory.

The maintenance of a state of tension and antagonism between third Powers had avowedly been one of the principal elements in Bismarck's political combinations by which he first secured and then endeavoured to preserve the predominant position of Germany on the continent. It is now no longer denied that he urged England to occupy Egypt and to continue in occupation, because he rightly foresaw that this would perpetuate the antagonism between England and France. Similarly, he consistently impressed upon Russia that it would be to her interest to divert her expansionist ambitions from the Balkan countries to Central Asia, where he hoped both Russia and England would, owing to the inevitable conflict of interests, keep one another fully occupied. The Penjdeh incident, which nearly brought about a war, was the outcome of his direct suggestion that the moment was favourable for Russia to act. Prince Bismarck had also succeeded by all sorts of devices—including the famous reinsurance Treaty with Russia—in keeping France and Russia apart so long as he remained in office. The conclusion of the Franco-Russian alliance some time after Bismarck's fall filled Germany with concern and anxiety, and she never ceased in her efforts at least to neutralise it by establishing the closest possible relations with Russia for herself. From this point of view the weakening of Russia's general position presented simultaneously two advantages. It promised to free Germany for some time to come from any danger of aggression on her eastern frontier, and it deprived France of the powerful support which alone had hitherto enabled her to stand up to Germany in the political arena on terms of equality. It is only natural that the feeling of satisfaction derived from the relative accession of strength due to these two causes should have been somewhat rudely checked by the unexpected intelligence that France had come to an understanding with England.

It was, in fact, soon made apparent that, far from welcoming, as Prince Bülow pretended, an Anglo-French rapprochement, the Emperor's Government had been thoroughly alarmed at the mere disappearance of all causes of friction between the two Western Powers, and was determined to resort to any measures likely to bring about the dissolution of a fresh political combination, which it was felt might ultimately prove another stumbling-block in the way of German supremacy, as the Franco-Russian alliance had previously been regarded. Nor is it possible to be blind to the fact that Germany is bound to be as strongly opposed to a possible Anglo-Russian understanding; and, indeed, there is already conclusive evidence of German activity to prevent any such contingency from happening in the near future.

The German view on this subject cannot be better stated than was done by Herr von Tschirschky, now Foreign Secretary at Berlin, then Prussian Minister at Hamburg, in speaking on New Year's Day 1906 to His Majesty's Consul-General at that place. He said :—

> "Germany's policy always had been, and would be, to try to frustrate any coalition between two States which might result in damaging Germany's interests and prestige; and Germany would, if she thought that such a coalition was being formed, even if its actual results had not yet been carried into practical effect, not hesitate to take such steps as she thought proper to break up the coalition."

In pursuance of this policy, which, whatever its merits or demerits, is certainly quite intelligible, Germany waited for the opportune moment for taking action, with the view of breaking up, if possible, the Anglo-French *entente*. When Russia was staggering under the crushing blows inflicted by Japan, and threatened by internal revolution, the German campaign was opened. The object of nipping in the bud the young friendship between France and England was to be attained by using as a stalking-horse those very interests in Morocco which the Imperial Chancellor had, barely a year before, publicly declared to be in no way imperilled.

The ground was not unskilfully chosen. By a direct threat of war, for which France was known to be unprepared, she was to be compelled to capitulate unconditionally. England had, on being questioned officially, admitted that beyond the terms of the Agreement which bound her to give France her diplomatic support in Morocco she was not pledged to further co-operation. Her reluctance for extreme measures, even under severe provocation, had only recently been tested on the occasion of the Dogger Bank incident. It was considered practically certain that she would shrink from lending armed assistance to France, but if she did, care had been taken to inflame French opinion by representing through the channels of a venal press that England was in her own selfish interest trying to push France into a war with Germany, so revealing the secret intentions which had inspired her in seeking the *entente*.

We now know that this was the policy which Herr von Holstein with the support of Prince Bülow succeeded in imposing on the German Emperor. It promised at the outset to succeed. M. Delcassé fell; France, thoroughly frightened, showed herself anxious to make concessions to Germany, and ready to believe that England's friendship, instead of being helpful, was proving disastrous. It is difficult to say what would have happened if at this critical moment Germany, under the skilful guidance of a Bismarck, had shown herself content with her decided triumph, and willing in every way to smooth the path for France by offering a friendly settlement of the

Moroccan question in a sense that would have avoided wounding her national honour. Germany would, perhaps, have foregone some of the nominal advantages which she afterwards wrung from a reluctant and hostile France at the Algeciras Conference. This would not have hurt Germany, whose real interests, as Bismarck had long ago asserted, would be well served by France getting militarily and financially entangled in Morocco, just as England had got entangled in Egypt. On the other hand, a policy of graceful concessions on Germany's part, and the restriction of her demands to nothing more than the recognition of her existing rights in Morocco and the treatment of a friend, would have deepened the conviction which at this stage was forcing itself on the mind of the French Government, that the full enjoyment of benefits which the agreement concluded with England had been incapable of securing effectually, could be reaped from an amicable understanding with Germany.

At this point Herr von Holstein's policy overreached itself. The minatory attitude of the German Government continued. French overtures were left unanswered. A European Conference to be convoked under conditions peculiarly humiliating to France was insisted upon. Some manœuvres of petty crookedness were executed at Fez by Count Tattenbach, in matters of concessions and loans, which were thought to have been already settled in a contrary sense by special agreements reluctantly assented to in Paris. It became clear to the successors of M. Delcassé that he had been sacrificed in vain. His original policy reasserted itself as the only one compatible with national dignity and ultimate independence. With it revived the confidence that safety lay in drawing closer to England. A bold demand was frankly made for her armed alliance in case of a German attack. This was perhaps the most critical moment for the *entente*.

Would France listen to and appreciate the arguments which the British Government were bound to advance against the conclusion of a definite alliance at this moment? If she saw reason, would the perhaps unavoidable sense of immediate disappointment tend, nevertheless, to react unfavourably on the only just rekindled trust in the loyalty of England? If so, Germany's object would have come near realization. France would, however sorrowfully, have become convinced of the necessity of accepting unconditionally the terms for which Germany then held out, and which involved practically the recognition that French foreign policy must be shaped in accordance with orders from Berlin. The bitterness of such political abdication would naturally have engendered unmeasured hatred of the pretended friend who refused the helping hand in the hour of need.

The attitude adopted under these difficult conditions by His Majesty's Government has been justified by results. The difficulties in the way of there and then converting the *entente* into an alliance were frankly and firmly explained. At the same time Germany was explicitly warned, and the principal other Powers informed, that public opinion in England could not be expected to remain indifferent, and would almost certainly demand the active intervention of any British Government, should a quarrel be fastened upon France on account of her pursuing a policy in which England was under an honourable obligation to support her.

There can be no doubt that an element of bluff had entered into the original calculations of both Germany and France. M. Delcassé, who must be credited with sufficient foresight to have realized early in 1905, if not before, that his policy exposed his country to the resentment of its Teutonic neighbour, is proved, by his neglect to take military precautions, to have in his own mind discounted any German threats as unreal and empty of consequences. He had not counted on the capabilities for taking alarm and for working itself into a panic which reside in the nervous breast of an unprepared French public, nor on the want of loyalty characteristic of French statesmen in their attitude to each other. He paid for his mistake with his person.

Germany on her part had not really contemplated war, because she felt confident that France, knowing herself unprepared and unable to withstand an attack, would yield to threats. But she miscalculated the strength of British feeling and the character of His Majesty's Ministers. An Anglo-French coalition in arms against her

2 D

was not in her forecast, and she could not face the possible danger of it. It is now known that Herr von Holstein, and, on his persuasion, Prince Bülow, practically staked their reputation on the prophecy that no British Government sufficiently bullied and frightened would stand by France, who had for centuries been England's ubiquitous opponent, and was still the ally of Russia, England's "hereditary foe." So lately as the time when the International Conference was sitting at Algeciras, the German delegates, on instructions emanating from Prince Bülow, confidentially pressed upon the British representative in all seriousness the folly and danger of supporting France, and painting in attractive colours a policy of co-operation with Germany for France's overthrow. Even at that hour it was believed that England could be won over. So grave a misapprehension as to what a British Government might be capable of, manifested at such a juncture, shows better than many a direct utterance the estimation in which England has been held in responsible quarters at Berlin. The error eventually proved fatal to the persistent inspirer of this policy, because its admitted failure on the present occasion apparently made it necessary to find a scapegoat. When, contrary to Herr von Holstein's advice, Germany finally made at Algeciras the concessions which alone rendered the conclusion of an international treaty possible, he was ignominiously dismissed by Prince Bülow, who had up to then consistently worked on the same lines, and must have had the principal share in recommending the unsuccessful policy to the Emperor.

When the signature of the Algeciras Act brought to a close the first chapter of the conflict respecting Morocco, the Anglo-French *entente* had acquired a different significance from that which it had at the moment of its inception. Then there had been but a friendly settlement of particular outstanding differences, giving hope for future harmonious relations between two neighbouring countries that had got into the habit of looking at one another askance; now there had emerged an element of common resistance to outside dictation and aggression, a unity of special interests tending to develop into active co-operation against a third Power. It is essential to bear in mind that this new feature of the *entente* was the direct effect produced by Germany's effort to break it up, and that, failing the active or threatening hostility of Germany, such anti-German bias as the *entente* must be admitted to have at one time assumed, would certainly not exist at present, nor probably survive in the future. But whether the antagonism to Germany into which England had on this occasion been led without her wish or intention was but an ephemeral incident, or a symptomatic revelation of some deep-seated natural opposition between the policies and interests of the two countries, is a question which it clearly behoves British statesmen not to leave in any obscurity. To this point, then, inquiry must be directed.

The general character of England's foreign policy is determined by the immutable conditions of her geographical situation on the ocean flank of Europe as an island State with vast oversea colonies and dependencies, whose existence and survival as an independent community are inseparably bound up with the possession of preponderant sea power. The tremendous influence of such preponderance has been described in the classical pages of Captain Mahan. No one now disputes it. Sea power is more potent than land power, because it is as pervading as the element in which it moves and has its being. Its formidable character makes itself felt the more directly that a maritime State is, in the literal sense of the word, the neighbour of every country accessible by sea. It would, therefore, be but natural that the power of a State supreme at sea should inspire universal jealousy and fear, and be ever exposed to the danger of being overthrown by a general combination of the world. Against such a combination no single nation could in the long run stand, least of all a small island kingdom not possessed of the military strength of a people trained to arms, and dependent for its food supply on oversea commerce. The danger can in practice only be averted—and history shows that it has been so averted—on condition that the national policy of the insular and naval State is so directed as to harmonize with the general desires and ideals common to all mankind, and more particularly that it is closely identified with the primary and vital interests of a majority, or as many as possible, of the other nations.   Now, the first interest of all countries is the preservation of national independence. It follows that England, more than any other non-insular Power, has a direct and positive interest in the maintenance of the independence of nations, and therefore must be the natural enemy of any country threatening the independence of others, and the natural protector of the weaker communities.

Second only to the ideal of independence, nations have always cherished the right of free intercourse and trade in the world's markets, and in proportion as England champions the principle of the largest measure of general freedom of commerce, she undoubtedly strengthens her hold on the interested friendship of other nations, at least to the extent of making them feel less apprehensive of naval supremacy in the hands of a free trade England than they would in the face of a predominant protectionist Power. This is an aspect of the free trade question which is apt to be overlooked. It has been well said that every country, if it had the option, would, of course, prefer itself to hold the power of supremacy at sea, but that, this choice being excluded, it would rather see England hold that power than any other State.

History shows that the danger threatening the independence of this or that nation has generally arisen, at least in part, out of the momentary predominance of a neighbouring State at once militarily powerful, economically efficient, and ambitious to extend its frontiers or spread its influence, the danger being directly proportionate to the degree of its power and efficiency, and to the spontaneity or "inevitableness" of its ambitions. The only check on the abuse of political predominance derived from such a position has always consisted in the opposition of an equally formidable rival, or of a combination of several countries forming leagues of defence. The equilibrium established by such a grouping of forces is technically known as the balance of power, and it has become almost an historical truism to identify England's secular policy with the maintenance of this balance by throwing her weight now in this scale and now in that, but ever on the side opposed to the political dictatorship of the strongest single State or group at a given time.

If this view of British policy is correct, the opposition into which England must inevitably be driven to any country aspiring to such a dictatorship assumes almost the form of a law of nature. as has indeed been theoretically demonstrated, and illustrated historically, by an eminent writer on English national policy.

By applying this general law to a particular case, the attempt might be made to ascertain whether, at a given time, some powerful and ambitious State is or is not in a position of natural and necessary enmity towards England; and the present position of Germany might, perhaps, be so tested. Any such investigation must take the shape of an inquiry as to whether Germany is, in fact, aiming at a political hegemony with the object of promoting purely German schemes of expansion, and establishing a German primacy in the world of international politics at the cost and to the detriment of other nations.

For purposes of foreign policy the modern German Empire may be regarded as the heir, or descendant of Prussia. Of the history of Prussia, perhaps the most remarkable feature, next to the succession of talented Sovereigns and to the energy and love of honest work characteristic of their subjects, is the process by which on the narrow foundation of the modest Margraviate of Brandenburg there was erected, in the space of a comparatively short period, the solid fabric of a European Great Power. That process was one of systematic territorial aggrandizement achieved mainly at the point of the sword, the most important and decisive conquests being deliberately embarked upon by ambitious rulers or statesmen for the avowed object of securing for Prussia the size, the cohesion, the square miles and the population necessary to elevate her to the rank and influence of a first class State. All other countries have made their conquests, many of them much larger and more bloody. There is no question now, or in this place, of weighing or discussing their relative merits or justification. Present interest lies in fixing attention on the special circumstances which have given the growth of Prussia its peculiar stamp. It has not been a case of a King's love of conquest as such, nor of the absorption of lands regarded geographically or ethnically as an integral part of the true national domain, nor of the more or less unconscious tendency of a people to expand under the influence of an exuberant vitality, for the fuller development of national life and resources. Here was rather the case of the Sovereign of a small and weak vassal State saying: "I want my country to be independent and powerful. This it cannot be within its present frontiers and with its present population. I must have a larger territory and more inhabitants, and to this end I must organize strong military forces."

The greatest and classic exponent in modern history of the policy of setting out deliberately to turn a small State into a big one was Frederick the Great. By his sudden seizure of Silesia in times of profound peace, and by the first partition of Poland, he practically doubled his inherited dominions. By keeping up the most efficient and powerful army of his time, and by joining England in her great effort to preserve the balance of power in face of the encroachments of France, he successfully maintained the position of his country as one of the European Great Powers. Prussian policy remained inspired by the same principles under his successors. It is hardly necessary to do more than mention the second and the third partitions of Poland; the repeated attempts to annex Hanover in complicity with Napoleon; the dismemberment of Saxony, and the exchange of the Rhenish Provinces for the relinquishment of Polish lands in 1815; the annexation of Schleswig-Holstein in 1864; the definite incorporation of Hanover and Electoral Hesse and other appropriations of territory in 1866; and, finally, the reconquest of Alsace-Lorraine from France in 1871. It is not, of course, pretended that all these acquisitions stand on the same footing. They have this in common—that they were all planned for the purpose of creating a big Prussia or Germany.

With the events of 1871 the spirit of Prussia passed into the new Germany. In no other country is there a conviction so deeply rooted in the very body and soul of all classes of the population that the preservation of national rights and the realization of national ideals rest absolutely on the readiness of every citizen in the last resort to stake himself and his State on their assertion and vindication. With "blood and iron" Prussia had forged her position in the councils of the Great Powers of Europe. In due course it came to pass that, with the impetus given to every branch of national activity by the newly-won unity, and more especially by the growing development of oversea trade flowing in ever-increasing volume through the now Imperial ports of the formerly "independent" but politically insignificant Hanse Towns, the young empire found opened to its energy a whole world outside Europe, of which it had previously hardly had the opportunity to become more than dimly conscious. Sailing across the ocean in German ships, German merchants began for the first time to divine the true position of countries such as England, the United States, France, and even the Netherlands, whose political influence extends to distant seas and continents. The colonies and foreign possessions of England more especially were seen to give to that country a recognized and enviable status in a world where the name of Germany, if mentioned at all, excited no particular interest. The effect of this discovery upon the German mind was curious and instructive. Here was a vast province of human activity to which the mere title and rank of a European Great Power were not in themselves a sufficient passport. Here in a field of portentous magnitude, dwarfing altogether the proportions of European countries, others, who had been perhaps rather looked down upon as comparatively smaller folk, were at home and commanded, whilst Germany was at best received but as an honoured guest. Here was distinct inequality, with a heavy bias in favour of the maritime and colonizing Powers.

Such a state of things was not welcome to German patriotic pride. Germany had won her place as one of the leading, if not, in fact, the foremost Power on the European continent. But over and beyond the European Great Powers there seemed to stand the "World Powers." It was at once clear that Germany must become a "World Power." The evolution of this idea and its translation into practical politics followed with singular consistency the line of thought that had inspired the Prussian

Kings in their efforts to make Prussia great. "If Prussia," said Frederick the Great, "is to count for something in the councils of Europe, she must be made a Great Power." And the echo: "If Germany wants to have a voice in the affairs of the larger oceanic world she must be made a 'World Power.'" "I want more territory," said Prussia. "Germany must have Colonies," says the new world-policy. And Colonies were accordingly established, in such spots as were found to be still unappropriated, or out of which others could be pushed by the vigorous assertion of a German demand for "a place in the sun": Damaraland, Cameroons, Togoland, German East Africa, New Guinea, and groups of other islands in the Pacific. The German example, as was only natural, found ready followers, and the map of unclaimed territories was filled up with surprising rapidity. When the final reckoning was made up the actual German gain seemed, even in German eyes, somewhat meagre. A few fresh possessions were added by purchase or by international agreement—the Carolines, Samoa, Heligoland. A transaction in the old Prussian style secured Kiao-chau. On the whole, however, the "Colonies" have proved assets of somewhat doubtful value.

Meanwhile the dream of a Colonial Empire had taken deep hold on the German imagination. Emperor, statesmen, journalists, geographers, economists, commercial and shipping houses, and the whole mass of educated and uneducated public opinion continue with one voice to declare: We *must* have real Colonies, where German emigrants can settle and spread the national ideals of the Fatherland, and we *must* have a fleet and coaling stations to keep together the Colonies which we are bound to acquire. To the question, "Why *must?*" the ready answer is: "A healthy and powerful State like Germany, with its 60,000,000 inhabitants, must expand, it cannot stand still, it must have territories to which its overflowing population can emigrate without giving up its nationality." When it is objected that the world is now actually parcelled out among independent States, and that territory for colonization cannot be had except by taking it from the rightful possessor, the reply again is: "We cannot enter into such considerations. Necessity has no law. The world belongs to the strong. A vigorous nation cannot allow its growth to be hampered by blind adherence to the *status quo*. We have no designs on other people's possessions, but where States are too feeble to put their territory to the best possible use, it is the manifest destiny of those who can and will do so to take their places."

No one who has a knowledge of German political thought, and who enjoys the confidence of German friends speaking their minds openly and freely, can deny that these are the ideas which are proclaimed on the housetops, and that inability to sympathise with them is regarded in Germany as the mark of the prejudiced foreigner who cannot enter into the real feelings of Germans. Nor is it amiss to refer in this connection to the series of Imperial apothegms, which have from time to time served to crystallize the prevailing German sentiments, and some of which deserve quotation: "Our future lies on the water." "The trident must be in our hand." "Germany must re-enter into her heritage of maritime dominion once unchallenged in the hands of the old Hansa." "No question of world politics must be settled without the consent of the German Emperor." "The Emperor of the Atlantic greets the Emperor of the Pacific," &c.

The significance of these individual utterances may easily be exaggerated. Taken together, their cumulative effect is to confirm the impression that Germany distinctly aims at playing on the world's political stage a much larger and much more dominant part than she finds allotted to herself under the present distribution of material power. It would be taking a narrow view of the function of political criticism to judge this theory of national self-assertion as if it were a problem of morals to be solved by the casuistical application of the principles governing private conduct in modern societies. History is apt to justify the action of States by its general results, with often but faint regard to the ethical character of the means employed. The ruthless conquests of the Roman Republic and Empire are recognized to have brought about an organization of the world's best energies, which, by the characteristic and lasting impulse it gave to the civilization of the ancients, fully compensated for the obliqueness of the conquerors' political morals. Peter the Great and Katharine II are rightly heroes in the eyes of Russia, who largely owes to their unscrupulous and crafty policies her existence as a powerful and united nation. The high-handed seizure of Silesia by Frederick the Great, the low intrigues by which the first partition of Poland was brought about, the tortuous manœuvres by which Bismarck secured Schleswig-Holstein for Prussia are forgotten or condoned in the contemplation of a powerful Germany that has brought to these and all her other territories a more enlightened government, a wider conception of national life, and a greater share in a glorious national tradition than could have been their lot in other conditions. Germans would after all be only logical if they did not hesitate to apply to their current politics the lesson conveyed in such historical judgments, and were ready to leave to posterity the burden of vindicating the employment of force for the purpose of spreading the benefits of German rule over now unwilling peoples. No modern German would plead guilty to a mere lust of conquest for the sake of conquest. But the vague and undefined schemes of Teutonic expansion ("die Ausbreitung des deutschen Volkstums") are but the expression of the deeply rooted feeling that Germany has by the strength and purity of her national purpose, the fervour of her patriotism, the depth of her religious feeling, the high standard of competency, and the perspicuous honesty of her administration, the successful pursuit of every branch of public and scientific activity, and the elevated character of her philosophy, art, and ethics, established for herself the right to assert the primacy of German national ideals. And as it is an axiom of her political faith that right, in order that it may prevail, must be backed by force, the transition is easy to the belief that the "good German sword," which plays so large a part in patriotic speech, is there to solve any difficulties that may be in the way of establishing the reign of those ideals in a Germanized world.

The above very fragmentary sketch has given prominence to certain general features of Germany's foreign policy, which may, with some claim to impartiality, accuracy, and clearness, be deduced from her history, from the utterances and known designs of her rulers and statesmen, and from the unmistakable manifestations of public opinion. It remains to consider whether, and to what extent, the principles so elucidated may be said, on the one hand, to govern actual present policy, and, on the other, to conflict with the vital interests of England and of other independent and vigorous States, with the free exercise of their national rights, and the fulfilment of what they, on their part, may regard as their own mission in this world.

It cannot for a moment be questioned that the mere existence and healthy activity of a powerful Germany is an undoubted blessing to the world. · Germany represents in a pre-eminent degree those highest qualities and virtues of good citizenship, in the largest sense of the word, which constitute the glory and triumph of modern civilization. The world would be unmeasurably the poorer if everything that is specifically associated with German character, German ideas, and German methods were to cease having power and influence. For England particularly, intellectual and moral kinship creates a sympathy and appreciation of what is best in the German mind, which has made her naturally predisposed to welcome, in the interest of the general progress of mankind, everything tending to strengthen that power and influence—on one condition : there must be respect for the individualities of other nations, equally valuable coadjutors, in their way, in the work of human progress, equally entitled to full elbow-room in which to contribute, in freedom, to the evolution of a higher civilization. England has, by a sound instinct, always stood for the unhampered play and interaction of national forces as most in accord with Nature's own process of development. No other State has ever gone so far and so steadily as the British Empire in the direction of giving free scope to the play of national forces in the internal organization of the divers peoples gathered under the King's sceptre. It is perhaps England's good fortune, as much as her merit, that taking this view of the manner in which the solution of the higher problems of national life must be sought, she has had but to apply the same principle to the field of external policy in order to arrive at the theory and practice governing her action as one of the international community of States.

So long, then, as Germany competes for an intellectual and moral leadership of the world in reliance on her own national advantages and energies England can but admire, applaud, and join in the race. If, on the other hand, Germany believes that greater relative preponderance of material power, wider extent of territory, inviolable frontiers, and supremacy at sea are the necessary and preliminary possessions without which any aspirations to such leadership must end in failure, then England must expect that Germany will surely seek to diminish the power of any rivals, to enhance her own by extending her dominion, to hinder the co-operation of other States, and ultimately to break up and supplant the British Empire.

Now, it is quite possible that Germany does not, nor ever will, consciously cherish any schemes of so subversive a nature. Her statesmen have openly repudiated them with indignation. Their denial may be perfectly honest, and their indignation justified. If so, they will be most unlikely to come into any kind of armed conflict with England, because, as she knows of no causes of present dispute between the two countries, so she would have difficulty in imagining where, on the hypothesis stated, any such should arise in the future. England seeks no quarrels, and will never give Germany cause for legitimate offence.

But this is not a matter in which England can safely run any risks. The assurances of German statesmen may after all be no more genuine than they were found to be on the subject of the Anglo-French *entente* and German interests in Morocco, or they may be honestly given but incapable of fulfilment. It would not be unjust to say that ambitious designs against one's neighbours are not as a rule openly proclaimed, and that therefore the absence of such proclamation, and even the profession of unlimited and universal political benevolence are not in themselves conclusive evidence for or against the existence of unpublished intentions. The aspect of German policy in the past, to which attention has already been called, would warrant a belief that a further development on the same general lines would not constitute a break with former traditions, and must be considered as at least possible. In the presence of such a possibility it may well be asked whether it would be right, or even prudent, for England to incur any sacrifices or see other, friendly, nations sacrificed merely in order to assist Germany in building up step by step the fabric of a universal preponderance, in the blind confidence that in the exercise of such preponderance Germany will confer unmixed benefits on the world at large, and promote the welfare and happiness of all other peoples without doing injury to any one. There are, as a matter of fact, weighty reasons which make it particularly difficult for England to entertain that confidence. These will have to be set out in their place.

Meanwhile it is important to make it quite clear that a recognition of the dangers of the situation need not and does not imply any hostility to Germany. England herself would be the last to expect any other nation to associate itself with her in the active support of purely British interests, except in cases where it was found practicable as a matter of business to give service for counter-service. Nevertheless, no Englishman would be so foolish as to regard such want of foreign co-operation for the realization of British aims as a symptom of an anti-British animus. All that England on her part asks—and that is more than she has been in the habit of getting—is that, in the pursuit of political schemes which in no way affect injuriously the interests of third parties, such, for instance, as the introduction of reforms in Egypt for the sole benefit of the native population, England shall not be wantonly hampered by factious opposition. The same measure, and even a fuller measure, England will always be ready to mete out to other countries, including Germany. Of such readiness in the past instances are as numerous as they are instructive; and this is perhaps the place where to say a few words respecting the peculiar complexion of the series of transactions which have been characteristic of Anglo-German relations in recent years.

It has been so often declared, as to have become almost a diplomatic platitude, that between England and Germany, as there has never been any real clashing of material interests, so there are no unsettled controversies over outstanding questions. Yet for the last twenty years, as the archives of our Foreign Office show, German Governments have never ceased reproaching British Cabinets with want of friendliness and with persistent opposition to German political plans. A review of British relations during the same period with France, with Russia, and with the United States reveals ancient and real sources of conflict, springing from imperfectly patched-up differences of past centuries, the inelastic stipulations of antiquated treaties, or the troubles incidental to unsettled colonial frontiers. Although with these countries England has fortunately managed to continue to live in peace, there always remained sufficient elements of divergence to make the preservation of good, not to say cordial, relations an anxious problem requiring constant alertness, care, moderation, good temper, and conciliatory disposition. When particular causes of friction became too acute, special arrangements entered into succeeded as a rule in avoiding an open rupture without, however, solving the difficulties, but rather leaving the seed of further irritation behind. This was eminently the case with France until and right up to the conclusion of the Agreement of the 8th April, 1904.

A very different picture is presented by the succession of incidents which punctuate the record of contemporary Anglo-German relations. From 1884 onward, when Bismarck first launched his country into colonial and maritime enterprise, numerous quarrels arose between the two countries. They all have in common this feature—that they were opened by acts of direct and unmistakable hostility to England on the part of the German Government, and that this hostility was displayed with a disregard of the elementary rules of straightforward and honourable dealing, which was deeply resented by successive British Secretaries of State for Foreign Affairs. But perhaps even more remarkable is this other feature, also common to all these quarrels, that the British Ministers, in spite of the genuine indignation felt at the treatment to which they were subjected, in each case readily agreed to make concessions or accept compromises which not only appeared to satisfy all German demands, but were by the avowal of both parties calculated and designed to re-establish, if possible, on a firmer basis the fabric of Anglo-German friendship. To all outward appearance absolute harmony was restored on each occasion after these separate settlements, and in the intervals of fresh outbreaks it seemed true, and was persistently reiterated, that there could be no further occasion for disagreement.

The peculiar diplomatic methods employed by Bismarck in connection with the first German annexation in South-West Africa, the persistent way in which he deceived Lord Ampthill up to the last moment as to Germany's colonial ambitions, and then turned round to complain of the want of sympathy shown for Germany's " well-known " policy; the sudden seizure of the Cameroons by a German doctor armed with officially-obtained British letters of recommendation to the local people, at a time when the intention of England to grant the natives' petition for a British Protectorate had been proclaimed; the deliberate deception practised on the Reichstag and the German public by the publication of pretended communications to Lord Granville which were never made, a mystification of which Germans to this day are probably ignorant; the arousing of a profound outburst of anti-English feeling throughout Germany by Bismarck's warlike and threatening speeches in Parliament; the abortive German raid on St. Lucia Bay, only just frustrated by the vigilance of Mr. Rhodes; the dubious proceedings by which German claims were established over a large portion of the Sultan of Zanzibar's dominions; the hoisting of the German flag over vast parts of New Guinea, immediately after inducing England to postpone her already-announced intention to occupy some of those very parts by representing that a friendly settlement might first determine the dividing line of rival territorial claims; the German pretensions to oust British settlers from Fiji and Samoa : these incidents constitute the first experience by a British Cabinet of German hostility disguised as injured friendship and innocence. It was only England's precarious position resulting from the recent occupation of Egypt (carefully encouraged by Bismarck), the danger of troubles with Russia in Central Asia (directly fomented by a German special mission to

St. Petersburgh), and the comparative weakness of the British navy at the time, which prevented Mr. Gladstone's Government from contemplating a determined resistance to these German proceedings. It was, however, felt rightly that, apart from the offensiveness of the methods employed, the desires entertained by Germany, and so bluntly translated into practice, were not seriously antagonistic to British policy. Most of the territory ultimately acquired by Bismarck had at some previous time been refused by England, and in the cases where British occupation had lately been contemplated, the object had been not so much to acquire fresh provinces, as to prevent their falling into the hands of protectionist France, who would inevitably have killed all British trade. It seems almost certain that had Germany from the outset sought to gain by friendly overtures to England what she eventually secured after a display of unprovoked aggressiveness, there would have been no difficulty in the way of an amicable arrangement satisfactory to both parties.

As it was, the British Cabinet was determined to avoid a continuance of the quarrel, and having loyally accepted the situation created by Germany's violent action, it promptly assured her of England's honest desire to live with her on terms of absolute neighbourliness, and to maintain the former cordial relations. The whole chapter of these incidents was typical of many of the fresh complications of a similar nature which arose in the following years. With the advent of Lord Salisbury's administration in 1885, Bismarck thought the moment come for inviting England to take sides with the Triple Alliance. Repeated and pressing proposals appear to have been made thenceforward for some considerable time with this end.* Whilst the British Government was too prudent to abandon altogether the traditional policy of holding the balance between the continental Powers, it decided eventually, in view of the then threateningly hostile attitude of France and Russia, to go so far in the direction of co-operation with the Triple Alliance as to conclude the two secret Mediterranean Agreements of 1887. At the same time Lord Salisbury intimated his readiness to acquiesce in the German annexation of Samoa, the consummation of which was only shipwrecked owing to the refusal of the United States on their part to abandon their treaty rights in that group of islands in Germany's favour. These fresh manifestations of close relations with Germany were, however, shortly followed by the serious disagreements caused by the proceedings of the notorious Dr. Carl Peters and other German agents in East Africa. Dr. Peters' design, in defiance of existing treaties, to establish German power in Uganda, athwart the line of communication running from Egypt to the head-waters of the Nile, failed, but England, having previously abandoned the Sultan of Zanzibar to Germany's territorial ambitions, now recognised the German annexation of extensive portions of his mainland dominions, saving the rest by the belated declaration of a British protectorate. The cession of Heligoland sealed the reassertion of Anglo-German brotherhood, and was accompanied by the customary assurance of general German support to British policy, notably in Egypt.

On this and on other occasions England's spirit of accommodation went so far as to sacrifice the career of subordinate British officials, who had done no more than carry out the policy of their Government in as dignified a manner as circumstances allowed, and to whose conduct that Government attached no blame, to the relentless vindictiveness of Germany, by agreeing to their withdrawal as one of the conditions of a settlement. In several instances the German Government admitted that no fault attached to the British official, whilst the German officer alone was acknowledged to be at fault, but asked that the latter's inevitable removal should be facilitated, and the outside world misled, by the simultaneous withdrawal of his British colleagues. In one such case, indeed, a German Consul, after being transferred with promotion to another post, was

---

* For the whole of Lord Salisbury's two Administrations our official records are sadly incomplete, all the most important business having been transacted under the cover of " private " correspondence. It is not known even to what extent that correspondence may have been integrally preserved. A methodical study of our relations with Germany during that interesting period is likely to remain for ever impossible. [E. A. C.] [*ED. NOTE.*—Partly quoted in *Gooch & Temperley*, I and II, p. vii.]

only a few years afterwards reinstated on the scene of his original blunders with the higher rank of Consul-General without any British protest being made.

The number of British officials innocently branded in this manner in the course of some years is not inconsiderable, and it is instructive to observe how readily and *con amore* the German Government, imitating in this one of the great Bismarck's worst and least respectable foibles, habitually descend to attacking the personal character and position of any agents of a foreign State, often regardless of their humble rank, whose knowledge, honesty, and efficient performance of their duties are thought to be in the way of the realization of some particular, probably not very straightforward, piece of business. Such machinations were conspicuous in connection with the fall of M. Delcassé, but tales could be told of similar efforts directed against men in the service of the Spanish, Italian, and Austrian, as well as of the British Government.

It seems unnecessary to go at length into the disputes about the frontiers of the German Colonies in West Africa and the hinterland spheres of influence in 1903–1904, except to record the ready sacrifice of undoubted British treaty rights to the desire to conciliate Germany, notwithstanding the provocative and insulting proceedings of her agents and officials; nor into the agreement entered into between Germany and France for giving the latter access to the Niger, a transaction which, as the German Government blandly informed the British Embassy at Berlin, was intended to show how unpleasant it could make itself to England if she did not manifest greater alacrity in meeting German wishes.

It was perhaps partly the same feeling that inspired Germany in offering determined resistance to the scheme negotiated by Lord Rosebery's Government with the Congo Free State for connecting the British Protectorate of Uganda by a railway with Lake Tanganyika. No cession of territory was involved, the whole object being to allow of an all-British through communication by rail and lake steamers from the Cape to Cairo. It was to this that Germany objected, although it was not explained in what way her interests would be injuriously affected. She adopted on this occasion a most minatory tone towards England, and also joined France, who objected to other portions of the Anglo-Congolese Agreement, in putting pressure on King Leopold. In the end the British Government consented to the cancellation of the clauses respecting the lease of the strip of land required for the construction of the railway, and Germany declared herself satisfied.

More extraordinary still was the behaviour of the German Government in respect to the Transvaal. The special treaty arrangements, which placed the foreign relations of that country under the control of England, were, of course, well known and understood. Nevertheless, it is certain that Germany believed she might by some fortuitous circumstances hope some day to establish her political dominion over the Boers, and realize her dream of occupying a belt of territory running from east to west right across Africa. She may have thought that England could be brought amicably to cede her rights in those regions as she had done before in other quarters, but, meanwhile, a good deal of intriguing went on which cannot be called otherwise than actively hostile. Opposition to British interests was deliberately encouraged in the most demonstrative fashion at Pretoria, which went so far in 1895 that the British Ambassador at Berlin had to make a protest. German financial assistance was promised to the Transvaal for the purpose of buying the Delagoa Bay Railway, a British concern which had been illegally confiscated by the Portuguese Government, and was then the subject of an international arbitration. When this offer failed, Germany approached the Lisbon Cabinet direct with the demand that, immediately on the arbitration being concluded, Germany and Portugal should deal with the railway by common agreement. It was also significant that at the time of the British annexation of Amatongaland (1895), just south of the Portuguese frontier on the East Coast, Germany thought it necessary to warn England that this annexation was not recognised by the Transvaal, and that she encouraged the feverish activity of German traders to buy up all available land round Delagoa Bay. In the same year, following up an intimation that England's " opposition to German interests at Delagoa Bay "—interests of which no British Government had ever previously been informed—was considered by Germany as one of the legitimate causes of her ill-will towards England, the German Government went out of its way to declare the maintenance of the independence of the Transvaal to be a German national interest. Then followed the chapter of the Jameson raid and the Emperor's famous telegram to President Krüger. The hostile character of that demonstration was thoroughly understood by the Emperor's Government, because we know that preparations were made for safeguarding the German fleet in the contingency of a British attack. But in a way the most important aspect of the incident was that for the first time the fact of the hostile character of Germany's official policy was realized by the British public, who up to then, owing to the anxious care of their Government to minimize the results of the perpetual friction with Germany, and to prevent any aggravation of that friction by concealing as far as possible the unpleasant details of Germany's aggressive behaviour, had been practically unaware of the persistently contemptuous treatment of their country by their Teutonic cousins. The very decided view taken by British public opinion of the nature of any possible German intervention in South Africa led the German Government, though not the German public, to abandon the design of supplanting England at Pretoria. But for this "sacrifice" Germany, in accordance with her wont, demanded a price—namely, British acquiescence in the reversion to her of certain Portuguese Colonies in the event of their eventual division and appropriation by other Powers. The price was paid. But the manner in which Germany first bullied the Portuguese Government and then practically drove an indignant British Cabinet into agreeing in anticipation to this particular scheme of spoliation of England's most ancient ally, was deeply resented by Lord Salisbury, all the more, no doubt, as by this time he was fully aware that this new "friendly" settlement of misunderstandings with Germany would be no more lasting than its many predecessors. When, barely twelve months later, the Emperor, unabashed by his recent formal "abandonment of the Boers," threatened that unless the question of the final ownership of Samoa, then under negotiation, was promptly settled in Germany's favour, he would have to reconsider his attitude in the British conflict with the Transvaal which was then on the point of being submitted to the arbitrament of war, it cannot be wondered at that the British Government began to despair of ever reaching a state of satisfactory relations with Germany by continuing in the path of friendly concessions and compromises. Yet no attempt was even then made to seek a new way. The Agreement by which Samoa definitely became German was duly signed, despite the serious protests of our Australian Colonies, whose feelings had been incensed by the cynical disregard with which the German agents in the group, with the open support of their Government, had for a long time violated the distinct stipulations of the Samoan Act agreed to at Berlin by the three interested Powers in 1889. And when shortly after the outbreak of the South African war, Germany threatened the most determined hostility unless England waived the exercise of one of the most ancient and most firmly-established belligerent rights of naval warfare, namely, the search and citation before a Prize Court of neutral mercantile vessels suspected of carrying contraband, England once more preferred an amicable arrangement under which her undoubted rights were practically waived, to embarking on a fresh quarrel with Germany. The spirit in which this more than conciliatory attitude was appreciated at Berlin became clear when immediately afterwards the German Chancellor openly boasted in the Reichstag that he had compelled England by the display of German firmness to abandon her absolutely unjust claim to interference with the unquestioned rights of neutrals, and when the Emperor subsequently appealed to his nation to hasten on the building of an overwhelming German fleet, since the want of superior naval strength alone had on this occasion prevented Germany from a still more drastic vindication of Germany's interests.

A bare allusion must here suffice to the way in which the German Government at the time of the South African war abetted the campaign of odious calumny carried on throughout the length and breadth of Germany against the character of the British army, without any Government official once opening his mouth in contradiction; and this in the face of the faithful reports known to have been addressed to their Government by the German military officers attached to the British forces in the field. When the Reichstag proceeded in an unprecedented fashion to impugn the conduct of a British Cabinet Minister, it was open to Prince Bülow to enlighten his hearers as to the real facts, which had been grossly misrepresented. We know that he was aware of the truth. We have the report of his long interview with a distinguished and representative English gentleman, a fortnight after Mr. Chamberlain's famous speech, which was alleged to be the cause of offence, but of which a correct version revealing the groundlessness of the accusation had been reported in a widely-read German paper. The Prince then stated that his Government had at that moment no cause to complain of anything in the attitude of British Ministers, yet he descended a few days afterwards to expressing in the Reichstag his sympathy with the violent German outcry against Mr. Chamberlain's supposed statement and the alleged atrocities of the British army, which he knew to be based on falsehoods. Mr. Chamberlain's dignified reply led to extraordinarily persistent efforts on the Chancellor's part to obtain from the British Government an apology for the offence of resenting his dishonouring insinuations, and, after all these efforts had failed, he nevertheless intimated to the Reichstag that the British Government had given an explanation repudiating any intention on its part to imply any insult to Germany by what had been said.[1]

As if none of these things had happened, fresh German demands in another field, accompanied by all the same manifestations of hostility, were again met, though with perhaps increasing reluctance, by the old willingness to oblige. The action of Germany in China has long been distinctly unfriendly to England. In 1895 she tried to obtain from the Chinese Government a coaling station in the Chusan Islands, at the mouth of the Yang-tsze, without any previous communication with the British Government, whose preferential rights over the group, as established by Treaty, were of course well known. The manner in which Kiao-chau was obtained, however unjustifiable it may be considered by any recognized standard of political conduct, did not concern England more than the other Powers who professed in their Treaties to respect China's integrity and independence. But Germany was not content with the seizure of the harbour, she also planned the absorption of the whole of the large and fertile province of Shantung. The concession of the privileged rights which she wrung from the Chinese Government was obtained owing in no small degree to her official assurance that her claims had the support of England who, needless to say, had never been informed or consulted, and who was, of course, known to be absolutely opposed to stipulations by which, contrary to solemn British treaty rights, it was intended to close a valuable province to British trade and enterprise.

About this time Germany secretly approached Russia with a view to the conclusion of an Agreement, by which Germany would have also obtained the much desired foothold on the Yang-tsze, then considered to be practically a British preserve. These overtures being rejected, Germany wished at least to prevent England from obtaining what she herself had failed to secure. She proposed to the British Cabinet a self-denying Agreement stipulating that neither Power should endeavour to obtain any territorial advantages in Chinese dominions, and that if any third Power attempted to do so both should take common action.

The British Government did not conceal their great reluctance to this arrangement, rightly foreseeing that Germany would tacitly exempt from its operation her own designs on Shantung, and also any Russian aggression in Manchuria, whilst England would solemnly give up any chances she might have of establishing on a firm basis her well-won position on the Yang-tsze. That is, of course, exactly what subsequently did happen. There was no obvious reason why England should lend herself to this gratuitous tying of her own hands. No counter-advantage was offered or even suggested, and the British taste for these one-sided transactions had not been

---

[1] [This and the preceding paragraph were printed in *Gooch & Temperley*, Vol. I, pp. 276–7.]

stimulated by past experience. Nevertheless, the policy of conciliating Germany by meeting her expressed wishes once more triumphed, and the Agreement was signed—with the foreseen consequences : Russian aggression in Manchuria was declared to be altogether outside the scope of the stipulations of what the German Chancellor took care to style the "Yang-tsze" Agreement, as if its terms had referred specially to that restricted area of China, and the German designs on Shantung continue to this day to be tenaciously pursued.

But Germany was not content with the British renunciation of any territorial claims. The underhand and disloyal manœuvres by which, on the strength of purely fictitious stories of British plans for the seizure of various Chinese places of strategical importance (stories also sedulously communicated to the French Government), Germany wrung out of the Peking Court further separate and secret guarantees against alleged British designs, on the occasion of the termination of the joint Anglo-Franco-German occupation of Shanghae, betrayed such an obliquity of mind in dealing with her ostensible friends that Lord Lansdowne characterized it in the most severe terms, which did not prevent him from presenting the incident to Parliament in the form of papers from which almost every trace of the offensive attitude of Germany had been carefully removed, so as not to embitter our German relations. And this was after the reports from our officers had shown that the proceeding of the German troops in Northern China, and the extraordinary treatment meted out by the German General Staff to the British and Indian contingents serving, with a loyalty not approached by any of the other international forces, under the supreme command of Count Waldersee, had created the deepest possible resentment among all ranks, from the British General Commanding to the lowest Indian follower.[2]

Nor was any difficulty made by the British Government in shortly afterwards cordially co-operating with Germany in the dispute with Venezuela, and it was only the pressure of public opinion, which had gradually come to look upon such co-operation for any political purpose whatsoever as not in accord with either British interests or British dignity, that brought this joint venture to a very sudden and somewhat lame end.

It is as true to-day as it has been at any time since 1884, in the intervals of successive incidents and their settlements, that, practically every known German demand having been met, there is not just now any cause troubling the serenity of Anglo-German relations. So much so, that the German Ambassador in London, in reply to repeated inquiries as to what specific points his Government had in mind in constantly referring to its earnest wish to see those relations improved, invariably seeks refuge in the vaguest of generalities, such as the burning desire which consumes the German Chancellor to be on the most intimate terms of friendship with France, and to obtain the fulfilment of this desire through the good offices of the British Government.

Nothing has been said in the present paper of the campaign carried on against this country in the German press, and in some measure responded to in English papers. It is exceedingly doubtful whether this campaign has had any share whatever in determining the attitude of the two Governments, and those people who see in the newspaper controversy the main cause of friction between Germany and England, and who consequently believe that the friction can be removed by fraternizations of journalists and the mutual visits of more or less distinguished and more or less disinterested bodies of tourists, have not sufficiently studied—in most cases could not possibly be in a position to study—the records of the actual occurrences which have taken place, and which clearly show that it is the direct action of the German Government which has been the all-sufficient cause of whatever obstacle there may be to the maintenance of normally friendly relations between the two countries. If any importance is in this connection to be attributed to the German press, it is only in so far as it is manipulated and influenced by the official Press Bureau, a branch of the Chancellor's Office at Berlin of

[2] [This and the preceding three paragraphs were printed in *Gooch & Temperley*, Vol. II, pp. 152–3.]

which the occult influence is not limited to the confines of the German Empire. That influence is perceived at work in New York, at St. Petersburgh, at Vienna, at Madrid, Lisbon, Rome, and Cairo, and even in London, where the German Embassy entertains confidential and largely unsuspected relations with a number of respectable and widely-read papers. This somewhat unsavoury business was until recently in the clumsy hands of the late Chancellor of the Embassy, whose energies are now transferred to Cairo. But, by whomsoever carried on, it is known that the tradition of giving expression to the views of the German Government for the benefit of the British public, and even of the British Cabinet, by using other and less direct methods than the prescribed channel of open communication with the Secretary of State for Foreign Affairs, survives at Carlton House Terrace.

There is no pretence to completeness in the foregoing survey of Anglo-German relations, which, in fact, gives no more than a brief reference to certain salient and typical incidents that have characterized those relations during the last twenty years. The more difficult task remains of drawing the logical conclusions. The immediate object of the present inquiry was to ascertain whether there is any real and natural ground for opposition between England and Germany. It has been shown that such opposition has, in fact, existed in an ample measure for a long period, but that it has been caused by an entirely one-sided aggressiveness, and that on the part of England the most conciliatory disposition has been coupled with never-failing readiness to purchase the resumption of friendly relations by concession after concession.

It might be deduced that the antagonism is too deeply rooted in the relative position of the two countries to allow of its being bridged over by the kind of temporary expedients to which England has so long and so patiently resorted. On this view of the case it would have to be assumed that Germany is deliberately following a policy which is essentially opposed to vital British interests, and that an armed conflict cannot in the long run be averted, except by England either sacrificing those interests, with the result that she would lose her position as an independent Great Power, or making herself too strong to give Germany the chance of succeeding in a war. This is the opinion of those who see in the whole trend of Germany's policy conclusive evidence that she is consciously aiming at the establishment of a German hegemony, at first in Europe, and eventually in the world.

After all that has been said in the preceding paragraphs, it would be idle to deny that this may be the correct interpretation of the facts. There is this further seemingly corroborative evidence that such a conception of world-policy offers perhaps the only quite consistent explanation of the tenacity with which Germany pursues the construction of a powerful navy with the avowed object of creating slowly, but surely, a weapon fit to overawe any possible enemy, however formidable at sea.

There is, however, one obvious flaw in the argument. If the German design were so far-reaching and deeply thought out as this view implies, then it ought to be clear to the meanest German understanding that its success must depend very materially on England's remaining blind to it, and being kept in good humour until the moment arrived for striking the blow fatal to her power. It would be not merely worth Germany's while, it would be her imperative duty, pending the development of her forces, to win and retain England's friendship by every means in her power. No candid critic could say that this elementary strategical rule had been even remotely followed hitherto by the German Government.

It is not unprofitable in this connection to refer to a remarkable article in one of the recent numbers of the "Preussische Jahrbücher," written by Dr. Hans Delbrück, the distinguished editor of that ably conducted and influential magazine. This article discusses very candidly and dispassionately the question whether Germany could, even if she would, carry out successfully an ambitious policy of expansion which would make her follow in the footsteps of Louis XIV and of Napoleon I. The conclusion arrived at is that, unless Germany wishes to expose herself to the same overwhelming combinations which ruined the French dreams of a universal ascendency, she must make up her mind definitely and openly to renounce all thoughts of further extending her frontiers, and substitute for the plan of territorial annexations the nobler ambition of spreading German culture by propagating German ideals in the many quarters of the globe where the German language is spoken, or at least taught and understood.

It would not do to attribute too much importance to the appearance of such an article in a country where the influence of public opinion on the conduct of the affairs of State is notoriously feeble. But this much may probably be rightly gathered from it, that the design attributed by other nations to Germany has been, and perhaps is still being, cherished in some indeterminate way by influential classes, including, perhaps, the Government itself, but that responsible statesmen must be well aware of the practical impossibility of carrying it out.

There is then, perhaps, another way of looking at the problem : It might be suggested that the great German design is in reality no more than the expression of a vague, confused, and unpractical statesmanship, not fully realizing its own drift. A charitable critic might add, by way of explanation, that the well-known qualities of mind and temperament distinguishing for good or for evil the present Ruler of Germany may not improbably be largely responsible for the erratic, domineering, and often frankly aggressive spirit which is recognizable at present in every branch of German public life, not merely in the region of foreign policy ; and that this spirit has called forth those manifestations of discontent and alarm both at home and abroad with which the world is becoming familiar ; that, in fact, Germany does not really know what she is driving at, and that all her excursions and alarums, all her underhand intrigues do not contribute to the steady working out of a well conceived and relentlessly followed system of policy, because they do not really form part of any such system. This is an hypothesis not flattering to the German Government, and it must be admitted that much might be urged against its validity. But it remains true that on this hypothesis also most of the facts of the present situation could be explained.

It is, of course, necessary to except the period of Bismarck's Chancellorship. To assume that so great a statesman was not quite clear as to the objects of his policy would be the *reductio ad absurdum* of any hypothesis. If, then, the hypothesis is to be held sound, there must be forthcoming a reasonable explanation for Bismarck's conduct towards England after 1884, and a different explanation for the continuance of German hostility after his fall in 1890. This view can be shown to be less absurd than it may at first sight appear.

Bismarck suffered from what Count Schuvaloff called *le cauchemar des coalitions*. It is beyond doubt that he particularly dreaded the hostile combination against his country of France and Russia, and that, as one certain means of counteracting that danger, he desired to bring England into the Triple Alliance, or at least to force her into independent collision with France and Russia, which would inevitably have placed her by Germany's side. He knew England's aversion to the entanglement of alliances, and to any policy of determined assertion of national rights, such as would have made her a Power to be seriously reckoned with by France and Russia. But Bismarck had also a poor opinion of the power of English Ministers to resist determined pressure. He apparently believed he could compel them to choose between Germany and a universal opposition to England. When the colonial agitation in Germany gave him an opening, he most probably determined to bring it home to England that meekness and want of determination in foreign affairs do not constitute a policy ; that it was wisest, and certainly least disagreeable, for her to shape a decided course in a direction which would secure her Germany's friendship ; and that in co-operation with Germany lay freedom from international troubles as well as safety, whilst a refusal to co-operate brought inglorious conflicts, and the prospect of finding Germany ranged with France and Russia for the specific purpose of damaging British interests.

Such an explanation gains plausibility from the fact that, according to Bismarck's own confession, a strictly analogous policy was followed by him before 1866 in his dealings with the minor German States. Prussia deliberately bullied and made herself disagreeable to them all, in the firm expectation that, for the sake of peace and quiet, they would follow Prussia's lead rather than Austria's. When the war of 1866 broke out Bismarck had to realize that, with the exception of a few small principalities which were practically *enclaves* in the Kingdom of Prussia, the whole of the minor German States sided with Austria. Similarly he must have begun to see towards the end of his career that his policy of browbeating England into friendship had failed, in spite of some fugitive appearance of success. But by that time the habit of bullying and offending England had almost become a tradition in the Berlin Foreign Office, and Bismarck's successors, who, there is other evidence to show, inherited very little of his political capacity and singleness of purpose, seem to have regarded the habit as a policy in itself, instead of as a method of diplomacy calculated to gain an ulterior end. Whilst the great Chancellor made England concede demands objectionable more in the manner of presentation than in themselves, treating her somewhat in the style of Richard III wooing the Lady Ann, Bismarck's successors have apparently come to regard it as their ultimate and self-contained purpose to extract valuable concessions from England by offensive bluster and persistent nagging, Bismarck's experience having shown her to be amenable to this form of persuasion without any risk of her lasting animosity being excited.

If, merely by way of analogy and illustration, a comparison not intended to be either literally exact or disrespectful be permitted, the action of Germany towards this country since 1890 might be likened not inappropriately to that of a professional blackmailer, whose extortions are wrung from his victims by the threat of some vague and dreadful consequences in case of a refusal. To give way to the blackmailer's menaces enriches him, but it has long been proved by uniform experience that, although this may secure for the victim temporary peace, it is certain to lead to renewed molestation and higher demands after ever-shortening periods of amicable forbearance. The blackmailer's trade is generally ruined by the first resolute stand made against his exactions and the determination rather to face all risks of a possibly disagreeable situation than to continue in the path of endless concessions. But, failing such determination, it is more than probable that the relations between the two parties will grow steadily worse.

If it be possible, in this perhaps not very flattering way, to account for the German Government's persistently aggressive demeanour towards England, and the resulting state of almost perpetual friction, notwithstanding the pretence of friendship, the generally restless, explosive, and disconcerting activity of Germany in relation to all other States would find its explanation partly in the same attitude towards them and partly in the suggested want of definite political aims and purposes. A wise German statesman would recognise the limits within which any world-policy that is not to provoke a hostile combination of all the nations in arms must confine itself. He would realize that the edifice of Pan-Germanism, with its outlying bastions in the Netherlands, in the Scandinavian countries, in Switzerland, in the German provinces of Austria, and on the Adriatic, could never be built up on any other foundation than the wreckage of the liberties of Europe. A German maritime supremacy must be acknowledged to be incompatible with the existence of the British Empire, and even if that Empire disappeared, the union of the greatest military with the greatest naval Power in one State would compel the world to combine for the riddance of such an incubus. The acquisition of colonies fit for German settlement in South America cannot be reconciled with the Monroe doctrine, which is a fundamental principle of the political faith of the United States. The creation of a German India in Asia Minor must in the end stand or fall with either a German command of the sea or a German conquest of Constantinople and the countries intervening between Germany's present south-eastern frontiers and the Bosphorus. Whilst each of these grandiose schemes seems incapable of fulfilment under anything like the present conditions of the world, it looks as if Germany were playing with them all together simultaneously, and thereby wilfully concentrating in her own path all the obstacles and oppositions of a world set at defiance. That she should do this helps to prove how little of logical and consistent design and of unrelenting purpose lies behind the impetuous mobility, the bewildering surprises, and the heedless disregard of the susceptibilities of other people that have been so characteristic of recent manifestations of German policy.

If it be considered necessary to formulate and accept a theory that will fit all the ascertained facts of German foreign policy, the choice must lie between the two hypotheses here presented :—

Either Germany is definitely aiming at a general political hegemony and maritime ascendency, threatening the independence of her neighbours and ultimately the existence of England;

Or Germany, free from any such clear-cut ambition, and thinking for the present merely of using her legitimate position and influence as one of the leading Powers in the council of nations, is seeking to promote her foreign commerce, spread the benefits of German culture, extend the scope of her national energies, and create fresh German interests all over the world wherever and whenever a peaceful opportunity offers, leaving it to an uncertain future to decide whether the occurrence of great changes in the world may not some day assign to Germany a larger share of direct political action over regions not now a part of her dominions, without that violation of the established rights of other countries which would be involved in any such action under existing political conditions.

In either case Germany would clearly be wise to build as powerful a navy as she can afford.

The above alternatives seem to exhaust the possibilities of explaining the given facts. The choice offered is a narrow one, nor easy to make with any close approach to certainty. It will, however, be seen, on reflection, that there is no actual necessity for a British Government to determine definitely which of the two theories of German policy it will accept. For it is clear that the second scheme (of semi-independent evolution, not entirely unaided by statecraft) may at any stage merge into the first, or conscious-design scheme. Moreover, if ever the evolution scheme should come to be realized, the position thereby accruing to Germany would obviously constitute as formidable a menace to the rest of the world as would be presented by any deliberate conquest of a similar position by "malice aforethought."

It appears, then, that the element of danger present as a visible factor in one case, also enters, though under some disguise, into the second; and against such danger, whether actual or contingent, the same general line of conduct seems prescribed. It should not be difficult briefly to indicate that line in such a way as to command the assent of all persons competent to form a judgment in this matter.

So long as England remains faithful to the general principle of the preservation of the balance of power, her interests would not be served by Germany being reduced to the rank of a weak Power, as this might easily lead to a Franco-Russian predominance equally, if not more, formidable to the British Empire. There are no existing German rights, territorial or other, which this country could wish to see diminished. Therefore, so long as Germany's action does not overstep the line of legitimate protection of existing rights she can always count upon the sympathy and good-will, and even the moral support, of England.

Further, it would be neither just nor politic to ignore the claims to a healthy expansion which a vigorous and growing country like Germany has a natural right to assert in the field of legitimate endeavour. The frank recognition of this right has never been grudged or refused by England to any foreign country. It may be recalled that the German Empire owes such expansion as has already taken place in no small measure to England's co-operation or spirit of accommodation, and to the British principle of equal opportunity and no favour. It cannot be good policy for England to thwart such a process of development where it does not directly conflict either with British interests or with those of other nations to which England is bound by solemn treaty obligations. If Germany, within the limits imposed by these two conditions, finds the means peacefully and honourably to increase her trade and shipping, to gain coaling stations or other harbours, to acquire landing rights for cables, or to secure concessions for the employment of German capital or industries, she should never find England in her way.

Nor is it for British Governments to oppose Germany's building as large a fleet as she may consider necessary or desirable for the defence of her national interests. It is the mark of an independent State that it decides such matters for itself, free from any outside interference, and it would ill become England with her large fleets to dictate to another State what is good for it in matters of supreme national concern. Apart from the question of right and wrong, it may also be urged that nothing would be more likely than any attempt at such dictation, to impel Germany to persevere with her ship-building programmes. And also, it may be said in parenthesis, nothing is more likely to produce in Germany the impression of the practical hopelessness of a never-ending succession of costly naval programmes than the conviction, based on ocular demonstration, that for every German ship England will inevitably lay down two, so maintaining the present relative British preponderance.

It would be of real advantage if the determination not to bar Germany's legitimate and peaceful expansion, nor her schemes of naval development, were made as patent and pronounced as authoritatively as possible, provided care were taken at the same time to make it quite clear that this benevolent attitude will give way to determined opposition at the first sign of British or allied interests being adversely affected. This alone would probably do more to bring about lastingly satisfactory relations with Germany than any other course.

It is not unlikely that Germany will before long again ask, as she has so often done hitherto, for a " close understanding" with England. To meet this contingency, the first thing to consider is what exactly is meant by the request. The Anglo-French *entente* had a very material basis and tangible object—namely, the adjustment of a number of actually-existing serious differences. The efforts now being made by England to arrive at an understanding with Russia are justified by a very similar situation. But for an Anglo-German understanding on the same lines there is no room, since none could be built up on the same foundation. It has been shown that there are no questions of any importance now at issue between the two countries. Any understanding must therefore be entirely different in object and scope. Germany's wish may be for an understanding to co-operate for specific purposes, whether offensive or defensive or generally political or economical, circumscribed by certain geographical limits, or for an agreement of a self-denying order, binding the parties not to do, or not to interfere with, certain things or acts. Or the coveted arrangement might contain a mixture of any or all of these various ingredients. Into offensive or defensive alliances with Germany there is, under the prevailing political conditions, no occasion for England to enter, and it would hardly be honest at present to treat such a possibility as an open question. British assent to any other form of co-operation or system of non-interference must depend absolutely on circumstances, on the particular features, and on the merits of any proposals that may be made. All such proposals England will be as ready as she always has been to weigh and discuss from the point of view of how British interests will be affected. Germany must be content in this respect to receive exactly the same treatment as every other Power.

There is no suggestion more untrue or more unjust than that England has on any recent occasion shown, or is likely to show in future, a *parti pris* against Germany or German proposals as such, or displayed any unfairness in dealing strictly on their own merits with any question having a bearing on her relations with Germany. This accusation has been freely made. It is the stock-in-trade of all the inspired tirades against the British Government which emanate directly or indirectly from the Berlin Press Bureau. But no one has ever been able to bring forward a tittle of evidence in its support that will bear examination. The fact, of course, is that, as Mr. Balfour felt impelled to remark to the German Ambassador on a certain occasion, German communications to the British Government have not generally been of a very agreeable character, and, unless that character is a good deal modified, it is more than likely that such communications will in future receive unpalatable answers. For there is one road which, if past experience is any guide to the future, will most certainly not lead to any permanent improvement of relations with any Power, least of all Germany, and which must therefore be abandoned : that is the road paved with graceful British concessions—concessions made without any conviction either of their justice or of their being set off by equivalent counter-services. The vain hopes that in this manner Germany can be " conciliated " and made more friendly must be definitely given up. It may be that such hopes are still honestly cherished by irresponsible people, ignorant, perhaps necessarily ignorant, of the history of Anglo-German relations during the last twenty years, which cannot be better described than as the history of a systematic policy of gratuitous concessions, a policy which has led to the highly disappointing result disclosed by the almost perpetual state of tension existing between the two countries. Men in responsible positions, whose business it is to inform themselves and to see things as they really are, cannot conscientiously retain any illusions on this subject.

Here, again, however, it would be wrong to suppose that any discrimination is intended to Germany's disadvantage. On the contrary, the same rule will naturally impose itself in the case of all other Powers. It may, indeed, be useful to cast back a glance on British relations with France before and after 1898. A reference to the official records will show that ever since 1882 England had met a growing number of French demands and infringements of British rights in the same spirit of ready accommodation which inspired her dealings with Germany. The not unnatural result was that every successive French Government embarked on a policy of " squeezing " England, until the crisis came in the year of Fashoda, when the stake at issue was the maintenance of the British position on the Upper Nile. The French Minister for Foreign Affairs of that day argued, like his predecessors, that England's apparent opposition was only half-hearted, and would collapse before the persistent threat of French displeasure. Nothing would persuade him that England could in a question of this kind assume an attitude of unbending resistance. It was this erroneous impression, justified in the eyes of the French Cabinet by their deductions from British political practice, that brought the two countries to the verge of war. When the Fashoda chapter had ended with the just discomfiture of France, she remained for a time very sullen, and the enemies of England rejoiced, because they believed that an impassable gulf had now been fixed between the two nations. As a matter of fact, the events at Fashoda proved to be the opening of a new chapter of Anglo-French relations. These, after remaining for some years rather formal, have not since been disturbed by any disagreeable incidents. France behaved more correctly and seemed less suspicious and inconsiderate than had been her wont, and no fresh obstacle arose in the way which ultimately led to the Agreement of 1904.

Although Germany has not been exposed to such a rebuff as France encountered in 1898, the events connected with the Algeciras Conference appear to have had on the German Government the effect of an unexpected revelation, clearly showing indications of a new spirit in which England proposes to regulate her own conduct towards France on the one hand and to Germany on the other. That the result was a very serious disappointment to Germany has been made abundantly manifest by the turmoil which the signature of the Algeciras Act has created in the country, the official, semi-official, and unofficial classes vying with each other in giving expression to their astonished discontent. The time which has since elapsed has, no doubt, been short. But during that time it may be observed that our relations with Germany, if not exactly cordial, have at least been practically free from all symptoms of direct friction, and there is an impression that Germany will think twice before she now gives rise to any fresh disagreement. In this attitude she will be encouraged if she meets on England's part with unvarying courtesy and consideration in all matters of common concern, but also with a prompt and firm refusal to enter into any one-sided bargains or arrangements, and the most unbending determination to uphold British rights and

2 E 2

interests in every part of the globe. There will be no surer or quicker way to win the respect of the German Government and of the German nation.

E. A. C.

MINUTES.

Mr. Crowe's Memorandum should go to the Prime Minister, Lord Ripon, Mr. Asquith, Mr. Morley, Mr. Haldane, with my comment upon it.—E. G.

This Memorandum by Mr. Crowe is most valuable. The review of the present situation is both interesting and suggestive, and the connected account of the diplomatic incidents of past years is most helpful as a guide to policy. The whole Memorandum contains information and reflections, which should be carefully studied.

The part of our foreign policy with which it is concerned involves the greatest issues, and requires constant attention.—E. GREY. *January* 28, 1907.

The observations at p. 11 [*supra* p. 403] on the beneficial results of our free trade policy on our international position are very well put. The only other remark I make on this most able and interesting Memo[randum] is to suggest whether the restless and uncertain personal character of the Emperor William is sufficiently taken into account in the estimate of the present situation. There was at least method in Prince Bismarck's madness; but the Emperor is like a cat in a cupboard. He may jump out anywhere. The whole situation would be changed in a moment if this personal factor were changed, and another Minister like General Caprivi also came into office in consequence.—F.

APPENDIX B.

Memorandum by Lord Sanderson.

Sir C. Hardinge to Sir E. Grey.

(Private.)(¹)
Sir E. Grey, *Foreign Office, February* 25, 1907.

Some weeks ago I gave Lord Sanderson a copy of Mr. Crowe's mem[orandu]m on our relations with Germany which I thought might interest him.

Somewhat to my surprise he has taken up the cudgels for Germany and has weighed in with the accompanying mem[orandu]m which is of some interest as coming from the pen of an official whose duty it was to carry out for many years the policy of the F[oreign] O[ffice].

I submitted it to Mr. Crowe for his observations which he noted in the margin. I do not intend to show them to Lord Lansdowne or to do anything further with this memorandum.

C. H.

MINUTES.

It may all come to rest now.—E. G.

Mr. Crowe and Lord Sanderson on Prince Bismarck.—The question whether in the period 1880–85, Prince Bismarck was or was not guilty of *deception*, is largely verbal only. A person may enter on a certain course of action and thereby induce a friend to undertake liabilities. He then may suddenly enter on an exactly opposite course; disclaim his previous conduct; and leave his friend with the liabilities which the latter has incurred. Or he may be guilty of the false pretence of an existing fact, and thereby fraudulently obtain money.—In both these cases the person in question may be said to have "deceived." The chief difference is that in one case he would at most have exposed himself to a civil action while in the other he could be criminally prosecuted and convicted. The difference between Mr. Crowe and Lord Sanderson is: that Mr. Crowe thinks Prince Bismarck ought to have been prosecuted; while Lord Sanderson thinks he was only civilly liable.—F.

(¹) [Sir C. Hardinge's note and the minutes following exist only in the Grey MSS. (Vol. 53). The Memorandum printed here as Enclosure I exists in draft in Lord Sanderson's own hand among the Grey MSS. On this text Mr. Eyre Crowe wrote his marginal comments. The Memorandum and comments were printed in September 1908, as a separate confidential paper (8882*), and a copy was bound up in F.O. 371/257.]

F.O. 371/257.

Enclosure I.

Observations on printed Mem[orandu]m on Relations with France and Germany, January 1907.

Foreign Office,

Secret. February 21, 1907.

I.—*Page 5.*([1]) *German action in regard to Morocco.*

(1.) It must be remembered that in confidential conversations some years ago, Count Hatzfeldt distinctly intimated to Lord Salisbury that Germany took an interest in the eventual disposal of the Atlantic Coast of Morocco.

But subsequently Germany has repeatedly declared that she had no political ambitions, and only economical interests, in Morocco. [E. A. C.]

(2.) I do not think that Count Bülow's statement in the Reichstag at the announcement of the Anglo-French Agreement can be regarded otherwise than as an invitation to Great Britain and France to discuss in due course its bearings on German interests whenever these interests were likely to be effected. We were obliged to do so in order to obtain German assent to the Conversion of the Egyptian Debt, and the German Gov[ernmen]t were not in the end unreasonable. M. Delcassé, on the other hand, ignored Germany entirely when he commenced operations in Morocco. The action of France and her demands on the Sultan were undoubtedly much exaggerated and misrepresented. But in addition there is no doubt that M. Delcassé was steadily pursuing a series of manœuvres for the purpose of isolating Germany and weakening her alliances. The German Gov[ernmen]t and the German nation are extremely sensitive about being ignored or neglected in the discussion of important questions, and it is not surprising that on this occasion they should have been much exasperated, and determined on inflicting on France a severe humiliation. That they also wished to separate us from France, to prevent the Agreement from developing into an alliance, and to obtain any share they could in the eventual development of Morocco is no doubt also true. The methods adopted were characteristic of German policy, and as on some other occasions they failed.

See Mr. Mallet's memo[randum] A attached hereto. [E. A. C.]

The situation in Egypt and Morocco was different. The changes which the British Gov[ernmen]t contemplated in Egypt could not be carried out without Germany's consent unless her express treaty rights were to be violated. In Morocco France threatened no such rights. The German contrary assertion was based on the alleged list of demands said to have been presented to the Sultan by France in the terms of an ultimatum. France has categorically denied that any such demands were ever made, and all German attempts to disprove this have failed. [E. A. C.]

This presumably refers to the understanding arrived at by France with Italy which, *pro tanto*, weakens the policy embodied in the Triple Alliance. But the understanding dates back to about 5 years before the Morocco incident. [E. A. C.]

This is exactly what I have said in my memorandum. [E. A. C.]

II.—*Pages 21 and 22.*([2]) *Inception of German Colonial Policy.*

(3.) I cannot agree in the description of the inception of German colonial policy, nor of the acts of " direct and unmistakable

I believe it to be a fact that the acts were considered at the time so hostile that the question of resisting them by force was seriously discussed by the Cabinet.

([1]) [*v. supra*, p. 399.]
([2]) [*v. supra*, p. 408.]

Lord Ampthill up to the last moment assured Lord Granville that Bismarck would maintain his opposition to the colonial policy clamoured for by a noisy section of the German shipping interest. It is certain that the sudden annexation of Angra Pequena came as a complete surprise to Lord Granville. The despatch in which Bismarck afterwards alleged he had fully explained his view to the British Gov[ernmen]t is the famous bogey document which although published in the German White Book, was in fact never delivered. It is difficult to find a better word than "deception" for these proceedings.　　[E. A. C.]

I have developed my views about what is "deception" in a separate minute [v. supra, p. 420].　　　　F.

He was not thwarted. We immediately recognized all the German annexations, notwithstanding the offensive manner of their being effected.　　　　[E. A. C.]

Just so. I have endeavoured to supply an explanation of the ideas which probably inspired Bismarck's action. See p. 35 of my memorandum [v. supra, p. 415]. [E. A. C.]

There is however much evidence to support the statement. The present paragraph itself furnishes some, and seeks to justify the practice, which of course was not confined to the period of Lord Salisbury's administration. Lord Fitzmaurice's Life of Lord Granville gives numerous instances. I could quote several more myself.
　　　　[E. A. C.]

The Italian agreement of 1887 was certainly made privately, as I know from the text having fallen into my hands by mistake!　　　　C. H.

This is the negotiation referred to in Vol. II, p. 211, of my Life of Lord Granville. I ascertained, when writing this chapter, that there was no trace of the negotiation in the Foreign Office. I am aware of what has come to light since then on the subject, as mentioned by Lord Sanderson.　　　　F.

hostility to England" by which it is said to have been pursued.

(4.) There was not according to my recollection any deception practised on Lord Ampthill. Prince Bismarck was personally opposed to German colonisation, on the ground that it tended to weaken German military strength which would for some time to come be required to keep France in check, and frustrate schemes of revanche. He therefore encouraged us to make fresh annexations on the West Coast of Africa, to which we had been previously indisposed : hoping that the clamour for such annexations by Germany would subside. Suddenly he found that the movement was too strong for him, and that his only expedient, in order to avoid a crushing Parliamentary defeat, was to make friends with the party which urged the acquisition of Colonies. He went to Lord Ampthill, explained his dilemma, said he should have to take up the Colonial policy vigorously, and begged that we would give him our support. We countermanded some projects, but in other places we had already gone too far and could not draw back, and where Cape Colony was concerned we could do little in the way of concession. Prince Bismarck was furious at being thwarted and he had to justify to the German nation the very limited nature of his success. The natural expedient was to throw the blame upon us. The methods adopted were not always scrupulous, and his attitude was unreasonable. But we were by no means the only Country who had to complain on that score in those years.

III.—Page 23.(³) Mediterranean Alliances.

(5.) I dissent from the statement in the Note that during the two administrations of Lord Salisbury all the most important business was transacted under the cover of private correspondence.

The most important business is on record in the Foreign Office. But it is probable that several overtures which came to nothing were made in some verbal form for the express purpose of avoiding a record if the matter were dropped. I have quite recently heard that a proposal was made by Germany for an alliance with England in 1879. The overture was made verbally by the German Ambassador, with the express condition that, unless accepted, it was not to be officially recorded. and having been civilly declined the matter was not put on record.

Lord Sanderson's memory is at fault. In 1895 Count Hatzfeldt informed Lord Rosebery that he had for 8 years made "strenuous efforts to induce the gov[ernmen]t of Great Britain to come to a close understanding with the Triple Alliance." Presumably these are the instances referred to above (§ 5, page 7) which were not recorded. If so this would further confirm my statement on that point.

In 1901, however, the most important of these negotiations for the entry of England into the Triple Alliance *were* recorded. The papers were kept private. One or two only nominally made official by being numbered in the political series. But these were *not* placed in the archives nor properly entered in the registers and indices. The originals have mostly disappeared, but private copies were fortunately allowed by Lord Lansdowne just before he left office to be removed from his private papers and left in the hands of the Private Secretary, who allowed me to peruse them. Among these papers is a draft treaty prepared by Lord Sanderson (and in H[is] L[ordship's] own handwriting) as an alternative to the German proposal for our joining the Triple Alliance.   [E. A. C.]

I have been unable to find anything to confirm this statement. Perhaps it is another instance of Lord Salisbury's action by private letter?   [E. A. C.]

(6.) So far as I am aware there is no foundation for the statement that repeated and pressing proposals were made after 1885 for inviting England to take sides with the Triple Alliance. We have never known positively the conditions of that compact.

(7.) It is true however that Prince Bismarck's policy was directed towards assisting Austria and Italy in forming a league for the maintenance of the *status quo* in the Mediterranean and for checking aggressive designs of Russia on Bulgaria and Constantinople. Prince Bismarck would not join the League on behalf of Germany whom he declined to involve in the question of Constantinople. But he did his best to help Austria and Italy in their negotiations for the protection of their special interests. I do not think that Lord Salisbury required much urging to go as far in this direction as he thought the constitutional obligations of an English Foreign Minister would permit. He thought that England and Austria were both interested in preventing a seizure of Constantinople by Russia, though he declined to pledge the Government to material action for that object. He laid great stress on the importance of protecting Italy from being crushed by France, and in general questions (as he once said to me) he was disposed, when we were not directly interested, to follow the German game, because it was the strongest. To an alliance with Germany he was firmly opposed on the ground that we should gain nothing by it at all commensurate with our increased responsibilities. Such an alliance being outside the sphere of practical politics.

(8.) It was quite in accord with Prince Bismarck's policy and methods that he should encourage Russia to push on her advances in Central Asia. Such action on her part tended to diminish the risk of Germany being dragged into active support of Austria in South Eastern Europe, and in so far as it might be distasteful or menacing to us, it would render us more disposed to bargain for Austrian friendship and support.

IV.—*Page* 23.([4]) *Samoa.*

(9.) My recollection of the Samoan negotiations is not very precise but my impression is that we have not an absolutely clear record, and that Lord Salisbury while conceding any claims on our part did his best to rouse the opposition of the United States. It is not likely that the German Gov[ernmen]t were

([4]) [*v. supra*, p. 409.]

So far as I know only Sir C. Eliot can be said ever to have been so inclined. His opinion and judgment would hardly carry any great weight. The history of German proceedings in Samoa shows the German Gov[ernmen]t probably in its very worst light.

A reference to my memorandum will show that this is also my view. I pointed out that it was the German *method* of proceeding which was so offensive and that had she approached us in a friendly way, she could probably have obtained all she desired, without any friction.

I understand from Sir E. Grey that the German Gov[ernmen]t relied on an undertaking which they said had been given by Lord Salisbury. The latter, on being referred to, failed to recollect the alleged incident. Perhaps another instance of an unrecorded transaction?
[E. A. C.]

The German argument, if I remember rightly, was that in previous negotiations with them we had tried to obtain this strip, that they had explained their objections and we had deferred to them and by implication agreed to forgo the scheme.

It was King Leopold who claimed that the British East Africa Company had given him the Upper Nile and that Lord Salisbury was cognisant of the transaction and had not objected.
E. G.

unaware of this. They certainly always contended that we had not treated them fairly and some of our own Diplomatists were inclined to share that view.

V.—*Page 24.*(⁵) *Zanzibar.*

(10.) The main facts of the case were as follows :—Great Britain and France were bound to one another by a mutual engagement to respect the independence and integrity of Zanzibar. Germany was not so bound. She consequently stepped in and acquired a considerable portion of the Sultan's possessions on the mainland, and was in a position to do more. We were compelled by the force of circumstances to come to an arrangement with her on this and other questions, of which arrangement the cession of Heligoland formed part, and before we could proceed to a formal Protectorate over Zanzibar we had to come to a bargain also with France. The procedure of Germany was no doubt annoying to us, but we have no claim to a monopoly of acquisitions in Africa, and it can scarcely be contended that we have not obtained our full share.

VI—*Page 25.*(⁶) *German Objections to the Anglo-Congolese Agreement of 1894.*

(11.) The objection of Germany to Art. III of this Agreement was that it placed Great Britain on the Western frontier of German East Africa, in lieu of the neutral Congo Free State, Great Britain being already on the Northern and South Western frontiers. For a Government which is absorbed in strategical considerations the argument has naturally a good deal of importance.

VII.—*Pages 25–28.*(⁷) *German policy towards the Transvaal.*

(12.) The history of this question is briefly as follows :—

The German Gov[ernmen]t were by no means satisfied with their acquisitions in Africa; they looked upon them, perhaps rightly, as not very promising possessions, and they entertained the ordinary impression that an undertaking which was not giving good results in its actual shape, would be more successful if it assumed larger proportions. For the gratification of their wishes they

(⁵) [*v. supra*, p. 409.]
(⁶) [*v. supra*, p. 410.]
(⁷) [*v. supra*, p. 410–1.]

Yes, but only possible in antagonism to England.
[E. A. C.]

I cannot find any record of these discussions.
[E. A. C.]

That is to say, Germany was pursuing a course incompatible with respect for British treaty rights, for the purpose of embarrassing us sufficiently to make us pliable in regard to German demands in other quarters. Lord Sanderson confirms my theory of political blackmail. We bought off German hostility in the Transvaal by conceding a reversion to certain Portuguese Colonies.

The transaction was quite understood in this light at the time, Lord Salisbury, as well as Mr. Balfour considered the German demands most impertinent ; and refused for some time to have anything to say for them. But they eventually gave way in order to quiet Germany for the moment.
[E. A. C.]

looked forward to the dismemberment of the African possessions of Portugal, which seemed a not unremote contingency as the Portuguese Gov[ernmen]t were in great financial straits, and for the furtherance of this object the friendship, and possibly the alliance of the Transvaal was clearly desirable.

(13.) In 1895 Count Hatzfeldt initiated some secret discussions with Lord Kimberley as to the eventual disposal of the Portuguese African possessions on the East Coast, and claimed for Germany, if I remember rightly, the Coast down to the mouth of the Zambesi, with a special proviso that Delagoa Bay should be *neutralised*. Lord Kimberley became hot with indignation, and the discussions terminated somewhat abruptly. From that time forth the attitude of Germany towards the Transvaal became constantly more encouraging and sympathetic; and it was clear that unless we came to some arrangement with the German Gov[ernmen]t we should find them ranged against us in any questions which might ensue between us and the Boers. At the same time the financial needs of Portugal became more and more pressing, and there was imminent danger that she might be pressed and cajoled into some detrimental bargain, prejudicial to our interests. In these circumstances Mr. Balfour acting on behalf of Lord Salisbury concluded the Secret Convention with Germany, pledging the two Powers to act in accord in any financial assistance to Portugal, and specifying the Colonial possessions of that Country on which either Power might respectively establish a lien in consideration of such financial assistance. This arrangement reserved to Great Britain all the Portuguese possessions in the neighbourhood of the Transvaal. The German Gov[ernmen]t no doubt desired and expected that the Convention would bear immediate fruit, and that Portugal would shortly come under advances from them, and obligations to both Countries. That was not at all our wish, and I fancy that it has been an occasion of much disappointment and considerable soreness at Berlin that Portugal, with our openly expressed approbation, has succeeded in making her way without pledging any of her Colonial possessions.

(14.) But from the moment that the arrangement was concluded the friendship of the Transvaal had no longer any value for the German Gov[ernmen]t and President Krüger was left to his fate. The Boers are not a quick minded people, and they failed to grasp the significance of the change of attitude. Moreover the sympathy of the German public

Exactly. German hostility had been bought off. Germany's friendship was not obtained. [E. A. C.]

There is however the strongest doubt as to the correctness of this story. All the available evidence points to Germany having sounded the Russian and French governments as to the possibility of falling upon England. M. Delcassé has furnished information which cannot be explained in any other way. (See Mr. Mallet's memo. B annexed hereto.) [E. A. C.]

What I pointed out was that we readily made a waiver of our rights of search, as a friendly concession, but that Germany used this very concession as a peg on which to hang a further exceedingly hostile demonstration and political agitation against us, in which the Emperor and Count Bülow (as he then was) took a prominent and leading part. [E. A. C.]

was strongly with them, and it is very intelligible that the German Ministers, embarrassed by their previous professions of sympathy should have found it convenient to abstain from defending us against unjust aspersions. But their conduct towards us, though not particularly gracious, was perfectly correct. I see no reason to doubt that Germany declined Mouravieff's invitation to join a European League for the purpose of offering and pressing mediation. And the German Emperor altogether refused any encouragement to President Krüger when he came over to Europe. The protests of Germany against our method of exercising the right of search were no doubt rude, but not altogether without excuse. The almost simultaneous seizure of three large German mailships, laden with passengers and cargo, two of which were searched from top to bottom without finding the smallest evidence to justify the step, and the third of which was no doubt equally innocent, was an act which if practised on ourselves would have certainly been denounced as intolerable.

VIII.—*Page 29.*([8]) *German policy in China.*

(15.) My recollection of the negotiations which led to the Anglo-German Agreement of October 1900 does not altogether tally with that given in the Memorandum.

(16.) The Emperor William having obtained from the Emperor of Russia a promise that he would not oppose the acquisition by Germany of a Chinese port, suddenly and much to the disgust of the Russian Gov[ernmen]t seized Kiao-Chou in November 1897, and there seems little doubt, notwithstanding the assurances which were given us on that occasion that she succeeded as part of the arrangement made with China in extracting from the Chinese Gov[ernmen]t certain preferential and possibly exclusive rights in the province of Shantung, the exact nature and extent of which however we have never to my knowledge precisely ascertained.

(17.) Within a few months the Russian Gov[ernmen]t demanded and obtained the lease of Port Arthur.

(18.) As a countermove, and more or less at the suggestion of the Chinese Gov[ernmen]t we obtained a similar lease of Wei-hai-Wei, and in order to disarm German opposition, which would have been very inconvenient when we had Russia with France at her back in antagonism to us, we gave

([8]) [*v. supra,* p. 412. The following paragraphs (15)–(21) were printed in *Gooch & Temperley,* Vol. II, pp. 1–2, *note.*]

We had denied the existence of any special rights of Germany in Shantung. We spontaneously offered valuable assurances to her which she had not even asked for and had no right whatever to expect. Our action was altogether gratuitous, it tied our own hands for the future (as we now experience at Wei-hai-wei) and we neither asked for, nor got, anything whatever in return.　　[E. A. C.]

As I point out in my memorandum, we gave the desired undertaking, but we did *not* obtain Germany's general support, not even in regard to the very matters which we considered covered by the agreement. We held that the Russian seizure of Manchuria and German monopolization of Shantung were contrary to it, but Germany promptly repudiated this view and declared that the agreement applied solely to the Yangtsze. We were not supported but abandoned by Germany. This appears clearly on the facts as here stated by Lord Sanderson, which do not conflict with anything I have said.　　[E. A. C.]

Germany an assurance that we had no intention of interfering with her rights and interests in Shantung by this acquisition.

(19.) In 1899, the Russian Gov[ernmen]t having been seriously exercised by the grant to a British Company of a concession for a railway into Manchuria, we concluded an Agreement with Russia by which we precluded ourselves from obtaining for British subjects concessions for railways North of the Great Wall of China, and Russia renounced the right to obtain such concessions in the Yangtsze Valley. We had in Feb. 1898 obtained from the Chinese Gov[ernmen]t a public engagement that no territory should be alienated in the provinces adjoining the Yangtsze and the language of the English press indicated a tendency to regard the valley of that river as the proper sphere of English influence in any partition of interests. The Germans were keen to prevent our acquiring exclusive rights or privileges in this enormous and important tract of country and when in 1900 the seizure by Russia of the railway between Tientsin and Niuchwang and other acts brought us into a somewhat acute controversy with the Russian Gov[ernmen]t, the German Emperor told Sir F. Lascelles that he was ready to give us his general support provided we would engage to observe the policy of the open door in the Yangtsze valley. At that time our relations with Germany were decidedly friendly and a considerable section of the Cabinet were in favour of an alliance or at least of an agreement for joint policy—an idea to which as I have already said Lord Salisbury was never very favourable.

(20.) Shortly after the Emperor's conversation Count Hatzfeldt proposed the Agreement to Lord Salisbury which was eventually signed in Oct. 1900. In its original wording it applied only to the region of the Yangtsze. Lord Salisbury did not welcome the idea of a fresh Agreement with any enthusiasm, but he accepted the discussion. He objected altogether, however, to making the instrument applicable to one portion of the Chinese Empire in which Great Britain was specially interested, and Article I was worded so as to extend the principle of equal opportunities to ports on the littoral and in the rivers of China. Other Articles were added providing against the acquisition of territorial advantages in China by the Signatory or other Powers during the existing complications. The whole was regarded by Lord Salisbury as unnecessary but innocuous, and having a certain value in that it placed on record a community of policy between Great Britain

My point is that we made a gratuitous concession, most earnestly coveted by Germany, and got less than nothing in return.   [E. A. C.]

They were reported to us in a despatch from Sir C. (then Mr.) Hardinge from St. Petersburg, No. 126 of Nov. 2, 1900. The German Chargé d'Affaires at that place, in explaining away the significance of the so-called Yangtsze agreement with England, declared that it was not directed against Russia, and added that Germany had been driven to come to terms with England because Russia had declined to entertain the proposals made by Germany for assuring her (Germany's) position on the Yangtsze..

There was at one time a great fear lest Russia, by means of the Peking–Hankow railway, should instal herself firmly on the Upper Yangtsze.   [E. A. C.]

My memorandum appears to have stated the case quite correctly. It is not contradicted by anything said in the present paragraph.   [E. A. C.]

My memorandum gives a summary, but, I venture to maintain, accurate, statement of the principal instances of Anglo-German political discussions and transactions. My object in making that statement was not at all to portray a record of black deeds, but to show that the line of action followed by England with amiable persistency for 20 years did not in the end secure what she expected and bargained for : Germany's friendship and political support.
                                               [E. A. C.]

and Germany and any Powers who adhered to it. The German Gov[ernmen]t no doubt valued it mainly on the ground that it kept the Yangtsze open to German industrial enterprise. When later on the tendencies of Russia to monopolise Manchuria became evident, the German Gov[ernmen]t declared that they had never considered the Agreement to apply to Manchuria, which was outside the sphere of German interests and influence, a contention of which no trace could be found in the negotiations, and Count Bülow rather indirectly revealed in a Parliamentary speech the original intention with which it had been proposed by calling it "the Yangtsze Agreement."

(21.) The whole proceeding was no doubt shifty and not over creditable, but I do not see that the Agreement, to the principle of which France, Italy, Austria, Japan and the United States agreed, and to which even Russia expressed a certain gratified assent, was in any way detrimental to our interests.

(22.) I have no knowledge of the secret overtures mentioned in the Memorandum as made by Germany to Russia "by which she would have obtained the much desired foothold on the Yangtsze," nor do I understand how any agreement with Russia could have had that effect. I do not see why Russia should have opposed such a step, but Russia is not the Power to be reckoned with.

(23.) The conduct of the Germans in pressing the Chinese for fresh guarantees against hypothetical British designs on the withdrawal of European troops from Shanghae, mentioned on page 30 of the Memorandum([9]) was discreditable enough. It was rather typical of the German Foreign Office, which seems to me often to overreach itself by trying to be more subtle than is consistent with the Teutonic disposition, and to be constantly suspecting others of trickery by which I am afraid that it feels it would itself, under temptation, be capable. But the incident was more annoying than serious, and although Lord Lansdowne's strictures were justified and I think called for, it would have served no useful purpose to inflame the existing antipathy to Germany in this country by publishing them.

(24.) I have written these notes, partly because the circumstances themselves are of considerable interest, partly because they tend to show that the history of German policy towards this Country is not the unchequered record of black deeds which the Memorandum seems to portray. There have been many occasions on which we have worked comfortably in accord with Germany, and not a

(9) [v. supra, p. 413.]

Lord Sanderson does not quote these cases. [E. A. C.]

This is what I have illustrated by the analogy of the blackmailer. [E. A. C.]

But surely this is not an offence, but a duty. [E. A. C.]

I cannot recall any such instance. Venezuela and the Bagdad railway are the only two cases known to me where the foreign policy of H[is] M[ajesty's] G[overnment] seemed to be directly influenced by public opinion as expressed in the newspapers and magazines. As regards Venezuela events showed that co-operation with Germany was certainly not "desirable" in British interests. And the conditions offered to Lord Lansdowne for British participation in the Bagdad Railway were clearly unacceptable at the time. [E. A. C.]

few cases in which her support has been serviceable to us. There have been others in which she has been extremely aggravating, sometimes unconsciously so, sometimes with intention. The Germans are very tight bargainers, they have earned the nickname of " *les Juifs de la diplomatie.*" The German Foreign Office hold to a traditional view of negotiation that one of the most effective methods of gaining your point is to show how intensely disagreeable you can make yourself if you do not. They are surprised that the recollection of these methods should rankle, and speaking generally the North Germans combine intense susceptibility as regards themselves with a singular inability to appreciate the susceptibilities of others.

(25.) On the other hand it is undeniable that we have at times been compelled to maintain an attitude in defence of British interests which has been very inconvenient to German ambitions. And of late years while the British Gov[ernmen]t has remained calm and conciliatory, the press and public opinion here have interfered seriously with our working so much together as would otherwise have been desirable. It is not at all unnatural that the German Ambassador, who has seen better days, should feel this rather keenly.

(26.) In considering the tendencies and methods of German policy, we have to remember that the Empire took its present place among the Great Powers of Europe only 35 years ago, after some 50 years of helpless longings for united national existence. It was inevitable that a nation flushed with success which had been obtained at the cost of great sacrifices, should be somewhat arrogant and over-eager, impatient to realise various long-suppressed aspirations, and to claim full recognition of its new position. The Government was at the same time suffering from the constant feeling of insecurity caused by the presence on the East and West of two powerful, jealous and discontented neighbours. It is not surprising that with the traditions of the Prussian monarchy behind it, it should have shown itself restless and scheming, and have had frequent recourse to tortuous methods, which have not proved wholly successful.

(27.) It is not, I think, to be expected that Germany will renounce her ambition for oversea possessions, which shall assist and support the development of her commerce, and afford openings for her surplus population. But, as time goes on, her manner of pursuing these objects will probably be less open to exception, and popular opinion, which

This tendency is not observable at present and it would not be prudent to build any plans on its effective emergence in the immediate future.   [E. A. C.]

I do not quarrel with this characterization. Germany may be helpful as a friend. All I wish to recall is that Germany has not given us her friendship although she has repeatedly pocketed the price demanded for it.
[E. A. C.]

But this is exactly what we have so often done.
[E. A. C.]

in Germany is on the whole sound and prudent, will exercise an increasing amount of wholesome restraint. If the mere acquisition of territory were in itself immoral, I conceive that the sins of Germany since 1871 are light in comparison to ours, and it must be remembered that, from an outside point of view, a Country which looks to each change as a possible chance of self aggrandisement is not much more open to criticism than one which sees in every such change a menace to its interests, existing or potential, and founds on this theory continued claims to interference or compensation. It has sometimes seemed to me that to a foreigner reading our press the British Empire must appear in the light of some huge giant sprawling over the globe, with gouty fingers and toes stretching in every direction, which cannot be approached without eliciting a scream. The sentiment was aptly expressed by a member of a Deputation from South Africa who concluded an address to the late Lord Salisbury with the remark " My Lord, we are told that the Germans are good neighbours, but we prefer to have no neighbours at all." That is an attitude which no Government can successfully maintain, and it appears to me that Mr. Rhodes was better advised when in order to draw off the attention of the German Government from South African affairs, he mentioned to the Emperor William " that blessed word Mesopotamia," and suggested opportunities for the development of German energy in a different quarter of the globe.

(28.) The moral which I should draw from the events of recent years is that Germany is a helpful, though somewhat exacting, friend, that she is a tight and tenacious bargainer, and a most disagreeable antagonist. She is oversensitive about being consulted on all questions on which she can claim a voice, either as a Great Power or on account of special interests, and it is never prudent to neglect her on such occasions. Her diplomacy is, to put it mildly, always watchful, and any suspicion of being ignored rouses an amount of wrath disproportionate to the offence. However tiresome such discussions may be, it is, as a general rule, less inconvenient to take her at once into counsel, and to state frankly within what limits you can accept her views, than to have a claim for interference suddenly launched on you at some critical moment. It would of course be absurd to make to her any concessions of importance except as a matter of bargain and in return for value received. Her motto has always been " Nothing for nothing in this world, and

Gratitude among nations had better not be expected. We have for our continuous "friendly support" not only received from Germany no gratitude, but are undoubtedly the most cordially detested of her neighbours.

With the rest of the concluding paragraph I quite agree. I have said practically the same in my memorandum.

[E. A. C.]

very little for sixpence." But I do not think it can be justly said that she is ungrateful for friendly support. It is at all events unwise to meet her with an attitude of pure obstruction, such as is advocated by part of our press. A great and growing nation cannot be repressed. It is altogether contrary to reason that Germany should wish to quarrel with us though she may wish to be in a position to face a quarrel with more chances of success, than she can be said now to have. But it would be a misfortune that she should be led to believe that in whatever direction she seeks to expand she will find the British lion in her path. There must be places in which German enterprise can find a field without injury to any important British interests, and it would seem wise that in any policy of development which takes due account of those interests she should be allowed to expect our good will.

SANDERSON.

[ED. NOTE.—The following document from the private papers of Lord Salisbury has been communicated to the Editors by Lady Gwendolen Cecil.

[*The Marquess of Salisbury to the Queen.*]

Foreign Office, April 10th, 1900.

Lord Salisbury with his humble duty to Your Majesty respectfully thanks Your Majesty for Your gracious letter, and for the most affectionate and satisfactory letter from the German Emperor. There lingers in Lord Salisbury's mind a doubt whether a proposal for a combination against England was ever really made by France and Russia to Germany, but still it is very satisfactory to receive from the German Emperor such earnest expressions of his goodwill.

Some further papers on this subject will be published in a later volume.]

Enclosure 2.

Memorandum A by Sir L. Mallet.

(With reference to Lord Sanderson's memo., page 1, § 2.([1]))

Foreign Office, February 25, 1907.

I do not think that the Bülow speech can be regarded as an invitation to negotiate. His words were that Germany had "no cause to apprehend that the Agreement was levelled against any individual Power. It seemed to be an attempt to eliminate the points between France and England by an amicable understanding. From the point of view of German interests, they had nothing to complain of . . . . .([2]) As regards Morocco, they had a substantial economic interest there, but had no cause to fear that their economic interests would be disregarded or injured."

A year later, after Mukden, Bülow changed his tone, and in reply to Bebel's taunts about the Emperor's visit to Tangier and the alteration of German policy towards Morocco, admitted that "the language and attitude of a politician are governed by circumstances."

Moreover, the French Government were always willing to discuss the question with Germany.

Rouvier admitted in the Chamber that Delcassé had taken the initiative in this matter. He spoke to Radolin himself, and instructed Bihourd to make explanations in Berlin.

([1]) [*v. supra,* p. 421.]
([2]) [Thus in original.]

Rouvier came in prejudiced against Delcassé, and with the avowed object of arranging matters with Germany, but left Office convinced that Germany did not want to discuss the question.

The charge that Delcassé was trying to isolate Germany is often made by Germans, but it was certainly not Lord Lansdowne's view, and is only true in so far as the establishment of good relations between France, England, and Italy must naturally neutralise Germany's success as an "agent provocateur." But that Delcassé aimed especially at the isolation of Germany in these agreements is, I think, disproved by the whole trend of modern French foreign policy.

L. MALLET.

Memorandum B by Sir L. Mallet.

(With reference to Lord Sanderson's memo., page 19, § 14.([1]))

Charles Kinsky, of the Austrian Embassy at Petersburg showed Sir Charles Hardinge, who was then Secretary of Embassy there, a despatch from M. Koziebrodski, Austrian Chargé d'Affaires at Madrid, to Count Goluchowski stating that the German Ambassador at Madrid had proposed to the Spanish Government that they should join in a coalition against Great Britain, consisting of Russia, Germany and France.

Absolutely correct.—C. H.

This was corroborated from Paris.

I have notes of a conversation which I recently had with M. Delcassé in Paris upon this subject (annexed).

He was astonished that we were not aware of Germany's action, and said that it was known to every Chancery in Europe.*

L. MALLET.

Feb. 25, '07.

The following are some notes of a conversation which I had with Mr. Delcassé in Paris about a month ago.—L. M. *Dec[ember] 20, [19]05.*

From the moment M. Delcassé came into office the Emperor of Germany [sic] never missed an opportunity of trying to make bad blood between France and England, impressing upon France that England was the enemy. Directly after the outbreak of the Boer War he called personally upon M. de Noailles at the Embassy, and spoke violently against England, the English Royal Family (especially the then Prince of Wales) and the ruling classes. The war was "une occasion unique qui ne se représentera d'un siècle pour mettre une fin à l'arrogance et aux empiètements de l'Angleterre." He held the same language, but in still more violent terms, to M. de Noailles at a small supper which he gave in the Imperial box on the occasion of a representation by a French actress.

A few days later Prince Bülow had an interview with the French Ambassador, when he produced a map of the world. He pointed out that French and German interests clashed nowhere, whereas England stood in the path of both countries. They had only to combine and an end would be put to a state of things so disadvantageous to both countries.

At his interviews with M. de Noailles and Count Osten-Sacken, the Russian Ambassador, the Emperor always ended his tirades against England with the significant phrase "Enfin si on voulait me suivre!" These conversations, which M. de Noailles reported to Paris, made a great impression on M. Delcassé, but he was very suspicious of Germany and determined not to be drawn. He therefore telegraphed

([1]) [v. supra, pp. 425–6.]

* See also article in *National Review* for July 1908 by André Mévil, which bears every evidence of being inspired by M. Delcassé.

to M. de Noailles in the following words : " Je suis d'accord que la thèse de M. de Bülow peut se soutenir et mériterait d'être examinée, mais je constate que toutes les déclarations de l'Empereur et de Chancelier n'ont jamais jusqu'à présent amené le Gouvernement Impérial à faire des propositions sérieuses." M. de Bülow replied that he was delighted to hear that this was the view of M. Delcassé, and that the whole question would be examined. From that day no further communication was received from Prince Bülow.

At the beginning of March 1900, at the time of our greatest disasters, the language of the German Emperor became still more violent. He repeatedly said that the moment had now come to " step in." M. de Bülow, at his official reception, used the same language as the Emperor to M. de Noailles, insisting upon the necessity of steps being taken to stop the terrible " effusion de sang." M. de Noailles at last asked him what Germany really wanted—whether it was an " intervention amicale " and if so, he said he concluded that as Germany had hitherto taken the initiative in the matter, she would continue to lead and make definite proposals. Upon this M. de Bülow at once drew back. M. de Muravieff, who, although no longer in Paris, was in constant communication with M. Delcassé, raised the whole question with him, and they both came to the conclusion that the language of the Emperor and M. de Bülow throughout showed clearly that they wished to push France and Russia into action which would be most unfriendly to Great Britain, and then, when they had the proof of the intention of the two Powers to take such action, to make use of it in London and claim a reward for their noble action. M. Muravieff, in a letter to M. Delcassé, wrote in such a way as to incline the latter to the belief that he had given a hint to H[is] M[ajesty's] Government of what Germany was up to.

Margin notes: January? — This is quite true. It was well known at St. Petersburg at the time. —C. H.

L. MALLET.

APPENDIX C.

Extract from General Report on Germany for 1906.([1])

I.—GENERAL.

F.O. 371/260.   *Berlin, May 24, 1907.*

1. The year 1906 has been a remarkable one as regards Germany, as during the course of it the change which has come over public opinion in political questions, more especially in connection with the relations between the people and the Government, and even the Emperor himself, has become evident. No doubt this change has been gradual in its development, but it has only been in the course of this year that it has become apparent. When I first came to Berlin, eleven years ago, 1 was told that the attitude of an ordinary German in reading a newspaper was to ask whether the statements contained in it were official. If the answer was in the affirmative, he would read it with attention and respect; if in the negative he would attach but little importance to what he read. Now, anything published by authority is received with suspicion and closely criticized, and constant attacks have been made in newspapers, which might be expected to support the authorities, not only against the action of the Government, but also against the person of the Emperor. The first manifestations of this change came under my notice during the sittings of the conference at Algeciras, when I was astonished to hear people in society, to whose individual opinion no great weight was attached, openly criticizing the action of the Government. "What," they asked, "had Germany to seek in Morocco?" "Why did the Government insist on a conference which showed the position of isolation in which Germany was placed, when, after the triumph they had achieved by

([1]) [Enclosure in despatch No. 238 from Sir F. Lascelles.]

M. Delcassé's resignation, they might have come to terms with France by direct negotiation?" These, and similar questions, were symptomatic of a general feeling that the foreign affairs of Germany were not skilfully dealt with, and that the Moroccan question in particular had been woefully bungled. How far the responsibility for the action of the German Government with regard to Morocco, both before and during the Algeciras conference, the details of which I need not recapitulate, is attributable to the Emperor, is a question which I am unable to answer. I have been assured by two persons who accompanied His Majesty on his memorable voyage to Tangier in the spring of 1905, that, on his arrival at Lisbon, he had determined to give up his projected visit to Morocco, and that it was only in consequence of the reports from Berlin, which he received at Lisbon, that he decided to carry out his original intention. However this may be, the Emperor certainly took credit to himself for the signature of the convention, and he told me himself during the month of August that he had been obliged to send the most stringent instructions to his Representatives at Algeciras, who wanted to break up the conference without coming to an agreement. . . . .

The Emperor admitted to a friend of mine that he had made a great mistake in going to Tangier.—E. B.

VII.—The Emperor.([2])

109.   It is no easy matter, even for one who has been brought into somewhat close and occasionally even confidential relations with the Emperor, to attempt a description of His Majesty's personality, which is composed of various and sometimes contradictory qualities. Before taking up my post at Berlin in December 1895, I had been informed by the late Count Hatzfeldt, then German Ambassador in London, that I should certainly be impressed by the knowledge which the Emperor possessed on a vast number of subjects, and more especially by His Majesty's quickness of apprehension. It was not long before I was in a position to realize the accuracy of Count Hatzfeldt's description. The Emperor certainly possesses great and varied knowledge, and is very quick in grasping the meaning of what is said to him, but this quickness is not an unmixed advantage, as it not unfrequently causes His Majesty to jump at a conclusion without giving sufficient consideration to all the conditions of the case. It has been pointed out to me that when a question is submitted to His Majesty he is apt to at once express an opinion, and when the same question is again submitted from a different point of view he very probably may pronounce a very different opinion.

Many people believe it is rather varied than great.—E.A.C.

This would be impossible if there were real knowledge.—E.A.C.

110.   The well-known impulsiveness of the Emperor's character, coupled with the exaggeration in which he is in the habit of indulging in conversation, have given rise to an impression, which is very generally entertained, that his persistent activity in pushing German interests in all parts of the world, and in claiming for the German Empire a larger share of influence than the other Powers are disposed to admit, constitutes a danger for the peace of Europe. If His Majesty is judged by his words there would be ample justification for this impression, but it must be admitted that during the nineteen years he has now been on the throne, he has not broken the peace, although he might have taken an opportunity, or even created one himself on more than one occasion, of going to war if he had really wished it.

Not going to war with the reasonable certainty of winning.—E.A.C.

111.   Before coming to Berlin I had already had considerable experience, at the different diplomatic posts which I had had the honour of holding, of reporting conversations with the various sovereigns and statesmen with whom I had been brought into official relations, but I was not prepared for the great difficulty which I experienced in attempting to give an account of a conversation with the Emperor. I found that, with every wish to report all that His Majesty said, I should give a wrong impression of what he wished to convey if I repeated His Majesty's words without an explanation of the accompanying tone and gesture. This difficulty was in part due to the habit of exaggeration to which I have alluded above, and in part to his fondness for indulging in

([2]) [The marginal annotations to this section appear on the copy preserved in F.O. 371/260.]

jokes, which sometimes may be taken seriously by those who fail to see them. As an illustration of this I may state that on one occasion when, in obedience to the instructions of your predecessor, I made a communication to the Emperor of an agreeable nature, His Majesty replied in such a way that I was constrained to ask him whether he wished me to convey such a message to His Majesty's Government. "No," said His Majesty, "you surely know me well enough to translate what I say into diplomatic language." "In that case," I said, "I propose to report that your Majesty has received the communication with satisfaction." "Yes," replied His Majesty, "you may say, with great interest and great satisfaction," a meaning which even those intimately acquainted with His Majesty might easily have failed to gather from his original remark, which was, "The noodles seem to have had a lucid interval."

112. A characteristic of the Emperor, on which it is difficult to pronounce an opinion, but a reference to which is necessary to enable a just appreciation of his character to be formed, consists of the mysticism by which he is said to be influenced. I have been told on good authority that he interprets the words "King of Prussia by the grace of God" in a literal sense, and regards himself as placed in a very special manner under the direct protection of the Almighty. On the occasion of the centenary of the birth of the Emperor William I, His Majesty, in a speech delivered at a banquet in the "Weisse Saal," expressed the conviction that his grandfather was present in spirit, and added with some emphasis, "and he certainly paid a visit last night to the colours," which on the previous day His Majesty had himself deposited in the palace of the first Emperor which had remained uninhabited since his death in 1888. It was stated that the Emperor appointed himself for that special occasion aide-de-camp to his late grandfather, and whether this story is true or not, the credence it obtained is a proof of the belief that is generally entertained of His Majesty's leanings towards mysticism. The appointment of certain persons in his entourage, and the choice of some of his personal friends, are supposed to be due to the mystical tendencies of the particular individuals. It is possible that the belief in the sacredness of his position as King and Emperor has induced him to surround himself with an amount of pomp which some times verges on the theatrical, and for which it would be necessary to go back to the times of the first King of Prussia, 200 years ago, to find a parallel in the history of the Court of Berlin. On state occasions the Emperor is in the habit of assuming a very rigid attitude, and a severe, if not forbidding, expression of countenance. An acute observer, M. Jules Cambon, the newly-accredited French Ambassador, was struck by this attitude which the Emperor assumed during the official part of the audience at which he presented his credentials, and he came away with the impression that His Majesty had to make an effort, and a very great effort, to maintain the severe and dignified attitude befitting a sovereign, and that it was a relief to him, when the official part of the audience was over, to relax and indulge in agreeable and even jocose conversation which he believed to be more in consonance with His Majesty's real nature.

[NOTE.— A minute apparently by Sir E. Barrington is omitted here.]

113. How far the Emperor interferes directly in the affairs of state or with the conduct of the administration is a question on which great differences of opinion exist. It is generally believed abroad that the Emperor is directly responsible for the general lines ,if not the actual details, of the German policy, and the articles which appeared in the press during the autumn condemning the system of personal government prove that this opinion was largely shared in Germany. His Majesty's daily morning visits to Prince Bülow during his residence in Berlin have been taken to indicate the interest which he takes in the general administration of his country, and more especially in the conduct of its foreign relations, but doubts have been expressed as to whether these matutinal conversations usually went beyond those vague generalities in the expression of which Prince Bülow is so perfect a master. Herr von Mühlberg told me on one occasion, in speaking of the attacks in the press on the system of personal government, that it was a mistake to suppose that the Emperor interfered in affairs of State to the extent which was generally supposed. Indeed, His Majesty would not, as a

2 F 2

rule, be in a position to do so. He no doubt wished to be kept informed of what was going on, but he had a somewhat unfortunate habit of cutting short a conversation which was not entirely to his liking by the remark, "I do not admit that this is so," and his information is therefore often not complete enough to enable him to form a correct opinion. That the Emperor on occasions does exercise his direct authority is an indisputable fact, and as he told me himself, the signature of the Act of Algeciras was due entirely to the very precise instructions which he felt called upon to send in opposition to the opinion of his representatives on the spot, who would have preferred that the conference should have broken up without coming to an arrangement. I have been told that the Emperor himself has complained that whenever anything goes wrong the blame is thrown upon him personally, and the credit for any success which may have been achieved is invariably attributed to one of his advisers. I am inclined to think that the interference of the Emperor in affairs of state has been largely exaggerated, and that in many cases the actions or utterances of his representatives abroad—to which exception may have been taken on account of their unconciliatory and somewhat blustering character—have been due rather to the want of direction of affairs to which I have called attention in a former chapter of this report, rather than to the initiative of His Majesty.

In fact His Majesty's knowledge is not always "great."— [E.A.C.]

114. In one respect the Emperor may perhaps be considered as a typical German. Very shortly after my arrival in Berlin, M. Herbette, who was then the French Ambassador, described the Germans as being "inconscients," a word for which I am unable to find an exact equivalent in English. They were the most sensitive people in the world, and at the same time it would never enter into their heads that they could by any possibility be offensive themselves, although in reality they very often were. It was not long before I realized that the Emperor himself shared to a very large extent the sensitiveness which M. Herbette considered a characteristic of the German people generally. In the early days of my official intercourse with His Majesty I had frequently to listen to complaints about the want of consideration which was shown to the German Empire by foreign countries in general and by England in particular, who seemed to regard her as a *quantité négligéable*. He had frequently made advances to England which had been rejected, but some day no doubt we should see our mistake in alienating the sympathies of the most powerful military Empire in the world. Then came the celebrated telegram to President Krüger on the occasion of the Jameson raid. The Emperor was certainly unprepared for the outburst of indignation which this telegram called forth in England, and, as he told me himself at the time, he could not understand why so much abuse should be lavished upon him for expressing an opinion upon a proceeding which His Majesty's Government themselves had so strongly condemned. During the Boer war the violent anti-English articles in the German press, and the vile caricatures in which even the person of Queen Victoria herself was not spared, excited intense and just indignation in England, and I more than once heard the Emperor very strongly criticized for not putting a stop to these abominable publications. On two occasions Prince Bülow, or rather Count Bülow as he was then, urged me to address a formal application to His Majesty to prosecute the editors of these papers, explaining that the German Government had no legal power to proceed against a paper on account of abuse of a foreign sovereign except upon the demand of the diplomatic representative of that sovereign. Count Bülow said that the Emperor was so annoyed and distressed at the caricatures of the Queen that he hoped I would apply for a prosecution. I persistently declined, on the ground, firstly, that my sovereign was far too exalted to be touched by such scurrilous slanders; and, secondly, that in the excited state of public opinion in Germany it was doubtful whether a conviction would be obtained, and that I should be only giving an extra advertisement to the papers in question. At the time of the death of Queen Victoria the Emperor seemed to have produced a most favourable impression on English public opinion by the devotion which he displayed for the memory of Her Majesty. But this phase did not last long. The Boer war had not been concluded, and the mutual animosity

fomented by certain organs of the press in both countries reached a high pitch of intensity. It must, however, I think, be admitted that the attitude of the Emperor himself during the Boer war was, to say the least, correct. On the 3rd March, 1900, His Majesty informed me in a private note that he had refused an invitation from the Imperial Russian Government to take part with them and France in a collective intervention for the Boers to bring England to make peace, and on the 11th of the same month His Majesty again wrote to me that, "like a thunderbolt the sudden request of the Boer Republics for intercession and peace negotiations had fallen upon me," and that he had declined "as long as Great Britain does not express by her own accord and free will the same wish to me." I understand that documentary evidence exists at the Foreign Office which has given rise to the belief that the Emperor had himself instigated intervention on behalf of the Boers, but, however this may be, I cannot believe, after making every allowance for his usual exaggeration of expression, that His Majesty would have put his hand in writing to two deliberate misstatements of fact, and I think that therefore he is entitled to the claim which has been put forward on his behalf that, at all events on two occasions, he declined to take part in intervention. Then, again, the Emperor on two occasions ran the risk of incurring unpopularity with his subjects: firstly, by refusing to receive President Krüger, who had come as far as Cologne on his way to Berlin, and turned back on hearing that His Majesty declined to see him; secondly, by his refusal to receive the Boer generals after the war unless they should be formally presented by His Majesty's Ambassador—a condition which he must have known could not be complied with, as the generals, after publishing a most offensive proclamation, were then engaged in making a tour through Europe, which in itself was a reproach to England.

[margin note: This is rather hard on our press, who surely had the right to resent the campaign of unexampled calumny carried on in Germany against England.— E.A.C.]

115. It has been my fate to converse with the Emperor on matters of high political importance, and sometimes on matters of an intimate and delicate nature. As a rule His Majesty's cordiality and amiability recalled to memory the wonderful personal charm of the Empress Frederick, which to a certain degree he has inherited. Sometimes, when his temper has been somewhat ruffled, a conversation with His Majesty has been far from an agreeable experience, and on one occasion I felt it incumbent upon me, as His Majesty's Ambassador, to express somewhat strongly my resentment at his personal discourtesy. Had I been called upon some years ago to express an opinion of the Emperor's character, it would probably have coincided with that which I believe to be generally held in England. I should have described him as a man possessed of great knowledge and ability, and endowed with remarkable personal charm, but impulsive, rash, with an undue sensitiveness as to the recognition of the position which he considers the German Empire ought to occupy in the world, and a personal desire to be considered as the most important personage in Europe. A man, in fact, to whom Pope's [sic] description of Buckingham might not be inaptly applied—

[margin note: Our evidence is however too substantial to admit of doubt.— E.A.C.(³)]

> " A man so various that he seemed to be
> Not one, but all mankind's epitome;
> Fixed in opinion, ever in the wrong,
> Was all by fits and starts, and nothing long."

116. Further knowledge and more ample opportunities of intercourse with His Majesty have made me feel much more diffident in expressing an opinion which a slighter acquaintance would perhaps have induced me to pronounce without hesitation, and now I am inclined to share the opinion which is gradually gaining ground, that, in spite of his habit of twirling his moustache and rattling his sabre (I trust that this sentence may be taken in its metaphorical and not in its literal sense, for, as a matter of fact, I have never either seen him twirl his moustache or heard him rattle his

(³) [Cf. statement by Lord Salisbury, supra p. 431, and Sir L. Mallet's memoranda pp. 432–3.]

That Germany kept the peace is not due to the pacific character of the Emperor but to the armaments of the countries which Germany would have to fight.—E.A.C.

sword), which he may think a befitting attitude for the ruler of a mighty Empire, he is really animated by the most pacific sentiments, and that his great ambition now is that his name should be handed down to posterity as that of the German Emperor who kept the peace. It would seem that this is the estimate which the Emperor has formed of his own character, as in a recent conversation with Prince Radolin he said he was at a loss to understand how, with his well-known peaceful intentions, he had come to be looked upon as a disturbing element—an instance, perhaps, of that "inconscience" which M. Herbette considered a characteristic of the German nation, and concluded with the almost pathetic sentence, "Ich bin doch kein böser Mensch."

APPENDIX D.

Note de l'Etat-Major général français en Réponse à la Note de l'Etat-Major général anglais en date du 22 Janvier 1906.

W.O. Liaison III.
Secret.   *Londres, le 13 Février 1906.*

I.—*Composition de l'Armée—Effectifs.*

Aucune observation à formuler.

II.—*Mobilisation—Embarquement et Débarquement.*

Aucune observation à présenter au tableau de débarquement des unités fourni par l'Etat-major anglais, ni aux propositions relatives à l'organization des camps. Les troupes pourront être facilement enlevées dans les conditions prévues pour leur débarquement; mais, à Cherbourg, quelques-uns des éléments pourront avoir une étape de 15 à 20 kilomètres à faire avant d'être embarqués en chemin de fer.

L'Etat-major français demande que le nombre des unités débarquées à Cherbourg ne soit pas augmenté (bataillons d'infanterie montée).

III.—*Parc d'Artillerie.*

L'Etat-major français juge indispensable que les parcs d'artillerie de corps d'armée soient organisés *sur roues*, en raison des consommations de munitions très grandes qu'il y a lieu de prévoir; il estime qu'on ne disposera jamais de trop de moyens pour assurer le ravitaillement en munitions, et que 500 coups transportés sur roues est un minimum, au dessous duquel il pourrait être dangereux de descendre.

IV.—*Convois.*

L'Etat-major français estime qu'il serait désirable que les convois de corps d'armée fussent mobilisés et attelés. L'armée anglaise se trouverait ainsi approximativement dans les mêmes conditions que les troupes françaises qui portent, tant sur elles que dans leurs voitures, environ 8 jours de vivres.

V.—*Ligne de Communication—Services de l'Arrière.*

1. Il y aura une ligne de communication spéciale, complètement réservée à l'armée anglaise, aboutissant aux deux ports de Calais et de Boulogne. Il n'est pas possible de la déterminer actuellement d'une manière définitive, en raison des éventualités d'ordres divers qui pourront se présenter au début de la guerre; mais le réseau ferré français permettra, en tout état de cause, d'en adapter très facilement une appropriée aux conditions spéciales du moment. Le port de Calais semble

particulièrement bien outillé comme base d'opération, en raison des docks considérables qu'il possède, et où la plus grande partie des approvisionnements de l'armée pourront trouver place.

2, 3 et 7. Il paraît utile de mobiliser les éléments de ligne de communication indiqués au tableau, sauf les suivants :

> 1 état-major du service des chemins de fer ;
> 2 état-majors de sections de chemin de fer,

le service des voies ferrées devant être assuré uniquement par l'exploitation française.

1 compagnie de sapeurs de chemin de fer pourrait être mobilisée, pour aider aux réparations et éventuellement aux destructions à exécuter sur les voies ferrées ; s'il devenait nécessaire, les 2 autres pourraient être appelées ultérieurement ; elles pourraient donc être tenues prêtes à partir, sans toutefois être transportées dès le début.

Les 3 état-majors de commissions de gare pourraient ne comprendre qu'un officier avec un interprète ; leur rôle serait d'assurer la liaison entre le Commandement anglaise et les autorités françaises des chemins de fer.

La compagnie de télégraphie d'étapes ne paraît utile à transporter que si elle peut être utilisée pour le service de première ligne ; pour les services de l'arrière, il semble préférable de ne pas mélanger les unités anglaises et les unités similaires françaises, en raison des différences existant dans les règles d'exploitation.

Le matériel des 4 trains sanitaires serait très utile, à la condition toutefois qu'il puisse s'adapter sans grosse modification au matériel des chemins de fer français.

5. Les prévisions relatives à l'organizations du service des vivres n'ayant été établies qu'en vue des effectifs français, il serait à désirer que l'armée anglaise pût assurer elle-même son réapprovisionnement en vivres, principalement en ce qui concerne la viande et la farine. Des dépôts pourraient être organisés à Calais et Boulogne, d'où les denrées seraient transportés journellement par voie ferrée aux points de livraison convenables. En cas de nécessité, l'administration française fournirait celles qui feraient défaut.

Le droit de réquisition est naturellement accordé aux autorités militaires anglaises. Les réquisitions importantes seraient, pour en faciliter l'exécution, transmises aux autorités civiles françaises par l'intermédiaire des officiers français accrédités auprès des troupes anglaises ; pour celles de faible importance, il sera remis des carnets de réquisition établis et visés par l'autorité militaire française, et que les autorités anglaises n'auront qu'à remplir et signer au moment du besoin.

6. Les dépôts de munitions seront primitivement établis à Calais et Boulogne ; on déterminera ensuite, s'il y a lieu, des dépôts intermédiaires dont il n'est pas actuellement possible de fixer les emplacements.

8. Les autorités militaires anglaises auront le droit de réquisitionner des montures dans le pays en cas d'urgence ; mais les ressources en chevaux disponibles après la mobilisation seront des plus limitées. Il paraît donc prudent de ne compter que dans une très faible mesure sur ce mode de remplacement qui ne donnera que des résultats aléatoires et probablement très insuffisants.

9. Les Troupes anglaises jouiront, en ce qui concerne les cantonnements, absolument des mêmes droits que les troupes françaises.

10. Il paraît désirable que l'armée anglaise conserve, au point de vue des services de l'arrière, son organization propre et son autonomie complète, sauf en ce qui concerne l'exploitation *technique* des voies ferrées qui ne peut être exécutée que par du personnel français.

VI.—*Presse.*

L'intention de l'Etat-major français est de prendre les mesures les plus complètes les plus rigoureuses pour assurer le secret des opérations ; elles seront communiqués à l'Etat-major anglais dès le début des opérations.

Il ne sera pas possible d'autoriser les correspondants militaires des journaux à utiliser les lignes télégraphiques de l'armée.

VII.—*Service des Renseignements.*

L'Etat-major français sera très heureux que l'Etat-major anglais continue son service spécial d'informations pendant toute la durée les différents points de débarquement, avec leur effectif probable en hommes, chevaux et voitures (à 4 ou à 2 roues), afin que l'Etat-major français puisse dès maintenant prévoir la composition et l'organisation des trains destinés à les enlever.

La présente note a été soumise le 10 Février 1906 au Chef d'Etat-major général de l'armée française, qui l'a approuvée.

Londres, le 13 Février 1906.

L'Attaché Militaire,
A. HUGUET.

Erratum.

Page 169, *Ed. Note*, para. 1, last line ...　　... For "pp. 176–7, No. 216 (*a*)" read "pp. 178–9, No. 217 (*a*)."

INDEX OF PERSONS.

SHOWING WRITERS OF DESPATCHES, &C., AND OFFICIAL POSITIONS OF THE PRINCIPAL PERSONS MENTIONED IN THE TEXT.

———

H.R.H. PRINCE ARTHUR, DUKE OF CONNAUGHT.
Conversation with the German Emperor, 357 (No. 415), 357 (No. 416).
Visit to German Army Manœuvres, 1906, 390 (No. 440).
Appointed Field-Marshal by German Emperor, 390 (No. 440).

AUNAY, COMTE LE PELETIER D', French Senator, Ambassador at Berne, 1907–11.
Speech by, 16 (No. 13).

AYERBE, MARQUIS DE, Spanish Ambassador at St. Petersburgh, 1905–7.
Conversation with M. Isvolsky, 343–4 (No. 407).

BACHERACHT, M. B. DE, Russian Minister at Tangier, 1898–1906; 2nd Representative at Conference at Algeciras, 1906; Minister at Berne, 1906–16.
Conversation with Sir A. Nicolson, 205–6 (No. 224).
Appointed representative at Conference at Algeciras, 204 (No. 222).
Morocco police reform proposals of, 205–6 (No. 224), 214 (No. 233), 285–6 (No. 330).

BALFOUR, MR. A. J. (since 1922, 1ST EARL OF), British First Lord of the Treasury, 1895–1905; Prime Minister, 1902–5.
Conversation with German Ambassador, 418–9 (*Appendix* A).

BARNARDISTON, LIEUT.-COL. N. W., British Military *Attaché* at Brussels and The Hague, 1902–6; at the Courts of Denmark, Sweden and Norway, 1903–6.
To Maj.-Gen. J. M. Grierson, 170 (*note*), 187–200 (No. 221 (*c*) (1), (2), (4), (6), (7), (9)–(12)).
To Sir E. C. Phipps, 179–80 (No. 218).
Conversations with Gen. Ducarne, 187–201 (No. 221 (*c*) (1)–(14)), 203 (*ed. note*).

BARRÈRE, M. CAMILLE, French Ambassador at Rome, 1897–1924.
Conversation with Sir E. Egerton, 71 (No. 88), 95 (No. 122), 213 (No. 232).
Conversation with Signor Tittoni, 66 (No. 78).

BARRINGTON, SIR ERIC, Private Secretary to the Marquess of Lansdowne, 1900–5; Assistant Under-Secretary of State for Foreign Affairs, 1906–7.
Minutes by, 272 (No. 308), 282 (No. 322), 299 (No. 342), 334 (No. 398), 341 (No. 404), 343 (No. 405), 355 (No. 413), 358 (No. 416), 360 (No. 419), 373 (No. 429), 395 (No. 444), 434 (*Appendix* C).

BEBEL, HERR AUGUST, Member of the Reichstag.
Speech by, in Reichstag, 348 (No. 412, *note*), 431 (*Appendix* B).

BECKHOVEN, M. VAN, Belgian War Office.
Articles by, in *Bulletin de la Presse*, 194 (No. 221 (*c*) (7)).

BERNSTORFF, COUNT VON, 1st Secretary to the German Embassy at London, 1902–6; Consul-General at Cairo, 1906–8.
Conversation with Prince Bülow, 79 (No. 97).

BERTIE, SIR F. (since 1915, 1ST BARON; 1918, 1ST VISCOUNT), British Ambassador at Rome, 1903–4; at Paris, 1905–18.
To Sir E. Grey, 151 (No. 194), 158–9 (No. 195), 163–5 (No. 204), 174–6 (No. 213), 224 (No. 242), 226 (No. 245), 252 (No. 282), 281 (No. 322), 292 (No. 336), 296–7 (No. 340), 309–10 (No. 361), 317–8 (No. 375), 327–8 (No. 387), 330–1 (No. 395), 362–3 (No. 421), 385–8 (No. 437), 393 (No. 441), 394–5 (No. 443).
To the Marquess of Lansdowne, 17–18 (No. 15), 60 (No. 67), 68 (No. 84), 74 (No. 92), 74 (No. 93), 78 (No. 96), 84 (No. 101), 90 (No. 111), 91 (No. 114), 140 (No. 182).
Communication to M. Delcassé, 73–4 (No. 91 and *note*), 175 (No. 213).
Communication to M. Rouvier, 158–9 (No. 195 and *encl.*).
Conversation with M. Bourgeois, 307 (No. 358), 317–8 (No. 375), 330–1 (No. 395), 362–3 (No. 421).
Conversation with M. Clemenceau, 307 (No. 357), 307 (No. 358).
Conversation with M. Delcassé, 60 (No. 67), 68 (No. 84), 74 (No. 92), 74–5 (No. 93), 78 (No. 96), 175 (No. 213), 309 (No. 361).
Conversation with M. Étienne, 307 (No. 358).
Conversation with Signor Fusinato, 17–8 (No. 15).
Conversation with M. Louis, 158 (No. 195).
Conversation with M. Pichon, 393 (No. 441).
Conversation with M. Rouvier, 140 (No. 182), 163 (No. 204), 292 (No. 336), 296–7 (No. 340).
Relations with Prince Radolin, 385 (No. 436).
Private Letters and Telegrams—
To Sir E. Grey, 284 (No. 327), 306 (No. 355), 306 (No. 356), 307 (No. 358).

449

GRANVILLE, 2ND EARL, British Secretary of State for the Colonies, 1868-70; for Foreign Affairs, 1870-74, and 1880-5.
408 (*Appendix* A), 422 (*Appendix* B).

GRANVILLE, 3RD EARL, Secretary of British Embassy at Berlin, 1904-5.
Conversation with M. Bihourd, 374 (No. 431), 375-6 (No. 433), 376 (No. 434).
To Sir E. Grey, 373 (No. 429).

GREY, SIR EDWARD (since 1916, 1ST VISCOUNT GREY OF FALLODON), Secretary of State for Foreign Affairs, 11 December, 1905-11 December, 1916.
To Lord Acton, 343-4 (No. 406).
To Sir F. Bertie, 160 (No. 197), 170-1 (No. 210 (*a*)), 177 (No. 215), 180-2 (No. 219), 213-5 (No. 233), 225 (No. 244), 250-1 (No. 280), 255-6 (No. 286), 278 (No. 319), 289 (No. 333), 303 (No. 350), 304 (No. 352), 308-9 (No. 360), 329 (No. 391), 331 (No. 396), 361-2 (No. 420), 373 (No. 428), 373 (No. 430), 393-4 (No. 442).
To Sir M. de Bunsen, 285 (No. 329), 316 (No. 372).
To M. Paul Cambon, 373 (No. 428).
To Mr. Cartwright, 271 (No. 307).
To Sir M. Durand, 317 (No. 374), 318 (No. 377).
To Sir E. Egerton, 166 (No. 206), 262 (No. 295).
To Sir E. Goschen, 276-7 (No. 316), 315-6 (No. 371), 318 (No. 378).
To Sir C. Hardinge, 209 (No. 228).
To Sir F. Lascelles, 209-11 (No. 229), 211-2 (No. 230), 225 (No. 243), 240 (No. 264), 254-5 (No. 285), 263-4 (No. 296), 301 (No. 347), 302 (No. 348), 358 (No. 417), 363-4 (No. 422), 372 (No. 427).
To Mr. Lowther, 339 (No. 403).
To Sir A. Nicolson, 151 (No. 193), 160 (No. 196), 162 (No. 201), 215 (No. 234), 239 (No. 261), 251-2 (No. 281), 261 (No. 293), 269 (No. 302), 285 (No. 327, *note*), 292 (No. 335), 299-300 (No. 343), 300 (No. 344), 304 (No. 351), 329 (No. 389), 329 (No. 390).
To Colonel Repington, 169 (*ed. note*).
To Mr. Spring-Rice, 246 (No. 274), 264 (No. 297), 270 (No. 304).
To Mr. Whitehead, 160-1 (No. 198).
Conversation with M. Paul Cambon, 160 (No. 197), 162 (No. 201), 170-1 (No. 210 (*a*)), 171 (No. 210 (*b*)), 173 (No. 212, *encl.*), 174 (No. 213), 177 (No. 215), 178-9 (No. 217 (*a*)), 180-2 (No. 219), 182-3 (No. 220 (*a*)), 184 (No. 220 (*b*)), 203 (*ed. note*), 213-5 (No. 233), 225 (No. 244), 255-6 (No. 286), 278 (No. 319), 289 (No. 333), 300 (No. 344), 304 (No. 352), 307 (No. 357), 329 (No. 391), 331 (No. 396), 393-4 (No. 442).
Conversation with M. Geoffray, 361 (No. 420).
Conversation with Count Mensdorff, 315-6 (No. 371), 318-9 (No. 378).
Conversation with Count Metternich, 160-1 (No. 198), 181 (No. 219), 182 (No. 220 (*a*)), 209-11 (No. 229), 218 (No. 237), 240 (No. 264), 254-5 (No. 285), 263-4 (No. 296), 266-7 (No. 299), 270 (No. 304), 301 (No. 347), 302 (No. 348), 304 (No. 351), 363-4 (No. 422), 367 (No. 425).
Conversation with Signor A. Pansa, 166 (No. 206).
Conversation with Señor Polo de Bernabé, 215 (No. 234).
Conversation with M. Sazonow, 264-5 (No. 297).
Conversation with Herr von Stumm, 358 (No. 417).
Conversation with Austrian *Chargé d'Affaires*, 276 (No. 316).
Conversation with Spanish *Chargé d'Affaires*, 316 (No. 372).
Memorandum by (to M. P. Cambon), 226 (No. 244, *encl.*).
Memorandum by (Morocco), 266-7 (No. 299).
Minutes by, 172 (No. 210 (*b*)), 174 (No. 212, *encl.*), 176 (No. 213), 184 (No. 220 (*a*), (*b*)), 209 (No. 227), 224 (No. 240), 241 (No. 265), 272 (No. 308), 282 (No. 322), 299 (No. 342), 343 (No. 405), 358 (No. 416), 359 (No. 418), 360 (No. 419), 381 (No. 435), 389 (No. 439), 392 (No. 440), 395 (No. 444), 420 (*Appendix* A), 420, 424 (*Appendix* B).
Private Letters—
To Sir F. Bertie, 177-8 (No. 216), 304-5 (No. 353), 307 (No. 357).
To Sir A. Nicolson, 161 (No. 199), 162 (No. 200), 248-9 (No. 278), 258 (No. 288).
To Lord Tweedmouth, 203 (*ed. note*).
Statement in House of Commons (1910), 383 (No. 435, *min.*).

GRIERSON, MAJOR-GENERAL SIR J. M., Director of Military Operations, British War Office, 1904-6.
To Lt.-Col. N. W. Barnardiston, 170 (*ed. note*), 179 (No. 217 (*b*)), 190, 192, 196, 200-1 (No. 221 (*c*), (3), (5), (8), (13), (14)).
To Lord Sanderson, 172-3 (No. 211).
Conversation with M. Huguet, 172 (No. 211), 186 (No. 221 (*b*)).
Authorisation of, 174 (No. 212, *min.*), 176-7 (No. 214), 177 (No. 215), 178 (No. 216), 179 (*ed. note*), 186 (No. 221 (*b*)).
Conversation with Lord Sanderson, 171 (No. 210 (*b*)).

[15869]   2 G

2 G 4

RICHTHOFEN, OSWALD, BARON VON, German Secretary of State for Foreign Affairs, 1900–6.
   Conversation with M. Bihourd, 69 (No. 86), 106 (No. 133), 154, 156 (No. 194, *encl.*).
   Conversation with Count di Lanza, 106 (No. 133).
   Conversation with Sir F. Lascelles, 86–7 (No. 104), 207–8 (No. 226), 211 (No. 230).
   Conversation with Mr. Whitehead, 113 (No. 142).

RODRIGUEZ SAN PEDRO, SEÑOR, Spanish Minister for Foreign Affairs, 1903–4.
   Conversation with Sir E. Egerton, 34 (No. 35), 38 (No. 43), 43 (No. 51), 44 (No. 52).
   Speech by, 37 (No. 42).

ROGHI, EL (BU I'AMARA), Pretender in Morocco, 1905, 1906.
   Condition of Morocco and, 337 (No. 401).
   Suppression of, 148 (No. 190), 153 (No. 194, *encl.*), 250 (No. 280), 347 (No. 412, *encl.*).

ROMAN, SEÑOR SANCHEZ, Spanish Minister for Foreign Affairs, 1905–6.
   Conversation with M. J. Cambon, 111 (No. 138).
   Conversation with Sir A. Nicolson, 109–10 (No. 136), 114 (No. 144), 120 (No. 154).
   Conversation with Herr von Radowitz, 111 (No. 138).

ROOSEVELT, MR. THEODORE, President of the U.S.A., 1901–9.
   To German Emperor, 97 (No. 126).
   Communication from the German Emperor, 67 (No. 82).
   Morocco Conference and, 256 (No. 286).

ROOT, MR. ELIHU, U.S. Secretary of State, 1905–9.
   To Baron Speck von Sternburg, 312 (No. 365); *Text*, 313–4 (No. 367, *encl.*).
   To Mr. H. White, 320–1 (No. 380).
   Conversation with Sir M. Durand, 320 (No. 380), 321 (No. 381).
   Morocco Conference and, 217 (No. 236).

ROSEN, DR. F., German Foreign Office, 1901–5; Minister at Tangier, 1905–10.
   Conversation with Sir F. Lascelles, 86 (No. 104).
   Conversation with Mr. Lowther, 147–9 (No. 190).
   Conversation with M. Rouvier, 141 (No. 183), 158 (No. 195), 237 (No. 259).
   Agreement with M. Révoil, 143–4 (No. 184, *encl.* 2), 148 (No. 190).
   Visit to Paris, September 1905, 156 (No. 194, *encl.*).

ROTENHAN, BARON VON, German Under-Secretary of State for Foreign Affairs, 1890–7.
   381 (No. 435, *min.*).

ROTHSCHILD, 2ND BARON.
   Conversation with Count Metternich, 280 (No. 321 and *encl.*).

ROUVIER, M. C., French Minister at Lisbon, 1898–1906.
   Conversation with Sir M. Gosselin, 31 (No. 31).

ROUVIER, M. MAURICE, French Finance Minister, 1902–5; Prime Minister, Finance Minister and Minister for Foreign Affairs, 1905–6.
   Circular despatch of (June 8, 1905), 153–4 (No. 194, *encl.*).
   To M. Bihourd, 142 (No. 183), 154–6 (No. 194, *encl.*, *passim*), 159 (No. 195).
   To M. Paul Cambon, 119–20 (No. 153).
   To M. Jonnart, 153 (No. 194, *encl.*).
   To Prince von Radolin, 133–5 (No. 174 (*b*)), 155–7 (No. 194, *encl.*, *passim*), 259 (No. 290).
   Conversation with Sir F. Bertie, 140 (No. 182), 163 (No. 204), 292 (No. 336), 296–7 (No. 340).
   Conversation with Sir M. de Bunsen, 281 (No. 322, *encl.*), 282 (No. 322, *min.*), 285 (No. 327, *note*).
   Conversation with H.M. King Edward VII, 284 (No. 327).
   Conversation with Sir C. Hardinge, 226–7 (No. 245).
   Conversation with Mr. R. Lister, 107–8 (No. 134).
   Conversation with Prince von Radolin, 96 (No. 124), 97 (No. 126), 105–6 (No. 133), 110 (No. 137), 112 (No. 139), 119 (No. 153), 154 (No. 194, *encl.*), 255–6 (No. 286), 259 (No. 290), 288 (No. 331).
   Conversation with Dr. Rosen, 141 (No. 183), 158 (No. 195), 237 (No. 259).
   Conversation with *Times* correspondent, 90 (No. 111).
   Conversation with the Marquis Visconti Venosta, 230 (No. 249).
   Communication to Prince von Radolin (June 21, 1905), 217 (No. 235, *encl.*).
   Communication to Dr. Rosen, 159 (No. 195), 259 (No. 290).
   Communiqué to Press (Morocco), 115 (No. 146).
   Agreement with Prince von Radolin (Programme of Conference), 115–6 (No. 147), 143 (No. 184, *encl.*), 146 (No. 188, *encl.*).
   Instructions to M. Révoil, 214 (No. 233), 220–2 (No. 239), 225 (No. 244), 260 (No. 291), 304 (No. 352).
   Policy of, 108 (No. 134).

Subject Index.

ABYSSINIA.
Abyssinian Bank and Germany, 79 (No. 97).
Ethiopian Railway Scheme,
Anglo-French proposed agreement on, 356 (No. 414).
Sir E. Grey on, 356 (No. 414).
Italy and,
M. Bourgeois on, 356 (No. 414).
Signor Tittoni and, 356 (No. 414).
Tripartite Agreement,
M. Paul Cambon and Sir E. Grey, on, 393–4 (No. 442).

AFGHANISTAN.
Anglo-Russian negotiations *re*, 367 (No. 425).

AFRICA, GENERAL.
German aspirations in,
Mr. Cartwright on, 372 (No. 426).

AFRICA, EAST, BRITISH.
East Africa Company and King Leopold and Upper Nile, 424 (*App.* B).
East Africa Protectorate Liquor Ordinance, 1902, 1903, 339 (No. 403).

AFRICA, EAST, GERMAN.
Dr. C. Peters and, 409 (*App.* A).

AFRICA, EAST, PORTUGUESE.
v. sub Portugal, African colonies.

AFRICA, SOUTH, BRITISH.
Cape to Cairo railway, 410 (*App.* A).
Germany and, 422, 430 (*App.* B).
South African War,
Germany and, general, 79 (No. 97), 334 (No. 398, *min.*), 367 (No. 425), 433 (*App.* B, *annex*).
British statesmen on, Sir E. Crowe, 426 (*App.* B); Sir F. Lascelles, 436 (*App.* C); Lord Sanderson, 426 (*App.* B).
Contraband, hostility over, 411 (*App.* A); Press and, 436 (*App.* C).
German Emperor and, 378 (No. 435), 432–3 (*App.* B, *annex*), 436–7 (*App.* C).
Alleged intervention by Russia and France,
German Emperor and, 426 (*App.* B), 437 (*App.* C); Sir E. Crowe on, 437 (*App.* C, *min.*); Sir C. Hardinge on, 433 (*App.* B, *annex*).
Count Muravieff and, 426 (*App.* B), 433 (*App.* B, *annex*).
Lord Salisbury on, 431 (*ed. note*).

AFRICA, SOUTH-WEST, GERMAN.
Annexed by Prince Bismarck, 408 (*App.* A).
Frontier, disputes and campaigns, 361 (No. 420), 410 (*App.* A), 363 (No. 422), 367 (No. 425), 378 (No. 435),

AFRICA, WESTERN AND CENTRAL (FRENCH).
Anglo-French convention, 8 April, 1904 (*v.* Anglo-French Convention, Treaties).
French advantages obtained in,
M. Delcassé on, 12 (No. 9).

AFRICA, WEST, GERMAN, CAMEROONS.
Prince Bismarck and, 408 (*App.* A), 422 (*App.* B).
Germany and,
Sir E. Crowe on, 355 (No. 413), 408 (*App.* A).
Lord Granville and, 408 (*App.* A).

AKABA QUESTION.
British appreciation of French support,
Sir E. Grey on, 355 (No. 414).

ALGECIRAS.
Acte Général of Conference (*v.* sub Conference of Powers).
Conference of Powers at (*v. sub* Conference of Powers).

ALGERIA.
Frontier, French interests, 32 (No. 32), 104 (No. 132 (*b*)), 107 (No. 134, 115–6 (No. 147), 152 (No. 194, *encl.*), 174–6 (No. 213), 181 (No. 219).
M. Paul Cambon on, 171 (No. 21 (*a*)).
M. Delcassé on, 12 (No. 9).
Germany and, 107 (No. 134), 148 (No. 190).
Sir E. Monson on, 54 (No. 63).
Policing of, 152 (No. 194, *encl.*), 164 (No. 204), 218 (No. 237), 226 (No. 244, *encl.*), 227 (No. 245), 228 (No. 247), 233 (No. 252), 237 (No. 259), 250 (No. 280), 325 (No. 385).
Germany and, 93 (No. 117), 107 (No. 134), 148 (No. 190), 255 (No. 285).

ALLIANCES.
Great Britain against, 415 (*App.* A).
Sir E. Grey on, 177–8 (No. 216), 181 (No. 219).
Specific,
Anglo-French, alleged offensive and defensive (*v.* also France),
Prince Bülow on, 79 (No. 97), 81 (No. 98).
M. Cambon on, 120–1 (No. 210 (*a*)), 173 (No. 212, *encl.* 2).
Sir E. Crowe on, 399 (*App.* A).
King Edward, minutes by, 79 (No. 97), 81 (No. 98).
Entente and defensive alliance, 181 (No. 219), 182 (No. 220 (*a*)).
Herr von Holstein on, 81 (No. 98).
Marquess of Lansdowne on, 76 (No. 94, *min.*), 82 (No. 99), 86 (No. 104), 399 (*App.* A).
Sir F. Lascelles on, 79 (No. 97), 81 (No. 98).
Count Metternich on, 83 (No. 99).

CONFERENCE OF POWERS AT ALGECIRAS—*(continued)*.

Course of negotiations—(continued).

State Bank,

Bank censors, formulas of, 328 (No. 388).

Discussions on, 259 (No. 289), 283 (No. 326), 286 (No. 330).

Establishment of, suggested, 120 (No. 153), 149 (No. 190), 210 (No. 229).

Franco-German discussions, 236 (No. 257), 236–7 (No. 259), 239 (No. 261), 285 (No. 328).

French concessions suggested, 289 (No. 332), 294 (No. 338).

M. Bourgeois on, 309 (No. 360).

M. Révoil on, 319–20 (No. 379).

M. Rouvier on, 284 (No. 327).

Count Welsersheimb, 319–20 (No. 379).

German proposal for compromise, 311–2 (No. 364).

French proposals, 303 (No. 349).

Sir A. Nicolson on, 275 (No. 312).

M. Rouvier on, 284 (No. 327).

Austrian suggestion of concessions, 319 (No. 379).

Germany and, 262 (No. 295), 269 (No. 301).

Great Britain to support, 262 (No. 295).

Spanish views on currency, 269 (No. 301).

German concessions to France,

Sir A. Nicolson on, 233 (No. 251), 234 (No. 254), 265 (No. 298).

M. Révoil on, 231 (No. 250), 231 (No. 251), 237 (No. 259).

Plenary sitting, question reserved, 282 (No. 323), 282 (No. 324).

Reforms,

Financial : Great Britain proposes to include taxation, 122 (No. 153); German comments on French proposals, 133 (No. 174 (*a*)), 148 (No. 190); French proposals for, 156 (No. 194, *encl.*).

General : French proposals, 216 (No. 235, *encl.*).

Claim to European mandate, 216 (No. 235, *encl.*); M. Delcassé on, 216 (No. 235, *encl.*); Count Tattenbach on, 216 (No. 235, *encl.*); Moorish Government and, 216 (No. 235, *encl.*).

France, special position of, Sir E. Grey on, 211 (No. 230).

German proposals, 155 (No. 194, *encl.*), 207–8 (No. 226).

International or one-Power basis, 207 (No. 226), 211 (No. 230), 223 (No. 240); Baron Richthofen on, 207 (No. 226), 211 (No. 230); Sir F. Lascelles on, 207 (No. 226).

Morocco and Ben Sliman on, 338 (No. 402).

CONFERENCE OF POWERS AT ALGECIRAS—*(continued)*.

Course of negotiations—(continued).

Reforms—(continued).

Moroccan basis suggested, Sir F. Lascelles on, 223 (No. 240); Herr von Holstein on, 223 (No. 240).

Morocco, Sultan of, acceptance by, Sir E. Grey on, 299 (No. 343); Sir A. Nicolson on, 301 (No. 346), Herr von Radowitz on, 301 (No. 346); Mr. Lowther on, 337 (No. 401).

Slavery, 328 (No. 388), 330 (No. 392), 330 (No. 393).

Status quo and, 227 (No. 245, *encl.*).

Treatment of Jews, 328 (No. 388), 330 (No. 392).

Contraband at sea, suppression of, 131 (No. 173), 136 (No. 175), 132 (No. 174 (*a*)), 134 (No. 174 (*b*)), 148 (No. 190), 208 (No. 227), 214 (No. 233), 227 (No. 246), 229 (No. 248).

Mr. Lowther on, 148 (No. 190).

Dr. Rosen on, 148 (No. 190).

Neutralization of Morocco, German proposal,

Señor Moret on, 233 (No. 253).

M. Rouvier on, 233 (No. 253).

Economic questions,

Open door,

German desire for, 218 (No. 237); Sir E. Grey on, 210 (No. 229); Count Metternich and, 210 (No. 229), 226 (No. 244, *encl.*), 227 (No. 246), 229 (No. 248), 241 (No. 265), 254 (No. 285).

British support for, 229 (No. 248), 251 (No. 281), 254 (No. 285).

French support for, 229 (No. 248), 254 (No. 285); Sir A. Nicolson on, 241 (No. 265); Count Tattenbach on, 241 (No. 265).

Customs duties, taxation, Germany and, 164 (No. 204); increase of, Sir E. Grey on, 239 (No. 261), 261 (No. 293).

Custom house control, 148 (No. 190), 328 (No. 388).

Economic guarantees, 254–5 (No. 285), 263 (No. 296), 264 (No. 297).

Liquor traffic question, Sir E. Grey on, 339 (No. 403).

Procedure and meetings,

Order of procedure, 214 (No. 233), 225 (No. 244), 227 (No. 246), 250 (No. 280), 259 (No. 289), 282 (No. 323), 283 (No. 326), 286 (No. 330), 337 (No. 401).

Duke of Almodovar on, 208 (No. 227).

Sir A. Nicolson on, 208 (No. 227).

Special commissions at, 13 (No. 232).

Meetings,

Election of Duke of Almodovar as President, 227 (No. 246), 229 (No. 248)

Termination of, 328 (No. 388), 329 (No. 392).

MADEIRA.
German concession in, Sir E. Grey on, 361 (No. 420).
Sanatorium, question, 371 (No. 426).

MADRID CONFERENCE, 1880 (v. also sub Treaties).
Señor de Villa-Urrutia as secretary, 150 (No. 192).

MANCHESTER CHAMBER OF COMMERCE.
Marquess of Lansdowne's letter, July 3, 1905, to, 112 (No. 140).

MANCHURIA.
British railway concession in, 427 (App. B).
Russia and, 412 (App. A), 427–8 (App. B).

MARNIA.
Proposed carriage road and telegraph line, 153 (No. 194, encl.).

MAZAGAN.
Police at, 291 (No. 334, encl.).

MEKONG VALLEY.
M. Delcassé on, 17 (No. 14).

MELILLA.
Development of resources of, 325 (No. 385).
Erection of fortifications, 25 (No. 24), 27 (No. 26), 53 (No. 61).
Harbour works at, 396 (No. 445).
Police question, 242 (No. 267).
French sphere of influence, 32 (No. 32).
Spanish fortress at, 31 (No. 32).
Spanish sphere of influence, 29 (No. 28), 31 (No. 32), 33 (No. 34), 34 (No. 36), 35 (No. 38), 36 (No. 39).

MESA, RIVER.
Spanish sphere of influence, 35 (No. 36), 35 (No. 38).

MOGADOR.
Police at, 244 (No. 270), 291 (No. 334, encl.).
German proposals, 208 (No. 227), 212 (No. 231); Sir E. Grey on, 208 (No. 227, min.); Señor Moret on, 212 (No. 231).
Suggested concession of, to Germany, 70 (No. 86).

MONTENEGRO.
Possibility of attack on Servia; German Emperor on, 391 (No. 440).

MOROCCO (v. also sub Conference of Powers at Algeciras, Madrid Convention (1880), Treaties, Anglo-French Agreement of April 8, 1904).
Anglo-French policy re,
Germany and, 67 (No. 82).
Mr. Taft on, 67 (No. 82).
Conditions of,
Sir A. Nicolson on, 109–110 (No. 136).
Lord Lansdowne on, 117 (No. 150).
Mr. Lowther on, 337 (No. 401), 347 (No. 412, encl.).
Necessity for police, Count Tattenbach on, 242 (No. 267); Sir A. Nicolson on, 242 (No. 267).

[15869]

MOROCCO—(continued).
Anti-Christian feeling in, 124 (No. 165).
Army,
Condition of, 102 (No. 131).
France not to use as a recruiting ground, Dr. Rosen on, 148 (No. 190).
French personnel to take service in, 152 (No. 194, encl.).
French reorganisation of, 121 (No. 156), 147 (No. 190), 153–5 (No. 194, encl.).
Military force contemplated by Sultan, 101 (No. 130).
Bank, State, creation of, M. Taillandier on, 152 (No. 194, encl.).
Joint establishment of by the Powers, 155 (No. 194, encl.).
Meetings to be held in Paris, May, 1907, 345 (No. 410); Hadj Dris Benjelun, Moorish Representative and, 345 (No. 410).
British and Moorish Agreement, March 13, 1895, Cape Juby, territory in neighbourhood of,
Lord Lansdowne's memo. to M. Paul Cambon, 27th April, 1904, Text, 32 (No. 33).
British commerce, security for, 20 (No. 18).
Sir A. Nicolson and "open door," 241 (No. 265).
Commercial Liberty in,
Commerce in, 59 (No. 66), 62 (No. 71), 69 (No. 86); Prince Bülow on, 80 (No. 97).
Commercial equality in, 27 (No. 26), 111 (No. 137).
Commercial rights and privileges, 65 (No. 75), 69 (No. 86).
Customs Duties, French Agents appointed, 1904, 152 (No. 194, encl.).
Finance and Taxation,
Financial condition of, Mr. Lowther on, 337 (No. 401), 346 (No. 412, encl.).
Taxation, Foreign protection, 101 (No. 130), 102 (No. 131); Count Tattenbach on, 102 (No. 131); Mr. Lowther on, 102 (No. 131).
Treaty rights of Powers, 103 (No. 132 (b)).
France and,
Franco-German accord favoured by France, 155 (No. 194, encl.).
Franco-German policies in, Lord Sanderson on, 185 (No. 220 (b)).
Franco-German relations concerning, 155 (No. 194, encl.); possibility of war, 108 (No. 134).
Franco-Spanish economic participation, 41 (No. 47); M. Delcassé on, 41 (No. 47); M. P. Cambon on, 41 (No. 47).
French entanglements in, 401 (App. A).
French financial assistance to, 26 (No. 24), 27 (No. 26), 38 (No. 43), 41 (No. 47).
Loan by French Syndicate, 1903, 1904, 152 (No. 194, encl.).
Monopoly for France, Prince Radolin on, 106 (No. 133).
French influence in, Duc de Mandas on, 39 (No. 44).

2 I 3

2 I 4